THE
FOREIGN CORRUPT
PRACTICES ACT
HANDBOOK

A Practical Guide for
Multinational General Counsel,
Transactional Lawyers and
White Collar Criminal Practitioners

THE
FOREIGN CORRUPT
PRACTICES ACT
HANDBOOK

A Practical Guide for
Multinational General Counsel,
Transactional Lawyers and
White Collar Criminal Practitioners

Robert W. Tarun

AMERICAN BAR ASSOCIATION
Defending Liberty
Pursuing Justice

Printed in the United States of America.

14 13 12 11 10 5 4 3 2

Cataloging-in-Publication Data is on file with the Library of Congress.

The Foreign Corrupt Practices Act Handbook: A Practical Guide for Multinational
    General Counsel, Transactional Lawyers, and White Collar Criminal Practitioners
Robert W. Tarun
ISBN: 978-1-60442-951-0

This book is dedicated to my children
Abigail, Aimee, Parker, and Tyler

Contents

Preface

Enforcement of the Foreign Corrupt Practices Act (FCPA) has in the past five years increased dramatically. The United States Department of Justice and the Securities and Exchange Commission are conducting over 140 investigations of U.S. and foreign companies,[1] their joint ventures, employees,, and third-party contractors for alleged improper payments around the world. There is no reason to believe this trend will subside in the United States or elsewhere. Indeed, there is now clear momentum and a clear incentive among foreign governments to investigate bribery and related conduct under various international conventions.

The era of mysterious "one man" consultancies, extravagant behind-the-curtain gifts to foreign officials, minimal due diligence of foreign agents, or willful blindness to the conduct of joint venture partners is coming to a close. Corporate directors and officers can no longer ignore or rationalize unusually large foreign sales budgets, lucrative consultancies, or extravagant entertainment with shadowy or unknown figures with the words, "This is the way it is done in that part of the world." While there remain some lax foreign states that knowingly permit their citizens to engage in corrupt practices in distant countries, they are a minority, their world is shrinking, and they will likely have to reform if they wish to remain members of an increasingly transparent international business community. Transparency is becoming the governing watchword in multinational mergers, acquisitions, joint ventures, and corporate transactions and is all the more critical in challenging economic times.

Increased FCPA enforcement means increased responsibilities for boards of directors, general counsel, and transactional lawyers—and new and uncharted waters for white-collar criminal prosecutors and defense lawyers. "Preventative law" in the form of proactive counseling and director, officer, and employee training is the smart way for corporations to manage risk in an area where missteps can be very costly. Quality anti-bribery and recordkeeping training along with comprehensive, recorded due diligence on the front end of mergers, acquisitions, joint ventures, and third-party contracts and follow-on due diligence can minimize criminal liability and avoid lengthy investigations, serious fines, substantial legal fees, and damage to corporate and executive reputations. There is no substitute for live anti-bribery training of officers and employees responsible for foreign sales, finances, and accounting. As important, thorough pre-acquisition due diligence may be the most compelling defense to expensive successor criminal liability.

Professor Julie R. O'Sullivan of Georgetown Law Center has correctly and insightfully observed:

> FCPA work is a vital area of white-collar criminal practice because lawyers are consulted not just when a potentially corrupt payment is uncovered by the government, but also at every stage leading up to that point. Thus, FCPA practitioners consult with companies, among other things: on how to put in place systems to prevent such violations; on companies' potential exposure under the FCPA were they to engage in proposed mergers, acquisitions, joint ventures, contracts, consulting arrangements, and the like; on structuring transactions and contracts to avoid FCPA problems; on whether and how to conduct a corporate investigation of allegations of wrongdoing; on how to avoid an enforcement action by the SEC or a criminal prosecution by the Justice Department; and on how to settle or litigate such cases if they are brought.
>
> The challenge of [an] FCPA practice lies in part in the fact that there is little in the way of public precedents on the subject, and the FCPA itself is complex and, in many areas, vague. Much of this practice is conducted under the legal waterline: "success" means that counsel has put in place an effective system to avoid FCPA problems or, if such problems arise, has dealt with the matter in such a way as to avoid any governmental interest or enforcement. Thus, FCPA practitioners' expertise depends more on experience in similar cases and consultations among lawyers who do FCPA work than on reading law reports. The practice is also extremely challenging for many of the reasons that white-collar practice in general is challenging, including the potential that a client will be facing potential liability on a number of fronts simultaneously (civil enforcement action, criminal prosecution, private or shareholder litigation, etc.)[2]

THE FOREIGN CORRUPT PRACTICES HANDBOOK is based on over 20 years' experience of working with and representing multinational companies in sensitive payment investigations, as well as sharing best practices and compliance ideas with corporate counselors and white-collar criminal lawyers. Its guidance stems from investigating and prosecuting white-collar crimes for a decade and defending the often misunderstood in the same vineyard for twice as long. This book is intended, above all, to be a *practical* resource for three audiences—general counsel, transactional lawyers, and white-collar criminal lawyers—not a treatise detailing legislative history or domestic bribery precedent nor a definitive compilation of every FCPA investigation, prosecution, or enforcement action ever brought. The handbook is also not intended to serve as a substitute for corporate counsel regularly consulting FCPA experts or retaining experienced litigators to represent their companies in significant

FCPA investigations. Because there are few cases directly interpreting the FCPA and because the statute is complex, the handbook necessarily offers interpretation of the FCPA's unique, broad, and often undefined terms and the 100-plus Department of Justice (DOJ) plea agreements and Securities and Exchange Commission (SEC) settlements with companies and individuals the past decade.

Chapter 1 covers the elements and defenses under the FCPA's anti-bribery regime and its accounting provisions—recordkeeping and internal controls—that also subject companies and individuals to criminal liability. The chapter also addresses conspiracy and other offenses often charged in FCPA prosecutions as well as the potential penalties, fines, and other sanctions. It discusses the five-year statute of limitations and the three-year suspension available to the DOJ to secure foreign evidence, FCPA opinion releases, and the collateral litigation that may follow FCPA investigations and prosecutions.

Chapters 2 and 3 examine the expansive jurisdiction of the FCPA and other anti-bribery conventions, including the increasingly important Organization for Economic and Cooperative Development (OECD) Convention. Chapter 4 reviews the important responsibilities of boards of directors and how compliance programs of multinational companies can be tailored to FCPA and related issues. Live FCPA training of multinational officers and key employees in high-risk countries is arguably the most important component of an effective compliance program. Chapter 5 covers the frequent transactional third-party issues that have resulted in many FCPA prosecutions and enforcement actions involving agents, consultants, subcontractors, distributors, and joint venture partners. It also addresses the importance of conducting risk profiles for foreign acquisitions, identifies 15 key FCPA risks, lists documents necessary for a quality review, and emphasizes that a thorough acquisition due diligence record is the best defense to successor liability. Chapter 6 addresses gift, travel, lodging, and entertainment issues and the importance of securing quality written legal opinions from FCPA counsel. Chapter 7 discusses and offers practical advice on the potentially thorny issues of foreign charitable donations and political contributions.

Chapter 8 is dedicated to conducting FCPA investigations and discusses disclosure and cooperation options, reflecting the fact that today many management teams, boards, or audit committees elect to conduct thorough bribery investigations, implement constructive remedial measures, and voluntarily disclose and cooperate with the hope of obtaining substantial credit from the DOJ and SEC. While managements may elect in the wake of misconduct to promptly discipline employees, institute reforms, and improve internal controls. the imposition of mammoth, crippling fines on cooperative public companies, particularly during a global recession, too often punishes innocent shareholders and jeopardizes the jobs of tens of thousands of decent employees. Chapter 8 recommends a five-step investigative process first outlined 17 years ago in Webb, Tarun, and Molo, Corporate Internal Investigations (Law Journal Press 1993–2010). The template has in large part stood the test of time and sensitive investigations in 40 countries. This chapter includes a working chronology and interview outline for a hypothetical FCPA scenario to illustrate key components of the investigation process.

Chapter 9 focuses on the defense of companies and individuals that are the subjects and targets of DOJ investigations. It covers the DOJ and SEC charging criteria and lists 30 potential defenses to FCPA charges. The chronology and type of interview outline discussed in Chapter 8 are equally applicable and important to coordinating an aggressive defense of corporations or its officers.

Chapter 10 summarizes significant DOJ and SEC foreign bribery and FCPA accounting provision cases—a list certain to grow in the coming decade—and highlights a variety of effective remedial measures to combat improper payment schemes. Because there is little FCPA case law, practitioners are guided by the challenging statutory language and legislative history, but also by the DOJ and FCPA resolutions and FCPA opinions issued the past five years. This final chapter gives counsel practical advice on how to interpret FCPA settlements and strategize the legal and factual challenges in an FCPA investigation.

I am grateful for the insights of my Baker & McKenzie partners and especially my colleagues John F. McKenzie of San Francisco, whose knowledge of the U.S. export laws and the Foreign Corrupt Practices Act is encyclopedic, and William Joseph Linklater of Chicago, whose prismatic issue analysis is always keen. I also wish to thank Jay G. Martin, Vice President, Chief Compliance Officer, and Senior Deputy General Counsel, Baker Hughes, Inc., whose experience with and study of FCPA compliance is second to none, for his most generous review of and comments on the draft manuscript. I welcome the comments and suggestions of other practitioners and scholars for future editions. Finally, I wish to acknowledge and thank Ms. Linda Braggs of Oakland for her tireless patience, professionalism, and attention to detail in helping me bring this handbook to completion.

Robert W. Tarun
San Francisco
March 1, 2010

NOTES

1. Dionne Searcey, *U.S. Cracks Down on Corporate Bribes*, Wall St. J., May 26, 2009, at A1.

2. David Luban, Julie O'Sullivan & David Stewart, *Corruption*, ch. 14 in International and Transnational Criminal Law (Aspen 2009).

Introduction

Enacted in 1977 in the wake of a series of overseas and domestic bribery scandals involving 400 major corporations and payments of over $300 million, the Foreign Corrupt Practices Act (FCPA) (Appendix 1) originally prohibited U.S. corporations and nationals from making improper payments to foreign officials, parties, or candidates, in order to assist a company in obtaining, retaining, or directing business to any person.[1] The Act also imposes recordkeeping and internal controls requirements on all companies subject to United States Securities and Exchange Commission (SEC) jurisdiction.[2]

As a result of amendments in 1998, the FCPA is largely no longer solely the concern of U.S. companies and citizens. The amendments greatly expanded the jurisdiction of the U.S. government to prosecute foreign companies and nationals who cause, directly or through agents, an act in furtherance of a corrupt payment to take place within the territory of the United States. U.S. parent corporations may also be liable for the acts of foreign subsidiaries where they have authorized, directed, or controlled the activity of U.S. citizens or residents who are employed by or acting on behalf of foreign incorporated subsidiaries.

The Department of Justice (DOJ) has primary responsibility for enforcing the anti-bribery provisions of the Act while the SEC is a civil law enforcement authority that generally enforces the accounting (books and records and internal controls) provisions. Both have authority to seek permanent injunctions against present and future violations.[3] Criminal and civil penalties for violating the FCPA can be severe for corporations as well as individual officers, employees, and agents. In addition to large DOJ and SEC monetary sanctions, including, routinely, disgorgement of profits, FCPA investigations can spawn shareholder litigation, government debarment and suspension proceedings, and parallel investigations in foreign jurisdictions.

FCPA actions by the DOJ and SEC in the past five years have concentrated on the aerospace, energy, technology, engineering and construction, medical and pharma, telecom, and food and agriculture sectors. Foreign governments often represent the largest and most influential purchasers of capital equipment and support services in their countries. Even if they do not directly purchase substantial goods and services, many governments regulate or oversee certain sectors such as energy, telecom, and pharmaceuticals where potential FCPA issues abound. Perhaps as important, the future for many multinationals lies in emerging markets where legal systems are immature or less developed and government agencies wield broad discretion. Compliance, training, and risk analyses by multinationals are often relatively new to and lacking in the Third World. While the recent geographical pattern of FCPA actions has pointed toward Asia, Latin America, and Africa as having the most serious corruption problems, there have been major DOJ and SEC bribery prosecutions involving multinationals doing business in Europe and the Middle East (e.g., BAE Systems plc, Siemens AG). The BRIC countries (Brazil, Russia, India, and China) of course remain in the FCPA spotlight due to their large markets, growth potential, perceived corruption problems, and Transparency International rankings.

At least five new trends have emerged in recent FCPA enforcement actions.[4] First, FCPA mega settlements ($100 million plus fines) have now been filed and are not likely to subside.[5] In December 2008, Siemens AG, a German corporation with operations in over 100 countries, and three of its subsidiaries pled guilty to violations of and charges related to a six-year, $1.36 billion bribery scheme, and the parent agreed to pay a combined total of more than $1.6 billion in fines, penalties, and disgorgement of profits to U.S. and foreign authorities.[6] In February 2009, Kellogg Brown & Root LLC pled guilty to participation in a decade-long scheme to bribe Nigerian officials to obtain engineering, procurement, and construction (EPC) contracts, and agreed to pay a $402 million criminal fine and $177 million in disgorgement of profits relating to the bribery scheme.[7] In February 2010, BAE Systems plc agreed to pay $400 million to the DOJ for improper payment activity over the past decade repeatedly involving *inter alia* princes in the Kingdom of Saudi Arabia.[8]

As important as these mega settlements are in conveying how high the *ceiling* can be for DOJ and SEC enforcement penalties in extended bribery schemes, cases such as the often-neglected SEC case of *In the Matter of Delta & Pine Land Company and Turk Deltapine, Inc.*[9] are equally important in guiding multinational general counsel and their outside counsel about the *floor* for FCPA misconduct. In 2007 the SEC settled with the above two Mississippi-based companies that had made improper payments totaling $43,000 in Turkey over a five-year span. Notwithstanding their voluntary disclosure, full cooperation, and the comparatively small amount of improper payments, Delta & Pine Land Company and Turk DeltaPine were fined $300,000 by the SEC. The FCPA resolution with these two companies, which were soon acquired by Monsanto, establishes a low SEC floor for FCPA violations by a public company or a foreign subsidiary—a floor surprising to some multinational general counsel who view $8,600 a year as *de minimis* improper payments.

The second recent trend is increased multi-jurisdictional interest and cooperation in coordinating multinational investigations and simultaneously prosecuting corporations for bribery conduct. In Siemens, the U.S. and German governments worked closely together and announced a combined $1.6 billion plus in fines or restitution the same day. In the February 2010 BAE matter, the British government's Serious Fraud Office (SFO) joined the DOJ and secured a $50 million fine against BAE for misconduct in Tanzania.[10] Today global anti-bribery enforcement is at the point that international cartel enforcement was a decade ago: other nations' law enforcement agencies are learning from and working with U.S. authorities to combat a corruption pandemic, are filing similar bribery charges, and are beginning to seek unprecedented fines in their respective jurisdictions. As a result, multi-jurisdictional bribery investigations, multinational responses, and corporate fines may parallel if not exceed the dramatic rise of the same that anti-cartel enforcers witnessed the past decade.

The third recent trend is the U.S. indictment of former foreign government officials, utilizing federal statutes that, unlike the FCPA, permit the charging of foreign officials. In January 2010 the United States unsealed a 2009 indictment in Los Angeles charging Juthamas Siriwan, the former senior procurement officer for the Tourism Authority of Thailand, with accepting bribes in connection with the Bangkok Film Festival.[11] Specifically, Siriwan was charged with money laundering but not with FCPA violations. In 2009, the DOJ also charged in Florida Robert Antoine and Jean Rene Duperval, former directors for international relations at state-owned Haiti Telco, with conspiracy to commit money laundering[12] in order to obtain various business advantages, including preferred telecommunications rates. Foreign officials should be less sanguine that their misconduct will escape U.S. prosecution, particularly if they travel to and conduct any business in the United States. The U.S. prosecution of foreign officials is likely to increase the spotlight on public corruption in these officials' home lands and, in turn, foster more joint or collaborative U.S.-foreign investigative scrutiny.

The fourth trend is the expansion of SEC liability theories as illustrated by two 2009 enforcement actions. In July 2009, the SEC, in *SEC v. Nature's Sunshine Products, Inc.*, applied the control person doctrine to hold parent senior executives liable for $1 million in improper payments that a Brazilian-based subsidiary made to Brazilian customs agents.[13] Douglas Faggioli and Craig Huff were charged, *inter alia*, with, directly or indirectly, as control persons, failing to make and keep accurate books and records and maintain adequate internal controls for the Brazilian subsidiary, even though the two executives were neither aware of the subsidiary's misconduct nor directly responsible for its records and filings.[14] In December 2009, the SEC, in *SEC v. Bobby Benton*, charged as one theory that a former manager of a subsidiary of a U.S. drilling company offered bribes and that Benton, in an effort to conceal bribes from internal and external auditors, redacted references to the Venezuelan payments in an action plan responding to an internal audit report.[15] Signally, the SEC did not allege that Benton was aware of the improper payments at the time they were made by another in Venezuela or authorized them. Rather, the SEC alleged that Benton did not inform Pride International's management, legal department, or internal auditors of the matter and allowed the false records to remain on the parent's books and records. Both *Nature's Sunshine Products* and *Benton* signal that the SEC is willing to charge parent senior executives with the misdeeds of foreign subsidiary managers, to wit: failing to establish sufficient controls to record transactions properly or allowing false records to remain on a subsidiary's books, even though the executives were not aware of the improper payments at the time and did not authorize them.[16]

The fifth and perhaps most startling trend became apparent in January, 2010 when twenty-two executives and employees of companies in the military and law enforcement products industry were arrested as part of an elaborate FBI undercover sting operation for engaging in schemes to bribe foreign government officials to obtain and retain military and law enforcement equipment business.[17] One undercover agent posed as a representative of the Minister of Defense of a country in Africa. A second undercover agent posed as a procurement officer for Country A's Ministry of Defense who purportedly reported directly to the Minister of Defense.[18] All but one of the defendants were arrested in Las Vegas while attending an industry trade show.[19] The 16 indictments represent the largest single investigation and prosecution against individuals in the history of DOJ's enforcement of the FCPA. In connection with these indictments, approximately 150 FBI agents executed 14 search warrants in locations across the country, including Bull Shoals, Ark.; San Francisco; Miami; Ponte Vedra Beach, Fla.; Sarasota, Fla.; St. Petersburg, Fla.; Sunrise, Fla.; University Park, Fla.; Decatur, Ga.; Stearns, Ky.; Upper Darby, Penn.; and Woodbridge, Va. In addition, the United Kingdom's City of London Police executed seven search warrants in connection with their own investigations into companies involved in the foreign bribery conduct that formed the basis for the American indictments. This type of near year-long sting operation requires enormous law enforcement resources and demonstrates the DOJ's commitment to ferret out foreign bribery, to charge executives and to work with other governments.

The above matters and trends further illustrate how multinational corporations condoning sensitive foreign payments face very costly U.S. and cross-border government investigations, corporate felony convictions, massive fines, disgorgement of profits, and injunctive relief requiring independent monitors.[20] Individuals in the United States and abroad face the increased prospect of FBI sting operations, extradition, prosecution, and very serious incarceration terms. To avoid FCPA liability, general counsel and transactional lawyers need to conduct heightened due diligence for mergers and acquisitions and contracts with third parties, including joint venture partners, agents, consultants, and distributors. The cases also illustrate how especially important compliance and internal controls are in both reducing the risk of improper payments and reducing the fines and penalties if a company is found to have engaged in misconduct.

To effectively represent a client facing potential liability, counsel conducting an FCPA internal investigation or defending a DOJ or SEC investigation must understand the scope of the FCPA and, often, foreign bribery statutes; promptly conduct a thorough but focused investigation, with the flexibility to expand where appropriate; develop appropriate legal and factual defenses; institute appropriate remedial measures; and execute a comprehensive well-planned global strategy. A public company should, upon discovering improper conduct, also weigh the potential benefits of timely voluntary disclosure to and cooperation with the DOJ and SEC and foreign government agencies.

NOTES

1. Foreign Corrupt Practices Act of 1977, Pub. L. No. 95-213, 91 Stat. 1494 (codified as amended at 15 U.S.C. §§ 78m, 78dd-1 to -2, 78ff (1994)) [hereinafter FCPA], as amended by International Anti-Bribery and Fair Competition Act of 1998, 15 U.S.C.A. §§ 78dd-1 to -3, 78ff (1999).

2. 15 U.S.C. § 78m(b)(2)(A), (B).

3. *See* 15 U.S.C. § 78dd-2(d) (injunctions sought by the Attorney General); 15 U.S.C. § 78u(d)(1) (injunctions sought by the SEC).

4. *See also* Ch. 10, I: FCPA Prosecution and Enforcement Action Trends.

5. *See, e.g.,* David Voreacos, Justin Blum and Joshua Gallu, "Daimler Said to Agree to Pay $200 million over Probe." Bloomberg Wire Service, February 12, 2010; and Press Release, Technip Charge for Potential Resolution of the TSKJ Nigeria matter in the U.S. Q4-09 Operating Performance above Expectations (Paris, February 12, 2011) (disclosing exceptional charge of 245 million to resolve TSKJ matter with the U.S. Department of Justice). http://www.technip.com/english/press/articles/2010/2010-02-12.htm.

6. *United States v. Siemens AG*, No. 08-OR-367 (Filed December 15, 2008) (D.D.C. 2008).

7. *United States v. Kellogg, Brown & Root LLC*, H-09-071 (S.D. Tx. February 17, 2009).

8. *United States v. BAE Systems plc.*, 1:10-cr-00035-JDB-1 U.S.D.C. D.D.C. (filed February 5, 2010).

9. SEC Release No. 56138, Administrative Proceeding File No. 3-12712 (July 26, 2007); *SEC v. Delta & Pine Land Co.,* No. 1:07-CV-01352 (RWR) (D.D.C.) (July 25, 2007).

10. Press Release, United Kingdom Serious Fraud Office, BAE Systems plc (February 5, 2010), http://www.sfo.uk/press-room/latest-press-releases/press-releases-2010/bae-systems-plc.

11. *United States v. Juthamas Siriwan and Jittisopa Siriwan,* CR0900081 U.S.D.C. C.D. Cal. (filed January 28, 2009).

12. Press Release, U.S. Dept. of Justice, Two Florida Executives, One Florida Intermediary and Two Former Haitian Government Officials Indicted for Alleged Participation in Foreign Bribery Scheme (December 7, 2009), http://www.justice.gov/pr/December/90-crm-1307-html.

13. *SEC v. Nature's Sunshine Products, Inc., Douglas Faggioli and Craig D. Huff,* Civil No. 2:09CV0672, U.S.D.C. D. Utah. *See* http:www.sec.gov/litigation/complaints/2009/1R21162.htm, Fifth Cause of Action, Control Person Liability for Books and Records Violations and False Filing with the Commission.

14. *SEC v. Bobby Benton,* Civil Action No. 4:09-cv-03963 (S.D. Texas Dec. 11, 2009), SEC Lit. Release No. 21335 (Dec. 14, 2009); http://www.sec.gov/litigation/litreleases/2009/lr21335.htm.

15. *SEC v. Bobby Benton, supra,* Complaint at ¶ 3. *See* http://www.sec.gov/litigation/litreleases/2009/lr21335.htm.

16. *See* notes 13 and 14.

17. Press Release, U.S. Dept. of Justice, Twenty-Two Executives and Employees of Military and Law Enforcement Products Companies Charged in Foreign Bribery Scheme (January 19, 2010), http://www.justice.gov/opa/pr/2010/January/10-crm-048.html.

18. *See, e.g., United States v. Andrew Bigelow,* CR-09-346, U.S.D.C. D.D.C. (J. Leon) Sealed December 11, 2009 indictment at ¶¶ 4-5 filed in open court in January 2010.

19. Diana B. Henriques, *FBI Snares Weapons Executives in Bribery Sting,* N.Y. Times, Jan. 21, 2010, at A3.

20. See Ch. 10, I. *supra* for general FCPA Prosecution and Enforcement Action Trends.

CHAPTER 1

Foreign Corrupt Practices Act Overview

The Foreign Corrupt Practices Act (FCPA)[1] contains two types of provisions: anti-bribery provisions, which prohibit corrupt payments to foreign officials, parties, or candidates to assist in obtaining or retaining business or securing any improper advantage; and recordkeeping and internal controls provisions, which impose certain obligations on all companies whose securities are registered in the United States or that are required to file reports with the Securities and Exchange Commission, regardless of whether or not the companies have foreign operations.

I. ANTI-BRIBERY

A. Application

The FCPA's anti-bribery provisions apply to three categories of persons: (1) "issuers"[2] (or an agent thereof); (2) "domestic concerns"[3] (or an agent thereof); and (3) foreign nationals or businesses[4] (or an agent or national thereof) who take any action in furtherance of a corrupt payment while within the territory of the United States. "Issuer" means any company whose securities are registered in the United States or that is required to file periodic reports with the SEC.[5] "Domestic concern" and "any officer, director, employee or agent of such domestic concern or any stockholder thereof acting on behalf of such domestic concern" mean any individual who is a citizen, national, or resident of the United States and any corporation, partnership, association, joint-stock company, business trust, unincorporated organization, or sole proprietorship that has its principal place of business in the United States, or that is organized under the laws of a state of the United States, or a territory, possession, or commonwealth of the United States.[6] The third category significantly increases the liability of non-U.S. companies and their employees or agents as the FCPA now covers foreign persons who commit bribery on U.S. territory, regardless of whether the person is a resident or does business in the United States.[7]

Issuers and domestic concerns may be held liable for violating the anti-bribery provisions of the FCPA whether or not they took any action in the United States in furtherance of the corrupt foreign payment. Prior to the 1998 FCPA amendments, only issuers and domestic concerns could be held liable, and only if they used the U.S. mails or instrumentalities of interstate commerce in furtherance of the illicit foreign payment. The 1998 amendments expanded the FCPA's jurisdiction to cover corrupt foreign payments outside the United States by U.S. persons without any link to interstate commerce; the FCPA amendments make it illegal for any United States person to violate the FCPA "irrespective of whether such United States person makes use of the mails or any means or instrumentality of interstate commerce in furtherance of [the illegal foreign activity]."[8] Thus, a U.S. company or issuer can be liable for the conduct of overseas employees or agents, even if no money was transferred from the United States and no U.S. person participated in any way in the foreign bribery.

Until 1998, foreign persons were not subject to the anti-bribery provisions unless they were issuers or domestic concerns. The amendments, however, expanded the FCPA to allow for the prosecution of any (foreign) person who takes any act in furtherance of a corrupt payment while in the territory of the United States.[9] The 1998 amendments were passed to implement the Organization for Economic and Cooperative Development (OECD) Convention on Combating Bribery of Foreign Officials in International Business Transactions (the OECD Convention). The legislative history of the 1998 FCPA amendments provides that "the territorial basis for jurisdiction should be broadly interpreted so that an extensive physical connection to the bribery act is not required."[10]

B. Elements

A violation of the anti-bribery prohibition by a person as defined above consists of five elements:

1. A payment, offer, authorization, or promise to pay money or anything of value, directly or through a third party;
2. To (a) any foreign official, (b) any foreign political party or party official, (c) any candidate for foreign political office, (d) any official of a public international organization, or (e) any other person while "knowing" that the payment or promise to pay will be passed on to one of the above;
3. Using an instrumentality of interstate commerce (such as telephone, telex, e-mail, or the mail) by any person (whether U.S. or foreign) or an act outside the United States by a domestic concern or U.S. person, or an act in the United States by a foreign person in furtherance of the offer, payment, or promise to pay;

4. For the corrupt purpose of (a) influencing an official act or decision of that person, (b) inducing that person to do or omit doing any act in violation of his or her lawful duty, (c) securing an improper advantage, or (d) inducing that person to use his influence with a foreign government to affect or influence any government act or decision;

5. In order to assist the company in obtaining or retaining business for or with or directing business to any person.[11]

C. Key Concepts

1. *Offers, Payments, Promises to Pay, or Authorizations of Payments*

A company or person can be liable under the FCPA not only for making improper payments, but also for an offer, promise, or authorization of a corrupt payment, even if the employees or agents do not ultimately make a payment. In other words, a bribe need not actually be paid, and a corrupt act need not succeed in its purpose.

2. *Recipients*

The FCPA prohibition extends only to corrupt payments (or offers, promises to pay, or authorizations of payment) to a foreign official, foreign political party, party official, or a candidate for foreign political office, and any other person while the payer "knows" that the payment or promise to pay will be passed on to one of the above.

a. Foreign Official

The term "foreign official" is defined under the FCPA as "any officer or employee of a foreign government or any department, agency or instrumentality thereof, or of a public international organization, or any person acting in an official capacity or on behalf of any such government, department, agency or instrumentality or for, or on behalf of, any such public international organization."[12] This broad definition is normally considered to encompass executive branch employees, elected legislators or parliamentarians, managers, and, in the view of the Department of Justice and the Securities and Exchange Commission, employees of state-owned enterprises and officials of quasi-governmental entities. For example, the U.S. government charged Dow Chemical with making payments to a key member of a committee in India that determined when certain chemical products would receive government registrations[13] and Monsanto with improper payments to obtain governmental licenses and permits in Indonesia.[14] No court has addressed the breadth of the term "foreign official" in the FCPA context.

The 1998 amendments added "public international organization officials" to the definition of "foreign official." A "public international organization" is defined as "(1) an organization that is designated by Executive Order pursuant to section 288 of title 22; or (2) any other international organization that is designated by the President by Executive Order for the purposes of this section."[15] Examples include the World Bank, the Organization of American States (OAS), and the African Union. The FCPA has long been interpreted to preclude prosecution of foreign officials, party officials, or candidates who are recipients of bribes.[16]

b.   Foreign Political Party, Political Party Official, or Candidate

The FCPA prohibits an illicit offer and payment not only to a foreign official but also to a foreign political party, an official of a foreign political party, or a candidate for foreign office. A potential problem can arise where a U.S. person's foreign agent or partner makes political campaign contributions to persons in the country where they are doing business. A U.S. company should consider instituting a policy that prohibits its foreign agents, partners, or consultants from making any political contributions whatsoever for or on behalf of their venture or relating in any way to a venture. Absent a blanket corporate prohibition, proposed foreign political contributions by an agent, consultant, or employee should be reviewed in advance on a formal, case-by-case basis by a company's legal department or outside counsel.

3.   Money or Anything of Value

The FCPA prohibits paying, offering, or promising to pay (or authorizing to pay or offer) money or making a gift of anything of value. Although neither has the statute defined nor has any FCPA decision addressed the concept of a "thing of value," it certainly includes cash equivalents and other forms of valuable inducements such as travel and travel-related expenses, jewelry, housing expenses, country club memberships, cars, entertainment, shopping excursions, and the hiring of relatives. Federal courts addressing similar domestic bribery statutes have construed the term broadly to include tangible and intangible property such as "information,"[17] the testimony of a witness,[18] loans and promises of future employment,[19] a college scholarship,[20] and sports equipment.[21] In *United States v. King*, the Eighth Circuit found that the planned payment of a $1 million "kiss payment" or "closing cost" to senior Costa Rican officials and political parties to obtain land concessions on which a port development was to be built satisfied the "thing of value" requirement.[22] The FCPA contains no de minimis exception.

4.   Corrupt Intent

To violate the FCPA's anti-bribery provisions, a payment, offer, or promise to pay or making of a gift must be made corruptly. Although the FCPA does not define "corruptly," the legislative history indicates there must be an "evil motive" or purpose or intent to wrongfully influence the recipient to "misuse his official position" in order to wrongfully direct, obtain, or retain business.[23] The history indicates that the motive or purpose is the same as that required under 18 U.S.C. § 201(b), which prohibits domestic bribery.[24]

In *United States v. Liebo*,[25] the Eighth Circuit affirmed the following jury instruction definition of the term "corruptly":

> [T]he offer, promise to pay, payment or authorization of payment, must be intended to induce the recipient to misuse his official position or to influence someone else to do so. . . . [A]n act is "corruptly" done if done voluntarily [a]nd intentionally, and with a bad purpose of accomplishing either an unlawful end or result, or a lawful end or result by some unlawful method or means.[26]

In 2007 the Fifth Circuit upheld the *Liebo* jury instruction definition in *United States v. Kay* (Kay III) and further held that the prosecution must prove both that the defendant knew he was doing something generally "unlawful" and that his misconduct was willful.[27] Willfulness, however, does not require a defendant to have known that he was violating the specific provisions of the law, that is, the FCPA.[28]

Prosecutors invariably look in bribery cases to see if a recipient has personally benefited or whether a target or subject has personally benefited. While there is no such requirement under the FCPA anti-bribery provision, the DOJ in at least one FCPA opinion release has declined to take enforcement action where a recipient has not personally benefited. As to the businessperson paying foreign officials or authorizing a payment, travel, or gift, the DOJ routinely concludes that these subjects or targets maintained their employment, earning a good salary or a bonus, and thus personally benefited. The lack of any personal benefit to the recipient rather than to the businessperson is usually a more successful defense argument.[29]

Although officers and employees routinely reject any suggestion that they acted corruptly or with an evil motive in offering or giving money or things of value to foreign officials, a review of the facts, circumstances, transparency, and motivations surrounding payments or gifts to foreign officials usually proves troublesome. For example, an employee will have difficulty explaining or justifying a substantial cash voucher and payment or gift to a midlevel foreign government official whom he has only met once or twice in his life. Still, there are many gift, travel, lodging, and entertainment investigations involving relatively small amounts of cash or gifts where lack of a corrupt intent may be the most viable defense to otherwise indisputable periodic gifts or significant payments to local officials.

5.   *Business Purpose Test*

The FCPA prohibits payments, offers, or promises to pay made in order to assist a company in obtaining or retaining business for or with, or directing business to, any person. Business to be obtained or retained does not need to be with a foreign government or foreign government instrumentality. As a result of the 1998 amendments, the FCPA now prohibits payments to foreign officials for the purpose of securing "any improper advantage" in obtaining or retaining business. Although it remains unclear what conduct falls within the scope of this language, it certainly can include payments to foreign customs and tax officials.

The leading FCPA business purpose decision is *United States v. Kay*[30] (Kay II), in which the Fifth Circuit reversed a district court dismissal of an indictment that charged a businessman with bribing a Haitian official to understate customs duties and sales taxes on rice shipped to Haiti, to assist American Rice, Inc. in obtaining or retaining business. The district court ruled that as a matter of law, illicit payments to foreign officials to avoid portions of customs duties and sales taxes were not the type of bribes that the FCPA criminalizes. On appeal, the Fifth Circuit found that such bribes *could* (but do not necessarily) come within the ambit of the FCPA, but "[i]t still must be shown that the bribery was intended to produce an effect—here, through tax savings—that would assist in obtaining or retaining business."[31] In other words, bribes need not, in order to obtain or retain business, be direct payments to government officials to win contracts. Local bribes to tax or customs officials that enable companies to compete with other companies can satisfy the "retain business" language of the FCPA.

In remanding the case, the Fifth Circuit indicated that the prosecution would have to prove that the defendant intended for the foreign official's anticipated conduct in consideration of a bribe (the "quid pro quo") to produce an anticipated result, in this case a diminution of customs duties and sales taxes that would assist in obtaining or retaining business.[32] The United States filed a superseding indictment repeating the original twelve counts but also charging both defendants with conspiracy to violate the FCPA and one defendant with obstruction of justice for making false statements to the SEC during its investigation. A jury found defendants guilty on all counts. On appeal, the Fifth Circuit held that the defendants failed to establish that the FCPA and the district court's application of it did not provide them fair notice of the proscribed conduct, and upheld the convictions (Kay III).[33]

6.   *Knowledge*

The FCPA does not require proof of actual knowledge that a payment to or promise to pay an intermediary will be passed on to a foreign official. A person may be liable on the basis of constructive knowledge. In addressing the knowledge requirement, the FCPA states:

> (2)(A) A person's state of mind is "knowing" with respect to conduct, a circumstance, or a result if—
>
> (i) such person is aware that such person is engaging in such conduct, that such circumstance exists, or that such result is substantially certain to occur; or
>
> (ii) such person has a firm belief that such circumstance exists or that such result is substantially certain to occur.[34]

When knowledge of the existence of a particular circumstance is required for an offense, such knowledge is established if a person is aware of a high probability of the existence of such circumstance, unless the person actually believes that such circumstance does not exist.[35]

The FCPA's legislative history speaks of "willful blindness," "deliberate ignorance" and taking a "head-in-the-sand" attitude as constituting knowledge under the statute. Individuals or corporations who consciously disregard or deliberately ignore known circumstances that should have put them on notice of an improper payment may be prosecuted for knowing that a payment would be passed on to a foreign official. The requisite state of mind in light of the legislative history requires either direct or actual knowledge, or a "conscious purpose to avoid learning the truth."[36]

7.   *Use of Third Parties*

A company may be liable for a payment by an agent or third party if the company authorized such payment or if it "knew" the improper payment would be made. Many companies regularly employ or contract with third parties, such as sales or marketing agents, consultants, joint venture partners, consortium partners, freight forwarders, customs agents, law firms, accountants, distributors, and resellers. These relationships can greatly increase FCPA risks, which usually arise in one of two ways: (1) a third party makes improper payments to government officials, or (2) a third party is owned by or affiliated with a government official.[37]

A company is deemed to have knowledge of an offer, promise to pay, or payment if it is aware of a "high probability" that such an offer, promise, or payment will be made.[38] This risk of vicarious liability means that companies and employees subject to the FCPA must undertake significant steps to minimize the risks of becoming liable due to actions by agents or third parties.

8. Instrumentalities

The FCPA defines a foreign official as "any officer or employee of a foreign government or any department, agency or *instrumentality* thereof."[39] It further prohibits payments to foreign officials to induce them to use their influence with a foreign government or *instrumentality* thereof to affect or influence any act or decision of such government or *instrumentality*.[40] (Emphases supplied.)

a. Instrumentality

Nowhere does the statute define "instrumentality" or provide guidance about what types of partially state-owned entities are foreign government "instrumentalities" such that their employees are foreign officials. Multinational companies often deal with foreign government partners, for example, joint ventures doing business with state-owned enterprises including oil, steel, telecommunication, and transportation companies.[41] For example, it is currently estimated that 75 percent of all oil and gas reserves in the world are owned in whole or in part by state-owned entities. Further, some foreign governments are investing in minority interests in foreign ventures, muddling the instrumentality issue even further, while other governments are investing in second- or third-tier state-owned subsidiaries. In the current economic crisis where governments are assuming majority interests in financially strapped major banks, it is very possible that improper payments to heretofore private banking officials may come within the jurisdiction of the FCPA. Neither the DOJ nor the SEC has distinguished between foreign companies that are majority owned or controlled by foreign governments and those that are minority owned. Whether the latter should be considered an instrumentality under the FCPA remains an open and untested question.[42]

Another foreign-conduct-directed statute and the U.S. anti-boycott regulations give some guidance on the likely breadth of the term "instrumentality." First, the Foreign Sovereign Immunities Act of 1976,[43] enacted one year before the FCPA, defines "an agency or instrumentality of a foreign state" as an entity that is "a separate legal person or otherwise," and "which is an organ of a foreign state or political subdivision thereof, or a majority of whose shares or other ownership interest is owned by a foreign or political subdivision thereof."[44]

Second, under the U.S. anti-boycott regulations, a state-owned enterprise will be presumed governmental if:

- The foreign government entity owns or controls, directly or indirectly, more than 50 percent of the voting rights;
- The foreign government owns or controls 25 percent or more of the voting securities, and no other entity or person owns or controls an equal or larger percentage;

- A majority of members of the board are also members of the governing body of the government department;
- The foreign government has the authority to appoint the majority of the members of the board; or
- The foreign government has the authority to appoint the Chief Operating Officer.

An entity majority-owned or controlled by a foreign government will very likely be considered an "instrumentality" for FCPA purposes.[45]

b.   Sovereign Wealth Funds

A sovereign wealth fund (SWF) is a state-owned investment fund composed of financial assets such as stocks, bonds, property, precious metals, or other financial instruments. The original SWF is the Kuwait Investment Fund, an entity created in 1953 from vast oil revenues. SWFs are typically created for governments with surpluses and little or no international debt. Major SWFs include the Abu Dhabi Investment Authority, the Government Pension Fund of Norway, Government of Singapore Investment Corporation, Kuwait Investment Authority, China Investment Corporation, Singapore's Temasek Holdings, and Qatar Investment Authority. Investment goals, internal checks and balances, and disclosure of relationships are of concern with SWFs for FCPA purposes. Absent exceptional facts or circumstances, an SWF will be deemed an instrumentality under the FCPA.

9.   Authorization

The FCPA prohibits the "authorization of the payment of any money, or offer, gift, promise to give, or authorization of the giving of anything of value"[46] to foreign officials for improper purposes. This language applies to issuers, domestic concerns and individuals, and foreign firms or individuals who engage in acts in furtherance of improper payments while in the territory of the United States. The statute does not define "authorization," but the legislative history makes clear that authorization can be either implicit or explicit. Authorization issues frequently arise when U.S. companies fund overseas operations, approve budgets, and take similar actions with respect to foreign subsidiaries or joint ventures. In suspicious circumstances, U.S. directors and managers should disavow any possible improper payments and take affirmative steps to avoid even the appearance of acquiescence.[47]

10.   Permissible Payments and Affirmative Defenses

a.   Facilitating Payment Exception for Routine Governmental Actions

As a result of the 1998 amendments, the FCPA provides an exception for so-called "facilitating," "expediting," or "grease" payments to low-level foreign officials who perform "routine governmental actions."[48] The purpose of this exception is to avoid FCPA liability where small sums are paid to facilitate certain routine, nondiscretionary government functions such as the processing of permits, licenses, visas, work orders, or other official documents; providing police protection, power and water supply, cargo handling, or protection of perishable products; and scheduling inspections associated with contract performance or transit of goods across the country.[49] "Routine governmental actions" do not include decisions by foreign officials to award new business or to continue business with a particular party.[50] While the FCPA may exempt facilitating payments, many foreign countries do not, and some multinational companies have decided as a matter of policy to bar all facilitating payments.

b.   Affirmative Defenses

The 1998 FCPA amendments incorporated two affirmative defenses to the anti-bribery provisions. First, the FCPA provides an affirmative defense where the payment, gift, offer, or promise of anything of value at issue was permitted by the written laws of the foreign official's or political candidate's country.[51] Second, an affirmative defense exists where a payment, gift, offer, or promise of anything of value was for "reasonable and bona fide" expenditures related to the execution or performance of a contract with a foreign government or agency thereof, or the promotion, demonstration, or explanation of products or services.[52] For each of these affirmative defenses, the company or its officers or employees bears the burden of establishing in the first instance facts underlying the affirmative defense.

i. Written Laws of Foreign Country   A person charged with an anti-bribery violation may assert as an affirmative defense that the payment was lawful under the written laws and regulations of the foreign country. Expatriates frequently assert that bribery is permitted and recognized in the host or work country. However, no country's laws expressly permit bribery, and absent a written law or regulation, this affirmative defense fails.

The issue of what constitutes a payment permissible under the laws of a country to a commercial agent or government official can, in select circumstances, be a matter of significant debate. Although no country has "written laws" permitting bribery, it is far less clear whether a payment to a government official who can, under local law, undertake commercial activities constitutes a permissible payment under the FCPA. Similarly, a political contribution that is legal under foreign law may make a payment permissible. However, if an actor makes a foreign political contribution with a corrupt intent, for example, to obtain or retain business, the mere fact that a sizeable political contribution is lawful in the foreign country will not negate an offense under U.S. law. The extent of a transaction or payment's transparency will in many cases determine whether the DOJ prosecutes or the SEC files an enforcement action.

ii. Reasonable and Bona Fide Expenditures   An affirmative defense to an anti-bribery violation also exists where a payment, offer, or promise of anything of value was a reasonable and bona fide expenditure, such as travel and lodging expenses incurred by or on behalf of a foreign official, party official, or candidate, and was related to the promotion, demonstration, or explanation of products or services; or the execution or performance of a contract with a foreign government or agency.

Thus, a company may pay the reasonable, necessary, and bona fide expenses of government officials who are brought to a corporate location to inspect equipment or facilities in connection with a potential sale of the equipment or facilities. Similarly, U.S. persons may cover the reasonable expenditures involved in bringing foreign officials to review and/or approve contractual work (e.g., fabrication of equipment at other locations). A side trip to a resort en route to a corporate location, or payment for the travel of a foreign official's spouse, is not reasonable, necessary, or bona fide.

The reasonable expenses affirmative defense does not give companies carte blanche to pay travel expenses for government officials. In a 1999 civil enforcement action, the DOJ took the position that a U.S. company, Metcalf & Eddy, Inc., violated the FCPA by providing an Egyptian official and his family with first-class air travel to the United States and with food, lodging, and other expenses because the purpose of the visit allegedly was to influence the official to use his authority to help direct a United States Agency for International Development contract award to Metcalf & Eddy. The DOJ alleged, among other things, that the Egyptian official received 150 percent of the estimated per diem expenses in a lump-sum payment and then was not required to pay for any of his expenses while in the United States. Metcalf & Eddy settled the case with a consent decree, without admitting or denying culpability, and agreed to pay a $400,000 civil fine as well as $50,000 to reimburse the U.S. government for the cost of the investigation.[53]

Counsel for companies considering the payment of travel expenses for foreign government officials should scrutinize the proposed travel carefully to ensure that it falls within the confines of this affirmative defense and is not a disguised attempt to provide compensation for help in securing business. Some companies compare the proposed government travel expense to their own employee travel reimbursement policies and only approve foreign government official travel expenses that are consistent with employee travel policies.

D. Commercial Bribery

The FCPA anti-bribery provisions do not govern or prohibit bribes paid to officers or employees of wholly private, nongovernmental entities. The provisions apply only to improper payments made, directly or indirectly, to a foreign official, foreign political party or official thereof, or foreign political candidate in order to obtain or retain business or to direct business to any business or to secure an improper advantage.[54] However, commercial bribery payments that are mischaracterized or undercharacterized on the books and records of a public company may constitute FCPA books and records or internal controls violations. In addition, the DOJ has charged private improper payments or kickbacks along with public official bribes in FCPA cases[55] under the general conspiracy statute[56] and the Travel Act.[57] It has also required in some deferred prosecution agreements that the company not engage in acts of commercial bribery.

II. RECORDKEEPING AND INTERNAL CONTROLS

In addition to the anti-bribery provisions, the FCPA imposes recordkeeping and internal controls requirements on issuers (not on domestic concerns or other persons). Essentially, these requirements mandate that publicly traded companies keep accurate books and records and sound systems of internal controls. Neither the recordkeeping nor the internal controls provisions limit themselves to transactions above a certain amount or impose a materiality requirement. The FCPA accounting provisions are primarily enforced by the SEC,[58] but the DOJ can bring criminal charges of knowing circumvention of internal controls as well as the knowing falsification of books, records, and accounts.[59] The SEC can bring civil accounting provision enforcement actions where the burden of proof is preponderance of the evidence and there is no scienter requirement. While the DOJ has exclusive jurisdiction to prosecute criminal violations of the FCPA, both the DOJ and the SEC may obtain injunctive relief to prevent bribery and recordkeeping violations of the Act.[60]

The rationale behind the books and records and internal controls provisions being complementary to the anti-bribery provisions was explained by Stanley Sporkin, the former federal judge and SEC Enforcement Director who played a major role in drafting the FCPA legislation in the 1970s. According to Judge Sporkin, the SEC proposed the recordkeeping and financial control provisions because investigations had revealed that companies that paid bribes overseas never accurately recorded the illicit transactions on their books. Instead, companies had concealed the bribes by falsely describing the payments as other transactions. Judge Sporkin theorized "that requiring the disclosure of all bribes paid would, in effect, foreclose that activity."[61]

A. Application

The recordkeeping and internal controls provisions of the FCPA apply to issuers, those companies whose securities are registered with the SEC, or those who are required to file reports with the SEC, pursuant to the Securities Exchange Act of 1934, regardless of whether they have any foreign operations.[62]

B. Recordkeeping Provisions

1. *"Records"*

The FCPA requires every issuer to "make and keep books, records, and accounts which, in reasonable detail, accurately and fairly reflect the transactions and dispositions of the assets."[63] The Act broadly defines "records" to include "accounts, correspondence, memorandums, tapes, discs, papers, books, and other documents or transcribed information of any type."[64] "Reasonable detail" means such level of detail as would satisfy prudent officials in the conduct of their own affairs.[65] There is no materiality requirement for a books and records violation.[66] An individual or entity may be criminally liable if he knowingly falsifies a book, record, or account.[67] However, inadvertent mistakes will not give rise to enforcement actions or prosecutions.[68]

In *United States v. Jensen,*[69] the Northern District of California rejected a defendant's argument that the "books and records" statute was too vague and did not give a person of ordinary intelligence fair notice of what is proscribed. The defendant, a corporate human-resources director, had falsified minutes of a committee meeting during which stock option grants had been discussed. In dismissing the "void for vagueness" argument as applied to these facts, the district court ruled that "helping to create false committee meeting minutes that have the effect of understating corporate expenses constitutes the falsification of a record that 'reflects the transactions and dispositions of the assets of the issuer.'"[70]

Recordkeeping violations normally involve three types of offenses:

1. Records that simply fail to record improper transactions at all, for example, off-the-books transactions such as bribes and kickbacks;
2. Records that are falsified to disguise aspects of improper transactions otherwise recorded correctly; and
3. Records that correctly set forth the quantitative aspects of transactions but fail to record the qualitative aspects of the transactions that would reveal their illegality or impropriety, such as the true purpose of particular payments to agents, distributors, or customers.[71]

To establish an FCPA violation, it is not necessary that the inaccurately recorded transactions in question be material under federal securities laws.

2. *Examples of Transactions That Accounting Records May Fail
    to Adequately or Accurately Disclose*

- Substantial payments to mid- or high-level foreign government officials
- "Facilitating payments" to low-level foreign government officials
- Commercial bribes or kickbacks
- Political contributions
- Charitable contributions
- Smuggling activities
- Income tax violations
- Customs or currency violations
- Extraordinary gifts

3. *Foreign Subsidiaries*

An issuer can violate the books and records provisions if a majority-owned foreign subsidiary creates false records to conceal an illicit payment, and the issuer parent then incorporates the subsidiary's information into its books and records. For example, in 2000 the SEC brought a books and records action against IBM Corp. related to "presumed illicit payments" to foreign officials by one of IBM's wholly owned subsidiaries. The SEC alleged that IBM-Argentina paid money to a subcontractor, which payment in turn was given to certain foreign officials. The SEC charged that IBM-Argentina's then-senior management overrode IBM procurement and contracting procedures and fabricated documentation to conceal the details of the subcontract. IBM-Argentina allegedly recorded the payments to the subcontractor as third-party subcontractor expenses, and IBM incorporated this information into the Form 10-K it filed with the SEC in 1994. Without admitting or denying the SEC's allegations, IBM consented to the entry of a cease-and-desist order and agreed to pay a $300,000 civil penalty.[72] The IBM settlement with the SEC was unusual in that it did not include an internal controls violation. The accounting provisions of the FCPA do not normally apply when the issuer holds 50 percent or less interest in the foreign entity.[73] However, when an issuer holds 50 percent or less interest, it must "proceed in good faith to use its influence to the extent reasonable under the circumstances to cause [the affiliate] to devise and maintain a system of internal controls"[74] consistent with the accounting and recordkeeping provisions. Where it demonstrates good-faith efforts to influence the internal controls system of the affiliate, it enjoys a conclusive presumption that it has complied with books, records and accounting provisions of the statute.[75]

C. Internal Controls

The FCPA's internal controls provisions codify existing auditing standards[76] and require issuers to devise and maintain a system of internal accounting controls sufficient to provide reasonable assurances that:

(1) transactions are executed in accordance with management's general or specific authorization;

(2) transactions are recorded as necessary:

    (a) to permit preparation of financial statements in conformity with generally accepted accounting principles or any other criteria applicable to such statements; and

    (b) to maintain accountability for assets;

(3) access to assets is permitted only in accordance with management's general or specific authorization; and

(4) the recorded accountability for assets is compared with the existing assets at reasonable intervals and appropriate action is taken with respect to any differences.[77]

"Reasonable assurances" means such degree of assurance as would satisfy prudent officials in the conduct of their own affairs.[78]

Signally, the FCPA does not mandate "any particular kind of internal controls systems."[79] Rather, the test for compliance is "whether a system, taken as a whole, reasonably meets the statute's specified objectives."[80] Because there are no specific standards by which to evaluate the sufficiency of controls, any evaluation is a highly subjective process.[81]

Still, in conducting an FCPA controls assessment, one should evaluate: (1) the industry(ies) the company is in; (2) the countries where the company does business; (3) whether customers in those countries are state-owned or state-controlled entities; and (4) the company's business model.[82]

Certain industries, such a energy, health, and chemicals industries, have long presented anti-bribery challenges. However, recent DOJ and SEC enforcement actions make clear that no industry is immune from FCPA investigation or prosecution. Importantly, multinational companies must examine not only their own industry, but also the nature of the logistics services it requires and the companies that provide such services, as there is risk that multinationals may knowingly use vendors and service providers to handle more problematic local government tasks.

Companies that do business in geographic locations where corruption risks are high require a stronger level of internal controls for those operations. The *Transparency International* Corruption Perception Index ranks each of 180 countries from 1 to 10 (see Chapter 5), and multinationals must consider the countries or regions where corruption risk profiles are substantial. Controls for countries or regions with high-risk profiles require greater oversight of accounting and purchasing functions. Internal audits and FCPA audits should also be undertaken with greater frequency in high-risk countries.

Many multinational companies such as pharmaceuticals or energy companies find foreign governments their largest customers or partners in certain regions. Where potential customers or partners are state-owned or state-controlled entities, companies must be not only careful in the direct procurement process, but also with travel, lodging, and entertainment related to customer product or services demonstrations. Controls should be established to identify all government-related customers, to identify customers' expenses, and to ensure appropriate advance authorizations and proper recordkeeping.

A company's particular business model may necessitate additional internal controls. For example, if a company employs a limited sales force and relies largely on distributors, it will have to address the distributor risks and evaluate their background, draft contracts with FCPA warranties and representations, and monitor their activities on an ongoing basis. If it uses consultants or marketing personnel as "agents" to help develop business, that model significantly increase FCPA risks. Policies and procedures for conducting thorough due diligence and the retention of consultants, agents, and distributors should be developed and implemented. A due diligence file should be created to ensure and record a solid understanding of the background of the agent, contractor, distributor, or vendor engaged to represent the company. Ongoing due diligence is also an important internal control. For example, documentation of payments to agents (such as banking details) should be compiled during contracting and compared to payment instructions received with invoices from the third party to ensure discrepancies do not exist.

If a company's business model invoices substantial customer travel and entertainment, such budgets and related policies must be carefully reviewed and monitored (see Chapter 4). Other practices occasionally unique to certain industries, such as charitable or political contributions, should consider prior approval and monitoring of related general ledger accounts (see Chapter 7).

If a company operates in a highly regulated industry, e.g., pharmaceuticals or state-owned telecommunications, specific internal controls should be implemented regarding licenses, permits, and other approvals (see Chapter 5). Companies that regularly engage in mergers and acquisitions must implement detailed due diligence practices and preserve a record of the same. Day One Compliance plans should be organized well in advance for any new acquisitions or joint venture operations.

The senior management of companies committed to compliance analyze their particular risks and their industry's risks, implement controls to reduce the same, consider the "best practice" internal controls of others in the industry(ies), constantly reassess their control environment, and establish clear controls for mergers and acquisitions.

A person or entity may be criminally liable if he or it knowingly circumvents or knowingly fails to implement an internal accounting controls system.[83] No criminal liability, however, is imposed for insignificant or technical accounting errors.[84] One highly respected FCPA commentator, Stuart H. Deming, has observed that the internal controls provisions will always be applied in hindsight, where they are rarely found to be adequate.[85] Where an issuer holds 50 percent or less of the voting power with respect to a foreign or domestic firm, the FCPA requires only that the issuer proceed in good faith to cause the affiliate to devise and maintain a system of internal accounting controls to the extent reasonable under the circumstances.[86]

III.   CONSPIRACY

A.   General Conspiracy Statute: 18 U.S.C. § 371

The DOJ's Fraud Section frequently includes a conspiracy count in FCPA prosecutions under the federal general conspiracy statute (18 U.S.C. § 371). The statute provides:

> If two or more persons conspire either to commit any offense against the United States, or to defraud the United States, or any agency thereof in any manner or for any purpose, and one or more of such persons do not act to effect the object of the conspiracy, each shall be fined under this title or imprisoned not more than five years, or both.
>
> If, however, the offense, the commission of which is the object of the conspiracy, is a misdemeanor only, the punishment for such conspiracy shall not exceed the maximum punishment for such misdemeanor.[87]

This statute addresses two types of conspiracies: (1) conspiracies to commit violations of specific federal statutes (the "offense clause"), and (2) conspiracies to defraud the United States (the "defraud clause"). In the FCPA area the United States typically charges the "offense clause" conspiracy, and specifically, a conspiracy to violate the anti-bribery section of the FCPA. On occasion, the United States will charge a conspiracy to violate the FCPA and another statute, such as the wire fraud statute.[88]

B.   Elements

The four elements of the general conspiracy statute are:

1. An agreement by two or more persons,
2. To commit the unlawful object of the conspiracy,
3. With knowledge of the conspiracy and with actual participation in the conspiracy, and
4. At least one co-conspirator committed one overt act in furtherance of the conspiracy.[89]

To sustain a conviction, the government must prove that a defendant knew of the conspiracy and its essential objective(s). The essence of the crime of conspiracy is the agreement and not the commission of an objective substantive crime.[90] The government need not prove that the victim of the conspiracy lost money or that the defendant intended that the victim lose money.[91]

C. Agreement

The essence of a conspiracy is an agreement to commit an unlawful act.[92] The offense of conspiracy necessarily involves an agreement by at least two persons.[93] The courts are split over whether a corporation may conspire with its officers and employees.[94] A corporation may be indicted as a co-conspirator,[95] and the acquittal of a corporation's employee of conspiracy does not require acquittal of the corporation.[96] Proof of conspiratorial conduct is frequently established by circumstantial evidence.[97]

D. Overt Act

The crime of general conspiracy[98] is not complete until an overt act has been committed.[99] The overt act need not be a crime.[100] For example, it may consist of merely purchasing office supplies, opening a bank account, or transmitting an e-mail as long as that act is in furtherance of the conspiracy.

E. Government Advantages in Charging the General Conspiracy Statute

The government gains considerable advantage by including a conspiracy count in a criminal case. First, the ongoing nature of conspiracy lends itself to expansive drafting, particularly in temporal terms. Conspiracies frequently are alleged to have continued for years and occasionally decades. Second, the breadth and vagueness of a conspiracy count allow the admission of much proof that might otherwise be inadmissible. Third, a conspiracy count enables the government to broadly join persons and allegations. A conspiracy can allege an agreement to defraud multiple entities, individuals, and companies or both the government (e.g., the Securities and Exchange Commission) and private entities and individuals. Fourth, evidentiary rules with respect to co-conspirator declarations enlarge the admissibility of often-damaging statements in conspiracy trials.[101] Fifth, because conspiracy is a continuing crime, its five-year statute of limitations does not begin to run until either the conspiracy's objectives are met,[102] the conspiracy is abandoned,[103] its members affirmatively withdraw,[104] or the last overt act committed in furtherance of the conspiracy occurs.[105]

IV. OTHER FEDERAL STATUTES USED BY THE FRAUD SECTION OF THE CRIMINAL DIVISION IN FCPA ENFORCEMENT INVESTIGATIONS

The DOJ Fraud Section not only charges the FCPA and the federal conspiracy statute,[106] but has also used the false statements,[107] money laundering,[108] mail fraud,[109] and wire fraud[110] statutes in FCPA prosecutions. In addition, it increasingly corroborates with the Antitrust Division to investigate price-fixing or bid-rigging violations[111] and also pursues tax[112] and export[113] violations. The conspiracy statute in particular enables the government to charge relevant conduct five or more years old.

V. STATUTE OF LIMITATIONS

A. General Five-Year Statute

The statute of limitations for most noncapital federal offenses,[114] including mail and wire fraud,[115] securities fraud,[116] and the FCPA is five years.[117] General conspiracy charges[118] have a five-year limitation unless the alleged conspiracy involves a substantive offense that has a different limitation provision.[119] A charge of conspiracy to commit a substantive offense cannot have a longer statute of limitations from that provided for the substantive offense itself.[120]

B. Conspiracy

The most important "continuing offense doctrine" exception involves conspiracy prosecutions. FCPA indictments typically include a conspiracy count.[121] A conspiracy ends when the central criminal purpose of the conspiracy has been attained.[122] The Supreme Court has held that in these prosecutions, "the period of limitation must be computed from the dates of the overt act rather than the formation of the conspiracy . . . where, during the existence of the conspiracy, there are successive acts, the period of limitation must be computed from the last of them."[123] The fact that the conspiracy began outside the limitations period will not prevent prosecution as long as at least one overt act in furtherance of the conspiracy occurred within five years of the indictment.[124]

Acts of concealment, without more, will generally not "extend the life of the conspiracy after its main objective has been obtained."[125] In addressing statute of limitations challenges, many courts, particularly in Sherman Act prosecutions, have focused on and upheld conspiracies through the point of receipt of economic benefits.[126] Courts have attempted to distinguish between overt acts in furtherance of a conspiracy and the result of a conspiracy.[127] To escape continuing liability for a conspiracy, a co-conspirator must unequivocally and affirmatively withdraw.[128] Mere cessation of participation is not enough to constitute withdrawal.[129] The burden of proof is generally on a defendant to establish withdrawal.[130]

C. Potential Three-Year Suspension of Limitations to Obtain Foreign Evidence

If in an FCPA criminal investigation the DOJ seeks evidence located in a foreign country, the running of the statute of limitations may be suspended for a period of up to three years.[131] The United States may, before the return of an indictment, apply to the grand jury supervisory court to suspend the running of the statute of limitations. To suspend the statute, the district court must find by a preponderance of the evidence that an official request has been made for evidence located in a foreign country and that it reasonably appears, or reasonably appeared at the time the request was made, that such evidence is, or was, in a foreign country.[132]

The period of suspension begins when the official request is made and ends when the foreign court or authority takes final action on the request. In no event may the suspension exceed three years, or extend the period within which a criminal case must be initiated for more than six months if all foreign authorities take final action on the request before the period would expire.[133] "Official request" as used in this context means a letter rogatory, a request under a treaty or convention, or any other request for evidence made by a court of the United States or an authority of the United States having criminal law enforcement responsibility, to a court or other authority of a foreign country.[134]

D. Extensions of the Statute of Limitation

Near the eve of the expiration of a statute of limitations, prosecutors often will advise defense counsel that in the absence of a written waiver and tolling agreement, the government will file a complaint or return an indictment against the client. Under such threat, counsel must evaluate all facts and circumstances of the investigation and the prosecutor's intentions and decide whether a waiver or tolling agreement is appropriate. If a company is generally cooperating with the DOJ, it will be difficult for it to refuse an extension of the statute of limitations, as often the government will have sufficient evidence to return a charge against the company based on the conduct of one or more employees or agents. For this reason, companies usually accede to a government request for a limited or reasonable extension of the statute.

However, if counsel concludes that the government has not conducted anywhere near an adequate investigation and probably is not likely to file charges despite the threat, an individual client may elect to refuse to enter into a tolling agreement. If counsel concludes that the government remains truly open about whether to file criminal charges, the client may be wise to consent to an extension. By agreeing to a limited waiver, a target or subject may establish goodwill with the government and pave the way for a noncriminal disposition of the case.

From an evidentiary point of view, an extension generally will not disadvantage a client, because the passage of time generally favors the defense.[135] If a client agrees to execute a limited waiver or extension, it should not agree to any waiver of defenses that may exist as of the date of execution of the tolling agreement.

VI.   PENALTIES, FINES, AND OTHER SANCTIONS

A. Criminal Penalties

The FCPA is a criminal statute for which sentences of individuals and corporations are considered in the context of the United States Sentencing Guidelines.[136] Individuals who commit willful violations of the FCPA anti-bribery provisions may be punished by up to $250,000 in fines and/or five years of imprisonment.[137] Individuals who violate the FCPA accounting provisions may be fined up to $5,000,000 and imprisoned for up to 20 years.[138] Corporations may be fined up to $2,500,000 per violation of the FCPA accounting provisions[139] and $2,000,000 for violation of the FCPA anti-bribery provisions.[140] Moreover, under the Alternative Fines Act, fines for both individuals and corporations can be much higher: the fine may be up to twice the amount of loss to the victim or benefit the defendant obtained or sought to obtain by making the corrupt payment.[141] In practice, Alternative Fines Act fines often exceed the statutory maximum fine in significant FCPA cases.

The 1998 amendments eliminated a disparity in penalties between U.S. nationals who are employees or agents of issuers or domestic concerns and foreign nationals who are employees or agents of issuers or domestic concerns. Previously, foreign nationals were subject only to FCPA civil penalties. Now, both U.S. and foreign persons may be prosecuted and face criminal penalties.[142]

Any property, real or personal, "which constitutes or is derived from proceeds traceable to a violation of the FCPA, or a conspiracy to violate the FCPA," may be forfeited.[143] Fines imposed on individuals may not be paid by their employer or principal.[144] An unlawful payment under the FCPA is not deductible under U.S. tax laws as a business expense.[145]

B. Civil Penalties

The FCPA also allows a civil penalty of up to $10,000 against any firm that violates the anti-bribery provisions of the FCPA, and against any officer, director, employee, or agent of a firm who willfully violates the anti-bribery provisions of the Act.[146] The SEC may bring an enforcement action seeking an additional fine, depending on the circumstances, of up to $500,000 on the gain obtained as a result of the violation.[147]

C. Disgorgement of Profit and Prejudgment Interest

Beginning in mid-2004, the SEC began seeking disgorgement of profits and prejudgment interest in FCPA cases. The government first obtained this type of relief in an FCPA proceeding in *SEC v. ABB Ltd.*[148] where a Swiss-based global provider of power and automation technologies agreed to pay $5.9 million in disgorgement of profits. Since 2004, the SEC has regularly sought this relief from issuers, like ABB Ltd., that trade in the United States through American Depositary Receipts (ADRs).

D. Government Suspension and Debarment Sanctions

1. *United States*

Public procurement projects are a substantial revenue source for many multinational companies. A company found in violation of the FCPA may also be suspended or barred from federal programs such as Defense Department procurement programs, the Commodity Futures Trading Commission, and the Overseas Private Investment Corporation.[149] A suspension by one U.S. government agency generally has government-wide effect.[150] Indictment alone can lead to the suspension of the right to do business with the U.S. government. Other potential collateral consequences for FCPA violations include ineligibility to receive export licenses, and SEC suspension and debarment from the securities industry.[151]

2. *European Union—Article 45*

In 2004, the European Union implemented mandatory debarment provisions under its Public Procurement Directive.[152] Specifically, Article 45 provides that "any candidate or tenderer who has been the subject of conviction by final judgment of which the contracting authority is aware . . . shall be excluded from participation in a public contract."[153] It is widely believed that the record-setting Siemens $1.6 billion settlement with the U.S. and German governments carefully avoided a bribery conviction of the parent company and pleas by any European Community subsidiaries in order to avoid a corruption conviction and a mandatory debarment under Article 45 of the EU Directive.[154]

VII.   DOJ FCPA OPINION LETTERS

In 1980, the Department of Justice instituted an FCPA review or opinion procedure,[155] and in 1992 it published a final rule[156] that enables public companies and all domestic concerns to obtain an enforcement opinion of the Attorney General as to whether prospective conduct conforms with the DOJ's enforcement policy regarding the anti-bribery provisions of the FCPA. Under this procedure, a request must relate to an actual transaction and not a hypothetical one. It also must be prospective, that is, made prior to the requestor's commitment to proceed with a transaction.[157] The request must be specific and furnish "all relevant and material information bearing on the conduct . . . and on the circumstances of the prospective conduct."[158]

A favorable opinion from the DOJ creates a rebuttable presumption, applicable in any subsequent enforcement action, that the conduct described in the request conformed with the FCPA. In considering the presumption, a court will weigh all relevant factors, including whether the submission to the Attorney General was accurate and complete and whether the actual conduct diverged from that described in the request. An FCPA opinion provides a safe harbor only to the requestor and affords no protection to any party that did not join in the request.[159]

While many of the early FCPA opinions involved minor gifts or payments, a number of the opinions have addressed issues that multinational corporations routinely encounter, including marketing representative agreements with foreign state-owned enterprises,[160] payments to foreign officials during a leave of absence,[161] joint ventures with a foreign company that has numerous agent agreements,[162] and a foreign official as a shareholder and chairman or consortium member.[163] The opinions can provide guidance to companies entertaining mergers, acquisitions, or divestitures.[164] While the opinions provide protection only to specific requestors, many contain terms and language useful to contemplated contractual relationships with third parties.

Since 1980 the DOJ has released 51 opinions pursuant to this review procedure. The reluctance of corporations to use the FCPA opinion procedure has been attributed to the risk of the loss of confidentiality, the possibility of negative results, government delays in issuing opinions, and the risk of instigating further government investigation.[165] Although one might anticipate that the 1998 amendments would have spawned greater use of the FCPA opinion procedure as businesses sought clarification of the new provisions, there were, in fact, no opinions released in 1999 or 2005 and only fourteen opinions issued from 2000 through 2007.[166] In 2008, the DOJ issued three opinions. In 2009, the DOJ issued only one opinion. The prompt turnaround time on several recent opinion requests makes clear that the DOJ has recognized past criticism that it has been slow to respond to requests.

VIII. COLLATERAL LITIGATION

The FCPA does not expressly provide for a private cause of action, and most federal courts have held that the FCPA does not imply a private cause of action.[167] However, in the wake of a public company's disclosure of an FCPA investigation or the filing of a criminal or enforcement action, follow-on collateral litigation has been common. Derivative lawsuits or class action suits have been filed, and plaintiffs in collateral litigation have included shareholders, competitors, employees, sovereigns, and pension plans. Specifically, three types of civil actions are typically filed: (1) securities class actions against companies and directors alleging inaccurate disclosures in violation of Section 10(b) and Rule 10b-5 thereunder and Section 20(a) of the Exchange Act; (2) shareholder derivative actions brought on behalf of companies against their directors and officers for breach of fiduciary duties; and (3) class actions under Section 502 of the Employee Retirement Income Security Act (ERISA) on behalf of participants in and beneficiaries of a qualified ERISA plan against the company and its directors for breach of fiduciary duties. Although collateral litigation is beyond the scope of this handbook, counsel must advise clients who are considering voluntary disclosure or who will be charged by government authorities with FCPA violations of the likelihood of follow-on civil litigation.

IX. ADDITIONAL RESOURCES

- Brown, *Parent Subsidiary Liability Under the Foreign Corrupt Practices Act,* 50 BAYLOR L. REV. 1 (1998).
- Clark & Suprenant, *Siemens—Potential Interplay of FCPA Charges and Mandatory Debarment Under the Public Procurement Directive of the European Union,* ABA NAT'L INST. ON WHITE COLLAR CRIME (San Francisco, March 5-6, 2009).
- DONALD CRUWER, COMPLYING WITH THE FOREIGN CORRUPT PRACTICES ACT (ABA, 2d ed. 1999).
- STUART DEMING, THE FOREIGN CORRUPT PRACTICES ACT AND THE NEW INTERNATIONAL NORMS (ABA 2005).
- Deming, *The Potent and Broad-Ranging Implications of the Accounting and Record-Keeping Provisions of the Foreign Corrupt Practices Act,* 96 J. CRIM. L. & CRIMINOLOGY 465 (2006).
- Grime & Fischer, *Obvious and Not-So-Obvious Consequences from the Rise of FCPA Enforcement,* ABA NATIONAL INSTITUTE ON WHITE COLLAR CRIME (MARCH 2008).
- Grime & Rogers, *Why the Accounting Provisions of the Foreign Corrupt Practices Act Should Concern You,* ABA NATIONAL INSTITUTE ON WHITE COLLAR CRIME (March 2009).
- Martin, *Compliance with the Foreign Corrupt Practices Act and the Developing International Anti-Corruption Environment* (© 2009 Jay Martin) (unpublished manuscript on file at Baker Hughes, Inc.).

- Mendelsohn, *The Foreign Corrupt Practices Act: Current SEC and DOJ Enforcement Initiatives,* paper presented at the American Bar Association Conference, Washington, D.C., Sept. 11, 2008.
- Naftalis, *The Foreign Corrupt Practices Act,* 11(8) WHITE-COLLAR CRIME REPORTER 6 (Sept. 1997).
- O'MELVENY & MYERS, FOREIGN CORRUPT PRACTICES ACT: AN O'MELVENY HANDBOOK (6th ed. 2009).
- David Luban, Julie O'Sullivan & David Stewart, *Corruption, ch. 14 in* INTERNATIONAL AND TRANSNATIONAL CRIMINAL LAW (Aspen 2009).
- PBS/Frontline World, *The Business of Bribes* (Feb. 2009), http://www.pbs.org/frontlineworld/stories/bribe.
- Shearman & Sterling, FCPA DIGEST (March 2009) (comprehensive listing of every FCPA case since 1977), *available at* http://www.shearman.com.
- U.S. Dep't of Justice, *Lay-Person's Guide to FCPA* (2001).
- U.S. DEP'T OF JUSTICE, UNITED STATES ATTORNEY'S MANUAL, *available at* http://www.usdoj.gov.
- U.S. SECURITIES & EXCHANGE COMM'N, DIV. OF ENFORCEMENT, ENFORCEMENT MANUAL, *available at* http://www.sec.gov/divisions/enforce/enforcementmanual.pdf.
- Urofsky & Newcomb, *Recent Trends and Patterns in the Enforcement of the Foreign Corrupt Practices Act* (© 2009 Shearman & Sterling LLP), *available at* http://www.shearman.com.
- Roger Witten & Kimberly Parker, COMPLYING WITH THE FOREIGN CORRUPT PRACTICES ACT (6th ed. 2007).
- Witten, Partner & Koffer, *Navigating the Increased Anti-Corruption Environment in the United States and Abroad,* paper presented at the 20th Annual ACI Conference on the Foreign Corrupt Practices Act, Washington, D.C., Nov. 18, 2008.
- Don Zarin, DOING BUSINESS UNDER THE FOREIGN CORRUPT PRACTICES ACT (PLI 2007).

NOTES

1. Foreign Corrupt Practices Act of 1977, Pub. L. No. 95-213, 91 Stat. 1494 (codified as amended at 15 U.S.C. §§ 78m, 78dd-1 to -3, 78ff (1999)) [hereinafter FCPA].

2. 15 U.S.C. § 78dd-1(a)(3) (for issuers).

3. 15 U.S.C. § 78dd-2(a)(3) (for domestic concerns).

4. 15 U.S.C. § 78dd-3(a)(3) (for "any person").

5. 15 U.S.C. § 78dd-1(a).

6. 15 U.S.C. § 78dd-2(h).

7. 15 U.S.C. §§ 78dd-1(a), -2(a), -3(a).

8. 15 U.S.C. § 78dd-2(i)(l). *See also* 15 U.S.C. § 78dd-1(g) (setting forth the same rule for "Issuers").

9. 15 U.S.C. § 78dd-3(a).

10. S. Rep. No. 105-277, at 6 (1998) (quoting Commentaries on the Convention on Combating Bribery of Foreign Public Officials in International Business Transactions (OECD Commentary re: Article 41)).

11. 15 U.S.C. §§ 78dd-1(a), -2(a), -3(a). The text of the Act is appended hereto as Appendix 1.

12. 15 U.S.C. §§ 78dd-1(f)(l)(A), -2(h)(2)(A), -3(f)(2)(A).

13. *See SEC v. Dow Chem. Co.*, No. 07-336 (D.D.C. Feb. 12, 2007).

14. *See, e.g., United States v. Monsanto Co.*, No. 05-008 (D.D.C. Jan. 6, 2005); *SEC v. Monsanto Co.*, No. 05-014 (D.D.C. Jan 6, 2005).

15. 15 U.S.C. §§ 78dd-1((f)(l)(B), -2(h)(2)(B), -3(f)(2)(B).

16. *See, e.g., United States v. Castle*, 925 F.2d 831, 834 (5th Cir. 1999) (noting the "overwhelming evidence of a Congressional intent to exempt foreign officials from prosecution for receiving bribes").

17. *United States v. Sheker*, 618 F.2d 607, 609 (9th Cir. 1980).

18. *United States v. Zouras*, 497 F.2d 1115, 1121 (7th Cir. 1974).

19. *United States v. Crozier*, 987 F.2d 893, 901 (2d Cir. 1993); *United States v. Hare*, 618 F.2d 1085 (4th Cir. 1980).

20. *United States v. McDade*, 827 F. Supp. 1153 (E.D. Pa. 1993).

21. *Id.*

22. *United States v. King*, 351 F.3d 859, 863 (8th Cir. 2003).

23. S. Rep. No. 95-114, at 10 (1977).

24. H.R. Rep. No. 95-650, at 18 (1977); Chapter 4 of Don Zarin, Doing Business under the FCPA (2007), has thorough coverage of domestic bribery cases that provide precedent for the Department of Justice in the FCPA area.

25. 923 F.2d 1308 (8th Cir. 1991).

26. *Id.* at 1312.

27. 513 F.3d 461, 464 (5th Cir. 2007), *aff'g* 359 F.3d 738 (5th Cir. 2004), *cert. denied*, 2008 U.S. LEXIS 6775, 77 U.S.L.W. 3196 (U.S. Oct. 6, 2008).

28. 513 F.3d at 465.

29. FCPA Procedure Op., Release No. 82-03 (Apr. 22, 1982) (no expectation that any individual will personally benefit from the proposed agency relationship).

30. 359 F.3d 738 (5th Cir. 2004).

31. *Id.* at 756.

32. *Id.* at 740.

33. 513 F.3d at 466.

34. 15 U.S.C. § 78dd-1(f)(2)(A).

35. 15 U.S.C. §§ 78dd-1(f)(2), -2(h)(3), -3(f)(3).

36. Conference Report at 2116-17 citing United States v. Jacobs, 475 F.2d 270, 277–88 (2d Cir. 1973).

37. Roger M. Witten, Kimberly A. Parker & Thomas J. Koffer, *Navigating the Increased Anti-Corruption Environment in the United States and Abroad*, 20th

Annual ACI Conference on the Foreign Corrupt Practices Act, Nov. 18, 2008, Washington, D.C.

38. 15 U.S.C. §§ 78dd-1(f)(2)(B), -2(h)(3)(B).

39. 15 U.S.C. §§ 78dd-1(f)(1)(A), -2(h)(2)(A), -3(f)(2)(A).

40. 15 U.S.C. §§ 78dd-1(a), -2(a), -3(a).

41. *See, e.g., SEC v. Chandramoli Srinivasan*, Civil Action 1:07-CV-01699 (RBW) (D.D.C.); *United States v. Schnitzer Steel Indus., Inc.; SEC v. Philip*, No. CV 07-1836, SEC Litig. Release No. 20,397 (D. Or.), filed Dec. 13, 2007.

42. Joel M. Cohen, Michael P. Holland & Adam P. Wolf, *Under the FCPA, Who Is a Foreign Official Anyway?*, 63 Bus. Law. 1243 (Aug. 2008).

43. 28 U.S.C. §§ 1602–1611.

44. 28 U.S.C. § 1603(b)(2).

45. For a thoughtful discussion of "instrumentality" caselaw, see Zarin, *supra* note 24, at 4:4:2.

46. 15 U.S.C. §§ 78dd-1(a), -2(a), -3(a).

47. *See* H.R. Rep. No. 95-640, at 18 (1977) (Conf. Rep.).

48. 15 U.S.C. §§ 78dd-1(b), -2(b), -3(b).

49. 15 U.S.C. §§ 78dd-1(f)(3), -2(h)(4), -3(f)(4).

50. *Id.*

51. 15 U.S.C. §§ 78dd-1(c)(l), -2(c)(l), -3(c)(l).

52. *Id.* §§ 78dd-1 (c)(2), -2(c)(2), -3(c)(2).

53. *United States v. Metcalf & Eddy, Inc.*, No. 99 Civ. 12566 NG (D. Mass. 1999).

54. 15 U.S.C. §§ 78dd-1(a), -2(a).

55. *See, e.g.*, Press Release, U.S. Dep't of Justice, Schnitzer Steel Industries Inc.'s Subsidiary Pleads Guilty to Foreign Bribes and Agrees to Pay a $7.5 Million Criminal Fine (Oct. 16, 2006) (SSI Korea admitted that it violated the FCPA and the conspiracy and wire fraud statutes in connection with more than $1.8 million in corrupt payments paid over a five-year period to officers and employees of nearly all Schnitzer Steel's government-owned customers in China and private customers in China and South Korea to induce them to purchase scrap material from Schnitzer Steel.).

56. 18 U.S.C. § 371.

57. 18 U.S.C. § 1952.

58. 15 U.S.C. § 78m(a) (1994).

59. *See, e.g., United States v. Rothrock*, 4 FCPA Rep. 699.818801 (W.D. Tex. 2001) (plea to knowingly and willfully falsifying and causing to be falsified certain books, records, and accounts in violations of FCPA); *United States v. UNC/Leah Services*, 2 FCPA Rep. 600.050 (W.D. Ky.) (recording $140,000 payments to a subcontractor falsely as engineering fees).

60. 15 U.S.C. §§ 78dd-2(d)(l), 78u(d)(l).

61. Stanley Sporkin, *The Worldwide Banning of Schmiergeld: A Look at the Foreign Corrupt Practices Act on Its Twentieth Birthday*, 18 Nw. J. Int'l. L. Bus. 269, 274 (1998).

62. 15 U.S.C. § 78m(a).

63. Reasonableness, rather than materiality, is the threshold standard. Criminal liability under the accounting provisions requires that a person "knowingly" falsify its books and records and "knowingly" circumvent a system of internal accounting records. 15 U.S.C. §§ 78m(b)(4)-(5).

64. 15 U.S.C. § 78c(a)(37).

65. 15 U.S.C. § 78m(b)(7).

66. *See, e.g., SEC v. Collins & Aikman Corp.*, 524 F. Supp. 2d 477, 491 (S.D.N.Y. 2007).

67. 15 U.S.C. §§ 78m(b)(4)–(5).

68. *See* Harold Williams, Chairman, Securities and Exchange Comm'n, Address to the SEC Developments Conference of AICPA (Jan. 13, 1981), Exchange Act Release No. 17,500 (Jan. 29, 1981).

69. 532 F. Supp. 2d 1187 (N.D. Cal. 2008).

70. *Id.* at 1196–97.

71. Donald Cruwer, Complying with the Foreign Corrupt Practices Act (Am. Bar Ass'n, 2d ed. 1999).

72. *See SEC v. Int'l Business Machs. Corp.*, SEC Litig. Release No. 16,839 (Dec. 21, 2000).

73. 15 U.S.C. § 78m(b)(6).

74. *Id.*

75. *Id.*

76. Am. Inst. of Certified Pub. Accountants, Statement on Auditing Standard No. 1,320.28 (1973), *cited in* Report of the Securities and Exchange Commission on Questionable and Illegal Corporate Payments and Practices, May 12, 1976, at 12, *reprinted in* Sec. Reg. & L. Rep. (BNA), No. 353, Special Supp. (May 19, 1976).

77. 15 U.S.C. § 78m(b)(2).

78. 15 U.S.C. § 78m(b)(7).

79. Williams, *supra* note 68, at 11,545.

80. *Id.*

81. *SEC v. World-Wide Coin Inv., Ltd.*, 567 F. Supp. 724, 751 (N.D. Ga. 1983).

82. Gentenaur & Olsen, *"Controlling" FCPA Risk: Assessing Internal Controls to Ensure Risk Is Mitigated.* Corporate Compliance Insights (Aug. 10, 2009), http://www.corporatecomplianceinsights.com/2009/controlling_fcpa_risk_assessing_internal_controls.

83. 15 U.S.C. §§ 78m(b)(4)–(5).

84. 15 U.S.C. § 78m(b)(4) (1994).

85. Stuart H. Deming, *The Potent and Broad-Ranging Implications of the Accounting and Record-Keeping Provisions of the Foreign Corrupt Practices Act*, 96 J. Crim. L. & Criminology 465, 500 (2006).

86. 15 U.S.C. § 78m(b)(6).

87. 18 U.S.C. § 371.

88. 18 U.S.C. § 1343.

89. *See generally:* First Circuit: *United States v. Brandon,* 17 F.3d 409 (1st Cir.), *cert. denied sub nom. Granoff v. United States,* 513 U.S. 820 (1994); Second Circuit: *United States v. Svoboda,* 374 F.3d 471, 476 (2d Cir. 2003); *United States v. Ferrarini,* 219 F.3d 145, 155 (2d Cir. 2000); Fifth Circuit: *United States v. Parks,* 68 F.3d 860, 866 (5th Cir. 1995); *United States v. Williams,* 12 F.3d 452, 458 (5th Cir. 1994); *United States v. Medrano,* 836 F.2d 861, 863 (5th Cir.), *cert. denied,* 488 U.S. 818 (1988); Sixth Circuit: *United States v. Dolt,* 27 F.3d 235, 238 (6th Cir. 1994); *United States v. Reifsteck,* 841 F.2d 701, 704 (6th Cir. 1988); Seventh Circuit: *United States v. Jones,* 317 F.3d 363, 366 (7th Cir. 2004); *United States v. Gee,* 226 F.3d 885, 893 (7th Cir. 2000); *United States v. Knox,* 68 F.3d 990 (7th Cir. 1995); *United States v. Brown,* 31 F.3d 484, 488 (7th Cir. 1994); *United States v. Sophie,* 900 F.2d 1064, 1080 (7th Cir.), *cert. denied sub nom. Duque v. United States,* 498 U.S. 843 (1990); Eighth Circuit: *United States v. Powell,* 853 F.2d 601, 604 (8th Cir. 1988); Ninth Circuit: *United States v. Chong,* 419 F.3d 1076 (9th Cir. 2005); *United States v. Wright,* 215 F.3d 1020, 1028 (9th Cir. 2000); *United States v. Indelicato,* 800 F.2d 1482, 1484 (9th Cir. 1986); Tenth Circuit: *United States v. Daily,* 921 F.2d 994, 999 (10th Cir. 1991); *Nelson v. United States,* 406 F.2d 1136, 1137 (10th Cir. 1969); Eleventh Circuit: *United States v. Cure,* 804 F.2d 625, 628 (11th Cir. 1986); *United States v. Kammer,* 1 F.3d 1161, 1164 (11th Cir. 1993).

90. *United States v. Rabinowich,* 238 U.S. 78, 87–89, 35 S. Ct. 682, 59 L. Ed. 1211 (1915).

91. *United States v. Easton,* 54 Fed. Appx. 242 (8th Cir. 2002).

92. Supreme Court: *Inanelli v. United States,* 420 U.S. 770, 777, 95 S. Ct. 1284, 43 L. Ed. 2d 616 (1975); Second Circuit: *United States v. Savarese,* 404 F.3d 651 (2d Cir. 2005); *United States v. Mittelstaedt,* 31 F.3d 1208, 1218 (2d Cir. 1994); *United States v. Beech-Nut Nutrition Corp.,* 871 F.2d 1181, 1191 (2d Cir. 1989); Third Circuit: *United States v. Applewhaite,* 195 F.3d 679, 684 (3d Cir. 1999); Fifth Circuit: *United States v. Bright,* 630 F.3d 804 (5th Cir. 1980); Seventh Circuit: *United States v. Hooks,* 848 F.2d 785, 792 (7th Cir. 1988); Tenth Circuit: *United States v. Arutunoff,* 1 F.3d 1112, 1116 (10th Cir. 1993); Eleventh Circuit: *United States v. Chandler,* 376 F.3d 1303, 1314 (11th Cir. 2004); *United States v. Toler,* 144 F.3d 1423, 1425 (11th Cir. 1998); Dist. of Columbia Circuit: *United States v. Lam Kwong-Wah,* 924 F.2d 298, 303 (D.C. Cir. 1991).

93. *Morrison v. California,* 291 U.S. 82, 92, 54 S. Ct. 281, 78 L. Ed. 664 (1934).

94. Several courts have held that a corporation can conspire with its officers and employees. *See:* Fifth Circuit: *Alamo Fence Co. v. United States,* 240 F.2d 179, 181 (5th Cir. 1957); Sixth Circuit: *United States v. Ames Sintering Co.,* 916 F.2d 713 (6th Cir. 1990); *United States v. S & Vee Cartage,* 704 F.2d 914, 920 (6th Cir.), *cert. denied,* 464 U.S. 935 (1983); Eleventh Circuit: *McAndrew v. Lockheed Martin Corp.,* 206 F.3d 1031 (11th Cir. 2000); on the other hand, the Seventh Circuit, in *Pearson v. Youngstown Sheet & Tube Co.,* 332 F.2d 439, 442 (7th Cir. 1964), held that a corporation is not capable of conspiring with its own officers and employees.

95. *Joplin Mercantile Co. v. United States*, 213 F. 926, 936 (8th Cir. 1914), *aff'd*, 236 U.S. 531, 35 S. Ct. 291, 59 L. Ed. 705 (1915).

96. *United States v. Hughes Aircraft Co.*, 1994 U.S. App. LEXIS 12526 (9th Cir., Mar. 28, 1994).

97. *See, e.g.,* Supreme Court: *Glasser v. United States*, 315 U.S. 60, 80, 62 S. Ct. 457, 86 L. Ed. 680 (1942); Second Circuit: *United States v. Svoboda*, 374 F.3d 471, 476 (2d Cir. 2003); *United States v. Samaria*, 239 F.3d 228, 234 (2d Cir. 2001); Third Circuit: *United States v. Helbling*, 209 F.3d 226, 238 (3d Cir. 2000); *United States v. Carr*, 25 F.3d 1194 (3d Cir. 1994); Fourth Circuit: *United States v. Wilson*, 135 F.3d 291, 306 (4th Cir. 1998); *United States v. Whittington*, 26 F.3d 456, 465 (4th Cir. 1994); Sixth Circuit: *United States v. Salgado*, 250 F.3d 438, 447 (6th Cir. 2001); *United States v. Mullins*, 22 F.3d 1365, 1368 (6th Cir. 1994); Seventh Circuit: *United States v. Miller*, 405 F.3d 551 (7th Cir. 2005); *United States v. Viezca*, 265 F.3d 597 (7th Cir. 2001); *United States v. Redwine*, 715 F.2d 315 (7th Cir. 1973); Eighth Circuit: *United States v. Fletcher*, 322 F.3d 508 (8th Cir. 2003); *United States v. Hermes*, 847 F.2d 493, 495 (8th Cir. 1988); Ninth Circuit: *United States v. Daychild*, 357 F.3d 1082, 1097 (9th Cir. 2004); Tenth Circuit: *King v. United States*, 402 F.2d 289, 292 (10th Cir. 1968).

98. Compare RICO conspiracy (18 U.S.C. § 1962(d)), which has been interpreted by some courts as not requiring an overt act. *See, e.g., United States v. Barton*, 647 F.2d 224 (2d Cir.), *cert. denied*, 454 U.S. 857 (1981).

99. *See, e.g., United States v. Bayer*, 331 U.S. 532, 542, 67 S. Ct. 1394, 91 L. Ed. 1654 (1947).

100. Supreme Court: *Yates v. United States*, 354 U.S. 298, 334, 77 S. Ct. 1064, 1 L. Ed. 2d 1356 (1957); First Circuit: *United States v. Hurley*, 957 F.2d 1, 3 (1st Cir. 1992); *United States v. Tarvers*, 833 F.2d 1068, 1075 (1st Cir. 1987); *United States v. Medina*, 761 F.2d 12, 15 (1st Cir. 1985); Second Circuit: *United States v. Montour*, 944 F.2d 1019, 1026 (2d Cir. 1991); Sixth Circuit: *United States v. Reifsteck*, 841 F.2d 701, 704 (6th Cir. 1988); Seventh Circuit: *United States v. Crabtree*, 979 F.2d 1261, 1267 (7th Cir. 1992), *cert. denied*, 510 U.S. 878 (1993); Eighth Circuit: *United States v. Fletcher*, 322 F.3d 508 (8th Cir. 2003); *United States v. Hermes*, 847 F.2d 493, 496 (8th Cir. 1988).

101. *See* OTTO G. OBERMAIER & ROBERT G. MORVILLO, WHITE COLLAR CRIME: BUSINESS AND REGULATORY OFFENSES § 4.01 (1989); *see also Bourjaily v. United States*, 483 U.S. 171, 179-80, 107 S. Ct. 2775, 97 L. Ed. 2d 144 (1987); FED. R. EVID. 801(d)(2)(E).

102. Second Circuit: *United States v. Roshko*, 969 F.2d 9, 12 (2d Cir. 1992).

103. *Fiswick v. United States*, 329 U.S. 211, 67 S. Ct. 224, 91 L. Ed. 196 (1946).

104. Second Circuit: *United States v. Diaz*, 176 F.3d 52, 98 (2d Cir. 1999); *United States v. Cruz*, 797 F.2d 90, 96-97 (2d Cir. 1986); Fifth Circuit: *United States v. Mann*, 161 F.3d 840, 859-60 (5th Cir. 1998); Sixth Circuit: *United States v. Rogers*, 118 F.3d 466, 473-74 (6th Cir. 1997); Seventh Circuit: *United States v. Febus*, 218 F.3d 784, 796 (7th Cir. 2000); *United States v. Read*, 658 F.2d 1225,

1232 (7th Cir. 1981); Eleventh Circuit: *United States v. LaQuire*, 943 F.2d 1554, 1563 (11th Cir. 1991); *cert. denied*, 505 U.S. 1223 (1992).

105. Second Circuit: *United States v. Guerro*, 694 F.2d 898, 903 (2d Cir. 1982); Eighth Circuit: *United States v. Perry*, 152 F.3d 900, 904 (8th Cir. 1998); Ninth Circuit: *United States v. Koonin*, 361 F.3d 1250, 1254–55 (9th Cir. 2004), *vacated on other grounds*, 544 U.S. 945 (2005); Eleventh Circuit: *United States v. Anderson*, 326 F.3d 1319 (11th Cir.), *cert. denied*, 540 U.S. 825 (2003); *United States v. Butler*, 792 F.2d 1528, 1532 (11th Cir. 1986).

106. 18 U.S.C. § 371.

107. 18 U.S.C. § 1001.

108. 18 U.S.C. §§ 1956, 1957.

109. 18 U.S.C. § 1341.

110. 18 U.S.C. § 1343.

111. 15 U.S.C. § 1.

112. 26 U.S.C. §§ 7201 *et seq.*

113. 50 U.S.C. app. §§ 1701–1706 (2000).

114. For a thorough discussion of federal statute of limitation issues, see J. Anthony Chavez, *Federal Criminal Statutes of Limitations: Shifting the Balance Toward Punishment*, 1994 COMPLEX CRIMES J. 1.

115. *United States v. Eckhardt*, 843 F.2d 989, 993 (7th Cir.), *cert. denied*, 488 U.S. 839 (1988).

116. Second Circuit: *United States v. Scop*, 846 F.2d 135, 138 (2d Cir.), *modified in part on other grounds on reh'g*, 856 F.2d 5, 7 (1988); Fourth Circuit: *United States v. United Med. & Surgical Supply Corp.*, 989 F.2d 1390 (4th Cir. 1993); Tenth Circuit: *United States v. Jensen*, 608 F.2d 1349, 1355 (10th Cir. 1979).

117. 18 U.S.C. § 3282.

118. 18 U.S.C. § 371.

119. For example, the six-year statute of limitations provided in 26 U.S.C. § 6351(1) applies to conspiracies to commit tax fraud. *United States v. Fletcher*, 928 F.2d 495, 498 (2d Cir.), *cert. denied*, 502 U.S. 815 (1991).

120. *Bridges v. United States*, 346 U.S. 209, 223, 73 S. Ct. 1055, 97 L. Ed. 1557 (1952).

121. 18 U.S.C. § 371.

122. Supreme Court: *Grunewald v. United States*, 353 U.S. 391, 402–03, 77 S. Ct. 963, 1 L. Ed. 2d 931 (1957); Seventh Circuit: *United States v. McKinney*, 954 F.2d 471, 475 (7th Cir.), *cert. denied*, 506 U.S. 1023 (1992).

123. *United States v. Elliott*, 225 U.S. 392, 401, 32 S. Ct. 812, 56 L. Ed. 1136 (1912); *see also Fiswick v. United States*, 329 U.S. 211, 216, 67 S. Ct. 224, 91 L. Ed. 196 (1946).

124. Second Circuit: *United States v. Scop*, 846 F.2d 135, 139 (2d Cir.), *modified in part on reh'g on other grounds*, 856 F.2d 5, 7 (1988); Fourth Circuit: *United States v. Head*, 641 F.2d 174, 177 (4th Cir. 1981); Eighth Circuit: *United States v. Andreas*, 458 F.2d 491 (8th Cir.), *cert. denied*, 409 U.S. 848 (1972).

125. *Grunewald v. United States,* 353 U.S. 391, 405–06, 77 S. Ct. 963 1 L. Ed. 2d 931 (1957); *see also* Second Circuit: *United States v. Crozier,* 987 F.2d 893, 898 (2d Cir.), *cert. denied,* 510 U.S. 880 (1993); Seventh Circuit: *United States v. Eisen,* 974 F.2d 1362, 1368 (7th Cir.), *cert. denied,* 507 U.S. 1029 (1993); *but see United States v. Masters,* 924 F.2d 1362, 1368 (7th Cir.), *cert. denied,* 500 U.S. 919 (1991).

126. Supreme Court: *United States v. Lane,* 474 U.S. 438, 451–53, 106 S. Ct. 725, 88 L. Ed. 2d 814 (1986); Second Circuit: *United States v. Mennuti,* 679 F.2d 1032, 1035 (2d Cir. 1982); Fourth Circuit: *United States v. A-A-A Elec. Co., Inc.,* 788 F.2d 242, 244 (4th Cir. 1986); Fifth Circuit: *United States v. Girard,* 744 F.2d 1170, 1172 (5th Cir. 1984); Seventh Circuit: *United States v. Dick,* 744 F.2d 546, 552 (7th Cir. 1984); Eighth Circuit: *United States v. N. Improvement Co.,* 814 F.2d 540 (8th Cir.), *cert. denied,* 484 U.S. 846 (1987); Ninth Circuit: *United States v. Walker,* 653 F.2d 1343, 1350 (9th Cir. 1981), *cert. denied,* 484 U.S. 846 (1987); *United States v. Inryco, Inc.,* 642 F.2d 290, 293–94 (9th Cir. 1981), *cert. dismissed,* 454 U.S. 1167 (1982); Eleventh Circuit: *United States v. Helmich,* 704 F.2d 547, 549 (11th Cir.), *cert. denied,* 464 U.S. 939 (1983).

127. First Circuit: *United States v. Keohane,* 918 F.2d 273 (1st Cir. 1990), *cert. denied,* 499 U.S. 907; *United States v. Nazzaro,* 889 F.2d 1158 (1st Cir. 1989); *United States v. Doherty,* 867 F.2d 47 (1st Cir.), *cert. denied,* 492 U.S. 918 (1989); Third Circuit: *United States v. Anwar,* 714 F.2d 238, 253 (3d Cir.), *cert. denied,* 464 U.S. 936 (1983).

128. Supreme Court: *Hyde & Schneider v. United States,* 225 U.S. 347, 369, 32 S. Ct. 793, 56 L. Ed. 1114 (1912); Fourth Circuit: *United States v. Barsanti,* 943 F.2d 428, 437 (4th Cir. 1991); Seventh Circuit: *United States v. Andrus,* 775 F.2d 825, 850 (7th Cir. 1985).

129. *See, e.g., United States v. Bafia,* 949 F.2d 1465, 1477 (7th Cir. 1991), *cert. denied sub nom. Kerridan v. United States,* 504 U.S. 928 (1992).

130. Second Circuit: *United States v. Borelli,* 336 F.2d 376, 388 (2d Cir. 1964), *cert. denied,* 379 U.S. 960 (1965); Fifth Circuit: *United States v. Bradsby,* 628 F.2d 901, 905 (5th Cir. 1980); Eleventh Circuit: *United States v. Roper,* 874 F.2d 782, 787 (11th Cir.), *cert. denied,* 493 U.S. 867 (1989).

131. 18 U.S.C. § 3292.

132. 18 U.S.C. § 3292(a)(1).

133. 18 U.S.C. § 3292(c).

134. 18 U.S.C. § 3292(d).

135. Dan K. Webb, Robert W. Tarun & Steven F. Molo, Corporate Internal Investigations (1993–2009), § 15.09(1).

136. Sentencing for individuals who violate FCPA accounting provisions is considered under § 2B1.1. Sentencing for individuals who violate FCPA bribery provisions is determined under § 2B4.1. *See* U.S. Sentencing Guidelines Manual (2004). In *United States v. Booker,* 543 U.S. 220 (2005), the Supreme Court held that the guidelines were supervisory and not mandatory.

137. 15 U.S.C. §§ 78dd-2(g)(2)(A), 78dd-3(e)(2)(A), 78ff(c)(2)(A).

138. 15 U.S.C. § 78ff(a).

139. 15 U.S.C. §§ 78dd-2(g), -3(e).

140. 15 U.S.C. § 78ff(a) (accounting); 15 U.S.C. § 78dd-2(g)(1)(A) (bribery).

141. 18 U.S.C. § 3571(d).

142. *See* 15 U.S.C. §§ 78ff(c), 78dd-2(a), 78dd-3(a), 77d-1(a).

143. U.S. ATTORNEYS' MANUAL, Criminal Resource Manual § 1019; *see* 18 U.S.C. §§ 981(a)(i)(c), 1956(c)(7).

144. *See* 15 U.S.C. §§ 78dd-2(g)(3), 78dd-3(e)(3), 78ff(c)(3).

145. 26 U.S.C. § 162(c).

146. 15 U.S.C. §§ 78dd-2(g)(l)(B), 78dd-3(e)(l)(B), 78ff(c)(2)(C).

147. 15 U.S.C. § 78u(d)(3).

148. No. 1.04 CV 1141 [RBW] (U.S.D.C., D.D.C.).

149. 48 C.F.R. § 9.406-2(a)(3).

150. *See* Exec. Order No. 12,549,51 Fed. Reg. 6,370 (Feb. 18, 1986).

151. U.S. ATTORNEYS' MANUAL, Criminal Resource Manual § 1019.

152. Directive 2004/18/EC of the European Parliament of the Council of 31 March 2004 and coordination of procedures for the award of public work contracts, public supply contracts, and public service contracts. Recital 1, O.J. (L 134), 114–20.

153. *Id.*

154. Peter B. Clark & Jennifer A. Suprenant, *Siemens—Potential Interplay of FCPA Charges and Mandatory Debarment Under the Public Procurement Directive of the European Union*, 2009 ABA NAT'L INST. ON WHITE COLLAR CRIME (San Francisco, March 5–6, 2009).

155. U.S. ATTORNEYS' MANUAL tit. 9, ch. 9-47.110.

156. 28 C.F.R. 50.18. (Att'y Gen. Order No. 878-80).

157. The current DOJ opinion procedure is codified in 28 C.F.R. §§ 80.1, 80.6 (1993). DOJ opinions may be found in issues of *Foreign Corrupt Practices Act Reporter* (West) or online at http://www.usdoj.gov/criminal/fraud.

158. 28 C.F.R. § 80.6.

159. U.S. ATTORNEYS' MANUAL, Criminal Resource Manual § 1016.

160. FCPA Op., Release No. 96-2 (Nov. 25, 1996).

161. FCPA Op., Release No. 2000-1 (Mar. 29, 2000).

162. FCPA Op., Release No. 2001-01 (May 24, 2001).

163. FCPA Op., Release No. 2001-02 (July 18, 2001).

164. FCPA Op., Release Nos. 2003-01 (Jan. 15, 2003), 2004-02 (July 12, 2004).

165. Gary P. Naftalis, *The Foreign Corrupt Practices Act*, 11(8) WHITE-COLLAR CRIME REPORTER 6 (Sept. 1997) ("In connection with any request for an FCPA Opinion, the Department of Justice may conduct whatever independent investigation it believes appropriate.").

166. FCPA Opinion Procedure Releases, http://www.usdoj.gov/criminal/fraud/fcpa/opinion (last visited September 6, 2009).

167. *See, e.g., Lamb v. Phillip Morris, Inc.*, 915 F.2d 1024, 1029 (6th Cir. 1990); *J.S. Serv. Ctr. Corp. v. GE Tech. Servs.*, 937 F. Supp. 216, 226–27 (S.D.N.Y. 1996). *But see United States v. Young & Rubicain, Inc.*, 741 F. Supp. 334, 399 (D. Conn. 1990).

CHAPTER 2

The FCPA's Expansive Jurisdiction

I. ORIGINAL AND EXPANDED JURISDICTION

In enacting the Foreign Corrupt Practices Act in 1977, Congress originally limited its jurisdictional scope to U.S. companies and individuals.[1]
The 1998 amendments expanded the Act's jurisdiction to include foreign
individuals and corporations. In particular, Congress amended the FCPA
to implement the provisions of the Convention on Combating Bribery
of Foreign Officials in International Business Transactions adopted by
the Organization for Economic Cooperation and Development (OECD)
on December 17, 1997 (the OECD Convention). The OECD Convention,
which the United States Senate ratified on July 31, 1998, required signatories to conform their laws to its terms. The United States did so with
the International Anti-Bribery and Fair Competition Act of 1998, which
President William J. Clinton signed on November 10, 1998.[2]

Among its provisions, the OECD Convention called on signatories
to make it a criminal offense for "any person" to bribe a foreign public
official[3] and required them "to take such measures as may be necessary
to establish its jurisdiction over the bribery of a foreign public official
when the offense is committed in whole or in part in its territory."[4] As a
result, the FCPA had to be modified to conform to the OECD Convention by extending its anti-bribery provisions to cover any bribery committed by any person (not just issuers or domestic concerns) who commits
an offense, in whole or in part, in U.S. territory.

II. ENTITIES AND PERSONS COVERED BY THE ANTI-BRIBERY PROVISIONS

The following persons and entities are now covered by the Act's anti-
bribery provisions:

1. *Issuers of securities*—essentially, publicly traded companies: any corporation (domestic or foreign) that has registered a class of securities with the Securities and Exchange Commission or is required to file reports with the SEC, for example, any corporation with its stocks, bonds, or American Depository Receipts traded on a U.S. securities exchange;[5]

2. *Domestic concerns*—any individual who is a citizen, national, or resident of the United States and any corporation, partnership, association, joint stock company, business trust, unincorporated organization, or sole proprietorship that has its principal place of business in the United States, or that is organized under the laws of a State of the United States or a territory, possession, or commonwealth of the United States;[6]

3. *Persons*—a national of the United States (as defined in Section 101 of the Immigration and Nationality Act)[7] or any corporation, partnership, association, joint stock company, business trust, unincorporated organization, or sole proprietorship organized under the laws of the United States of any State, territory, possession or commonwealth of the United States, or any political subdivision thereof, who commits an act outside the United States in furtherance of a prohibited payment;[8]

4. *Foreign nationals and entities* (whether or not they are issuers) that commit any act in United States territory in furtherance of a prohibited payment;[9] and

5. *Any officers, directors, employees, or agents* of the entities or persons described in 1–4 above.[10]

III.   TERRITORIAL AND NATIONALITY JURISDICTION BASES

The traditional federal jurisdictional basis over U.S. companies and individuals has been territorial, that is, "the use of the mails or any means of instrumentality of interstate commerce in furtherance of 'an improper payment.'"[11] The interstate commerce element, which has long been broadly interpreted under the mail and wire fraud statutes,[12] is easily satisfied through the use of the U.S. mails, e-mails, computer transmissions, and telephone calls.

The 1998 amendments created an alternative jurisdictional basis of nationality. Issuers and domestic concerns may now be held liable under either territorial or nationality bases. Under the nationality principle, improper payments made by U.S. citizens and U.S. companies that take place wholly outside the United States may be prosecuted under the FCPA without any interstate commerce requirement.[13] Nationality jurisdiction has not been challenged under the FCPA, and a successful challenge is questionable given the availability of the broadly interpreted interstate commerce jurisdiction.

The 1998 amendments and recent Department of Justice prosecutions confirm that counsel may increasingly find themselves defending non-U.S. persons in FCPA investigations and cases. One issue that counsel for non-U.S. persons should keep in mind is the due process limitation on personal jurisdiction of United States courts. Even where a defendant falls within the broad subject matter jurisdiction of the amended FCPA, the due process clause may be a bar to U.S. courts exercising personal jurisdiction over a defendant in either criminal or civil FCPA actions.

A. Civil Cases: Minimum Contacts

The due process clause of the Constitution has been interpreted to provide that a United States court may exercise personal jurisdiction only over persons who have sufficient "minimum contacts" with the jurisdiction.[14] The exercise of such jurisdiction must not "offend 'traditional notions of fair play and substantial justice.'"[15] A defendant must have had sufficient activities in the forum jurisdiction to reasonably anticipate being brought into the forum court.[16] In an action brought under a federal statute, the due process inquiry generally turns on a defendant's contacts with the United States as a whole—not simply the state where the federal district court is located.[17]

Defense counsel may wish to consider a due process argument in contesting personal jurisdiction over a foreign person in an FCPA case where the defendant has little or no contact with the United States. Extraterritorial conduct that causes a substantial effect in the United States can create personal jurisdiction over a defendant who personally had no contact with the United States. A person committing such conduct should reasonably anticipate being brought into court in this country.[18] For example, U.S. authorities have asserted that telephone calls, e-mails, and even bank transfers briefly passing through the United States permit the DOJ and SEC to assert jurisdiction over foreign nationals and entities.[19]

De minimis consequences do not, however, suffice to create personal jurisdiction. For example, in the securities context, the Second Circuit has held that "not every causal connection between action abroad and ultimate injury to American investors will suffice.... ('[E]ven assuming ... some causal relation ... the test for in personam jurisdiction is somewhat more demanding'")[20] but found a foreign person who defrauds U.S. investors through illicit insider trading of the securities of a U.S. company traded exclusively in a U.S. stock exchange was plainly subject to U.S. jurisdiction.[21] The issue is much less clear in the case of a foreign person who pays a bribe to a foreign official, by money transfer from the United States, in circumstances that do not affect any U.S. investor or company. When a defendant has little or no contact with the United States, the strength of his personal jurisdiction argument will turn largely on the materiality (or lack thereof) of the U.S. consequences resulting from the foreign conduct.

B.   Criminal Cases: Sufficient Nexus

In criminal prosecutions, the due process analysis for personal jurisdiction is usually stated in terms of whether the defendant's extraterritorial conduct has sufficient nexus with the United States. As the Ninth Circuit observed, "The nexus requirement serves the same purpose as the 'minimum contacts' test in personal jurisdiction. It ensures that a United States court will assert jurisdiction only over a defendant who 'should reasonably anticipate being hauled into court' in this country."[22] Thus, foreign persons who plot terrorist acts to be committed in the United States are subject to jurisdiction of U.S. courts,[23] as are persons who conspire to smuggle drugs into the United States.[24]

The same is not necessarily true for a defendant with little or no contact with the United States, who causes an act in furtherance of a foreign bribe to take place in the United States, or who aids and abets foreign bribery by a U.S. person, particularly where the conduct at issue causes no material consequences in the United States. Where the U.S. government is relying primarily on an effects test to establish a substantial nexus, the strength of a substantial nexus defense will depend on the significance of the U.S. effects of the conduct at issue. Due process challenges will be filed more as the DOJ brings additional cases using the amended FCPA's broad provisions targeted at persons other than issuers and domestic concerns.

IV. CORPORATE CRIMINAL LIABILITY

In addition to the expansive geographic reach of the FCPA, parent companies not only face the traditionally broad principles of corporate criminal liability for the acts of their agents and employees but also various theories of criminal liability for the conduct of their foreign subsidiaries, agents, and employees.

A.   Parent Corporate Criminal Liability

In general, a corporation can be held criminally liable for any criminal act carried out by one of its agents or employees if that act occurs within the scope of his employment for the benefit of the corporation.[25] Low level employees, acting contrary to expressed directions, may create criminal liability for a corporation.[26] Liability may also be imposed on a corporation even if the individual employees involved in the criminal conduct are not indicted.[27] Only two requirements must be met to impute criminal liability of an agent or employee to the corporation. First, the conduct must occur within the scope of the agent or employee's employment. Second, the conduct must in some way be undertaken for the benefit of the corporation.

1.   Scope of Authority

The "scope of authority" requirement means that the agent or employee was exercising the duties and authority conferred upon him by his employment position. It does not mean that the corporation must actually have authorized the agent or employee to commit illegal acts. Indeed, often the agent's acts will have been *ultra vires* and contrary to express authority. Rather, "within the agent's scope of authority" means that the agent or employee must have committed the acts in the course of his ordinary duties. For example, an international salesman agreeing to bribe a foreign official in order to obtain or retain business will be deemed to be acting within the scope of his authority. The focus is on the function delegated to the agent or employee and whether the conduct falls within that general function.[28] So long as the agent or employee's acts are consistent with his general employment function, his employer may be held liable for those acts, even if they were contrary to express corporate policy.[29]

2.   Benefit of the Corporation

The "for the benefit of the corporation" requirement means an agent or employee's acts must be intended to benefit the corporation in some way.[30] The benefit to the corporation need not have been the sole reason for the agent or employee's acts nor must the corporation have received some actual benefit.[31] The corporate agent or employee committing the act almost always will receive some direct or indirect personal benefit. For example, increased sales may entitle an executive to a commission or better performance ratings entitling him to a bonus or raise. However, corporate liability will not be avoided merely because the primary motivation may have been the personal benefit to the agent or employee. So long as the motive includes a direct or ancillary benefit to the corporation—either realized or unrealized—a corporation will be accountable for the agent or employee's acts.[32]

B.   Foreign Subsidiaries

1.   Bribery Conduct

While the legislative history and one case indicate that foreign subsidiaries of U.S. companies acting on their own and not as agents of a U.S. parent are not subject to the anti-bribery provisions,[33] the DOJ's lay guidance on the FCPA asserts that U.S. parent corporations may be held liable "for corrupt payments by employees or agents acting entirely outside the United States, using money from foreign bank accounts, and without any involvement by personnel located within the United States.[34]

The FCPA does not specifically address foreign subsidiaries, and no court has addressed the Act's coverage of foreign subsidiaries. Still, FCPA settlements have charged parent companies and foreign subsidiaries, and there are numerous statutory and common law theories under which a U.S. parent company may be liable for the misconduct of a foreign subsidiary. First, a U.S. company may be liable for bribery under agency principles if it had knowledge of or was willfully blind to the misconduct of its subsidiary. Second, a U.S. parent corporation that authorizes, directs, or controls the wayward acts of a foreign subsidiary may be liable. Third, a U.S. company may be held liable under principles of *respondeat superior* where its corporate veil can be pierced. Fourth, a U.S. company that takes actions abroad in furtherance of a bribery scheme may be found liable under the Act's 1998 alternative theory of nationality jurisdiction. Finally, foreign subsidiaries may be liable if any act in furtherance of an illegal bribe took place in the United States territory.[35]

2.   *Accounting Misconduct*

The DOJ may charge a publicly traded parent company for FCPA accounting violations by a foreign subsidiary(ies) when the books and records of the parent and subsidiary(ies) are consolidated in SEC filings. Specifically, a parent may be criminally liable where it *knowingly* fails to keep accurate books and records or maintain internal controls sufficient to provide "reasonable assurances" that transactions are executed in a proper manner.[36] Companies may also be liable for books and records misconduct by the employees of foreign subsidiaries if the parent owns or controls more than 50 percent of a subsidiary's voting securities.[37]

V.   ADDITIONAL RESOURCES

- Brown, *Parent Subsidiary Liability Under the Foreign Corrupt Practices Act*, 50 BAYLOR L. REV. 1 (1998).
- Grime & Savage, *FCPA Jurisdiction Over Foreign Entities and Individuals: The Trend of Increasingly Aggressive Enforcement*, PLI FOREIGN CORRUPT PRACTICES ACT: COPING WITH HEIGHTENED ENFORCEMENT RISKS (PLI 2007).
- David Luban, Julie O'Sullivan & David Stewart, *Corruption,* ch. 14 in INTERNATIONAL AND TRANSNATIONAL CRIMINAL LAW (Aspen 2009).
- Sullivan & Grimes, Ch. XVIII, *Antitrust in Global Markets: The Extra Territorial Reach of Unilateral Rules; Comparative Antitrust; and*

Conflicting National Requirements and Bilateral and Multilateral Efforts to Resolve Them, THE LAW OF ANTITRUST: AN INTEGRATED HANDBOOK (2d Ed. 2006).

NOTES

1. Foreign Corrupt Practices Act of 1977, Pub. L. No. 95-213, 91 Stat. 1494 (codified as amended at 15 U.S.C. §§ 78m, 78dd-1 to -3, 78ff (1999)) [hereinafter FCPA].

2. Pub. L. No. 105-366.

3. OECD Convention, Article 1.

4. OECD Convention, Article 4.

5. *See* 15 U.S.C. § 78dd-1(a).

6. *See* 15 U.S.C. § 78dd-2(a).

7. 8 U.S.C. § 1101.

8. *See* 15 U.S.C. § 78dd-1(g).

9. 15 U.S.C. § 78dd-3.

10. 15 U.S.C. §§ 78dd-1(a), -2(a), -3(a).

11. 15 U.S.C. §§ 78dd-1(a), -2(a).

12. *See, e.g., Schmuck v. United States,* 489 U.S. 705 (1989).

13. International Anti-Bribery and Fair Competition Act of 1998, Pub. L. No. 105-366, § 4, 112 Stat. 3302, 3306 (1998) (codified at 15 U.S.C. §§ 78dd-1(g), -2(i)).

14. *Int'l Shoe Co. v. Washington,* 326 U.S. 310, 316 (1945).

15. *Id.* (quoting *Miliken v. Meyer,* 311 U.S. 457, 463 (1940)).

16. *World-Wide Volkswagen Corp. v. Woodson,* 444 U.S. 286, 297 (1980).

17. *See, e.g., Cent. States v. Reimer,* 230 F.3d 934, 946 (7th Cir. 2000); *U.S. v. Int'l Bhd. of Teamsters,* 945 F. Supp. 609, 620 (S.D.N.Y. 1996).

18. *SEC v. Unifund Sal,* 910 F.2d 1028, 1033 (2d Cir. 1990). Commentators and other countries have criticized the exercise of jurisdiction over foreign nationals based solely on the U.S. effects of overseas conduct. *See, e.g.,* H. Lowell Brown, *Extraterritorial Jurisdiction Under the 1998 Amendments to the Foreign Corrupt Practices Act: Does the Government's Reach Now Exceed its Grasp?,* 26 N.C. J. INT'L LAW & COM. REG. 239, 335 (Spring 2001) (discussing criticism).

19. *See, e.g., United States v. SSI Int'l Far East Ltd.,* No. 06-398 (D. Or. Oct. 10, 2006) (changing foreign subsidiary based on international wire transfers originating from the United States).

20. *SEC v. Unifund Sal,* 910 F.2d at 1033 (quoting *Bersch v. Drexel Firestone, Inc.,* 519 F.2d 974, 1000 (2d Cir. 1975).

21. *Id.*

22. *United States v. Klimavicius-Viloria,* 144 F.3d 1249, 1257 (9th Cir. 1998) (quoting *World-Wide Volkswagen,* 444 U.S. at 297)).

23. *United States v. Bin Laden,* 92 F. Supp. 2d 189, 219 (S.D.N.Y. 2000).

24. *See, e.g., United States v. Davis,* 905 F.2d 245 (9th Cir. 1990).

25. *Supreme Court:* United States v. Wise, 370 U.S. 405, 82 S.Ct. l354, 8 L.Ed.2d 590 (1962); New York Central & Hudson River Railroad Co. v. United States, 212 U.S. 481, 493.29 S.Ct. 304, 53 L.Ed. 613 (1909).

First Circuit: United States v. Potter, 463 F.3d 9 (1st Cir. 2006); United States v. Cincotta, 689 F.2d 238 (1st Cir. 1982).

Second Circuit: United States *v.* Koppers Co. Inc., 652 F.2d 290, 298 (2d Cir.), *cert. denied* 454 U.S. 1083 (1981); Granite Partners, L.P. Y. Bear, Stearns & Co., 17 F. Supp. 2d 275, 296 (S.D.N.Y. 1998).

Third Circuit: Mininshon v. United States, 101 F.2d 477 (3d Cir. 1939).

Seventh Circuit: United States v. Empire Packing Co., 174 F.2d 16 (7th Cir. 1949).

Ninth Circuit: United States v. Hilton Hotels Corp., 467 F.2d 1000 (9th Cir. 1972), *cert, denied sub nom.* Western International Hotels Co. v. United States, 409 U.S. 1125 (1973).

See generally Kathleen Brickey, Corporate Criminal Liability, Vol. 1, Ch. 3 (2d ed. 1991).

26. See cases holding that low-level employees may bind a corporation for purposes of imposing criminal liability, e.g.:

Supreme Court: United States v. Illinois Central Railroad, 303 U.S. 239, 58 S. Ct. 533,82 L. Ed. 773 (1938) (manual laborers; employee whose duty was unloading cattle for carrier).

First Circuit: St. Johnsbury Trucking Co. v. United States, 220 F.2d 393 (1st Cir. 1955) (rating clerk).

Second Circuit: United States v. George F. Fish, Inc., 154 F.2d 798 (2d Cir.), *cert. denied* 328 U.S. 869 (1946) (salesman).

Fourth Circuit: United States v. E. Brooke Matlack, Inc., 149 F. Supp. 814 (D. Md. 1957) (truck drivers).

Fifth Circuit: Steere Tank Lines, Inc. v. United States, 330 F.2d 719 (5th Cir. 1963) (truck driver).

Seventh Circuit: Zito v. United States, 64 F.2d 772, 775 (7th Cir. 1933) (sales agent).

Eighth Circuit: Riss & Co. v. United States, 262 F.2d 245 (8th Cir. 1958) (terminal log clerk).

Ninth Circuit: Dollar S.S. Co. v. United States, 101 F.2d 638 (9th Cir. 1939) (manual laborers; crew member emptying garbage); United States v. Wilson, 59 F.2d 97 (W.D. Wash. 1932) (sales manager).

Tenth Circuit: United States v. Harry L. Young & Sons, Inc., 464 F.2d 1295 (10th Cir. 1972) (truck driver); Texas-Oklahoma Express. Inc. v. United Stares. 429 F.2d 100 (10th Cir. 1970) (truck drivers).

See also United States v. Dye Construction Co., 510 F.2d 78, 82 (10th Cir. !975) (pipe-laying crew consisting of supervisor, foreman, and back hoe operator).

But see State of Ohio v. Black on Black Crime, Inc, 136 Ohio App. 3d 436, 444, 736 N.E.2d 962, 968 (2000) (business entity is guilty of criminal act only if it was approved, recommended or implemented by high managerial personnel who make basic corporate policies).

27. State of Ohio v Black on Black Crime, Inc., 136 Ohio App. 3d 436, 444, 736 N.E.2d 962, 968 (2000).

28. See K. Brickey, *Corporate Criminal Liability: A Primer for Corporate Counsel,* 40 Bus. Lawyer 129, 131 (1984). *See also* C.J.T. Corp. v. United States, 150 F.2d 85, 89 (9th Cir. 1945).

29. *See e.g.:* United States v. Portac, Inc., 869 F.2d 1288, 1293 (9th Cir. 1989); United States v. Hilton Hotels Corp., 467 F.2d 1000 (9th Cir. 1972), *cert. denied sub nom.* Western International Hotels Co. v. United States, 409 U.S. 1125 (1973).

30. *See generally:*

Supreme Court: New York Central & Hudson River Railroad Co. v. United States, 212 U.S. 481, 493, 29 S. Ct. 304, 53 L.Ed. 613 (1909).

First Circuit: United States v, Cincotta, 689 F.2d, 238, 241–242 (1st Cir. 1982).

Second Circuit: United States v. Georgopoulos, 149 F.3d 169, 171 (2d Cir. 1998), *cert. denied* 525 U.S. 1139, 119 S. Ct. 1029, 143 L. Ed. 2d 38 (1999); United States v. Jacques Dessange. Inc., 103 F. Supp. 2d 701, 706 (S.D.N.Y. 2000), *aff'd* 4 Fed. Appx. 59 (2d Cir. 2001).

Third Circuit: United States v. American Standard Radiator & Standard Sanitary Corp., 433 F.2d 174 (3d Cir. 1970).

Fifth Circuit: United States v. Ridglea State Bank, 357 F.2d 495 (5th Cir. 1966); Steere Tank Lines, Inc. v. United States. 330 F.2d 719 (5th Cir. 1963); Standard Oil Co. of Texas v. United States, 307 F.2d 120, 128 (5th Cir. 1962).

Sixth Circuit: Trollinger v. Tyson Foods, Inc., 2007 WL 1091217 (E.D. Tenn. April 10, 2007); United States v. Carter, 311 F.2d 934, 941–942 (6th Cir), *cert. denied* 373 U.S. 915 (1963).

Seventh Circuit: United States v. One Parcel of Land, 965 F.2d 311, 316 (7th Cir. 1992); United States v. One 1997 E35 Ford Van, 50 F. Supp. 2d 789, 796 (N.D. Ill. 1999).

Eighth Circuit: Egan v. United States, 137 F.2d 369, 380 (8th Cir.), *cert. denied* 320 U.S. 788 (1943).

Ninth Circuit: Magnolia Motor & Logging Co. v. United States, 264 F.2d 950 (9th Cir.), *cert. denied* 361 U.S. 815 (1959); United States v. Banco Internacional/Bital, 110 F. Supp. 2d 1272 (C.D. Cal. 2000).

Tenth Circuit: United States v. Harry L. Young and Sons, Inc., 464 F.2d 1295 (10th Cir. 1972).

District of Columbia Circuit: United States v. Sun-Diamond Growers of California, 138 F.3d 961 (D.C. Cir 1998), *aff'd on other grounds* 526 U.S. 398, 119 S. Ct. 1402, 143 L. Ed. 2d 576 (1999).

See also Kathleen Brickey, Corporate Criminal Liability, Vol. 1, § 4.02 (2d ed. 1991).

31. *Fourth Circuit:* Old Monastery Co. v. United State,. 147 F.2d 905 (4th Cir.). *cert. denied* 326 U.S. 734 (1945).

Sixth Circuit: United States v. NHML, Inc., 225 F.3d 660 (6th Cir. 2000); United States v. Rhoad, 36 F. Supp. 2d 792, 792 (S.D. Ohio 1998).

Ninth Circuit: United States v. Beusch, 596 F.2d 871, 877–878 (9th Cir. 1979).

Eleventh Circuit: United States v. Gold, 743 F.2d 800, 823 (11th Cir. 1984), *cert. denied* 469 U.S. 1217 (1985).

See, e.g. United States v. Sun-Diamond Growers of California, 138 F.3d 961, 970 (D.C. Cir. 1998), *aff'd on other grounds,* 526 U.S. 398, 119 S. Ct. 1402, 143 L. Ed. 2d 576 (1999) (finding corporate liability even though the employee's scheme "came at some cost to [the corporation]" because it "also promised some benefit.").

See also Kathleen Brickey, Corporate Criminal Liability, Vol. 1, § 4.02 (2d ed. 1991); Burgess and Stein, *Carrots, Sticks and Criminal Penalties.* Arizona Attorney, p. 32 (Feb. 2001).

32. United States v. Automated Medical Laboratories, 770 F.2d 399 4th Cir. 1985).

33. *See* H.R. Conf. Rep. No. 95-831, at 15 (1977); *J. Dooley v. United Techs. Corp.,* 803 F. Supp. 428, 439 (D.D.C. 1992).

34. U.S. Dept. of Justice, *Lay-Person's Guide to FCPA,* www.usdoj.gov/criminal/fraud/docs/dojdocb.html.

35. This discussion reflects the analysis of Professor Julie O'Sullivan of Georgetown Law Center in David Luban, Julie O'Sullivan & David Stewart, International and Transnational Criminal Law, ch. 14 *Corruption* (Aspen 2009).

36. 15 U.S.C. § 78m(b)(4).

37. *See generally* Howard Brown, *Parent Subsidiary Liability Under the Foreign Corrupt Practices Act,* 50 Baylor L. Rev. 1-29 (1998).

CHAPTER 3

Anti-Bribery Conventions

Companies doing business internationally must be aware of the increasing global focus on prosecuting foreign bribery of government officials. This focus is evident from a number of major international treaties directed against these practices and legislation in the signatory nations implementing these pacts. The increased presence of multijurisdictional government investigations may require companies to engage international law firms or a team of law firms to handle the often conflicting interests, privacy, laws, and demands of U.S. and foreign authorities.

I. THE ORGANIZATION FOR ECONOMIC AND COOPERATIVE DEVELOPMENT CONVENTION

A. Background

The Organization for Economic and Cooperative Development (OECD) Convention on Combatting Bribery of Foreign Officials in International Business Transactions was signed on December 17, 1997.[1] This treaty requires all signatories to take steps to criminalize the payment of bribes to foreign public officials and to establish appropriate sanctions on firms and individuals guilty of violating these provisions. The Convention does not eliminate the tax deductibility of bribes permitted by some countries and does not generally apply to bribes made to political parties. The U.S. State Department has called the OECD Convention "a major milestone in U.S. efforts over more than two decades to have other major trading nations join us in criminalizing the bribery of foreign public officials in international business transactions."[2]

B. The OECD Convention and Domestic Legislation

The OECD Convention is the narrowest of the multilateral treaties and, like the Foreign Corrupt Practices Act, focuses only on transnational active bribery (Appendix 2).[3] There are 38 signatories to the OECD Convention, with Israel becoming the 38th signatory in September 2008.[4] In the United States, the International Anti-Bribery and Fair Competition Act of 1998 amended the FCPA to implement the OECD Convention.[5] Other countries have similarly adopted legislation, which varies widely on many significant points. As a result, corporations conducting international business must carefully scrutinize the law in each OECD country where they do business.

The OECD Convention has not yet achieved the goal of leveling the playing field between U.S. persons subject to the FCPA and their foreign competitors. In 2004 a State Department report found many deficiencies in the implementing legislation of the signatories, including, among others, France, Japan, and the United Kingdom.[6] The report noted, however, that many of the deficient countries are in the process of considering, or implementing, amendments to their legislation that may put more teeth in their enforcement programs.[7] Persons engaged in international commerce, and their counsel, are wise to stay abreast of these developments.

C. The Main Provisions of the OECD Convention

In general, the OECD Convention requires signatory nations to adopt "effective, proportionate, and dissuasive criminal sanctions" to those persons who bribe foreign public officials.[8] It calls for each nation to exercise its full jurisdictional powers to punish foreign bribery where the offense is committed in whole or in part on its soil, or is committed by its nationals abroad.[9] Like the FCPA, it contains both anti-bribery and recordkeeping provisions. Other significant points of the OECD Convention include the following:

1. Active Bribery Only

The Convention criminalizes only "active bribery," which involves offering or giving a bribe. "Passive bribery," or the act of soliciting a bribe, is not addressed on the basis that this is presumably already a criminal offense in most countries.

2. Definition of Bribery

"Active bribery" is defined as a bribe offered or given "in order to obtain or retain business or other improper advantage in the conduct of international business." As with the FCPA, small facilitation payments made with the intention of expediting or securing the performance of a routine governmental action are excluded from the definition of improper payments under the Convention. By referring to "other improper advantage," the Convention intends to address situations where a payment is made to obtain something to which the company is clearly not entitled (e.g., an operating permit for a factory that failed to meet local health and safety standards). The Convention also requires signatories to prohibit the use of off-the-book accounts and other practices used to conceal bribes made to public officials.

3. Public Officials

The Convention defines "public official" as follows: "any person holding a legislative, administrative or judicial office of a foreign country, whether appointed or elected; any person exercising a public function or involved in a public agency or public enterprise; and any official or agent of a public international organization." According to an OECD report of the negotiating conference, the term "public official" does not encompass political parties, persons on the verge of being elected or appointed to public office, or private sector corruption.[10]

4. Civil Liability If Not Criminal

The Convention recognizes that in countries like Brazil, Japan, and Germany, legal entities (e.g., corporations) generally cannot be criminally responsible under domestic law. However, Article 2 of the Convention requires all signatories to hold legal entities liable for the bribery of foreign public officials without specifying whether such liability is to be criminal or civil. Article 3.2 further requires that in countries that do not impose criminal liability on legal persons, "effective, proportionate, and dissuasive non-criminal sanctions, including monetary sanctions" should be imposed.

5. Reliance on Domestic Laws

The Convention seeks to impose general standards rather than detailed prohibitions. Though it provides a definition of the offense criminalized, the Convention also relies on the fact that its signatories' domestic laws regarding the issue of internal bribery or their rules pertaining to criminal law will be extended so as to address the bribery of foreign public officials.

6. Legal Assistance

The Convention requires members to give "prompt and effective" legal assistance to other parties in connection with investigations and proceedings brought by a party to the convention. Dual criminality is not required.

D. Significant Enforcement

In 2008 Transparency International issued a report in which it concluded there is now "significant enforcement" in sixteen countries: Argentina, Australia, Belgium, Denmark, Finland, France, Germany, Hungary, Italy, Korea, the Netherlands, Norway, Spain, Sweden, Switzerland, and the U.S.[11]

II. UNITED NATIONS CONVENTION AGAINST CORRUPTION

On December 14, 2005, the United Nations Convention Against Corruption (UNCAC) entered into force and currently has 140 state parties.[12] UNCAC is the broadest and most comprehensive of all the multilateral corruption conventions. This convention does not explicitly exclude facilitating agents, but its definition of "bribe" is thought to exclude such payments.[13] The United States ratified the UN Convention on October 30, 2006. The UN Convention covers commercial bribery and not simply bribes of government officials. It also addresses embezzlement, money laundering, obstruction of justice, corporate recordkeeping, extradition, and international law enforcement cooperation.

III. REGIONAL CONVENTIONS

A. The Organization of American States Inter-American Convention Against Corruption

The Organization of American States (OAS) Inter-American Convention Against Corruption (IACAC), which entered into force on March 6, 1997, was the first multilateral treaty to address corruption.[14] Twenty-eight countries have signed the convention,[15] which is considered a model for laws on jurisdiction, extradition, legal assistance cooperation, bank secrecy, and tax deductibility of international bribes.[16] Similar to the FCPA, the convention requires parties to criminalize the bribery of foreign officials.[17] To serve its purpose of preventing, detecting, punishing, and eradicating corruption, the OAS Convention calls for cooperation among countries in the fight against domestic and transnational corruption in the Western Hemisphere.[18] The convention requires that member states afford one another the "widest measure of mutual assistance" in the criminal investigation and prosecution of such acts.[19] As a result, parties must extradite individuals who violate another country's anti-corruption laws.[20] Moreover, member states cannot invoke bank secrecy as a basis for refusing to assist another state.[21]

Parties are also required to update their domestic legislation to criminalize corrupt acts, such as transnational bribery, to prevent any national from bribing an official of another state, and illicit enrichment, to prohibit inexplicable increases in assets of government officials.[22] The United States, however, ratified the OAS Convention in September 2000 with the understanding that the United States would not establish a new criminal offense of illicit enrichment because it is constitutionally problematic.[23]

B. The Council of Europe Convention

The Council of Europe (CoE), founded in 1949, consists of 46 member countries whose aims include a solution to organized crime and corruption. This convention is more comprehensive as, unlike the OECD Convention or the IACAC, it seeks to criminalize active *and* passive bribery of domestic public officials (Arts. 2 and 3); foreign public officials (Art. 5); domestic public assemblies (Art. 4); foreign public assemblies (Art. 6); international or company officials (Art. 9); members of international parliamentary assemblies (Art. 10); judges and officials of international courts (Art. 11); and those in the private sector (Arts. 7 and 8).[24] Article 2 defines bribery as giving "any undue advantage" for an official "to act or refrain from acting in the exercise of his or her functions." This Convention makes no explicit exception for facilitating payments. The Group of States Against Corruption (GRECO), which is an enlarged partial agreement, was established in 1999 by the CoE to monitor states' compliance with the organization's anti-corrupt standards. Currently, GRECO has 46 member states (45 European states and the United States).[25] The convention criminalizes a wide range of corrupt practices in both the public and private sector, such as bribery of domestic and foreign public officials, active and passive bribery in the private sector, and money laundering of proceeds from corruption offenses.[26] Similar to the OAS Convention Against Corruption, the CoE convention calls for states to afford one another the "widest measure of mutual assistance" in investigating or prosecuting such acts.[27] Likewise, the CoE convention deems corrupt acts outlined in the convention as extraditable offenses.[28]

IV.   2008–2009 UNITED KINGDOM CORRUPTION ENFORCEMENT ACTIONS AND EXTRADITION COOPERATION

In fall 2008, United Kingdom authorities filed two separate corruption enforcement actions signaling a clear commitment to enforce foreign bribery laws. First, the Overseas Anti-Corruption Unit of the London Police Department charged a U.K. consulting firm managing director and a Ugandan official with bribery in a scheme under which the managing director's security firm paid the foreign official for a contract with the Ugandan Presidential Guard. Both pled guilty, and the Ugandan official was sentenced to a year in jail.[29] Second, the United Kingdom's Serious Fraud Office announced a $3.9 million civil settlement with the major construction firm Balfour Beatty PLC for unlawful accounting in connection with payment irregularities.[30] While these two cases do not begin to approach the magnitude of U.S. anti-corruption civil and criminal actions or fines, they signal a start by a country that has been criticized for lax corruption enforcement and highlight the conviction of a foreign government official—something unavailable to U.S. prosecutors under the FCPA. Whether the United Kingdom will actively prosecute corporations for corruption remains unclear.

Finally, in March 2009, the London Metropolitan Police arrested Jeffrey Tesler for his alleged role in the efforts of the engineering and construction firm KBR to bribe Nigerian officials in order to obtain engineering, procurement, and construction contracts. Tesler extradition efforts are just beginning, but U.S. and U.K. authorities likely agreed before the arrest to work together closely to extradite Tesler.[31] A full extradition hearing is underway.

V.   ADDITIONAL RESOURCES

- Witten, Parker & Koffer, *Navigating the Increased Anti-Corruption Environment in the United States and Abroad,* paper presented at the National Institute on White Collar Crime, San Francisco, March 5–6, 2009.
- David Luban, Julie O'Sullivan & David Stewart, *Corruption,* ch. 14 in INTERNATIONAL AND TRANSNATIONAL CRIMINAL LAW (Aspen 2009).
- Don Zarin, DOING BUSINESS UNDER THE FOREIGN CORRUPT PRACTICES ACT, ch. 13 (PLI 2007).

NOTES

1. The original signatories of the OECD Convention are Argentina, Australia, Austria, Belgium, Brazil, Bulgaria, Canada, Chile, the Czech Republic, Denmark, Finland, France, Germany, Greece, Hungary, Iceland, Ireland, Italy, Japan, Korea, Luxembourg, Mexico, the Netherlands, New Zealand, Norway, Poland, Portugal, the Slovak Republic, Slovenia, Spain, Sweden, Switzerland, Turkey, the United Kingdom, and the United States. The Organization for Economic Cooperation and Development Convention on Combatting Bribery of Foreign Officials in International Business Transactions, Dec. 18, 1997, OECD document DAFFE/IME/BR (97) 20, 37 I.L.M. 1 (1998).

2. *Id.* at v.

3. *See* DAVID LUBAN, JULIE O'SULLIVAN & DAVID STEWART, INTERNATIONAL AND TRANSNATIONAL CRIMINAL LAW at 24 (Aspen 2009) for a thorough discussion of the current multilateral conventions.

4. BATTLING INTERNATIONAL BRIBERY, *supra* note 1, at iii.

5. International Anti-Bribery and Fair Competition Act of 1998, Pub. L. No. 105-366, 112 Stat. 3302 (1998) (codified at 15 U.S.C. §§ 78dd-1 to -3, 78ff), amending the Foreign Corrupt Practices Act of 1977, Pub. L. No. 95-213, 91 Stat. 1494 (codified as amended at 15 U.S.C. §§ 78m, 78dd-1 to 78dd-2, 78ff (1994)) [hereinafter FCPA].

6. *Id.* at 12.

7. *Id.* at 14.

8. OECD Convention art. 3.

9. OECD Convention art. 4.

10. However, under the laws of some countries, bribes promised or given to a person anticipating to become a foreign public official may qualify

under the Convention. *See Commentaries on Convention on Combating Bribery, in* BATTLING INTERNATIONAL BRIBERY 2004, *supra* note 1, at B-6. Furthermore, there are some countries where certain individuals (such as political party officials in single-party states) are not formally recognized as public officials, but for their de facto performance of a public function. Under the legal principles of those states, such individuals may be considered public officials. *See id.* at B-7.

11. OECD Anti-Bribery Convention: Progress Reports 2008 at 11 at http://www.transparency.hu/files/Final%20Progress%ReportOECD2008.pdf.

12. *See* Signatories to the United Nations Convention Against Corruption, http://www.unodc.org/unodc/en/treaties/CAC/signatories.html.

13. O'SULLIVAN, *supra* note 3, at 51.

14. Alejandro Posadas, *Combating Corruption Under International Law*, 10 DUKE J. COMP. & INT'L L. 345, 384 (2000).

15. IACAC Signatory Countries, http://www.oas.org/juridico/English/Sigs/b-58.html.

16. Nora M. Rubin, *A Convergence of 1996 and 1997 Global Efforts to Curb Corruption and Bribery in International Business Transactions: The Legal Implications of OECD Recommendations and Convention for the United States, Germany, and Switzerland*, 14 A.M.U. INT'L L. REV. 257, 261–63 (1998).

17. *See* U.S. Dep't of State Fact Sheet, OAS Inter-American Convention Against Corruption, May 27, 1997.

18. *See* Inter-American Convention Against Corruption art. II.

19. *See id.* art. XIV.

20. *See id.* art. XIII.

21. *See id.* art. XVI.

22. *See id.* arts. VII–IX.

23. *See* U.S. Dep't of State, First Annual Report to Congress on the Inter-American Convention Against Corruption (Apr. 2001).

24. LUBAN, O'SULLIVAN & STEWART, *supra* note 3, at 47.

25. http://www.coe.int/t/dghl/monitoring/greco/general.

26. *See* Criminal Law Convention on Corruption ch. II.

27. *See id.* ch. IV, art. 26.

28. *See id.* art. 27.

29. Press Release, City of London Police, Government Official Guilty of Corruption (Sept. 22, 2008), http://www.cityoflondon.police.uk/CityPolice/Media/News/NewsArchive/2008/govermentofficialguiltyofcorruption.htm.

30. Press Release, Serious Fraud Office, Serious Fraud Office Successfully Obtains First Ever Civil Recovery Order Involving Major PLC. (Oct. 6, 2008), http://www.sfo.gov.uk/news/prout/pr_582.asp?id=582.

31. David Leigh & Rob Evans, *US Seeks to Extradite Briton in Nigerian Bribery Case*, GUARDIAN (UK), May 11, 2009.

CHAPTER 4

Board of Directors and Management Responsibilities

I. BOARD OF DIRECTORS RESPONSIBILITIES

A board of directors has a duty of care to the company that requires it to be informed of developments in the company's business and of possible liabilities. Certain categories of Securities and Exchange Commission investigations (including those raising issues of improper payments, false books and records, and circumvention of internal controls) may require directors to inform themselves of the underlying facts. This is especially true where senior management is alleged to have engaged in improper conduct.[1] A responsible multinational board of directors today must focus on anti-bribery issues, policies, and compliance.

II. *IN RE CAREMARK* AND DIRECTOR CORPORATE GOVERNANCE RESPONSIBILITIES

In re Caremark International Inc. Derivative Litigation[2] is a landmark decision that establishes a baseline for the corporate governance responsibilities of a board of directors. In this case the Delaware Chancery Court held that the failure of a board of directors to ensure that its company had an adequate corporate compliance information and reporting system in place could "render a director liable for losses caused by non-compliance with applicable legal standards." Commenting on the 1991 enactment of the Organizational Sentencing Guidelines, Chancellor William T. Allen emphasized: "Any rational person attempting in good faith to meet an organizational governance responsibility would be bound to take into account this development and the enhanced penalties and the opportunities for reduced sanctions that it offers."[3]

Further, the chancellor wrote: "The Guidelines offer powerful incentives for corporations today to have in place compliance programs to detect violations of law, promptly to report violations to appropriate public officials when discovered, and to take prompt, voluntary reme-dial efforts."[4] A company's compliance program should be "reasonably designed to provide to senior management and to the board itself timely, accurate information sufficient to allow management and the board, each within its scope, to reach informed judgments concerning both the corporation's compliance with the law and its business performance."[5]

Chancellor Allen concluded that "a director's obligation includes a duty to attempt in good faith to assure that a corporate information and reporting system, which the board concludes is adequate, exists, and that failure to do so under some circumstances may, in theory at least, render a director liable for losses caused by noncompliance with applicable legal standards."[6] Directors therefore have an affirmative duty to find and cor-rect illegal behavior by corporate employees. The most effective way to fulfill this duty is through an effective and regularly updated compliance program, including a methodology for identifying and addressing any violations of applicable laws or company policies.

III.   SARBANES-OXLEY CERTIFICATIONS BY PUBLIC COMPANY OFFICERS

Under the Sarbanes-Oxley Act of 2002, chief executive officers and chief financial officers of public companies must certify the accuracy of periodic filings with the SEC.[7] A CEO or CFO must certify that he has reviewed the report, that to his knowledge the report does not contain any mate-rial misstatements or omissions, and that the financial statements and other information contained in the report fairly represent in all material respects the company's financial condition and results of operations of the issuer for the periods presented in the reports.[8]

The CEO and CFO must also certify in each quarterly or annual report that they are responsible for establishing and maintaining internal con-trols[9] and have designed such internal controls to ensure that material information relating to the company and its consolidated subsidiaries is made known to such officers by others within those entities;[10] that they have evaluated the effectiveness of the company's internal controls within the past 90 days;[11] that they have presented in the report their conclusions about the effectiveness of their controls;[12] and that they have disclosed to the company's auditors and the audit committee all signifi-cant deficiencies in the design or operation of internal controls that could adversely affect the company's ability to record, process, summarize, and report financial data, and have identified for the auditors any material weaknesses in internal controls and any fraud, whether material or not, that involves management or other employees who have a significant role in the issuer's internal controls.[13]

Whoever certifies one of the above statements knowing that the periodic report does not comport with all the requirements can be fined up to $1,000,000 and imprisoned up to 10 years.[14] Whoever willfully certifies such a statement knowing it does not comport with the statute's requirements can be fined up to $5,000,000 and imprisoned up to 20 years.[15] Foreign Corrupt Practices Act investigations frequently trigger reporting or disclosure responsibilities and certification issues for publicly held companies and their CEOs and CFOs.

IV. COMPLIANCE PROGRAMS

Perhaps no other federal law enforcement area places a greater premium or penalty on compliance programs than the FCPA enforcement area. If a multinational company has a quality compliance program in place, identifies a problem, takes the steps to stop it (worldwide), and implements substantial remedial measures, the efforts will generally be rewarded. Conversely, if the company has no compliance program in place, poor internal controls, and does not address the issues in a timely and responsibly, it will be seriously punished when misconduct is discovered by the U.S. government.

The hallmarks of a quality corporate compliance program are a clear statement of the company's code of conduct or ethics policy (a written confirmation of the "tone at the top"), strong managers and compliance officers, clear written compliance materials, periodic live training and consulting, program monitoring, thorough due diligence, and periodic audits of specific work programs. Mere "paper" compliance programs will earn no credit for companies undergoing FCPA investigations by the SEC or the Department of Justice.

A. Effective Compliance and Ethics Programs

Corporations must bear in mind the relevant compliance program language in and commentary to the Organization section of the United States Sentencing Guidelines.[16] Although the Guidelines were designed to determine the appropriate punishment for convicted persons and corporations, their criteria have become the benchmark for U.S. corporations seeking to both satisfy corporate governance standards and to minimize sentencing exposure in the event of prosecution and conviction.

The organizational guidelines highlight seven minimum standards for an effective corporate compliance and ethics program. The commentary to the guidelines in essence provides that an organization must:

1. Establish "compliance standards and procedures . . . capable of reducing . . . criminal conduct";

2. Assign "high-level personnel" to "oversee compliance with such standards and procedures";
3. Not delegate "substantial discretionary authority" to personnel with "a propensity to engage in illegal activities";
4. "[C]ommunicate effectively its standards and procedures to all employees and other agents";
5. Take "reasonable steps to achieve compliance with its standards";
6. "[C]onsistently enforce[ ]" its compliance standards;
7. "[R]espond appropriately to" a legal violation and take steps "to prevent further similar" violations.[17]

In addition to following these minimum steps, company counsel should keep abreast of SEC enforcement actions and DOJ resolutions, as they can offer valuable guidance on compliance programs and evolving compliance standards.

B.   Preliminary Anti-Bribery/FCPA Risk Profile

Many multinational companies that have not experienced a government anti-bribery or FCPA investigation all too often presume that they have no corruption or compliance program problems and that their existing compliance programs would fare well if the companies were to become the subject or target of an anti-bribery or FCPA investigation.

Corporate counsel should conduct a Preliminary Anti-Bribery/FCPA Risk Profile test for their companies. Such tests afford multinational companies a preliminary assessment of whether they have standard or recommended compliance measures in place *and* how they would fare with an initial request by the DOJ and/or SEC for overall compliance program material, anti-bribery/FCPA oversight documentation, e.g., Board of Director and/or Audit Committee records and Anti-Bribery/FCPA training documentation. Appendix 3 is a sample preliminary Risk Assessment; it is preliminary in that it affords a company a quick snapshot assessment of a company's compliance commitment, but it is not a substitute for a deep dive analysis of a company's compliance program.

In addition to focusing on the underlying issue, for example, payment to a tax official in the Indonesian federal tax office, both the DOJ and SEC routinely request or subpoena compliance program, document retention, training, and internal audit materials. In the majority of FCPA prosecutions to date, charged companies have had weak compliance programs and often no FCPA training. The more compliance and FCPA-oriented materials a company can produce early in an investigation, the much better off it will be in avoiding a felony prosecution or serious enforcement action.

A simple, ten-minute Preliminary Multinational Compliance Risk Profile test is found in Appendix 3. This test is designed to evaluate the compliance roles and activities of the board of directors, the chief executive officer, chief financial officer, general counsel, and the internal audit staff; to review international contracts, FCPA training, and due diligence and acquisition practices; and to then weigh the multinational's country risks, regional and/or in-country management weaknesses, and prior enforcement history. While it is no substitute for an FCPA audit or consultation with FCPA counsel, an FCPA risk profile test can provide a company with a good idea of how it would fare in forming an important first impression in connection with an initial DOJ or SEC document request.

C. Tone at the Top

The overriding mantra of most compliance experts is that a good corporate citizen must have an affirmative, ethical "tone at the top." Senior executives who embrace this value repeatedly state it at annual meetings, in annual reports, in employee newsletters, and at management conferences, retreats, and large employee gatherings. As important, they take firm action when employees or colleagues blur or cross ethical lines. Of course, they must hold themselves to the same high ethical standards.

Virtually all CEOs and CFOs state that they embrace "tone at the top." In government FCPA investigations, experienced prosecutors and enforcement attorneys are not hesitant to test that commitment in interviews of senior officers, to explore employees' and subordinates' perceptions of the true "tone at the top," or to examine the company's existing compliance program. Prudent multinational companies can demonstrate a strong "tone at the top" by conducting FCPA training for the boards of directors and annually reviewing how often and effectively the company and its executives have communicated the importance of compliance to its constituents. They can also demonstrate "tone at the top" by having active FCPA oversight by a board committee such as an audit or ethics committee; establishing related management committees, for example, a compliance task force that meets quarterly; employing one or more full-time compliance officers; and having an engaged internal audit staff.

D. Codes of Conduct

Effective codes of conduct will both provide an organizational compliance structure and inform employees, officers, and directors of proscribed anti-bribery conduct in plain terms. A cover message from the chief executive officer or chief compliance officer can convey the company's commitment to ethical values and the importance of adherence to the code of conduct by all employees, and thereby establish a correct "tone at the top" and promote leadership among managers.

Some codes are formal, adopting statutory language, while others are conversational. The best codes of conduct are custom-made for the company and its business and recognize the particular challenges that officers, employers, and business units face in the regions where the company conducts business. They invariably address conflicts of interest, related-party interests, reporting of unusual activity, safety, accuracy of books and records, and disciplinary actions. For multinational companies, anti-bribery law and exports and imports violations should be addressed. Large organizations offer employees examples of problematic situations and appropriate guidance through short case studies or Frequently Asked Questions (FAQs).

Codes of conduct should address all appropriate and key risk areas for a company and its given industry or industries. They should offer a clear reporting mechanism and guidance to employees on how to seek help. Codes of conduct should be made available and distributed to all employees, officers, and directors, and should be translated into the languages of the countries where the company has significant operations. Many corporations require an annual certification that each employee has read and understands the code and is unaware of any violations in the past year.[18]

While broad and wide-ranging codes of conduct have become salutary and commonplace for U.S. companies, they can create risks for multinational companies in other jurisdictions. Global employment law expert Cynthia L. Jackson has cautioned that, in order to mitigate against foreign legal liabilities, U.S. multinationals should:

- Distinguish legally mandated from voluntary provisions in a Code of Conduct. If the company determines that voluntary policies are critical to its stakeholders, it should commit sufficient time and money to monitor, train, and ensure compliance.
- Understand and monitor for compliance with local legal requirements (e.g., wage and hour and other employment regulations, bribery, environmental, import-export, data privacy, and other local laws).
- Observe all local employment and privacy procedural prerequisites before rolling out the Code of Conduct.
- Not assume that "cause" to discipline in the U.S. will be "cause" in a local jurisdiction.
- Recognize that some countries, particularly within the E.U., restrict the types of violations that can be reported to the U.S. to, for instance, accounting, internal accounting controls, auditing matters, government bribery, banking, and financial matters.
- Recognize most E.U. countries permit, but discourage, anonymity. Some countries, such as Spain, prohibit anonymous hotlines.
- Consider deleting voluntary "feel good" policies, unless they are truly core to the company's culture and ingrained into corporate practice. In some jurisdictions, such as China, merely requiring

compliance with local law may require "raising the bar" significantly and constant training and reinforcement.

- Review of the Code of Conduct with the same precision as a proxy statement. Better to under promise and over deliver than the opposite.[19]

E.   FCPA Policies

Companies that operate in many foreign jurisdictions, employ a significant number of foreign nationals, or conduct business in countries perceived to be corrupt often conclude that a detailed FCPA policy is necessary both to emphasize the importance of compliance and to give employees operational guidance.

Practical FCPA policies will consider and address the countries or regions in which a company operates, the nature of a company's foreign government interface, and the risks of the particular industry. If a company operates in countries with a Transparency International Corruption Perceptions Index of less than 5 and has any interface with foreign government officials, it should have a standalone FCPA policy.

In 2001, the DOJ issued a *Lay-Person's Guide to FCPA*,[20] a very practical nine-page description of the anti-bribery provisions of the Act. Some corporations have made this guidance part of, or an appendix to, their FCPA policies. Many multinationals require all officers and heads of business units to certify compliance with the FCPA annually. As with corporate codes of conduct, FCPA policies should be written in plain terms and be available to all employees in the languages relevant to the company's operations. Posting FCPA policies on a company intranet is another way to convey to a workforce the importance of and commitment to the FCPA. Well-managed companies and legal departments will have a specific protocol for handling FCPA allegations.

F.   FCPA Training

Multinational companies should conduct periodic live FCPA training for country general managers, sales, legal, financial, accounting, and audit personnel. Custom training will address, inter alia, the company's greatest risks, for example, hospitality practices in China or petty cash practices in Nigeria, and particular functions, for example financial review of contracts, payment instructions, and invoices from consultants; and cover recent FCPA prosecution and enforcement actions.

While numerous companies provide online FCPA training packages to employees, most compliance experts consider live training essential to their officers', directors', and senior employees' thorough understanding of the statute's anti-bribery and accounting provisions. Live training permits interaction as well as the sharing of up-to-date FCPA developments. Online training may be sufficient for employees who have minimal authority or interface with foreign government officials, but it is no substitute for live training in the case of key employees and officers who regularly deal with foreign government officials and contract and purchasing personnel. Some companies have multitier training: general ethics awareness training for low-level employees, advanced training for managers, and comprehensive anti-bribery workshops for senior managers who interface with government officials. Companies should keep records of FCPA training attendance and copies of all presentations.

A quality FCPA training program will review the fundamental anti-bribery provision elements, the facilitating payment exceptions, the reasonable and bona fide expenditure and written law affirmative defenses, common myths (e.g., "it's a legal defense that everyone, including competitors in the country in question, makes substantial payments to foreign officials"), red flags, the types of FCPA scenarios most likely to confront managers in particular countries, and examples of recent FCPA cases. The training program should cover "books and records" issues and best recordkeeping practices. It should also address local logistics risks such as customs, taxes, visas, and freight-forwarding contractors. FCPA training should be mandatory for key managers, including sales, accounting, and financial personnel, and be periodically updated.

G. FCPA Audits

Multinational companies are stepping up FCPA audits of foreign operations, using attorneys and either internal audit staffs or regular outside auditors. If possible, attorneys should conduct interviews to best preserve applicable privileges and supervise or handle audit report writing. A company must ensure that its internal auditors have a clear audit plan and have received FCPA training before they participate in FCPA audits. Audits can focus on financial controls, consulting contracts, petty cash practices, travel and entertainment, joint ventures, charitable donations, campaign contributions, distributors, foreign government disputes, sales, commissions, agency relationships, gift practices, parastatals, and relationships with foreign government officials. Audits will customarily track or analyze the money flow and involve sample testing. A multinational may decide to prioritize its FCPA audits based on prior company problems, industry-wide investigations, books and records and internal controls issues, recent problems of other multinational companies in the industry, work countries or regions, and the Transparency International index ratings. Audits of large operations in high-risk countries can last four weeks or more, but experienced attorneys can complete the required interviews in a week.

In planning an FCPA audit, many experienced attorneys and auditors find it helpful to review risk profile factors or models at the outset. (See Appendix 3.) Models can serve to identify points of potential vulnerability in a sales organization and to better focus an FCPA audit. Tests of controls will commonly address the adequacy of policies and procedures; FCPA training; agent, representative, and distributor agreements and payments; payments to government employees and foreign officials; foreign entity financial statements; foreign bank account reconciliations; travel and entertainment expenses; accounts payable; and petty cash disbursements.

H. Regular FCPA Risk Assessments, or "Audit Lites"

Some multinational companies annually conduct one-week FCPA risk assessments or "audit lites" in a limited number of foreign countries. There are clear advantages to having outside FCPA legal experts conduct these mini audits, as they can frequently identify issues and present a set of fresh eyes that others who perform the regular audits may not. If mini or limited audits lead to improvements in the entire compliance program, they can save the company enormous costs and pain.

I. FCPA Opinion Release Procedure 2004-02 (July 12, 2004)

In July 2004, two subsidiaries of the Swiss company ABB Ltd.—ABB Vetco Gray, Inc., a U.S. subsidiary, and ABB Vetco Gray U.K., Ltd.—pled guilty to FCPA violations relating to commissions and referral payments made to officials in Angola, Nigeria, and Kazakhstan. Prior to the announcement of the criminal charges, investment groups seeking to acquire certain companies and assets from ABB relating to ABB's oil, gas, and petrochemical business requested an opinion on the acquisition, filed a copy of their ABB Preliminary Agreement with the DOJ and agreed to conduct a thorough investigation through separately engaged counsel. As part of the compliance, the successor companies agreed to adopt a rigorous anti-corruption compliance code designed to detect and deter violations of the FCPA and foreign anti-corruption laws.[21]

Newco's anti-bribery compliance code, which is detailed in FCPA Opinion Release Procedure 2004-02 (July 12, 2004), consisted of the following elements:

- A clearly articulated corporate policy against violations of the FCPA and foreign anti-bribery laws and the establishment of compliance standards and procedures to be followed by all directors, officers, employees, and all business partners, including, but not limited to, agents, consultants, representatives, and joint venture partners and teaming partners involved in business transactions, representation, or business development or retention in a foreign jurisdiction (respectively, "agents" and "business partners") that are reasonably capable of reducing the prospect that the FCPA or any applicable foreign anti-corruption law of Newco's compliance code will be violated;

- The assignment to one or more independent senior Newco corporate officials, who shall report directly to the compliance committee of the audit committee of the board of directors, of responsibility for the implementation and oversight of compliance with policies, standards, and procedures established in accordance with Newco's compliance code;

- The effective communication to all shareholders' representatives directly involved in the oversight of Newco and to all directors, officers, employees, agents, and business partners of corporate and compliance policies, standards, and procedures regarding the FCPA and applicable foreign anti-corruption laws, by requiring (1) regular training concerning the requirements of the FCPA and applicable anti-corruption laws on a periodic basis to all shareholders, directors, officers, employees, agents, and business partners and (2) annual certifications by all shareholders, directors, officers, employees, including the head of each Newco business or division, agents, and business partners certifying compliance therewith;

- A reporting system, including a "helpline" for directors, officers, employees, agents, and business partners to report suspected violations of the compliance code or suspected criminal conduct;

- Appropriate disciplinary procedure to address matters involving violations or suspected violations of the FCPA, foreign anti-corruption laws, or the compliance code;

- Clearly articulated corporate procedures designed to assure that all necessary and prudent precautions are taken to cause Newco to form business relationships with reputable and qualified business partners;

- Extensive pre-retention due diligence requirements pertaining to, as well as post-retention oversight of, all agents and business partners, including the maintenance of complete due diligence records at Newco;

- Clearly articulated corporate procedures designed to ensure that Newco exercises due care to assure that substantial discretionary authority is not delegated to individuals whom Newco knows, or should know through the exercise of due diligence, to have a propensity to engage in illegal or improper activities;

- A committee consisting of senior Newco corporate officials to review and to record, in writing, actions relating to (1) the retention of any agent or subagents thereof, and (2) all contracts and payments related thereto;

- The inclusion in all agreements, contracts, and renewals thereof with all agents and business partners of provisions: (1) setting forth anti-corruption representations and undertakings; (2) relating to compliance with foreign anti-corruption laws and other relevant laws; (3) allowing for internal and independent audits of the books and records of the agent or business partner to ensure compliance with the foregoing; and (4) providing for termination of the agent or business partner as a result of any breach of applicable anti-corruption laws and regulations or representations and undertakings related thereto;

- Financial and accounting procedures designed to ensure that Newco maintains a system of internal accounting controls and makes and keeps accurate books, records, and accounts; and
- Independent audits by outside counsel and auditors, at no longer than three-year intervals, to ensure that the compliance code, including its anti-corruption provisions, are implemented in an effective manner.

Although the DOJ did not expressly endorse the above measures, it conceded that these measures constituted "significant precautions" against future violations. The compliance code and procedures are likely the new minimum standard for a company seeking to persuade the DOJ and SEC that it has a solid compliance program and procedures.

J.   Siemens Corporate Compliance Program

In the wake of the largest corporate internal investigation ever undertaken and the uncovering of bribery conduct across the globe, Siemens AG agreed as a condition of its December 2008 plea agreement with the DOJ to appoint a monitor and to implement a compliance program with the following elements:

- A compliance code with a clearly articulated corporate policy against violations of the FCPA, including its anti-bribery, books and records, and internal controls provisions, and other applicable counterparts (collectively, the "anti-corruption laws").
- A system of financial and accounting procedures, including a system of internal accounting controls, designed to ensure the maintenance of fair and accurate books, records, and accounts.
- Promulgation of compliance standards and procedures designed to reduce the prospect of violations of the anti-corruption laws and Siemens AG's compliance code. These standards and procedures shall apply to all directors, officers, and employees and, where necessary and appropriate, outside parties acting on behalf of Siemens in foreign jurisdictions, including agents, consultants, representatives, distributors, teaming partners, and joint venture partners (collectively referred to as "agents and business partners").

- The assignment of responsibilities to one or more senior corporate officials of Siemens AG for the implementation and oversight of compliance with policies, standards, and procedures regarding the anti-corruption laws. Such corporate official(s) shall have the authority to report matters directly to the audit or compliance committee of Siemens AG's supervisory board.
- Mechanisms designed to ensure that the policies, standards, and procedures of Siemens regarding the anti-corruption laws are effectively communicated to all directors, officers, employees, and, where necessary and appropriate, agents and business partners. These mechanisms shall include (1) periodic training for all such directors, officers, employees, and, where necessary and appropriate, agents and business partners; and (2) annual certifications by all such directors, officers, employees, and, where necessary and appropriate, agents and business partners, certifying compliance with the training requirements.
- An effective system for reporting suspected criminal conduct and/or violations of the compliance policies, standards, and procedures regarding the anti-corruption laws for directors, officers, and, as necessary and appropriate, agents and business partners.
- Appropriate disciplinary procedures to address, among other things, violations of the anti-corruption laws of Siemens' compliance code by directors, officers, and employees.
- Appropriate due diligence requirements pertaining to the retention and oversight of agents and business partners.
- Standard provisions in agreements, contracts, and renewals thereof with all agents and business partners that are designed to prevent violations of the FCPA and other applicable anti-corruption laws, which provisions may, depending upon the circumstances, include (1) anti-corruption representations and undertakings related to compliance with the anti-corruption laws; (2) rights to conduct audits of the books and records of the agent or business partner to ensure compliance with the foregoing; and (3) rights to terminate an agent or business partner as a result of any breach of anti-corruption laws, and regulations or representations and undertakings related to such matters.
- Periodic testing of the compliance code and standards and procedures designed to evaluate its effectiveness in detecting and reducing violations of the anti-corruption laws and Siemens' internal controls system and compliance code.

These ten elements are not, of course, required or expected of all multinational companies, but general counsel and their counselors would be wise to review and consider what elements or parts of the Siemens compliance program might help their clients.

K. Common FCPA Compliance Program Failures

Failures of FCPA compliance efforts can significantly damage a corporate program's overall effectiveness and deprive the company of salutary benefits under the Organizational Sentencing Guidelines. Multinational companies can:

- Fail to adopt and fully distribute a clear, written code of conduct or ethics policy, and more particularly, written FCPA policies prohibiting proscribed conduct and policies establishing a methodology for the identification, selection, approval, and retention of foreign agents, consultants, distributors, or other third-party contractors in connection with foreign government procurement or other projects; and clear gift, travel, and entertainment policies for non-U.S. government officials.

- Fail to adequately undertake *and* document their due diligence efforts in evaluating and approving potential agents, consultants, distributors, joint venture partners, and other third parties. Decisions to decline a potential agent or consultant relationship should be memorialized in some fashion, as they can establish the company takes both the FCPA and related due diligence seriously.

- Fail to appoint company or regional compliance officers.

- Overload a compliance officer with other responsibilities.

- Fail to vet officers or key employees who are to be assigned or promoted to key positions of interface with government officials in high-risk countries; vetting should include a thorough personnel file review, interviews by the legal department, and an overall health assessment of such candidates.

- Delegate compliance to officers or employees who have no real understanding or training in FCPA requirements and issues. Similarly, companies mistakenly delegate compliance activities to persons who have an inherent conflict of interest, for example, having a marketing or project proponent undertake due diligence of proposed agents.

- Fail to make compliance a priority, with the result that, due to the press of other business matters, compliance efforts, training, and appropriate due diligence become a secondary priority.

- Fail to implement hotlines or other proper reporting mechanisms that offer no likelihood of retaliation.

- Take a "head in the sand" approach with agents, consultants, distributors, and partners and senior managers. For example, sales personnel erroneously assume that if they do not conduct due diligence on agents, consultants, and partners or if they disregard facts that should prompt them to make further inquiries, they will not face any liability.

- Take a laissez-faire attitude about FCPA-proscribed conduct, with senior managers or sales personnel rationalizing that other U.S. or foreign competitors engage in FCPA-proscribed conduct.
- Fail to require senior management or newly hired senior managers to undertake periodic ethics and FCPA training.
- Fail to conduct FCPA training using counsel or compliance experts experienced in such matters.
- Fail to rotate senior management financial and accounting personnel out of high-risk countries.
- Fail to work closely with their outside auditors to evaluate FCPA efforts annually and to modify audit work programs, policies, and training.
- Lack experienced internal auditors who understand, are trained in, and regularly focus on FCPA issues.
- Fail to implement internal administrative and financial controls that reduce risks of improper payments (e.g., check issuance, wire transfers, petty cash controls).
- Not adequately monitor the activities of foreign subsidiaries, distributors, or joint venture partners.
- Ignore their own compliance rules and policies due to business deadlines and time constraints, permitting senior managers or sales personnel to engage in questionable practices without advance compliance clearance or legal advice.
- Fail to translate into appropriate foreign languages their compliance codes, FCPA and ethics policies, forms, and questionnaires.
- Hire or appoint foreign nationals to run overseas operations without thoroughly training them on the specific requirements and prohibitions of the FCPA. Many foreign nationals erroneously assume they are not subject to FCPA liability.
- Fail to employ standard-form baseline contracts for foreign agents, joint ventures, sales representatives, consultants, and other contractors, or to enforce model uniform covenant, warranty, representation, and audit clauses. Random departures from the company's standard-form foreign agent consultant or representative agreements will raise questions about a company's commitment to compliance and internal controls.
- Fail to conduct due diligence of agents, consultants, distributors, and third parties *during* the life of the contract.
- Fail in their due diligence efforts to address local law issues that may be relevant to agency or consultant agreements, partnerships, distributorships, joint venture agreements, or employment relationships.
- Fail to monitor the public disclosures of competitors that can reveal an industry-wide investigation.

- Fail to take appropriate or sufficient disciplinary actions in the wake of FCPA misconduct.
- Fail to apprise and involve boards of directors or audit committees in a timely manner in sensitive payment allegations oversight roles.
- Fail to design and undertake FCPA audit plans.
- Fail to periodically monitor and update their ethics and FCPA compliance programs. In particular, in-house legal departments fail to regularly review, reevaluate, and modify compliance programs along with agent, consultant, third party, and joint venture agreements for FCPA-related issues, developments, and best practices.

Finally, even though the seventh and final original step to an effective compliance program is to take steps to prevent further violations, it is remarkable how often, after the completion of a thorough FCPA investigation and the identification and punishment of wrongdoers, well-intended companies will *not* take steps to prevent the recurrence of violations. This lapse is usually not willful, but a result of investigation fatigue and the press of new matters or business priorities. A company should maintain and adhere to a post-investigation action plan with objectives, action steps, responsible persons, and commitment dates. Otherwise, the original problems are likely to recur.

V. REASONS TO CONDUCT AN INTERNAL INVESTIGATION

There are often compelling legal, practical, and tactical reasons to conduct an internal investigation in the wake of potentially serious FCPA allegations. They include:

- To fulfill the legal duties of directors and management;
- To address any misconduct, adopt remedial measures, modify the compliance program, and take appropriate disciplinary actions so as to minimize the recurrence of improper acts or the risk of future prosecution;[22]
- To marshal the facts and prepare for the defense of a potential investigation by the DOJ, SEC, or foreign authorities, or litigation with shareholders and others;
- To review, reconsider, and revise accounting procedures and internal controls to make sure that adequate systems are in place;
- To assist the board of directors and company in determining whether the company has disclosure obligations or has made accurate disclosures;
- To respond to a Section 10(a) of the Exchange Act inquiry by external auditors;

- To respond to a shareholder demand in the nature of an actual or threatened derivative action;
- To persuade the government to forgo a separate or broader, more costly investigation;
- To obtain the benefit of prosecutorial discretion (e.g., declination, deferred prosecution agreement, nonprosecution agreement, reduced fines) by demonstrating that upon discovering misconduct, the company was proactive, investigated the matter, took appropriate disciplinary action, instituted remedial measures, or voluntarily disclosed to the government;
- To give a company conducting a credible investigation some opportunity to control the nature and scope of the government investigation;
- To reduce potential corporate sentencing exposure under the Organizational Guidelines (Chapter 8 of the United States Sentencing Guidelines); and
- To make recommendations and provide legal advice to management, audit committees, or boards of directors, consistent with the above objectives.

VI. SELECTION OF OUTSIDE FCPA INVESTIGATION OR DEFENSE COUNSEL

To highlight perhaps the obvious, management should not conduct an internal investigation, as they usually do not have investigative experience, they may be perceived as trying to minimize their role or involvement, *and* an investigation by management is not protected by any privilege.[23] For a variety of reasons, companies often turn to outside counsel to conduct internal investigations or to defend DOJ investigations involving FCPA allegations. These include:

- Outside counsel often have substantial FCPA investigation experience, DOJ and/or SEC backgrounds, and resources that inside counsel may not.
- Outside counsel generally enjoy at least a partial presumption of independence from management. Many companies find it prudent to retain or consult a law firm other than their regular primary outside corporate or litigation counsel to secure FCPA expertise, to demonstrate greater independence, or to avoid potential conflicts where the role or advice of regular outside counsel may be an issue. The DOJ and SEC can be expected to closely examine the relationship between the company and outside counsel chosen to investigate FCPA allegations. The DOJ and SEC expect sufficient independence to assure a full and rigorous examination and a reasonable and logical scope.

- Outside counsel may have more experience in designing and reviewing corporate compliance policies and procedures and internal controls, including FCPA-specific policies, procedures, and internal controls.
- An investigation by outside counsel will receive greater privilege protection from discovery by the DOJ, SEC, and others, including attorney work-product and attorney-client communication privileges, than one conducted by in-house counsel.[24]
- Outside FCPA counsel sometimes have more experience and contacts with forensic accounting firms trained in FCPA bribery investigation as well as related books and records and internal control issues. Forensic accounting personnel should similarly be committed to traveling to and conducting appropriate investigations with outside counsel in any country at issue.
- Outside counsel may have offices in foreign jurisdictions that are also focusing on alleged misconduct, and such counsel may be able to advise the company on foreign criminal, legal privileges, and data privacy laws.

For FCPA matters, it is usually wise and cost effective to retain outside counsel with substantial sensitive payment investigation background and overseas experience. A company, board of directors, or audit committee has the right to expect FCPA investigation or defense counsel to travel to and conduct appropriate investigations in any country at issue.

VII. WRITTEN LEGAL OPINIONS

Corporate managers and in-house counsel often request "quick advice on a simple hospitality issue" from outside FCPA counsel. In some cases the answer will be simple and straightforward; in other more complex or risky situations, the correct answer will be less immediately clear and it will be wise for both in-house and outside counsel to carefully gather and address relevant facts and issue(s) and for outside counsel to provide a written legal opinion to the client. The latter will save the client substantial costs in later reconstructing the relevant facts, analyzing the then-current law and applicable FCPA guidance, and defending any arguably wayward conduct in any U.S. government inquiry. By securing a written legal opinion after obtaining all relevant facts, the company will have in many circumstances established a credible advice of counsel defense.

A quality written legal opinion will state the issue, summarize the relevant known facts, and address the purpose of the contemplated activity and advise the client of the legality of its proposed conduct and any key conditions or limitations. As with any solid legal opinion and advice of counsel defense, the client must furnish all relevant facts. For example, if a multinational company seeks permission to sponsor trips to the

United States for Chinese employees of a state-owned enterprise, a legal opinion will recite the essential facts and will address the identity and titles of Chinese employees, their likely status as government officials, the purpose of the trip (e.g., to learn about U.S. products and to visit manufacturing facilities), the estimated time and costs of the trip, the potential authority of the visiting Chinese employees to award business, and the relationship of the Chinese employees to any government officials. In approving the travel and lodging expenses, FCPA counsel will provide a written opinion that contains cautionary guidance, including that payment for airline tickets should be made directly to the airline; that no side trips, for example, to Disneyland or Las Vegas, should be taken; that attendance sheets should be kept; that per diem coverage should be made to the recipient's employer rather than directly to the recipient; that no cash distributions should be made; and that foreign expenses should be consistent with the parent company's domestic travel and lodging expense policies.

An FCPA opinion addressing a potential bribery situation will very often consider false books and records and internal control implications. Even if a payment or thing of value is made or given lawfully to a foreign official, the person making the payment or giving the gift or thing of value may still be criminally liable if he/she fails to accurately record in reasonable detail a transaction in a public company's books or records. The opinion should further examine what the legal consequences of potential improper payments under the FCPA are under local law. In addition to reviewing local bribery laws, an inquiry could examine potential local tax consequences. For example, payments made to hospital personnel to assist in promoting products in the People's Republic of China could implicate two types of Chinese turnover taxes: (1) value-added taxes levied on the sale and importation of goods and the provision of processing services and repair and replacement services, and (2) business taxes levied on the provision of taxable services, the transfer of intangible assets, and the sale of improvable property. While not directly related to bribery, informal payments can create potential corporate liability for the client in the foreign country in a host of other areas. Therefore, an opinion should not be narrowly confined to the FCPA's anti-bribery and false books and records implications; it should also consider foreign law implications and exposure. The cost of securing and memorializing a quality written legal opinion can later save the client enormous investigative and defense costs and again provide a credible good faith defense..

VII.   ADDITIONAL RESOURCES

- KAY TATUM, FRANK BURKE & DAN GUY, AUDIT COMMITTEES: A GUIDE FOR DIRECTORS, MANAGEMENT, AND CONSULTANTS (CCH 2006).

- NANCY BARTON & STEPHEN RADIN, THE BUSINESS JUDGMENT RULE: FIDUCIARY DUTIES OF CORPORATE DIRECTORS (Prentice Hall 1989).
- Dean, *The Necessity of an Effective Anti-Corruption Compliance Policy, in* THE FOREIGN CORRUPT PRACTICES ACT 2008: COPING WITH HEIGHTENED ENFORCEMENT RISKS (Practising Law Institute 2008).
- Finnegan, *Briefly Speaking . . . The First 72 Hours of a Government Investigation,* 11(2) Nat'l Legal Center, Feb. 2007.
- JAMES HAMILTON & TED TRAUTMANN, SARBANES OXLEY ACT OF 2002 (CCH 2002).
- WILLIAM KNEPPER & DAN BAILEY, LIABILITY OF CORPORATE OFFICERS AND DIRECTORS (7th ed. 2002).
- Stewart Landefeld, Andrew Moore & Katie Ludwig (Perkins Coie), THE PUBLIC COMPANY HANDBOOK (Bowne, 2d ed. 2003).
- Pollack & Schrantz, *Conducting Internal Investigation After Sarbanes-Oxley: Best Practices,* SH083 ALI-ABA 8791 (2003).
- Tarun, *Tarun Preliminary Multinational FCPA Compliance Risk Profile* (© 2009 Robert W. Tarun); THE FOREIGN CORRUPT PRACTICES ACT 2009, *Coping with Heightened Enforcement Risks* (Seminar San Francisco, July 10, 2009).
- Tarun, *Tarun's Ten Commandments for Conducting Internal Investigations,* INTERNAL INVESTIGATIONS 2009 (PLI Course Handbook No.B-1745 2009) reprinted in *Ethisphere* Q3 2009 at 12.
- Tarun, *Ten Tips for Handling Sensitive Corporate Investigations: Practical Advice in the Sarbanes-Oxley Era,* 10 BUS. CRIMES BULL. 10 (Nov. 2003).

NOTES

1. *See Report of Investigation in the Matter of the Cooper Companies, Inc. as It Relates to the Conduct of Cooper's Board of Directors,* Exchange Act Release No. 34-35082, 1994 SEC Lexis 3975, at *18–20 (Dec. 12, 1994).

2. 698 A.2d 959 (Del. Ch. 1996).

3. *In re Caremark Int'l, Inc. Derivative Litig.,* 698 A.2d 959, 972 (Del. Ch. 1996).

4. *Id.*

5. *Id.*

6. *Id.*

7. 15 U.S.C. § 7241.

8. 15 U.S.C. § 7241(a)(1)–(3).

9. 15 U.S.C. § 7241(a)(4)(A).

10. 15 U.S.C. § 7241(a)(4)(B).

11. 15 U.S.C. § 7241(a)(4)(C).

12. 15 U.S.C. § 7241(a)(4)(D).

13. 15 U.S.C. § 7241(a)(5).

14. 18 U.S.C. § 1350(c)(1).

15. 18 U.S.C. § 1350(c)(2).

16. U.S. SENTENCING GUIDELINES MANUAL ch. 8. The Guidelines' Effective Compliance and Ethics Program Commentary is appended hereto as Appendix 11.

17. See Appendix 11 for the U.S. Sentencing Guidelines' discussion of effective compliance programs.

18. The Ethisphere Institute, an organization dedicated to business ethics, has identified eight critical components to benchmarking codes of conduct. *See 50 Codes of Conduct Benchmarked,* http://www.ethisphere.com.

19. Cynthia L. Jackson, *Overreacting Global Codes of Conduct Can Violate the Law,* LOS ANGELES AND SAN FRANCISCO DAILY JOURNAL (June7, 2006). Ms. Jackson is a principal at Baker & McKenzie LLP in Palo Alto, California.

20. FCPA Opinion Procedure Release 2004-02 (July 12, 2004), http://www.usdoj.gov/criminal/fraud/fcpa/opinion/2004/0402.html.

21. Attachment 1 Corporate Compliance Program. See http://www.usdoj.gov/opa/documents/siemens_ag_stmt_offense.pdf

22. *See* DAN K. WEBB, ROBERT W. TARUN & STEVEN F. MOLO, *Persuading the Government Not to Indict,* ch. 16 in CORPORATE INTERNAL INVESTIGATIONS (1993–2009).

23. *In re Grand Jury Subpoena,* 599 F.2d 504, 1510 (2d Cir. 1979).

24. *But see In re Steinhardt Partners, L.P,* 9 F.2d 230, 235–39 (2d Cir. 1993) (voluntary submission of report to SEC is disclosure to an adversary, waiving work product protection).

CHAPTER 5

Transaction Issues and Considerations

I. OVERVIEW

Persons transacting business internationally must always consider possible issues arising under the Foreign Corrupt Practices Act.[1] While these issues are particularly relevant in the context of the sale of goods or services to foreign governments and their instrumentalities, FCPA issues can arise as well in the context of purely private-sector transactions. For example, an improper payment to a foreign government official to obtain a license to commence or continue a business activity, such as a telecommunications license, may equally be an FCPA violation. General counsel and transaction counsel must be sensitive to FCPA issues in all international transactions, regardless of the direct or indirect role of any governmental entity.[2]

A second significant issue is that some transaction counsel mistakenly consider FCPA potential exposure only in situations of "intermediaries" (e.g., agents, commission sales representatives, or consultants) who could be possible conduits or payors of an improper payment. Multinational companies should also undertake appropriate review and due diligence in connection with potential mergers, acquisitions, and joint ventures. The March 2005 DOJ–SEC case against Titan Corporation demonstrated how a savvy suitor can protect itself through careful due diligence in connection with a merger (discussed in Chapter 10).[3] Similarly, Monsanto's acquisition of Delta & Pine demonstrated how an acquirer protected itself from successor criminal liability when it discovered improper payments by the target to Turkish Ministry of Agriculture officials.[4] FCPA issues arise in transactions comprising foreign investments or acquisitions, joint ventures, licensing arrangements, infrastructure projects, offset and countertrade agreements, and mergers. Also, a company may face FCPA liability for the actions of a joint venture partner or a subcontractor and its employees and agents. Increasingly, acquirers have urged targets to voluntarily disclose problematic payments to the Department of Justice and the Securities and Exchange Commission.

Companies operating internationally should implement procedures and steps to assure that FCPA and related compliance considerations are taken into account in every overseas transaction. General counsel and transactional counsel must ensure that the following elements are systematically included in reviewing and implementing all overseas transactions:

1. *Selection criteria.* Agents, consultants, customs clearing brokers, sales representatives, partners, professionals (attorneys and accountants), or other third-party contractors (collectively "third-party contractors") must be identified and selected on the basis of objective and written evaluation criteria; for example, a partner is selected on the basis of identifiable commercial and technical competence and not because he/she is the relative of an important government official.

2. *Reasonableness of price or compensation.* In reviewing an acquisition or other transaction, counsel should review the economics of the contemplated transaction or agency; for example, is the agency fee reasonable given the contemplated services? Unsupported general statements or folklore that "10 percent finder's fees are common in the industry or region" should be viewed with skepticism.

3. *Target of joint venturer's business with foreign governments.* In considering a target or joint venture partner, one should consider the volume and percentage of the acquiree's business derived from foreign government contracts as well as its countries of operation (see Transparency International's Corruption Perception Index).

4. *Due diligence and reputation check.* Third-party contractors should be objectively evaluated and due diligence undertaken into their contracts, business reputation, qualifications, ownership, and integrity. Depending upon the scope of the contemplated relationship and other factors, due diligence may include: (a) reviewing their government contracts; (b) checking sources of information (Internet, public databases); (c) checking business references provided by the potential third-party contractor; (d) interviewing the third-party contractor; (e) obtaining information from U.S. government sources (Department of Commerce business liaison and State Department desk office inquiries); and (f) obtaining information from institutions (banks, accounting firms, lawyers) in the third-party contractor's country of operations. Due diligence efforts should be memorialized.

5. *Contract provisions.* Written agreements with third-party contractors must be within the norm for and consistent with standard arrangements in the industry or geographic sector. The agreements should specify duties or services to be provided by agents, consultants, or contractors. The agreements must contain certain standard representations, warranties, covenants, and the like. The agreements should also provide for audit rights, annual or periodic FCPA cer-

tifications, and termination for breach of any representations, warranties, covenants, or other FCPA-related requirements.

6. *Related and unrelated agreements.* Transactional counsel must consider the big picture to assure that a third-party contractor is not possibly structuring the transaction and related or unrelated agreements so as to generate funds, with or without the company's explicit knowledge, and utilizing the funds to make improper payments. Particular business arrangements and structures may not make economic sense and should heighten concerns about funds being delivered to third-party contractors to facilitate improper payments. For example, SEC enforcement activity has evaluated unrelated offshore or third-country investment projects, offset and counter trade arrangements, inflated subcontracts, and contracts for "advisory" or other vaguely defined services.

7. *Relationship of directors, officers, or employees to foreign government officials.* Transactional counsel will want to determine whether employees, officers, or directors of a target company, joint venture, partner, or agent are relatives or close associates of foreign government officials.

8. *Subject of law enforcement investigations.* Transactional counsel will want to explore directly with the third party and through other sources whether the third party or its owners, directors, officers, or employees has been the subject of any DOJ, SEC, Interpol, or in-country law enforcement investigation or the recipient of any subpoena or correspondence from any of these law enforcement agencies.

9. *Red flags.* There are certain "signaling devices" or "red flags" that should put transactional counsel on notice to review a transaction carefully, since such signs are possible indications that improper payments may be intended by third-party contractors.

II.   EXAMPLES OF AGENT, CONSULTANT, AND OTHER THIRD-PARTY RED FLAGS

Certain signs or the lack of transparency in accounting records may suggest that improper payment activity has occurred or may be occurring. Standing alone, these red flags certainly do not prove the existence of illicit or improper activity. However, they may suggest the need for further inquiry and economic justification for certain business arrangements as well as greater vigilance and increased audit activity.

Twenty-five third-party warning signs that can portend FCPA problems are listed next. Although these red flags focus on agents and consultants, they apply equally to joint venturers, contractors, and other business partners.

1. The agent or consultant resides outside the country in which the services are to be rendered.

2. The commission payments to the agent or consultant are required to be made outside the country and/or to a country linked to money laundering activity.
3. Company wire transfers do not disclose the identity of the sender or recipient.
4. The agent or consultant demands an unusually high commission without a corresponding level of services or risk (e.g., an agent who bears financial risks on delivery of goods or performs substantial pre- or post-sales services may be entitled to greater compensation than a pure commission agent/broker).
5. The agent or consultant refuses to disclose its complete ownership, ownership structure, or other reasonable requested information.
6. The agent or consultant does not have the organizational resources or staff to undertake the scope of work required under the agreement (e.g., pre-award technical activities or logistical assistance, and post-award activities such as assistance with customs, permits, financing, and licenses).
7. The agent or consultant has a close family connection with or other personal or professional affiliation with the foreign government or official.
8. An agent or consultant's family members or relatives are senior officials in the foreign government or ruling political party.
9. The agent or consultant has been recommended to the company by a foreign official of the potential government customer.
10. The agent or consultant has undisclosed subagents or subcontractors who assist in his/her work.
11. The agent or consultant's commissions are greater than the range that is customary or typical within the industry and region.
12. The agent or consultant refuses to sign representations, warranties, and covenants that he/she has not violated and will not violate the requirements of the FCPA.
13. The agent or consultant requests or requires payment in cash.
14. The agent or consultant requests that payments be made to a bank located in a foreign country unrelated to the transaction, or be made to undisclosed third parties.
15. The agency or consultancy is headquartered in a country with a reputation for corruption.
16. The agent or consultant requests a substantial up front payment or fee.
17. The agent or consultant insists on the involvement of third parties who bring no apparent value.
18. The agent or consultant intends to or reserves the right to assign its rights or obligations to a third party.
19. The agency or consultancy is incorporated in a tax haven.

20. The agent or consultant requests that false invoices or other documents be prepared in connection with a transaction.
21. The transaction involves or takes place in a country with a general reputation for bribery and corruption.
22. There is a lack of transparency in expenses and/or accounting records.
23. A party to a contract requests that a cash or undisclosed campaign contribution be made to a foreign party candidate.
24. The agent or consultant has no established track record.
25. There is a rumor that the agent or consultant has a silent partner.

III. TRANSPARENCY INTERNATIONAL (TI) 2009 CORRUPTION PERCEPTION INDEX (CPI)

In October 2009, Berlin-based Transparency International (TI) released its twelfth Corruption Perception Index (CPI) survey, ranking 180 countries according to the extent they are internationally perceived to have corrupt business environments.[5] A CPI score indicates the perceived level of public sector corruption in the country/territory. In the most recent TI survey, CPI scores ranged from 1.1 (the most corrupt) to 9.4 (the least corrupt). A CPI score below 5.0 indicates a serious level of corruption. Somalia (1.1) ranked the worst followed by Afghanistan (1.3), Myanmar (1.4), Sudan (1.5), and Iraq (1.5). New Zealand (9.4) was the least corrupt followed by Denmark (9.3), Singapore (9.2), Sweden (9.2), and Switzerland (9.0). The United States ranked 19th in the 2009 survey with a CPI score of 7.5.

These rankings, while subjective at some level, can highlight business environment risks for multinationals and provide guidance on compliance programs and annual risk assessments. U.S. prosecutors and regulators are well aware of the Transparency International surveys and expect multinational companies to adopt global compliance measures, consistent with increased perceived corruption risks. Because law enforcement authorities may evaluate a company's controls environment, especially in countries with well-known corruption issues and correspondingly low CPI scores, in deciding which companies or individuals to prosecute, resolve civilly, or decline altogether, multinationals should monitor and analyze these surveys in the context of their ongoing foreign operations, acquisition targets, special international projects, and potential merger partners.

Historically, the harshest DOJ and SEC FCPA resolutions have involved multinationals that have had poor or little compliance programs and few or no internal controls. In order to be able to prove a current quality compliance and audit program, a multinational should keep and maintain memos and minutes of compliance meetings and related improvements so, if a federal grand jury convenes, the company can prove through its records a robust compliance program and argue that it should not be prosecuted for the wayward conduct of a few when good controls were in place and quality training had been implemented.

The Transparency International rankings are especially important to any contemplated international merger or acquisition and an evaluation of the corruption risks of a partner or target's foreign operations. Absent thorough due diligence, an acquirer risks both successor criminal liability and a risk that the target's corrupt obligations and payments may continue. In a close case, the DOJ may consider a weak due diligence effort that ignores TI-type corruption perception rankings in deciding whether to prosecute a company that acquires a company that has engaged in, or, far worse, continues to engage in, improper payments. It may also evaluate how quickly the acquirer implemented a new company-wide robust compliance program that reflects the parent company's values. For these reasons, a legal department in conjunction with a compliance officer or team should annually consider the TI survey rankings in light of the operations of any foreign-acquired companies or joint venture partners and the corporate business plans.

A.   2009 TI Rankings

The 2009 Transparency International rankings from least corrupt to most corrupt and CPI scores are as follows:

Rank	Country/Territory	CPI 2009 Score	Surveys Used	Confidence Range
1	New Zealand	9.4	6	9.1–9.5
2	Denmark	9.3	6	9.1–9.5
3	Singapore	9.2	9	9.0–9.4
3	Sweden	9.2	6	9.0–9.3
5	Switzerland	9.0	6	8.9–9.1
6	Finland	8.9	6	8.4–9.4
6	Netherlands	8.9	6	8.7–9.0
8	Australia	8.7	8	8.3–9.0
8	Canada	8.7	6	8.5–9.0
8	Iceland	8.7	4	7.5–9.4
11	Norway	8.6	6	8.2–9.1
12	Hong Kong	8.2	8	7.9–8.5
12	Luxembourg	8.2	6	7.6–8.8
14	Germany	8.0	6	7.7–8.3
14	Ireland	8.0	6	7.8–8.4

Rank	Country/Territory	CPI 2009 Score	Surveys Used	Confidence Range
16	Austria	7.9	6	7.4–8.3
17	Japan	7.7	8	7.4–8.0
17	United Kingdom	7.7	6	7.3–8.2
19	United States	7.5	8	6.9–8.0
20	Barbados	7.4	4	6.6–8.2
21	Belgium	7.1	6	6.9–7.3
22	Qatar	7.0	6	5.8–8.1
22	Saint Lucia	7.0	3	6.7–7.5
24	France	6.9	6	6.5–7.3
25	Chile	6.7	7	6.5–6.9
25	Uruguay	6.7	5	6.4–7.1
27	Cyprus	6.6	4	6.1–7.1
27	Estonia	6.6	8	6.1–6.9
27	Slovenia	6.6	8	6.3–6.9
30	United Arab Emirates	6.5	5	5.5–7.5
31	Saint Vincent and the Grenadines	6.4	3	4.9–7.5
32	Israel	6.1	6	5.4–6.7
32	Spain	6.1	6	5.5–6.6
34	Dominica	5.9	3	4.9–6.7
35	Portugal	5.8	6	5.5–6.2
35	Puerto Rico	5.8	4	5.2–6.3
37	Botswana	5.6	6	5.1–6.3
37	Taiwan	5.6	9	5.4–5.9
39	Brunei Darussalam	5.5	4	4.7–6.4
39	Oman	5.5	5	4.4–6.5
39	Korea (South)	5.5	9	5.3–5.7
42	Mauritius	5.4	6	5.0–5.9
43	Costa Rica	5.3	5	4.7–5.9
43	Macau	5.3	3	3.3–6.9
45	Malta	5.2	4	4.0–6.2
46	Bahrain	5.1	5	4.2–5.8
46	Cape Verde	5.1	3	3.3–7.0
46	Hungary	5.1	8	4.6–5.7
49	Bhutan	5.0	4	4.3–5.6
49	Jordan	5.0	7	3.9–6.1

Rank	Country/Territory	CPI 2009 Score	Surveys Used	Confidence Range
49	Poland	5.0	8	4.5–5.5
52	Czech Republic	4.9	8	4.3–5.6
52	Lithuania	4.9	8	4.4–5.4
54	Seychelles	4.8	3	3.0–6.7
55	South Africa	4.7	8	4.3–4.9
56	Latvia	4.5	6	4.1–4.9
56	Malaysia	4.5	9	4.0–5.1
56	Namibia	4.5	6	3.9–5.1
56	Samoa	4.5	3	3.3–5.3
56	Slovakia	4.5	8	4.1–4.9
61	Cuba	4.4	3	3.5–5.1
61	Turkey	4.4	7	3.9–4.9
63	Italy	4.3	6	3.8–4.9
63	Saudi Arabia	4.3	5	3.1–5.3
65	Tunisia	4.2	6	3.0–5.5
66	Croatia	4.1	8	3.7–4.5
66	Georgia	4.1	7	3.4–4.7
66	Kuwait	4.1	5	3.2–5.1
69	Ghana	3.9	7	3.2–4.6
69	Montenegro	3.9	5	3.5–4.4
71	Bulgaria	3.8	8	3.2–4.5
71	FYR Macedonia	3.8	6	3.4–4.2
71	Greece	3.8	6	3.2–4.3
71	Romania	3.8	8	3.2–4.3
75	Brazil	3.7	7	3.3–4.3
75	Colombia	3.7	7	3.1–4.3
75	Peru	3.7	7	3.4–4.1
75	Suriname	3.7	3	3.0–4.7
79	Burkina Faso	3.6	7	2.8–4.4
79	China	3.6	9	3.0–4.2
79	Swaziland	3.6	3	3.0–4.7
79	Trinidad and Tobago	3.6	4	3.0–4.3
83	Serbia	3.5	6	3.3–3.9
84	El Salvador	3.4	5	3.0–3.8
84	Guatemala	3.4	5	3.0–3.9
84	India	3.4	10	3.2–3.6
84	Panama	3.4	5	3.1–3.7

Rank	Country/Territory	CPI 2009 Score	Surveys Used	Confidence Range
84	Thailand	3.4	9	3.0–3.8
89	Lesotho	3.3	6	2.8–3.8
89	Malawi	3.3	7	2.7–3.9
89	Mexico	3.3	7	3.2–3.5
89	Moldova	3.3	6	2.7–4.0
89	Morocco	3.3	6	2.8–3.9
89	Rwanda	3.3	4	2.9–3.7
95	Albania	3.2	6	3.0–3.3
95	Vanuatu	3.2	3	2.3–4.7
97	Liberia	3.1	3	1.9–3.8
97	Sri Lanka	3.1	7	2.8–3.4
99	Bosnia and Herzegovina	3.0	7	2.6–3.4
99	Dominican Republic	3.0	5	2.9–3.2
99	Jamaica	3.0	5	2.8–3.3
99	Madagascar	3.0	7	2.8–3.2
99	Senegal	3.0	7	2.5–3.6
99	Tonga	3.0	3	2.6–3.3
99	Zambia	3.0	7	2.8–3.2
106	Argentina	2.9	7	2.6–3.1
106	Benin	2.9	6	2.3–3.4
106	Gabon	2.9	3	2.6–3.1
106	Gambia	2.9	5	1.6–4.0
106	Niger	2.9	5	2.7–3.0
111	Algeria	2.8	6	2.5–3.1
111	Djibouti	2.8	4	2.3–3.2
111	Egypt	2.8	6	2.6–3.1
111	Indonesia	2.8	9	2.4–3.2
111	Kiribati	2.8	3	2.3–3.3
111	Mali	2.8	6	2.4–3.2
111	Sao Tome and Principe	2.8	3	2.4–3.3
111	Solomon Islands	2.8	3	2.3–3.3
111	Togo	2.8	5	1.9–3.9
120	Armenia	2.7	7	2.6–2.8
120	Bolivia	2.7	6	2.4–3.1
120	Ethiopia	2.7	7	2.4–2.9

Rank	Country/Territory	CPI 2009 Score	Surveys Used	Confidence Range
120	Kazakhstan	2.7	7	2.1–3.3
120	Mongolia	2.7	7	2.4–3.0
120	Vietnam	2.7	9	2.4–3.1
126	Eritrea	2.6	4	1.6–3.8
126	Guyana	2.6	4	2.5–2.7
126	Syria	2.6	5	2.2–2.9
126	Tanzania	2.6	7	2.4–2.9
130	Honduras	2.5	6	2.2–2.8
130	Lebanon	2.5	3	1.9–3.1
130	Libya	2.5	6	2.2–2.8
130	Maldives	2.5	4	1.8–3.2
130	Mauritania	2.5	7	2.0–3.3
130	Mozambique	2.5	7	2.3–2.8
130	Nicaragua	2.5	6	2.3–2.7
130	Nigeria	2.5	7	2.2–2.7
130	Uganda	2.5	7	2.1–2.8
139	Bangladesh	2.4	7	2.0–2.8
139	Belarus	2.4	4	2.0–2.8
139	Pakistan	2.4	7	2.1–2.7
139	Philippines	2.4	9	2.1–2.7
143	Azerbaijan	2.3	7	2.0–2.6
143	Comoros	2.3	3	1.6–3.3
143	Nepal	2.3	6	2.0–2.6
146	Cameroon	2.2	7	1.9–2.6
146	Ecuador	2.2	5	2.0–2.5
146	Kenya	2.2	7	1.9–2.5
146	Russia	2.2	8	1.9–2.4
146	Sierra Leone	2.2	5	1.9–2.4
146	Timor-Leste	2.2	5	1.8–2.6
146	Ukraine	2.2	8	2.0–2.6
146	Zimbabwe	2.2	7	1.7–2.8
154	Côte d´Ivoire	2.1	7	1.8–2.4
154	Papua New Guinea	2.1	5	1.7–2.5
154	Paraguay	2.1	5	1.7–2.5
154	Yemen	2.1	4	1.6–2.5
158	Cambodia	2.0	8	1.8–2.2
158	Central African Republic	2.0	4	1.9–2.2

Rank	Country/Territory	CPI 2009 Score	Surveys Used	Confidence Range
158	Laos	2.0	4	1.6–2.6
158	Tajikistan	2.0	8	1.6–2.5
162	Angola	1.9	5	1.8–1.9
162	Congo Brazzaville	1.9	5	1.6–2.1
162	Democratic Republic of Congo	1.9	5	1.7–2.1
162	Guinea-Bissau	1.9	3	1.8–2.0
162	Kyrgyzstan	1.9	7	1.8–2.1
162	Venezuela	1.9	7	1.8–2.0
168	Burundi	1.8	6	1.6–2.0
168	Equatorial Guinea	1.8	3	1.6–1.9
168	Guinea	1.8	5	1.7–1.8
168	Haiti	1.8	3	1.4–2.3
168	Iran	1.8	3	1.7–1.9
168	Turkmenistan	1.8	4	1.7–1.9
174	Uzbekistan	1.7	6	1.5–1.8
175	Chad	1.6	6	1.5–1.7
176	Iraq	1.5	3	1.2–1.8
176	Sudan	1.5	5	1.4–1.7
178	Myanmar	1.4	3	0.9–1.8
179	Afghanistan	1.3	4	1.0–1.5
180	Somalia	1.1	3	0.9–1.4

Transparency International e.V. copyright © 1994–2009

Naturally, there are clear differences of opinion about any characterization of these (or any) countries as "most corrupt," insofar as the bribery reputation of the foreign country is a red flag. However, the Transparency International CPI and similar lists from other organizations may be useful to counsel in evaluating the potential risks of a proposed foreign transaction, handling an internal investigation, defending a government investigation, or prioritizing foreign operations for FCPA audits.

B.   The Three Most Vulnerable Industries: Energy, Healthcare and Pharmaceuticals, and Information Technology

For different reasons, three major industries in particular seem vulnerable to FCPA investigations and prosecutions for the mid- if not long-term: energy, health and pharmaceuticals, and information technology.

1.   Energy

Given global oil production demand and opportunities in high-risk business environments, large production sharing agreements (PSAs) with foreign governments and the proliferation of state-owned oil companies, the energy sector, and related industries have been the most fertile area for FCPA enforcement action the past decade. *See, e.g.*, Aibel Group, BJ Services, Baker-Hughes, Chevron, Halliburton, KBR, Flowserv and numerous Oil for Food Program cases, Paradigm, B.V., Statoil ASA, and Vetco Gray. China and Russia rank second and fifth among the leading oil producing nations;[6] they are also countries that have been the subject of numerous FCPA enforcement actions and ones with poor Transparency International corruption perception scores (2.1 and 3.6, respectively). Other leading oil producers, Saudi Arabia (4.3), Iran (1.8), Kuwait (4.1), Mexico (3.3), and Venezuela (1.9),[7] all rank low in the Transparency International corruption perception scores, and oil is the dominant export in those countries. The global demand for oil and natural gas is not likely to subside in the next decade nor is the U.S. government's interest in the sector.

2.   Health Care

In November 2009, Assistant Attorney General of the Criminal Division, Lanny A. Breuer, announced that health care would be a major FCPA investigative priority of the DOJ under the Obama Administration.[8] The medical device and pharmaceutical industries represent a ripe area for FCPA abuses, and the aging population makes health care an expanding sector. It is especially vulnerable to public corruption, as foreign governments typically regulate, operate, and finance health systems and state-owned hospitals in their countries. Close to $100 billion of pharma sales are generated outside the United States.[9] Due to the heavy regulation in many countries, nearly every aspect of the approval, manufacture, import, export, pricing, sale, and marketing can involve a "foreign official" in the broad meaning of the FCPA.[10] FCPA enforcement actions in the medical device and pharmaceutical sector have included AGA Medical, DPC-Tianjin, Micrus, and Schering Plough.

3.   Information Technology

Information technology is a dominant U.S. industry that outsources manufacturing and, of course, sells software as well as hardware worldwide. The Fraud Section has made it clear Silicon Valley is in need of strong FCPA compliance programs and subject to abuses as a result of its channel distribution model. The sector also presents complex export issues that can become intertwined with FCPA issues. As the leader in the global innovation index,[11] the United States will continue to globally offer computer hardware and software, with an increasing emphasis on untapped emerging markets. This still young sector is ripe for FCPA investigations and prosecutions.

4.   Other Risky Sectors

Three other sectors have historically presented substantial bribery problems: telecom (*see, e.g.,* Alcatel, Bell South, Congressman William Jefferson, Latinode, and Lucent Technologies), aerospace and defense (e.g., BAE Systems, Nexus Technologies), and infrastructure (Siemens), and none is likely to decline soon. Given that many financial institutions are now owned in part by foreign governments as a result of national efforts to stimulate the worldwide recession, the financial services industry now finds itself subject to increased FCPA exposure and scrutiny. Government-led stimulus efforts are likely to result in more FCPA investigations, as large infrastructure projects have historically spawned corruption.

C.   BRIC Countries and Beyond

1.   Macro View

The four BRIC countries—Brazil, Russia, India, and China—offer large, expanding markets that are marked by problematic Transparency International corruption perception scores:[12]

Country	GDP PPP $bn[13]	GDP PPP Rank	Annual Growth Rate[14]	CPI Score
Brazil	1,833	9th	4.2%	3.5
Russia	2,087	7th	8.5%	2.1
India	3,097	4th	10.2%	3.4
China	7,097	2nd	13.7%	3.6

The BRIC markets collectively represent over 2.798 billion consumers and have a weighted annual growth rate of over eight percent—double and, in some cases, triple other nations among the fifteen countries with the biggest purchasing power.

Examination of the remaining eleven of the fifteen biggest economies by purchasing power is instructive:

Country	GDP PPP $bn	GDP PPP Rank	Annual Growth Rate	CPI Score
United States	13,751	1st	2.9%	7.3
Japan	4,297	3rd	2.2%	7.3
Germany	2,830	5th	1.5%	7.9
United Kingdom	2,143	6th	2.8%	7.7
France	2,078	8th	2.0%	6.9
Italy	1,802	10th	1.2%	4.8
Mexico	1,485	11th	3.7%	3.6
Spain	1,416	12th	3.8%	6.5

Country	GDP PPP $bn	GDP PPP Rank	Annual Growth Rate	CPI Score
South Korea	1,202	13th	4.7%	5.6
Canada	1,181	14th	2.9%	8.7
Turkey	957	15th	7.9%	4.6

Thus, over half of the top fifteen largest economy countries have CPI scores below 5, indicating a serious likelihood of corruption. Excluding the United States, the Purchasing Power Parity (PPP) leader among the fifteen biggest economies, the combined purchasing power of the seven countries with CPI scores below 5.0 exceeds that of the seven countries with CPI scores above 5.0: $17,838 billion to $15,147 billion.

Given that Mexico's PPP ($1,485 billion) currently exceeds Brazil's ($1,313 billion) by eleven percent or $170 billion despite very close corruption perception indices (3.6 vs. 3.5), an argument can be made that an M should replace the B in BRIC (resulting in CRIM). However, two factors caution against any change in the acronym. First, Brazil's average annual growth the past five years has exceeded Mexico's 4.2% to 3.7%. Second, the award of the 2016 Olympic Games to Rio de Janeiro portends global competition for lucrative Olympic infrastructure projects, telecommunications, and transportation systems—all of which present bribery opportunities. Thus, Brazil can be expected to uphold first place in the BRIC acronym for the foreseeable future. For risk assessment purposes, multinationals, when analyzing Transparency International surveys, should examine the general growth patterns of the countries where they do business and any special major projects.

The annual economic growth rates for China and Russia during the period 2002–2007 were especially startling: 13.7% and 8.5% respectively. The consensus among economists is that by 2025 China's economy will replace the U.S.'s economy as the world leader. Absent an extraordinary corruption perception sea change, China will still likely have a CPI score well under 5.0 for the next decade. The three large markets where many multinationals most desire to expand and that present difficult bribery environments will remain, for the next decade, China, India, and Russia.

Below these three, another trio among the top fifteen economic purchasing powers—Brazil, Italy, and Turkey—presents corruption challenges according to the 2009 Transparency International rankings. Of course, the relatively recent Siemens, KBR-Halliburton, and BAE Systems FCPA resolutions make clear that serious corruption can be found in and has been orchestrated out of the U.K., Western Europe, and Japan, where TI's CPI figures have long indicated less corruption risk.

2.   Micro View

The macro analysis of course does not address the business challenges and goals of particular multinational companies. For example, an oil field services company will likely encounter serious bribery issues in petroleum-rich Eastern Europe and West Africa. Most multinational companies are focusing on emerging markets, which usually means greater corruption risks (low CPI scores) and higher rewards—and greater compliance challenges.

Also, a successful and safe marketing model in one large country may not work for another country of similar size. While Canada and China are remarkably close in terms of large land mass and thus confound parent managements for those countries over the optimum sales model (i.e., direct or channel), China has fourteen cities with over 3.3 million people while Canada has only two cities with 3.3 million people. China has 41 times as many people; Canada has the cleanest CPI score (8.7, ranking eighth in the world) of any country with a population of 30 million or more, while the most-populated country, China (1.331 billion), has a low CPI score of 3.6, ranking 79th in the world. Multinationals have to know and vet their sales agents, consultants, and distributors (*see, e.g.*, Invision, Willbros) and evaluate the risks of their sales and business models.

For these reasons, each multinational should on a micro level carefully design an anti-bribery compliance program geared to its particular products, markets, and special projects, and also one that recognizes the macro data utilized by international law enforcement authorities to identify and measure corruption risk. Well-managed companies and legal departments annually reevaluate their macro and micro risk analyses of Transparency International rankings in connection with their current business model and long-term business plans and markets.

IV. AGENT AND CONSULTANT INTERMEDIARIES

A. Liability

The "knowing" standard under the FCPA means that a company is equally liable whether an improper payment is made directly by the company's employees or through a third party, such as agents, consultants. or distributors. As a result of stronger codes of conduct and ethics policies at multinational companies, it is more likely that an agent, consultant, or other intermediary will make an improper payment than a company officer or employee directly. A company can be held responsible for the actions of an agent or other third party if it: (1) authorizes an agent or third party to make improper payments to foreign officials or (2) makes payments to an agent or third party, knowing that all or a portion of the money will be paid directly or indirectly to foreign officials. The FCPA clarifies that proof of knowledge is not required. Knowledge is satisfied when a person is aware of a high probability of the existence of a particular circumstance.[15] In short, companies and their employees may not consciously disregard or deliberately ignore suspicious facts before entering into or during a third-party contract.

B.   Agent, Consultant, and Other Third-Party Contracts

Many multinational companies routinely enter into arrangements with local agents, sales representatives, distributors, or consultants that assist in procuring foreign, private, or government business. While each company has its own particular approach to these contractual relationships, it is prudent for the multinational to provide clear direction to the local party concerning FCPA-proscribed behavior and to obtain the local party's written acknowledgment of these standards.[16] Typically, this direction and affirmation is and should be confirmed in written agreements. Counsel drafting agency, consulting, or other third-party agreements should consider the following principles, subjects, and terms.

1.   Description of Duties and Services

An agreement should specify as much as is practical the duties and services that will be undertaken and provided by the agent or consultant, as the more general the duties and description, the more questionable the role of or need for the agent or consultant. Further, the agreement should customarily limit the duties and services to a particular project or contract. Some agent and consultant contracts set forth limitations on duties, for example, the agent or consultant shall not obtain or procure information where procurement of such information is unauthorized, illegal, or unethical.

2.   Time Frames

Most agency or consulting agreements should be for a year or two, or the duration of a particular project or contract. Evergreen agency or consulting contracts should be cancelable with 90 days' notice, and they should be reevaluated annually.

3.   Representations and Warranties

Agreements should include the following representations and warranties:

- A representation about the identity of all shareholders, directors, officers, and other "stakeholders" of the agent or consultant.
- A representation that no shareholder, director, officer, or employee of an agent or consultant is a foreign official or is related to a foreign official (as defined in the FCPA).
- A representation that the agent or consultant has read and understands the company's code of conduct and that he/she/it will do nothing to violate the company's code of conduct.
- A representation that in respect of any business for which it provides or may have provided consulting services to the company, the agent or consultant has not paid, offered, or agreed to pay any political contributions or charitable donations. Alternatively, a rep-

resentation that the agent or consultant will disclose in writing and has no objection to the disclosure of all political contributions or charitable donations to the U.S. and/or foreign governments.

- A representation that the agent or consultant has no undisclosed subagents, subcontractors, or third parties who have any role in the agency or consultancy.
- A representation that the agent or consultant has not been convicted of or pled guilty to an offense involving fraud, corruption, or moral turpitude, and that it is not now listed by any U.S. or foreign government agency as debarred, suspended, proposed for suspension or disbarment, or otherwise ineligible for government procurement programs.
- A representation that the agent or consultant will not make and has not made directly or indirectly any payments or given anything of value to any foreign official, foreign political party, or foreign party candidate in connection with the company's activities or in obtaining or retaining business from any governmental agency or instrumentality (e.g., a parastatal).

4.   Covenants

An agreement should include covenants that all of the listed representations and warranties will remain true, accurate, and complete at all relevant times and that the agent or consultant will promptly notify the company in writing if any of them change (e.g., a shareholder becomes a foreign official).

5.   Annual Certifications re: FCPA Compliance and Understanding

The agent or consultant should agree to provide annual certifications to the company relating to its understanding of and compliance with the FCPA. The agent or consultant should also acknowledge that he/she/it has read and understands the U.S. Department of Justice *Lay-Person's Guide to FCPA* (Appendix 4).[17] This guide can be appended to an agreement so that the agent or consultant cannot later claim that he/she/it did not understand the U.S. law, had never read the law, or had never received any clear explanation of the law.

6.   Audit Rights

- The agent or consultant should permit the company, or an independent accountant, to audit its books and records annually to assure compliance with the FCPA.
- A provision permitting direct access to an agent or consultant's books and records is sometimes difficult to negotiate. Often, a third-party audit right conducted by an internationally recognized accounting firm is a reasonable compromise.

7. *Payments*

The company should make payments only upon receipt of an invoice from the agent or consultant that includes a clear description of services rendered, and only to an established bank account in the country where the business activities are taking place (payments in another offshore location should be limited to special cases that can be justified). Under no circumstances should significant payments be made in cash or to unknown third parties.

8. *Assignment*

The agent or consultant should not assign, transfer, or subcontract any of its rights or duties under the contract without the prior written approval of the company.

9. *Compliance with Applicable Laws*

The agent or consultant should certify that it is in compliance with all applicable laws relating to (1) its status as a legal entity; (2) its role as an agent for the company; (3) its scope of work for the company, including its appearance before governmental agencies and instrumentalities; and (4) its receipt of funds as set forth in the agreement.

10. *Termination*

A company should specify the grounds for agent or consultant termination. Grounds for cause shall include but not be limited to:

- Any material breach of the contract;
- Any false or misleading information provided by consultant or agent;
- Any failure to comply with the representations and warranties;
- Any failure to timely provide annual certifications;
- Any refusal to timely comply with the company's annual audit right;
- Any failure to comply with applicable U.S. and foreign laws;
- Any failure by the agent or consultant to notify the company within 30 days of a material change in a representation or warranty or any event that renders or materially alters a prior representation or warranty.

11. *Choice of Law*

U.S. companies will typically insist that an agency or consultant agreement be governed by, subject to, and interpreted under the laws of a U.S. state (e.g., Delaware or its principal state of business).

12. Disputes

In some circumstances, the parties may agree to international arbitration to resolve disputes. A condition that the arbitrator(s) be trained in U.S. law is preferable in an FCPA agent or consultant agreement.

Termination clauses are particularly important even though sometimes awkward to negotiate at the outset of a relationship. As Don Zarin, a most respected FCPA expert, has aptly pointed out, without clear and appropriate contract language, a company will be in a difficult position to ascertain the facts and be able to terminate a relationship.[18] For these reasons, transaction counsel must give considerable thought to the cause provisions and the rights to investigate and terminate in agency, consultant, joint venture, distributor, and other third-party agreements.

V. DISTRIBUTORS

A. Models

A distributor is usually a wholesaler who buys goods in bulk quantities for its own account from a manufacturer at a discount and independently resells the goods at a higher price to other dealers or retailers. Distributor models and contracts vary greatly. Some companies have substantial control over and knowledge of their distributors' activities. For example, they know their distributors' customers and resale policies and have contractual and supervisory control over the activities of the distributors. Other companies have little control or relationship with their distributors once the goods are shipped. Some companies, including telecommunications and technology companies, have two-tier distribution models under which they have a very strong relationship and structure with Tier 1 distributors and a much less formal relationship with Tier 2 distributors—often resellers.

B. Liability

Because of distributors' general independence and the customary transfer of title of goods from the manufacturer to the distributor, many companies mistakenly assume that distributors pose little or no risk to them under the FCPA. The fact is that the FCPA prohibits the use of an agent to violate the statute.[19] A distributor can itself be an "agent" of the manufacturer or supplier and thus subject the company to criminal liability if the company corruptly gives the distributor anything of value, for example, goods or a price discount, knowing that all or some of the things of value will be offered, given, or promised, directly or indirectly, to a foreign official to obtain or retain business.

If a distributor receives a substantial discount and the controlling company or supplier knows with a "high probability" that an improper payment may take place or has taken place, the latter may be held criminally liable. Under such circumstances, the independence of the distributor or the passage of title from the company to the distributor are irrelevant.[20] However, where a distributor makes payments to a foreign official to obtain or retain business, the DOJ will face a substantial burden to prove a "high probability of knowledge" on the part of the manufacturer.

C. Risk Reduction

To minimize FCPA exposure, many multinational companies recite relevant FCPA or anti-bribery language in their distributor agreements. Others require mandatory FCPA training for Tier 1 or large distributors. Some also impose audit rights whereby third-party auditors may annually examine the distributor's books and records in whole or in part.

Counsel should review the traditional red flags for agents and consultants to determine whether they prove or corroborate the requisite high standard of knowledge that establishes a violation in the distributor context. Recent DOJ or SEC FCPA distributor cases have included AGA Medical Corporation, DPC (Tianjin) Co. Ltd., Fiat, and InVision (see Chapter 10).

VI.   PRACTICAL AGENT, CONSULTANT, AND DISTRIBUTOR DUE DILIGENCE ADVICE

The following are practical due diligence steps counsel should consider with respect to agents, consultants, and distributors (hereafter "third party"):

- Obtain the full legal name of the third party, including any trade names.
- Obtain the principal business *street* address.
- Obtain the names and Web sites of any entities sharing the same business address, facilities, or employees as the client and state the nature of the business of such entities.
- Determine the number of years the third party has been in business using the above legal name and other names.
- Obtain the full names (first, middle, and last) of the third party's five most senior officers and the third party's three principal business contacts with the company.
- List the proposed countries in which the third party intends to represent the company.
- Determine the country under which the third party was incorporated and the legal form, for example, sole proprietorship, joint venture partnership, limited liability company.

- List all shareholders or owners of 10 percent or more of the outstanding shares.
- Identify the names and Web sites of other businesses owned or controlled by the 10 percent-plus shareholders (of the third party) and their family members.
- Identify any shareholders or family members of the third party who are foreign government officials, political party officials, or political party candidates and describe their financial interests or control in the business.
- Determine whether the third party has had anti-corruption or FCPA training.
- Obtain three business references of the third party (other than the client), contact them, and make a memorandum to a file incorporating the substance of their references.
- Have someone other than the sponsor or proposer of the agent or consultant conduct the due diligence and evaluate red flags and risks.
- Determine whether any officers or employees have been known or found by a court or government agency to have violated any laws prohibiting fraud, bribery, or other corruption in the last ten years.
- Direct the third-party applicant to provide a form and attest to the accuracy of its answer(s) to the above areas of inquiry.
- Draft an agreement that enables the company to obtain relevant facts of an FCPA issue or allegation or risk and to terminate the third party for misconduct or failure to fully cooperate in an internal inquiry or government investigation.
- Obtain a local background check of the company and conduct an Internet search of the third party's five most senior officers and three principal business contacts. Place a copy of all responsive downloaded information into a permanent, separate due diligence file.
- Print a copy of the third party's business Web site. Place a copy of all responsive downloaded information into a permanent due diligence file.
- Review the following U.S. government-published lists for the third party and its directors or five most senior officers: Denied Persons List, Unverified List, Entity List, Specifically Designated Nationals List, Debarred List, Nonproliferation Sanctions, and the World Bank List of Ineligible Firms.
- Prepare and maintain a separate, permanent written file memorializing and reflecting all due diligence efforts undertaken with respect to each third-party applicant—successful or otherwise.

Analyze the collected data for current and future risk and prepare a memorandum analyzing the risks.

Due diligence for major distributors will be more intensive than due diligence for second-tier distributors or resellers.

VII.   ACQUISITION DUE DILIGENCE

A.   Reasons to Conduct Acquisition Due Diligence

A company contemplating an acquisition or merger should conduct sufficient due diligence to assure itself that the target's employees or agents have not engaged in and/or do not intend to make improper payments to government officials in the performance of company business. A "check the box" approach or broad target representation that the company is unaware of any bribery-type conduct is simply no longer adequate. Justifications for thorough due diligence include good corporate citizenship; avoidance of ongoing obligations by the successor entity to make improper payments; overpayment of assets such as contracts that were obtained through foreign bribes; accounting and disclosure issues that can arise if there are material contracts or licenses obtained through bribery that may be void or voidable; damage to reputation from the investigation and prosecution of the acquired entity or its executives; and follow-on civil litigation.[21]

Perhaps the two most compelling reasons to conduct thorough due diligence of a foreign acquisition today are (1) to determine whether the acquisition is worth the business risk; and (2) to build a full record so that if an improper payment scheme does surface, the acquirer can demonstrate to the DOJ or SEC that it conducted comprehensive due diligence that did not disclose the problem and thus should not be criminally or civilly charged for misconduct by its predecessor.[22]

B.   FCPA Risk Assessment—15 Key Risk Factors

Certain foreign acquisition risk factors should cause an acquirer to conduct extra-careful, heightened due diligence or even reconsider the acquisition. Fifteen key risk factors for targets are:

1. A presence in a BRIC (Brazil, Russia, India, and China) country and other countries where corruption risk is high, for example, has a Transparency International CPI rating of 5 or less;
2. An industry that has been the subject of recent anti-bribery or FCPA investigations, for example, oil and energy sector, telecommunications, pharmaceuticals;
3. Significant use of third-party agents, for example, sales representatives, consultants, distributors, subcontractors, or logistics personnel (customs, visas, freight forwarders);

4. Significant contracts with a foreign government or instrumentality;

5. Substantial revenue from a foreign government or instrumentality;

6. Substantial projected revenue growth in the foreign country;

7. High amount or frequency of claimed discounts, rebates, or refunds in the foreign country;

8. Substantial system of regulatory approval, for example, for licenses and permits, in the foreign country;

9. History of prior government anti-bribery or FCPA investigations or prosecutions;

10. Poor or no anti-bribery or FCPA training;

11. Weak corporate compliance program and culture, in particular from legal, sales, and finance perspectives at the parent level or in the foreign country operations;

12. Significant issues in past FCPA audits;

13. The degree of competitive factors in the foreign country;

14. Weak internal controls at the parent or in foreign country operations; and

15. In-country managers who appear indifferent or uncommitted to U.S. laws, the FCPA, and/or anti-bribery laws.

Prudent legal departments will weigh risk factors relevant to their business operations and models and combine the individual rankings and arrive at low, middle, and high risk ranges. Composite or individual rankings can lead potential acquirers to pull out of a deal, step up the due diligence, or plan and enact a comprehensive "Day One" compliance program (see Section VII.G.2, *infra*).

C. Due Diligence Questionnaire

An acquirer should submit a thoughtful, custom due diligence questionnaire to a target. For example, have you ever been advised orally or in writing of a government inquiry into any of your operations, including foreign subsidiaries, regarding potential acts of bribery?; who are all the shareholders of your Nigerian affiliate holding 48.2%?; how often have you conducted anti-bribery training of your Middle Eastern sales team and who conducted the training? The due diligence questionnaire will be tailored to the operations, foreign government touch points, and risks of the target.

D. Document Review

An acquiring company should consider reviewing the following materials during its due diligence:

- Ownership records and interests of merger partners or acquisition candidates;
- Contracts with foreign governments;
- Local registration and other local public records;
- All consulting and agency agreements;
- All foreign commission agreements and books and records;
- Web sites for contractors, subcontractors, and vendors;
- Due diligence files for foreign business and/or joint venture partners;
- Due diligence files for agents and consultants;
- Due diligence files for distributors;
- Due diligence files for significant local vendors, for example, freight forwarders and customs agents;
- Leases and any related party interests or connections to government officials or family members;
- Protective contract language (audit rights, FCPA warranties, etc.);
- Manager compliance certification requirements;
- Contributions to foreign political candidates or parties;
- Employee and officer rotation policies;
- Internal controls;
- Overseas compliance training programs including FCPA training;
- All audits, particularly prior FCPA audits;
- Petty cash accounts;
- Charitable donations, activities, and gifts;
- Travel and entertainment records;
- In-country purchase records;
- In-country court files where the target is a party;
- The most recent Transparency International CPI of the countries in which the target company or its subsidiaries operate; and
- U.S. government-published lists: Denied Persons List, Unverified List, Entity List, Specifically Designated Nationals List, Debarred List, Nonproliferation Sanctions, and the World Bank List of Ineligible Firms.

The company should keep and maintain copies of all relevant and responsive document review materials. Some multinationals ask FCPA experts to spend a set number of hours in a data room to search for problematic relationships, contracts, or transactions.

E.   On-Site Visits and Interviews

Due diligence should include on-site visits to the target's business operations and sales offices. It will often include interviews of the target's foreign sales, accounting, financial, compliance and legal personnel, and third parties. Interviews will be appropriate where the target has operations in countries with high Transparency International CPIs; it competes in an industry known for corruption or abuses (e.g., oil, health care and pharmaceuticals, telecommunications); or has weak compliance, poor books and records, and few or inconsistent internal controls.

F. Overall Assessment of Target's Operations and Books and Records

Due diligence should include a review of the target's books and records. The acquirer should assess the general quality of the target's books and records, for example, are they readily accessible and organized? Has the target demonstrated a commitment to financial transparency? Does the target have entertainment and travel and expense reports that describe employees' activities in reasonable and sufficient detail? Is any training of foreign customer personnel directly related to the performance of a contract? Are there questionable side trips of foreign officials visiting the U.S. to inspect plant operations? Have all third-party contracts been kept and secured in one place? Do foreign books and records generally comply with GAAP-type practices? Is back-up documentation complete? Are consulting or agency contracts signed and annual certifications current? Do they contain clear anti-bribery language? Are cash vouchers reasonable and appropriate under the circumstances? Are the recordkeeping practices of U.S. and foreign operations consistent? Are relevant books and records policies translated into the appropriate foreign languages?

G. Proceeding to Acquire a Target with FCPA Issues

Upon discovering FCPA problems, an acquirer must weigh the legal and business risks. Several acquirers have encouraged targets to voluntarily disclose and resolve FCPA matters before closing, such as GE, Syncor International, ABB Vetco Gray (2004), and Paradigm. Others have stumbled at the altar, for example, Lockheed-Titan, with the result that target shareholders lost substantial value. Still others have conducted inadequate merger and acquisition due diligence and paid substantial sums later, for example, Delta & Pine Land Co., Baker Hughes, and Latin Node. FCPA expert Lucinda Low cautions that in certain scenarios an acquisition may be a violation itself: for example, where it is known that a portion of the purchase price will be used to make an improper payment, such as to secure government approvals; or where a company provides benefits to shareholders who are foreign government officials in return for discretionary action.[23]

1. Four Critical Acquirer Steps

If a company elects to pursue an acquisition in the face of some red flags, one well-respected FCPA expert, Margaret Ayres, recommends that the acquirer take the following four steps:

1. Obtain appropriate representations, warranties, and indemnifications in the purchase agreement coupled with the possible disclosure to the DOJ and SEC;
2. Develop and implement a comprehensive plan to terminate the FCPA-related misconduct;
3. Develop and implement an effective compliance program for the target, the program to commence immediately upon closing; and
4. In the case of an "issuer," correct any inaccurate books and records (bribes and facilitating payments) of the target *before* the close of its fiscal year.[24]

Ayres further cautions the acquirer to preserve any evidence or books and records relating to illegal bribes and facilitating payments.[25] If a company makes facilitating or expediting payments consistent with the "routine governmental action" exemption, it must ensure that these payments are accurately recorded in reasonable detail.

2. "Day One" Compliance

FCPA due diligence expert Gary DiBianco has written of "Day One" compliance, recommending a post-closing compliance framework that includes (1) written policies that address governing anti-corruption laws; (2) revised reporting procedures; (3) compliance resources for sales personnel and other relevant employees; (4) training; and (5) an audit function to review compliance.[26] A post-closing compliance program should have a short, firm deadline, and remedial steps should be addressed as early as the signing of a letter of intent.[27]

H. Safe Harbor for Acquirers: FCPA Opinion Procedure Release 2008-02 (June 13, 2008)

In June 2008, the DOJ responded to a three-part request from Halliburton and its controlled subsidiaries. Halliburton, a U.S. issuer, was considering making a bid for a United Kingdom target that operates internationally in the upstream oil and gas industry. A competitor was also bidding to acquire the target.

Halliburton asked the DOJ whether (1) the acquisition would violate the FCPA; (2) Halliburton would "inherit" FCPA liability for any unlawful pre-acquisition conduct by the target; and (3) Halliburton would be held criminally liable for any post-acquisition conduct by the target prior to Halliburton's completion of its FCPA and anti-corruption due diligence, when such conduct was identified and disclosed to the DOJ within 180 days of closing. Halliburton effectively argued that a competing foreign bidder could underbid Halliburton's negotiation by not imposing any FCPA contingency term or by ignoring any anti-bribery due diligence. Halliburton also detailed the legal reasons why it did not have sufficient time to conduct due diligence before closing, and proposed a post-closing action plan of investigations and disclosures in order to avoid any potential FCPA violations.[28]

Specifically, within 10 days of closing, Halliburton agreed to provide a comprehensive, risk-based FCPA and anti-corruption work plan that would address:

- Relationships with distributors, sales agents, consultants, and other third parties who could be used to facilitate improper payments;
- Commercial dealings with state-owned customers;
- Joint venture, teaming, or consortium arrangements;
- Customs and immigration issues;
- Tax issues; and
- Government licenses and permits.

As the target does business in Africa, Asia, the Middle East, South America, and the former Soviet Union, the risk profile of this acquisition was substantial.

The DOJ stated that it did not presently intend to take any enforcement action against Halliburton based on the three points Halliburton described in its request. The DOJ was careful to note that its opinion took the particular circumstances into account, and reserved the right to take enforcement actions against Halliburton for violations beyond the scope of the three questions.[29]

This opinion is significant because it affords acquirers some measure of safe harbor as they compete to acquire a target under challenging due diligence deadlines and with competitors that are less interested in FCPA compliance. At the same time the opinion placed multiple restrictions upon Halliburton as the requestor to comply with numerous disclosure obligations and due diligence milestones. The DOJ can use the disclosed information in a prosecution of the target.

I.   DOJ FCPA Opinion Releases

When significant FCPA concerns arise during due diligence, an acquirer may wish to consider seeking an FCPA opinion from the DOJ in order to avoid the risk of successor criminal liability. An index of all the DOJ FCPA opinions issued to date is found in Appendix 5. The turnaround time of the DOJ on such opinions has historically been slow and can be impractical in a transaction context. However, the DOJ has recently responded to such criticisms by issuing opinions more quickly. For example, Opinion Release 08-03 relating to approval of journalist travel expenses in China was released just four days after it was requested.

J.   Practical Acquisition Due Diligence Advice

- Explain to the executive team the risks and costs of a failed due diligence effort of a wayward target or partner (e.g., damage to reputation, lengthy government investigations of the company and its officers, disclosure obligations, decrease in share value, and substantial legal and accounting fees). Describe the problematic acquisition cases of Titan and InVision. (See Chapter 10).
- Consider the present value of an acquisition if it were discovered that the price was based in significant part on contracts procured by bribes or improper payments to local customs, tax officials, or other regulators who may soon enforce and investigate potential regulatory infractions.
- Visit the target's foreign business offices and facilities, including sales offices and major agents, consultants, or distributors, and examine whether other businesses in the same buildings appear to be related in business or to employ some of the target's employees.
- Conduct a criminal records search and review all prior U.S. and foreign government investigations of the target, its executives, key managers, and owners.
- Review the local public records of the target and conduct a thorough Internet search of the target, its executives, and its key managers and employees.
- Secure warranties and representations, indemnification agreements, and closing conditions that protect the acquisition.
- Review all government contracts, relationships, or touch points (e.g., with customs, taxes, visas, licenses, permits).
- Review all third-party contracts (e.g., with agents, consultants, distributors, joint venture partners, freight forwarders, customs brokers).
- Review the target's historic due diligence files for third parties (e.g., agents, consultants, distributors, joint venture partners, freight forwarders, customs brokers).
- Assess the quality of the target's books and records, internal controls and compliance codes, policies, and culture.
- Review potential red flags and resolve them before signing any agreement.
- Keep track of remedial measures and all Day One Compliance efforts.

It is critical that the acquisition due diligence file be kept.

Resolution may include disclosing potential FCPA violations to the DOJ and SEC before closing or securing an agreement with the DOJ to further timely disclose after closing and a plan to immediately stop any improper practices and, in the case of issuers, correct any inaccurate books and records before the end of the target's fiscal year.

A sample FCPA Acquisition Due Diligence Checklist is in Appendix 6.

VII.   JOINT VENTURES

A.   Foreign Joint Ventures

FCPA issues can arise in joint venture transactions. U.S. companies seeking to sell goods or services in other countries will frequently enter into joint ventures for various commercial, legal, or financial reasons. In many countries, it is a legal requirement that foreign parties have a local partner to undertake certain projects. In other cases, it will be essential, as a matter of operational necessity, that a foreign company have a local partner in order to access local labor, equipment, financing, and other resources. In large infrastructure projects, the requirements of different forms of input (construction, equipment, labor), level of financing, and risk allocation may require the formation of a joint venture company to undertake such projects.

A joint venture can be as simple as a contractual agreement relating to a particular project, with each party agreeing to undertake certain activities and receive certain benefits and compensation in return. More typically, a joint venture will consist of the formation of a new legal entity under the laws of the country in question, with its equity ownership, board of directors, steering committee, and day-to-day management shared between the partners. In considering a potential joint venture, a partner will consider whether it wishes an active or passive role. An active role will give a partner greater influence on compliance and finance and controller functions. Voting rights—unanimous, supermajority, or majority—as well as blocking rights are very important considerations. Whatever the form, the joint venture partner should adopt the same due diligence procedures and methodology of its partners described for mergers and acquisitions in this chapter to minimize the risk of past or future FCPA anti-bribery violations.

B.   Common Joint Venture Scenarios

There are two common joint venture scenarios whereby issuers or persons face potential FCPA criminal risk for anti-bribery conduct. The first involves a joint venture partnership with a state-owned entity, under which the issuer or subsidiary has a substantial operation in the foreign

state and customarily half of the directors are foreign government officials. The second involves a joint venture partnership of a U.S. issuer or
person, such as a manufacturer, and a privately owned foreign entity
whereby the latter manufactures under license the product for the often
U.S.-based issuer or its foreign subsidiary. Each scenario presents substantial and unique commercial and FCPA risks.

1.   Joint Venture with a State-Owned Entity

FCPA exposure frequently arises in joint ventures between companies
subject to the FCPA and foreign state-owned entities. The first priority
is to confirm that the structure and relationship are legal under the local
laws. Many foreign countries encourage, if not require, joint ventures,
and in certain industries use of a joint venture agreement (JVA) is common. For example, in the energy sector it is common for the petroleum
or natural resource government authority to enter into a JVA and a production sharing agreement (PSA) whereby a resource extraction company
and the foreign government contract over how much of the resource (e.g.,
oil) extracted from the country each will receive. The private company
typically provides management and technical services while the foreign
government provides natural resources. In the oil and gas industry the
extraction company is customarily allowed to recover capital and operational expenses, known as "cost oil," first. The remaining money is known
as "profit oil" and is split between the company and the government—
usually 20 percent–80 percent.

To the extent the directors of the joint venture knowingly authorize
improper payments to foreign government officials, they, as well as the
venture itself and the U.S. shareholder, may be found criminally liable.
A potential major FCPA issue is the payment of directors' fees, as the
state-owned entity's directors[30] can not only award business but can also
influence other government entities, for example, customs and taxes,
that can otherwise impede the joint venture's business. To avoid potential improper "influence" accusations, it is better for each partner to pay
its own directors, to cover travel and lodging for its respective directors,
and to handle similar expenses whenever possible. Transparency and disclosure of all foreign government approvals, agency relationships, and
transactions are essential where state-owned entities partner with issuers
and U.S. companies and subject their managing employees and directors
to the jurisdiction of the FCPA.

2.   Joint Venture with a Foreign Private Entity

As indicated above, many U.S. companies enter into joint venture agreements with foreign private companies to secure lower manufacturing
and labor costs in foreign countries. As with foreign distributors, U.S.
companies often mistakenly assume that far-away joint ventures pose

little FCPA risk absent direct payments by an in-country U.S. manager to local officials. Issuers, directors, and the joint venture face FCPA criminal liability under various provisions of the Act.[31] Where the foreign partner has the operating responsibilities and employs only foreign nationals, it is oftentimes more difficult for the U.S. partner and its directors to know the in-country activities and, in particular, any improper activities there. Still, their authorization of payments and acts while in the territory of the United States can put them in peril. The traditional red flags that apply to agents and consultants should be considered with joint venture partners. Multiple red flags may establish the highly likely knowledge of the improper payments standard necessary for a criminal prosecution. Joint venture partners are wise to require FCPA/anti-bribery training of their staffs, to conduct regular audits, and to enforce a strong "tone at the top."

C. Issuer, Director, and Joint Venture Liability

1. Issuer

There are usually two scenarios under which an issuer faces FCPA anti-bribery liability for a foreign joint venture. First, it is unlawful for any issuer or any stockholder thereof acting on behalf of the issuer, that is, a joint venture, to make use of the mails or any means or instrumentality of interstate commerce corruptly in furtherance of an offer, payment, promise to pay, or *authorization* of the payment of any money, offer, gift, promise to give, *or authorization of the giving of anything of value* to any foreign official for purposes of influencing any act or decision of such foreign official in his or her official capacity or inducing such foreign official to do or omit to do any act in violation of the lawful duty of such official.[32] Second, it is unlawful for any stockholder acting on behalf of a foreign firm *while in the territory of the United States* corruptly to make use of the mails or any means or instrumentality of interstate commerce or *to do any other act in furtherance of any offer, payment, promise to pay, or authorization of the payment of any money, offer, or gift* for the aforementioned purposes.[33]

2. Directors

U.S. directors often compose half of a joint venture's board and can be subject to FCPA criminal liability under all three substantive anti-bribery provisions—15 U.S.C. § 78dd-1, 78dd-2, and 78dd-3. First, directors can be liable as employees or agents of an issuer if they make use of the mails or interstate commerce corruptly in furtherance of an offer, payment, promise to pay, or authorization of the payment of any money, or offer, gift, promise to give, or *authorization of the giving of anything of value to foreign officials* for the aforementioned purposes.[34] Second, they can either be liable as a domestic concern (any individual who is a citizen, national, or resident of the United States), or as employees of a corporation with its principal place of business in the United States if they make use of the mails or any means of instrumentality corruptly in furtherance of any offer, payment, promise to pay, or *authorization of the payment of any money, offer, gift, or promise to give* for the above-mentioned purposes.[35] Third, directors can be directors or agents of a foreign firm while in the territory of the United States corruptly to make use of the mails or do any other act in furtherance of an offer, payment, promise to pay, or *authorization of the giving of anything of value to any foreign official* for the above-mentioned purposes.[36] U.S. directors of joint ventures invariably engage in many acts while in U.S. territory, but whether any of their acts are in furtherance of an improper offer, promise to pay, or gift becomes the real issue in some investigations.

3.   Joint Venture

A joint venture itself may be liable if it as a foreign firm has a stockholder or agent on its behalf *while in the territory of the United States* corruptly make use of the mails or do any other act in furtherance of an offer, payment, promise to pay, or *authorization of the payment of any money, offer, gift*, promise to give, or authorization of the giving of anything of value to a foreign official.[37] The United States generally takes a very expansive view of "acts in furtherance" of improper payments, for example, wiring funds or e-mailing authorizations. The DOJ or SEC will also look closely at the circumstances surrounding any authorization of expenses and any relevant red flags at the time of the improper payments or giving of things of value. The DOJ has to date preferred to charge the U.S. joint venture partner—as opposed to the joint venture itself.[38]

D. Internal Controls

Under the FCPA, an issuer that holds 50 percent or less of the voting power with respect to a foreign firm is required only to proceed in good faith to use its influence to the extent reasonable under the issuer's circumstances to cause such foreign firm to devise and maintain a system of internal controls that satisfies the Act's internal control standards.[39] Such circumstances shall include the relative degree of the issuer's ownership of the foreign firm and the laws and practices governing the business operations of the country in which the firm is located. An issuer that demonstrates good faith efforts to use such influence shall be conclusively presumed to have complied with the FCPA's internal controls provisions.[40]

E. Joint Venture Due Diligence

1.   Practical Joint Venture Due Diligence Advice

Joint ventures are common in international business transactions, and in some countries required by law. Before entering into an international joint venture, a company should conduct due diligence into the qualifications of the partner:

- The ownership of the proposed joint venture partner;
- The prior business experience of the proposed joint venture partner;
- The presence of any owners, managers, directors, officers, or their family members, who are foreign government officials;
- Its corporate compliance programs;
- Its familiarity, policies, and training in FCPA, OECD, and related anti-bribery conventions;
- Any prior criminal record, litigation, and local administrative history of the proposed joint venture partner;
- Any audit opinions and history;
- The transparency of its financial statements;
- The qualifications and experience of its senior management; and
- Review of U.S. government lists as described in Section VI, *supra*.

It is also important to examine any underlying agency or consulting relationships; the payment procedure and history; the due diligence conducted with respect to current and past agents and consultants; and compensation structure for agents and consultants (e.g., success fee, hourly fee).

Upon confirming that there are no ongoing FCPA problems, counsel will want to focus on securing strong warranties and representations and indemnification rights for the final joint venture agreement and insert anti-bribery controls and inspection rights in the venture's governing documents.[41]

2.   FCPA Opinion Procedure Release 2001-01 (May 24, 2001)

U.S. companies forming joint ventures with other foreign companies under which each party will contribute preexisting contracts to the venture should be aware of potential FCPA issues relating to the contracts procured by the foreign company prior to formation of the venture. In May 2001, the DOJ addressed this subject through its opinion release procedure when a U.S. company sought guidance concerning its plans to enter into a joint venture with a French company.[42] Both companies planned to contribute preexisting contracts to the venture, including contracts procured by the French company before the effective date of the new French Law No. 2000-595 Against Corrupt Practices. In indicating that it would not take any enforcement action under the facts and circumstances there presented, the DOJ raised several important issues.

The U.S. company requesting the opinion letter informed the DOJ that the French company had represented that none of the contracts and transactions to be contributed by the French company were procured in violation of applicable anti-bribery or other laws. In response, the DOJ noted that it specifically interpreted this representation to mean that all the contracts the French company was bringing to the joint venture were obtained in compliance with all applicable anti-bribery law—not just French law. The DOJ then stated that if the French company's representation was "limited to violation of then-applicable French law, the Requestor, as an American company, may face liability under the FCPA if it or the joint venture knowingly takes any act in furtherance of a payment to a foreign official with respect to previously existing contracts irrespective of whether the agreement to make such payments was lawful under French law when the contract was entered into."[43] Thus, a U.S. company can be held liable if it takes any act in furtherance of a payment (e.g., payment of a commission due an agent who had previously assisted in obtaining a contract for the foreign partner) to a foreign official in violation of the anti-bribery provisions of any country.

FCPA Opinion Release 2001-01 also allowed the DOJ to state its view concerning the appropriate termination provision for the joint venture. The joint venture agreement provided that the U.S. company could opt out of the venture or terminate its obligations if "(i) the French company is convicted of violating the FCPA; (ii) the French company enters into a settlement with an admission of liability under the FCPA; or (iii) the Requestor learns of evidence that the French company violated anti-bribery laws and that violation, even without a conviction or settlement, has a material adverse effect upon the joint venture."[44] The DOJ objected to the "material adverse effect" standard, which it called "unduly restrictive," and warned, "Should the Requestor's inability to extricate itself result in the Requestor taking, in the future, acts in furtherance of original acts of bribery by the French company, the Requestor may face liability under the FCPA."[45] As a result, the DOJ specifically declined to endorse the "materially adverse effect" standard. This opinion highlights for transaction counsel the importance of structuring joint ventures and acquisitions so that "FCPA-tainted" assets or contracts will not result in liability for the U.S. party.

IX.   SAMPLES AND THE GOVERNMENT PROCUREMENT PROCESS

Foreign governments are very often major customers of multinational companies. In tenders for government purchases, it is not uncommon for foreign government officials to request samples as part of technical performance evaluations. FCPA issues can arise when there is a request for samples in connection with a product that has both commercial and personal uses and when an official requests or is offered manufacturer samples of personal products that are not part of the proposed tender. Providing samples for the personal use or benefit of a government official or family members presents clear risks.

In August 2009, the DOJ issued Opinion Procedure Release 09-01,[46] which reviewed the request of a U.S. domestic concern that manufactured a specific type of medical device and sought approval to provide sample devices to foreign government health centers for evaluation of its technology, measured outcomes, and feedback from the top physicians. A senior official had explained that the foreign government was not familiar with its products, that it would only endorse products that it had technically evaluated with favorable results, and that it had already found competitors qualified. The foreign government and the requestor jointly determined that the optimal sample size for an evaluation study was 100 units distributed among ten experienced health centers each receiving ten devices at $19,000 per device, or $1.9 million for all 100 units.

Both the manufacturer and its potential government customer undertook a series of steps to make the provision of expensive samples to government health centers fair and transparent. The 100 recipients were to be selected from a list of candidates provided by the participating medical centers and were to be culled from long lists of candidates based on certain objective criteria outlined in a letter of request. All candidates were required to present a certificate of economic difficulty from the relevant local government authority establishing the candidates' inability to pay. The recipients were to be selected from the list of candidates by a working group of healthcare professionals familiar with the type of medical device and the requestor's country manager who had received FCPA training.

The names of the 100 recipients were to be published on the government agency's website for two weeks. Close family members of government officials were ineligible, unless (1) the government-employed relatives of such recipient held low-level positions and were not in positions to influence either the selection or the testing process; (b) the government-employed relatives of such recipient clearly met the requisite economic criteria; and (c) the recipient is determined to be a more suitable candidate than candidates who were not selected based on technical criteria. Further, the requestor's country manager was to review the selection of any immediate family members of any other government official (e.g., those unaffiliated with the medical device project or the government agency) to make certain that the criteria were properly and fairly applied and would report his determination to Requestor's legal counsel. A favorable evaluation under this process would only make the requestor's products eligible for the government's subsidized medical device program and not necessarily result in the award of business.

The evaluation of the donated medical devices was to be based on objective criteria that are standard for this type of medical device and that have been provided to the Department. The results of the evaluation were to be collected by the Country Manager, who would enlist the help of two other medical experts to review the results and provide an overall report, as well as individual objective results, to a senior health official in a foreign country who would share his assessment with the government agency. The government agency was to then evaluate the results of the evaluation and the report by the Country Manager, along with the senior health official's assessments, to determine the suitability of Requestor's technology for the medical device program. If the results of the evaluation were favorable, Requestor's devices would be identified by the government agency as eligible for the subsidized medical device program, along with the devices of Requestor's competitors, which had already been declared eligible. The foreign government has advised the Requestor that none of the company's devices would be promoted by the foreign government above any of the other qualified devices.

Requestor represented that more than thirty government health centers throughout the country would receive the evaluation results, which would in large part determine whether those centers would purchase the requestor's products as part of the government's medical device program. As a result of the anticipated success of the proposed evaluation, Requestor expected that its products would meet all technical criteria for this program and that its opportunities for participation in the program would be greater as a result of the awareness among government physicians of the performance of Requestor's devices. Finally, the requestor represented to the DOJ that it had no reason to believe that the senior official who suggested providing the medical devices to the government would personally benefit from the donation of the devices and related items and services.

The DOJ approval of this opinion request rested largely on the fact that the proposed provision of 100 medical devices fell outside the scope of the FCPA in that the donated products were to be provided to the government—and not to government officials—for ultimate use by patient recipients. While the decision is not surprising in light of the absence of anything of value being given to a government official, Opinion Procedure Release No. 09-01 nonetheless provides very useful guidance on the detailed and lengthy prophylactic measures a company can and should take when it considers offering samples to potential government customers.

X. ONGOING AGENCY OR CONSULTANCY DUE DILIGENCE

Companies must not only conduct due diligence prior to an agency or consultancy, but also review and document the agent or consultant's performance of its duties *during* the life of the contract.[47] To that end, companies should require third parties to detail the nature of goods or services in invoices and explain any charges for goods or services that raise questions. They should also be prepared to cancel any contracts with third parties that unreasonably refuse to provide documentation of ongoing goods and services or submit to an audit.

XI. ADDITIONAL RESOURCES

Ayres, Pelayo & Hipp, *FCPA Considerations in Mergers and Acquisitions*, in THE FOREIGN CORRUPT PRACTICES ACT 2007: COPING WITH HEIGHTENED ENFORCEMENT RISK (PLI Course Handbook No. B-1619, 2007).

Ayres & Hipp, *M&A and Third-Party Transactions under the FCPA*, in THE FOREIGN CORRUPT PRACTICES ACT: COPING WITH HEIGHTENED ENFORCEMENT RISK (PLI Course Handbook 2008).

Brown, *Steps to an Effective Foreign Corrupt Practices Act Compliance Program*, 20 COMM. ON CORP. COUNS. NEWSL. (Summer 2006).

DiBianco & Pearson, *Anti-Corruption Due Diligence in Corporate Transactions: One Size Does Not Fit All*, Feb. 2009, *available at* http://www.skadden.com.

DiBianco, Due Diligence of Business Partners and Agents, paper presented at ACI FCPA Boot Camp, San Francisco (June 4–5, 2007).

Friedenberg et al., *Joint Ventures, in* SUCCESSFUL PARTNERING BETWEEN INSIDE AND OUTSIDE COUNSEL, ch. 50 (Haig, ed., West Group 2008).

Low & Best, *Addressing FCPA Risk in Mergers and Acquisitions: At What Price Safety?, in* THE FOREIGN CORRUPT PRACTICES ACT 2009: COPING WITH HEIGHTENED ENFORCEMENT RISKS (PLI Course Handbook No. B-1737, 2009).

Muck, Kevane, Donohue & O'Lellana, *Avoiding FCPA Risk in Dealing with Agents, Consultants and Other Third Parties, in* THE FOREIGN CORRUPT PRACTICES ACT 2009: COPING WITH HEIGHTENED ENFORCEMENT RISKS (PLI Course Handbook No. B-1737, 2009).

Sokenu, *DOJ Again Clarifies FCPA Due Diligence Expected in Business Combinations*, 40(34) SEC. REG. & LAW REP., August 25, 2008.

Transparency International, http://www.transparency.org.

Turza, *The Foreign Corrupt Practices Act: Elements, Due Diligence and Affirmative Defenses—A Practical Guide, in* ABA FOREIGN CORRUPT PRACTICES ACT 2006 (ABA 2006).

DON ZARIN, DOING BUSINESS UNDER THE FOREIGN CORRUPT PRACTICES ACT, ch. 9 (PLI 2007).

NOTES

1. Foreign Corrupt Practices Act of 1977, Pub. L. No. 95-213, 91 Stat. 1494 (codified as amended at 15 U.S.C. §§ 78m, 78dd-1 to -3, 78ff (1999)) [hereinafter FCPA].

2. In investigating FCPA issues, counsel must often master international transaction agreements and practices, including joint venture agreements, shareholder agreements, merger and acquisition agreements, operating and management agreements, transfer of technology and license agreements, production sharing agreements (PSAs), and joint operation agreements (JOAs), as well as commercial agency agreements, distribution agreements, commission sales representation agreements, consulting contracts, and so forth.

3. *United States v. Titan Corp.,* No. 05 CR 0314 BEN (S.D. Cal. Mar. 1, 2005); *SEC v. Titan Corp.,* Civil Action No. 05-0411 (D.D.C.) (JR) (filed Mar. 1, 2005).

4. *In the Matter of Delta & Pine Land Co. & Turk Daltapine Inc.,* SEC Release No. 56,138, Admin. Proceeding File No. 3-12712 (July 26, 2007).

5. http://www.transparency.org/layout/set/print/policy-research/surveys_indices/cpi/2009/cpi.

6. Source: THE ECONOMIST, *Pocket World in Figures* (2010 Ed.) at p. 55.

7. *Id.*

8. Assistant Attorney General Lanny A. Breuer, U.S. Dept. of Justice Keynote Address, 10th Annual Pharmaceutical Regulatory and Compliance Congress and Best Practices Forum (Nov. 12, 2009), http://www.justice.gov/criminal/prl/speeches/2009/11/11-12-09.breuerpharmaspeech.pdf.

9. *Id.*

10. *Id.*

11. THE ECONOMIST, *Pocket World in Figures* (2010 Ed.) at p. 62.

12. THE ECONOMIST, *Pocket World in Figures* (2010 Ed.) at p. 9.

13. GDP means Gross Domestic Product; PPP means Purchasing Power Parity.

14. Annual growth rate in real GDP 2002–2007. Source: THE ECONOMIST, *Pocket World in Figures* (2010 Ed.).

15. 15 U.S.C. §§ 78dd-l (f)(2), -2(h)(3), -3(f)(3).

16. *See* DON ZARIN, DOING BUSINESS UNDER THE FCPA (PLI 2007), ch. 9.

17. *Available at* http://www.usdoj.gov/criminal/fraud/docs/dojdocb.html.

18. *See* ZARIN, *supra* note 16, at ch. 6, § 6.2.2.

19. 15 U.S.C. §§ 78dd-1(a), -2(a), -3(a).

20. ZARIN, *supra* note 16, at 62.2.

21. Margaret M. Ayres & Bethany K. Hipp, *Third-Party Transactions Under the FCPA, in* THE FOREIGN CORRUPT PRACTICES ACT 2008: COPING WITH HEIGHTENED ENFORCEMENT RISKS 163 (PLI 2008).

22. *See* Gary DiBianco & Wendy E. Pearson, *Anti-Corruption Due Diligence: One Size Does Not Fit All* (Feb. 2009), *available at* http://www.skadden.com.

23. Lucinda Low & Thomas R.L. Best, *Addressing FCPA Risk in Mergers and Acquisitions: At What Price Safety?, in* THE FOREIGN CORRUPT PRACTICES ACT 2009: COPING WITH HEIGHTENED ENFORCEMENT RISKS (PLI COURSE HANDBOOK NO. B-1737 2009).

24. Margaret M. Ayres & Bethany K. Hipp, *FCPA Considerations in Mergers and Acquisitions, in* THE FOREIGN CORRUPT PRACTICES ACT: COPING WITH HEIGHTENED ENFORCEMENT 17–18 (PLI 2007 Course Handbook No. B-1619).

25. *Id.* at 19.

26. *See* DiBianco & Pearson, *supra* note 22.

27. *Id.*

28. *See* FCPA Opinion Procedure Release 2008-02 (June 13, 2008), http://www.usdoj.gov/criminal/fraud/fcpa/opinion/2008/0802.html.

29. *Id.*

30. *See* FCPA Opinion Procedure Release No. 93-01 (Apr. 20, 1993).

31. Ellen S. Friedenberg et al., *Joint Ventures, in* SUCCESSFUL PARTNERING BETWEEN INSIDE AND OUTSIDE COUNSEL (Robert Haig ed., 2008).

32. 15 U.S.C. § 78dd-1(a).

33. 15 U.S.C. § 78dd-3(a).

34. 15 U.S.C. § 78dd-1(a).

35. 15 U.S.C. § 78dd-2(a).

36. 15 U.S.C. § 78dd-3(a).

37. 15 U.S.C. § 78dd-3.

38. *See, e.g., United States v. Kellogg Brown & Root,* Chapter 10 § VI.KK.

39. 15 U.S.C. § 78m(b)(2).

40. 15 U.S.C. § 78m(b)(6).

41. Roger M. Witten, Kimberly A. Partner & Thomas J. Koffer, Navigating the Increased Anti-Corruption Environment in the United States and Abroad, paper presented at the 20th Annual ACI Conference on the Foreign Corrupt Practices Act, Washington, D.C. (Nov. 18, 2008).

42. *See* FCPA Opinion Procedure Release 2001-01 (May 24, 2001).

43. *Id.*

44. *Id.*

45. *Id.*

46. *See FCPA Opinion Procedure Release,* No. 09-01 (Aug. 3, 2009)

47. Mark Mendelsohn, Acting Chief Fraud Section, Criminal Div., U.S. Dep't of Justice, Remarks at the ABA White Collar Crime Institute, San Francisco (Mar. 5, 2009).

CHAPTER 6

Gifts, Travel, Lodging, and Entertainment

I. INTRODUCTION

Gifts, travel, lodging, and entertainment for non-U.S. government officials present the most common or day-to-day Foreign Corrupt Practices Act issues for multinational companies and their counsel. If a company has clear written policies and procedures for such requests, most of the issues will resolve themselves without any substantial risk. Thoughtful written policies and internal controls can reduce the risk of FCPA anti-bribery, books and records, and internal controls violations; establish sound guidance for managers; and deter some potential wrongdoers.

Some multinational companies prohibit all forms of gifts, hospitality, or entertainment. Many rely largely on a two- or three-paragraph summary of the FCPA in their Code of Company Conduct to guide employees. Still others that operate in challenging countries provide specific written FCPA guidance to employees utilizing a reasonableness standard—often tied to the magnitude of the gift, travel, or entertainment. Because the FCPA has no de minimis exclusion for gifts, travel, lodging, or entertainment expenditures, the analysis often reverts to the Act's use of the word "corrupt" (see Chapter 1 at I.C.4).[1] Most well-managed multinational companies conduct some form of annual FCPA training—live, or at least online—that addresses gifts, travel, lodging, and entertainment, among other topics.

For many gift, travel, lodging, and entertainment issues, it is often helpful to consider the simple question: How would the host officer or employee feel about being pictured with the donee or beneficiary in the local newspaper, and the gift, travel, or entertainment and supporting invoice(s) were next featured in a front-page story of *The New York Times?*

Because the FCPA expressly covers certain types of travel, lodging, and entertainment but does not directly address gifts anywhere, the topics are here addressed separately.[2]

II. GIFTS

Most business gifts are simply that: gifts designed to promote products or services and thus business and business relationships. Under the FCPA, the term "corruptly" connotes an evil motive or purpose, and only a gift with an intent to wrongfully influence the recipient in awarding or retaining business or gaining an improper business advantage should provide the basis for a bribery charge. A gift or entertainment that is provided to create a favorable business climate with only a generalized hope or expectation of ultimate benefit to the donor lacks the benefit of a quid pro quo for the award of business.[3]

A. Nature, Value, and Transparency

In general, the nature, value, and transparency of a gift to a non-U.S. government official will determine whether the gift is *corruptly* motivated. Some of the questions and factors that should be considered in determining whether a gift is proper under the FCPA include:

1. The nature of the gift:
   - Is the gift business-appropriate?
   - Would a donor be at all embarrassed if the fact of the gift were to be publicly disclosed?
   - Is the gift something a donor would be comfortable accurately describing on an expense voucher?
   - Is the gift a memento of a business occasion, for example, a bowl with an engraved corporate logo to commemorate a joint venture opening?
   - Is the gift cash or one involving something not appropriate for a business, for example, adult entertainment?
   - Is the gift a one-time event to a recipient, or has the recipient received repeated gifts over time?
   - Does the recipient or a close friend or relative have any decision-making authority with respect to the donor's business, bid, award, or contract?
2. The value of the gift:
   - Is the value of the gift excessive and likely to be interpreted as able to influence the recipient?
   - Is the value of the gift consistent or at odds with the donor company's domestic gift policy?
   - Is the value of the gift substantial when compared to the annual income of the recipient or the annual per capita income of the country?
3. The transparency of the gift:
   - Will the gift be given openly to the intended recipient?

- Is the gift to be presented to the intended recipient at a group setting, or one-on-one?
- Is the gift to be presented directly to the intended recipient?
- Has the intended recipient requested the gift?
- What is the intended recipient's role in any current or upcoming business award or approval process?
- Has the donor provided multiple gifts of value to one recipient for the recipient to distribute to others?
- Is the gift reciprocal (e.g., has a visiting group presented a gift to the host and is it a custom and practice in the country in question for the host to reciprocate and present a similar gift)?
- Does the recipient's government, company, or organization have any written policies governing gifts and does the gift in question conform to or violate that policy?
- Has the donor consulted his/her supervisor and obtained advance approval to give the gift?
- Has the donee consulted his/her supervisor and obtained advance approval to receive the gift?

B.   Practical Gift Advice

Some rules of thumb or policies that can minimize the risk that a gift to a non-U.S. government official may be corruptly construed include the following:

- No cash gifts of any kind should be permitted.
- No direct per diem payments to the recipient should be permitted— that is, per diem payments should be made by check to the intended recipient's employer, which may then reimburse the employee.
- No gift should be offered or given that violates either the donor company or the donee agency or organization's written policies.
- No gift other than a modest public gift (e.g., of a value of $100 or less) should be made to a foreign official unless there is advance written disclosure of the nature, amount, and purpose of the gift to the foreign official's immediate supervisor.
- No gift should be offered or given to a foreign official that violates the local written laws and regulations of the country.
- Any gift to a foreign official of other than nominal value should require at least one supervisory prior approval by the donor company.
- Any gift to a foreign official should not exceed the maximum amount permitted by the company in a comparable domestic setting.
- Any gift to a foreign official should be accurately described in the company's books and records including the name and title of the recipient, the value, the purpose, and the date of the gift.

- Gifts should be infrequent.
- Multiple gifts should not be permitted to one recipient in a one-year period without approval of the legal department. Alternatively, a maximum annual limit for any recipient should be established.
- Determination of the value of the gift should be from the recipient's point of view (e.g., a $1,000 gift to a recipient who has a $9,000 annual salary).

III.   TRAVEL, LODGING, AND ENTERTAINMENT

A.   Permissible Travel, Lodging, and Entertainment

The FCPA permits companies to provide certain types of entertainment or travel to non-U.S. government officials, to the extent the travel or entertainment expenses are (1) reasonable and bona fide, and related to certain marketing and contracting activities; and (2) lawful under applicable local law. A company may pay for reasonable travel and lodging expenses for a foreign official that *directly* relate to the promotion, demonstration, or explanation of products or services, or to the execution or performance of a contract with a foreign government or agency.[4]

A travel or entertainment expenditure that is lawful under the written laws and regulations of a foreign official's country similarly provides an affirmative defense under the FCPA. No written laws condone bribery. However, foreign campaign contribution laws may permit substantial campaign contributions to a local political party or candidate and thus create a defense to an otherwise improper payment. As to the propriety of other travel and entertainment expenses not expressly covered by the FCPA, the issue is invariably whether things of value were provided to a foreign official for a corrupt purpose and to obtain or retain business or gain an improper advantage.

B.   Three Leading FCPA Travel and Entertainment Cases

Since 1977, numerous FCPA settlements have included travel and entertainment misconduct, but only two have exclusively addressed questionable travel and entertainment practices. In 2009 the DOJ and SEC settled with UTStarcom for misconduct that primarily involved travel and entertainment abuses in connection with purported foreign government customer training in the United States.

1.   United States v. Metcalf & Eddy[5]

In December 1999, Metcalf & Eddy, Inc., of Wakefield, Massachusetts, as successor to Metcalf & Eddy, International, Inc., agreed to a civil judgment as a result of the payment of excessive travel and entertainment expenses for an Egyptian government official and his family. Metcalf &

Eddy had promised to pay travel, lodging, and entertainment expenses to the chairman of the Alexandria General Organization for Sanitary Drainage (AGOSD). In exchange the chairman, an official of the Egyptian government, would use his influence to have AGOSD support contracts between the United States Agency for International Development (USAID) and Metcalf & Eddy. AGOSD was the beneficiary of these contracts. The AGOSD chairman did not directly participate in the selection of bidders, but the contract to operate and maintain wastewater treatment facilities managed by AGOSD was ultimately awarded to Metcalf & Eddy. The chairman, along with his wife and two children, traveled to the United States twice as guests of Metcalf & Eddy. The first trip included visits to Boston, Washington, D.C., Chicago, and Disney World. The second trip took the AGOSD chairman and his family to Paris, Boston, and San Diego. The chairman was paid 150 percent of his estimated per diem expenses and his airline tickets were upgraded to first class by Metcalf & Eddy.

The civil judgment permanently enjoined Metcalf & Eddy from further violations of the FCPA, and the company agreed to pay a $400,000 civil fine; no criminal charges were filed. Further, as part of the settlement, the U.S. Department of Justice required Metcalf & Eddy to adopt an 11-point compliance and ethics program (detailed in Chapter 10, Section VI.A).[6]

2. United States Department of Justice–Lucent Technologies Inc. Agreement;[7] SEC v. Lucent Technologies Inc.[8]

In a two-year nonprosecution agreement also significant for its travel and entertainment guidance, Lucent Technologies Inc. agreed in 2007 to pay the DOJ a $1 million fine to resolve allegations of bribery violations of the FCPA[9] and a $1.5 million civil penalty to the Securities and Exchange Commission. In 2002 and 2003 alone, Lucent paid for 24 presale trips for Chinese government customers. Of these trips, at least 12 were primarily for sightseeing. Lucent spent over $1.3 million on at least 65 presale visits between 2000 and 2003. Significantly, these "business trips" were actually for entertainment purposes, including the destinations of Disneyland and the Grand Canyon. In addition to the fines, Lucent was required to adopt new or modify existing internal controls, policies, and procedures with the objective of ensuring that Lucent makes and keeps true and accurate books, records, and accounts, as well as rigorous anti-corruption compliance code standards and procedures designed to detect and deter FCPA violations and other applicable anti-corruption laws.

3. United States Department of Justice UTStarcom Inc. Agreement; SEC v. UTStarcom

In December 2009, UTStarcom Inc. (UTSI) entered into a non-prosecution agreement with the DOJ (*United States v. UTStarcom, Inc.*),[10] agreeing to pay a $1.5 million fine for violations of the FCPA by providing travel and other things of value to foreign officials, specifically employees at state-owned telecommunications companies in the People's Republic of China (PRC). The same day, the SEC obtained a $1.5 million penalty and permanent injunctive relief (*SEC v. UTStarcom*).[11] UTSI, a publicly traded Delaware-based corporation headquartered in California, is a global telecommunications company that designs, manufactures, and sells network equipment and handsets and has historically done most of its business in China with government-controlled municipal and provincial telecommunications companies through its wholly owned subsidiary UT Starcom China, Co. Ltd. (UTS-China). Most of the alleged misconduct specifically involved travel and entertainment abuses.

The SEC alleged that UTStarcom's wholly owned subsidiary in China paid nearly $7 million between 2002 and 2007 for hundreds of overseas trips by employees of Chinese government-controlled telecommunications companies that were customers of UTStarcom, purportedly to provide customer training. It is part of UTS-China's standard practice to include as part of its internal sales contracts for wireless networks a provision for UTS-China to pay for some of the customer's employees to attend the purported training overseas after installation of the network. In reality, the trips were entirely or primarily for sightseeing popular tourist attractions in the United States, including Hawaii, Las Vegas, and New York City. Most trips lasted two weeks and cost $5,000 per customer employee. Further, the trips were supposed to be for training at UTSI training facilities when UTSI had no training facilities at the purported training locations and conducted no training.

The SEC also alleged that on at least seven occasions between 2002 and 2004, UTSI paid for executive training programs at U.S. universities that were attended by managers and other employees of government customers in China. The programs covered general management topics and were not specifically related to UTSI's products or business. UTSI paid for all expenses associated with the program, which totaled more than $4 million and included travel, tuition, room and board, field trips to tourist destinations, and a cash allowance of between $800 and $3,000 per person. UTSI accounted for the cost of the programs as "marketing expenses." The company's senior management believed that the executive training programs helped it obtain or retain business.

Finally, as part of the travel and entertainment abuses, the SEC alleged that in 2004, UTSI submitted a bid for a sales contract to a government-controlled telecommunications company in Thailand. While its bid was under consideration, UTSI's general manager in Thailand spent nearly $10,000 on French wine as a gift to agents of the government, including rare bottles that cost more than $600 each. The manager also spent $13,000 for entertainment expenses to secure the same contract. UTSI's former chief executive officer and executive vice president of UTS China approved the payments. UTSI reimbursed the expenditures and accounted for them as marketing expenses.

The *UTStarcom* case highlights the not uncommon travel and entertainment expenses associated with service contracts, product inspection, and training where foreign customers of state-owned entities visit U.S. manufacturers or service companies request or are offered side trips, car allowances, and expensive entertainment. In some cases, the visits become annual excursions or junkets that result in not only improper payments or the provision of things of value to obtain and retain business, but lead to voluminous false books and records violations. The purposes of these trips must be consistent with the limited exceptions permitted under the FCPA, and books and records entities for such trips must be scrupulously accurate.

C. Quid Pro Quo

In essence, one must ascertain whether under the particular travel, lodging, and entertainment facts and circumstances, there is a quid pro quo. Thoughtful stand-alone written company FCPA policies are more likely to provide a safe haven for a company and its employees alike. In such policies, "reasonableness"—borrowing from the statute's travel and entertainment language relating to certain marketing and contracting activities—should be the governing standard and is best met and assured under policies where prior written approval is required.

D. Practical Travel, Lodging, and Entertainment Advice

Rules of thumb or policies for travel and entertainment of non-U.S. government officials include the following:

- All travel, lodging, and entertainment expenses must be accurately reported.
- All travel, lodging, and entertainment expenses must be "reasonable and necessary"—and not lavish.
- All lodging should be in business-class hotels and not first-class hotels.
- No general advancement of travel, lodging, and entertainment expenses should be permitted (e.g., the company should provide a nonexchangeable transportation ticket to the foreign government).
- No travel, lodging, or entertainment expenses should exceed the amounts under the donor company's corresponding written domestic travel, lodging, and entertainment policy for customers (e.g., the donor company should not host guests in a manner more lavish than it hosts comparable personnel at the parent company).

- No travel, lodging, or entertainment should be extended to an official in a position to award or influence an award without advance legal department written approval.
- No travel, lodging, or entertainment should be extended for events that are not completely or substantially business-related.
- No travel, lodging, or entertainment should be offered or provided that violates the local laws of the foreign country or the internal policies and regulations of the recipient's employer.
- No travel, lodging, or entertainment should be provided to a foreign official recipient's spouse, significant other, or family members that is not promptly and accurately reimbursed.
- Daily incidental expenses should be supported with receipts.
- No travel, lodging, or entertainment should be offered for a trip whose purpose could be accomplished in the official's own country.
- No side travel, lodging, or entertainment by the foreign official to another city, resort, or entertainment venue (e.g., Paris, Las Vegas, Disney World) should be allowed or permitted absent appropriate and timely reimbursement.
- The value of the travel, lodging, and entertainment should be determined from the recipient's point of view (e.g., is a trip to Disney World an expensive, once-in-a-lifetime event for the recipient and guest?).
- Per diem advances, if necessary, should be made to the guest's employer or agency for distribution to the employee.
- It is usually wise to have the foreign government agency select any travel and lodging recipients rather than the host company.

IV. BOOKS AND RECORDS AND INTERNAL CONTROLS

All gifts, travel, lodging, and entertainment for foreign officials must be accurately and timely recorded in the books and records of the company. Expense vouchers should accurately relate the date, event, amount, recipient, and attendees and should be no less rigorously enforced than vouchers submitted in the company's domestic operations. If an officer or employee who intends to make a gift or host a foreign official is reluctant to accurately record the event or transaction, that is very likely an indication that something may be improper. The more thoughtful and custom-made the FCPA policies for companies operating in challenging countries are, the better such companies are able to defend a "failure to maintain adequate internal controls" allegation or inquiry by the SEC or DOJ.

V. TRADITIONAL RED FLAGS

In all gift, travel, lodging, and entertainment situations, a company and its employees must remain mindful of traditional FCPA red flags, including the following:

- The country in which the gift or hospitality has a reputation for significant corruption under the Transparency International Index or ranking of a similar organization.
- A foreign bank account or foreign bank is involved in any way.
- A relative of the intended recipient is a foreign government official, foreign political party representative, or foreign political candidate.
- There has been suspicious conversation or behavior (e.g., "The Minister will need an advance in the amount of $15,000, and his staff will handle the travel details and payments"; "A $25,000 diamond necklace is insignificant in value compared to His Excellency's net worth/annual income"; "There are no direct commercial flights available from Dubai to Miami").
- An intended recipient has requested inappropriate things of value in connection with this event or in the past (e.g., "Our chief of state has been customarily provided a Rolex by visitors and would likely be insulted if your company does not recognize his Office with an appropriate goodwill gesture"; "The Deputy always has her family and staff travel with her, and they will all of course require an advance per diem").
- An intended recipient is unwilling or unable to obtain prior written approval for a gift, travel, or entertainment from his/her government or agency.

VI. EFFECTIVE GIFT, TRAVEL, LODGING, AND ENTERTAINMENT COMPLIANCE PROGRAMS

A. General

In drafting FCPA policies, a company should consider the corruption reputation of the countries in which it does business, the customs and practices in the countries in which it operates, the local laws of the countries, and the likely gift, travel, lodging, and entertainment situations that its employees face abroad in order that the policies provide employees real-world guidance. For example, if a company is in an industry that offers customers substantial entertainment (e.g., golf, hunting trips, sporting events), conducts business in countries where there are widespread gift traditions (e.g., red packets in China), or has operations in countries where there are substantial cash economies (e.g., Nigeria), the FCPA policies should address these practices and issues in forthright, practical fashion. Prudent companies will retain experienced FCPA counsel to vet FCPA policies, practices, and issues.

A compliance program for a company with significant operations abroad that is simply left to the "good judgment" or "common sense" of employees is in most circumstances not adequate. Under no circumstance should in-house counsel simply cut and paste other companies'

FCPA policies, procedures, or forms. Specific FCPA policies provide the additional benefit of giving foreign-based employees and foreign nationals who face awkward circumstances an "out"—something in writing that explains to potential "donees" why a gift or donation is not appropriate and cannot be made under a clear company policy.

B.   Emergency Circumstances

There are invariably short-notice or emergency circumstances where a host officer or employee is unable to secure the requisite prior written approval of a gift, travel, or entertainment under company policies. These situations are best addressed by policies that require the donor officer or employee to notify the legal department in writing within a certain time (e.g., 72 hours) of the offer of any gift, travel, lodging, or entertainment or face serious disciplinary action for failure to do so.

C.   Tiered Authorizations

Many multinational companies employ a multitiered authorization system for approving gifts, travel, lodging, and entertainment. For example, a one-time gift of a value of $100 or less to a non-government official requires no approval; gifts of a value of $100–$400 require one supervisory authorization; gifts exceeding $400 require two supervisory authorizations; and gifts above $1,000 require prior legal department approval. Tiered authorization systems for gifts, travel, lodging, or entertainment purposes should require advance written approval for any significant levels.

D.   Request Forms and Questionnaires

A request for travel or entertainment expenditures will routinely require the names, titles, and employers of those attending or traveling to an event; the destination(s) and starting and ending dates of the events or travel; and the proposed expenditures in detail (flights, rental cars, hotels, and entertainment costs). State of the art compliance programs will in addition list questions that make the requestor consider the FCPA. For example, Baker Hughes' guidelines for travel and entertainment of a non-U.S. government official contain the following questions:

- Why is the particular venue or destination chosen?
- Is there a contract with a government entity that requires the proposed expenditure?
- Is the purpose of the proposed expenditure for training?
- Please explain in detail the purpose and business justification for this proposed expenditure.

- Have any of the proposed guests or travelers been entertained or traveled at the company's expense before? If so, please provide the details below.
- Is there any additional relevant information relating to the proposed expenditures that has not been discussed in this form?
- Are there any stopovers en route (other than stopovers of less than one day necessary to make an airline or other transportation connections) or indirect routing of transportation?
- Signature and details of person requesting expenditures.
- Approval signatures.

This type of request-form procedure will often discourage requests for travel or entertainment that are problematic under the FCPA.

E. Training

Annual FCPA training is recommended for appropriate personnel (e.g., sales personnel, controllers, financial officers, and accounting personnel) of a company that does business regularly with foreign governments, has joint ventures with foreign governments, or has expatriate personnel who regularly interface with foreign government employees (e.g., immigration, environmental, customs, tax)—in short, multinational companies that have foreign sales or manufacturing operations. FCPA training is particularly critical for foreign employees who are not U.S. citizens, who speak a language other than English, or who are not familiar with U.S. laws. Annual FCPA training will address gifts, travel, lodging, and entertainment and include any recent FCPA opinions or relevant DOJ or SEC policy statements. All ethics and FCPA training must emphasize the importance of accurate books and records.

F. Chinese Lodging and Hospitality Guidance: FCPA Opinion Procedure Release 2008-03 (July 11, 2008)

In 2008, the DOJ responded to a request submitted by TRACE International, Inc., an Annapolis, Maryland-based anti-bribery organization. TRACE had submitted a request just four days earlier, on July 7, proposing to pay for expenses (transportation, lodging, and incidentals) for 20 journalists employed by the People's Republic of China (PRC) media outlets, so that the journalists could attend a TRACE Shanghai press conference. The press conference was scheduled to coincide with an international anti-corruption conference at the same hotel. The journalists are "foreign officials" under the FCPA because the media outlets are owned by the PRC.

TRACE requested a determination of the DOJ's present intent to bring an enforcement action against such conduct, and the Department responded that it had no such intent.[10] The DOJ concluded that the stipend and expenses, as detailed by TRACE, fell within the FCPA's promotional expenses affirmative defense.[11] As is customary, the DOJ limited this opinion to TRACE and stated that it has no binding application on other parties. However, this opinion does afford some guidance to multinational companies doing business in China, where generous hospitality has long been a tradition.

NOTES

1. Foreign Corrupt Practices Act of 1977, Pub. L. No. 95-213, 91 Stat. 1494 (codified as amended at 15 U.S.C. §§ 78m, 78dd-1 to -3, 78ff (1999)) [hereinafter FCPA].

2. Facilitating payments that may be interpreted as gifts are not addressed in this section. Facilitating payments should only be for nondiscretionary actions and should always be modest. They must always be accurately recorded in the books and records of the company.

3. DON ZARIN, DOING BUSINESS UNDER THE FOREIGN CORRUPT PRACTICES ACT 6–7 (PLI 2007).

4. U.S.C. §§ 78 DD-1(c)(1) and (2), 78 DD-2(c)(1) and (2), and 78 DD-3 (c)(1) and (2).

5. *United States v. Metcalf & Eddy, Inc.*, No. 99 Civ. 12566 (D. Mass. Dec. 14, 1999).

6. *Consent and Undertaking of Metcalf & Eddy, Inc.*, No. 99 Civ. 12566-NG (D. Mass. filed Dec. 14, 1999).

7. http://www.usdoj.gov/opa/pr/2007/December/07-crm_1028.html.

8. No. 07-CV-02301 (D.D.C. 2007).

9. Press Release, U.S. Dep't of Justice, Lucent Technologies, Inc. Agrees to Pay $1 Million Fine to Resolve FCPA Allegations (Dec. 21, 2007), http://www.usdoj.gov/opa/pr/2007/December/07_crm_1028.html.

10. Press Release, U.S. Dept. of Justice, *UTStarcom Agrees to Pay $1.5 Million Penalty for Acts of Foreign Bribery in China* (December 31, 2009), www.justice .gov/opa/pr/2009/ December/09-CRM-1390.html.

11. *Securities and Exchange Commission v. UTStarcom Inc.*, Case No. CV/09 6094 (JSW), U.S.D.C. N.D. Cal., Lit. Rel. No. 21357 (December 31, 2009), www .sec.gov/litreleases/ 2009/lr 21357.htm.

12. FCPA Opinion Procedure Release 2008-03 (July 11, 2008), http://www.usdoj.gov/criminal/fraud/fcpa/opinion/2008/0803.html.

13. *See* 15 U.S.C. § 78dd-2(c)(2)(A).

CHAPTER 7

Charitable Donations and Political Contributions

I. INTRODUCTION

There have been few Foreign Corrupt Practices Act charitable donation and political contribution cases brought by the U.S. Department of Justice or the Securities and Exchange Commission, with the notable exceptions of *In re Schering Plough* and *United States v. Titan, infra*. There have also been few FCPA Opinion Releases in this area. Still, contribution and donation issues arise not infrequently for brand-name multinational companies because many publicize their corporate generosity and good citizenship, because they operate in challenging countries, and, to some degree, because they are perceived as having deep pockets. These three potential problem areas are best protected by clear global policies and a clear message to foreign managers that such global corporate policies govern these issues. Many companies benefit by requiring that all political donations and campaign contributions above a certain amount (e.g., $500) have advance written approval from the corporate law department.

II. CORPORATE POLICY AND LOCAL LAWS

In-country managers of foreign operations or subsidiaries are from time to time approached about making local charitable donations and political contributions. The first consideration is whether the parent company has a uniform charitable or political contribution policy that governs the request. The second consideration is whether local laws permit, prohibit, or cap charitable donations or political contributions. The inquiry is not what local practice or custom is, but what the *written* local law is. Assuming that a proposed donation or contribution is permitted by corporate policy and under written local law, the third common and most critical consideration is whether the contemplated donation or contribution has a *corrupt* motive. Obviously, a modest annual contribution to a local youth football organization team will not pose an FCPA problem. What approaches a risky charitable donation or political contribution will depend on a number of factors.

III.   CORRUPT MOTIVES

A.   Political Contributions

In evaluating a possible corrupt motive surrounding a proposed or completed campaign contribution, counsel will want to consider:

- The amount or value of the political contribution;
- The nature of the political contribution, for example, check, use of a company facility, office equipment, vehicle, or plane, or hosting a reception;
- The authority or ability of the recipient/candidate to award business to the company, retain business for the company, or to influence local licenses, taxes, customs duties, or other regulatory approvals;
- The timing of the contribution, for example, whether it coincides with the award of a bid opening or contract;
- The entity receiving the contribution, that is, whether it is clear that the actual recipient is a foreign candidate or foreign political party as opposed to an individual or shell organization not implicitly tied to a campaign or candidate, and whether there will be a local public record of the contribution, for example, whether the donor, candidate's name, and size of the contribution will be on file locally;
- The overall propriety of the contribution, for example, whether the company's contributor would be embarrassed to be pictured with the political candidate in a local newspaper;
- Whether the requestor—a candidate, a member of a campaign staff, or a government official—is connected to a bid or regulatory process and;
- Requests by the political party or candidate to limit or conceal the political contribution, or otherwise involve suspicious circumstances.

Under no circumstances should a company endorse or approve cash contributions to a foreign political candidate or party.

B.   Charitable Donations

In evaluating the possible corrupt motive surrounding a proposed or completed charitable donation, counsel will want to consider:

- The amount or value of the charitable donation;
- The relationship of the charitable organization to the donor company, that is, whether the charity is logically associated with or

related to the company's principal business—for example, a medical device company contributing to a local children's hospital;

- The authority or ability of the recipient or a relative to award business to the company or to influence local licenses, taxes, customs duties, or other regulatory approvals;
- The public record of the contribution, for example, whether there is a local filing requirement by the candidate or party;
- The deductibility of the charitable contribution, for example, whether the charitable donation is deductible under local law, and whether the company will exercise the deductibility;
- Evidence of receipt—is the charitable organization reluctant to issue a receipt that fully and accurately describes the donation?

Under no circumstances should a company endorse or approve cash charitable donations. Sometimes, employees or officers view donations in kind, for example, use of a corporate jet, computers, office space, or business facilities, as less troubling or problematic. Neither the DOJ nor the SEC shares this view.

IV. CONTRACTS CONTAINING CHARITABLE DONATION TERMS

In some countries a bid will request a contribution to a worthy local cause, for example, construction of a clinic or school. In this circumstance, counsel should confirm that this condition or term is uniform to all bidders and is contained in the local bid documents available to the public. Further, any contractual donation should be made payable to a governmental body and earmarked for the intended purpose. The more public the donation, the better and the safer for the donor. For example, a pharmaceutical company might be wise to require a plaque on a children's hospital facility that reads, "Premier Pharmaceutical Prenatal Care Center. This Facility Is Made Possible Through a Donation of Premier Pharmaceutical, September 15, 2009."

V. TRANSPARENCY OF DONATIONS OR CONTRIBUTIONS

As with all transactions implicated by the FCPA, transparency is the cornerstone. If the donor or donee is hesitant about the company's recording of or the eventual or potential disclosure to the public of the contribution or donation, counsel and management will want to understand the reasons. As with all books and records entries, the description of the contribution or donation should be in reasonable detail, that is, such level of detail that would satisfy prudent officers in the conduct of their own affairs. Companies that have formal approval procedures and forms in place for both domestic and foreign political contributions or charitable donations substantially reduce the risk of corrupt or improper payments.

VI. TWO LEADING FCPA CHARITABLE AND POLITICAL DONATION CASES

A. *In re* Schering Plough

In June 2004, Schering-Plough Corporation, headquartered in New Jersey, settled an SEC complaint alleging improper payments made by Schering-Plough Poland (S-P Poland), a branch office of a wholly owned subsidiary of the company's Swiss division, to a charitable organization called the Chudow Castle Foundation.[1] The parent company agreed to pay a civil penalty of $500,000 for violations of the FCPA's books and records and internal controls provisions[2] and to retain an independent consultant to review its internal controls and financial reporting policies and procedures.

The Foundation was headed by an individual who was director of the Silesian Health Fund, a Polish governmental body that, among other things, provided money for the purchase of pharmaceutical products and influenced the purchase of those products by other entities such as hospitals. The complaint alleged that S-P Poland paid $76,000 to the Foundation over a three year period to induce its director to influence the health fund's purchase of S-P Poland pharmaceutical products. The complaint alleged that S-P Poland paid more money to the Foundation than any other recipient of promotional donations.

Signally, the SEC complaint did not allege that the parent company knew of any improper payments. Indeed, according to the complaint, the payments were structured at or below the local Schering-Plough manager's approval limit so that the parent would not detect or disclose the true nature of the payments, which were recorded on the books and records as "medical donations."

The SEC asserted that the parent company should have been alerted to FCPA issues by the following:

1. The Foundation was not a healthcare-related entity;
2. The magnitude of the payments to the Foundation in relation to the company's budget for such donations;
3. The structuring of certain payments by the manager, which allowed him to exceed his authorized limits; and
4. The director was the founder and chairman of the Foundation and also a Polish government official with the ability to influence formulary payments.

The DOJ did not file criminal charges.

B.   *United States v. Titan*

In March 2005, Titan Corporation, a San Diego, California, defense contractor, pled guilty to three FCPA criminal violations: one count of violating the anti-bribery provision; one count of falsifying the books and records provision; and one felony tax count; it also agreed to pay a record FCPA criminal fine of $13 million.[3] Combined with its agreement with the SEC to pay $15.5 million in disgorgement and prejudgment interest,[4] Titan paid over $28.5 million to resolve the FCPA investigation. The company was also required to retain a consultant to review the company's FCPA compliance and procedures and to adopt and implement the consultant's recommendations.

The military intelligence and communications company did not contest that from 1999 to 2001 it paid $3.5 million to its agent in Benin, Africa, who was then known by Titan to be the president of Benin's business advisor. The complaint alleged that Titan failed to conduct any meaningful due diligence into the background of this agent. Much of the money funneled to Titan's African agent went to the election campaign of Benin's then incumbent president. The complaint alleged that some of these funds were used to reimburse Titan's agent for the purchase of T-shirts adorned with the president's picture and instructions to vote for him in the upcoming election. A former senior Titan officer also directed that payments be falsely invoiced as consulting services and that actual payment of the money be spread over time and into smaller increments.[5]

VII.   FCPA OPINIONS

As indicated at the beginning of the chapter, very few of the FCPA opinions have dealt with charitable donations or campaign contributions. The three opinions below represent the major opinion guidance in the area.

A.   FCPA Opinion Procedure Release No. 95-01 (January 11, 1995): Charitable Donation for Substantial Medical Facility

In 1995, a requestor addressed the situation where a formal contract contemplated a very large charitable contribution for a medical facility, and the DOJ approved the prospective donation:

> The Department has reviewed the FCPA Opinion request by a U.S.-based energy company. The requestor plans to acquire and operate a plant in a country in South Asia that lacks modern medical facilities in the region where the plant is located.

A modern medical complex is presently under construction near the requestor's future plant. Costs for the medical facility are projected to run to hundreds of millions of dollars. If the acquisition of the plant is completed, the requestor plans to donate $10 million in a public ceremony to the medical facility for construction and equipment costs. The donation will be made through a charitable organization incorporated in the United States and through a public limited liability company located in the South Asian nation. Because the medical facility will be open to the public, the requestor's employees and affiliates may use the facility when it is completed.

The requestor has represented that, before releasing any funds, it will require certifications from all officers of the U.S. charitable organization and the foreign limited liability company that none of the funds will be used, promised or offered in violation of the FCPA. The requestor further represents that none of the persons employed by or acting on behalf of the charitable organization or the limited liability company are affiliated with the foreign government. The requestor also represents that it will require audited financial reports from the U.S. charitable organization, accurately detailing the disposition of the donated funds.

Based on all the facts and circumstances, as represented by the requestor, the Department does not presently intend to take any enforcement action with respect to the prospective donation for the construction and equipment of the medical facility described in this request.[6]

B. FCPA Opinion Procedure Release No. 97-02 (November 5, 1997): Charitable Donation for Elementary School

In 1997, a requestor sought permission to donate $100,000 to a proposed elementary school construction project, and the DOJ indicated that under the circumstances it would not take any enforcement action.

The Department has reviewed the FCPA Opinion Request by a U.S.-based utility company. The requestor has commenced construction of a plant in a country in Asia that lacks adequate primary-level educational facilities in the region where the plant is under construction.

An elementary school construction project has been proposed near the location of the requestor's plant. Construction and supply costs of the elementary school will exceed $100,000. The requestor plans to donate $100,000 to this proposed school construction project. The donation will be made by the company directly to the government entity responsible for the construction and supply of the proposed elementary school.

The requestor has represented that, before releasing any funds, it will require a written agreement from the government entity that the funds will be used solely to construct and supply the elementary school. The written agreement will set forth other conditions to be met by the government entity, including: guaranteeing the availability of land, teachers, and administrative personnel for the school; guaranteeing timely additional funding of the school project in the event of any financial shortfall; and guaranteeing provision of all funds necessary for the daily operation of the school.

As the requestor's donation will be made directly to a government entity—and not to any foreign government official—the provisions of the FCPA do not appear to apply to this prospective transaction.

Based on all the facts and circumstances, as represented by the requestor, the Department does not presently intend to take any enforcement action with respect to the proposed transaction described in this request.[7]

C. FCPA Opinion Procedure Release No. 06-01 (October 16, 2006): $25,000 Contribution to Improve Local Law Enforcement

In 2006, a requestor sought permission to contribute $25,000 to a regional customs department of an African country and was advised by the DOJ that it would not take enforcement action based on the disclosed facts.

> The Department has reviewed the FCPA Opinion Procedure request of a Delaware corporation with headquarters in Switzerland (hereinafter the "Requestor"). The Requestor seeks to contribute $25,000 to a regional Customs department or the Ministry of Finance (collectively, the "Counterparty") in an African country as part of a pilot project to improve local enforcement of anti-counterfeiting laws. The Requestor seeks to make the monetary contribution to the Counterparty in order for the agency to fund incentive awards to local customs officials to improve local enforcement relating to seizures of counterfeit products bearing the trademarks of the Requestor and its competitors.
>
> The letter of request states that counterfeiting has become "a serious issue" for manufacturers such as the Requestor and the issue "is often not a major priority for Customs authorities (particularly in developing countries)[.]" According to the Requestor, the African country selected for this "anti-counterfeiting coalition" serves

as a major transit point for illicit trade in counterfeit products, including the products of the Requestor and its competitors. The Requestor states that currently a transit tax is collected on all goods transiting the country, even those that are contraband or counterfeit. The Requestor notes that the salaries of local customs officials include a small percentage of any transit tax they collect, again, whether on authentic or counterfeit products. Thus, there is a financial disincentive for thorough inspection by local customs officials of goods for counterfeit products. The Requestor asks for a determination of the Department's present enforcement intention under the FCPA with respect to the proposed $25,000 contribution.

The Requestor represents, among other things, that in connection with its proposed $25,000 contribution, it would execute a formal memorandum of understanding (hereinafter "MOU") with the Counterparty in the African country to:

- encourage the mutual exchange of information related to the trade of counterfeit products bearing the trademarks of the Requestor and its competitors;
- establish procedures for an incentive compensation fund for the payment of awards to local Customs officials who detain, seize, and destroy counterfeit products ("Award Candidates");
- establish eligibility criteria for the calculation of awards and the methods and frequency of distribution; and
- provide that the awards be given to Award Candidates directly by the Counterparty or given to local customs offices to distribute to their qualified Award Candidates.

The Requestor further represents that it would establish "a number of procedural safeguards designed to assure that the funds made available by the [Requestor's] contribution were, in fact, going to provide incentives to local customs officials for the purposes intended." The Requestor will ensure that the Ministry of Justice in the African country is aware of the pilot program and that all aspects of the program are consistent with local laws, including but not limited to the following procedural safeguards:

- First, the Requestor will make its contribution to the incentive compensation fund by electronic transfer to an official government bank account in the African country controlled by and in the name of the Counterparty, and will require written confirmation that the account is a valid government account, subject to periodic internal audit by the relevant government authorities.

- Second, the Requestor will be notified, upon a seizure of suspected counterfeit items by local customs officials, and will examine the suspect goods to confirm they are in fact counterfeit. The Requestor further represents that payments to Award Candidates will not be distributed unless and until destruction of the counterfeit goods is confirmed by delivery of a destruction certificate to the Counterparty (a copy of which would be sent to the Requestor).
- Third, the Requestor will have no part in choosing the Award Candidates, and the Counterparty will have sole control over, and full responsibility for, the appropriate distribution of funds. The Requestor, however, will require written evidence that its entire contribution was used only to pay identified Award Candidates and that the awards were based upon a predetermined award eligibility criteria and calculation method.
- Fourth, the Requestor will monitor the efficacy of the incentive program and discuss with the Counterparty during periodic reviews whether changes or refinements are necessary. As part of its monitoring effort, the Requestor will monitor the number of notices received from local Customs officials relating to relevant seizures during each six-month period and follow the progression of such seizures.
- Fifth, the Requestor will require as part of its MOU with the Counterparty that the Counterparty will retain for five years the records of the distribution and receipt of funds, and shall permit inspection of such records by the Requestor upon request during the life of the pilot project and for three years thereafter.

The Requestor states in its letter of request that its pending business activities in the African country are relatively small and "entirely unrelated to the current request for an advisory opinion." The Requestor further states that its future business in the African country is not dependent upon the existence of the proposed incentive program, and that the program is not intended to influence any foreign official to obtain or retain business. Finally, the Requestor states that if the program were to be successful, the Requestor would continue to fund the central account on an as-needed basis to ensure that there would be no interruption in merited awards to local customs officials, and that the Requestor would seek, both initially and over time, to encourage its competitors to contribute funds to the effort as well.

Based upon all of the facts and circumstances, as represented by the Requestor, the Department does not presently intend to take any enforcement action with respect to the proposed $25,000 payment described in this request.

This Opinion, however, is subject to the following important caveats:

- The Department's Opinion should not be deemed to endorse the proposed language of the MOU or the methodology for selection of the proposed Award Candidates and distribution of funds, as neither the language of the MOU nor any proposed methodology was submitted to the Department. This Opinion likewise should not be deemed to address any possible expansion of the program within or outside the African country. Rather, this Opinion is limited to consideration of the $25,000 contribution to the particular African country set forth in the letter of request.
- This Opinion does not apply to any monetary payments made by the Requestor for purposes other than those expressed in the letter of request; nor does it apply to any individuals involved in authorizing or distributing the monetary awards to the Award Candidates.

The FCPA Opinion Letter and this release have no binding application to any party which did not join in the request, and can be relied upon by the Requestor only to the extent that the disclosure of facts and circumstances in its request is accurate and complete and remains accurate and complete.[8]

Each of the above requestors was very fact specific and the DOJ assurance of taking no enforcement action under the FCPA Opinion procedure is predicated on any disclosure being complete and accurate.

VIII. PRACTICAL POLITICAL CONTRIBUTION AND CHARITABLE DONATION ADVICE

A. Political Contributions

- Make clear in the company's code of conduct and/or political contribution policy that all foreign political contributions must be approved in advance, in writing, by the parent company legal or compliance department.
- Determine what, if any, local laws govern or limit foreign political party or candidate contributions. Even if local laws permit campaign contributions by a foreign company, subsidiary, affiliate, or officer, a political contribution may still have a corrupt motive and violate the FCPA.
- Determine whether the foreign operation or subsidiary's political contribution policies and written procedures are consistent with

the parent company's written policies and procedures for political contribution. Absent unique circumstances, the two should be the same or very similar in their objectives, limits, eligibility, and approval procedures.

- Ascertain what the in-country manager or requesting officer or employee specifically knows about the foreign candidate or campaign and the circumstances surrounding any requests for a contribution.
- Ascertain why the requesting officer or employee wishes to support the foreign candidate and what the purpose of the political contribution is.
- Determine from the requesting officer or employee whether there is any pending or forthcoming contract or award that the foreign candidate or political party might directly or indirectly influence.
- Question any pattern of repeat contributions to one foreign candidate, political party, or campaign.
- Consider whether the company is better off with a simple ban of all foreign political contributions—or at least a maximum or cap on any one foreign candidate or party in a given year.
- Make sure the company's code of conduct or political contribution policy does not adopt solely U.S. terminology, for example, "Congress" or "PAC," if the company intends the policy to be universal or global. Otherwise, foreign employees or expats may misinterpret the policy as applying only to U.S. political candidates, political parties, or campaigns.
- Determine whether the contemplated foreign political contribution will be transparent in both the host country and parent country, and if not, why not.
- Obtain a legitimate contemporaneous receipt for any political contribution.
- Make sure all political contributions are recorded accurately and in sufficient detail in the company's or subsidiary's books and records.
- Prepare a legal memorandum analyzing the facts and circumstances and confirming the propriety of any significant political contribution.

B.   Charitable Donations

- Make clear in the company's code of conduct and/or charitable donation policy that all foreign charitable donations must be approved in advance, in writing, by the parent company's legal or compliance department.
- Determine what, if any, local laws govern or limit foreign charitable donations. Even if local laws permit or are silent about charitable

contributions by a foreign company, subsidiary, or officer, a charitable donation may still have a corrupt motive and violate the FCPA.

- Consider whether the company's charitable donation policy should confine the type of charities the company will consider for significant contributions to those related to the company's principal business, for example, a pharmaceutical company's donation might be limited to oncology care or to related research and development.
- Determine whether the foreign operation or subsidiary's charitable donation policies and written procedures are consistent with the parent company's written policies and procedures for charitable donations. Absent unique circumstances, the two should be the same or very similar in their objectives, limits, eligibility, and approvals.
- Ask what the in-country manager or requesting officer or employee specifically knows about the charitable organization.
- Ask the requesting officer or employee why he/she wishes to support the particular charitable organization and what the purpose of the charitable donation is.
- Ask the requesting officer or employee whether there is any pending or forthcoming contract or award that the charitable organization or its officers might directly or indirectly influence.
- Question what assurance there is that the charitable donation will go to a specific end, for example, bricks and mortar as opposed to a general administrative fund, and seek to ensure that the specific purpose is memorialized in advance in writing.
- Question any pattern of repeat donations to one charitable organization and insist that any request for a donation address cumulative charitable donations to the entity.
- Obtain a legitimate, contemporaneous receipt for any charitable donation.
- Consider publicizing the charitable donation to promote and confirm transparency.
- Make sure all charitable donations are recorded accurately and in sufficient detail in the company's or subsidiary's books and records.
- Prepare a legal memorandum analyzing the facts and circumstances and confirming the propriety of any significant charitable contribution.

IX. ADDITIONAL RESOURCES

Witten, Parker & Koffer, *Navigating the Increased Anti-Corruption Environment in the United States and Abroad,* paper presented at the

National Institute on White Collar Crime 2009 (San Francisco, Mar. 5-6, 2009).

Sokenu, *Government Tackles the Thorny Issue of Travel and Entertainment under the FCPA, in* THE FOREIGN CORRUPT PRACTICES ACT 2008: COPING WITH HEIGHTENED ENFORCEMENT RISKS (PLI 2008).

NOTES

1. *In re Schering Plough,* Exchange Act Release No. 49838, 82 SEC Docket 3644 (June 9, 2004).

2. 15 U.S.C. §§ 78m (b)(2)(A) and (B) (1999).

3. *United States v. Titan Corp.,* CR No. 05 314 (S.D. Cal. 2005).

4. SEC Litig. Release No. 19-107 (Mar. 1, 2005).

5. *Id.*

6. FCPA Opinion Procedure Release No. 95-01 (January 11, 1995). http://www.usdoj.gov/criminal/fraud/fcpa/opinion/1995/9501.html.

7. FCPA Opinion Procedure Release No. 97-02 (November 5, 1997). http://www.usdoj.gov/criminal/fraud/fcpa/opinion/1997/9702.html.

8. FCPA Opinion Procedure Release No. 06-01 (October 16, 2006). http://www.usdoj.gov/criminal/fraud/fcpa/opinion/2006/0601.html.

CHAPTER 8

Conducting a Foreign Corrupt Practices Act Investigation

The basic steps and best practices of conducting an internal investigation are largely the same whether for the board of directors, the audit committee, a special committee, or senior management. Today, the emphasis on corporate governance means that the board or a committee is more likely to engage special counsel to perform a Foreign Corrupt Practices Act investigation and report the results to the entire board or a board committee.

I. BASIC STEPS OF AN FCPA INTERNAL INVESTIGATION AND RELATED ACTIONS

A. Five Basic Steps and Logical Lines of Inquiry

The five basic steps of an FCPA internal investigation[1] are:

1. Determine the nature of the allegation(s) (e.g., bribery payments through business advisors to a foreign official in Brazil; substantial payments to a consultant whose services coincide with an oil concession in Qatar; corporate sponsorship of U.S. visits of Chinese governmental officials; payment to an Indonesian tax official to reduce an assessment) and establish the preliminary scope of the allegation(s);

2. Develop the facts through U.S. and foreign document reviews and thorough interviews—and prepare a Working Chronology;

3. Retain experts as necessary, including in particular forensic accountants for evaluating books and records and internal controls practices, and making constructive control recommendations;

4. Analyze the legal elements, issue(s), and permissible payments and affirmative defenses of the Foreign Corrupt Practices Act, for example, corrupt intent, knowledge, foreign official status *and* relevant local laws; and

5. Synthesize the facts and law to serve the client's objective, e.g., to defend the company in a grand jury FCPA investigation; to provide legal advice to a board of directors, audit committee, special committee, or management as part of an internal investigation, including recommendations on compliance programs, disciplinary actions, and corporate policies; to voluntarily disclose to the DOJ and SEC in order to obtain leniency or avoid criminal damages; and so on.

In determining what questions to logically pursue in interviews and what documents to review as a result of an FCPA bribery allegation, counsel will, in addition to being mindful of the elements of the anti-bribery offense outlined in Chapter 1, wish to review the red flag and due diligence steps and issues discussed in previous chapters. For example, if an agent is alleged to have made an improper payment through a relative in a foreign government, the investigation will focus in part on the due diligence for that agent, any warranties and representatives in the agency Agreement, Internet searches of the agent and relative, business references, descriptions of services on agency invoices, and of course hard and electronic correspondence between the agent and the company. Answers to the interview questions or telltale documents may establish the requisite knowledge on the part of the company or a strong defense.

In some cases the record of payments, gifts, or travel will be beyond dispute, and criminal liability will turn on corrupt intent—an "evil motive" or purpose or intent to wrongfully influence the recipient to "misuse his official position" in order to wrongfully direct, obtain, or retain business.[2] In other cases, the issue may be whether any government official ever received anything of value; such cases can still be prosecuted on an offer or conspiracy theory but are much less attractive to a jury. For example, in the numerous U.N. Oil for Food Program cases the Iraq government, not Iraqi government officials, received kickbacks and the DOJ elected to proceed with books and records violations—not bribery charges. Still, in other cases a U.S. company's conduct can appear to be driven more by the negligence or incompetence of employees than a corrupt motive and thereby negate the requisite criminal knowledge standard.

Whatever the improper payment allegation, counsel will want to examine not only the basic bribery elements and permissible payments and affirmative defenses, but also the red flags and due diligence factors outlined in earlier chapters as they can frequently bear on ultimate issues of corrupt intent, knowledge, and authorization and will be factors that U.S. law enforcement agencies will likely examine if the matter is disclosed to them or they otherwise learn of the allegations.

B. Scoping

Often, the general counsel, business unit manager, or regional counsel will have the best overall understanding of the nature of the allegation(s) and will be able to identify those employees likely to have relevant knowledge. The scope of the investigation should focus on the *time* period and *geography* and remain flexible, depending on what is uncovered. For example, if a regional manager is responsible for Countries A, B, and C, and is found to have authorized a series of bribes in Country A in Years 1, 2, and 3, his conduct in Countries B and C should be examined for Years 1, 2, and 3. Government agencies including the DOJ or SEC will be skeptical of a corporate internal investigation that has an unduly narrow engagement scope or does not pursue logical paths of inquiry. It is prudent for all involved—client and counsel—to think carefully about the language used in the engagement letter, a board of directors resolution, or an audit committee resolution, as government lawyers may later review them and insert some expansion language if circumstances and investigation so warrant. At some point, the U.S. government may seek to determine whether the company, the board, or a committee committed to discovering the truth in its investigation.

C. Document Review, Forensic Teams, Witness Interviews, and Working Chronology Overview

Document review and witness interviews will often be conducted both in the United States and in foreign countries. Promptly securing and preserving electronic data is essential to a thorough internal investigation—and to establishing credibility with both the Department of Justice and the Securities and Exchange Commission. Counsel, while being mindful of applicable data privacy laws, should take steps to secure electronic storage facilities such as hard drives, network backup tapes, and floppy disks. The DOJ and SEC, when evaluating a company's cooperation, will look to see how promptly and thoroughly management moved to secure both documentary and electronic evidence. Of course, the responsibility of preserving such evidence is even greater when responding to a formal government subpoena.

Forensic accounting firms and investigators often assist investigation counsel in sensitive payment investigations. They can gather and secure electronic evidence, deal with encrypted data, conduct searches for sensitive terms (e.g., *bribe, sunshine money, kickback, gift, взямка, oil, grease, comisión confidencial, caisse noire*), identify books and records and internal controls issues, and assist in recommending and formulating remedial measures. These forensic specialists should normally be independent and not the company's regular outside accounting or auditing firm. Since there is no federal accountant-client privilege, investigation counsel—not the client—should retain the accounting firm under a clearly defined scope of work set forth in an engagement letter. Investigation counsel should carefully monitor the scope of the accountant or investigation engagement, the work plan, interviews, and progress. Whenever non-lawyers are assigned responsibilities, they should perform under the direction of and report to counsel in order to maintain the attorney-client privilege and work product protection.[3] Counsel should determine early on what types of memoranda forensic accountants or investigations will prepare and if they will remain in draft form.

Of course, focused interviews, preferably in the country in question, are the sine qua non of any corporate internal investigation and are particularly challenging in an FCPA investigation given the cultural and language challenges. It is useful for counsel to prepare and update a comprehensive Working Chronology that not only tracks and analyzes key underlying conduct and meetings but identifies key players (and their counsel), questionable payments, hot documents, false books and records, potential red flag issues, due diligence steps, disciplinary actions, disclosure to one or more agencies, cooperation efforts, internal controls issues, remedial measures, and other important events or mitigating factors. Without a continuously updated chronology, it is usually difficult to recall and understand the relationship and timing of key events and documents in a lengthy, multicountry investigation. Chronologies can be particularly helpful in tracking the activities of employees or agents in several countries, ventures, or operations. Finally, they are helpful in recalling key documents, preparing for important interviews, and drafting internal reports, position papers, Wells submissions, and PowerPoint presentations for both boards of directors and government authorities.

Legal issue development will obviously focus on the statutory provisions, the legislative history, the FCPA case law, FCPA criminal prosecutions, SEC enforcement actions,[4] deferred prosecution agreements, nonprosecution agreements (NPAs), foreign law, and any relevant FCPA opinions issued by the Department of Justice. It can include review of analogous statutes such as domestic bribery statutes, applicable conventions (as implemented), and related case law.

II. PRELIMINARY INVESTIGATION ISSUES AND PRACTICES

A. Identification of the Client

An important early question to decide is: Who is the client—the corporation, the board of directors, the audit committee, or a special committee? The answer will in part be determined by the company's structure and whether the investigation involves alleged wrongdoing by any members of senior management. Retainer letters and agreements should specify whom counsel represents.[5]

B. Use of In-House or Outside Counsel

At the outset, a company or its general counsel will decide whether an FCPA allegation should be handled internally by the legal department. It is unwise to allow internal audit staff or non-lawyers to review any significant FCPA allegation as there is usually no legal privilege. Sometimes an FCPA allegation can be ably handled by in-house attorneys. Other times, due to limited corporate legal resources, the scope of the allegation(s), in-house counsel's advice or participation in the transaction at issue, the awkwardness of interviewing senior management, or in-house counsel's lack of DOJ or SEC experience, companies or a board will retain independent outside counsel.

If the allegation is credible and indicates any pattern of improper payments and/or approval by senior management and there is likely a disclosure obligation by a public company, it is usually wise to retain a law firm expert in FCPA and white-collar criminal defense representation. If the matter has a potential to become substantial and disclosure is likely, the DOJ and SEC will want to be sure credible and experienced independent counsel are conducting the investigation. In the current and foreseeable regulatory environment, independent counsel—without a substantial or regular outside counsel company role—are more likely to be credited by prosecutors, regulators, and private counsel (e.g., when justifying settlement of a class or derivative lawsuit).[6]

C. Legal Representation

Issues of legal representation can arise, especially in dealing with officers and employees.

- In representing the company or an audit committee, investigative counsel will come into contact with many mid- and low-level employees. These individuals may assume that outside counsel represents them personally and offer self-incriminating information. ABA Model Rule 1.13(d) requires an attorney who represents only a company or committee to ensure that employees understand at the outset of interviews that only the company or committee is the client and that the employees may wish to seek separate counsel.
- Counsel should also advise employees that the interview is privileged, that the privilege belongs to the company or committee, which alone retains the right to waive it, and that the company may decide to share the results of the interview with government agencies such as the DOJ or SEC.[7]
- Employees may be warned that the company may take action against them later based on the information learned in the interview.
- Counsel should control who attends interviews of employees. The presence of a non-attorney at an interview can result in a waiver of the attorney-client privilege.[8]
- Counsel should avoid tape-recording or transcribing verbatim interviews. Tape-recorded interviews are less likely to enjoy the status of opinion work product because they do not reflect counsel's mental processes. Also, unless counsel is prepared to tape-record

every interview, the decision to record some interviews but not others will be questioned.

- Counsel and the client should consider whether "pool counsel" for a group of nonconflicted mid- and low-level employees is appropriate.

D. Legal Privileges

Oftentimes, a company will opt for the least expensive review without first considering the privilege implications. Unless the attorney-client and attorney work product privileges are carefully protected, a written report or PowerPoint presentation and/or underlying work product may become discoverable.[9] The work product of an internal audit department, accounting firm, or a forensic firm is going to have far less privilege protection than a law firm.

E. Communications with Outside Auditors

A company conducting an internal investigation will need to decide when and whether to disclose the nature and findings of an FCPA investigation to its regular outside auditor. The latter will be concerned inter alia about the accuracy of prior public financial statements, the adequacy of internal controls, and the integrity of management representation letters. Inasmuch as the regular outside auditor has a vested interest in the accuracy and integrity of past and future public filings, the quality of an FCPA internal investigation is critically important to it. The outside auditor will want to see any hot documents; understand who will be or has been interviewed and, in particular, any members of senior management who made representations; what search terms are to be employed; whether hard and soft data/documents have been preserved; and what type of report findings will be forthcoming. Informal exchange of necessary information can usually be negotiated by responsible professionals. While the regular outside auditor should not guide an independent FCPA investigation, it is usually wise to have early and ongoing communication with the regular outside auditor so that its engagement partner, national office, and risk group have trust in the integrity and thoroughness of the investigation and continued confidence in senior management. What an outside auditor neither wants nor needs is notification of a completed internal investigation on the eve of a public filing.

Any disclosure to an auditor raises waiver issues, and the courts are split on whether the disclosure of investigation results to a company outside auditor waives work product protection. In *Medinol Ltd. v. Boston Scientific Corp.*,[10] Medinol provided internal investigation information to its outside auditors in connection with their audit of the company's litigation exposure. A Southern District of New York judge found that the disclosure of meeting minutes of the Special Litigation Committee to Ernst & Young (E&Y) waived the protection of the work product doctrine. The court found that, as an outside auditor, E&Y's interests were not necessarily united with those of Boston Scientific and that the disclosure served a litigation purpose.

In *Merrill Lynch & Co., Inc. v. Allegheny Energy Inc.*,[11] the Southern District of New York in 2004 reviewed the disclosure of the internal investigation reports (conducted by and under the supervision of in-house and outside counsel) to outside auditors Deloitte & Touche. Allegheny Energy sought to obtain the reports, contending that the disclosure to outside auditors constituted a waiver of any applicable privilege. The district court found that Merrill Lynch and Deloitte & Touche were not adversaries as contemplated by the work product doctrine. Specifically, any business between an auditor and a corporation that arises from an auditor's need to scrutinize and investigate a corporation's records and bookkeeping practices simply is not the equivalent of the adversarial relationship contemplated by the doctrine.

The *Merrill Lynch* district court observed that a business and its auditor can and should be aligned insofar as they both seek to prevent, detect, and root out corporate fraud. Without access to information regarding internal controls that directly relate to the reliability of financial information and legality of corporate behavior, auditors would likely fail in the fulfillment of their important public trust. The district court concluded that to construe a company's auditor as an adversary and to find a blanket rule of waiver of the applicable work product privilege could and would discourage companies from conducting critical self-analysis and addressing the fruits of such inquiries with appropriate actions. Other courts have since adopted the *Merrill Lynch* rationale and now the majority view is that disclosure to independent auditors does not waive work product protection.[12]

III. AMERICAN COLLEGE OF TRIAL LAWYERS' RECOMMENDED PRACTICES FOR INTERNAL INVESTIGATIONS

In February 2008, the American College of Trial Lawyers published a best internal investigation practices report entitled *Recommended Practices for Companies and Their Counsel in Conducting Internal Investigations* (Appendix 7). The report addresses factors to consider when evaluating whether to commence an internal investigation, the role of the board and management in conducting and overseeing an investigation, the need for independent outside counsel, and the appropriate scope of the inquiry. It also covers the mechanics of a litigation hold, document collection and review, and witness interviews. This "best practices" report should be read by both the general counsel and investigation counsel of companies undertaking FCPA internal investigations as well as counsel representing officers or employees in these investigations.

IV. DOCUMENTS

A. Nondestruction Memorandum

As soon as counsel and the client determine there is a credible FCPA allegation and a possible violation, the company should take prompt steps to ensure that relevant documents—hard and electronic—are preserved. This invariably means issuance of a timely, formal nondestruction memorandum to all relevant officers and employees, including domestic and foreign information technology personnel. If the matter becomes public or investigated by U.S. prosecutors or regulators, one of their first questions will concern what the company did to secure and preserve all relevant documents. How well a company answers this question can determine its credibility with the board, audit committee, prosecutors, and regulators. Companies and counsel should take precautions to make sure that persons whose conduct may be the subject of the investigation are not responsible for gathering and preserving documents. Often, counsel, forensic accountants, or paralegals can perform this function.

B. Security of Documents and Databases[13]

Corporate internal investigations present challenging security implications because investigations often deal with information that is very sensitive and may never become public. This is particularly true of FCPA investigations where different security issues may arise by virtue of the documents' location on foreign soil, including issues raised by foreign data privacy laws.

Counsel should implement proper security issues at the outset of any document-gathering process for several reasons. First, the documents may contain sensitive business information. Second, although the documents may not be sensitive on their face, their designation as "relevant to the investigation" can make them de facto sensitive. Third, proper security can enhance the efficiency of storage, organization, and retrieval. Fourth, proper security will decrease the chance of loss or destruction of critical documents and lessen the likelihood of the company being party to an obstruction of justice investigation.

Whether the documents consist of hard copies stored in boxes, or computer data stored electronically, or both, care must be taken to prevent unauthorized persons from having access to them. Counsel should limit access to investigative documents on a "need to know" basis. Whether the documents are stored in a locked drawer in counsel's office or in a warehouse off site, the premises should be kept secure, knowledge about the storage of the data should be limited, and access should be restricted. Depending upon the nature of the investigation, the number of documents, and the site of storage, counsel may implement sign-in or key-card procedures to limit and track access.

Although automated data support systems can be advantageous to investigating counsel, they can also make it possible for unauthorized third parties to quietly access large volumes of records, possibly off site. Confidential passwords for system access and data encryption during any electronic transmission are easily available and usually inexpensive. Encryption generally renders the data useless to persons gaining unauthorized access.[14] How much or how little metadata to transmit will depend on the mandate of the investigation. If data is being stored electronically, counsel should also take appropriate measures to reduce the chances of electronic or system problems that can cause the loss of data. Anti-virus programs and other preventive measures will lessen the chance of a computer virus creating havoc with the data.[15] Quality surge protectors and an uninterruptible power supply will minimize the risk of problems caused by electric surges, lightning strikes, and short circuits.[16]

Document security can take different forms. Object-based security systems in electronic review platforms allow for restrictions on the objects (tags, folders, etc.) and metadata elements that reviewers can see. Since many of the objects used in a document review reflect privileged attorney work product, restricting certain reviewers from access to work product is often appropriate. Document-based security systems limit reviewers' access to specific sets of documents. Feature-based security systems can be used to restrict users from using certain features, for example, restricted download or redaction features. Most electronic document review vendors can provide review groups with different levels of security.

C. Foreign Document Preservation and Review

Because FCPA investigations extend beyond the borders of the United States, counsel should pay particular attention to foreign laws and treaties governing access to documents relevant to investigation. In some countries, the code law is inconsistent with unwritten local custom and practice. Close collaboration with local counsel and personnel is usually essential to the success of an FCPA investigation. If the company intends to cooperate with U.S. authorities, the DOJ or SEC will want and expect the company or its investigative counsel to preserve appropriate chains of custody for evidence.

D. Data Protection or Data Privacy Laws

"Data protection" or "data privacy" laws govern the use of personal information relating to an identified or identifiable individual and have been adopted internationally in often haphazard fashion. There is significant variance among countries in the scope of personal information that qualifies for legal protection, the necessity for the individual's consent for the review of such information, the nature of actions that can legally be performed with the information, and the rights and remedies afforded to both the individual and the investigating counsel. Other countries—notably, the United States—do not have a comprehensive data protection regime.

The most well-known data protection regime is that adopted by nations of the European Union, set forth in Directive 95/46/EC of the European Parliament and of the Council on the Protection of Individuals with Regard to the Processing of Personal Data and on the Free Movement of Such Data. Many other regions also have data protection regimes. Some regional regimes are formalized, such as the Asia Pacific Economic Cooperation (APEC) area's common data principles for Asia.[17] Others are informal, consisting of similarities between the data protection laws of the countries within the region. Still others are specific to individual countries and are not common at all to a region. The regional variations of data protection regimes necessarily influence the practical mechanics of integrating data protection considerations into data collection, processing, and review.

1. Elements of Data Protection Regimes

Data protection regimes have two key elements: (1) the definition of data subject to protection; and (2) the definition of circumstances under which certain actions with respect to such data are permissible.

a. Definition of Personal Data

Generally, data subject to protection includes any information relating to an identified or identifiable natural person.[18] Most regimes have an extraordinarily broad approach to defining personal data, with many regimes, for example the European Union countries, even expressly including the individual's name within the scope of personal data.[19] Moreover, certain individual data is deemed even more worthy of special protection, such as data relating to the custodian's race or ethnic background, sexual and criminal history, and political, philosophical, religious, and trade union affiliations, and may be subject to even more stringent regulations—including, in some circumstances, a complete bar on the processing of such data even with the custodian's consent. For that reason, investigating counsel must take data protection law into account with almost any collection or interview undertaken in a data protection jurisdiction.

b.   Data Processing Restrictions

The second element of data protection is the restriction on certain types of data processing under certain circumstances. "Data processing" is generally defined—equally broadly—as any action taken with respect to personal data, including its collection, review, replication, transmission, export, modification, or deletion. The key difference between data protection regimes lies in the precise actions that can be performed with personal data, and the circumstances under which they are permissible. For instance, many data protection regimes, including Europe's, prohibit the export of personal data to countries that do not assure a similar level of data protection.[20] That prohibition certainly includes the United States, which has no comprehensive data privacy regime. (Note, however, that a limited exception to that prohibition exists pursuant to the safe harbor self-certification program between the EU and the United States, which allows export to companies that participate in the program.)[21]

Other restrictions may include those on transferring personal data to "third parties," which may or may not include the company's outside counsel, auditors, and consultants, and which may even encompass other legal entities within the company's corporate group. In case of a multinational corporation, the company's parent organization may thus be precluded from reviewing its employees' personal data. Investigating counsel must be mindful of such restrictions and take them into account when planning the international portion of the investigation.

2.   *Consent of Data Subject*

The most challenging aspect of data protection law compliance, from the standpoint of conducting a foreign investigation, is the necessity to obtain consent of the affected individual ("data subject") before processing the data. Most data protection regimes generally require the consent of the data subject before any data processing begins.[22] The need to obtain a data subject's consent, if not handled correctly, can pose a problem to the investigating counsel—particularly where the data subject's documents may contain information damaging to the data subject, as is often the case in an internal investigation, the data subject will have every incentive to withhold consent. Moreover, the company may be precluded from disciplining or threatening to discipline the data subject on these grounds: many regimes provide that consent must be "freely given," and some expressly prohibit termination on such grounds.[23] Although data protection regimes sometimes provide exception to the consent requirement, such exceptions may be insufficient for the performance of a proper investigation. Accordingly, investigating counsel must design the investigation in such a manner as to either maximize the likelihood of obtaining consent, or find an exception to the consent requirement.

a.   Consent as a Condition of Employment

The best approach is prevention—in this case, of the need to secure an uncooperative data subject's consent, or an exception to the consent requirement, in the middle of the investigation. Such consent is best obtained at the time the data subject becomes an employee of the company, when the data subject may be required to provide it as a condition of employment, and, not yet having done anything improper, is unlikely to have a vested interest in withholding it. An advance consent must be both specific enough to comply with the consent specificity requirements and broad enough to encompass any data relating to the data subject, whether maintained by the company or by the data subject himself or herself, that might become relevant in an investigation.

Relatively few companies have an advance consent provision in place when the need for an FCPA investigation arises. Some companies may have a consent requirement that is insufficiently broad; others' may be legally questionable. In some cases, investigating counsel, in coordination with the company, may offer the data subject "immunity," or guarantee that no adverse action will result from the investigation, in exchange for the data subject's cooperation in the investigation. This tactic may be useful in an internal investigation targeting higher-level misconduct, particularly where it is likely that the data subject may have relevant information, and where the review of such information would not violate the rights of others. In cases where this is not possible, investigating counsel must devise a strategy to proceed with the investigation, without obtaining the data subject's consent, but in compliance with the local data privacy law.

b.   Use of In-House Personnel

One strategy is to make substantial use of in-house company personnel or contract lawyers in executing the review, at least in the initial stages. While investigating counsel may be prohibited from engaging in any data processing due to lack of consent, the company itself may not be. The company's in-house legal, compliance, or control personnel can be key in performing functions that require access to the data subject's personal data. For example, they may be tasked with performing the first-level review of the unconsenting data subject's files. They can then communicate their findings, or even specific documents, to the investigating counsel, provided that personal data is redacted. Specific data subjects and other individuals may be assigned code names or numbers, and investigating counsel may use such code names and numbers to keep track of documents, request additional information, and designate specific individuals for further action (such as an additional collection or an interview).

In circumstances where in-house personnel who can be trusted with this responsibility are not available (for example, in a multinational corporation's small subsidiary lacking its own legal or compliance function, or where such personnel may have been compromised), local laws may permit an arrangement whereby outside personnel or lawyers may be seconded to the company to temporarily work as the company's own employees. Under such circumstances, the seconded personnel (which can come from the investigating counsel's firm, a consulting firm, or elsewhere) will act just like in-house personnel with respect to preventing the investigating counsel from seeing anything that may be deemed "personal data."

E.   Document Preservation Mechanics in FCPA Investigations

1.   *Physical Presence*

Since data may be governed both by the law of the jurisdiction in which the original data controller is located and the law of the jurisdiction to which the data is to be exported, the physical scope of the data collection is relevant to the choice of data collection and processing vendor. Under the European Directive, for example, data export to a country without "adequate" data protection laws may be prohibited. As a practical matter, counsel should consider not only the formal data protection safeguards a vendor has in place, but also whether the vendor has sufficient reach to collect the data in all of the relevant locations, or good relationships with qualified local subvendors who can do so. Subvendors may be desirable in some locations because they may have experience with obscure hardware and local operating systems, as well as with local data archival practices, and may be helpful in planning the scope of the collection effort. A vendor should provide technical specifications for the types of load files it needs to process the data. If documents are to be collected from several locations, it may be useful to collect, process, and review samples of data from each location to ensure that the process is working correctly before fully committing to it.

2.   *Server Location and Cross-Border Data Flows*

Counsel should also consider the physical location of the server that will host the data to be collected and reviewed. A client may feel safer if counsel hosts its data within the company itself (which is often unfeasible without compromising the investigation) or within outside counsel's firm, especially if the law firm is certified as a safe harbor, rather than with an outside vendor. In other circumstances, it may be advantageous to physically store the data within the jurisdiction of collection, in order to obviate cross-border data transfer issues in jurisdictions that impose such restrictions.

3.   *Data Transfer Agreements and Data Subject Consent*

Even where the law does not require a data transfer agreement or data subject consent, counsel may consider obtaining them anyway, to the extent it can be done without compromising the investigation. It is not always easy to determine at the beginning of an FCPA investigation all of the countries to which the data might need to be exported, or which might host a portion of the custodian's data. Obtaining consent early in an investigation can avoid delay.[24]

4.   Foreign Language Documents

Documents and data located in foreign countries are often in languages other than English. Sometimes even a single document may contain several languages (e.g., an e-mail where a custodian corresponds with a colleague in Spanish, and another person replies with history in English; or a contract prepared in multiple languages simultaneously). The languages involved in an investigation will affect the selection of the vendor or vendors to process the data and the system used to store and review the data. Many U.S.-based electronic data vendors and review systems use only the American Standard Code for Information Interchange (ASCII). These vendors cannot process special characters used in other languages. The best format for supporting a multilingual review is Unicode, as it will process diacritical marks (such as accents, umlauts, diereses, and cedillas) and special characters in Latin alphabets (such as Eszett (ß) and Ethel (œ)), as well as characters from languages not written in the Latin alphabet, for example, Chinese and Arabic. Additionally, language recognition systems vary across vendors. Accordingly, counsel should also consider language issues when selecting a vendor.

5.   Search Terms for Foreign Language Documents

Search terms play an essential role in data processing by trimming the amount of data to export, host, and review, and therefore limiting expense and data export issues. Counsel and client will want to use search terms that are relevant and appropriate for the country in question, for example, "red packets" in China. Search terms will be more successful if they address language-specific characters and modifications (for example in German, writing terms with "ss" in addition to "ß" or "ue" in addition to "ü") and account for various word forms, such as conjugation and cases, through the use of wildcards. Local company personnel and vendors may be able to provide information on these common issues; however, investigating counsel should take care to ensure that the vendor offers the ability to arrange the search terms accordingly.

6.   Multilingual Data Reviewers

Depending on the scope of an FCPA investigation, it may be necessary to employ contract attorneys who read foreign languages. Many countries lack markets for contract attorneys; therefore, somewhat counterintuitively, investigating counsel may have an easier time finding contract attorneys with specific language skills in major international centers than in the "home country." Lead investigation counsel should conduct overview presentations for contract attorneys in order to introduce them to the hot topics and alert them to the categories of hot documents.

F. Electronic Evidence

Electronic evidence may be divided into two broad categories: (1) structured electronically stored information (ESI) and (2) unstructured ESI. Structured ESI is contained in databases, such as financial or accounting databases (e.g., general ledger, accounts payable, and payroll, and other databases). Unstructured ESI includes e-mails, documents (e.g., Word and Excel, instant messaging logs, and voicemail). Too often internal investigations focus on structured data at the expense of unstructured data and, in particular, e-mails, which can be the source of evidence that bears heavily on search for intent.

Data mining is an analytic technique that involves searching through large amounts of data to identify relevant information, patterns, trends, and differences indicative of fraud. Electronic evidence experts Ben Hawksworth and Jennifer Hadsell have observed:

> Typically, 80% of data collected during an investigation is e-mail and other unstructured data. Investigators should consider the use of alternative search methods, such as concept clustering, social network analysis, and thread analysis, in order to facilitate the discovery of important evidence. Concept clustering groups data into sets with similar scenes. Social network analysis captures the pattern and frequency of communications between custodians, and thread analysis groups together e-mails that are part of a chain so that the investigator can more easily understand the entire conversation.[25]

Clients often understandably question the cost of collection and analysis of large volumes of electronic evidence. However, to the extent that the government, an outside auditor, or other third parties will review an internal investigation and be expected to credit and rely on the work, an investigation that does not review and analyze relevant unstructured data is likely to be given little weight.

V. SOURCES OF IN-COUNTRY INFORMATION

In conducting an internal investigation of a foreign operation, there are many sources of information that can help determine whether it is more likely than not that a certain event occurred, or was a factor in a questionable transaction. Many sources are the same that transactional lawyers use in conducting the due diligence for a foreign transaction. Helpful foreign sources and records include:

1. In-Country Records
   a. Consulting Contracts and Agency Agreements
   b. Joint Venture Agreements
      i. Partner Shareholders
      ii. Partner Director, Officer, and Key Employee Background
      iii. Government Relationships
      iv. Partner Contracts
      v. Minutes
      vi. Anti-Corruption Training Programs
      vii. Audits
      viii. Anti-Corruption Warranties and Representations
      ix. Books and Records Warranties and Representations
   c. Electronic Databases
   d. General Ledgers
   e. Local Bank Account Statements
   f. Subcontracts
   g. Vendor Lists and Aging Accounts
   h. Expense Reports (e.g., Travel and Entertainment)
   i. Correspondence Files
   j. Petty Cash Accounts
   k. Purchase Records
   l. Professional Service Fees and Expenses
      i. Attorneys
      ii. Accountants
   m. Off-the-Books Records
   n. Charitable Contributions
   o. Gift Lists
   p. Cash Vouchers
   q. Leases
   r. Court Records
      i. Federal
      ii. State
2. In-Country Employees
   a. General Managers or Managing Directors
   b. Financial Officers
   c. Sales and Marketing Personnel
   d. Accounting and Bookkeeping Personnel
   e. Operations Personnel
   f. Legal Personnel
   g. Information Technology Personnel
   h. Purchasing Department Personnel
   i. Project Managers, Superintendents, and Engineers
   j. Project Estimators
   k. Security Personnel
3. Former Employees

4. Subcontractors
5. Agents
6. Periodicals and Publications
   a. Transparency International Reports and Surveys
   b. International Company Profiles (ICPs) of the U.S. Commerce Department
   c. Local and Regional Business and Trade Journals
   d. Dun & Bradstreet Reports
   e. Local Government Publications, Circulars, or Gazettes
7. Local Law Firms
8. Local Accounting Firms
9. American Local Chambers of Commerce[26]
10. Banking References
11. Local Industry Associations
12. U.S. Embassies or Consulates (Commercial Attaché)
13. Internet Sites of Vendors, Consultants, Agents, and Others
14. State Department and Commerce Department Desk Officers
15. Trace International Reports
16. Local Registrations
17. Private Investigators

None of these sources will likely be dispositive but a combination can help one draw conclusions.

VI. INTERVIEWS

FCPA investigations are the most challenging of all corporate investigations because the potential misconduct is serious, many countries in which most misconduct may have occurred are distant and tolerant of corruption, interviewees are frequently hostile and indifferent to U.S. laws, and, in limited cases, there is personal risk to investigating counsel. A first-rate FCPA investigation requires a comprehensive chronology, *infra*, that covers witness backgrounds, legal issues, factual issues, hot documents, and key events and meetings. Counsel should have strong interview skills, knowledge of the FCPA and local laws and practices—and patience, persistence, and discretion. The goal should be to conduct fair, firm, and focused interviews where persons are able to provide their best and most accurate recollections and express opinions. The object of the investigation is to obtain as much accurate and reliable information from knowledgeable witnesses as quickly and efficiently as possible.

A. Hot Documents

To conduct quality interviews, counsel should secure key hot documents in advance and, where appropriate, have documents translated. Most often, interviews are conducted by subject and/or in chronological order. Counsel (in coordination with forensic teams) will often conduct extensive electronic searches in order to best capture relevant documents among databases containing hundreds of thousands (or more) of documents. Concurrent with the review of documents to determine whether improper payments occurred will be a review of a company's or subsidiary's books and records for false entries. Where numerous false books and records are uncovered, there may be an internal controls weakness. It is recommended, where practical, that witnesses be provided key documents in advance, including e-mails, invoices and other company books and records.[27]

B. In-Country

Almost without exception, FCPA investigations and interviews should be conducted in the countries where the employees or witnesses worked during the alleged conduct in question. This usually enables counsel to interview a number of knowledgeable persons at once in-country and to be able to easily gather original additional documents that may have not been secured or even contemplated initially. Employees or witnesses often prefer an off-site interview location (e.g., local law office, hotel conference room) where there are fewer employment distractions and others may not observe the interview(s). Another advantage of in-country interviews is that bilingual lawyers or investigators may be more accessible and less expensive; the former may also be able to properly opine on local written laws and language idioms. Where interviewees do not speak or understand English well, professional translators will be necessary. Counsel will usually want to have a colleague present since a second lawyer can help clarify unclear statements, prepare memoranda of interviews, and be able to confirm the essence of the interview, if necessary later.

C. Third-Party Interviews

Investigation counsel will usually have the authority to require current employees to submit to an interview or face termination. Former employees and third parties present a different challenge as there is often no control or leverage to make them submit to interviews. In some instances, cooperation clauses in agency or consulting agreements may compel agents or consultants to submit to interviews, and severance packages may require former employees to cooperate. Some third parties and former employees who have joined or advise competitors may use knowledge of the investigation or information gleaned during an interview to their or the new company's business advantage. Counsel will in such situations have to weigh the potential benefits and costs of third-party interviews to the client and act in its best interest.

D. *Upjohn* Warning

At the outset, counsel should give an interviewee an *Upjohn* warning[28] and make clear whom he represents, the purpose of the interview, and that the interview is privileged. If the interviewing lawyer represents a corporation, a board of directors, an audit committee, or a special committee and is interviewing an employee, he should make clear the identity of the company or entity he represents and equally clear that he does not represent the employee. Often, employees or officers mistakenly assume company counsel also represents them. Counsel should further explain that the client controls the privilege and confidentiality of the communication, and that only the corporate client may elect to waive and disclose the communication to others. If a company is in fact cooperating with the U.S. government or a foreign government, the employee should be apprised of that fact and told that waiver of the privilege is probable, likely, or certain. The employee or witness should be asked if he or she has any questions and be directed not to discuss the interview with other employees.

E. Order and Methodology

FCPA investigation interviews may not be as orderly as desired due to employees being engaged in assignments elsewhere, being on vacation, or having schedule conflicts. Usually, there is a company lawyer or manager who can give an overview of the operation in question and sensitive issues. This person may have valuable insight into not only the issues, but the likely biases, candor, cooperation, and reliability of employees to be interviewed. The overview person may also have input into the most effective order of interviews, including who may have the most firsthand knowledge, who may be the most forthright, or who may try to intimidate or influence other employees or witnesses. Ordinarily, preliminary overview managers should not be present for interviews since their presence may lessen the candor or cooperation of the employee and, as important, vitiate privileges.

Absent unique circumstances, each witness should be interviewed separately. Further, each witness should be instructed not to discuss the substance of the interview with anyone (other than counsel). Otherwise, there is a risk others will claim that the company or counsel got witnesses together to get their story right. In many cases, it is advantageous to interview lower-level employees first and to work up to senior personnel. Sometimes, schedules do not permit investigating counsel this order, and flexibility or adaptability by all is required.

F. Clarification and Omnibus Questions

Before the conclusion of an interview, counsel can ask the employee or witness if he or she wishes to add or clarify any topic and pose an omnibus question that covers the central subject(s), for example, "Are you aware of any (other) improper payments, gifts or vacations, paid for by Alpha, directly or indirectly, to government officials or employees in Angola?" To the extent the company is cooperating with U.S. authorities who may conduct later interviews, the omnibus question can be expected to be asked by prosecutors or SEC staff. It is better for the company and its counsel to know the answer to any omnibus questions in advance. With some long-time employees or senior managers, it can also be instructive at the end of the interview to ask if they have any remedial suggestions or ideas as to who else should be interviewed. Their answers may form what remedial measures or new controls may be practical or helpful.

G. Memoranda of Interviews

Ordinarily, memoranda of interviews should be prepared or at least drafted within 72 hours of the interview(s). Lawyers will best remember the substance of the interview if a memorandum is promptly dictated or written shortly after the interview. This practice reduces the risk of misrecalling a witness statement or confusing a witness with another interviewee near the same time. The memorandum should contain mental impressions of its author and address legal theories, thereby preserving the work product privilege. The memorandum should identify, if not append for easy convenience, any central or hot documents covered in the interview. It is usually best for one person to take notes and draft the memorandum of interview. Above all, the interview memorandum should be clear, fair, and accurate. There is an increased risk today that investigation counsel will be called as a witness in either civil or criminal litigation to summarize a witness's statement—usually for impeachment purposes. Therefore, counsel ought to take extra care to be sure the work product is clear, fair, and accurate.

H. Potential Remedial Action Lists

If problematic conduct is uncovered in an investigation, a running list of potential remedial actions—for example, rotation of ex pats or other personnel, new FCPA policies, correction of false books and records, increased FCPA audits, and implementation of FCPA training for local managers, accounting, and finance staff—will be helpful. It is best to promptly note possible remedial actions during the investigation and resulting from interviews lest they be forgotten later. In some situations counsel can test on location the in-country practicality or efficacy of potential remedial measures with employees or managers.

VII. HYPOTHETICAL FCPA INTERVIEW OUTLINE

The interviews of each investigation will vary depending upon the sensitive issue(s), and each interview may differ depending upon the employee's possible connection to or knowledge of the alleged bribery, books and records, or internal controls issues. The nature of the interview of the persons at corporate headquarters may differ substantially from those at foreign operation locations. In-country topics for one employee may be irrelevant to the interview of an accounting manager in the United States. It can be helpful in an outline to italicize exhibits to be shown to the witness or areas for follow-up or corroboration. An abbreviated FCPA hypothetical interview outline in an investigation into alleged improper payments in Angola[29] follows:

Owen Officer
(This interview outline is a work of fiction. Names, characters, places, and incidents are products of the author's imagination or are used fictitiously. Any resemblance to actual events, locales, or persons living or dead is entirely coincidental.)

1. *Upjohn* Warning
    Explanation of the nature of the inquiry or investigation
    Representation of company and not any individuals
    Privileged nature of the interview and sole right of company to waive the privilege
    Importance of telling the truth and distinguishing between what you know and are speculating
    Request you do not discuss the substance of interview with other employees
2. Background
    Birthplace and age
    Nationality
    Language proficiency (Rank English skills 1 to 10: _____)
    Education
        Apprenticeships or degrees and dates
        Degrees and advance degrees and dates
        Relevant continuing education and dates
    Work history
        Current Alpha-Angola position and dates and responsibilities
        Supervisors—direct and dotted line
        Subordinates

Interface with U.S. parent corporation or headquarters
Current organization chart
Prior titles/positions with Company (e.g., sales, finance, procurement)
  2007 –
  2004 – 2007
  2000 – 2004
Original hiring and interviews in 2007
Employee Personnel File
Relevant Travel
  To Luanda
  To Cabinda
  To Geneva
  To US Headquarters (Houston)
Prior employment history
  Titles/positions/dates
  Locations
  Reporting chain/interfaces
  Anti-bribery or FCPA training
Computer Practices
  Desktop
  Laptop
  Other
Licenses (e.g., CPA, CFA)
  Determine whether the company used a recruiter or conducted any due diligence and reference checks

3. Alpha Compliance and Training
"Tone at the Top" messages
Company Code of Business Conduct
  Receipt of Code of Business Conduct
Ethics training
FCPA or anti-bribery training
  3/09 Annual Sales Meeting
  2/08 Madrid Sales Meeting
Conflicts of interest coverage
  Receipt
Related party interests coverage
Ascertain whether there is documentary proof that interviewee attended FCPA or anti-bribery training

4. Key Topics
Alleged improper payments for offshore Cabinda, Block Zero, Area R
  Cash receipts
    Detail
    Internal controls

Meetings at cabinda
  Personal calendars
  Dates
  Documents
  Expense Reports
  Contract bids and awards and dates
  Books and records entries
7/21/07 Award of Cabinda, Block Zero Area A to Petroangola–China Oil JV
7/27/08 Award to Alpha of Cabinda, Block Zero Area Q EPC
  Contract
  Confirm signatures on contract
Rumors re: Cabinda Award
  Conversations with Bodkin
  Conversations with Flagler
  Phone records to Cabinda
  E-mails to Cabinda July 1–29, 2008
Gifts to Petroangola officials in Luanda
  Dollar value
  - Given as a group or to an individual
  - Government official status
  - Requisition forms to purchase gifts
    - *Title, employer Web site check*
    - *Transparency of gifts in subsidiary books and recods*
  - *Description*
  - *Dollar value*
  - *Recipients*
  - Authority of recipients to award or retain business (e.g., Block Zero Areas D and E contracts)
  - Block Zero Area B
  - Contract award date
    - *Approval of gifts by Finance Dept.*
Cash Payments to local police to part-time guard ex-pats' compound and provide transportation to and from work
  U.S. Embassy's cash payments for protection services of embassy personnel (counter argument)
  Cash economy in Angola (e.g., gasoline stations, hotels, restaurants)
Consultant Conrad Flagler
  CV and engineering background of Conrad Flagler
  Warranties and representations of his London-based company, Conrad Flagler Ltd. (CFL)
  Brochures of CFL
  Letters of reference from Congo, Dubai, and Qatar government officials

Other businesses and entities

Knighthood in 2004

2/03/08 *Financial Times* article re: "Flagler's Growing Ex-Minister
  Network in Western Africa"

Familiarity with CFL

Due diligence on CFL

- *7/1/08 Recommendation of Petroangola official that
  Alpha retain Flagler as consultant*
- *Interview*
- *Bank*
- *Trace International*

Due diligence files

- Where?
- Who is responsible for EMEA (Europe, Middle
  East, and Africa) files?
- Legal department input?

Other consultants considered for this project?

CFL reference checks

- Tobias Freeman
- Foreign Minister Miguel Ilanguo

CFL local representation

Other CFL projects/clients in Angola or West Africa

Offices and staff of CFL

- Luanda office
- London office
- Experience in oil and gas
- Other multinational CFL customers
- Visits to CFL offices

Awareness of consulting contract

- *CFL "Success Fee"*
- *Discussions*
- *Negotiation*
- *10 percent figure*
- *"Payable Immediately" term when contract is three
  years*

Payments to Swiss bank accounts

- Who approved?
- Who at CFL requested?

Retention known only to select subsidiary officers

CFL industry or energy sector history

Meetings with Conrad Flagler and the employees of
  CFL before award of CFL consulting contract

Flagler contacts with Sonangol

- Due diligence of consulting services

Invoices

Witness any efforts/successes of CFL
Contract performance
Any regular record of Alpha ongoing due diligence?
- Circumvention of consultant contract approval procedure

No approval signatures
No forwarding of consultant contract to legal department
- No audit rights clause

Finance Department
- Payment of services under a general contract
- No copy of CFL contract in records dept. files
- No audit rights
- *Fourteen hot documents*

7/22/08 Deletion of audit rights clause by CFL on Consultants Draft Agreement

7/26/08 Request for $250,000 political campaign contribution to MPLA (ruling Angola political party)

7/29/08 Conrad Flagler e-mail from Cabinda re: need to approve Consultancy Agreement ASAP and for $1 million advance

7/26/08 e-mail of Alpha-Angola CFO to Flagler re: authorization for "extra expenses"
- Acts in the United States and other U.S. Contacts

Travel to and purpose
E-mails
Telephone calls
Wire transfers
- Electrical fire

Security of storage facility
First awareness of fire
10/16/08 Internal Security Report
5. Parent Company Audits
   Frequency
   EMEA
   Angola—2007
   - Poor books and records finding
   - No petty cash controls

   Findings
6. Related Party Interests
   Angola Dive
   Luanda Trucking Ltd.
   Determine whether local registrations exist and who are listed as owners

7. Clarification and Omnibus Questions
    Is there anything you wish to clarify about what we
        have discussed today with respect to Alpha-Angola?
    Is there any other information you have with respect to
        possible improper payments by Alpha-Angola that
        you can share with us?
8. Potential Remedial Actions (Optional)
    Based on your experience in the EMEA region, how
        would you go about ensuring that no improper
        payments are made by Alpha, or reducing the risk of
        such payments?

An FCPA interview outline can cover a host of key topics, such as facilitating payments, corrupt intent, evidence of transparency, acts by foreign employees while in the United States, state-owned enterprises, tours of overseas plants, local laws, and the detail of books and record entries. While proof of bribery conduct may be lacking, proof of books and records and internal controls violations may still exist, and such evidence should be addressed in interviews as well. When the U.S. government lacks proof of bribery conduct, it often tries to establish and file books and records and internal controls violations.

VIII. THE WORKING CHRONOLOGY

A. Overview

A Working Chronology is, at its essence, a privileged detailed record of both the underlying events and the FCPA investigation (internal and/or government) as it unfolds.[30] This key memorandum will provide counsel with a comprehensive overview of the documentary and interview evidence gathered in the investigation. Counsel will continually refer to the chronology to check dates, hot documents including e-mails, travel and entertainment records, and descriptions of events, and to compare new information from document reviews and interviews against facts discovered previously.

The Working Chronology is often customized for the specifics or needs of the investigation. It may begin with a section that identifies the corporate hierarchy, listing key officers and employees of particular foreign operations. It can identify and break down the central legal issues to be addressed. Many investigating counsel include separate sections for Investigation Team Contacts, U.S. Government Attorneys (e.g., DOJ and SEC) and FBI Agents, Legal Theories, Foreign Government Attorneys, Potential Remedial Measures, and a To-Do List. Sections addressing important consulting contracts, questionable vendors, due diligence files, prior internal audits, financial performance at the parent or subsidiary level, applicable data privacy laws, or other facts bearing on relevant FCPA issues can also be inserted in a Working Chronology for easy and quick reference.

The actual chronology section itself will begin with the earliest known date relevant to the underlying issues. Any significant event, meeting, communication, or document should be noted with a brief description following the date. Counsel may review and include memoranda of interviews, diaries, calendars, general correspondence, telephone records, regulatory filings, facsimile transmissions, financial records, audit data, travel records, expense reports, correspondence with foreign government agencies, and other documents to help develop a thorough and accurate timeline. The source of each key document, event, or conversation should be noted (e.g., 2/12/08 Employment Contract of J.D. Bodkin (see Bonus Clause re: Cabinda Offshore, Block Zero, Areas E-H Contract Awards); 10/15/08 Electrical Fire (source: Internal Security)). Counsel can employ an asterisk system in the left margin of the Working Chronology to weigh particular facts, events, red flags, or developments, for example, one asterisk to denote a significant event, four asterisks to identify a seminal event or action.

This timeline of the Working Chronology consists of two sections and should not simply end with the last date relevant to the underlying events. Rather, it should continue with the dates and descriptions of key investigation events—for example, the dates on which document preservation memoranda were issued, specific witnesses were interviewed, DOJ or SEC subpoenas were served, documents were produced, meetings with prosecutors or regulators were held, and the like.

The Working Chronology will track the company's FCPA investigation as well as any parallel U.S. and foreign government investigations and usually do it all in one easy-to-view document. In complex investigations, counsel may draft separate chronologies to address topics, allegations, or countries. For example, there may be separate chronologies for Angola and for China, or separate chronologies for improper cash payments and for hospitality issues.

The Working Chronology should be distributed among counsel only. Otherwise, its privilege protection may be waived. It should contain a legend describing its purpose and limiting its circulation. Because the Working Chronology is a work product memorandum, under no circumstances should it be shown to a client or potential witness, since the Federal Rules of Evidence[31] may require production and disclosure of any writing *used* to refresh a witness' memory.[32] Often, a Working Chronology in a simple investigation will be 30 pages or less. However, in complicated FCPA investigations, a Working Chronology can be 100 pages or longer.

B.   Hypothetical FCPA Working Chronology

This is a simple, much abbreviated hypothetical Working Chronology for an audit committee investigation of alleged payments by a U.S. oil company's foreign subsidiary in Luanda, Angola, to government officials there.

ALPHA CORP – ANGOLA

WORKING CHRONOLOGY

(This Working Chronology is a work of fiction. Names, characters, places and incidents are products of the author's imagination or are used fictitiously. Any resemblance to actual events, locales, or persons living or dead, is entirely coincidental.)

This Working Chronology is the attorney work product of [Name of Outside Counsel] and is privileged and confidential investigative and trial preparation material. This composite summary of events, documents, transactions, and meetings relating to an internal investigation by ALPHA CORPORATION and a federal grand jury investigation of ALPHA CORPORATION in the Southern District of Texas and Washington, D.C., of alleged improper payments in Angola, contains mental impressions, conclusions, and legal theories of its author(s).

UNDER NO CIRCUMSTANCES SHOULD THIS WORKING CHRONOLOGY BE FURNISHED OR SHOWN TO A POTENTIAL WITNESS. The distribution of this memorandum or revisions thereto is to be limited to the following persons:

Lead Outside Counsel

(Firm name):   [Name]

General Counsel of

Alpha Corporation: [Name]

Associate General Counsel: [Name]

Outside Counsel (Law Firm):   [Name]

Deputy General Counsel: [Name]

unless express permission is obtained from [Name]. The holders of this memorandum are requested to destroy earlier editions of this memorandum as revised editions are distributed.

I.   ALPHA CORPORATION

World Headquarters:	Alpha Corporation, Inc. 1000 Oil Patch Way Houston, TX (714) 555-5555 www.alpha.corp
Angola Office:	Alpha-Angola SARL 123 Cabinda Way Luanda, Angola
Audit Committee: (Names and contact information)	1. AC Chair: 2. AC Committee Member: 3. AC Committee Member:
Alpha Management: (Houston, TX) (E-mail addresses, office phones, and cell phones)	Chair/CEO: [Names] Admin. Asst.: General Counsel: Admin. Asst.: Deputy General Counsel: Admin. Asst.: Chief Operating Officer: Chief Financial Officer: Director of Internal Audit:
Alpha EMEA	Managing Director: Legal Manager: Director of Worldwide Procurement: IT Director:

Alpha-Angola	Managing Director:
(Luanda):	Administrator:
(E-mail addresses and mobile phone numbers)	Controller:
	Local Shareholders:
	Finance Director:
	V.P. Sales:
	Admin. Asst.:

II. PRELIMINARY ALLEGATIONS AND ISSUES

1. Whether consultant Conrad Flagler Ltd. (CFL) of Luanda and London was used in Angola to indirectly pay Angolan federal government officials to award contracts to Alpha-Angola.
2. Whether overstated expense accounts (e.g., fuel) were used by Alpha-Angola to generate funds to pay local officials in Cabinda.
3. Whether U.S. persons in Houston, TX approved, facilitated, or participated in improper payments by the West African subsidiary.
4. Whether dividends to local Angolan shareholders were used to make payments to government officials in Luanda to obtain or retain Alpha-Angola business.
5. Whether monthly cash payments to military police in Angola (FAA—Forcas Armadas Angolans) for police protection in guarding Alpha-Angola personnel from separatist guerillas (FLEC-FAC) and transporting Alpha-Angola managers and employees to and from home in Cabinda constitute improper payments, that is, corrupt intent.
6. Whether Conrad Flagler or CFL made a $1,000,000 political contribution to MPLA, the leading Angolan political party.
7. Whether local freight forwarder AEC made improper payments with Alpha-Angola's knowledge or authorization to reduce Angolan customs duties and speed up inspections.
8. Whether new country manager J.D. Bodkin had undisclosed party interests and a kickback relationship with local officials or vendors, making Alpha a victim of his conduct.

9. What Alpha due diligence and background check was conducted into the background of J.D. Bodkin prior to his hiring as Angola country manager.
10. Whether there are any false books and records entries.
11. Whether internal controls in Luanda are adequate or can be improved to (a) prevent improper payments or (b) vet local consultants or other vendors.
12. Whether Alpha has sufficient financial controls over Alpha-Angola and other EMEA operations.

III. ALPHA AUDIT COMMITTEE INVESTIGATIVE TEAM

A. Law Firm
   [Names and contact information]
B. Forensic Accounting Firm
   [Names and contact information]
C. Contract Lawyers
   [Names and contact information]

IV. U.S. GOVERNMENT ATTORNEYS

Main Justice—Fraud Section
[Names]
Department of Justice—Fraud Section
1400 New York Ave., 4th Floor
Washington, D.C. 20005
(202) 514-7023
E-mail addresses:

U.S. Attorney—Southern District of Texas
AUSAs [Names]
U.S. Attorney's Office
P.O. Box 61129
Houston, TX 77208
(713) 567-9000

Securities and Exchange Commission
[Enforcement Division attorney names]
U.S. Securities and Exchange Commission
Fort Worth Regional Office
Burnett Plaza, Ste. 1900
801 Cherry Street, Unit 18
Fort Worth, TX 76102
(817) 978-3821

U.S. Securities and Exchange Commission Headquarters
100 F Street, NE
Washington, D.C. 20549
(202) 942-8088

Investigative Agencies
[Lead agent name]
FBI
Arlington, VA
(301) 555-5555

U.S. Embassy/Consulate
[Names]
United States Embassy
Rua Houari Boumedienne, 32-Miramar
Luanda, Angola
Telephone: 244 222 641 1222
Web Site: http://luanda.usembassy.gov

V.   OTHER

A. Petroangola: A national oil company of Angola
B. Alpha-Angola SARL: 50 percent-owned Subsidiary opened following cessation of 27-year Angolan civil war
C. The Republic of Angola: The West African country is widely viewed as one of the last major oil frontiers
D. MPLA: Party of the President of the Republic of Angola
E. AEC: Angola Expedited Customs Ltd. is a local freight forwarder in Luanda

VI.   CHRONOLOGY

Date	Event
2007	
7/21/07 **	Alpha-Angola SARL lost bid in award of Cabinda Block Zero, Area P to Petroangola-China Oil JV
2008	
2/12/08 **	J.K. Bodkin hired away from Chinese competitor to firm Alpha-Angola's senior officer effective 4/1/08
4/1/08 **	J.K. Bodkin appointed Managing Director of Alpha EMEA Region/Priority: Previously beat Russian and Indian competition in Angola and Cabinda offshore blocks

4/3/08 ***	Alpha-Angola received "recommendation" from Petroangola to retain Conrad Flagler of London as project consultant: A. Doala 4/03/08 private e-mail to jkbodkin@alpha.corp: *J.K., CFL awaits your call re: Area Q at Dorchester. Proceed now. Time of essence. A.D.*
7/4/08 ****	U.S.-based Alpha CEO received very vague handwritten note about J.K. Bodkin, new Angola Country Manager, and villa in Cannes
7/27/08	Alpha-Angola awarded $258 million government contract for offshore Cabinda Block Zero, Area Q
7/30/08	CFL directed Alpha-Angola to wire $25.8 million success fee to a numbered account at UBS, Geneva
8/7/08	E-mail from S. Luango to J.K. Bodkin, *When can friends expect Swiss cheese?*
9/15/08	Special Dividend to two local shareholders Reijos and Castillo declared
10/01/08 ***	General Counsel of Alpha Corporation receives a detailed anonymous letter alleging (1) improper payments by a consultant in Angola to local government officials to obtain a contract; (2) improper payments funneled by the two local Angola shareholders to MPLA Party; (3) CFO contribution to MPLA on eve of Area Q award; (4) phony fuel bills; and (5) use of a local freight forwarder to make improper payments
10/15/08 ****	Electrical fire at Alpha-Angola records storage area
10/28/08 ***	Anonymous note re: $1 million wire to account of J.K. Bodkin, UBS, Zurich
11/24/08	Audit Committee engagement of outside law firm to conduct internal investigation (AC Resolution 11/21/08) • Review of FCPA statute • Discussion of scope of investigation and voluntary disclosure option
11/25/08 *	Nondestruction Memorandum and Imaging coordinated by IT Director J.D. Dork for Angola, and for management and accounting personnel in Houston
12/01/08	Memorandum re: Data Privacy Structure and Issues
12/02/08	Memorandum re: Angolan Bribery Laws. Republic of Angola Statute 666

12/02/08	Global retention of XYZ Forensic, Inc., NY, NY • Preliminary list of 112 search terms in English, Portuguese • Sample audit of 500 transactions and analysis of same by 2/01/09
12/07/08	Overview by Deputy GC of Operations and Personnel Initial Angola interview schedule • Ubjo—Cabinda • Bodkin—Luanda • Abubu—Cabinda • Soros—Luanda • Paralegal Document Review Teams assigned for Angola U.S. per 37 search terms
12/9/08 ***	J.K. Bodkin refused to be interviewed by outside counsel absent Alpha indemnification and release for all liability
12/10/08 **	Bodkin terminated per letter from Alpha General Counsel
12/11/08	Ubjo interviewed in Luanda and a consulting local lawyer to determine whether to make personal and bank records available to outside law firm
12/12/08 **	Termination of CFL consulting contract
12/12/08	Zurich counsel for Bodkin filed for International Arbitration re: Employment Contracts in London
12/12/08	Legal Issue Memorandum: Elements of 18 U.S.C. § 371; FCPA Bribery; Facilitating Payments; Recent FCPA Angola Enforcement Actions-U.S. DPA Trend
12/13/08	Alpha Audit Committee Status Report: Committee updated
12/13/08 ***	Interview of Alpha-Angola CFO Juan Soros • Bodkin told Soros he had disclosed his related party interests to Alpha's General Counsel in February 2008 and stated "the Chinese play the game"
2009	
2/22/09	Federal Grand Jury Subpoena Duces Tecum served on Alpha Corp. returnable 3/22/09: 1. All consulting, contracts, memoranda, agreements, and correspondence relating to Conrad Flagler Ltd. Consulting (London)

	2. All employment agreements, salary and bonus information, background and due diligence checks, severance agreements, stock options, and other remuneration relating to J.K. Bodkin 3. Any and all correspondence, findings, memoranda, and disciplinary actions relating to the company's Angolan investigation 4. All e-mails to or by management including but not limited to CEO, CFO, CAO, and Internal Audit from 2007 to present relating to CFL Consulting of Luanda 5. All Alpha FCPA audits or other internal audits for Angola, Brazil, Russia, and India
2/26/08	RWT contact of Fraud Section attorney Mark Miller and SEC enforcement attorney Laura Smith
2/28/09	Alpha and Audit Committee Telephonic Conference. Report on Angola Investigation and likely DOJ and SEC Investigations and U.S. interviews
3/02/09	Alpha Full Board of Directors meeting
3/10/09	RWT obtains extension of time to provide documents to FGJ until 5/30/09
3/15/09	RWT contact of SEC Ft. Worth Regional Office
3/17/09	RWT meeting with DOJ Fraud Section attorney Mark Miller, Washington, D.C. re: FCPA FGJ
3/30/09	10Q due to be filed by Alpha Corporation, Inc.
5/30/09	Extended Grand Jury return date for Alpha Corporation
7/12–15/09	Live Alpha FCPA HQ training

VII. ALPHA REMEDIAL MEASURES

- Implemented live FCPA and Export Controls Training in APAC (Asia Pacific), EMEA (Europe, Middle East, Africa), and HQ (Houston) by 7/30/09.
- Draft Alpha Worldwide FCPA Policy (effective 1/02/09).
- Moved all Alpha-Angola SARL records to secure location.
- Eliminated direct reporting line from Alpha-Angola CFO to Alpha-Angola Managing Director and made local CFO report to Alpha CFO (Houston) (12/18/08).
- Terminated J.K. Bodkin 12/10/08.
- Terminated Alpha-Angola SARL-CFL Consultants of Luanda, Inc. Agreement (12/12/08).
- Suspended Angolan CFO Juan Soros 12/15/08.
- Translated Code of Conduct and new FCPA Policy into four foreign languages (12/22/08), including Portuguese.

VIII. TO DO

- Review Alpha-Angola Block Zero, Areas Q and R Budget Analyses.
- Consider rotation policy for Alpha foreign subsidiary, country managers and CFOs—every five years.
- Determine what due diligence was conducted for CFL, what coordination was with U.S. (Houston), and what due diligence has been conducted in EMEA for consultants.
- XYZ Forensics to analyze internal controls, petty cash, and vendor due diligence procedures for Alpha-Angola.
- Review anonymous note to CEO in context of phony fuel bills.
- Organize Alpha Consultant and Agent Due Diligence procedures worldwide.
- Re-interview CEO re: 4/3/05 and 7/4/08 CFL Consulting e-mails.
- Interview freight forwarder and invoices.
- Update AC and BOD 4/05/09.
- Evaluate benefits of voluntary disclosure.
- Consult with Alpha's securities disclosure counsel.
- Confer with Alpha's outside auditors.
- Institute annual FCPA audits in Angola, India, and China through 2013.
- Draft new local Shareholder Agreements with anti-bribery warranty and representations and access to bank records provisions.
- Alpha-Angola Investigation PowerPoint Presentation to DOJ 4/09.

IX. REPORTS AND RECOMMENDATIONS TO MANAGEMENT, BOARDS OF DIRECTORS, AUDIT COMMITTEES, OR SPECIAL COMMITTEES

A written report simplifies presentation to a board, audit committee, or management and memorializes counsel's work, conclusions, and recommendations. However, it also increases the danger of waiver and exposes the company to litigation over discovery of the report. The company may also run a risk of appearing noncooperative if it refuses to share a written report with the government.[33] Increasingly, PowerPoint presentations to boards or committees are an effective and sound compromise between oral presentations and written reports.

Because the results of an internal investigation report or presentation may be disclosed at some point, careful draftsmanship is critical in either form. Counsel should draft a report bearing in mind the worst-case scenario—that is, that customers, vendors, employees, lenders, regulators, prosecutors, private litigants, competitors, shareholders, or the media will read it. Inartful phrasing can mislead important constituents or even result in unintended allegations that give rise to libel claims.[34]

At the conclusion of an FCPA investigation into improper payments, problematic books and records, or inadequate internal controls, counsel will likely make recommendations to the client to correct problems, including changing policies and procedures, hiring additional compliance and audit personnel, modifying audit work programs, instituting or increasing FCPA training, disciplining wrongdoers, and conducting periodic FCPA audits in foreign jurisdictions where the company does business, where there are substantial corruption perception indices, or where the company has encountered FCPA-type problems.

Recommendations must be constructive and reasoned: if they are minor, too rigid, too numerous, or overly burdensome, there is a risk that they will not be implemented. However, recommendations should not be rejected simply because they might embarrass management or prove costly. The company will likely face more serious consequences if the DOJ or SEC later discovers problematic conduct and learns that the company previously declined to implement remedial measures and better controls.

When making recommendations, it is generally useful to set reasonable deadlines for implementation of the recommendations and to assign specific responsibility to managers, lawyers, or compliance officers. If not, other business priorities can intervene, and the recommendations will not be implemented timely or ever. The board of directors, audit committee, shareholders, or prosecutors and regulators may then draw the harmful but possibly appropriate conclusion that compliance is not very important to management.

X. VOLUNTARY DISCLOSURE

A. Advantages

The benefits of voluntary disclosure and cooperation vary case by case and are rarely fully known at the time of a company's disclosure decision. While the DOJ has encouraged and trumpeted the benefits of voluntary disclosure and cooperation, it has issued no comprehensive policy clarifying when such disclosure and cooperation will lead to nonprosecution, deferred prosecution, or other favorable treatment.[35] A review of recent DOJ-SEC resolutions can give counsel a range of possible outcomes and trends, but each case is fact-dependent.

The DOJ and SEC need companies to voluntarily disclose because their resources are limited. The purported government "carrot" is twofold: the ultimate DOJ criminal and/or SEC enforcement sanctions will be less severe, and the cooperative path to resolution is much less onerous, costly, and distracting to management. For public companies whose senior officers are now required to certify the accuracy of corporate financial statements and attest to the company's internal controls, the decision to voluntarily disclose may be one that accelerates what would be filed in a quarterly or annual filing. For a number of companies, prompt, voluntary disclosure to the DOJ has avoided indictment and resulted instead in deferred prosecution agreements or no charges at all.

B. Disadvantages

Voluntary disclosure has both legal and practical ramifications. On the legal side, there is a risk that counsel's disclosure will constitute a statement against interest or an admission.[36] As important, civil litigants may try to gain access to disclosure materials in parallel civil proceedings, including private or civil litigation by shareholders, competitors, and foreign governments. Also, disclosure can dilute defenses and enable the government to attack the defenses before any court proceedings.[37] In general, disclosure of an attorney-client privileged communication as to one entity, for example, a department or agency of the government, waives the privilege as to all. While the elements of the work product doctrine are different and somewhat more protective of the privilege,[38] counsel need to carefully consider the implications of disclosure of privileged work product as well.

As for practical disadvantages, voluntary disclosure is never a simple, quick act of contrition. It usually is long, expensive, distracting, embarrassing, and, unfortunately, uncertain in benefits.[39] It can also lead to foreign enforcement and expansion of the scope of the company's original investigation. Although many executives question the time, resources, and costs associated with voluntary disclosure and cooperation, the costs of defending an FCPA investigation initiated by the DOJ or SEC are usually far greater. Before a company or a board elects to voluntarily disclose improper payments, counsel should fully advise it of potential adverse legal and practical consequences.[40]

C. Disclosure Mechanics

Voluntary disclosure should be timely, informative, and continuing. There is no prescribed form of disclosure. Many companies elect to contact the Fraud Section through counsel, set up a meeting, and provide in person a detailed oral overview of the known facts to DOJ attorneys and, in some instances, FBI agents. If the company is publicly held, it usually makes sense to schedule a similar disclosure meeting with SEC enforcement attorneys. Because the DOJ and SEC work closely on such matters, a joint meeting can often be arranged. It is best to stick to the facts, and not to leave copies of any presentations or privileged material with the government.

The DOJ and SEC will want to know who investigated the facts (inside counsel, outside counsel, the board of directors, a special committee), who the key participants in the wrongdoing were, what the likely potential magnitude of the improper payments is, what efforts have been made to secure and preserve both electronic evidence and hard copy records, what disciplinary actions have been taken, and what remedial measures are underway. The DOJ and SEC are especially interested in the *process* the company, board, or audit committee employed once it learned of the allegations. The DOJ and SEC will invariably examine how independent and thorough any internal investigation has been.

In general, the DOJ does not expect a company to report immediately an FCPA allegation. It understands that the board, the audit committee, or management and its counsel need a reasonable period of time to verify an allegation and to gather facts, particularly given that the alleged operative events have usually occurred in a foreign country. The DOJ welcomes disclosure early enough to allow covert investigative techniques. In certain instances, the DOJ may prefer and even request that cooperating wrongdoers remain on a company payroll for a reasonable time. In contrast, the SEC generally does not become involved in a company's employment actions or termination decisions.

D. Follow-up

The DOJ and SEC will expect a disclosing company and its counsel to continue any necessary investigation, to secure and provide documents, to make cooperating employees available for interviews in the United States or elsewhere, and to keep the DOJ and/or SEC apprised in real time of any material developments. The DOJ and SEC often schedule conferences or telephone calls to understand events and transactions and to be kept informed of any company investigation progress. To the extent a company's investigation indicates or uncovers more misconduct elsewhere, the government expects the company, board of directors, or audit committee to expand the scope of its investigation.

Given their limited resources and the number of companies discovering and disclosing FCPA violations, the DOJ and SEC welcome and need companies to cooperate and to conduct investigations with law enforcement monitoring or oversight. Government attorneys, of course, retain the right to formalize an investigation, that is, to subpoena documents and witnesses, to execute search warrants, and so on, if they determine that a company's investigation and cooperation are inadequate. Particularly in the wake of the December 2006 McNulty Memorandum and the August 2008 Filip Amendment to the Department of Justice Manual, the DOJ and SEC have become less insistent about requiring a waiver of the corporate attorney-client privilege as long as a company makes reasonable efforts to communicate essential facts and leads, and to advance the government investigation.

E. Cooperation Log

The government may keep a cooperation log that records what documents and witnesses the company has provided or made available and any other requests that have been accommodated. It is useful for company counsel to maintain a similar log, to record and quantify company's cooperative efforts during the investigation, and to seek credit for these acts when negotiating a resolution.

F. Siemens's Exceptional Cooperation and Corporate Amnesty and Leniency Programs

In reaching a $1.6 billion settlement with Siemens in December 2008, the Department of Justice commended as exceptional "Siemens' wide-ranging cooperation efforts throughout this investigation, which included a sweeping internal investigation, the creation of innovative and effective amnesty and leniency programs, and exemplary efforts with respect to preservation, collection, testing, and analysis of evidence."[41]

1. Manpower Commitment and Document Preservation

The Siemens internal investigation involved over 1.5 million hours of billable time by its audit committee's outside law firm and forensic professionals. Their investigative work took place in 34 countries and included over 1,750 interviews and 800 informational meetings. Over 100 million documents were collected and preserved, many of which were searched or reviewed for evidence relevant to the investigation. Siemens, either directly or through its outside law firm, produced to the Department of Justice over 24,000 documents, amounting to over 100,000 pages. Siemens also established a Project Office at headquarters staffed by 16 full-time employees who facilitated interviews and document collection. To facilitate visits to regional companies by the investigation team, the Project Office communicated with regional management to explain and prepare them for the interviews and other investigative work.

2. Corporate Amnesty and Leniency Programs

In consultation with the DOJ, Siemens designed and implemented a unique company-wide amnesty program to facilitate the internal investigation. The four-month amnesty program provided that all but the most senior employees who voluntarily disclosed to the law firm truthful and complete information about possible violations of relevant anti-corruption laws would be protected from unilateral employment termination and company claims for damages. The policy that implemented the amnesty program made clear that it was in no way binding on any prosecutors or regulators, including the DOJ and the SEC, but provided that

Siemens would bring an employee's cooperation to the attention of such authorities if he or she were the subject of a government investigation.

For employees too senior to qualify for the amnesty program, as well as those employees who did not come forward during the amnesty program period, Siemens established a leniency program that provided for individualized leniency determinations for cooperating employees. The creation of these two programs was an effective way to further the investigation. Over 100 employees provided information in connection with the two programs, including numerous employees who previously provided incomplete or less than truthful information and employees who had not come forward previously.

Shortly after the amnesty program began, the DOJ and the SEC identified various individuals and projects for more extensive debriefings, referred to by the parties as "deep dives." The amnesty and leniency programs were essential to obtaining the types of detailed information needed for the deep dives. These deep dive sessions enabled the DOJ to evaluate the overall case, properly target its limited resources, and develop the evidence necessary to bring charges. Siemens represents the most thorough bribery investigation ever necessitated by serious compliance lapses and misconduct. Its global cooperation led to a lesser penalty. Large multinationals uncovering serious misconduct will need to consider the cooperative efforts of Siemens and its unique amnesty and leniency programs, which should be carefully vetted with DOJ in advance. Whether Siemens employees who cooperated under the internal amnesty or leniency programs are prosecuted by governments will determine whether that proves a wise and fair strategy for other companies and their officers.

XI. UNIQUE ASPECTS OF FCPA INVESTIGATIONS AND MULTINATIONAL OPERATIONS

A. In-Country Visits and Interviews

In-country interviews and investigation are *essential* to a full understanding of a company or an agent's, consultant's, or contractor's operations and procedures in a foreign country and related FCPA issues. They can strengthen the facts and arguments that a company's officers or employees did not have reason or a high probability to know that improper payments to foreign officials would or did occur. Conversely, they can dispel a claim that payments were for a charitable organization rather than a government official's spouse. To the extent a company elects to voluntarily disclose or otherwise cooperate with the U.S. authorities, foreign visits, on-site interviews, and document preservation at the locations of the alleged improper activity will enhance the credibility of an investigation and any final report. In many cases the U.S. government will not have the ability to travel to the foreign country and will not have the advantage defense counsel has in evaluating first-hand the overseas business and legal practices and foreign witnesses.

As a rule, investigation counsel will seek to maintain a low profile when reviewing documents and interviewing company personnel and other witnesses in foreign locations.[42] Foreign nationals frequently question the authority of U.S. counsel or investigators to interview or look into local payments or books and records practices. They sometimes disclose the identity of or visit by FCPA investigation counsel to persons in the foreign countries whose conduct has been problematic or worse. Such disclosure can subject investigation counsel to personal risk. Finally, FCPA investigations may require translation of documents not in English and use of interpreters for witnesses who do not speak English.

B. Claims That the Payments or Practices in Question Are Common and Necessary

Employees, agents, and consultants, while sometimes conceding that payments or related practices have occurred, frequently contend that the corrupt payments were necessary to do business and customary in the country in question. The United States government does not recognize this response as a defense; DOJ attorneys reply routinely that Congress was well aware of corrupt customs and practices in foreign countries when it enacted the FCPA in 1977 and criminalized such payments.

C. Foreign Data Privacy Laws

Many foreign jurisdictions have enacted privacy, data protection, wiretapping, state secrecy, bank secrecy, blocking, and other local laws or requirements that apply to data and documentation collection activities.[43] Violations of these laws can lead to private rights of action by the affected individuals, risk of foreign enforcement actions against companies by data protection authorities (and corresponding fines and injunctive relief), and potential criminal liability for the company and corporate officers.[44]

Foreign privacy and data protection laws restrict the collection, handling, and transfer of any personally identifiable information about individuals. Perhaps the most important foreign privacy laws relevant to FCPA investigations were enacted in 1995 by the European Union on the Protection of Individuals with Respect to the Processing of Personal Data.[45] This EU directive is implemented through the national laws of each EU member country and often applies to FCPA investigations.

For example, the collection, use, and transfer of a document or e-mail that contains the name of a foreign subsidiary employee, personal financial information, data about payments made or received by the employee, and the name of the third-party payee or payor would implicate personal data concerning both the employee and the third party.[46] The collection, use, or transfer of this type of personal data could trigger a range of data protection requirements for the foreign subsidiary, including obligations to: (1) ensure that there is a "legitimate" purpose to collect and use such data; (2) provide a sufficient privacy notice to the affected individuals; (3) obtain consent in certain cases; (4) maintain reasonable measures to protect the security and confidentiality of the personal data; (5) complete a filing with the foreign data protection authority describing the data collection and processing activities; and (6) confirm that any international transfers of the personal data to the United States or other non-EU locations are properly subject to "adequate protection."[47]

In some instances a parent company's global privacy policy and compliance program will have effectively addressed these issues. Depending on the country, it may be necessary to obtain employee consents to searches with the condition that the reviewing personnel not review personal data. A company or board of directors with counsel will in most cases have to evaluate the types of data at issue, company operations, potential penalties, and the company's risk tolerance at the outset of an investigation.[48]

Other foreign statutes and laws that need to be considered in internal investigations include wiretapping and electronic communication, bank secrecy, and common law confidentiality and blocking statutes.

D. Local Labor Laws

In many countries, local labor laws greatly favor foreign nationals. For example, a local executive's refusal to cooperate in an investigation may not be grounds for termination. Privacy laws may also affect the ability of a multinational to secure and review electronic data. Local laws or a Worker's Council in Europe may also impede a company's desire to take swift remedial measures, including disciplinary actions. Notwithstanding suspicious conduct, termination packages that favor local executives or employees may be necessary. If a company has voluntarily disclosed misconduct and is cooperating with U.S. authorities, it is often wise to promptly advise the U.S. government of local labor law issues, termination or severance agreements, and related developments.

Investigative counsel can often benefit from the advice of experienced local partners or counsel, not only on local employment law, but also on local anti-bribery laws, local campaign laws, the reputation of local parties or consultants, and local self-reporting practices.

E. Relevant Local Laws

In FCPA investigations, local laws can be relevant in at least two respects. First, the written local law may provide an affirmative defense. Second, it may not exempt certain practices, for example, facilitating or expediting payments, that are permitted by the FCPA, thereby creating a conflict with U.S. law. Often the law and legal systems in third-world countries are undeveloped, as legislative history, case precedent, and enforcement are scant. Compounding the undeveloped law scenario is that the executive branch agencies in foreign countries often wield enormous administrative discretion and authority. Local counsel in FCPA investigations will commonly assist in analyzing local anti-corruption, conflicts of interest, data privacy, and money laundering laws and in advising whether facilitating payments are lawful and enforced.

F.   Separate Sets of U.S. and In-Country Books and Records

Multinational companies sometimes keep and maintain separate sets of financial records for U.S. and in-country operations. For example, overseas companies may have joint ventures with major competitors for which it would be inappropriate for a parent corporation or subsidiary to share all financial information. In these circumstances it can be appropriate or necessary to keep separate financial records. Internal controls of a foreign operation that do not include independent audits of consultants or third parties or that do not require keeping all copies of all consulting agreements only at the subsidiary will likely be viewed with skepticism by the DOJ and SEC.

G.   Access to Third-Party Foreign Bank Records

Absent an express contractual provision that a foreign agent, consultant, or partner must provide bank records to a company, its counsel, or an independent accountant, a company or its investigation counsel will normally have no access to third-party foreign bank records. This can limit the ability of a company to determine whether a joint venture partner, agent, consultant, or business partner has made improper payments to a foreign official. In very limited circumstances, local law may provide judicial remedies to obtain access to bank accounts and trace the disposition of funds from these accounts.

H.   Pressure to Enter into an Overseas Commercial Agreement

Foreign governments vary a great deal in the manner and timing of offering investment opportunities and contract awards to international companies. Moreover, many overseas project opportunities are subject to local and foreign political pressures, including, in the case of developing countries, pressures from favored allies or ex-colonial powers, bilateral financing entities, and lending agencies. Unique procedural requirements and delays in project announcements and competitive bidding are not uncommon. Occasionally, foreign investment opportunities are substantially altered, restructured, or accelerated by the host governments for political and financial reasons. Accordingly, multinational companies, with layered levels of review approval, must often rush to meet a newly announced deadline, leading to a lack of a complete paper trail and inadequate due diligence compared to what might occur in a purely domestic transaction.

Large investments and ventures with foreign partners or contractors can also be informally documented in a manner contrary to the custom and practice of such companies and their counsel. Moreover, until such time as a company is assured of a project award, it may not wish to enter into full-blown, properly documented arrangements. In some cases, a company may never enter into such detailed documentation, due to the priority of other ongoing projects. Seemingly negligent failures to document significant projects need to be understood in context. Examples occur in small as well as large projects, including major resource exploitation, infrastructure, and privatization projects. The more thorough the due diligence record, the more likely a company that inherits a bribery problem can avoid the conclusion by U.S. authorities that it intentionally closed its eyes to facts that should have prompted inquiries.

I.   Third-Party Motivations to Disparage a Multinational Company

From time to time, multinational companies receive FCPA allegations and quickly conclude that the allegations are the product of disgruntled employees, foreign competitors, subcontractors and agents, or foreign government officials or candidates who may have strong political and economic motivation to disrupt and disparage the operations. Notwithstanding questionable motives, many disgruntled employees or others with an incentive to harm companies have alleged corruption and been proven right. No allegation can be dismissed without some level of review, and it is reasonable to, whenever possible, locate and determine the source of the allegation to evaluate preliminarily its legitimacy before commencing a full-scale investigation. Regardless of the merits of the allegation, it is usually prudent for company counsel to memorialize the efforts undertaken to address even minor FCPA allegations, the facts learned, and any actions taken. Many companies as a matter of course also report even minor FCPA allegations to their audit committees and their review of same.

J.   Forensic Investigators

In substantial FCPA investigations, law firms often engage qualified forensic accountants or investigators to retrieve, image, and recover computer and electronic evidence, to search electronic databases, and to assist in internal control analyses and recommendations. Forensic services are routinely expected by the DOJ and SEC staff in both large FCPA investigations and monitorships. Sometimes companies try to use internal information technology and audit staff for these purposes. Absent the availability of fully qualified in-house IT personnel and audit personnel, it is prudent for an investigative law firm to engage outside forensic investigators in substantial investigations. Forensic firms should provide details of their work plans and meaningful budgets before any engagement.

K.   Books and Records and Internal Controls Issues

In most FCPA investigations, the primary focus is understandably on potential improper payments to foreign officials. Still, counsel must focus on the accounting provisions of the FCPA—the books and records and internal controls provisions. If a company is making lawful "facilitating payments" under the FCPA in a foreign country, these expenses should be identified and recorded as "facilitating payments," e.g., "facilitating payments to Nigeria Electric Power Authority (NEPA) Utility Clerk in Port Harcourt." Otherwise, the company may have a false books and records violation.

L.   Other Potential Criminal Violations

Investigation counsel must be mindful of other potential criminal violations including money laundering, false statements to the U.S. government, bid rigging, commercial bribery, and export violations.

XII.   POTENTIAL REMEDIAL MEASURES

It is best for company counsel to plan and, where possible, to promptly implement appropriate remedial measures—certainly in advance of any voluntary disclosure. Law enforcement agencies have a strong interest in ensuring that wrongful acts or conduct do not recur and that management understands the seriousness of the misconduct and has taken and will take appropriate steps to reduce any possibility of recurrence.

FCPA remedial measures can include:

- Disciplinary actions, including demotion, transfer, suspension, and termination of employees who engaged in wrongdoing or failed to adequately supervise those who engaged in wrongdoing;
- Increased FCPA training—for employees, officers, and directors;
- FCPA audits and testing;
- Implementation of stand-alone FCPA policies;
- Appointment of new financial and accounting personnel;

- Improved financial controls;
- Revised reporting chains of command;
- Expatriate country rotation policies;
- Certifications of compliance (by employees, business partners, and consultants);
- New or revised travel and entertainment policies and procedures;
- New or revised charitable or educational contribution policies;
- New or revised consultant, partner, and local agent approval policies and procedures;
- New or revised gift-giving policies;
- Appointment of regional or in-country compliance and/or ethics officers;
- Heightened due diligence requirements for joint venture partners and for mergers and acquisitions;
- Heightened due diligence of agents and consultants including third-party vetting and Web-based tools;
- Increased reporting to the audit committee and board of directors regarding compliance training and remedial efforts;
- Increased compliance oversight role responsibility of the board of directors;
- Coordination of corporate compliance in legal, internal audit, compliance, and finance departments; and
- Reduction of the number of company bank accounts.

Of course, some remedial measures will not be obvious or available at early stages. Others, such as the need for FCPA training, may be readily apparent and should be conducted promptly or concurrently with the investigation.

XIII.   EFFECTIVE REMEDIAL MEASURES

Two recent DOJ and SEC FCPA settlement resolutions have specially praised the remedial efforts of companies that have discovered bribery misconduct. Willbros, a Texas-based oil pipeline company, discovered wrongdoing by a senior officer, and its audit committee conducted an investigation. Willbros then self-disclosed the problematic conduct to both the DOJ and SEC and promptly implemented a host of remedial actions. Siemens AG, a German conglomerate, was the subject of dawn raids in Germany and then instituted a massive global investigation that, along with its remedial program, has been heralded as a model response for large multinational companies. The responses and actions described below provide guidance to midsize and large companies discovering bribery conduct.

A. Model Willbros Group Inc. Remedial Measures

In *United States v. Willbros Group Inc. & Willbros International Inc.*,[49] a pipeline company was able to obtain a deferred prosecution agreement (DPA) and avoid a felony as a result of prompt and exceptional cooperation and remedial measures notwithstanding egregious bribery conduct in three countries under the direction of a senior officer.

Upon discovering misconduct by a senior officer in Bolivia, Willbros undertook numerous remedial steps enabling it to obtain a DPA, including:

- Commencing a thorough audit committee internal investigation within 24 hours of notice of allegations of corporate tax fraud committed by employees and purported consultants working on behalf of the Willbros subsidiary's Bolivian subsidiary;
- Quickly expanding the scope of the internal investigation, which included extensive forensic analysis, into alleged misconduct in other international locations, primarily Nigeria and Ecuador, and promptly and voluntarily reporting the results of its investigation to the DOJ and the SEC;
- Severing its employment relationship with a senior international executive within 10 days of receiving allegations of his involvement in the Bolivian tax scheme, and seizing from him critical encrypted electronic evidence at the time of his severance;
- Taking prompt and appropriate disciplinary actions, without regard to rank, against 18 additional employees;
- Voluntarily agreeing, as to the DOJ only, to a limited waiver of attorney-client privilege with respect to certain specific subject matters important to the DOJ's understanding of the internal investigation;
- Promptly terminating commercial relationships with purported "consulting" companies based in Nigeria, which companies Willbros suspected of assisting in making improper payments to Nigerian government officials;
- Promptly reporting the misconduct of certain Willbros International employees who, along with others, made additional improper payments in Nigeria after Willbros Group Inc. and the government had begun investigations, which reporting was a substantial factor in causing the guilty pleas of two of the responsible individuals;
- Upon conclusion of the internal investigation, continuing to cooperate with the DOJ and SEC in their parallel investigations, which cooperation included making numerous current and former employees available for interviews and testimony in the United States and abroad, and responding promptly to requests for documentary evidence, much of which was located in remote international locations;

- Expanding, enhancing, and, where appropriate, centralizing its worldwide legal, accounting, and international audit functions;
- Issuing an enhanced, stand-alone FCPA policy and conducting worldwide training upon implementation of that policy;
- Retaining new senior management with substantial international experience and understanding of FCPA requirements;
- Acknowledging responsibility for the misconduct; and
- Delaying pursuit of civil remedies against certain former employees so as not to prejudice the DOJ's criminal investigation of the individuals.

The above cooperative and remedial steps were specifically recognized in the Willbros DPA and represent the most comprehensive list of remedial or cooperation steps to date by a midsize company discovering and promptly investigating FCPA misconduct. The Willbros resolution offers important guidance on how midsize companies uncovering very serious misconduct by senior management can promptly institute strong remedial measures and manage to avoid a felony conviction for the parent company and subsidiaries.

Because FCPA settlements with the DOJ and the SEC have increasingly featured independent monitors for terms of three years and, in the case of Siemens, four years, some companies under investigation have attempted to line up independent consultants to review and oversee their compliance reforms in advance and thereby influence the government's selection of a monitor in a DOJ or SEC settlement.[50]

B. Siemens Response to Munich Dawn Raids and Lessons Learned for Large Multinational Companies

In response to raids at multiple Siemens offices and the homes of Siemens employees in Munich, Germany, in November 2006, Siemens commenced, in the words of U.S. authorities, a "sweeping global investigation"[51] of possible bribery of foreign public officials and falsification of corporate books and records. This investigation uncovered what SEC Enforcement Director Linda Thomsen described as a "pattern of bribery unprecedented in scale and geographic reach." The company's follow-on cooperation was "exceptional and its reforms real."[52] While few multinational companies have 400,000 employees or operations in 191 countries, let alone uncover tens of millions of dollars of bribes, there are important compliance lessons from the *Siemens* resolution for large multinational companies.

As part of its remedial response, Siemens:

- Terminated members of senior management implicated in the misconduct.
- Reorganized the company to be more centralized from both a business and compliance perspective, with measures including the

creation of a new position on the managing board with responsibility for legal and compliance matters.

- Overhauled and expanded its compliance organization, with more than 500 full-time compliance personnel worldwide.
- Vested control and accountability for all compliance matters in a chief compliance officer, who, in turn, reports directly to the general counsel and the chief executive officer.
- Reorganized its audit department, which is now headed by a chief audit officer, who reports to the company's audit committee.
- Requested that every member of its 450-person audit staff reapply for their jobs.
- Enacted a series of anti-corruption compliance policies, including a new anti-corruption handout, sophisticated Web-based tools for due diligence and compliance matters, a confidential communications channel for employees to report irregular business practices, and a corporate disciplinary committee to impose appropriate disciplinary measures for substantial misconduct.
- Organized a working group devoted to fully implementing new compliance initiatives, consisting of eight employees from Siemens' finance and compliance departments and outside professionals from a major accounting firm. The working group developed a step-by-step guide on the new compliance program and improved financial controls known as the "Anti-Corruption Toolkit." The toolkit and its accompanying guide contain clear steps and timelier requirements on local management to ensure full implementation of the global anti-corruption program and enhanced controls. Over 150 people, including outside accounting professionals, provided support in implementing the toolkit at 162 Siemens entities. Dedicated support teams spent six weeks on the ground at 56 of those entities deemed to be "higher risk," assisting management in those locations with all aspects of the implementation. The total external cost to Siemens for these remediation efforts has exceeded $150 million.
- Imposed a moratorium on entering into new business consulting agreements or making payments under existing business consulting agreements until a complete collection and review was undertaken of all such agreements. The company also initiated, and has nearly completed, a review of all third-party agents with whom it has agreements. This has resulted in a significant reduction in the number of business consultants used by Siemens.
- Enhanced its review and approval procedures for business consultants. The new state-of-the-art system requires any employee who wishes to engage a business consultant to enter detailed information into an interactive computer system, which assesses the risk of

the engagement and directs the request to the appropriate supervisors for review and approval.

- Increased corporate-level control over company funds, centralizing and reducing the number of company bank accounts and outgoing payments to third parties.

The DOJ described Siemens' reorganization and remediation efforts as extraordinary and setting a "high standard for multinational companies to follow." Absent discovery of serious corruption problems, few multinational companies will be expected to employ hundreds of full-time compliance personnel or enact most of these measures, but multinational companies in risky industries or regions will review the Siemens measures and adopt ideas or measures as appropriate.

XIV. LOGISTICAL ADVICE IN CONDUCTING FOREIGN INVESTIGATIONS[53]

There is no substitute for conducting FCPA interviews, if at all possible, in-country at the site of the alleged wrongful conduct. An interview of a foreign national tied to a gratuity to a foreign tax official or an informal meeting with U.S. Department of Commerce officers at a U.S. embassy can enable a lawyer to paint a vivid picture and possibly persuade American prosecutors or regulators that an FCPA bribery charge is inappropriate.

The opportunity to interview (let alone re-interview) foreign witnesses is usually limited, and many foreign nationals, unaccustomed to the detailed nature of American litigation or white-collar criminal investigations, will understandably seek to avoid a second meeting. When counsel is considerate of overseas witnesses and staff and well prepared in initial interviews, the likelihood of a productive follow-up meeting or telephone conference is greatly enhanced. As often as not, company counsel will have earlier and greater access to documents and witnesses than U.S. authorities will.

A. Logistics

In representing a corporate client and coordinating logistics, investigation counsel will want to work closely with the general counsel, an assistant general counsel, or his or her designate. Usually the client will have an in-country manager or regional lawyer who can facilitate document preservation and imaging, and line up document reviews and interviews a week or two before the trip. This person often has helpful insights into the matters under review and the factual perspectives of certain practices and potential witnesses. He or she can often provide useful documents in advance, such as the local organization chart, accounts payable procedures, the audit plan, or the storage plan, and can also guide investigation counsel on what to wear at interviews or on a plant tour. An overseas contact can normally secure work space on company premises or another convenient location such as a law office or quality hotel conference room.

An unnecessarily broad request from American counsel to review every in-country file or transaction and interview dozens of employees can create a crisis atmosphere before counsel even arrives. While the company should take all appropriate steps to preserve all relevant documents—hard and electronic—at the outset, it usually helps to narrow initial interview and document requests and expand the requests after counsel has a better on-the-ground understanding of the value of witnesses and scope of relevant records. In planning meetings, counsel should be mindful of foreign holidays and travel schedules of interviewees. The order of the document review and witness interviews, as well as their location, can be important.

Foreign counsel can be very helpful in familiarizing U.S. counsel with local laws and customs. They also can advise where necessary, on how to deal with third-party sources of information or government officials. Logistics will also customarily include visa procurement, drivers, lodging reservations, airport and customs assistance, copying and fax services, and arrangements for weekend and evening support services.

B.   Documents

U.S. and foreign document reviews will normally precede in-country interviews. This process can often take weeks or even months depending on the volume or translation requirements. This review should search hot or key documents and sort them by witness and topic and incorporate them into each witness's interview outline. Important documents—particularly e-mails—are found through a quality electronic search with carefully thought-out search terms. Of course, any relevant U.S.-based documents should be addressed in the outline and interview, as well. Key domestic and foreign documents will usually be described and analyzed in a privileged Working Chronology, *supra*.

Many foreign-based corporate documents are in English. If there are key documents in foreign languages, counsel must plan ahead for translation services. Particularly where documents are sensitive, one should retain a trustworthy interpreter. Many multinational companies have experienced translators on call. If work product and copies of documents may be couriered back to the States, counsel should determine the legality of the transfer of documents outside the country, what overseas services are available, and the delivery schedules for time-sensitive documents. Counsel will want to consider whether there are compelling legal reasons—American or foreign—for not copying or removing documents from distant locations.

C. Interviews

Most foreign legal systems do not offer the intense experience of U.S.-litigation-style interviews or depositions. How one treats foreign employees and witnesses will often determine the success of FCPA interviews and the overall investigation. The more senior the officer or employee, the more likely he or she will speak English. If not, an interpreter or a colleague who speaks the foreign language and understands the culture at issue can bridge many substantive and cultural gaps. Counsel should be prepared to be far more patient with foreign employees and witnesses than with U.S. employees and witnesses.

Counsel may wish at the outset to provide employees and witnesses an overview or idea of what will be covered. Counsel should normally start with general noncontroversial topics such as background, that is, work history and schooling, and save more sensitive matters for later. Even when the foreign witness speaks English, counsel should allow almost twice as much time for the interview as for one with a person whose first language is English. Counsel should also schedule time overseas to review and supplement work product. A week or two later, one's recollection of five or more whirlwind interviews will usually be muddled.

Above all, counsel must try to appreciate the culture of the employees and witnesses and the likelihood that a detailed interview is a very different experience for them. Counsel should always bring an ample supply of business cards. In most countries it is customary to exchange professional cards at the outset of a meeting, and a formal presentation, as is the custom in Japan, can establish or advance the necessary initial professional rapport. Having carefully explained the privileged nature and purpose of the interview, counsel may be able to test important theories and the knowledge of these officers and employees about sensitive practices. Thoughtful foreign officers and ex-pats often present relevant scenarios and business practices that American lawyers may not anticipate. They invariably appreciate a team approach and consideration of their experience and views.

Counsel frequently elect to conduct interviews away from the client's business offices. Some clients find interviews at their offices disruptive and attention drawing and will ask counsel to use a conference room at a nearby hotel. Even that may not assure the desired confidentiality, as many hotels are reportedly bugged (for example, in Middle Eastern and former Soviet Republic countries). Counsel may need to be creative in selecting safe interview locations.

If counsel foresees the need for sworn statements, he should predetermine what the particular countries' practices are, as they differ widely. Some countries require notaries to review each line of a declaration or affidavit with the affiant. Some countries require the local filing of official statements; counsel may conclude for confidentiality purposes that a less official statement will suffice. He may want to prearrange a notary (or the foreign equivalent overseas) as they may be scarce in foreign countries.

D. Forensic Accountants and Investigators

Forensic accountants can be most helpful to a financial fraud or accounting investigation. Most large accounting firms have forensic groups consisting of former law enforcement officers, certified public accountants, and certified fraud examiners. Experienced forensic investigators can assist not only in the gathering and imaging of and electronic searching for relevant evidence but also in the logical organization and presentation of complex transactions. The work of accountants and others under the direction of counsel must be protected by the applicable privilege(s) since U.S. federal law, for example, does not recognize an accountant-client privilege.

In large FCPA investigations, the number of countries or questionable transactions may make the cost of a review of all transactions prohibitive. In these cases, forensic teams can design an audit using a representative random sample whereby the investigation team reviews initially a limited number of files for either liability or fine purposes. For example, counsel and the forensic team may review 500 possibly improper payments, files, or accounting transactions out of a five-year universe of 20,000 or more. If the company is cooperating with the DOJ or SEC, it is wise to consult in advance U.S. authorities to define a representative sample and sampling criteria, for example, by country, by year, or by sensitive practices.

U.S. and foreign investigators can be helpful and cost effective in FCPA investigations. Counsel will want to carefully oversee investigation planning, communications, and expectations. At the outset, counsel should discuss what types of memoranda, analyses, or work papers will be created, which particular team members will prepare them, and what kind of detail or commentary will be expected in any written product. Counsel will want to make sure that any retained investigators conduct investigations or interviews in a legally compliant and ethical way and understand the company's related policies and values.

E. Experts

Experts can be important to a full understanding of an alleged business crime scenario and can be especially important in FCPA investigations. They can tip the scales in close white-collar criminal investigations. For example, in-country lawyers can opine on whether certain conduct is legal under the written laws of the country. Counsel should anticipate the types of experts in the foreign locale that could assist the investigation and explore with the in-country counsel or contact possible sources of witnesses. An in-country expert conversant with English may be much more effective and credible in rendering an opinion on a business issue or practice in his country than an American counterpart would be. He will also usually be less expensive. Counsel should explore with both lay employees and experts whether there are any helpful in-country or regional books, treatises, brochures, or articles. A foreign publication may bring a different and helpful perspective to an FCPA investigation.

Foreign experts frequently view themselves as consultants rather than as trial witnesses. They may view their role at most as providing an affidavit. Therefore, if counsel envisions a need for their testimony, near the outset he will want to obtain the expert's full commitment to travel and give live testimony when and where necessary. As with all court experts, these witnesses need to be thoroughly prepared for cross-examination—frequently a new and challenging experience for foreign nationals.

F. Computers and Support Services

A laptop is essential for lengthy trips or distant investigation work. It is the most effective way to memorialize interviews quickly and communicate with clients, colleagues, and secretaries many time zones away. An airplane adapter kit and extra battery pack also may be useful. It is wise to check out in advance if the overseas client, contact, or law office has a compatible word-processing system and have a contingency plan. Counsel should keep a laptop not in use in a generic bag.

G. Cameras

There is hardly an FCPA investigation that cannot benefit from a digital 35-mm camera (with a modest zoom lens). Photos can capture a manufacturing operation in a dangerous country, a modest office building, or the grandiose headquarters of a tyrannical local bureaucrat. Investigation counsel will want to consult local counsel to see if there are any local or cultural issues with photographing persons or buildings. Quality photographs can portray a foreign business operation or client in a favorable light that an American jury or prosecutor might not otherwise draw.

H. Mobile Phones

In many foreign countries landlines have become extinct, and everyone uses mobile phones. Counsel have four choices overseas: (1) use an international credit card; (2) rent a mobile phone; (3) arrange for the client to lend you one; and (4) buy a mobile with worldwide calling capability. For both business and legal reasons, counsel should be circumspect or, at most, generally descriptive in overseas calls.

I.   Security

The increased risks of foreign travel by U.S. counsel require thought. With relatively few exceptions, Americans enjoy a much higher standard of living than other citizens of the world, and that fact is well known to the less advantaged. In many countries, counsel should carefully think about what they say, what they wear, what they pull out of their pockets (e.g., blue American passport), how and what time of day they venture out, and what they truly need to carry on their person. Lawyers should be particularly cautious about mentioning in public the name of the client or witnesses they are meeting. In third-world countries, American counsel should normally wear comfortable, nondescript clothing and avoid jewelry. One should typically avoid wearing client-logo or USA-marked apparel. Counsel may also want to leave large document carriers or computer bags with the law firm's name and logo back home.

J.   Travel, Lodging, Passport, Vaccinations, and Medicines

Counsel should ensure his passport is current and find out what visas are required and how long they last for the countries to be visited. Some countries will not permit visitors whose passports expire in less than six months. One also needs to check on any recommended or required vaccinations before departure, mindful that some do not take effect for a week or more. Counsel should pack all necessary common and prescription medicines for a trip.

Counsel should be on time for departures as many FCPA investigation destinations have limited flights. Airline clubs are helpful for at least three reasons. First, they are normally cleaner and quieter than the public areas of foreign (and American) airports. Second, they often have business facilities including conference rooms. Third, clubs at many international airports have shower facilities. Ideally, counsel will arrive at a distant destination a day in advance to adjust for the time change, meet the country manager, and be fully prepared and rested.

What matters most for hotel selection are safety, proximity to the client, and business services. A fitness center and a decent restaurant are welcome, but personal security should be foremost in a lodging choice. Hotels and multinational companies routinely have on staff or lists of reliable and knowledgeable drivers who can take one to destinations efficiently and ensure safety.

It is easy and wise to familiarize oneself with host countries, regions, or cities one is visiting. The *Economist* Pocket Series on the world and its regions includes Africa, Asia, Europe, Latin America and the Caribbean, and the Middle East and North Africa. It also publishes detailed county reports that feature political and economic analyses and forecasts and cross-country comparisons (http://www.eiu.com). The CIA and State Department have Web sites with country profiles and travel advisories (http://www.cia.gov and http://www.travel.state.gov). Counsel should also review the Web sites of the foreign governments.

Effective representation in sensitive international investigations requires thorough preparation, patience, persistence, and discretion. The most valuable lessons are often basic, but a misstep in one of them by a partner or associate can quickly derail the objectives of an investigation.

XV. TEN COMMANDMENTS FOR CONDUCTING INTERNAL INVESTIGATIONS OF PUBLIC COMPANIES[54]

The following are ten lessons learned in conducting internal investigations that apply equally to FCPA investigations.

One: Thou Shalt Fully Consider the Scope and Independence of the Client Engagement and Investigation, and Reevaluate as Necessary.

Two: Thou Shalt Take Immediate Steps to Secure and Preserve All Potentially Relevant Documents—Hard and Electronic—and to Make Sure All Appropriate Personnel Are Advised of the Importance of Not Destroying Potentially Relevant Documents.

Three: Thou Shalt Keep the Client Regularly Informed of the Law and the Likely Course, Progress, and Results of an Investigation.

Four: Thou Shalt Take Prompt and Effective Measures to Stop Illegal Conduct.

Five: Thou Shalt Advise Employees and Others of Whom Counsel Represents, to Whom the Attorney-Client Privilege Belongs, and Who May Waive It.

Six: Thou Shalt Be Firm and Fair in Conducting Witness Interviews.

Seven: Thou Shalt Review and Respect All Relevant Laws and Policies.

Eight: Thou Shalt in Representing the Client Remain Mindful of All Audiences and Constituents in Draft Presentations or Reports and Making Recommendations.

Nine: Thou Shalt Discipline Wrongdoers.

Ten: Thou Shalt Implement Effective Remedial Measures and Regularly Review the Progress of Their Implementation.

It can be helpful to revisit and examine these commandments during an investigation.

XVI. ADDITIONAL RESOURCES

American College of Trial Lawyers, *Recommended Practices for Companies and Their Counsel in Conducting Internal Investigations* (Feb. 2008) (Appendix 7).

Block & Barton, *Implications of the Attorney-Client Privilege and Work Product Doctrine*, INTERNAL INVESTIGATIONS (Brian & O'Neill eds., ABA 3rd ed. 2007).

BRIAN & O'NEILL (EDS.), INTERNAL INVESTIGATIONS (ABA 3rd ed. 2007).

The Economist "Pocket" series (2010) (economic and political profiles of regions of the world). *The Economist* also publishes informative country profiles for over 100 countries that can be very helpful in understanding the local government, political, and economic conditions.

Ernst & Young, THE GUIDE TO INVESTIGATING BUSINESS FRAUD (American Institute of Certified Public Accountants 2009).

Finnegan, *Briefly Speaking . . . The First 72 Hours of a Government Investigation*, 11(2) NAT'L LEGAL CTR. (Feb. 2007).

Gaydos, *Gathering and Organizing Relevant Documents: An Essential Task in Any Investigation*, in INTERNAL INVESTIGATIONS (Brian & O'Neill eds., ABA 3rd ed. 2007).

GOLDEN, SKALAK & CLAYTON, A GUIDE TO FORENSIC ACCOUNTING INVESTIGATION (Wiley 2006).

Hengesbaugh & Mensik, *Global Internal Investigations: How to Gather Data and Documents Without Violating Privacy Laws*, 8(7) BNA WORLD DATA PROT. REP. (July 2008).

Muller & Moosmayer, *Responding to a Multi-Jurisdictional Government Investigation: How to Deal with Enforcement Agencies, Minimize Cost and Management Distraction*, presentation at the 20th Annual ACI Conference on the Foreign Corrupt Practices Act Conference, Washington, D.C. (Nov. 18, 2008).

Tarun, *Tarun's Ten Commandments for Conducting Internal Investigations*, in INTERNAL INVESTIGATIONS 2009 (PLI Course Handbook No. B-1745, 2009).

Tarun, *Thirty Countries Later: Lessons of an International Business Crimes Lawyer*, BUS. CRIMES BULL. (Dec. 2001, Jan. 2002).

Turk, *The Interview Process*, in INTERNAL INVESTIGATIONS (Brian & O'Neill eds., ABA 3rd ed. 2007).

Urgenson, *Voluntary Disclosures: Criteria to Determine When to Disclose or Not*, presentation at the 20th Annual ACI Foreign Corrupt Practices Act Conference, Washington, D.C. (Nov. 19, 2008).

WEBB, TARUN & MOLO, CORPORATE INTERNAL INVESTIGATIONS (Law Journal Press 1993–2009).

Winer, Chilton & Virginkar, *International Investigations and the Foreign Corrupt Practices Act*, in THE FOREIGN CORRUPT PRACTICES ACT: COMPLYING WITH HEIGHTENED ENFORCEMENT RULES (PLI Course Handbook 2007).

Young & Nall, *Considerations When Conducting an Internal Investigation*, in THE FOREIGN CORRUPT PRACTICES ACT 2008: COMPLYING WITH HEIGHTENED ENFORCEMENT RISKS (PLI Course Handbook B-1665 2008).

NOTES

1. Dan K. Webb, Robert W. Tarun & Steven F. Molo, *Duties of Management* (ch. 3), *Developing and Implementing a Strategy* (ch. 4), *The Grand Jury* (ch. 12) & *Persuading the Government Not to Indict* (ch. 16), *in* Corporate Internal Investigations (1993–2009).

2. H.R. Rep. No. 95-640, at 18 (1977); Chapter 4 of Don Zarin, Doing Business under the FCPA (2007) has thorough coverage of domestic bribery cases that provide precedent for the Department of Justice in the FCPA area.

3. *See In re John Doe Corp.*, 675 F.2d 482 (2d Cir. 1983) (investigation by accounting firm as part of its audit is not privileged); *In re Grand Jury Subpoena*, 599 F.2d 504, 510 (2d Cir. 1979) (Investigation by management is not privileged).

4. Peter Romatowski & Geoffrey Stewart, *Basics of SEC Investigations: What Every Criminal Lawyer Should Know,* presentation at the National Institute on White Collar Crime 1992, San Francisco (Mar. 2–3, 1992).

5. *See, e.g., SEC v. Gulf & W. Indus. Inc.*, 518 F. Supp. 675, 680–82 (D.D.C. 1981).

6. Am. Coll. of Trial Lawyers, *Recommended Practices for Companies and Their Counsel in Conducting Internal Investigation* (Feb. 2009) (Appendix 7).

7. *See Upjohn Co. v. United States*, 449 U.S. 391, 394–95 (1981) (holding that communications between corporate counsel and tower-level employees for the purpose of seeking legal advice were protected as privileged attorney-client communications).

8. *In re Six Grand Jury Witnesses*, 979 F.2d 939 (2d Cir. 1992).

9. *See In re Salomon Bros. Treasury Litig.*, Fed. Sec. L. Rep. (CCH) 97,254 at 95, 146 (S.D.N.Y. 1992).

10. 214 F.R.D. 113 (S.D.N.Y. 2002).

11. 229 F.R.D. 441 (S.D.N.Y. 2004).

12. *See, e.g., Region Fin. Corp. & Subsidiaries v. United States*, No. 06-00895, 2008 U.S. Dist. LEXIS 41,940 at §§ 27–28 (N.D. Ala., May 8, 2008); *Lawrence E. Jaffe Pension Plan v. Household Int'l, Inc.*, 237 F.R.D. 176, 183 (N.D. Ill. 2006).

13. Substantial parts of this data protection laws discussion come from my colleagues at Baker & McKenzie, Michael Mensik and Brian Hengesbaugh, who authored *Global Internal Investigations: How to Gather Data and Documents without Violating Privacy Laws,* 8 World Data Protection Rep. (BNA) No. 7 (July 2008), *in* The Foreign Corrupt Practices Act: Coping with Heightened Enforcement (PLI 2007 Course Handbook No. B-1619).

14. Ronald W. Staudt & J. Keane, Litigation Support Systems § 6:53 (1992).

15. *Id.* § 6:53.

16. *Id.* § 6:53.

17. *See* Caslon Analytics, *Asia Privacy Guide*, http://www.caslon.com.au/privacyguide6.htm#apec.

18. Directive 95/46/EC § 1.2(a).

19. Russian Federation Law 152-FX, Art. III, Sec. 1 (July 27, 2006).

20. Directive 95/46/EC art. 25.

21. *See* 65 Fed. Reg. 45,666 (July 24, 2000).

22. *Id.* at § 7(a).

23. *See, e.g.,* Russian Federation, Labor Code Art. 81 (listing 14 statutorily permissible causes of termination, of which the refusal to grant consent to personal data processing is not one).

24. *See, e.g.,* European Commission, Model Contracts, http://ec.europa .eu/justice_home/fsj/privacy/modelcontracts/index_en.htm.

25. Hawksworth and Hadsell, "Electronic Evidence" in Ernst & Young, THE GUIDE TO INVESTIGATING BUSINESS FRAUD 160 (AICPA 2009).

26. Counsel must understand the customs and practices of the country in question. For example, a due diligence check with the in-country Chamber of Commerce might strike many Americans as of little value. Yet under the laws of Colombia, the Chamber of Commerce is recognized by statute as the official business registry of the country.

27. *See* Appendix 7.

28. The *Upjohn* warning stems from *Upjohn Co. v. United States,* 449 U.S. 383 (1981).

29. A related hypothetical Working Chronology is at section VIII.B of this chapter.

30. WEBB, TARUN & MOLO, *supra* note 1, at ch. 4, § 4.05[3].

31. FED. R. EVID. 612.

32. *See Redvanly v. Nynex Corp.,* 152 F.R.D. 460 (S.D.N.Y. 1993); *Berkey Photo, Inc. v. Eastman Kodak Co.,* 74 F.R.D. 613, 616 (S.D.N.Y. 1977), *aff'd in part, rev'd in part,* 603 F.2d 263 (2d Cir. 1979), *cert. denied,* 444 U.S. 1093 (1980).

33. *See, e.g.,* Pedowitz, *Conducting and Protecting Internal Corporate Investigations,* BUS. CRIMES BULL.: COMPLIANCE & LITIG. 9 (Mar. 1994).

34. *Id.*

35. The Antitrust Division has issued corporate amnesty policy with clear incentives and rewards.

36. FED. R. EVID. 801(d)(2)(c).

37. Thomas E. Holliday & Charles J. Stevens, *Disclosure of Results of Internal Investigations to the Government or Third Parties, in* INTERNAL INVESTIGATIONS (Brian & McNeil eds., 2d ed. 2003).

38. *See, e.g., In re Subpoena Duces Tecum* (Fulbright & Jaworski), 738 F.2d 1367, 1369.

39. Lawrence Urgenson, Voluntary Disclosures: Criteria to Determine When to Disclose or Not, remarks to the 20th Annual ACI Foreign Corrupt Practices Act Conference, Washington, D.C. (Nov. 19, 2008).

40. *Id.*

41. Press Release, U.S. Dept. of Justice, Siemens AGW Three Subsidiaries Plead Guilty to Foreign Corrupt Practices Act. Violatotions and Agree to Pay $450 million in Combined Criminal Fines (Dec. 15, 2008), www .usdoj-gov/opa/pr/2008/December108-crm-1105.html.

42. *See* Robert W. Tarun, *Thirty Countries Later: Lessons of an International Business Crimes Lawyer*, BUS. CRIMES BULL. I (Dec. 2001–Jan. 2002).

43. Brian Hengesbaugh & Michael Mensik, *Global Internal Investigations: How to Gather Data and Documents Without Violating Privacy Laws*, 8(7) WORLD DATA PROT. REP. (BNA) (July 2008).

44. *Id.*

45. Directive 95/46/EC.

46. Hengesbaugh & Mensik, *supra* note 43.

47. *Id.*

48. *Id.*

49. *SEC v. Willbros Group Inc.*, Civil Action No. 4:08-CV-01494, Litig. Release No. 20,571, (U.S.D.C./S.D. Tex. (Houston Div.), May 14, 2008); *see* Press Release, U.S. Dep't of Justice, Willbros Group Inc. Enters Deferred Prosecution Agreement and Agrees to Pay $22 Million Penalty for FCPA Violations (May 14, 2008), http://www.usdoj.gov/opa/pr/2008/May/08-crm-417.html.

50. *SEC v. Dow Chem. Co.*, Litig. Release No. 20,000, Civil Action No. 07 CV 0033 (D.D.C.) (Feb. 13, 2007).

51. Press Release, U.S. Dep't of Justice, Transcript of Press Conference Announcing Siemens AG and Three Subsidiaries Plead Guilty to Foreign Corrupt Practices Act Violations (Dec. 15, 2008), http://www.usdoj.gov/opa/pr/2008/December/08-opa-1112.html.

52. U.S. Dep't of Justice Sentencing Memorandum filed Dec. 12, 2008, *United States v. Siemens AG*, 1:08-cr-00367-RJL (D.D.C.), *available at* http://www.usdoj.gov/opa/documents/siemens-sentencing-memo.pdf.

53. Much of this advice was first published in a two-part article, *Thirty Countries Later: Lessons of an International Business Crimes Lawyer*, 8(11) BUS. CRIMES BULL. (Dec. 2001) and 9(1) BUS. CRIMES BULL. (Jan. 2002).

54. This section is reprinted with permission of the Practicing Law Institute. Robert W. Tarun, *Tarun's Ten Commandments for Conducting Internal Investigations, in* INTERNAL INVESTIGATIONS 2009 (PLI Course Handbook, Chicago and San Francisco, June 2009) and Ethisphere, which printed a version of the same in its Q3/2009 Issue.

CHAPTER 9

Defending an FCPA Investigation

I. U.S. GOVERNMENT INVESTIGATIONS

The Department of Justice and the Securities and Exchange Commission may jointly or separately initiate and conduct a Foreign Corrupt Practices Act investigation. They are increasingly conducting joint or parallel civil and criminal investigations of the same FCPA allegations and have substantially increased resources dedicated to enforcement of the statute. It has become common for the DOJ and SEC to announce settlements of FCPA investigations simultaneously or within a day or so of each other.

A. Department of Justice

The DOJ is solely responsible for the criminal enforcement of the FCPA. Allegations of FCPA criminal violations are generally investigated by the Federal Bureau of Investigation. The Fraud section of the DOJ's Criminal Division in Washington, D.C, has FCPA expertise and frequently coordinates with the SEC on FCPA matters. The FBI is required by internal regulation to bring alleged FCPA violations to the Fraud Section of the Criminal Division of the DOJ. No prosecution of alleged FCPA violations may be instituted without the express permission of the DOJ Criminal Division in Washington, D.C.[1]

Grand juries have broad latitude and "can investigate merely on suspicion that the law is being violated."[2] Individual clients need to understand, particularly in weighing whether to testify before a grand jury, that decisions to charge a company or its officers and employees with a criminal FCPA violation will be made by the Fraud Section of the Criminal Division in Washington, D.C., not by a grand jury. Justice William O. Douglas most succinctly captured the reality of the grand jury when he observed: "Any experienced prosecutor will admit he can indict anybody at any time for almost anything before any grand jury."[3]

Grand jury investigations normally proceed first with the issuance of subpoenas *duces tecum* for records followed by subpoenas *ad testificandum* for the testimony of witnesses. However, if the government secures early cooperation from a company or individuals, it may ask cooperating companies to voluntarily provide documents and cooperating individuals to meet and record others covertly, and such cooperation may not be immediately public. In criminal investigations it is the custom and practice of the DOJ to advise counsel whether a client is a subject or target. If an individual client is considered a subject or target, the conventional wisdom is he or she should assert a Fifth Amendment privilege in a grand jury proceeding and also decline to be interviewed.[4] This privilege protects individuals and sole proprietorships but not corporations, partnerships, and other business entities. If subpoenaed, corporations will in most investigations have to produce a broad range of documents, subject to primarily the attorney-client privilege.

B.   Securities and Exchange Commission[5]

The Securities and Exchange Commission is the primary regulator of the nation's securities markets. Allegations of civil violations of the antibribery and recordkeeping provisions are investigated by the SEC's Division of Enforcement. In August 2009, the SEC Enforcement Division annouced the creation of a specialized unit dedicated to FCPA enforement. The specialized unit is headed by a Unit Chief and is staffed around the country by SEC staff who already have FCPA expertise as well as new hires who have FCPA experience from the private sector.[6]

The SEC has the authority to bring an action in federal court or before an administrative law judge when it concludes an FCPA violation has occurred and that enforcement is appropriate. The Division and its staff employ attorneys, accountants, and analysts and may proceed on their own initiative to informally investigate without subpoena power, or with subpoena power through a "formal order of investigation" issued privately by the Commission. In 2008 the SEC published an Enforcement Manual, which is available on its Web site at http://www.sec.gov/divisions/enforce/enforcement_manual.pdf.

In informal investigations, SEC enforcement staff ask companies and employees to provide information on a voluntary basis. Interviews can be in person or by telephone and on or off the record. Informal investigations can include extensive document production and sworn testimony. The Division staff may request compilation of data or counsel may elect to submit to the SEC a chronology or similar data. Counsel should understand that while the SEC staff have no authority to compel the production of such data, the voluntary submissions will likely be deemed admissible. [7]

Staff requests for orders for formal investigations are routinely granted by the Commission and are used whenever the staff need subpoena authority to obtain the testimony of persons who are reluctant to appear or production of documents that cannot be obtained voluntarily, such as telephone and bank records. The formal order will describe the investigation in general terms and the suspected statutory violations.

The various federal securities laws grant broad authority to the Commission to conduct investigations.[8] A challenge to the SEC's right to investigate a public company has virtually no chance of success.[9] However, a challenge to the breadth of documents the SEC initially requests or subpoenas has some possibility of success. The scope of such requests is often negotiable with SEC staff. SEC civil enforcement matters may lead to a criminal referral to the Criminal Division.[10] Full access to SEC files is routinely granted to federal prosecutors by the SEC Director of the Division of Enforcement. A U.S. Attorney may independently request access to SEC files.[11]

SEC staff do not use the "subject" or "target" terminology common to federal prosecutors. Defense counsel should normally ask SEC attorneys whether prosecutors have been granted access to SEC files—unless there is a slim likelihood and a concern that merely raising the question could prompt the staff to refer the matter to DOJ. Given the increase in parallel government proceedings, it is today prudent to assume a referral to the DOJ and to ask the question.

Unlike in grand jury proceedings, witnesses who testify in SEC investigative proceedings are entitled to copies of their transcripts upon payment of a fee.[12] Witnesses in SEC proceedings also have a right to assert attorney-client, attorney work product, and Fifth Amendment privileges. However, the Commission may draw an adverse inference from an individual's assertion of the Fifth Amendment privilege, and such an assertion makes an enforcement action highly probable. Still, in most if not all cases, an SEC civil enforcement action is preferable to a DOJ criminal charge. However, when bribery is the subject or focus of an investigation, dual enforcement proceedings by the DOJ and SEC are far more common.

In considering whether to bring an enforcement action, the SEC will ask: "Did the company commit to learn the truth, fully and expeditiously? Did it do a thorough review of the nature, extent, origins, and consequences of the conduct and related behavior?" A public company conducting an internal investigation that is either cooperating with the SEC or intends to disclose the investigation to the SEC should be mindful of this standard.[13]

II.   SOURCES OF ALLEGATIONS

Potential sources of FCPA and, in particular, bribery allegations are many and include:

- Former or current employees
- Public filings
- Investigations of one FCPA matter that leads to discovery of another FCPA matter

- Competitors—often cooperating with one or more governments
- Agents
- Subcontractors
- Foreign government officials or party representatives
- Joint venture partners
- Internal audits
- Federal agency audits (e.g., Department of Defense, Inspector General)
- Media reports tracked through Google searches
- Internet surveillance
- Department of State and Embassy staff
- Acquisition due diligence

Occasionally, an FCPA investigation arises from the federal investigation of another offense, for example, antitrust or money laundering violations.[14]

III.   FACTUAL AND LEGAL DEFENSES TO THE FCPA

A.   The Statute

The FCPA is one of the most convoluted statutes in the federal criminal code and one that in three decades has had remarkably little judicial interpretation. For this reason, there are more untested defense arguments for clients facing FCPA charges than with many other federal statutes. Under the FCPA, defense counsel must pay particular attention to *who* is covered and *in what circumstances* such persons are covered.[15]

The defense strategy may well differ depending on whether counsel represents an issuer, a domestic concern, a foreign firm or citizen, an officer, a director, a stockholder, an employee, or an agent. In representing an issuer, a U.S. corporation, or a foreign company before the DOJ, the broad principles of corporate criminal liability apply, meaning that a corporation is criminally responsible for the acts carried out by its agents within the scope of the agent's employment for the benefit of the corporation.[16] For nonissuers, the SEC will have no jurisdiction.

After identifying under what section(s) a client may face liability, counsel will turn to the *particular facts and circumstances*. Because the statute is complex, convoluted, and without much precedent, and turns on who is acting and the specific facts and circumstances, there remains a significant number of legal and factual defenses available to companies and individuals.

B.   Beyond a Reasonable Doubt

In every criminal prosecution the government has the burden of proving *each* element of the alleged offense(s) beyond a reasonable doubt. If the defense can demonstrate that the government will likely fail to prove any single element beyond a reasonable doubt, it will in most instances be able to dissuade the DOJ from charging the client with the violation. Because most conduct in an FCPA investigation has taken place in a foreign country, and many relevant witnesses and documents are not in the United States, the DOJ's ability to secure reliable, admissible evidence before a U.S. grand or petit jury is usually difficult.

C.   "The Search for Intent"

While defense counsel will attempt to challenge the DOJ's ability to prove every element of a contemplated charge, the element most important to the government in FCPA cases, and the most overriding one if there is questionable or inconclusive evidence, is corrupt intent or evil motive. The legendary Washington, D.C. trial lawyer Robert S. Bennett has aptly described white-collar crime as a "search for intent."[17] In FCPA investigations and trials, it is a search for *corrupt* intent, which search will frequently turn on the transparency of a payment or relationship, direct or indirect, with a foreign government official. While some transactions or relationships will be fully concealed and thus likely corroborative of a corrupt plan or scheme, others will reveal a mixture of visibility and secrecy that can defeat a conclusion of evil motive.

Related books and records entries will often be telltale: a willful mischaracterization of a payment or expense on the company's books can confirm an improper payment scenario. Conversely, a fair or reasonable description of a payment on the company's books and records can belie a criminal motive by a payer or donor. In some investigations the DOJ and SEC cannot establish the payment of a bribe to a foreign official, but they can prove that a related or underlying expense in the books and records of the company is misleading, false, or did not occur, resulting in a "false books and records" charge and resolution. If defense counsel can undermine the corrupt intent proof, it will be a major step in avoiding an FCPA bribery prosecution and possibly books and records and internal controls charges.

D. Outline of FCPA Defenses

Defenses to the FCPA's three central anti-bribery provisions, its false books and records and internal controls provisions, as well as the federal conspiracy statute, are outlined below with the particular defenses italicized.

1.   Defenses Available Under 15 U.S.C. §§ 78dd-1 (Issuers), 78dd-2 (Domestic Concerns), and 78dd-3 (Persons Other than Issuers on Domestic Concerns)

- Lack of *corrupt* intent:
  - _ *Good faith*;
  - _ *Advice of counsel*;[18]
  - _ *Thorough due diligence* of the company in contracting with a third party or acquiring a target;
- Insufficient proof of *"conscious purpose to avoid learning the truth"*;
- Insufficient proof of *direct or actual knowledge*
- Insufficient proof of a payment, gift, offer, or promise of anything of value to a *foreign official, party, party official, or candidate*;
- Insufficient proof of a payment, gift, offer, or promise of anything of value to a *foreign official, foreign political party, or foreign party candidate*;
- Insufficient proof of a payment, gift, offer, or promise of anything of value to a foreign official, party, party official, or candidate for *purposes* of:
  - *(1) Influencing any act or decision of such foreign official in his official capacity; inducing such foreign official to do or omit to do any act* in violation of the lawful duty of the foreign official; *or securing any improper advantage;* or
  - *(2) Inducing a foreign official to use his influence with a foreign government or instrumentality to affect or influence any act or decision* of such government official, in order to assist such person in obtaining or retaining business for or with, or directing business to any person;
- Insufficient proof of a *business nexus* between the bribe *and* obtaining or retaining business;
- Insufficient proof that an *intermediary in fact made a payment, gift, offer, or promise of anything of value* to a foreign official;
- Insufficient proof of *authorization* of payment, gift, offer, or promise of anything of value;
- "Routine government action" exception *(facilitating or expediting payment)*;
- Affirmative defense that the payment, gift, offer, or promise of anything of value that was made was *lawful under the written laws and regulations of the foreign country*;
- Affirmative defense that the payment, gift, offer, or promise of anything of value that was made was *a reasonable and bona fide expenditure*, such as travel and lodging expenses, incurred by or on behalf of a foreign official, party, party official, or candidate and *was directly related to*:
  - *(1) the promotion, demonstration, or explanation of products or services;*
  - *(2) the execution or performance of a contract with a foreign government or agency thereof;*
- Insufficient proof that an *instrumentality* of a foreign government is involved;
- Insufficient proof that a company officer or employee *knew a payment would be passed on to a foreign official, foreign political party or party*

official, or candidate for foreign political office—that is, an awareness that an intermediary was engaging in misconduct, that such circumstance exists or that such result is substantially certain to occur, or that such person has a firm belief that such circumstance exists or that such result is substantially certain to exist;

- *Economic extortion.*[19]

2. **Defenses Available Under 15 U.S.C. § 78dd-3 (Persons Other than Issuers or Domestic Persons)**

- Insufficient proof of a person *while in the territory of the United States* corruptly using the mails or any means of instrumentality of interstate commerce or doing any other act in furtherance of an offer, payment, promise to pay, or authorization of the payment of money, or offer, gift, promise to give, or authorization of the giving of anything of value.

3. **Defenses Available Under 15 U.S.C. § 78m(b)(2)(A) (False Books and Records)**

- Insufficient proof that any book, record, or account was *false*;
- Insufficient proof that a person *knowingly* falsified any book, record, or account;
- The person merely committed *a technical violation*;
- The books and record entries contained *reasonable detail* about the transactions or disposition of assets;
- *Non-public company or issuer.*

4. **Defenses Available Under 15 U.S.C. § 78m(b)(2)(B) (Circumvention or Failure to Implement Internal Controls)**

- Insufficient proof that a person *knowingly circumvented* a system of internal accounting controls;
- Insufficient proof that a person *knowingly failed to implement* a system of internal accounting controls;
- *Non-public company or issuer.*

5. **Defenses Available Under 18 U.S.C. § 371 (Conspiracy)**

- Insufficient proof of an *agreement* by two or more persons to violate the FCPA;
- Insufficient proof of an *overt act in furtherance* of a conspiracy;
- Insufficient proof of a person's *knowing joinder* of a conspiracy;
- *Withdrawal* from the conspiracy.

6. **Statute of Limitations Defenses (All Offenses)[20]**

- Failure to charge *within five years*;
- Failure to *timely obtain a three-year extension* of the statute of limitations to obtain foreign evidence.

IV. NOTICE OF U.S. GOVERNMENT INVESTIGATION

Companies learn of U.S. government investigations in a variety of ways. Occasionally, company officials will learn informally that an employee or officer has been contacted by FBI agents or an SEC staff attorney. Sometimes an internal audit or outside auditors will uncover a problem. Still other times a company can learn of an investigation through the media. Or the company may be served by law enforcement with a federal grand jury subpoena *duces tecum*. Or perhaps most startling, a company may learn that its employees have been arrested at a trade show as a part of an FBI sting operation. The SEC is more likely to serve an informal request on the company, but in some instances the SEC staff will at the outset seek and obtain a formal order from the Commission to begin an investigation. Under any of these scenarios, prudent corporate counsel will respond promptly, preserve company records, gather facts in a privileged fashion so as to fully understand the risks, design a careful and thoughtful strategy, and, as appropriate, implement constructive remedial actions.

V. NOTIFICATION OF EMPLOYEES

When a company is not voluntarily cooperating with the government, it is entitled to advise employees of the possibility of contact by government authorities. Specifically, it can apprise them of the possibility that federal agents may attempt to contact them at work or at home, that they may speak to the agent or refuse to speak to the agent, that they may ask for counsel, that the company may provide them with individual counsel, and that if they choose to speak, they should tell the truth but also not speculate or guess. Most employees have not had the experience of being interviewed by federal law enforcement and are not aware of their rights. Therefore, it usually makes sense to advise officers and employees who are likely to be contacted by federal agents or attorneys of their rights.

VI. BASIC INTERNAL INVESTIGATION STEPS

The five basic steps that apply to a board or audit committee internal investigation of an FCPA allegation (see Chapter 8 at I.A) apply equally to the defense of a grand jury or SEC investigation. The DOJ or SEC can be expected to look into the legal elements and red flags and due diligence step issues discussed at the beginning of Chapter 8. Defense counsel should review not only the same legal elements but also the defenses enumerated in this chapter. The Working Chronology described in the previous chapter is equally helpful in defending a DOJ or SEC investigation. There may, in a defensive context, be a need to meet, coordinate, and consider sharing information with counsel for other officers and employees or entities that may be subjects, targets, or witnesses in a government investigation.[21] The sharing of information and possible strategies is protected under joint defense or common interest privilege case law.[22]

The timetable for the planning and completing of a defense of a company is sometimes accelerated because the fallout of a public FCPA criminal charge or enforcement action can be very serious and the government may impose a short prosecution or deal deadline. The large volume of government FCPA investigations has made this less of a problem recently. Counsel for multinational companies are able in most instances to more quickly and successfully interview employees and foreign third parties and obtain relevant documents than U.S. government agencies. However, this traditional advantage has become less certain with the proliferation of treaties, increased informal cooperation between U.S. and foreign law enforcement agencies, and the incentives of competitors to cooperate with U.S. or foreign governments.

VII. JOINT DEFENSE AGREEMENTS

It is wholly appropriate for a company and officers or employees of a company under an FCPA investigation by the DOJ or SEC to enter a joint defense or common interest agreement whereby they share information and work product in anticipation of litigation. Counsel for a company should however first determine whether there is in fact a common interest with potential parties.

VIII. DEPARTMENT OF JUSTICE CHARGING POLICIES

The ultimate challenge and goal of defense counsel is to persuade the Department of Justice not to indict the client. To do so one must know the factors that federal prosecutors weigh when determining whether to charge individuals and corporations.

In 1980 the Department of Justice first published its *Principles of Federal Prosecution*, which provided uniform charging criteria to federal prosecutors who were considering charges against individuals. In the decade that followed, relatively few corporations were prosecuted. As a result of enhanced corporate criminal penalties and promulgation of the Organizational Sentencing Guidelines in 1990, federal prosecutors began to aggressively pursue corporate malefactors in the 1990s. In February 2000, the DOJ announced its first corporate charging criteria, *infra*, which proved more problematic and controversial. Since then, corporate charging criteria have evolved as a result of both case law and congressional concerns over prosecutorial overreaching. In particular, DOJ corporate charging criteria have been controversial in two respects: invasion of the attorney-client privilege and government interference with the ability of corporate executives to defend themselves.

A. *Federal Principles of Prosecution* (Individuals) (1980)

In deciding whether to charge individuals, federal prosecutors have since 1980 considered: the sufficiency of the evidence, the likelihood of success at trial, the probable deterrent, rehabilitative, and other consequences of conviction, and the adequacy of noncriminal approaches.[23] These factors were first identified in a formal policy statement entitled *Federal Principles of Prosecution*. Defense lawyers for individuals routinely address the above criteria when seeking to avoid charges.

B. Evolution of the DOJ Corporate Prosecution Policy

In February 2000 the Department of Justice issued a Federal Prosecution of Corporations policy that outlined eight factors federal prosecutors should consider in deciding the proper treatment of corporate targets. In January 2003, it clarified its corporate prosecution policy under a revised policy entitled *Federal Prosecution of Business Organizations*[24] with respect to (1) charging employees responsible for misconduct; (2) cooperation of the corporation; (3) alternatives to criminal prosecution; and (4) compliance programs.

In December 2006, then Deputy Attorney General Paul J. McNulty issued the McNulty Memorandum, which superseded and replaced some of the guidance in the *Principles of Federal Prosecution of Business Organizations*.[25] Notably, the McNulty Memorandum addressed the controversial waiver of the corporate attorney-client privilege, which in the view of some defense counsel had often been the driving prerequisite for substantial corporate cooperation credit. The guidance stated that waiver of attorney-client and work product protections was not a prerequisite to a finding that the company has cooperated in a government investigation. The policy made clear that prosecutors might request waiver of attorney-client or work product protections only when there was a legitimate need for the privileged information to fulfill their law enforcement obligations. Signally, a legitimate need was not established by concluding that it was merely desirable or convenient for the DOJ to obtain privileged information. The McNulty Memorandum distinguished witness statements and purely factual interview memoranda (Category I information) from legal advice given to the corporation before, during, and after the underlying misconduct occurred (Category II information). The latter category could be sought by federal prosecutors only in rare circumstances. Criticism of the erosion of the attorney-client privilege led in 2008 to a discontinuation of Category II information subject to narrow exceptions and formal amendment and inclusion of the corporate charging in the *Department of Justice Manual*.[26]

C.   Amendments to *DOJ Manual* 9-28.000 (2008)

In August 2008, then Deputy Attorney General Mark R. Filip addressed criticisms of DOJ attorney-client privilege waiver demands and interference with the right to and payment of counsel, and further refined prior DOJ corporate charging criteria by announcing future revisions.[27] The nine current DOJ corporate charging criteria that are formal amendments to the *DOJ Manual* are:

1.   The nature and seriousness of the offense, including the risk of harm to the public, and applicable policies and priorities, if any, governing the prosecution of corporations for particular categories of crime;
2.   The pervasiveness of wrongdoing within the corporation, including the complicity in, or the condoning of, the wrongdoing by corporate management;
3.   The corporation's history of similar misconduct, including prior criminal, civil, and regulatory enforcement actions against it;
4.   The corporation's timely and voluntary disclosure of wrongdoing and its willingness to cooperate in the investigation of its agents;
5.   The existence and effectiveness of the corporation's preexisting compliance program;
6.   The corporation's remedial actions, including any efforts to implement an effective corporate compliance program or to improve an existing one, to replace responsible management, to discipline or terminate wrongdoers, to pay restitution, and to cooperate with the relevant government agencies;
7.   Collateral consequences, including whether there is disproportionate harm to shareholders, pension holders, employees, and others not proven personally culpable, as well as influence on the public arising from the prosecution;
8.   The adequacy of the prosecution of individuals responsible for the corporation's malfeasance; and
9.   The adequacy of remedies such as civil or regulatory enforcement actions.[28]

The complete *DOJ Manual* amendments and commentary are contained in Appendix 8.

IX. SECURITIES AND EXCHANGE COMMISSION CHARGING POLICIES

A.   October 2001 SEC Statement on the Relationship of Cooperation to Agency Enforcement Decisions (*Seaboard*)

The SEC has similarly issued a charging policy that provides companies and their counsel a better understanding of its civil enforcement charging criteria. Specifically, in October 2001, the SEC issued a Statement on the Relationship of Cooperation to Agency Enforcement Decisions, which set forth the civil law enforcement agency's policy for evaluating the impact of a company's cooperation in determining whether or not to bring an enforcement action.[29] The policy, announced in a 21(a) report popularly known now as the *Seaboard* Report, applies to all matters within SEC jurisdiction, including the FCPA. Companies considering self-reporting any matter to the SEC should consider carefully the implications of this SEC policy. In the *Seaboard* opinion, the SEC identified 13 criteria it will consider in determining whether, and how much, to credit self-policing, self-reporting, remediation, and cooperation:

1. What is the nature of the misconduct involved? Did it result from inadvertence, honest mistake, simple negligence, reckless or deliberate indifference to indicia of wrongful conduct, willful misconduct, or unadorned venality? Were the company's auditors misled?

2. How did the misconduct arise? Is it the result of pressure placed on employees to achieve specific results, or a tone of lawlessness set by those in control of the company? What compliance procedures were in place to prevent the misconduct now uncovered? Why did those procedures fail to stop or inhibit the wrongful conduct?

3. Where in the organization did the misconduct occur? How high up in the chain of command was knowledge of, or participation in, the misconduct? Did senior personnel participate in, or turn a blind eye toward, obvious indicia of misconduct? How systemic was the behavior? Is it symptomatic of the way the entity does business, or was it isolated?

4. How long did the misconduct last? Was it a one-quarter, or one-time, event, or did it last several years? In the case of a public company, did the misconduct occur before the company went public? Did it facilitate the company's ability to go public?

5. How much harm has the misconduct inflicted upon investors and other corporate constituencies? Did the share price of the company's stock drop significantly upon its discovery and disclosure?

6. How was the misconduct detected and who uncovered it?

7. How long after discovery of the misconduct did it take to implement an effective response?

8. What steps did the company take upon learning of the misconduct? Did the company immediately stop the misconduct? Are persons responsible for any misconduct still with the company? If so, are they still in the same positions? Did the company promptly, completely, and effectively disclose the existence of the misconduct to the public, to regulators, and to self-regulators?

Did the company cooperate completely with appropriate regulatory and law enforcement bodies? Did the company identify what additional related misconduct is likely to have occurred? Did the company take steps to identify the extent of damage to investors and other corporate constituencies? Did the company appropriately recompense those adversely affected by the conduct?

9. What processes did the company follow to resolve many of these issues and ferret out necessary information? Were the audit committee and the board of directors fully informed? If so, when?

10. Did the company commit to learn the truth, fully and expeditiously? Did it do a thorough review of the nature, extent, origins, and consequences of the conduct and related behavior? Did management, the board, or committees consisting solely of outside directors oversee the review? Did company employees or outside persons perform the review? If outside persons, had they done other work for the company? Where the review was conducted by outside counsel, had management previously engaged such counsel? Were scope limitations placed on the review? If so, what were they?

11. Did the company promptly make available to our staff the results of its review and provide sufficient documentation reflecting its response to the situation? Did the company identify possible violative conduct and evidence with sufficient precision to facilitate prompt enforcement actions against those who violated the law? Did the company produce a thorough and probing written report detailing the findings of its review? Did the company voluntarily disclose information our staff did not directly request and otherwise might not have uncovered? Did the company ask its employees to cooperate with our staff and make all reasonable efforts to secure such cooperation?

12. What assurances are there that the conduct is unlikely to recur? Did the company adopt and ensure enforcement of new and more effective internal controls and procedures designed to prevent a recurrence of the misconduct? Did the company provide our staff with sufficient information for it to evaluate the company's measures to correct the situation and ensure that the conduct does not recur?

13. Is the company the same company in which the misconduct occurred, or has it changed through a merger or bankruptcy reorganization?[30]

These criteria are nonexhaustive or limiting on the SEC.[31] Moreover, the fact that a company has satisfied all of the criteria does not guarantee that the SEC will refrain from taking enforcement action. Instead, the SEC has stated, "there may be circumstances where conduct is so egregious and harm so great that no amount of cooperation or other mitigating conduct can justify a decision not to bring any enforcement action at all.[32] The *Seaboard* criteria will be used to determine how much credit to give a company for its cooperation "from the extraordinary step of taking no enforcement action to bringing reduced charges, seeking lighter sanctions, or including mitigating language in documents [used] to announce or resolve actions."[33]

As with the DOJ, one of the most sensitive issues related to the SEC's cooperation policy involves the potential waiver of the attorney-client and/or work product privileges with respect to a company's internal investigation materials. Once a company crosses that threshold, it may be very difficult to limit the scope of the waiver. To illustrate, privileged materials turned over to the SEC will routinely be turned over to other law enforcement agencies, like the DOJ, and may be available to civil plaintiffs through discovery. The SEC has recognized this issue, and has gone so far as to advocate that disclosure of privileged information to the SEC does not constitute a waiver of privilege as to third parties.[34] Still, serious doubts remain as to whether federal courts will accept a limited waiver argument.

The SEC's *Seaboard* policy raises a number of important issues for companies that have discovered potential corporate misconduct. In each case, the decision to cooperate and voluntarily disclose sensitive information to the government requires careful and thorough analysis of the legal issues (including the potential criminal, enforcement, and private litigation exposure) and as complete an understanding of all relevant facts as possible. Because the benefits of cooperation can decrease in time, management and counsel must move quickly upon the discovery of potential misconduct to put themselves in a position to make fully informed disclosure and cooperation decisions.

B. January 2010 SEC Policy Statement Concerning Cooperation by Individuals in Its Investigations and Related Enforcement Actions.[35]

1. *Overview*

In January 2010, the Securities and Exchange Commission announced a series of measures to strengthen its enforcement program by encouraging greater cooperation from individuals and companies in the agency's investigations and enforcement actions.[36] The SEC cooperation initiative clarifies incentives for individuals and companies to cooperate and assist with SEC investigations and enforcement actions and is intended to achieve early assistance in identifying the scope, participants, victims, and ill-gotten gains associated with fraudulent schemes.

To improve the quality, quantity, and timeliness of information and assistance it receives, the SEC approved several measures. First, the Division of Enforcement authorized its staff to use various tools to encourage individuals and companies to report violations and provide assistance to the agency. The tools are laid out in a revised version of the Division's enforcement manual[37] in a new section entitled "Fostering Cooperation." The SEC acknowledges that similar cooperation tools have been used by the DOJ in investigations and prosecutions. The cooperation tools, not previously formally recognized or available in SEC enforcement matters, include:

- Cooperation Agreements—Formal written agreements in which the Enforcement Division agrees to recommend to the Commission that a cooperator receive credit for cooperating in investigations or related enforcement actions if the cooperator provides substantial assistance such as full and truthful information and testimony.[38]
- Deferred Prosecution Agreements—Formal written agreements in which the Commission agrees to forego an enforcement action against a cooperator if the individual or company agrees, among other things, to cooperate fully and truthfully and to comply with express prohibitions and undertakings during a period of deferred prosecution.[39]
- Non-Prosecution Agreements—Formal written agreements, entered into under limited and appropriate circumstances, in which the Commission agrees not to pursue an enforcement action against a cooperator if the individual or company agrees, among other things, to cooperate fully and truthfully and comply with express undertakings.[40]

Second, the SEC streamlined the process for submitting witness immunity requests to the DOJ for witnesses who have the capacity to assist in its investigations and related enforcement actions. Specifically, the Commission has delegated authority to the Director of the Division of Enforcement to submit witness immunity order requests to the DOJ for witnesses who have provided or have the potential to provide substantial assistance in SEC investigations.

Third, the Commission stated, for the first time, the way in which it will evaluate whether, how much, and in what matter to credit cooperation by individuals to ensure that potential cooperation arrangements maximize the Commission's law enforcement interests. This pronouncement is similar to the so-called "Seaboard Report," *supra*, that was issued in 2001 and detailed the factors the SEC considers when evaluating cooperation by companies.

In the January 2010-issued policy statement, the SEC identified four general considerations:

- The assistance provided by the cooperating individual.
- The importance of the underlying matter in which the individual cooperated.

- The societal interest in ensuring the individual is held accountable for his or her misconduct.
- The appropriateness of cooperation credit based upon the risk profile of the cooperating individual.

2.   Four Cooperation Credit Consideration Factors.[41]

The Policy Statement recognizes there is an array of options available to the SEC to encourage, facilitate, and reward cooperation by individuals, ranging from taking no enforcement action to pursuing reduced charges and sanctions in connection with enforcement actions. Although the evaluation of cooperation requires a case-by-case analysis of the specific circumstances presented, the Commission announced that its general approach will be to determine whether, how much, and in what manner to credit cooperation by individuals by evaluating four considerations: (1) the assistance provided by the cooperating individual in the Commission's investigation or related enforcement actions ("Investigation"); (2) the importance of the underlying matter in which the individual cooperated; (3) the societal interest in ensuring that the cooperating individual is held accountable for his or her misconduct; and (4) the appropriateness of cooperation credit based upon the profile of the cooperating individual. The specific criteria to be utilized in evaluating these four considerations are:

(a) *Assistance provided by the individual.* The Commission assesses the assistance provided by the cooperating individual in the investigation by considering, among other things:

(1) The value of the individual's cooperation to the investigation including, but not limited to:

  (i) Whether the individual's cooperation resulted in substantial assistance to the investigation;

  (ii) The timeliness of the individual's cooperation, including whether the individual was first to report the misconduct to the Commission or to offer his or her cooperation in the investigation, and whether the cooperation was provided before he or she had any knowledge of a pending investigation or related action;

  (iii) Whether the investigation was initiated based on information or other cooperation provided by the individual;

  (iv) The quality of cooperation provided by the individual, including whether the cooperation was truthful, complete, and reliable; and

  (v) The time and resources conserved as a result of the individual's cooperation in the investigation.

(2) The nature of the individual's cooperation in the Investigation including, but not limited to:

    (i) Whether the individual's cooperation was voluntary or required by the terms of an agreement with another law enforcement or regulatory organization;

    (ii) The types of assistance the individual provided to the Commission;

    (iii) Whether the individual provided non-privileged information; which information was not requested by the staff or otherwise might not have been discovered;

    (iv) Whether the individual encouraged or authorized others to assist the staff who might not have otherwise participated in the investigation; and

    (v) Any unique circumstances in which the individual provided the cooperation.

(b) *Importance of the underlying matter.* The Commission assesses the importance of the Investigation in which the individual cooperated by considering, among other things:

(1) The character of the Investigation including, but not limited to:

    (i) Whether the subject matter of the Investigation is a Commission priority;

    (ii) The type of securities violations;

    (iii) The age and duration of the misconduct;

    (iv) The number of violations; and

    (v) The isolated or repetitive nature of the violations.

(2) The dangers to investors or others presented by the underlying violations involved in the Investigation including, but not limited to:

    (i) The amount of harm or potential harm caused by the underlying violations;

    (ii) The type of harm resulting from or threatened by the underlying violations; and

    (iii) The number of individuals or entities harmed.[42]

(c) *Interest in holding the individual accountable.* The Commission assesses the societal interest in holding the cooperating individual fully accountable for his or her misconduct by considering, among other things:

(1) The severity of the individual's misconduct assessed by the nature of the violations and in the context of the individual's knowledge, education, training, experience, and position of responsibility at the time the violations occurred;

(2) The culpability of the individual, including, but not limited to, whether the individual acted with scienter, both generally and in relation to others who participated in the misconduct;

(3) The degree to which the individual tolerated illegal activity including, but not limited to, whether he or she took steps to prevent the violations from occurring or continuing, such as notifying the Commission or other appropriate law enforcement agency of the misconduct or, in the case of a violation involving a business organization, by notifying members of management not involved in the misconduct, the board of directors or the equivalent body not involved in the misconduct, or the auditors of such business organization of the misconduct;

(4) The efforts undertaken by the individual to remediate the harm caused by the violations including, but not limited to, whether he or she paid or agreed to pay disgorgement to injured investors and other victims or assisted these victims and the authorities in the recovery of the fruits and instrumentalities of the violations; and

(5) The sanctions imposed on the individual by other federal or state authorities and industry organizations for the violations involved in the Investigation.

(d) *Profile of the individual.* The Commission assesses whether, how much, and in what manner it is in the public interest to award credit for cooperation, in part, based upon the cooperating individual's personal and professional profile by considering, among other things:

(1) The individual's history of lawfulness, including complying with securities laws or regulations;

(2) The degree to which the individual has demonstrated an acceptance of responsibility for his or her past misconduct; and

(3) The degree to which the individual will have an opportunity to commit future violations of the federal securities laws in light of his or her occupation—including, but not limited to, whether he or she serves as: a licensed individual, such as an attorney or accountant; an associated person of a regulated entity, such as a broker or dealer; a fiduciary for other individuals or entities regarding financial matters; an officer or director of public companies; or a member of senior management—together with any existing or proposed safeguards based upon the individual's particular circumstances.

3. Five Cooperation Tools

The Policy Statement recognizes five cooperation tools and discusses the basics, procedures, considerations, and related consideration for each of the five tools. Below are the SEC's basic definitions and considerations for each:

a.   Proffer Agreements[43]

A proffer agreement is a written agreement providing that any statements made by a person, on a specific date, may not be used against that individual in subsequent proceedings, except that the Commission may use statements made during the proffer session as a source of leads to discover additional evidence and for impeachment or rebuttal purpose if the person testifies or argues inconsistently in a subsequent proceeding. The Commission also may share the information provided by the proffering individual with appropriate authorities in a prosecution for perjury, making a false statement, or obstruction of justice. The Policy Statement expresses the following consideration with regard to Proffer Agreements:

- In most cases, the SEC staff will require a potential cooperating individual to make a detailed proffer before selecting and utilizing other cooperation tools.
- The Commission may use information provided at a proffer session to advance its investigation or to generate leads to new evidence that the staff might not have otherwise discovered.
- To avoid potential misunderstandings regarding the nature of proffers sessions; with few exceptions, proffer sessions will be conducted pursuant to written proffer agreements.
- The SEC staff uses a standard proffer agreement, and modifications to the standard agreement will normally only be made after consultations with staff in the Office of Chief Counsel or the Chief Litigation Counsel.
- If the SEC staff conducts a joint proffer session with the DOJ or other criminal authorities, the staff will address any potential substantive or procedural issues with his or her supervisors, as well as the Assistant United States Attorney or state prosecutor on the case, before the proffer begins. In cases where the SEC staff participates in a proffer with the criminal authorities and the cooperating individual has not asked for a proffer letter from the Commission, the staff is directed to remind the individual that the proffer agreement with the criminal authorities does not apply to the Commission.

The SEC Enforcement Manual contains a sample proffer agreement.[44]

b.   Cooperation Agreements[45]

A cooperation agreement is a written agreement between the Division of Enforcement and a potential cooperating individual or company prepared to provide substantial assistance to the Commission's investigation and related enforcement actions. Specifically, under a cooperation agreement, the Division agrees to recommend to the Commission that the individual or company receive credit for cooperating in its investigation and related enforcement actions and, under certain circumstances, to make specific enforcement recommendations if, among other things: (1) the Division concludes that the individual or company has provided or is likely to provide substantial assistance to the Commission; (2) the individual or company agrees to cooperate truthfully and fully in the Commission's investigation and related enforcement actions and waive the applicable statute of limitations; and (3) the individual or company satisfies his/her/its obligations under the agreement. If the agreement is violated, the SEC staff may recommend an enforcement action to the Commission against the individual or company without any limitation. The Policy Statement expresses the following considerations with respect to cooperation agreements:

> In addition to the standard cooperation analysis in the SEC Enforcement Manual, when assessing whether to recommend that the Division enter into a cooperation agreement with an individual or company, the staff is to consider:

- Whether other means of obtaining the desired cooperation are available and likely to be timely and effective; and
- Whether the individual or company has entered into or is likely to enter into a plea agreement with criminal prosecutors that will require the individual or company to cooperate in the Commission's investigation and related enforcement actions.

The staff advises potential cooperating individuals or companies that cooperation agreements entered into with the Division do not bind the Commission and that the Division cannot, and does not, make any promise or representation as to whether or how the Commission may act on enforcement recommendations made by the Division.

- Cooperation agreements will generally include the following terms:
    - The cooperating individual or company agrees to cooperate truthfully and fully, as directed by the Division's staff, in investigations and related enforcement proceedings, including, but not limited to, producing all potentially relevant non-privileged documents and materials to the Commission, responding to all inquiries, appearing for interviews, and testifying at trials and other judicial proceedings as requested by the staff, and waiving the territorial limits on service contained in Rule 45 of the Federal Rules of Civil Procedure;
    - The cooperating individual or company agrees to waive the applicable statute of limitations period;
    - The cooperating individual or company agrees not to violate the securities laws;

- The cooperating individual or company acknowledges that the agreement does not constitute a final disposition of any potential enforcement action;
- The Division will bring the assistance provided by the cooperating individual or company to the attention of the Commission and other regulatory and law enforcement authorities requested by the cooperating individual or company; and
- The cooperating individual or company acknowledges that, although the Division has discretion to make enforcement recommendations, only the Commission has the authority to approve enforcement dispositions and accept settlement offers.

- If the Division agrees to make a specific enforcement recommendation to the Commission, the staff is to consider the settlement terms of other similar cases to identify prior precedent involving similar alleged misconduct and include the following terms in the cooperation agreement:
  - The federal securities laws alleged to have been violated;
  - The cooperating individual or company agrees to resolve the matter without admitting or denying the alleged violations;
  - The specific enforcement recommendation the Division expects to make if the cooperating individual or company satisfies the terms of the agreement; and
  - Any agreement to make a specific enforcement recommendation to the Commission shall be conditioned upon the Division's assessment that the cooperating individual or company has rendered substantial assistance in a Commission investigation or related enforcement action.
- The Division uses a standard form of cooperation agreement that is adapted to the specific circumstances of the investigation or related enforcement action.

c. Deferred Prosecution Agreements[46]

A deferred prosecution agreement (DPA) is a written agreement between the Commission and a potential cooperating individual or company in which the Commission agrees to forego an enforcement action against the individual or company if the individual or company agrees to, among other things: (1) cooperate truthfully and fully in the Commission's investigation and related enforcement actions; (2) enter into a long-term tolling agreement; (3) comply with express prohibitions and/or undertakings during a period of deferred prosecution; and (4) under certain circumstances, agree either to admit or not to contest underlying facts that the Commission could assert to establish a violation of the federal securities laws. If the agreement is violated during the period of deferred prosecution, the staff may recommend an enforcement action to the Commission against the individual or company without limitation for the original misconduct as well as any additional misconduct. Furthermore, if the Commission authorizes the enforcement action, the staff may use any factual admissions made by the cooperating individual or company to file a motion for summary judgment, while maintaining the ability to bring an enforcement action for any additional misconduct at a later date.

The Policy Statement expresses the following considerations with respect to DPAs:

- To determine whether to recommend that the Commission enter into a deferred prosecution agreement, the staff should use the standards cooperation analysis set forth in the SEC Enforcement Manual.
- An admission or an agreement not to contest the relevant facts underlying the alleged offenses generally is appropriate and should be carefully considered for the following:
  - Licensed individuals, such as attorneys and accountants;
  - Regulated individuals, such as registered brokers or dealers;
  - Fiduciaries for other individuals or entities regarding financial matters;
  - Officers and directors of public companies; and
  - Individuals or companies with a prior history of violating the securities laws.
- A deferred prosecution agreement will generally include the following terms:
  - The cooperating individual or company agrees to cooperate truthfully and fully, as directed by the Division's staff, in investigations and related enforcement proceedings including, but not limited to, producing all potentially relevant non-privileged documents and materials to the Commission, responding to all inquiries, appearing for interviews, and testifying at trials and other judicial proceedings as requested by staff, and waiving the territorial limits on service contained in Rule 45 of the Federal Rules of Civil Procedure;
  - The cooperating individual or company agrees to toll the applicable statute of limitations period;
  - The cooperating individual or company agrees not to violate the securities laws;
  - The cooperating individual or company shall make any agreed upon disgorgement or penalty payments;
  - If the cooperating individual or company satisfies the terms of the deferred prosecution agreement during the term of the agree-

ment, the Commission will not pursue any further enforcement action concerning the matter referenced in the agreement;

- If the individual or company violates the agreement during its term, the Division may recommend and the Commission may pursue an enforcement action against the individual or company without limitation;

- The cooperating individual or company agrees that the Commission may use statements, information, and materials provided pursuant to the agreement against him/her/it if the individual or company violates the terms of the agreement; and

- Additional prohibitions and undertakings designed to protect the investing public.

- The term of a deferred prosecution agreement will normally not exceed five years. In determining the appropriate term, the staff is to consider whether there is sufficient time to ensure that the undertakings in the agreement are fully implemented and the related prohibitions have adequately reduced the likelihood of future securities law violations.

d. Non-Prosecution Agreements[47]

A non-prosecution agreement (NPA) is a written agreement between the Commission and a potential cooperating individual or company, entered into in limited and appropriate circumstances, that provides that the Commission will not pursue an enforcement action against the individual or company if the individual or company agrees to, among other things: (1) cooperate truthfully and fully in the Commission's investigation and related enforcement actions; and (2) comply, under certain circumstances, with express undertakings. If the agreement is violated, the staff retains its ability to recommend an enforcement action to the Commission against the individual or company without limitation.

The Policy Statement expresses the following considerations with respect to NPAs.

- In virtually all cases, for individuals who have previously violated the federal securities laws, non-prosecution agreements will not be appropriate and other cooperation tools should be considered.

- Non-prosecution agreements should not be entered into in the early stages of an investigation when the role of the cooperating individuals or companies and the importance of their cooperation are unclear.

- In addition to the standard cooperation analysis set forth in the SEC Enforcement Manual, when attempting to determine whether to recommend that the Commission enter into a non-prosecution agreement, the staff should consider:

- Whether the individual or company has entered into or is likely to enter into a plea agreement with criminal prosecutors that will require them to cooperate in the Commission's investigation and related enforcement actions; and
- Whether other means of obtaining the desired cooperation are available and likely to be timely and effective.
- A non-prosecution agreement will generally include the following terms:
  - The cooperating individual or company agrees to cooperate truthfully and fully, as directed by the Division's staff, in investigations and related enforcement proceedings including, but not limited to, producing all potentially relevant non-privileged documents and materials to the Commission, responding to all inquiries, appearing for interviews, and testifying at trials and other judicial proceedings as requested by the staff, and waiving the territorial limits on service contained in Rule 45 of the Federal Rules of Civil Procedure;
  - The cooperating individual or company shall make any agreed-upon disgorgement or penalty payments;
  - Additional undertakings designed to protect the investing public; and
  - If the individual or company violates the agreement, the Division may recommend and the Commission may pursue an enforcement action against the individual or company without limitation and not subject to the applicable statute of limitations; and
  - The cooperating individual or company agrees that the Commission may use statements, information, and materials provided pursuant to the agreement against him/her/it if the individual or company violates the terms of the agreement.

e.   Immunity Requests[48]

In many circumstances, individuals may not be willing to provide testimony or cooperate without receiving protection against criminal prosecution. Experienced defense counsel will seek this protection before a client makes a statement of cooperation. To obtain testimony and/or facilitate cooperation that will substantially assist in the enforcement of the federal securities laws, the SEC staff may seek immunity orders or letters in order to obtain testimony and/or witness cooperation.

When witnesses assert their Fifth Amendment privilege against self-incrimination in enforcement proceedings, the Commission may seek one of two types of immunity: statutory immunity or letter immunity. Statutory immunity permits the Commission, pursuant to 18 U.S.C. Sections 6001–6004, to seek a court order compelling the individual to give testimony or provide other information that may be necessary to the public interest, if the request is approved by the U.S. Attorney General. In contrast, letter immunity is immunity conferred by agreement between the individual and a U.S. Attorney's Office. Both types of immunity prevent the use of statements or other information provided by the individual, directly or indirectly, against the individual in any criminal case, except for perjury, giving a false statement, or obstruction of justice. Neither an immunity order nor an immunity letter, however, prevent the Commission from using the testimony or other information provided by the individual in its enforcement actions, including actions against the individual for whom the immunity order or letter was issued. The staff are encouraged to seek a proffer from potential immunity candidates.

The Policy Statement provides the following considerations with respect to immunity:

- As a general rule, immunity orders or letters will not be requested in the early stages of an investigation when the role of the cooperating individuals and the benefits of their cooperation may be unclear.
- Pursuant to 18 U.S.C. Sections 6001–6004, an immunity order will be sought only if:
  - The testimony or other information from the witness may be necessary to the public interest; and
  - The witness has refused, or is likely to refuse, to testify or provide other information on the basis of his or her privilege against self-incrimination.
- When attempting to determine whether to recommend that an immunity order or letter be sought, the staff will conduct the standard analysis set forth in the SEC Enforcement Manual.
- Since the Supreme Court has interpreted the Fifth Amendment privilege against self-incrimination to include the act of producing business records by a sole proprietorship, the Commission may request immunity for the limited purpose of obtaining such documents. *United States v. Doe*, 456 U.S. 605 (1984). However, the witness immunity request form submitted to the DOJ should expressly state the purpose of the application.

Both DPAs and NPAs must be approved by the Commission. The Commission has again delegated responsibility for securing immunity from the DOJ to the Director of the Division of Enforcement.

f.   Publicity

Under the new policy, the SEC staff are urged to provide sufficient information to the public about the nature of the Commission's cooperation program and its significant benefits. However, the staff retains discretion regarding whether and how to disclose the fact, manner, and extent of an individual or company's cooperation in documents filed or issued by the Commission in connection with an enforcement action.

4. Conclusion

The January 2010 SEC Policy Statement on Cooperation defines and formalizes "tools" or incentives that have long been recognized and utilized in DOJ investigations of individuals. To the extent that many FCPA investigations of public companies are joint or parallel investigations of the DOJ and SEC, it is useful for both to have similar definitions of tools or incentives they can offer individuals and to avoid past situations where some SEC staff were uncomfortable discussing cooperation guidelines with defense counsel. The policy statement is likely to reduce the stalemates where SEC staff have been able to offer less assurance on policies than their DOJ counterparts to defense counsel representing individuals in joint proceedings. It will also expedite immunity requests where both DOJ prosecutors and SEC staff desire to offer individuals immunity. Finally, as with DOJ charging policies, this SEC policy gives defense counsel a clear set of criteria to address and satisfy in order to secure favorable treatment for clients, e.g., non-prosecution agreement or immunity.

X. WELLS SUBMISSIONS, POSITION PAPERS, AND POWERPOINT PRESENTATIONS

At the conclusion of a DOJ or SEC investigation, a company or its officers will often submit a position paper outlining why no prosecution or enforcement action is necessary or appropriate. This filing with the SEC is known as a Wells submission.[49] Within the Department of Justice and U.S. Attorney's offices, preindictment submissions are commonly called white papers or position papers. In complex criminal or enforcement matters, these submissions commonly exceed 50 pages. In such instances, three-to-five-page executive summaries are recommended.

A. Wells Submissions

The SEC rules provide that its enforcement staff may "advise [defendants] of the general nature of the investigation, including the indicated violations as they pertain to them, and the amount of time that may be available for preparing and submitting a statement prior to the presentation of a staff recommendation to the Commission for the commencement of an administrative or injunction proceeding."[50] The deadlines can be short. Unlike position papers with Department of Justice attorneys, Wells submissions are made in a context different from offers of settlement and negotiations and may be used as evidence in a subsequent proceeding.

The original Wells release in 1972 envisioned that the submissions would focus on questions of policy and occasionally questions of law,[51] because the Commission carefully considers the legal implications and messages to the securities marketplace that each enforcement action communicates. Still, the practice has become that many Wells submissions to the SEC address factual issues, credibility of witnesses, and evidentiary matters, as well as policy and legal implications. Counsel will customarily address in a Wells submission the nature of relief that the SEC is likely seeking.

B. Position Papers

Position papers can persuade federal prosecutors to decline criminal cases, bring less serious charges, or offer deferred prosecution or non-prosecution agreements. DOJ attorneys typically agree that a written presentation will not waive applicable privileges and will not be used directly against a later defendant as an admission. There are no specific guidelines on position papers. What most defense counsel review in these papers are the charging criteria addressed in the *Federal Principles of Prosecution* and the *DOJ Manual* combining the most recent corporate charging criteria (Appendix 8). Most responsible prosecutors are willing to share their legal theories and view of the government evidence at the conclusion of an investigation and to give defense counsel an opportunity to make an oral or written presentation outlining why charges should not be brought or why more lenient charges are appropriate.

C. PowerPoint Presentations

Where a group of DOJ or SEC supervisors is considering the prosecutorial or enforcement merits of a matter under investigation, counsel representing a company or an executive under investigation may wish to offer a PowerPoint presentation to the DOJ and/or SEC. A 20-to-30-slide presentation with charts or graphs can highlight key defense themes, factual weaknesses, problematic legal issues, and remedial measures. A visual presentation often will better sustain the attention of a large audience. As with all PowerPoint presentations, careful and accurate wording, thoughtful organization, and powerful graphics will improve the impact. A position paper or letter can follow and address issues raised by the DOJ or SEC during a PowerPoint presentation.

D. General Advice

Before submitting a Wells submission to the SEC or a position paper to the Fraud Section, or offering an FCPA PowerPoint or oral presentation, counsel for the company or executives must (1) determine what issues remain at the forefront for the prosecutors or regulators so as to address them and only them; and (2) again ascertain whether the government attorneys have an "open mind" about the issues and the merits of an enforcement action or prosecution. If they do not, there may be no advantage in detailing or foretelling the company's strategy or defense theory. If the underlying investigation has been thorough and focused, counsel for the company or individuals will normally have as great a mastery of key witnesses, documents, and in-country issues as the government attorneys. It is wise during a government investigation to outline or draft a Wells submission or position paper early since the DOJ and SEC may give the defense a short opportunity to submit views and arguments—and counsel should assume there will be only one real opportunity to present.

An effective presentation will usually marshal factual, legal, and policy arguments as to why a DOJ prosecution or an SEC enforcement action is inappropriate in a particular case.[52] In addressing the alleged FCPA transactions and activities at issue, the factual component will frequently focus on the knowledge element of the participants, that is, whether the company's employees knew with a high probability that a payment or offer would be made, whether there existed corrupt intent, and so on. The presentation may also discuss the transaction documentation, due diligence efforts, the absence of red flags, and the presence of an effective compliance program—all of which may defeat the "high probability of knowledge" threshold set forth in the FCPA.

E.   Timing

The timing of a presentation to the Fraud Section or SEC is important. If it is too early, the government will say it is premature, and counsel may address matters not at issue or, worse yet, raise problems unknown to the government. If it is too late, it may fall on deaf ears. One has to carefully track the progress of the grand jury investigation and maintain communication with prosecutors in order to determine the optimal time to address the real remaining issues. Defense counsel should maintain a dialogue with Fraud Section attorneys in Washington, D.C., in order to understand what they consider the central factual and/or legal FCPA issues. Those key issues should be addressed in the defense presentation along with other legal and factual defenses the government may not have fully considered.

F.   The "Bribery Is Accepted and Routine There" Defense

In FCPA investigations, in-country managers often assert "the company conducted business in a foreign country where corrupt practices are routine and long established, and there was no other practical way to do business and compete." This argument simply will not succeed, with either the DOJ or SEC. The uniform government response is that Congress was fully aware of foreign customs and practices where bribery payments were the norm when it enacted the FCPA three decades ago, and it sought to establish ethical business practices for U.S. companies doing business overseas. Foreign policy or national security considerations may in limited circumstances be relevant, persuasive, or mitigating.

G. Corporate Compliance Programs

A quality corporate compliance program decreases the chances that improper payments will occur. If improper conduct is discovered, a proactive company that has effective policies in place will be in a better position, when an FCPA investigation arises, to dissuade prosecutors from bringing serious criminal charges or the SEC staff from bringing an enforcement action and seeking serious sanctions. Moreover, even if a company's programs were mediocre or worse at the time of the events in question, counsel should make every effort to implement or overhaul the compliance program and FCPA policies *before* negotiations with the SEC or DOJ begin. In many instances, government attorneys will credit quality compliance programs or enhanced policies.

XI. PERSUADING THE DEPARTMENT OF JUSTICE NOT TO INDICT

The technical legal standard for indictment is, of course, whether the prosecutor has established probable cause to believe a crime has been committed.[53] Notwithstanding all the criteria and principles of prosecution that prosecutors are urged to consider, the principal standard for indictment, applied by line federal prosecutors and supervisors across the country, is whether the prosecution believes that the defendant(s) can be convicted on admissible evidence. Responsible prosecutors do not indict cases they do not believe they can win.

An overriding reason why many federal prosecutors decline to charge a company or its officers is that defense counsel persuade them that they are not likely to win their case for factual or legal reasons. Losing a case is a clear and understandable fear of the Department of Justice. Federal prosecutors, who have broad discretion in selecting whom and what to charge, are expected to win most of their cases. That expectation is even greater in high-profile business crime prosecutions. Because of the attendant publicity and often heightened expectations of conviction in major white-collar criminal cases, defeats or acquittals can be devastating to the government and affect the reputation of the offices or the prosecutors who bring the charges. Defense counsel must, above all, convey to the Department of Justice that the likelihood of prosecutorial success in the particular case is doubtful. If counsel perceives that an indictment may be avoided, he or she should outline for the Fraud Section all factual, legal, and policy reasons why FCPA charges should not be brought and present those arguments at the appropriate time.

While evidence supporting one or more of the factual or legal defenses outlined in Section III of this chapter may alone not warrant a declination, a combination of these defenses along with prompt effective remedial measures may persuade the DOJ to decline prosecution. In this context, counsel will want to assure the government that the likelihood of a recurrence of the problem is minimal and that the client's management is seriously committed to a quality compliance program. Policy reasons alone will normally not deter a prosecutor from instituting a case, but they can, in combination with significant factual or legal arguments and prompt remedial measures, convince a prosecutor not to indict and to resolve the matter in a civil enforcement action.

In deciding whether to attempt to persuade the DOJ not to indict, counsel must fully assess whether the "collective government audience" has an open mind. If it is clear that the DOJ or Fraud Section attorneys or supervisors have already reached a decision to return charges, there may be no point in advancing legal or factual defense theories in a preindictment context. An exception may be where counsel and the client conclude a conviction is inevitable, and there is an opportunity to obtain a more favorable plea agreement by highlighting evidentiary or legal weaknesses along with recent remedial measures. In general, however, if the DOJ attorneys have a closed mind and the client intends to go to trial, it is better to save persuasive legal and factual arguments for a judge or jury.

If a company intends to try to persuade the DOJ not to indict, the decision of whether to do so orally or in writing must be made. An oral presentation often has the advantage of allowing an exchange of issues and ideas, and allows the opportunity to follow up with a written position. On the other hand, the permanent nature of a detailed written submission makes it more likely that all arguments will be fully and carefully considered by supervisors or the ultimate decision makers.

XII.   FCPA PLEAS, DEFERRED PROSECUTION AGREEMENTS, NONPROSECUTION AGREEMENTS, AND CONSENT DECREE RESOLUTIONS

In major FCPA investigations, public companies, officers, and employees frequently face separate but parallel investigations by the DOJ and SEC involving the same underlying allegations. The optimum outcome for the company or individuals is of course to avoid any criminal indictment or enforcement action. Short of that outcome, corporate and officer targets will seek to avoid criminal charges, to obtain a deferred prosecution agreement or nonprosecution agreement from the DOJ and/or SEC, to enter into civil consent decrees whereby the parties neither admit nor deny any liability, and to minimize fines, disgorgement, and injunctive relief. An SEC books and records consent decree will in virtually all circumstances be preferable to a DOJ indictment or an SEC bribery complaint.

Although they are not a prerequisite, DOJ position papers and SEC Wells submissions frequently lead to settlement discussions with the agencies. The vast majority of both SEC and DOJ matters are resolved short of trial and in advance of the filing of criminal or civil charges, and solid legal or equitable arguments in a Wells submission or position paper can result in a compromise.

In enforcement matters, the SEC routinely agrees to settle with the defendant or respondent neither admitting nor denying the Commission's allegations of wrongdoing. Federal Rule of Evidence 408 provides that a settlement or compromise "is not admissible to prove liability for or invalidity of the claim or its amount." Additional reasons to settle with the SEC include the time and expense of litigation; the potential effect of Enforcement Division litigation on a company's relations with other SEC divisions, for example, the Division of Corporate Finance; the impact of continuing negative publicity on a company during government litigation; the need of senior management to devote substantial time to litigation; the uncertainty of ongoing government litigation on a company's stock price;[54] and the need for a company to return its attention to its core businesses.

DOJ resolutions raise different issues. The burden of proof in a criminal case is beyond a reasonable doubt, and the collateral consequences of a felony plea as opposed to a consent decree are far greater. A corporate plea is generally admissible in subsequent civil and criminal matters, may lead to debarment and suspension of government contractors, and may also affect lending covenants and the ability to raise capital. A deferred prosecution agreement (DPA), *supra*, can avoid a formal guilty plea, but the defendant corporation will not be able to assert its innocence or deny the filed charges. A DPA will signal corporate responsibility and a resolution of the matter to important audiences like concerned lenders, investors, and customers; nonetheless, a DPA can lead to an onerous three-year monitor requirement and result in substantial fines, *infra*.

The Organizational Sentencing Guidelines, whether a company and the government are considering a plea, a DPA, or some other resolution, are customarily the starting point for the DOJ when calculating the possible corporate fine. The Alternative Fines Act, in particular, can subject corporations to staggering 10-figure fines.[55] Counsel must study the potential fines under the guidelines to evaluate maximum corporate exposure before any negotiations with DOJ begin.

Although the sentencing guidelines were declared discretionary by the Supreme Court in *United States v. Booker*,[56] it remains unclear how much district courts will stray from guidelines that have been in place and familiar to federal judges for three decades. Prosecution difficulties in securing proof to meet the criminal burden of "beyond a reasonable doubt" may in certain cases lead the DOJ to not file criminal charges and to permit the company or individuals to accept responsibility through an SEC consent decree. Many of the factors listed above that favor settlement in SEC matters apply equally to resolution of criminal issues. If a settlement is the best possible resolution for the company and its officers, counsel will want to secure a global settlement that simultaneously concludes all DOJ and SEC matters.

XIII. MULTIJURISDICTIONAL GOVERNMENT INVESTIGATIONS

As a result of more U.S. anti-bribery investigations and prosecutions, increased international cooperation between U.S. and foreign law enforcement authorities, and the potential for mammoth FCPA corporate fines, the likelihood of a multijurisdictional government investigation is far greater today than in the past. Multijurisdictional government investigations have recently taken place at Siemens, Halliburton, Volvo AB, Statoil, BAE Systems plc, and Panalpina, and are likely to increase. Companies facing these investigations will need either an international law firm with offices in the countries in question or a team of law firms to handle multijurisdictional government investigations.

Highly respected white-collar criminal lawyer Scott W. Muller has written that the challenges in cross-border or global government investigations include:

- Different data privacy laws;
- Different labor laws;
- Local law restrictions;
- Different legal systems that may or may not impose corporate or individual criminal liability;
- Different attorney-client privilege laws;
- Different information technology infrastructure;
- Different language and culture;
- Different extradition principles and policies;
- Different or lack of corporate cooperation incentives; and
- Different or lack of reciprocity of mutual assistance between regulators, for example, Mutual Legal Assistance Treaties.[57]

The defense of a company facing multijurisdictional government investigations requires close client and counsel coordination and careful management of the often conflicting requirements of national and foreign law enforcement agencies.

XIV. ADDITIONAL RESOURCES

- DOJ MANUAL 9-28.000 (Appendix 8).
- 17 C.F.R. § 20012 (Appendix 12)
- Mahoney, et al., *The SEC Enforcement Process and Procedure in Handling an SEC Investigation After Sarbanes-Oxley*, 77-2nd C.P.S. (BNA).
- Memorandum from Craig S. Morford, Acting Deputy Att'y Gen., U.S. Dep't of Justice, to Heads of Department Components and United States Attorneys, Selection and Use of Monitors in Deferred Prosecution Agreements and Non-Prosecution Agreements with Corporations (Mar. 7, 2008), http://www.usdoj.gov/dag/morford-useofmonitorsmemo-03072008.pdf (Appendix 9).
- MORVILLO ET AL., SECURITIES INVESTIGATIONS: CRIMINAL, CIVIL AND ADMINISTRATIVE (Practising Law Institute 2009).
- Muller, *Recent Developments in Corruption Cases: Multi-Jurisdictional Government Investigations,* NATIONAL INSTITUTE ON WHITE COLLAR CRIME 2009 (ABA March 5-6, 2009, San Francisco).
- DAVID LUBAN, JULIE O'SULLIVAN & DAVID STEWART, *Corruption,* ch. 14 in INTERNATIONAL AND TRANSNATIONAL CRIMINAL LAW (Aspen 2009).
- Report of Investigation Pursuant to Section 21(a) of the Securities Exchange Act of 1934 and Commission Statement on the Relationship of Cooperation to Agency Enforcement Decisions (Exchange Act Release No. 44969, Accounting and Auditing Enforcement Release No. 1470, October 23, 2001) ("Cooperation Statement") (*Seaboard* Opinion). (Appendix 10).
- Romatowski & Stewart, *Basics of SEC Investigations: What Every Criminal Lawyer Should Know,* NATIONAL INSTITUTE ON WHITE COLLAR CRIME 1992 (ABA March 2-3, 1992 San Francisco).
- UNITED STATES SENTENCING GUIDELINES § 8b2.1, Effective Compliance and Ethics Program (Appendix 11).
- WEBB, TARUN & MOLO, CORPORATE INTERNAL INVESTIGATIONS, ch. 15, 16 (Law Journal Press 1993-2009).

NOTES

1. U.S. ATTORNEYS' MANUAL, CRIMINAL RES. MANUAL § 9-47.110.
2. *United States v. R. Enter,* 498 U.S. 292 (1991).
3. *United States v. Mara,* 410 U.S. 19, 23 (1973).

4. Dan K. Webb, Robert W. Tarun & Steven F. Molo, Corporate Internal Investigations (1993–2009).

5. For an excellent detailed review of the SEC enforcement process, see Colleen P. Mahoney, *The SEC Enforcement Process: Practice and Procedure in Handling an SEC Investigation After Sarbanes-Oxley*, 77-2nd C.P.S. (BNA).

6. http://www.net/public/resources/documents/WSJ_Khuzani_Spch 090805.pdf

7. *See SEC v. First City Fin. Corp.*, 890 F.2d 1215, 1225 (D.C. Cir. 1989) (chronology submitted to SEC was admissible).

8. *See, e.g.*, Securities Act of 1933 § 20(a), 15 U.S.C. § 77t(a); Securities Exchange Act of 1934 § 21(a)(l), 15 U.S.C. § 78u(a); *SEC v. Jerry T. O'Brien, Inc.*, 467 U.S. 735 (1984).

9. *See, e.g., SEC v. Arthur Young & Co.*, 584 F. 2d 1018, 1022–28 & n.45 (D.C. Cir. 1978), *cert. denied*, 439 U.S. 1071 (1979), quoting *United States v. Morton Salt Co.*, 338 U.S. 632, 652 (1950).

10. 15 U.S.C. § 78u(d)(1).

11. 17 C.F.R. § 202.5(b).

12. Commission Rule 6. But the Commission may, for good cause shown, deny a request.

13. Report of Investigation Pursuant to Section 21(a) of the Securities Exchange Act of 1934 and Commission Statement on the Relationship of Cooperation to Agency Enforcement Decisions, Exchange Act Release No. 44,969, Accounting and Auditing Enforcement Release No. 1470 (Oct. 23, 2001) [hereinafter the *Seaboard* Report or Cooperation Statement]. The SEC issued the Cooperation Statement in the context of announcing that it was commencing and settling a cease-and-desist proceeding against the former controller of a public company's subsidiary for misstating financial information. The SEC stated that it was not taking any action against the parent company because of its extensive cooperation with the investigation, and, in the process, the SEC took the opportunity to state its general criteria for evaluating a company's cooperation (printed as Appendix 10).

14. *See United States v. Misao Hioki*; select DOJ matters discussion, *infra*.

15. *See* David Luban, Julie O'Sullivan & David Stewart, International and Transnational Criminal Law (Aspen 2009), ch. 14, at 4.

16. *United States v. N.Y. Cent. & Hudson River R. Co.*, 212 U.S. 481 (1909).

17. E-mail from Robert S. Bennett to author (Sept. 1, 2009).

18. *See, e.g., Stichting v. Schreiber*, 327 F.3d 173 (2d Cir. 2003).

19. *See* Philip Urofsky, *Extortionate Demands Under the Foreign Corrupt Practices Act*, BNA White Collar Crime Rep., Dec. 19, 2008.

20. 18 U.S.C. §§ 3282, 3292.

21. *See* Webb, Tarun & Molo, *supra* note 4, at ch. 7, *Multiple Representation and Joint Defense Agreements*.

22. *See Cont'l Oil v. United States*, 330 F.2d 347 (9th Cir. 1964); *United States v. McPartlin*, 595 F.2d 1321(7th Cir. 1978); *Hunydee v. United States*, 355 F.2d 183 (9th Cir. 1965).

23. *See* U.S. ATTORNEYS' MANUAL § 9-27.220.

24. This policy is printed in its entirety as Appendix 8.

25. Memorandum from Paul J. McNulty, Deputy Att'y Gen., U.S. Dep't of Justice, to Heads of Department Components and United States Attorneys, Principles of Federal Prosecution of Business Organizations (Dec. 2006).

26. *DOJ Manual* 9-28.300 (Appendix 8 at pp. 411–412).

27. Memorandum from Mark R. Filip, Deputy Att'y Gen., U.S. Dep't of Justice, to Heads of Department Components and United States Attorneys, Principles of Federal Prosecution of Business Organizations (Aug. 28, 2008), *available at* http://www.usdoj.gov/opa/documents/corp-charging-guidelines. pdf.

28. *DOJ Manual* 9-28.300 (Appendix 8 at pp. 411–412).

29. Exchange Act Release No. 44969 (October 23, 2001) Report of Investigation Pursuant to Section 21(a) of the Securities Exchange Act of 1934 and the Commission Statement or the Relationship of Cooperation to Agency Enforcement Decisions.

30. *Id.*

31. *Id.*

32. *Id.*

33. *Id.*

34. *Id.* at n. 3 (citing Brief of SEC as Amicus Curiae, McKesson HBOC, Inc. No. 99-C-7980-3 (Ga. Ct. App. filed May 13, 2001).

35. 17 C.F.R. 202.12 (2010).

36. Press Release, U.S. Securities and Exchange Commission, *SEC Announces Initiative to Encourage Individuals and Companies to Cooperate and Assist in Investigations* (January 13, 2010) http://www.sec.gov/news/press/2010/ 2010-6.htm.

37. Securities and Exchange Commission Division of Enforcement, Enforcement Manual ("SEC Enforcement Manual") 6.2 (January 13, 2010).

38. *Id.* at 6.2.2.

39. *Id.* at 6.2.3.

40. *Id.* at 6.2.4.

41. 17 C.F.R. Part 202.12; Release No. 34-61340.

42. The Commission noted that cooperation in Investigations that involve priority matters or serious, ongoing, or widespread violations will be viewed most favorably.

43. SEC Enforcement Manual at 3.3.5.4, 6.2.1 (2010) available at www .sec.gov/divisions/enforcementmanual.

44. *Id.* at 3.3.5.4 Proffer Agreements.

45. *Id.* at 6.2.2 Cooperation Agreements.

46. *Id.* at 6.2.3 Deferred Prosecution Agreements.

47. *Id.* at 6.2.4 Non-Prosecution Agreements.

48. *Id.* at 6.2.5. Immunity Requests.

49. Securities Act Release No. 5310, Fed. Sec. L. Rep. (CCH) 79,010 (Sept. 27, 1972).

50. 17 C.F.R. § 202.5(c).

51. Securities Act Release No. 5310, Fed. Sec. L. Rep. (CCH) 79,010 (Sept. 27, 1972).

52. *See* WEBB, TARUN & MOLO, *supra* note 4, §16.07.

53. *See id.* at 11(B).

54. Colleen Mahoney et al., *The SEC Enforcement Process and Procedure in Handling an SEC Investigation After Sarbanes-Oxley*, 77-2nd C.P.S. (BNA).

55. 18 U.S.C. § 3571(d).

56. 125 S. Ct. 738 (2005).

57. *See* Scott Muller & Dr. Klaus Moosmayer, *Responding to a Multi-Jurisdictional Government Investigation: How to Deal with Enforcement Agencies, Minimize Cost and Management Distraction*, presentation at the 20th Annual ACI Conference on the Foreign Corrupt Practices Act Conference, Washington, D.C. (Nov. 18, 2008).

CHAPTER 10

Recent SEC Enforcement Actions and DOJ Prosecutions

Federal Corrupt Practices Act investigations and cases have increased dramatically in the past five years. The increase is likely attributed to Sarbanes-Oxley officer certifications, corporate governance reforms, increased international cooperation among law enforcement agencies, and a very committed Fraud Section at the Department of Justice that is responsible for and oversees these matters nationwide. This chapter discusses some of the trends emerging from recent FCPA U.S. Department of Justice prosecutions and Securities and Exchange Commission enforcement actions, and then summarizes select recent cases.

I. FCPA PROSECUTION AND ENFORCEMENT ACTION TRENDS

A. Larger Corporate Penalties

The December 2008 Siemens $1.6 billion anti-bribery settlement demonstrates how massive and serious criminal and civil penalties can be. This landmark resolution with the German and U.S. governments follows the $44 million Baker Hughes DOJ-SEC settlement; the $32 million Willbros DOJ-SEC settlement; and the $30 million Titan DOJ settlement. In February 2009, in the wake of the Siemens disposition, the U.S. government filed a DOJ criminal information and plea agreement and SEC consent decree with Kellogg, Brown & Root LLC that included penalties totaling $579 million. In March 2010, BAE Systems plc pled guilty to FCPA-related violations and agreed to pay a DOJ fine of $400 million and a U.K. fine of $50 million.[1] The Baker Hughes settlement demonstrates that repeat offenders can expect to face fines two to three times as stiff as first-time offenders.

B. More FCPA Prosecutions of Individuals

The Department of Justice has dramatically increased its efforts to prosecute culpable individuals. In 2009, the DOJ prosecuted 44 individuals, nearly quintupling the 2008 figure of 9. In recent years the DOJ has criminally charged a U.S. congressman in connection with bribes in Nigeria;[2] a director of sales who conspired to bribe the UK Ministry of Defense to secure contracts with the UK Royal Air Force;[3] telecommunications sales executives who bribed state-owned telecommunications carriers officials;[4] a Korean national who paid employees of government-owned customers in China to induce them to purchase scrap metal;[5] a U.S. general manager who paid Nigerian officials to obtain pipeline contracts with joint ventures partially owned by the Nigerian government; and three Taiwanese executives and one Korean executive in the global LCD cartel investigation.[6] In January 2010, the FBI arrested twenty-two executives and employees of companies in the military and law enforcement products industry in an FBI sting operation involving a scheme to pay bribes to the purported minister of defense for a country in Africa. The sixteen related indictments represent the largest single investigation and prosecution against individuals in the history of DOJ's enforcement of the FCPA.[7]

The trend toward more individual prosecutions is unmistakable. As Mark F. Mendelsohn, Deputy Chief of the DOJ Fraud Section responsible for FCPA enforcement, has stated, "The number of individual prosecutions has risen, and that is not an accident. It is our view that to have a credible deterrent effect, people have to go to jail."[8] The United States is also willing to extradite foreign nationals for FCPA violations. The substantial increase in the number of individuals charged will very likely lead to more FCPA trials and challenges to DOJ legal theories.

C. Joint DOJ-SEC Investigations and Global Resolutions

Increasingly in FCPA matters, the DOJ and SEC conduct parallel or joint investigations and file simultaneous criminal charges, civil complaints, and/or deferred prosecution agreements. The pleadings are commonly detailed and accompanied by a lengthy press release and conference. The filing of a criminal information in contrast to the return of an indictment by a grand jury is usually a clear signal that the charged company or individual is cooperating with the U.S. government. A simultaneous global resolution with both the DOJ and the SEC is usually in a corporation's interest. Moreover, the *Siemens* prosecution confirms that U.S. law enforcement authorities are willing to coordinate investigations and return criminal charges with foreign authorities.

D. Deferred Prosecution Agreements and Nonprosecution Agreements

The Fraud Section of the Department of Justice, which reviews all FCPA criminal matters, has recently made it clear that fulfillment of the voluntary disclosure and prompt remedial action criteria can in certain circumstances enable a corporation to sign a nonprosecution agreement (NPA) and avoid criminal charges (e.g., *Statoil ASA, BJ Services Company, InVision, Micrus,* and *Wabtech*) or to enter into a more formal court-filed deferred prosecution agreement (DPA) (e.g., *United States v. Monsanto*[9]). For companies that have provided valuable and prompt cooperation in FCPA investigations, the DPA holds out the promise that DOJ criminal charges may be held in abeyance and will not be admissible in civil matters. A recent trend has been to reward public companies that have provided exceptional cooperation with a DPA for the parent or issuer and a felony plea by a subsidiary (e.g., *Baker Hughes Services International* and *Schnitzer Steel Industries Inc.*). In May 2008, despite improper payments by a senior executive in three countries for years *and* the payment of a million-dollar bribe by a country manager during the DOJ-SEC investigation, Willbros Group Inc. was able to obtain a DPA for itself and its international subsidiary because of what the DOJ described as "exemplary cooperation." In late 2007, Ingersoll-Rand Company and its subsidiaries entered into a DPA arising out of its participation in an illegal U.N. Oil-for-Food program.[10] York Corporation also received a DPA for its participation and role in the same program.[11] In some cases, the DOJ takes no action and the SEC files an enforcement proceeding, and the entire matter is simply resolved by a civil consent decree.[12]

In most DPAs an independent monitor is appointed for a period of three years. The negotiated DPA will govern the monitor's duties, reporting responsibilities, and authority. Monitors have included former federal prosecutors and judges who propose compliance. There is no privileged relationship between the company and the monitor. The company has a right to challenge any monitor findings or recommendations in its report. Monitors will typically focus on the product line and type of misconduct that led to the misconduct at issue. Monitors will often prepare three reports and submit them to the Department of Justice.

A breach of a DPA can result in the government pursuing the original prosecution, a conviction, and substantial sentencing exposure. The company as part of the original agreement agrees not to contest the underlying charges in the event of a breach, and thus a felony conviction is virtually a certainty. The 2008 prosecution of *Aibel Group Ltd.* illustrates that the DOJ will revoke a DPA and heavily fine a corporate recidivist.[13]

In select matters where the improper payments usually total less than $1 million, voluntary disclosure is timely made, and the cooperation and remedial measures are prompt and extensive, the DOJ may offer a company an NPA whereby if the company meets certain obligations for a prescribed period, for example, 18 months, the DOJ will not bring criminal charges. *SEC v. Chevron* is an exception to the fines being under $1 million. The U.N. Oil-for-Food program payments totaled $20 million and the combined disgorgement and fine against Chevron was $30 million.

The U.N. Oil-for-Food program investigation resulted in a large number of false books and records and internal controls resolutions—in large part because payments were made to the Iraqi government rather than to government officials, political parties, or party candidates as required by the anti-bribery provisions.

Usually, an NPA is publicized by the DOJ. Often, the fine is significant, a multiple—three to five times—of the improper payments. The voluntary disclosure for an NPA must be completely voluntary, that is, normally a matter the U.S. government would not otherwise have discovered, and the cooperation must be exceptional (e.g., *United States Department of Justice—Paradigm BV Agreement* and *SEC v. Chevron, infra*).

E.   Independent Monitors

1.   *Trend*

Independent monitors or consultants have been required in many FCPA settlements with the DOJ and/or SEC including *Siemens, Syncor, DPC (Tianjin), Monsanto, Titan, Vetco, Schnitzer Steel Industries Inc., Delta & Pine Land Company*, and *Baker Hughes Services International, infra*. The monitors usually have a mandate to review all remedial measures in addition to the problematic foreign operations of the companies. Typically, monitors serve three-year appointments and submit two or three annual reports to the Department of Justice. In the *Siemens* case a four-year monitorship was imposed, and the monitor is a German national. In at least one case the DOJ has agreed to an independent consultant. More recently, monitors have not been automatically imposed; where the misconduct is isolated and does not include parent activity, a monitor can be avoided. See *Hemerlich & Payne* and *Wabtech*.

2.   *DOJ FCPA Monitor Requirements*

In general, candidates for FCPA monitorships must meet the following four qualifications:

1. Demonstrated expertise with respect to the FCPA, including experience counseling on FCPA issues;
2. Experience designing and/or reviewing corporate compliance policies and procedures and internal controls, including FCPA-specific policies, procedures, and internal controls;
3. The ability to access and deploy resources as necessary to discharge the monitor's duties under the agreement with the DOJ; and
4. Sufficient independence from the company to ensure effective and impartial performance.

The DOJ customarily retains the discretion to accept or reject a monitor proposed by a settling company.

3.   The Morford Memorandum

In March 2008, the Department of Justice issued a policy memorandum (the "Morford Memorandum") titled Selection and Use of Monitors in Deferred Prosecution Agreements with Corporations[14] (Appendix 9). In addition to requiring merit selection and addressing potential conflict issues, the policy sets forth six principles with respect to the scope of a monitor's duties:

1. A monitor is an independent third party, not an employee or agent of the corporation or of the government.
2. A monitor's primary responsibility should be to assess and monitor a corporation's compliance with those terms of the agreement that are specifically designed to address and reduce the risk of recurrence of the corporation's misconduct, including, in most cases, evaluating (and, where appropriate, proposing) internal controls and corporate ethics and compliance programs.
3. In carrying out his or her duties, a monitor will often need to understand the full scope of the corporation's misconduct covered by the agreement, but the monitor's responsibilities should be no broader than necessary to address and reduce the risk of recurrence of the corporation's misconduct.
4. Communication among the government, the corporation, and the monitor is in the interest of all the parties. Depending on the facts and circumstances, it may be appropriate for the monitor to make periodic written reports to both the government and the corporation.
5. If the corporation chooses not to adopt recommendations made by the monitor within a reasonable time, either the monitor or the corporation, or both, should report that fact to the government, along with the corporation's reasons. The government may consider this conduct when evaluating whether the corporation has fulfilled its obligations under the agreement; and
6. The agreement should clearly identify any types of previously undisclosed or new misconduct that the monitor will be required to report directly to the government. The agreement should also provide that as to evidence of other such misconduct, the monitor will have the discretion to report this misconduct to the government or the corporation or both.

Companies that may be facing the appointment of a monitor should carefully review the entire DOJ policy memorandum on monitors and commentary. (See Appendix 9.)

4.   Selection of a Monitor

The appointment of a monitor is an important event for a company that has likely endured a trying multiyear government investigation(s) and already implemented a host of remedial measures. The monitor should be independent, knowledgeable about the FCPA, committed to quality compliance, an effective communicator, and someone practical and mindful of the shareholders' interests. Monitors are expected to be knowledgeable in the design and implementation of quality compliance programs. Quality monitors will offer practical, constructive suggestions that add value and efficacy to the compliance program and controls of a company. In most cases, the monitors have had legal backgrounds and careers—frequently as former federal prosecutors or judges. In the case of Siemens, a former German Minister of Finance was appointed to serve a four-year monitorship.

In considering monitor candidates, a company should request a preliminary work plan and three-year budget for both the monitor candidate *and* any forensic accounting firm that will support the monitor. The latter may be more expensive than the monitor and his staff. The work plan will include a de novo review of the issues that led to the prosecution or enforcement action but not involve a reinvestigation of the underlying matter. The work plan will include interviews of senior management, internal audit staff, the compliance offers, and the outside company that conducted the investigation, and usually include periodic visits to the countries where the problem arose and possibly others that present a number of potential FCPA challenges. The monitor will issue two or three annual reports. Above all, the independent monitor should be fair and willing to listen—to management and to the government.

F.   Merger and Acquisition Cases

FCPA cases have resulted from multinational acquisition due diligence. For example, the *Titan* case, which led to a $28,500,000 fine and penalty, stemmed from merger and acquisition due diligence activity by Lockheed, the suitor of Titan. Lockheed abandoned the target when it uncovered improper overseas payments, and Titan responded slowly. The deal collapsed, the DOJ and SEC proceeded to charge Titan and secured then record penalties; in time, L3 Communications bought Titan at a significant discount.

In the *General Electric/InVision* matter, *infra*, General Electric, in conducting due diligence of target InVision, investigated and urged the target to disclose to the DOJ improper payments in China, the Philippines, and Thailand. The careful planning, disclosure, and comprehensive remedial measures overseen by General Electric resulted in the government not bringing any charges against the target or acquirer. Similarly, in the SEC's *In re Delta & Pine Land Company and Turk Deltapine, Inc.*, *infra*, improper payments in Turkey were discovered during the due diligence by acquirer Monsanto, and both avoided criminal charges through coordinated disclosure efforts. It is clear that companies looking to acquire foreign operations but failing to conduct thorough due diligence can face successor criminal liability.

G. Industry Investigations

From time to time, the DOJ and SEC focus on an industry—often as a result of one investigation of a company leading to the discovery of problematic conduct by others in the same industry. Sometimes, an investigation will spawn an investigation of a vendor or other third party that serves the industry. For example, the DOJ prosecution of Vetco Gray in Nigeria led to the investigation of almost a dozen companies in the oil and gas industry that used the same major international freight forwarding and customs clearance company.[15] This crossover trend suggests that in-house counsel should keep abreast of FCPA investigations not only in their industry but in suppliers to the industry and company.

H. Self-Reporting

The past decade witnessed an increase in self-reporting by public companies. While both the DOJ and SEC claim they credit early disclosure and substantial cooperation, there appears to now be a slight trend towards public companies electing not to self-report where possible.

II. FACTORS THE DOJ AND SEC WEIGH IN PROSECUTORIAL AND REGULATORY DECISIONS

In determining whether to file civil or criminal FCPA charges, what types of charges to file (e.g., bribery versus a books and records violation), whether to impose substantial fines, and whether to require ongoing monitoring of a company, the DOJ and SEC consider various FCPA factors including the following:

- The total amount of improper payments;
- The number of improper payments;
- The amount of business or revenue obtained as a result of the improper payments;
- The number of countries or geographic region(s) in which improper business payments occurred;
- The length of time over which improper payments occurred;
- The seniority of foreign government officials who received improper payments, for example, ministries;
- The seniority of corporate officers or employees who paid or authorized improper payments;
- The nature of the payments, for example, travel and entertainment versus cash payments to secure a large contract;

- The aggravating nature of any payments, for example, bribes of the judiciary;
- The pervasiveness of improper conduct at the company or in one or more subsidiaries, divisions, or business units;
- The role of the parent corporation or senior management in authorizing, approving, or sanctioning improper payments or misconduct;
- The company's overall perceived tolerance of improper payments;
- The nature of the transmission of payments (cash, wire transfer, cashier's check, bearer document, etc.);
- Red flags senior management saw or should have seen;
- The efforts of the company to conceal the nature of the payment (disguised records, elaborate bank transfers, foreign bank accounts, fictitious entities, and so on);
- The number of false books and records entries;
- The presence or absence of adequate internal controls;
- The nature and extent of a company's compliance program and anti-bribery training at the time of the misconduct;
- Prior enforcement action and criminal history of the company;
- The length of time it took the company to respond to the improper payment or practices allegations;
- The quality of the response of the board of directors and senior management to the discovery of potential FCPA problems;
- Any voluntary disclosure or self-reporting to the DOJ and/or SEC;
- The extent and promptness of corporate cooperation (providing the government original documents, securing electronic databases and computer hardware, identifying wrongdoers, making domestic and foreign employees available as potential witnesses, providing privileged materials or the substance of same to the government, and so on);
- The quality and scope of the remedial efforts by the company, including prompt disciplinary action of wrongdoers, the breadth of the investigation, and modifications to the corporate compliance program; and
- The value of the company's cooperation in making cases against individual wrongdoers and/or other companies.

In addition to these factors, counsel should consult the *Principles of Federal Prosecution of Business Organization* (Appendix 8) and the SEC's *Seaboard* factors (Appendix 10), which govern that agency's enforcement charging criteria.

III.   CORPORATE GOVERNANCE CHECKLIST

In resolving an FCPA problem, the DOJ and SEC want as much assurance as practicable that a public company will not repeat the misconduct at issue or engage in similar misconduct. To that end, counsel should examine various aspects of the company's corporate governance. Pricewater-houseCoopers has identified the following as key elements of corporate governance:

- An independent board composed of a majority of directors who have no material relationship with the company;
- An independent chairperson of the board *or* an independent lead director;
- An audit committee that actively maintains relationships with internal and external auditors;
- An audit committee that includes at least one member who has financial expertise, with all members being financially literate;
- An audit committee that has the authority to retain its own advisors and launch investigations as it deems necessary;
- Nominating and compensation committees composed of independent directors;
- A compensation committee that understands whether it provides particularly lucrative incentives that may encourage improper financial reporting practices or other behavior that goes near or over the line;
- Board and committee meetings regularly held without management and CEO present;
- Explicit ethical commitment ("walking the talk") and a tone at the top that reflects integrity in all respects;
- Prompt and appropriate investigation of alleged improprieties;
- Internally publicized enforcement of policies on a "no exception" or "zero tolerance" basis;
- The board and/or audit committee's reinforcement of the importance of consistent disciplinary action of individuals found to have committed fraud;
- Timely and balanced disclosure of material events concerning the company;
- A properly administered hotline or other reporting channels, independent of management;
- An internal audit function that reports directly to the audit committee without fear of being "edited" by management (CEO, CFO, controller, et al.);
- Budgeting and forecasting controls;
- Clear and formal policies and procedures; updated in a timely manner as needed;
- Well-defined financial approval authorities and limits;
- Timely and complete information flow to the board.[16]

Because the DOJ and SEC will be looking at the corporate governance culture overall of a company seeking credit or leniency in connection with a resolution, the above is a useful summary checklist for counsel to consider prior to advancing settlement negotiations.

IV. STATED OR IMPLIED TERMS OF FCPA DOJ PLEAS, DEFERRED PROSECUTION AGREEMENTS, AND SEC CONSENT DECREES

In DOJ pleas or other resolutions and SEC consent decrees, stated or implied terms include the following:

- Charging books and records and internal controls violations in lieu of bribery charges;
- Deferred prosecution agreements (DPAs);
- Nonprosecution agreements (NPAs);
- The charging of a subsidiary rather than a parent corporation;
- Charging a business entity rather than employees or other individuals;
- Disgorgement of ill-gotten gain;
- Reduced fines;
- Periodic payments of fines for companies in poor financial condition;
- Periodic FCPA audits;
- Improvements to compliance programs, including training;
- The appointment of independent monitors, compliance experts, or consultants;
- The term of any monitoring requirement;
- No debarment or suspension from U.S. government business;
- Voluntary production of contemporaneous documents, records, or other tangible evidence;
- Access to outside accounting and legal consultant work product;
- Not asserting a claim of attorney-client or work product privilege as to any memoranda of witness interviews (including exhibits thereto) and documents created contemporaneously with and related to the foreign transactions or events underlying the subject matter;
- Ongoing cooperation in the investigation and prosecution of employees and others; and
- Flexibility in issuing public statements.

Both the DOJ and SEC Web sites publish helpful press releases and copies of FCPA complaints, consent decrees, indictments, informations, DPAs, NPAs, plea agreements, and detailed statements of facts (http://www.usdoj.gov/criminal/fraud/fcpa and http://www.sec.gov). Shearman & Sterling has on its Web site (http://www.shearman.com) the most comprehensive list of FCPA matters going back to the 1970s. Founded by Danforth Newcomb, the *FCPA Digest* lists all foreign bribery criminal prosecutions, foreign bribery civil actions instituted by the

DOJ under the FCPA, SEC actions relating to foreign bribery, DOJ FCPA Opinion Releases, and ongoing investigations under the FCPA.

In sections V and VI, as follows, select DOJ and SEC actions are summarized in chronological order, and applicable countries, FCPA misconduct, and salient factors are highlighted with a short summary of the case. The vast majority of the 50-plus listed cases involve DOJ and/or SEC settlements, and in some cases posit jurisdictional theories that have yet to be tested in court. Nonetheless, these resolutions give the reader guidance on what the DOJ and the SEC have agreed upon as appropriate resolutions in various factual scenarios. Section VII offers practical pointers on how to read and interpret DOJ and SEC settlements. Emerging FCPA prosecution trends and enforcement policies are often discernable as much from what is not stated as they are for what is stated in these public documents.

V.   SELECT SEC ENFORCEMENT ACTIONS

A.   SEC v. IBM Corp.[17]

▶ **Misconduct Category:**	False "third-party contractor" expenses (bribes)
▶ **Country:**	Argentina
▶ **Foreign Government Officials:**	Unclear
▶ **Improper Payment Dollar Value:**	$4.5 million
▶ **Combined Penalties:**	$300,000
▶ **Other:**	Foreign subsidiary's false records entries incorporated into parent's Form 10-K

In December 2000, the SEC settled with International Business Machines Corporation (IBM) for violations of the books and records provision, Section 13(b)(2)(A) of the Securities Exchange Act of 1934, relating to bribes paid by former senior officers of its Argentine subsidiary. During 1994 and 1995, senior management of IBM-Argentina, S.A., a wholly owned subsidiary, entered into a subcontract with Capacitacion Y Computacion Rural, S.A. (CCR). Money that IBM-Argentina paid to CCR was subsequently given to Argentine government officials. IBM's senior management did not follow procurement and contracting procedures when it provided false documentation and reasons why CCR had been hired. Payments to CCR were recorded by IBM-Argentina as "third-party subcontractor expenses" and were then incorporated into the parent corporation's 1994 Form 10-K. IBM agreed to an injunctive order prohibiting future violations of the books and records provision along with a $300,000 penalty.

B. *In re* Baker Hughes Inc.;[18] SEC v. KPMG & Siddartha, Siddartha & Harsino;[19] SEC v. Mattson & Harris[20]

▶ **Misconduct Category:** Use of accounting firm to make improper payments to tax official to reduce tax liability

▶ **Country:** Indonesia

▶ **Foreign Government Official:** Tax official

▶ **Improper Payment Dollar Value:** $75,000

▶ **Combined Penalties:** N.A.

▶ **Other:** First time that the DOJ and SEC filed a joint civil FCPA injunctive action

In September 2001, the SEC settled with Baker Hughes Inc., a Texas-head-quartered oilfield services company, with respect to a $75,000 improper payment to an Indonesian tax official. In March 1999, Baker Hughes's CFO and controller, Eric Mattson and James Harris, authorized an illegal payment through its accounting firm agent, KPMG Indonesia (Siddartha, Siddartha & Harsino), to the tax official despite warnings by both Baker Hughes's FCPA advisor and its general counsel that a payment would violate the FCPA. KPMG created and sent a false invoice for $143,000 to PT Eastman Christiensen (PTEC), an Indonesian corporation controlled by Baker Hughes, and PTEC paid the invoice. Baker Hughes was aware that KPMG Indonesia intended to give all or part of the $143,000 to the official as a bribe to influence the official's decision to reduce Baker Hughes's tax liability. Senior managers at Baker Hughes had also authorized payments to agents in Brazil in 1995 and India in 1998, without making the proper inquiries to assure that the payments were not bribes. All three transactions were inaccurately recorded as routine business expenditures and therefore violated the books and records and internal controls provisions of the Exchange Act.

Upon learning that the Indonesian bribe had been authorized, Baker Hughes's general counsel and FCPA advisor attempted to stop the company's payment to the KPMG agent in Djakarta, and in turn that agent's payment to the tax official; took steps to issue a true and accurate invoice; and implemented new FCPA policies and procedures. No criminal charges were filed against Baker Hughes. The company was ordered to cease and desist from committing or causing future books and records violations by keeping books, records, or accounts with sufficient detail that truly represented the transactions and disposition of the assets. Baker Hughes agreed to an injunctive order prohibiting future internal controls violations by devising and maintaining a system of internal accounting controls that will provide reasonable assurances that transactions are executed with the approval of management and that the transactions are recorded to properly prepare financial statements in conformity of accepted accounting practices as well as to maintain accountability for assets.

Mattson and Harris moved to dismiss the complaint on the grounds that the payments were extorted by the local tax official and they did not assist Baker Hughes in obtaining or retaining business. The district court agreed, but this argument was rejected by the Fifth Circuit in *United States v. Kay*. In 2006, Baker Hughes uncovered improper payments exceeding $4 million to a Kazakh official, which led in 2007 to the then largest monetary sanction—$44 million—in FCPA enforcement history, *infra*. The large fine was no doubt imposed in part because the U.S. government viewed Baker Hughes as a recidivist.

C. *In re* Chiquita Brands International, Inc.[21]

▶ **Misconduct Category:**	Payments for license renewal
▶ **Country:**	Colombia
▶ **Foreign Government Officials:**	Customs officials
▶ **Improper Payment Dollar Value:**	$30,000
▶ **Combined Penalties:**	$100,000
▶ **Other:**	No criminal charges were filed

In October 2001, the SEC settled charges of books and records and internal controls violations with Chiquita Brands International, Inc. of Cincinnati, Ohio. Employees of Banadex, Chiquita's Colombian subsidiary, authorized payments equaling $30,000 to local customs officials in exchange for a renewal license at Banadex's Turbo, Colombia, port facility. The internal audit staff at Chiquita found the two incorrectly identified installment payments and after an internal investigation took corrective measures, including terminating the responsible parties at Banadex. Chiquita agreed to an injunctive order prohibiting further violations of the books and records and internal controls provisions of the Exchange Act and to a $100,000 civil penalty. No criminal charges were filed against the company.

D. *In re* Bell South Corp.[22]

▶ **Misconduct Category:**	Payment of lobbyist fees to spouse of legislator
▶ **Countries:**	Nicaragua, Venezuela
▶ **Foreign Government Official:**	Legislator
▶ **Improper Payment Dollar Value:**	$60,000

▶ **Combined Penalties:** $150,000

▶ **Other:**   SEC settlement—no DOJ charges were
                                   filed

In January 2002, BellSouth Corporation settled with the SEC over the conduct of BellSouth International (BSI), an indirectly wholly owned subsidiary that in 1997 began to acquire majority ownership of Telcel, C.A., a Venezuelan corporation, and Telefonia Celular de Nicaragua, S.A., a Nicaraguan corporation. Former Telcel senior management authorized payments to six offshore companies totaling $10.8 million between September 1997 and August 2000. The payments were recorded as disbursements based on fictitious invoices for professional, computer, and contracting services that were never provided. BellSouth was unable to determine why the payments were made or to identify the ultimate recipients.

In 1997, BellSouth owned a 49 percent share in Telefonia with an option to acquire an additional 40 percent. Nicaraguan law prohibited foreign companies from acquiring a majority interest in local telecommunications companies. BellSouth needed the Nicaraguan legislature to repeal the law in order to exercise their option. In October 1998, Telefonia hired the wife of the chairman of the Nicaraguan legislative committee with telecommunications oversight to lobby their cause. The wife had prior telecommunications experience, but did not have any legislative experience. Telefonia and the lobbyist agreed to a three-month trial period at a monthly salary of $6,500. The legislator/husband drafted the proposed repeal while his wife lobbied for Telefonia. The legislator/husband initiated hearings for the repeal in April 1999. The lobbyist was terminated in May 1999, and the following month she received a payment of $60,000 for consulting services and severance. In December 1999, the Nicaraguan National Assembly voted to repeal the restriction, and BellSouth exercised its 40 percent option six months later. BSI acquired operational control of Telefonia and therefore was responsible for causing Telefonia's failure to comply with the FCPA by recording payments to the wife as consulting services.

BellSouth agreed to injunctive relief prohibiting future violations of the books and records and internal controls provisions of the Exchange Act. BSI disciplined and terminated employees involved in the case and also initiated an FCPA compliance program and internal auditing regime. No criminal charges were filed against BellSouth.

E. *In re* BJ Services Company[23]

▶ **Misconduct Category:**   Use of third-party agent and false
                                   amortization of fixed costs

▶ **Country:**   Argentina

▶ **Foreign Government Officials:**   Customs officials

▶ **Improper Payment Peso Value:**   75,000 pesos

▶ **Combined Penalties:**   None

▶ **Other:**   No criminal charges were filed and
no fines were imposed as a result of
full internal investigation and prompt
remedial actions

In March 2004, BJ Services Company, a Houston, Texas, provider of oil field services, products, and equipment, settled with the SEC after B.J. Services, S.A. (BJSA), its wholly owned Argentinean subsidiary, made questionable payments of approximately 72,000 pesos to Argentinean customs officials in 2001. The controller of BJSA had learned that the equipment they were waiting for to begin work with a customer had been improperly imported under Argentinean customs laws. The Argentine customs official had offered to release the equipment and overlook the import violation for 75,000 pesos. If he was not paid the money, he would deport the equipment and BJSA would lose the 71,575 pesos that it had already paid in import taxes, pay a penalty of one to five times the cost of the equipment, and pay importation taxes again when the equipment was properly imported. The controller contacted the country manager of BJ Services, who contacted the regional manager. The country manager told BJ's Argentine controller that the payment had been approved and directed him to negotiate for a lower payment with the customs official. A third-party agent, previously used by BJSA to assist with customs matters, negotiated a 65,000 peso payment with the customs agent. The amount was improperly characterized as Amortization—Fixed Costs.

Also, in September 2001, BJSA's former treasury and purchasing manager authorized payments of 7,000 pesos to an Argentinean customs official to overlook customs violations. The customs official drafted falsified documents to cover up the violation in exchange for the money. BJSA improperly recorded the payment as import duties paid to a third-party customs agent. The same BJSA employee approved a 10,994 peso payment in October 2000 to an official in Argentina's Secretary of Industry and Commerce. The payment was made to expedite the approval process and was recorded as an importation cost.

In June 2002, BJ Services's senior management learned of the improper payments and began a full internal investigation. BJ Services learned that 151,406 pesos in additional payments had been made from January 1998 through April 2002. BJ Services notified the SEC and fully cooperated with the agency's investigation. It also replaced management in Latin America, arranged for proper classification of the equipment, changed the account procedures for payments, and expanded the corporate internal audit department, placing a manager in Latin America who reported directly to the BJ Services internal audit director. Finally, BJ Services retained an independent forensic auditor for the books and records of Argentina as well as expanded its FCPA education and prevention program. The SEC ordered BJ Services to cease and desist from committing or causing any future violations of the books and records and internal controls provisions of the Exchange Act. As a result of its full investigation and prompt remedial actions, BJ Services was not charged criminally.

F.   *In re* Schering-Plough Corp.[24]

▶ **Misconduct Category:**	Payments to charitable foundation
▶ **Country:**	Poland
▶ **Foreign Government Official:**	Spouse of director of Silesian Health Fund who purchased formulary for government-owned hospitals
▶ **Improper Payment Dollar Value:**	$76,000
▶ **Combined Penalties:**	$500,000
▶ **Other:**	Parent books and records and internal FCPA controls settlement; leading FCPA charitable contribution case

In June 2004, Schering-Plough Corporation, headquartered in New Jersey, settled a complaint with the SEC relating to improper payments made by a foreign subsidiary, Schering-Plough Poland (S-P Poland), to a charitable organization called the Chudow Castle Foundation. The Foundation was headed by an individual who was Director of the Silesian Health Fund, a Polish governmental body that, among other things, provided money for the purchase of pharmaceutical products and influenced the purchase of those products by other entities such as hospitals. The complaint alleged that S-P Poland paid $76,000 to the Foundation over a three-year period to induce its director to influence the health fund's purchase of S-P Poland pharmaceutical products.

The books and records and internal controls settlement included a $500,000 civil penalty by the parent corporation, the retention of an independent consultant required to provide a written report to both the SEC and the company, and an injunctive order prohibiting future violations of the books and records and internal controls provision of the Exchange Act. No criminal charges were filed against the company, and the SEC complaint did not allege that the parent company knew of or was in any way involved in the approval or authorization of the payments by the Polish subsidiary to the Chudow Castle Foundation.

G.   *In re* Oil States International, Inc.[25]

▶ **Misconduct Category:**	Kickback payments by consultant through inflated invoices; use of subsidiary to make payments

▶ **Country:**	Venezuela
▶ **Foreign Government Officials:**	State-owned oil company employees
▶ **Improper Payment Dollar Value:**	$348,000
▶ **Combined Penalties:**	None
▶ **Other:**	Cease and desist order: avoidance of bribery charge despite substantial payments due to effective remedial measures (restitution to victim, termination of consultant contract, correction of books and records) and voluntary disclosure

In April 2006 the SEC filed a cease and desist order against Oil States International Inc.,[26] a Houston-based oil and gas specialty provider, alleging FCPA books and records and internal controls violations arising from $348,350 in payments made through a subsidiary, Hydraulic Well Control Ltd. (HWC) to employees of state-owned Petroleos de Venezuela, SA (PdV). The payments were recorded as "ordinary business expenses" by the subsidiary and were consolidated onto the books and records of the parent company. The subsidiary HWC constituted approximately 1 percent of Oil States' consolidated revenues at the time.

HWC retained a Venezuela consultant to provide translation services and to assist in invoice submissions, but not to solicit business. Several PdV employees approached the consultant about a kickback scheme, and the consultant agreed to inflate bills for "lost rig time" and chemical costs in order to cover the kickbacks. As part of an annual budgeting process, HWC's senior management noticed narrower profit margins and brought the discrepancy to the attention of the parent's audit committee. The audit committee initiated an internal investigation and, as a result, terminated the contract with the Venezuelan consultant, disciplined the responsible employees, corrected the books and records, reimbursed the Venezuelan state-owned oil company for inflated billings, enhanced the company's controls, and voluntarily disclosed its findings to the DOJ and SEC.

Despite the substantial dollar value ($348,000), Oil States International was able to avoid SEC anti-bribery charges, any DOJ prosecutorial action, disgorgement of profit, and appointment of a monitor. This favorable cease and desist order outcome is likely the result of the parent's prompt remedial actions—an internal investigation, termination of a consultant, correction of the books and records, reimbursement of the victim, and voluntary disclosure to and full cooperation with U.S. authorities. The other two noticeable lessons of this case are that it confirms the U.S. government's position that state-owned oil company officers can be "public officials" under the FCPA and that the consultant did not pay anyone to obtain business. Rather, the payments were made to avoid work stoppage or delays by the state-owned oil company and, thus, retain business.

H. SEC v. Dow Chemical Co. [27]

▶ **Misconduct Category:**	Use of fictitious invoices and contractors; $37,600 for gifts, travel, entertainment
▶ **Country:**	India
▶ **Foreign Government Officials:**	Central Insecticides Board official; sales tax officials; excise tax officials; customs officials
▶ **Improper Payment Dollar Value:**	$200,000
▶ **Combined Penalties:**	$325,000
▶ **Other:**	Voluntary disclosure and engagement of consultant rather than monitor; improper payments through a fifth-tier subsidiary; no DOJ prosecution

In February 2007 the Dow Chemical Company of Midland, Michigan, settled a civil action alleging that a fifth-tier subsidiary in India violated the books and records and internal controls provisions of the FCPA in connection with an estimated $200,000 in improper payments to Indian government officials from 1996 to 2001. The complaint alleged that a crop protection subsidiary made approximately $39,700 in corrupt payments to an official in India's Central Insecticides Board (CIB) to expedite the registration of three pesticide products. Most of the payments were made through agreements with contractors, which added fictitious charges on their bills or issued false invoices to the subsidiary. The contractors in turn paid the CIB official.

The complaint further alleged that the subsidiary made an estimated $37,600 in gifts, travel, entertainment, and other items to Indian government officials; $19,700 to government business officials; $11,800 to sales tax officials; $3,700 to excise tax officials; and $1,500 to customs officials. Thus, between 1996 and 2001, the Dow subsidiary distributed an estimated $200,000 through federal and state channels in India. None of these payments were accurately reflected on Dow's books and records, and the company's system of internal controls failed to prevent the payments. The SEC issued a cease and desist order against findings that Dow violated the books and records and internal controls provisions of the Act in connection with the subsidiary's improper payments. Dow was also fined $325,000.

Dow voluntarily disclosed the payments to the SEC after an extensive internal investigation, took prompt disciplinary actions, trained relevant employees, and restructured its global compliance program. After it hired an independent consultant to review its FCPA compliance program, Dow was not required to have a three-year independent monitor appointed by the U.S. government. Dow's voluntary disclosure, the age of the payments, the involvement of a fifth-tier subsidiary, and its remedial actions appear to have avoided any DOJ prosecution.

I.   *In re* Delta & Pine Land Company and Turk Deltapine, Inc.[28]

▶ **Misconduct Category:** $43,000 in cash, air conditioners, computers, office furniture, and travel and hotel expenses

▶ **Country:**   Turkey

▶ **Foreign Government Officials:**   Ministry of Agricultural and Rural Affairs

▶ **Improper Payment Dollar Value:** $43,000 over five years

▶ **Combined Penalties:** $300,000

▶ **Other:**   Low-dollar SEC threshold for enforcement action ($8,600/year) over five years; appointment of independent consultant; acquisition due diligence case; voluntary disclosure; prior weak internal investigation

In July 2007, the SEC settled a civil action with Delta & Pine Land Company and its subsidiary Turk Deltapine, Inc., alleging that the two Scott, Mississippi, corporations violated the anti-bribery, internal controls, and books and records provisions of the 1934 Act with respect to improper payments to Turkish government officials. Delta & Pine was primarily engaged in the breeding, production, conditioning, and marketing of cotton planting seed. Turk Deltapine was a wholly owned subsidiary engaged in the production and sale of cottonseed in Turkey.

Without admitting or denying the Commission's allegation, the respondents consented to an order that requires them to cease and desist from committing violations of the anti-bribery, internal controls, and books and records provisions of the 1934 Act and to the appointment of an independent consultant to review and evaluate their internal controls, recordkeeping, and financial reporting policies and procedures. The parent is required to provide the independent consultant with access to its files, books, records, and personnel as normally requested for the review. The SEC order found that:

- From 2001 to 2006, Turk Deltapine made payments valued at approximately $43,000 (including cash, payments of travel and hotel expenses, air conditioners, computers, office furniture, and refrigerators) to multiple officials of the Turkish Ministry of Agricultural and Rural Affairs (MOA). Turk Deltapine made the

payments in order to obtain governmental reports and certifications that were necessary for Turk Deltapine to operate in Turkey.

- Prior to May 2004, payments to MOA officials were made in part
using revenue generated from the sale of Turk Deltapine waste
products and products for waste allowance. The sales and payments were not recorded in the books, records, and accounts of the
respondents. In the case of Turk Deltapine, some payments were
recorded as "Porter Fees" paid to nonexistent persons.

- In May 2004, Delta & Pine officers in the United States learned that
Turk Deltapine was making payments to MOA officials. Delta &
Pine reviewed the circumstances but did not receive all facts concerning the payments from Turk Deltapine employees. Instead of
halting the payments, Delta & Pine arranged going forward to have
the payments made to MOA employees by a chemical company
supplier to Turk Deltapine. The chemical company charged Turk
Deltapine the improper payment sums plus a 10 percent handling
fee. The post-May 2004 improper payments were similarly not
recorded in the books, records, and accounts of Turk Deltapine
or Delta & Pine. Moreover, an internal memorandum noted that
there were "no effective controls to put in place to monitor this
process."

- Turk Deltapine's payments to MOA officials did not cease until
2006, when the payments came to light in connection with due
diligence being performed by a potential acquirer of Delta &
Pine.

In addition, the SEC contemporaneously filed a complaint in the U.S.
District Court for the District of Columbia charging the respondents
with anti-bribery and accounting violations and seeking a $300,000 civil
penalty.[29] Delta & Pine and Turk Deltapine consented to the entry of a
final judgment that required them to pay the penalty jointly and severally. Delta & Pine was acquired by Monsanto in June 2007.

J.   SEC v. Textron, Inc.[30]

▶ **Misconduct Category:**	Kickback payments as "after-sales service fees"
▶ **Countries:**	Bangladesh, Egypt, India, Indonesia, United Arab Emirates
▶ **Foreign Government Officials:**	Iraqi government
▶ **Improper Payment Dollar Value:**	$765,544
▶ **Combined Penalties:**	$4,664,940
▶ **Other:**	Oil-for-Food program; NPA

In August 2007, the SEC filed books and records and internal controls charges against Textron Inc., a Rhode Island-based industrial equipment company, in the U.S. District Court for the District of Columbia. The SEC's complaint alleged that from approximately 2001 through 2003, two of Textron's David Brown French subsidiaries authorized and made approximately $650,539 in kickback payments in connection with its sale of humanitarian goods to Iraq under the U.N. Oil-for-Food program. The kickbacks were made in the form of "after-sales services fees"; however, no bona fide services were actually rendered. The program was intended to provide humanitarian relief for the Iraqi population, which faced severe hardship under international trade sanctions. Iraq was allowed to purchase humanitarian goods through a U.N. escrow account. However, the SEC alleged that the kickbacks paid by Textron's subsidiaries bypassed the escrow account and were instead paid by third parties to Iraqi-controlled accounts. The contracts submitted to the United Nations did not disclose that the cost of the illicit payments was included in the inflated contract price. The SEC also alleged that Textron's subsidiaries made illicit payments of $114,995 to secure 36 contracts in Bangladesh, Egypt, India, Indonesia, and the United Arab Emirates from 2001 to 2005.

Textron agreed to a consent decree and order of disgorgement of $2,284,579 in profits, plus $450,461.68 in prejudgment interest and a civil penalty of $800,000. Textron is also required to pay a $1,150,000 fine pursuant to an NPA with the DOJ.

K. *In re* Bristow Group Inc.[31]

▶ **Misconduct Category:** Payment to reduce local tax assessments

▶ **Country:** Nigeria

▶ **Foreign Government Officials:** State government officials

▶ **Improper Payment Dollar Value:** $423,000

▶ **Combined Penalties:** None

▶ **Other:** Cease and desist order

In September 2007, the SEC settled with Bristow Group Inc., a Houston-based and New York Stock Exchange-listed helicopter transportation services and oil and gas production facilities operation company, for violations of the FCPA. Without admitting or denying the Commission's allegations, Bristow Group consented to an order that requires it to cease and desist from committing violations of the anti-bribery, internal controls, and books and records provisions of the 1934 Act. The SEC Order found that:

- Since at least 2003, and through approximately the end of 2004, Bristow Group's Nigerian affiliate Pan African Airlines Nigeria Ltd. (PAAN) made improper payments totaling approximately $423,000 to employees of the governments of two Nigerian states, to influence them to improperly reduce the amount of expatriate employment taxes payable by PAAN to the respective Nigerian state governments.
- PAAN was responsible for paying an annual expatriate "Pay as You Earn" (PAYE) tax to the Nigerian state governments in each state where PAAN operated. At the end of each year, the government of each Nigerian state assessed a tax on the salaries of PAAN employees in that state and sent PAAN a demand letter. PAAN then negotiated with the government tax officials to lower the amount assessed. In each instance, the PAYE tax demand amount was lowered and a separate cash payment amount for the tax officials was negotiated. Once PAAN paid the state government and the tax officials, each state government provided PAAN with a receipt reflecting only the amount payable to the state government.
- During the same time period, Bristow Group underreported PAAN's and another Bristow Group Nigerian affiliate's payroll expenses to certain Nigerian state governments. As a result, Bristow Group's periodic reports filed with the Commission did not accurately reflect certain of the company's payroll-related expenses.

Additionally, the order found that during the same time period, Bristow Group lacked sufficient internal controls and had mischaracterized the improper payments as legitimate payroll expenses. Bristow Group cooperated with the Commission's investigation and took a number of remedial steps.

L.   SEC v. Srinivasan;[32] *In re* Electronic Data Systems Corp.[33]

▶ **Misconduct Category:**	Fictitious invoices by outside accountant
▶ **Country:**	India
▶ **Foreign Government Officials:**	Senior employees of state-owned enterprise
▶ **Improper Payment Dollar Value:**	$720,000
▶ **Combined Penalties:**	$560,902
▶ **Other:**	Payments made in part to avoid cancellation of customer contracts, that is, to retain business

In September 2007, the SEC settled with Chandramowli Srinivasan, the former president of A.T. Kearney India (ATKI), which at the time was a subsidiary of Electronic Data Systems Corp. (EDS), relating to his role in a bribery scheme. The Commission alleged that between early 2001 and September 2003, ATKI made at least $720,000 in illicit payments to senior employees of Indian state-owned enterprises to retain its business with those enterprises. ATKI made these payments at the direction of Srinivasan after the senior employees threatened to cancel the contracts with ATKI. Srinivasan consented to the entry of a final judgment enjoining him from violating Sections 13(b)(5) and 30A of the 1934 Act and ordering him to pay a $70,000 penalty.

In a separate but related action, the Commission instituted administrative proceedings against EDS for various violations of the issuer reporting and books and records provisions of the federal securities laws. The Commission Order found that EDS engaged in the following misconduct:

- EDS failed to disclose the cost of certain derivatives contracts for the first and second quarters of 2002, and then selectively disclosed the cost and early settlement in the third quarter of 2002.
- EDS failed to adequately disclose in its Form 10-Q for the second quarter of 2002 an extraordinary transaction that composed over 25 percent of EDS's operating cash flow in the first six months of 2002.
- EDS maintained inaccurate books and records by employing certain inaccurate assumptions in accounting models used to estimate revenues and expenses for the company's multibillion-dollar Navy/Marine Corps Intranet contract.
- The improper payments made by Srinivasan caused EDS to maintain inaccurate books and records.

EDS was also ordered to pay $358,800 in disgorgement and $132,102 in prejudgment interest.[34]

M. SEC v. Chevron Corp.[35]

▶ **Misconduct Category:**	Third-party contractors used to pay kickbacks and illegal surcharges
▶ **Country:**	Iraq
▶ **Foreign Government Officials:**	Iraqi government
▶ **Improper Payment Dollar Value:**	$20 million
▶ **Combined Penalties:**	$30 million, including disgorgement of $25 million in profits and $2 million OFAC penalty
▶ **Other:**	Oil-for-Food program; two-year NPA with the Southern District of New York U.S. Attorney's Office and the District Attorney of New York County

In November 2007, the SEC settled with Chevron Corporation of San Ramon, California, for $30 million regarding charges that third-party contractors of Chevron paid approximately $20 million in illegal kickbacks to Iraq in 2001–2002. These kickbacks were allegedly related to Chevron's purchases of oil under the U.N. Oil-for-Food program.

In 2000 the Iraqi government began requiring companies wishing to sell humanitarian goods to government ministries to pay a kickback, often mischaracterized as an "after-sales service fee," to the government in order to be granted a contract. The amount of that fee was usually 10 percent of the contract price. Such payments were not permitted under the Oil-for-Food program or other sanction regimes then in place.

The SEC alleged that:

- Chevron knew or should have known that portions of the premiums it received from its oil purchases were being used by third parties to pay illegal surcharges to Iraq;
- Chevron failed to create and maintain an internal accounting controls system to detect and prevent illegal payments;
- Chevron's accounting for its Oil-for-Food program transactions did not accurately record its third-party payments;
- In January 2001, Chevron learned of surcharge demands by Iraq's State Oil Marketing Organization and adopted a company-wide policy prohibiting their payment. This policy required that traders obtain written approval before any Iraqi oil purchases, and it required that management review each proposed Iraqi oil deal;
- From April 17, 2001, to May 6, 2002, pursuant to 36 third-party contracts, Chevron purchased 78 million barrels of crude oil from Iraq. However, Chevron traders did not follow the policy, and management did not enforce it.

Chevron did not admit or deny these allegations. It consented to the entry of a final judgment permanently enjoining it from future books and records and internal controls violations and ordering it to disgorge $25 million in profits and pay a $3 million civil penalty. Chevron will also pay the U.S. Department of Treasury's Office of Foreign Asset Controls a penalty of $2 million. Since it was approached by the SEC, Chevron cooperated with the U.S. government investigation. It entered into a two-year NPA with the U.S. Attorney's office for the Southern District of New York and the District Attorney of New York County, New York.

N. SEC v. Akzo Nobel, N.V.[36]

▶ **Misconduct Category:**   Kickback payments disguised as "after-sales service fees"

▶ **Country:**   Iraq

▶ **Foreign Government Officials:**	Iraqi government
▶ **Improper Payment Dollar Value:**	$279,491
▶ **Combined Penalties:**	$2,947,363
▶ **Other:**	Oil-for-Food program; NPA

In December 2007, the SEC filed FCPA books and records and internal controls charges against Akzo Nobel N.V., a Netherlands-based pharmaceutical company, in the U.S. District Court for the District of Columbia. The SEC complaint alleged that from 2000 to 2003, two of Akzo Nobel's subsidiaries made $279,491 in kickback payments in connection with their sales of humanitarian goods to Iraq under the U.N. Oil-for-Food program. The kickbacks were characterized as "after-sales service fees" (ASSFs), but no bona fide services were performed. The program was intended to provide humanitarian relief for the Iraqi population, which faced severe hardship under international trade sanctions. It allowed the Iraqi government to purchase humanitarian goods through a U.S. escrow account. The kickbacks paid in connection with Akzo Nobel's subsidiaries' sales to Iraq bypassed the escrow account and were paid by third parties to Iraqi-controlled accounts in Lebanon and Jordan.

Akzo Nobel's subsidiary Intervet International B.V. entered into one program contract involving a kickback payment of $38,741. Akzo Nobel's subsidiary N.V. Organon entered into three contracts that involved the payment of $240,750 in ASSF payments. The SEC alleged the parent knew or was reckless in not knowing that illicit payments were either offered or paid in connection with all of these transactions. Akzo Nobel failed to maintain an adequate system of internal controls to detect and prevent the payments. Akzo Nobel's accounting for these transactions failed properly to record the nature of the company's payments, and characterized the ASSFs as legitimate commission payments to the agent.

Akzo Nobel agreed to a consent decree on order of disgorgement of profits of $1,647,363, including $584,150 in prejudgment interest and a civil penalty of $750,000. Akzo Nobel entered into an NPA with the DOJ. Akzo Nobel's former subsidiary agreed to enter into a criminal disposition with the Dutch public prosecutor pursuant to which it agreed to pay an $800,000 fine.

O. SEC v. Con-Way Inc.[37]

▶ **Misconduct Category:**	Hundreds of small payments to customs officials to reduce customs fines and shipping charges
▶ **Country:**	Philippines
▶ **Foreign Government Officials:**	State-owned airlines, Bureau of Customs

▶ Improper Payment Dollar Value:	$417,000
▶ Combined Penalties:	$300,000
▶ Other:	Cease and desist order; no criminal charges

In August 2008, Con-way Inc., a San Mateo, California, international freight transportation company, paid a $300,000 civil penalty and accepted a cease and desist order to settle an FCPA enforcement action with the SEC. Con-way violated the books and records and internal controls provisions of the FCPA through a Philippines-based subsidiary, Emery Transnational, which made hundreds of small payments to Philippine customs officials and to officials at 14 state-owned airlines. These payments were made between 2000 and 2003, and totaled at least $417,000. The purpose and effect of these payments was to, inter alia, influence the foreign officials to violate customs regulations, settle customs disputes, and reduce or not enforce otherwise legitimate fines for administrative violations. Con-way failed to record these payments accurately on its books and records and knowingly failed to implement or maintain a system of effective internal accounting controls.

In early 2003, Con-way discovered potential FCPA issues at Emery. Its subsidiary, Menlo Worldwide Forwarding, Inc., initiated steps to improve Emery's internal reporting requirements. After a broader review, Con-way imposed heightened financial reporting and compliance requirements upon Emery, Menlo terminated a number of employees who had engaged in misconduct, and Con-way provided additional FCPA training and education to its employees and strengthened its regulatory compliance program.

P.   SEC v. ITT Corporation[38]

▶ Misconduct Category:	Improper Payment Through Third Party Agent or Subsidiary Employees to Influence Chinese Government Purchasing Decisions for Large Infrastructure Projects
▶ Countries:	China
▶ Foreign Government Officials:	Design Institute Officials and Other State-Owned Entity (SOE) Employees
▶ Improper Payment Dollar Value:	$200,000 plus
▶ Combined Penalties:	$1,679,670
▶ Other:	Disguised commissions; improper use of chinese design institutes

In February 2009, the SEC settled with ITT Corporation, a New York-based global multi-industry company, alleging FCPA violations in connection with improper payments to Chinese government officials by ITT's wholly owned Chinese subsidiary Nanjing Goulds Pumps Ltd. ("NGP") of the company's Fluid Technology Division. This subsidiary distributed a variety of water pump products that are sold to power plants, building developers and general contractors throughout China. The SEC complaint alleged that from 2001 through 2005, NAG, directly through certain employees or indirectly through third-party agents, made illicit payments totaling approximately $200,000 to state-owned entities (SOEs) to influence the purchase of NGP water pumps for large infrastructure projects in China. NGP made payments to employees of Design Institute, some of which were SOEs, that assisted in the design of the projects to ensure that the Design Institute recommended NGP water pumps to the project SOEs. The NGP payments were disguised as increased commissions in NGP's books and records. The improper NGP entries were consolidated and included in ITT's financial statements, which contained SEC filings for the company's fiscal years 2001 through 2005.

ITT, without admitting or denying the allegation, consented to entry of a final judgment permanently enjoining it from future violations of the books and records and internal controls provisions of the FCPA. The company agreed to pay disgorgement of $1,042,112 together with prejudgment interest of $387,558 and to pay a $250,000 civil penalty. In agreeing to this resolution, the SEC considered that ITT self-reported, cooperated with the investigation, and instituted subsequent remedial actions. The allegation arose from an anonymous complaint from wholly owned subsidiary NGP employees to ITT's Corporate Compliance Ombudsman.

Q. SEC v. Nature's Sunshine Products, Inc.,[39] Douglas Faggioli and Craig D. Hall[40]

▶ **Misconduct Category:**	Brazilian subsidiary's payments to customs officials to import product into country and purchase of false documentation to conceal the nature of the payments
▶ **Country:**	Brazil
▶ **Foreign Government Officials:**	Customs officials
▶ **Improper Payment Dollar Value:**	Unknown
▶ **Combined Penalties:**	First Section 20A of the exchange act "control person liability theory" against officers in an FCPA case; no criminal charges; no independent compliance monitor

In July 2009, Nature's Sunshine Products, Inc. (NSP), a Utah manufacturer of nutritional and personal care products, paid a $600,000 civil

penalty and accepted a cease and desist order to settle an FCPA books
and records and internal controls enforcement action with the SEC.
The SEC complaint alleged that, faced with changes to Brazilian regulations that resulted in classifying many of NSP's products as medicines,
NSP's Brazilian subsidiary made a series of cash payments to customs
officials to import into that country and then purchased false documentation to conceal the nature of the payments. It also alleged that this
conduct violated the Foreign Corrupt Practices Act, and, in particular,
antifraud, issuer reporting, book and records, and internal controls provisions of the federal securities laws. It further alleged that NSP failed to
disclose the payments to Brazilian customs agents in its filings with the
Commission.

Signally, the complaint alleges that Faggioli and Huff, in their
capacities as control persons, violated the books and records and internal controls provisions of the securities laws in connection with the
Brazilian cash payments. Specifically, the SEC invoked Section 20A of
the Exchange Act, which provides for central person liability under the
theory that the CEO, Faggioli, who was at the time COO, had overall
responsibility for the operations of the company and that Huff, as former
CEO, had responsibility for internal controls and books and records. The
SEC complaint suggests that there were red flags to the U.S. parent from
the Brazil subsidiary, including substantial customers payments that put
Faggioli and Huff on notice, and such notice made the senior officers'
conduct reckless. The purpose and effect of these payments was to *inter
alia* influence the foreign officials to violate customs regulations, settle
customs disputes, and reduce or not enforce otherwise legitimate fines
for administrative violations. NSP also failed to record these payments
accurately on its books and records and knowingly failed to implement
or maintain a system of effective internal accounting controls.

R.   SEC v. Avery Dennison Corporation[41]

▶ **Misconduct Category:**   Kickbacks using consulting fees;
excessive gifts; sightseeing trips; use of
government official's relative; improper
use of a distributor and customs
broker; customs and tax official bribes;
use of petty cash funds disguised as
"travel" to pay monthly bribes; poor
acquisition due diligence; and improper
post-acquisition payments in China,
Indonesia, and Pakistan

▶ **Countries:**   China, Indonesia, Pakistan

▶ **Foreign Government Officials:**   Ministry of Public Security—Traffic Management Research Institute (China); customs and tax officials (China, Indonesia, and Pakistan)

▶ **Improper Payment Dollar Value:** $100,000+

▶ **Combined Penalties:** $518,470

▶ **Other:**   Proactive 27-country global trade compliance review and 10-country comprehensive FCPA review; no independent monitor

In July 2009, the SEC settled two enforcement proceedings against Avery Dennison, a Pasadena, California corporation, alleging FCPA violations in connection with improper payments and provisions to foreign officials by Avery's Chinese subsidiary and several entities Avery had acquired. The federal civil suit filed in the U.S. District Court for the Central District of California charged Avery with books and records and internal control violations, and Avery agreed to pay a civil penalty of $200,000. The SEC administrative proceedings alleged the same violations and ordered the company to cease and desist from these violations and to disgorge $273,213 together with $45,257 in prejudgment interest.

Both actions charged that from 2002 through 2008, the Reflectives Division of Avery (China) Co. Ltd. paid or authorized the payments of kickbacks, sightseeing trips, and gifts to officials of the Chinese Ministry of Public Security and, in particular, its Traffic Management Research Institute in Wuxi, Jiangu Province (Wuxi Institute). In January 2004, an Avery China sales manager gave Wuxi Institute Chinese officials each a pair of shoes worth a combined value of $500. Three months later, Avery China hired a former Wuxi Institute official as a sales manager because his wife was an official in charge of two projects that Avery China wished to pursue.

In August 2004, Avery China was awarded two government contracts through the Wuxi Institute to install new graphics on approximately 15,400 police cars for two Chinese government entities. The Reflectives China National Manager obtained these contracts by agreeing to artificially increase the sales price and then refund that amount back to the Wuxi Institute as a "consulting fee." In doing so, he knew at least a portion of that refunded amount would be for the benefit of Wuxi Institute officials. The total sales under the two contracts were $677,494, and Avery China profited by approximately $363,953. However, Avery's Asia Pacific Group discovered the kickback scheme before any illegal payment was made, thereby avoiding illegal payments totaling approximately $41,138, or 6% of the total sales.

Further, in December 2002, another Reflectives Division salesman proposed, and the Reflectives China National Manager approved, hosting a sightseeing trip for five government officials with a budget of about RMB 35,000, or $4,227. Two reimbursement requests were used to conceal the expenses for the trip. Also, in August 2004, the Reflectives China National Manager approved a kickback payment to an official in Henan Luqiao, a state-owned enterprise, to secure a sales contract worth approximately $106,562, for which Avery China profited by $61,381. However, Avery China discovered the kickback arrangement and never made the promised $2,415 payment to the Henan Luqiao official.

From May to June 2005, an Avery Reflectives Division sales manager negotiated a sale to a state-owned end user. To secure the sale, the manager agreed to pay a commission to a project manager at the end user. He then asked a distributor to fill the order and fund the agreed upon commission out of what ordinarily would have been the distributor's profit. The transaction was booked as a sale to the distributor, rather than to the end user. The distributor claimed to have paid the project manager approximately $24,752 out of its own profit margin. The total sales in the transaction were $466,162, and Avery China profited by $273,213.

In late 2005, during a sales conference that Avery China sponsored in a famous Chinese tourist destination, the successor to the Reflectives China National Manager paid for sightseeing trips for at least four government officials. The national manager later attempted to cover up both his role in planning the trip and the sightseeing during the conference. He altered the conference invoice by reallocating the sightseeing expenses to other expense categories and had the travel agency submit the changed invoice to Avery China for payment. The changed invoice did not contain any sightseeing expenses; rather, they were buried in expenses for rooms, meals, and transportation. The total cost from the 40-plus attendee conference was $15,000.

In 2005, Avery integrated the operations of an Indonesian contractor it had acquired. The contractor operated out of a bonded zone in Indonesia, and had a practice of paying approximately $100 each to three customs officials who regularly visited its warehouse to inspect goods. The contractor continued the practice post-acquisition. To obtain cash for the payments, an employee of the acquired subsidiary obtained $10 petty cash on a daily basis for the $300 needed each month, and the accounting entry reflected $10 of travel expense each day for the employee.

In June 2007, Avery acquired Paxar Corporation, a NYSE-listed company. In September 2007, through a whistleblower, Avery discovered the Paxar employees in Indonesia made illegal payments to customs and tax officials to obtain bonded zone licenses and to overlook bonded zone regulatory violations, and that the former general manager of Paxar

Indonesia directed employees to fabricate fake invoices to conceal illegal payments. An internal audit review also uncovered payments to customs officials in Pakistan made by Paxar Pakistan through its customs broker.

In April 2008, Avery commenced a global trade compliance review in 27 countries, which included an FCPA review. Three months later, it began a more comprehensive FCPA review in ten high-risk countries, including China. Beyond the illicit payments identified at Paxar Indonesia and Paxar Pakistan, the ten country review also identified problematic payments in Paxar China. In all three locations, illicit payments were made both before and after the acquisition, with the latest illicit payment occurring in January 2008. The improper post-acquisition payments amounted to $5,000, $30,000, and $16,000 at Paxar Indonesia, Paxar Pakistan, and Paxar China, respectively.

The Avery Dennison matter illustrates a host of common FCPA problems: kickbacks through improper consultation arrangements; use of a government official's relative; inadequate acquisition due diligence; improper payments through a distributor or customs broker; post-acquisition improper payments; local tax and customs bribes; and travel and entertainment abuses. The SEC did not impose an independent monitor requirement; the SEC resolution suggests that, in the wake of problematic FCPA conduct in multiple countries, voluntary disclosure, a thorough global trade compliance review (27 countries), and a comprehensive FCPA review in high-risk countries (10 countries) may help a company avoid more severe sanctions. Avery Dennison highlights the importance of promptly integrating a parent company's internal controls into the operations of acquired companies, particularly where the target's books and records are consolidated with the parent company's.

S. SEC v. Bobby Benton[42]

▶ **Misconduct Category:**	Use of Consultant to Pay State-Owned Oil Company Official to Obtain Extensions of Drilling Contracts
▶ **Countries:**	Mexico, Venezuela
▶ **Foreign Government Officials:**	Customs Officials and State-Owned Oil Company Officials
▶ **Improper Payment Dollar Value:**	$409,000
▶ **Combined Penalties:**	Unknown
▶ **Other:**	Concealment of Bribes from Internal and External Auditors Through Redaction of References to Venezuelan Payments in an Action Plan Responding to an Internal Audit Report

In December 2009, the SEC charged Bobby Benton, Pride International, Inc.'s former Vice President for Operations, Western Hemisphere, in the Southern District of Texas, with violations relating to bribes paid to foreign officials in Mexico and Venezuela. Pride International of Houston, Texas, is one of the world's largest offshore drilling companies.

The complaint alleged that in December 2004, Benton authorized the payment of $10,000 to a third party, knowing all or a portion would go to a Mexican customs official in return for favorable treatment regarding customs deficiencies identified during an inspection of a supply boat. The complaint further alleged that Benton had knowledge of a second bribe of $15,000 paid to a different Mexican customs official the same month to ensure that the export of a rig would not be delayed due to customs violations. It is also alleged that from approximately 2003 to 2005, a manager of a Pride subsidiary in Venezuela authorized payments totaling approximately $384,000 to third party companies, knowing that all or a portion of the funds would be given to an official of Venezuela's state-owned oil company in order to secure extensions of three drilling contracts. Benton, in an effort to conceal these payments, redacted references to bribery in an action plan responding to an internal audit report and signed two false certifications in connection with audits and reviews of Pride's financial statements, denying any knowledge of bribery. But for Benton's false statements, Pride's management and internal and external auditors would have discovered the bribery schemes and the corresponding false books and records entries. The SEC's complaint sought a permanent injunction, a civil penalty, and the disgorgement of ill-gotten gains plus prejudgment interest. The SEC acknowledged the assistance and cooperation of the Department of Justice and the FBI in the continuing investigation.

T.   SEC v. NATCO Group Inc.[43]

▶ **Misconduct Category:**	Improper Payments to Avoid Expatriate Deportation; False Documentation to Obtain Visas
▶ **Countries:**	Kazakhstan
▶ **Foreign Government Officials:**	Kazakh Immigration Prosecutors
▶ **Improper Payment Dollar Value:**	$125,000
▶ **Combined Penalties:**	$65,000
▶ **Other:**	Extortionate threats of imprisonment and deportation

In January 2010, the SEC filed a settled civil action in the United States District Court for the Southern District of Texas charging Houston-based oil field services provider NATCO Group Inc. (NATCO) with violations of the books and records and internal controls provisions of the FCPA. According to the complaint, TEST Automation & Controls, Inc. (TEST), a wholly owned subsidiary of NATCO Group Inc., maintained a Kazakhstan branch office where it won a contract to provide instrumentation and electrical services. To perform the services, TEST Kazakhstan hired both expatriates and local Kazakh workers. Kazakhstan law requires TEST to obtain immigration documentation before any expatriate worker entered the country; its immigration authorities periodically audit immigration documentation of TEST Kazakhstan and other companies operating in the country for compliance with local law.

In 2007, Kazakh immigration prosecutors conducted audits and claimed that TEST Kazakhstan's expatriate workers were working without proper immigration documentation. The prosecutors threatened to fine, jail, or deport the workers if TEST Kazakhstan did not pay cash fines. Believing the prosecutors' threats to be genuine, employees of the Kazakhstan subsidiary sought guidance from TEST's senior management in Louisiana, who authorized the payments. The TEST Kazakhstan employees used personal funds to pay the prosecutors $45,000 and then obtained reimbursement from TEST.

TEST Kazakhstan used consultants to assist it in obtaining immigration documentation for its expatriate employees. One of the consultants did not have a license to perform visa searches, but maintained close ties to an employee working at Kazakh Ministry of Labor, the entity issuing the visas. The consultant requested cash from TEST Kazakhstan to help him obtain the visas. Kazakh law requires companies seeking to withdraw cash from commercial bank accounts to submit supporting invoices, and the subsidiary presented $80,000 worth of false invoices from the consultant to Kazakh banks to withdraw the requested cash.

TEST created and accepted false documents while paying extorted immigration fines and obtaining immigration visas in the Republic of Kazakhstan. NATCO's system of internal accounting controls failed to ensure that TEST recorded the true purpose of the payments, and NATCO's consolidated books and records did not accurately reflect these payments. Without admitting or denying the allegations in the Commission's complaint, NATCO agreed to pay a $65,000 civil penalty.

The *NATCO* case addresses the not infrequent circumstance where foreign government officials threaten to fine or deport workers of a foreign subsidiary. The FCPA legislative history limits the duress defense to true extortion situations and offers as an example that a payment to a foreign official to keep an oil rig from being dynamited would negate the requisite corrupt intent.[44] It is telltale that the DOJ chose not to file criminal charges under these facts and the SEC sought only a modest fine of $65,000.

VI.   SELECT DOJ MATTERS

A.   United States v. Metcalf & Eddy[45]

▶ **Misconduct Category:**   Travel, lodging, and entertainment

▶ **Country:**   Egypt

▶ **Foreign Government Officials:**   Alexandria General Organization for
                                  Sanitary Drainage

▶ **Improper Payment Dollar Value:**   Unspecified

▶ **Combined Penalties:** $400,000

▶ **Other:**   Early FCPA Guidance re: Effective
                                  Compliance Programs

In December 1999, Metcalf & Eddy, Inc. of Wakefield, Massachusetts, as successor to Metcalf & Eddy, International, Inc., agreed to a civil judgment as a result of the payment of excessive travel and entertainment expenses for an Egyptian government official and his family. Metcalf & Eddy promised to pay travel, lodging, and entertainment expenses to the chairman of the Alexandria General Organization for Sanitary Drainage (AGOSD). In exchange the chairman, an official of the Egyptian government, would use his influence to have AGOSD support contracts between the United States Agency for International Development and Metcalf & Eddy. AGOSD was the beneficiary of these contracts. The AGOSD chairman did not directly participate in the selection of bidders, but the contract to operate and maintain wastewater-treatment facilities managed by AGOSD was ultimately awarded to Metcalf & Eddy. The chairman along with his wife and two children traveled to the United States twice as guests of Metcalf & Eddy. The first trip included visits to Boston, Washington, D.C., Chicago, and Disney World. The second trip took the AGOSD chairman and his family to Paris, Boston, and San Diego. The chairman was paid 150 percent of his estimated per diem expenses and his airline tickets were upgraded to first class by Metcalf & Eddy.

As part of the settlement, the DOJ required the defendant to adopt a compliance and ethics program for the purpose of preventing future FCPA violations.[46] The terms of the program set forth in the consent decree have been interpreted as signaling what the DOJ views as the components steps of an effective compliance program. These components include the following:

- A clearly articulated corporate policy prohibiting violations of the FCPA and the establishment of compliance standards and procedures to be followed by the company's employees, consultants, and agents that are reasonably capable of reducing the prospect of violations;
- The assignment to one or more senior corporate officials of the responsibility of overseeing the compliance program and the

authority and responsibility to investigate criminal conduct of the company's employees and other agents, including the authority to retain outside counsel and auditors to conduct audits and investigations;

- Establishment of a committee to review and conduct due diligence on agents retained for business development in foreign jurisdictions as well as foreign joint venture partners;
- Corporate procedures to ensure that the company does not delegate substantial discretionary authority to individuals who the company knows, or should know, have a propensity to engage in illegal activities;
- Corporate procedures to ensure that the company forms business relationships with reputable agents, consultants, and representatives for purposes of business development in foreign jurisdictions;
- Regular training of officers, employees, agents, and consultants concerning the requirements of the FCPA and of other applicable foreign bribery laws;
- Implementation of an appropriate disciplinary mechanism for violations or failure to detect violations of the law or the company's compliance policies;
- Establishment of a system by which officers, employees, agents, and consultants can report suspected criminal conduct without fear of retribution or the need to go through an immediate supervisor;
- In all contracts with agents, consultants, and other representatives for purposes of business development in foreign jurisdictions, inclusion of warranties that no payments of money or anything of value will be offered, promised, or paid, directly or indirectly, to any foreign official public or political officer to induce such officials to use their influence with a foreign government or instrumentality to obtain an improper business advantage for the company;
- In all contracts with agents, consultants, and other representatives for purposes of business development in a foreign jurisdiction, inclusion of a warranty that the agent, consultant, or representative shall not retain any subagent or representative without the prior written consent of the company; and
- In all joint venture agreements where the work will be performed in a foreign jurisdiction, inclusion of similar contractual warranties regarding no payments to foreign officials and no hiring of subagents or representatives without prior written permission.[47]

The civil judgment permanently enjoined Metcalf & Eddy from further violations of the FCPA, and the company agreed to pay a $400,000 fine. No criminal charges were filed.

B. United States v. Sengupta;[48] United States v. Basu [49]

▶ **Misconduct Category:**	Consultant (Sweden) used to steer World Bank contracts
▶ **Country:**	Kenya
▶ **Foreign Government Official:**	Government official
▶ **Improper Payment Dollar Value:**	$177,000
▶ **Combined Penalties:**	$133,000
▶ **Other:**	World Bank contracts; Swedish prosecution of consultants

In 2002, Ramendra Basu and Gautam Sengupta, World Bank task managers, were charged with steering World Bank contracts to consultants obtaining kickbacks in return, and with assisting a contractor in bribery of a foreign official in violation of the FCPA.[50] Basu admitted that he conspired with a Swedish consultant, among others, to steer World Bank contracts for business in Ethiopia and Kenya to certain Swedish companies, obtaining kickbacks in the amount of $127,000. Additionally, Basu assisted Swedish consultants in bribing a Kenyan government official, arranging for a $50,000 wire transfer to an account outside the United States for the government official's benefit.

In April 2008, Basu, a national of India and permanent legal resident alien of the United States, was sentenced to 15 months in prison, two years' supervised release, and 50 hours of community service. Basu had previously cooperated with American and Swedish authorities, pleading guilty in December 2002,[51] then moving unsuccessfully to withdraw his guilty plea. Basu's co-conspirator Sengupta pled guilty in 2002 to the same charges in a related case.[52] Sengupta was also a national of India and a permanent legal resident alien of the United States. He was sentenced in February 2006 to two months in jail and a fine of $6,000. The Swedish consultants were prosecuted and convicted by the Swedish government.

C. United States v. Syncor Taiwan, Inc.;[53] SEC v. Syncor International Corp.; SEC v. Fu

▶ **Misconduct Category:**	Cash commissions to doctors
▶ **Country:**	Taiwan
▶ **Foreign Government Officials:**	Hospital officials
▶ **Improper Payment Dollar Value:**	$344,110
▶ **Combined Penalties:**	$2.5 million

▶ **Other:**   Merger due diligence led to discovery of cash commissions; premerger disclosure by target to DOJ and internal investigation; independent consultant appointed; reorganization of internal controls for recordkeeping

In November 2002, Syncor Taiwan, Inc., a Taiwanese subsidiary of Syncor International Corporation of Woodlands Hills, California, pled guilty to a one-count information alleging that over a four-year period the foreign subsidiary paid $344,110 in commissions to doctors who controlled the purchasing decisions for nuclear medicine departments, including hospitals owned by Taiwanese legal authorities, for the purpose of obtaining or retaining business. The cash payments were authorized by the chairman of the board of Syncor Taiwan while he was traveling in the United States. The payments were recorded as promotional and advertising expenses.

As part of its plea agreement, the Taiwanese subsidiary agreed to pay a $2 million fine. In December 2002, Syncor settled with the SEC by consenting to a cease and desist order preventing future violations of the FCPA as well as a $500,000 civil penalty.[54] Syncor's board of directors was also required to appoint an independent consultant to review and reorganize Syncor's internal controls for recordkeeping and financial reporting purposes.

While conducting due diligence for a merger, Cardinal Health, Inc. uncovered improper payments by Syncor Taiwan. Cardinal Health brought the problem to the attention of Syncor. After being notified by Cardinal Health, Syncor promptly disclosed the improper payments to the DOJ and engaged outside counsel to conduct a thorough investigation.

In September 2007, Monty Fu, the founder of Syncor International, settled with the SEC under a consent decree by which he agreed to a permanent injunction against books and records violations and to pay a $75,000 civil penalty.[55] Fu was Syncor's chief executive officer from 1985 to 1989 and chairman of the board from 1985 to November 2002, when he went on paid leave. He resigned from Syncor in December 2002.[56]

D. United States v. Giffen;[57] United States v. Williams[58]

▶ **Misconduct Category:**   Payments through shell companies and use of Swiss bank accounts

▶ **Country:**   Kazakhstan

▶ **Foreign Government Officials:**   Ministry of Oil officials

▶ **Improper Payment Dollar Value:** $78 million

| ▶ **Combined Penalties:** | Civil forfeiture action |
| ▶ **Other:** | FCPA, tax evasion, and money laundering charges; assertion of public authority (CIA) defense |

In March 2003, James H. Giffen, the chairman and principal shareholder of Mercator, Inc., a small merchant bank with offices in New York and the Republic of Kazakhstan, was charged with conspiracy to violate the FCPA in a scheme that awarded oil and gas rights contracts in Kazakhstan, and with money laundering. Mercator and the Kazakh Ministry of Oil and Gas Industries entered into an agreement to help develop a strategy for foreign investment in the oil and gas sector in 1994. The strategy included coordinating and negotiating several oil and gas transactions with foreign parties. Mercator would receive success fees only if the transactions closed. In 1995 the president of Kazakhstan named Giffen his counselor, a position that enabled him to influence matters of gas and oil transactions involving Mobil, Texaco, and Phillips Petroleum. Mercator received $67 million in success fees from 1995 to 2000. Giffen allegedly diverted $70 million of various oil companies' money to secret Swiss bank accounts that he controlled. From these two sources, the indictment charged, Giffen paid more than $78 million to two Kazakh government senior officials who had the power to determine if Giffen and Mercator would retain their positions. The indictment further alleged that Giffen himself kept millions of dollars from the oil transactions to buy jewelry and a speedboat and to pay for a daughter's tuition. After four years of foreign discovery disputes and unsuccessful efforts to obtain classified CIA documents, the *Giffen* case awaits trial in the southern District of New York in 2010.

In April 2003, Williams, a former senior Mobil executive, was charged with conspiring to defraud the United States, tax evasion, and five counts of filing false tax returns. Williams negotiated Mobil's $1 billion purchase of a 25 percent interest in the Tengiz oil field in 1996. When the deal died, Mobil paid $41 million to a New York merchant bank that represented the Republic of Kazakhstan in the transaction. The merchant bank's president kicked back $2 million to Williams's Swiss bank accounts. Williams pled guilty to conspiracy and tax evasion and was sentenced to 46 months' incarceration.

E.   United States v. Bodmer[59]

| ▶ **Misconduct Category:** | Cash and wire transfers; percentage of profits from privatization of state-owned oil company; jewelry; and medical, travel, and gift expenses |

▶ Country:	Azerbaijan
▶ Foreign Government Officials:	Officials of state oil company
▶ Improper Payment Dollar Value:	Millions
▶ Combined Penalties:	None to date
▶ Other:	Privatization of state-owned oil company; co-conspirators awaiting trial; money laundering charges

In August 2003, Hans Bodmer, a Swiss citizen and lawyer with the law firm von Meiss Blum & Partners, was charged with conspiracy to violate the FCPA in connection with a plan to bribe Azerbaijani officials to be able to invest in the privatization of oil enterprises. Bodmer acted as an agent for Oily Rock Group, Ltd., a British Virgin Islands corporation with its primary place of business in Baku, Azerbaijan; Minaret Group, Ltd., another BVI corporation based in Baku; Omega Advisors, Inc., a Delaware corporation with its principal place of business in New York; and various other members of the investment consortium. As an agent for the consortium, Bodmer paid bribes and authorized payments of bribes to Azeri officials in an attempt to convince the officials to allow the investment consortium to participate in the privatization auctions of the State Oil Company of the Azerbaijan Republic (SOCAR) and to acquire a controlling interest in SOCAR. In October 2004 Bodmer pled guilty to a money laundering conspiracy charge.[60] He has yet to be sentenced.

F. United States v. ABB Vetco Gray Inc.;[61] SEC v. ABB Ltd.[62]

▶ Misconduct Category:	Cash payments, automobiles; shopping excursions
▶ Countries:	Angola, Kazakhstan, Nigeria
▶ Foreign Government Official:	National Petroleum Investment Management Services official
▶ Improper Payment Dollar Value:	$1.1 million
▶ Combined Penalties:	$16.4 million
▶ Other:	First SEC-FCPA disgorgement of profits requirement case ($5.9 million); retention of independent consultant to review FCPA compliance policies and procedures; SEC jurisdiction under American Depository Receipts

In July 2004, ABB Vetco Gray Inc., a U.S. subsidiary, and ABB Vetco Gray U.K. Ltd., a UK subsidiary, of the Swiss company ABB Ltd. each pled guilty to a two-count information in connection with commissions and referral payments made to officials in Nigeria, Angola, and Kazakhstan. ABB Vetco Gray U.S. and ABB Vetco Gray UK, from 1998 through 2001, paid bribes and authorized the payment of bribes to Nigerian officials in the government program known as National Petroleum Investment Management Services (NAPIMS). NAPIMS was responsible for reviewing and awarding bids to potential contractors for oil exploration projects in Nigeria. ABB Vetco Gray UK hired a Nigerian agent to perform consulting work related to marketing and goodwill. ABB Vetco Gray UK used this agent to pay some of the bribes to NAPIMS officials. The bribes were in exchange for information regarding competitors' bids and to help secure contract awards. Six contract bids won by ABB had bribes attached to them, including automobiles, shopping excursions, country club memberships, and housing expenses, as well as cash payments. Pursuant to the plea agreement, each ABB subsidiary agreed to pay a criminal fine of $5,250,000.

In a separate action, the SEC, which had conducted a parallel investigation, filed a complaint against the Swiss parent company ABB Ltd., the stock of which is traded in the United States through American Depository Receipts (ADRs). Pursuant to a settlement, the SEC enjoined ABB Ltd. from future violations of the FCPA, and ABB Ltd. agreed to pay $5.9 million in disgorgement of profits and prejudgment interest and a $10.5 million civil penalty. The latter penalty was deemed satisfied by the payment of the ABB subsidiaries' criminal fines totaling the same amount. ABB Ltd. also agreed to retain an independent consultant to review its FCPA compliance policies and procedures. See also *United States v. Vetco Gray Controls Inc., Vetco Gray U.K. Ltd. & Vetco Gray Controls Ltd.*, discussed *infra* at section VI.P.

G.   United States v. Monsanto;[63] SEC v. Monsanto[64]

▶ **Misconduct Category:**   Bribe to repeal a government decree

▶ **Country:**   Indonesia

▶ **Foreign Government Officials:** 140 Ministry of Environment officials

▶ **Improper Payment Dollar Value:** $700,000

▶ **Combined Penalties:** $1.5 million

▶ **Other:**   DPA; discovery through international audit; voluntary disclosure to DOJ and SEC; appointment of independent consultant; likely avoidance of government suspension or debarment

In January 2005, Monsanto Company of St. Louis, Missouri, settled charges, under a DPA, with the Department of Justice in connection with improper payments to a senior Indonesian government environmental official. A senior Monsanto manager, based in the United States, had authorized payments to a senior Indonesian Ministry of Environment official in an attempt to influence the official to repeal a law that had an adverse effect on Monsanto. The bribe was made, but the law was not repealed. The senior Monsanto manager attempted to cover up the payment by creating false invoices that were submitted to Monsanto and approved for payment. From 1997 to 2002, Monsanto also made approximately $700,000 in improper payments to 140 current and former Indonesian government officials and their families under a bogus product registration scheme. The payments were inaccurately recorded or not recorded at all in Monsanto's books and records.

Under the DPA, Monsanto accepted and acknowledged that it was responsible for the acts of employees set forth in a detailed Statement of Facts. In return, the DOJ Fraud Section agreed that prosecution of Monsanto under the filed false books and records information would be deferred for three years and that it would dismiss with prejudice the information if Monsanto complied with the terms of the agreement for three years. Monsanto agreed to pay a $1,000,000 penalty, to retain an independent consultant to review its FCPA compliance policies and procedures, and to the entry of an injunction barring it from any future violations of the FCPA. There was no indication that Monsanto, under the DPA, would be suspended or barred from U.S. government contracts. In a related proceeding, the SEC charged Monsanto with anti-bribery, books and records, and internal controls violations for the same FCPA misconduct. Under the SEC settlement, Monsanto agreed to pay a $500,000 civil penalty.

H. U.S. Department of Justice—InVision Agreement;[65] SEC v. InVision[66]

▶ **Misconduct Category:**	Use of agents and distributors
▶ **Countries:**	China, Philippines, Thailand
▶ **Foreign Government Officials:**	Midlevel officials and political party members
▶ **Improper Payment Dollar Value:**	Approximately $100,000
▶ **Combined Penalties:**	$1.3 million, plus disgorgement of $589,000 in profits
▶ **Other:**	Discovery of payments during acquisition due diligence; use of distributors to make payments; disgorgement of profit

In February 2005, the Department of Justice entered into an NPA with InVision Technologies, Inc., a Newark, California, public company, in connection with its sales or attempted sales of airport security explosive detection products to airports owned by the governments of Thailand, China, and the Philippines. InVision through its employees and agents authorized bribes to government officials in order to facilitate or retain business. In China and the Philippines, InVision employees paid agents who in turn gave the bribes to foreign officials. In Thailand, a manager and executive of InVision set up a company masked as an InVision distributor. The distributor used the price differential of the equipment to pay Thai government officials and political party members.

InVision voluntarily disclosed the conduct and related conduct to the Department of Justice and also prevented the improper payment in Thailand. InVision's cooperation and prompt disciplinary action and absence of prior FCPA-related charges led to the DOJ decision not to file criminal charges against the company, finding that InVision had accepted responsibility for the actions of its employees and their failure to maintain internal controls with respect to foreign transactions. InVision also agreed to pay a penalty of $800,000. At the time of the investigation InVision was merging with General Electric, which agreed to take the responsibility for assuring future compliance with FCPA policies and procedures. The agreement also required ongoing cooperation by General Electric and allowed the United States to investigate and prosecute individuals and other entities.

I.   United States v. Titan Corp.;[67] Report of Investigation Pursuant to Section 21(a) of the Securities Exchange Act of 1934 and Commission Statement on Potential Exchange Act Section 10(b) and Section 14(a) Liability; SEC v. Titan Corp.;[68] United States v. Head[69]

▶ **Misconduct Category:**   Consultant; campaign contributions

▶ **Country:**   Benin

▶ **Foreign Government Official:** President of Benin

▶ **Improper Payment Dollar Value:** $13.5 million

▶ **Combined Penalties:** $28.5 million

▶ **Other:**   Campaign funding (president of Benin); discovery of improper payments by potential acquirer during due diligence; lack of internal controls; no due diligence files on 120 agents and consultants; SEC Guidance on disclosure to investors under Section 21(a) report

In March 2005, Titan Corporation of San Diego, California, pled guilty to three FCPA criminal violations: one count of violating the anti-bribery provision, one count of falsifying the books and records provision, and one felony tax count; it also agreed to pay a record FCPA criminal fine of $13 million. The military intelligence and communications company did not contest that from 1999 to 2001 it paid $3.5 million to its agent in Benin, Africa, who was then known by Titan to be the president of Benin's business advisor. Much of the money funneled to Titan's African agent went to the election campaign of Benin's then incumbent president. A former senior Titan officer directed that payments be falsely invoiced as consulting services and that actual payment of the money be spread over time and into smaller increments.

Also in March 2005, the SEC brought an enforcement action against Titan that alleged violations of the anti-bribery, internal controls, and books and records provisions of the FCPA.[70] Under a consent decree, Titan agreed to pay the $13 million penalty to the Department of Justice; to pay approximately $15.5 million in disgorgement and prejudgment interest; and to retain an independent consultant to review the company's FCPA compliance procedures and to adopt and implement the consultant's recommendations. The SEC stated that despite utilizing over 120 agents and consultants in over 60 countries, Titan never had a formal company-wide FCPA policy, had disregarded or circumvented the limited FCPA policies and procedures in effect, had failed to maintain sufficient due diligence files on its foreign agents, and had failed to have meaningful oversight over the foreign agents.

The background that led to the criminal and SEC enforcement case against Titan is as follows: in September 2003, Titan became a party to a merger agreement in which Lockheed-Martin agreed to acquire Titan pending certain contingencies. Titan affirmatively represented in that merger agreement that "to the knowledge of Titan, neither the Company nor any of its Subsidiaries, nor any director, officer, agent or employee of the Company or any of its Subsidiaries has . . . taken any action which would cause the Company or any of its Subsidiaries to be in violation of the FCPA."[71] This representation was publicly disclosed and disseminated by Titan. As a result of due diligence by Lockheed-Martin, the acquisition fell apart. In 2005, L-3 Communications acquired Titan in a separate buyout valued at $2.65 billion.

Titan's inclusion of the Lockheed merger agreement containing its affirmative FCPA representation in public disclosures, including a proxy statement filed with the SEC, also led the SEC to issue a Section 21(a) report to provide guidance concerning potential liability under the anti-fraud and proxy provisions of the federal securities laws for publication of materially false or misleading disclosures in merger and other contractual agreements.[72]

In June 2006, former Titan Africa president Steven L. Head pled guilty to a single count of falsifying a false invoice for consulting services in

Benin. While Head, the former assistant to Titan CEO Gene Ray and later president of Titan Africa, was subject to 10 years in prison and a $1 million fine, his substantial assistance and cooperation resulted in a September 2007 sentence of six months in prison, three years' supervised release, and a $5,000 fine.[73]

J.   U.S. Department of Justice—Micrus Corp. Agreement

▶ **Misconduct Category:**   False stock options, honoraria, and commissions

▶ **Countries:**   France, Germany, Spain, Turkey

▶ **Foreign Government Officials:**   Doctors of publicly owned hospitals

▶ **Improper Payment Dollar Value:** $105,000

▶ **Combined Penalties:** $450,000

▶ **Other:**   Voluntary disclosure; two-year NPA

In March 2005, Micrus Corporation, a privately held company based in Sunnyvale, California, that develops and sells embolic coils, medical devices that allow minimally invasive treatment of neurovascular diseases, agreed to resolve its criminal liability associated with potential FCPA violations by paying $450,000 in penalties to the United States and cooperating fully with the DOJ investigation.

The investigation revealed that Micrus, through the conduct of certain officers, employees, agents, and salespeople, paid more than $105,000—disguised in Micrus's books and records as stock options, honoraria, and commissions—to doctors employed at publicly owned and operated hospitals in France, Turkey, Spain, and Germany in return for the hospitals' purchase of embolic coils from Micrus. Micrus had also made an additional $250,000 in payments for which the company did not obtain the necessary prior administrative or legal approval as required under the laws of the relevant foreign jurisdictions. The DOJ investigation followed the voluntary disclosure to the DOJ by Micrus of facts obtained in its internal investigation into the potential FCPA violations.

The term of the Micrus NPA with the government was two years. As a result of Micrus's cooperation commitment, its remedial actions, and voluntary disclosure of the wrongdoing, the Department of Justice agreed not to file criminal charges stemming from the investigation for the two-year period. If Micrus fails to fully comply with the terms of the agreement during that two-year period, the DOJ will charge Micrus with violations of the FCPA.

In exchange for the DOJ's agreement not to prosecute Micrus for the conduct disclosed by Micrus to the Department, Micrus agreed, among other things, to accept responsibility for its conduct; fully and affirmatively disclose to the Department activities that Micrus believes may violate the FCPA and continue to cooperate with the Department in its investigation; agree that a statement of facts summarizing the subject transactions was materially accurate and further agree not to contradict those facts; pay a monetary penalty to the United States of $450,000; adopt an FCPA compliance program, where previously it had none, as well as a set of internal controls designed to prevent violations in the future; and retain an independent compliance expert for a period of three years to ensure the company's compliance program and internal controls are effective.[74]

K.   United States v. DPC (Tianjin) Co.;[75] *In re* Diagnostic Products Corp.[76]

▶ **Misconduct Category:**	Illegal "commissions" (bribes)
▶ **Country:**	People's Republic of China
▶ **Foreign Government Officials:**	Physicians and laboratory personnel of government-owned hospitals
▶ **Improper Payment Dollar Value:**	$1.6 million
▶ **Combined Penalties:**	$4.8 million
▶ **Other:**	Chinese subsidiary DOJ plea; SEC disgorgement of profit against parent company

In May 2005, the United States charged DPC (Tianjin) Co., the Chinese subsidiary of Los Angeles-based Diagnostic Products Corporation (DPC), with violating the FCPA in connection with the payment of approximately $1.6 million in bribes in the form of illegal "commissions" to physicians and laboratory personnel employed by government-owned hospitals in the People's Republic of China. DPC, a producer and seller of diagnostic medical equipment, agreed to plead guilty to a single charge, adopt internal compliance measures, and cooperate with ongoing criminal and SEC civil investigations. An independent compliance expert was appointed to audit the company's compliance program and monitor its implementation of new internal policies and procedures. DPC Tianjin also agreed to pay a criminal penalty of $2 million.

The bribes were allegedly paid from late 1991 through December 2002 for the purpose and with the effect of obtaining and retaining business with the Chinese hospitals. According to the criminal information and a statement of facts filed in court, DPC Tianjin made cash payments to laboratory personnel and physicians employed in certain hospitals in the People's Republic of China in exchange for agreements that the hospitals would obtain DPC Tianjin's products and services. This practice, authorized by DPC Tianjin's general manager, involved personnel who were employed by hospitals owned by the legal authorities in the People's Republic of China and, thus, "foreign officials" as defined by the FCPA.

In most cases, the bribes were paid in cash and hand-delivered by DPC Tianjin salespeople to the person who controlled purchasing decisions for the particular hospital department. DPC Tianjin recorded the payments on its books and records as "selling expenses." DPC Tianjin's general manager regularly prepared and submitted to DPC its financial statements, which contained sales expenses. The general manager also caused approval of the budgets for sales expenses of DPC Tianjin, including the amounts DPC Tianjin intended to pay to the officials of the hospitals in the following quarter or year. The "commissions," typically between 3 percent and 10 percent of sales, totaled approximately $1,623,326 from late 1991 through December 2002, and allowed DPC to earn approximately $2 million in profits from the sales.

Simultaneously with the criminal charge, the SEC filed an FCPA enforcement proceeding against DPC Tianjin's parent company, DPC. The SEC ordered the company to cease and desist from violating the antibribery, internal controls, and books and records provisions of the FCPA and to disgorge approximately $2.8 million in ill-gotten gains, representing its net profit in the People's Republic of China for the period of its misconduct plus prejudgment interest.[77]

L.   United States v. Viktor Kozeny, Frederic Bourke & David Pinkerton [78]

▶ **Misconduct Category:**	Investment scheme: cash and wire transfers to Azeri officials and family members; SOCAR privatization profit and issuance of $300 million worth of Oily Rock shares
▶ **Country:**	Azerbaijan
▶ **Foreign Government Officials:**	State-owned oil company officials
▶ **Improper Payment Dollar Value:**	To be determined
▶ **Combined Penalties:**	To be determined
▶ **Other:**	Failure to timely extend statute of limitations to gather foreign evidence; dismissal as to Pinkerton; jewelry, medical, travel, and gift expenses; government sought $100 million forfeiture; possible extortion defense pre-trial opinion; "conscious avoidance" issues at trial

In October 2005, the United States charged in a 27-count indictment Viktor Kozeny, Frederic Bourke, and David Pinkerton with, inter alia, participating in a conspiracy to bribe senior government officials in Azerbaijan to ensure that those officials would privatize the State Oil Company of the Azerbaijan Republic (SOCAR) and allow the three and others to share in the anticipated profits arising from that privatization and resale of its shares in the market. The Southern District of New York indictment charged that Kozeny, an Irish citizen and resident of the Bahamas, on behalf of the co-defendants and others made a series of corrupt payments to four Azeri officials. Payments allegedly included more than $11 million to the Azeri officials or their family members and sought $300 million worth of a controlled company's shares. Pinkerton filed a successful motion to dismiss all FCPA counts on the basis that the government did not timely move to extend the statute of limitations to collect foreign evidence. Bourke filed a motion to dismiss all but the false statements charges on statute of limitations grounds. The district court granted the motion, and the Second Circuit affirmed the dismissal of select charges against Bourke.[79] Three others, Thomas Farrell, Clayton Lewis, and Hans Bodmer (*supra*), have in related cases pled guilty in connection with their participation in the bribery scheme.

Bourke proceeded to trial in June 2009 and was convicted of conspiracy to defraud the United States and making false statements, but was acquitted of money laundering charges, thereby avoiding a $100 million forfeiture. In November 2009 he was sentenced to a year and a day incarceration over the strong objection of the DOJ. Bourke intends to appeal his conviction on, among other grounds, conscious avoidance issues.[80]

M. United States v. Sapsizian[81]

▶ **Misconduct Category:**   Use of consultant

▶ **Country:**   Costa Rica

▶ **Foreign Government Official:**   Board director of state-run telecommunications company

▶ **Improper Payment Dollar Value:** $2.5 million

▶ **Combined Penalties:** $261,500

▶ **Other:**   French citizen; 30 months in jail; forfeiture of $261,500

In 2006, Christian Sapsizian, a former Alcatel CIT executive, and Edgar Valverde Acosta, a Costa Rican citizen who was Alcatel's senior country officer in Costa Rica, were charged with conspiracy with others between February 2000 and September 2004 to make more than $2.5 million in bribe payments to Costa Rican officials to obtain a telecommunications contract on behalf of Alcatel. According to information and plea documents, the payments were made to a board director for Instituto Costarricense de Electricidad (ICE), the state-run telecommunications authority in Costa Rica, which was responsible for awarding all telecommunications contracts. Sapsizian also admitted that the ICE official was an advisor to a senior Costa Rican government official and that the payments were shared with that senior official. The payments, funneled through one of Alcatel's Costa Rican consulting firms, were intended to cause the ICE official and the senior government official to exercise their influence to initiate a bid process that favored Alcatel's technology, Sapsizian admitted, and to vote to award Alcatel a mobile telephone contract. ICE awarded a mobile telephone contract to Alcatel in August 2001 valued at $149 million.

Sapsizian, a 62-year-old French citizen, pled guilty to two counts of violating the FCPA. As part of his plea, Sapsizian agreed to cooperate with U.S. and foreign law enforcement officials in the ongoing investigation. Until November 30, 2006, Sapsizian was employed by Alcatel, a French telecommunications company whose American depository receipts (ADRs) were traded on the New York Stock Exchange.

In September 2008, Sapsizian was sentenced to 30 months in prison for engaging in an elaborate bribery scheme to obtain a mobile telephone contract from the state-owned telecommunications authority in Costa Rica by making more than $2.5 million in corrupt payments to Costa Rican officials. He was also ordered to forfeit $261,500, to serve three years of supervised release, and to pay a $200 special assessment. Acosta is a fugitive.

N. United States v. Statoil ASA;[82] *In re* Statoil ASA[83]

▶ **Misconduct Category:**	Use of Turks and Caicos consultant
▶ **Country:**	Iran
▶ **Foreign Government Officials:**	National oil company; son of a former president of Iraq
▶ **Improper Payment Dollar Value:**	$5.2 million
▶ **Combined Penalties:**	$21 million
▶ **Other:**	DPA; first FCPA enforcement action against a foreign company: jurisdiction based on ADRs traded on NYSE; appointment of an independent compliance consultant

In October 2006, the DOJ and SEC announced that Statoil ASA, an international oil company in Norway whose ADRs are traded on the New York Stock Exchange, had agreed to pay a total of $21 million to settle criminal and administrative charges for violating the FCPA's anti-bribery and accounting provisions. Pursuant to a DPA, Statoil agreed to a $10.5 million criminal penalty and the appointment of an independent compliance consultant who will review and report on Statoil's FCPA compliance. In the parallel SEC administrative proceeding, Statoil consented to the entry of an administrative order requiring the company to cease and desist from committing any future FCPA violations, and to pay disgorgement of an additional $10.5 million.

O. United States v. SSI Korea; *In re* Schnitzer Steel Industries, Inc.;[84] SEC v. Philip[85]

▶ **Misconduct Category:**	Commissions, refunds, and gratuities to both public and privately owned steel mills
▶ **Countries:**	China, Japan, Korea
▶ **Foreign Government Officials:**	Government-owned steel mill
▶ **Improper Payment Dollar Value:**	$1.8 million (only $200,000 to foreign officials)
▶ **Combined Penalties:**	$15.2 million
▶ **Other:**	Commercial bribery or bribery of privately owned companies included in DOJ settlement; criminal plea by Korean subsidiary; DPA with U.S. parent

In October 2006, the DOJ and SEC announced a plea and settlement with Schnitzer Steel Industries, Inc., based in Portland, Oregon, and its foreign subsidiary, SSI Korea. In the plea documents, SSI Korea admitted that it violated the FCPA's anti-bribery provisions by making more than $1.8 million in corrupt payments over a five-year period to managers of a government-owned steel mill in China. SSI Korea made the payments to induce the steel mill managers to purchase scrap metal from Schnitzer Steel. The bribes, which took the form of commissions, refunds, and gratuities via off-book bank accounts, led to a substantial increase in business. In addition, the SEC alleged that Schnitzer Steel violated the FCPA's books and records and internal controls provisions.

To settle the criminal and administrative charges levied against it for violating the FCPA, Schnitzer Steel agreed to pay a total of $15.2 million. In the criminal proceeding, the company's wholly owned subsidiary, SSI Korea, pled guilty to violations of the FCPA's anti-bribery and books and records provisions. SSI Korea agreed to pay a $7.5 million criminal fine. A DPA was entered into with Schnitzer Steel, the parent corporation, in which Schnitzer Steel accepted responsibility for the conduct of its employees and agreed to enhance its internal compliance measures. The DPA also provided for the appointment of an independent compliance consultant to review Schnitzer Steel's compliance program and monitor the implementation of new internal controls related to the FCPA. In a parallel SEC administrative proceeding, the U.S. parent Schnitzer Steel consented to the entry of a cease and desist order and agreed to pay $7.7 million in disgorgement.

In December 2007, the SEC charged Robert W. Philip, the former chairman and CEO of Schnitzer Steel, with violating the FCPA anti-bribery provision by approving cash payments and other gifts to Chinese government officials of the government-owned steel mills.[86] According to the SEC complaint, Philip authorized payments of more than $200,000 in cash bribes and other gifts to mill managers. Philip agreed to disgorge $169,863 in salary and bonuses he had received, to pay $16,536 in pre-judgment interest, to pay a $75,000 civil penalty, and to enter into an order enjoining him from future FCPA violations.

P.   United States v. Vetco Gray Controls Inc., Vetco Gray UK Ltd. & Vetco Gray Controls Ltd.[87]

▶ **Misconduct Category:**	Payments to secure preferential treatment in customs handling— "express courier services," "interventions," and "evacuations"
▶ **Country:**	Nigeria
▶ **Foreign Government Officials:**	Customs Service
▶ **Improper Payment Dollar Value:**	$2 million
▶ **Combined Penalties:**	$26 million
▶ **Other:**	Recidivism a factor in large fine; independent monitor (see FCPA opinion release no. 04-02); use of major international freight forwarder as intermediary; any purchaser of company to be bound by the compliance and monitoring terms

In February 2007, the United States charged Vetco Gray Controls Inc., Vetco Gray Controls Ltd., and Vetco Gray UK Ltd., wholly owned subsidiaries of Vetco International Ltd. of London, United Kingdom, with violating the anti-bribery provisions of the FCPA. Vetco International was acquired from ABB Ltd. in 2004 by private equity firms, but improper payments continued after the 2004 plea. The companies pled guilty to violations of the anti-bribery provisions of the FCPA, as well as conspiracy to violate the FCPA. Additionally, Aibel Group Ltd., another wholly owned subsidiary of Vetco International, simultaneously entered into a DPA with the Justice Department regarding the same underlying conduct. As part of the plea and DPAs, it was agreed that Vetco Gray Controls Inc., Vetco Gray Controls Ltd., and Vetco Gray UK Ltd. would pay criminal fines of $6 million, $8 million, and $12 million, respectively, for a total of $26 million.

Specifically, the United States charged that beginning in February 2001, Vetco Gray UK began providing engineering and procurement services and subsea construction equipment for Nigeria's first deepwater oil drilling project, the Bonga Project. Several Vetco Gray UK affiliates, including Aibel Group Ltd., Vetco Gray Controls Inc., and Vetco Gray Controls Ltd., supplied Vetco Gray UK with employees and manufacturing equipment for the project. From at least September 2002 to at least April 2005, each of the defendants engaged the services of a major international freight forwarding and customs clearing company and, collectively, authorized that agent to make at least 378 corrupt payments totaling approximately $2.1 million to Nigerian Customs Service officials to induce those officials to provide the defendants with preferential treatment during the customs process.

This is the second time since July 2004 that Vetco Gray UK has pled guilty to violating the FCPA. On July 6, 2004, Vetco Gray UK, then named ABB Vetco Gray UK Ltd., and an affiliated company pled guilty to violating the anti-bribery provision of the FCPA in connection with the payment of more than $1 million in bribes to officials of NAPIMS, a Nigerian government agency that evaluates and approves potential bidders for contract work on oil exploration projects. ABB Vetco Gray UK Ltd. was renamed Vetco Gray UK Ltd. after a group of private equity entities acquired the upstream oil and gas businesses and assets of its parent corporation, ABB Handels-und Verwaltungs AG (ABB). The July 12, 2004, acquisition included the sale of Vetco Gray UK and the predecessors to the two other Vetco International subsidiaries that pled guilty. In anticipation of the July 12, 2004, acquisition, the private equity acquirers requested and the DOJ issued an FCPA Opinion Release (No. 2004-02). The Opinion Release required the acquirers to effectively institute and implement a compliance system, internal controls, training, and other procedures sufficient to have deterred and detected violations of the FCPA, among other obligations. The corrupt payments underlying the guilty pleas continued unabated from the period prior to the acquisition until at least mid-2005, notwithstanding the acquirer's commitments to the DOJ under the Opinion Release.

The sale to new owners, the prior directives issued by the DOJ, and Vetco Gray UK's prior FCPA conviction were all taken into account under the U.S. Sentencing Guidelines in calculating the $12 million criminal fine against Vetco Gray UK Ltd. The resolution of the criminal investigation of Vetco International and its subsidiaries resulted, in large part, from the actions of Vetco International in voluntarily disclosing the matter to the DOJ and Vetco International's subsidiaries' agreement to take significant remedial steps. In addition to the criminal fines, the plea agreements also require the defendants to (1) hire an independent monitor to oversee the creation and maintenance of a robust compliance program; (2) undertake and complete an investigation of the companies' conduct in various other countries as originally required under FCPA Opinion Release No. 2004-02; and (3) ensure that in the event any of the companies are sold, the sale shall bind any future purchaser to the monitoring and investigating obligations.

Q. United States v. Baker Hughes Services International Inc.;[88] SEC v. Baker Hughes Inc. & Roy Fearnley[89]

▶ **Misconduct Category:**	Consulting payments; consultants in Isle of Man and Angola
▶ **Countries:**	Angola, Indonesia, Kazakhstan, Nigeria, Russia
▶ **Foreign Government Officials:**	Government official; state-owned oil company official
▶ **Improper Payment Dollar Value:**	$15 million
▶ **Combined Penalties:**	$44 million
▶ **Other:**	Recidivist factor in large fine; plea by subsidiary, and DPA by parent company; disgorgement of profits and prejudgment interest ($23 million); largest FCPA fine at the time; model compliance program today

In April 2007, the United States charged Baker Hughes Services International Inc. (BHSI), a wholly owned subsidiary of Texas-headquartered Baker Hughes Incorporated, with violating the FCPA anti-bribery provisions, conspiracy to violate the FCPA, and aiding and abetting the falsification of the books and records of Baker Hughes Inc. in connection with improper payments to a Kazakh official. The parent company simultaneously entered into a DPA with the DOJ regarding the same underlying conduct and accepted responsibility for the conduct of its employees. The subsidiary agreed to pay an $11 million criminal fine, serve a three-year probation, and adopt a comprehensive anti-bribery program.

In a related matter, Baker Hughes Inc. reached a settlement with the SEC whereby it agreed to pay $10 million in civil penalties and more than $24 million in disgorgement of all profits it earned in connection with the Kazakh projects, including prejudgment interest. In the same civil complaint, the SEC charged Roy Fearnley, a former business development manager for Baker Hughes, with violating the FCPA and aiding and abetting his employer in doing so. Fearnley has not reached any settlement with the Commission.[90]

Subsidiary BHSI admitted that it paid approximately $4.1 million in bribes over two years to an intermediary whom the company understood and believed made the improper payments to an official of Kazakhoil, the state-owned oil company. The payments were made through an Isle of Man consulting firm that the parent retained as an agent in connection with a major oil field services contract. The payments were made from the subsidiary's bank account in Houston to a London bank account in the consultant's name.

The large monetary sanction—$44 million[91]—and DPA for the parent company likely balanced the fact that Baker Hughes Inc. had been subject to an FCPA cease and desist order in 2001 arising from improper payments to an Indonesian tax official and that it voluntarily disclosed to the DOJ the improper Kazakh payments of over $4.1 million, conducted an extensive and thorough internal investigation of its business practices in Kazakhstan and throughout its high-risk global operations, and implemented significant remedial steps and control enhancements.[92]

R. United States v. William J. Jefferson[93]

▶ **Misconduct Category:** Misuse of Congressional Office to Obtain Business Delegations to Africa

▶ **Countries:** Nigeria, Ghana, Equatorial Guinea, Botswana, Congo

▶ **Foreign Government Officials:** Officials of NITEL, Nigerian Telecommunications Service Provider

▶ **Improper Payment Dollar Value:** Unknown

▶ **Combined Penalties:** 13 years imprisonment

▶ **Other:** First prosecution of U.S. Congressman in an FCPA context; storage of $90,000 in cash in freezer

In June 2007, Congressman William J. Jefferson (D., La) was charged in the Eastern District of Virginia with a conspiracy to commit bribery, wire fraud, and to violate the FCPA, along with substantive bribery, fraud, and RICO counts. Two co-conspirators, Vernon L. Jackson, a Louisville, Kentucky, businessman, and Brett M. Pfeffer, a former Jefferson congressional staff member, pled guilty before Jefferson's trial. Jackson was sentenced to 87 months in jail and Pfeffer to 96 months in prison.

In June 2009, Jefferson proceeded to trial where the DOJ proved *inter alia* that from 2000 to 2005, Congressman Jefferson performed a wide range of official acts in return for things of value, including leading official business delegations to Africa; corresponding with U.S. and foreign government officials; and utilizing congressional staff meetings to promote businesses and business persons. The business ventures the Congressman promoted included telecommunications deals in Nigeria, Ghana, and elsewhere; oil concessions in Equatorial Guinea; satellite transmissions contracts in Botswana, Equatorial Guinea, and the Republic of Congo; and development of different plants and facilities in Nigeria. In November 2009, Jefferson was sentenced to thirteen years in jail.[94]

S.   U.S. Department of Justice—Paradigm B.V. Agreement[95]

▶ **Misconduct Category:**   Commission payments; improper payments to "internal consultants" of state-owned entities

▶ **Countries:**   China, Indonesia, Kazakhstan, Mexico, Nigeria

▶ **Foreign Government Officials:**   Representatives of state-owned oil companies

▶ **Improper Payment Dollar Value:** $100,000–$222,250

▶ **Combined Penalties:** $1 million

▶ **Other:**   First FCPA enforcement action involving an initial public offering (IPO); no original consultant due diligence; due diligence in connection with an IPO uncovered FCPA problems and led to voluntary disclosure; NPA; retention of outside compliance counsel

In September 2007, DOJ entered into an agreement with Houston-based Paradigm, B.V. involving improper payments to government officials in China, Indonesia, Kazakhstan, Mexico, and Nigeria. Paradigm identified misconduct in January 2007 in connection with its anticipated initial public offering and responded by conducting an investigation through outside counsel, voluntarily disclosing its findings to the DOJ, cooperating fully with the Department, and instituting extensive remedial compliance measures.

Paradigm, a private limited liability provider of enterprise software to the global oil and gas exploration and production industry, admitted to the payment of $22,250 into the Latvian bank account of a British West Indies company recommended as a consultant by an official of a KazMunaiGas, Kazakhstan's national oil company, to secure a tender for geological software. In connection with the consultant, Paradigm performed no due diligence on the British West Indies company, did not enter into any written agreement with the company, and did not appear to receive any services from the company. Paradigm also admitted using an agent in China to make commission payments to representatives of a subsidiary of the China National Offshore Oil Company (CNOOC) in connection with the sale of software to the CNOOC subsidiary. In addition, Paradigm directly retained and paid employees of Chinese national oil companies or state-owned entities as so-called internal consultants to evaluate Paradigm's software and to evaluate their employer's software and to influence their employer's procurement divisions to purchase Paradigm's products. Finally, Paradigm acknowledged similar conduct in dealings in Mexico, Indonesia, and Nigeria. The corrupt payments in Nigeria were between $100,000 and $200,000 and made through an agent to Nigerian politicians in order to obtain a contract to perform services and processing work for a subsidiary of the Nigerian National Petroleum Corporation.

As a result of Paradigm's thorough due diligence and investigation by outside counsel in the course of an IPO, voluntary disclosure before it sought to go public, full cooperation with the DOJ, and institution of extensive remedial compliance measures, the company would not be prosecuted if it satisfies obligations for 18 months, including ongoing cooperation, adoption of rigorous internal controls, retention of outside compliance counsel, and the payment of a $1 million penalty.

T. U.S. Department of Justice—Ingersoll-Rand Company, Ltd. Agreement;[96] SEC v. Ingersoll Rand Co.[97]

▶ **Misconduct Category:**	Kickbacks to government; side trips to Florence, Italy; $8,000 in pocket money to government officials in connection with visit to manufacturing facility
▶ **Country:**	Iraq
▶ **Foreign Government Officials:**	Iraqi government
▶ **Improper Payment Dollar Value:**	$850,000
▶ **Combined Penalties:**	$6.7 million
▶ **Other:**	Oil-for-Food program; parent and Irish and Italian subsidiaries receive DPA

In October 2007, the Ingersoll-Rand Company, Ltd. of Montvale, New Jersey, agreed, as part of a DPA with the U.S. government, to pay a $2.5 million fine. Charges had been brought against two subsidiaries of the company, Thermo King Ireland Limited and Ingersoll Rand Italiana SpA, in connection with an ongoing investigation of the U.N. Oil-for-Food Program. Ingersoll-Rand subsidiary Thermo King Ireland Limited was charged with conspiracy to commit wire fraud, and subsidiary Ingersoll-Rand Italiana SpA was charged with conspiracy to commit wire fraud and to violate the books and records provisions of the FCPA.[98]

The Justice Department has agreed to defer prosecution of criminal charges against Ingersoll-Rand and its subsidiaries for three years, because Ingersoll-Rand has thoroughly reviewed the improper payments and implemented enhanced compliance policies. If Ingersoll-Rand abides by the terms of the DPA, the Justice Department will dismiss the charges. According to the DPA, Ingersoll-Rand has acknowledged that its subsidiaries paid the Iraqi government kickbacks to obtain contracts to provide road construction equipment, air compressors and parts, and refrigerated trucks. The Iraqi government began requiring such illegal kickbacks in 2000, frequently portraying them incorrectly as "after-sales services fees."

Simultaneously, Ingersoll-Rand reached a settlement with the SEC in a related complaint.[99] It agreed to pay $1.95 million in civil penalties and approximately $2.27 million in disgorgement of all profits, including prejudgment interest. Subsidiaries of Ingersoll-Rand generated these profits in connection with contracts for which they paid kickbacks to the Iraqi government.

U. U.S. Department of Justice—York International Corp. Agreement[100]

▶ **Misconduct Category:**	Bribes and kickbacks to obtain government contract work
▶ **Countries:**	Bahrain, Egypt, India, Iraq, Turkey, United Arab Emirates
▶ **Foreign Government Officials:**	Iraqi government and others
▶ **Improper Payment Dollar Value:**	$647,000
▶ **Combined Penalties:**	$12 million
▶ **Other:**	Oil-for-Food program; DPA; three-year independent monitor

In October 2007, the Justice Department agreed to defer the prosecution of York International Corporation (York) of York, Pennsylvania, for three years. As part of this agreement, York must pay $10 million, its compliance program and procedures must be reviewed by an independent monitor, and it must fully cooperate with the Justice Department's ongoing investigation of the U.N. Oil-for-Food Program.

According to a criminal information filed October 1, 2007, York is charged with conspiracy to commit wire fraud and to violate the books and records provision of the FCPA.[101] York has acknowledged that it is responsible for the actions of two subsidiaries, York Air Conditioning and Refrigeration, and York Air Conditioning and Refrigeration FZE. Employees and agents of these subsidiaries paid approximately $647,000 in kickbacks to the Iraqi government to obtain contracts with Iraqi ministries. They also paid kickbacks and bribes related to other government contract work in Bahrain, Egypt, India, Turkey, and the United Arab Emirates.

The Justice Department has agreed to defer prosecution for three years, because York:

- Discovered the kickback payments early and reported them;
- Thoroughly reviewed those payments;

- Discovered and reviewed improper payments made in other countries;
- Implemented enhanced compliance policies and procedures;
- Was willing to undergo a three-year review of its compliance policies and procedures by an independent monitor.

If York abides by the terms of the DPA for three years, the Justice Department will not pursue the charges.

A settlement has also been reached in a related SEC matter.[102] Under the terms of this settlement, York consented to the filing of a complaint and agreed to pay $2 million in civil penalties and approximately $10 million in disgorgement of profits, including prejudgment interest. Subsidiaries of York paid kickbacks to the Iraqi government and other governments in order to win the contracts that generated these profits.

V. United States v. Steph;[103] United States v. Tillery & Novak[104]

▶ **Misconduct Category:**	Consultants; cash payments
▶ **Countries:**	Bolivia, Ecuador, Nigeria
▶ **Foreign Government Officials:**	High-ranking executive branch officials; tax officials; officials of state-owned oil company
▶ **Improper Payment Dollar Value:**	$6 million
▶ **Combined Penalties:**	None imposed yet
▶ **Other:**	Steph cooperating; U.S. State Department cancellation of Novak's passport led to deportation from South Africa to U.S.; Novak is awaiting trial while Tillery remains at large

In November 2007, Jason Edward Steph pled guilty to conspiracy to violate the FCPA by bribing Nigerian government officials with over $6 million. Steph was a Nigerian-based employee of Willbros International Inc., a subsidiary of Willbros Group Inc., a construction and engineering oil and gas services company. Steph was general manager of Willbros International Inc.'s onshore operations in Nigeria from 2002 to April 2005, and had been a Willbros employee since 1998.

Steph admitted that he agreed in late 2003 to make a series of corrupt payments totaling over $6 million to help to win a major gas pipeline construction contract in Nigeria. He made this agreement with a senior Willbros International Inc. executive, two of its "consultants," and certain Nigeria-based employees of a German engineering and construction firm. The $6 million in payments were offered to officials of the Nigerian state-owned oil company and its subsidiary, a Nigerian political party, and a senior employee in the executive branch of the Nigerian federal government. He also agreed that in furtherance of this conspiracy, he arranged for the payment of $1.8 million in cash to Nigerian government officials. He did this with former Willbros International Inc. executives. The maximum sentence for conspiring to violate the FCPA is five years in prison and a fine of $250,000. Steph is cooperating with an ongoing government investigation. In January 2010, he was sentenced to fifteen months in jail.

In January 2008, J. Kenneth Tillery, a former Willbros executive vice president, and Paul Novak, a Willbros consultant, were charged in connection with a conspiracy to pay more than $6 million in bribes to government officials in Nigeria and Ecuador. The four-count indictment charged Tillery and Novak with one count of conspiracy to violate the FCPA, two FCPA violations for specific corrupt payments to officials in Nigeria, and one count of money laundering.

The indictment returned in January 2008 was sealed until December 2008, when Novak was arrested upon his arrival in Houston. He had returned to the United States from South Africa after his U.S. passport was revoked. In November 2009, Novak pled guilty to a conspiracy to violate the FCPA count and a substantive FCPA count and is cooperating with the government.[105] Tillery remains at large.[106]

W. U.S. Department of Justice—Lucent Technologies Inc. Agreement;[107] SEC v. Lucent Technologies Inc.[108]

▶ **Misconduct Category:**	Travel and entertainment for 315 trips of over 1,000 Chinese officials to the United States, including Disneyland and Grand Canyon visits
▶ **Country:**	China
▶ **Foreign Government Officials:**	Employees of Chinese state-owned or state-controlled telecommunications enterprises
▶ **Improper Payment Dollar Value:**	Arguably several million dollars
▶ **Combined Penalties:**	$2.5 million
▶ **Other:**	Leading China travel and entertainment guidance; DPA

In December 2007, Lucent Technologies Inc., then a Murray Hill, New Jersey-based[109] global communications solutions provider, agreed under a DPA with the DOJ to pay a $1 million fine to resolve allegations of bribery violations of the FCPA.[110] From at least 2000 to 2003, Lucent paid millions of dollars for approximately 315 trips for Chinese government officials. While these trips were actually primarily for leisure, entertainment, and sightseeing, Lucent improperly recorded them in its books and records, in violation of the FCPA. Lucent typically characterized the trips as "factory inspections" or "training" even though, by 2001, Lucent no longer had any factories to tour as it had outsourced most of its manufacturing. In fact, the trips had little or no business content and were to destinations such as the Grand Canyon and Disneyland. Lucent's most senior Chinese officials requested and approved these trips, with support from Lucent employees in the United States, including Lucent's New Jersey headquarters. Lucent failed to provide internal controls to adequately monitor the provision to Chinese officials of travel and other things of value.

Lucent admitted to this conduct and agreed to pay a $1 million criminal fine. It also agreed to enhance its internal controls policies and procedures to ensure that Lucent keeps accurate books and records, develops a rigorous anti-corruption compliance code, and implements standards and procedures designed to detect and deter violations of the FCPA and other anti-corruption laws.

In a related matter and in connection with related conduct, the SEC filed a settled complaint against Lucent in December 2007.[111] The SEC's complaint asserts that Lucent spent $10 million on the trips discussed above, and that at least 1,000 Chinese government officials were involved. Lucent consented to the entry of a final judgment permanently enjoining it from future violations of books and records and internal controls provisions and agreed to pay a civil penalty of $1.5 million.

X. U.S. Department of Justice—Westinghouse Air Brake Technologies Corp. Agreement;[112] SEC v. Westinghouse Air Brake Technologies Corp.[113]

▶ **Misconduct Category:**	Payments to have bids for government business awarded or considered; monthly $31.50 facilitating payments to stop frequent governmental audits
▶ **Country:**	India
▶ **Foreign Government Officials:**	Railway Board, 16 Zonal Railways, Central Board of Excise and Customs
▶ **Improper Payment Dollar Value:**	$137,400
▶ **Combined Penalties:**	$677,000
▶ **Other:**	NPA; disgorgement of profits; self-investigation, voluntary disclosure, full cooperation and remedial efforts; low threshold for improper "facilitating payments"; SEC permits independent compliance consultant for 60 day review of compliance program

In February 2008, Westinghouse Air Brake Technologies Corporation (Wabtech) entered into an NPA with the Department of Justice regarding payments to Indian government officials, in violation of the FCPA.

Wabtech's business includes the manufacture of brake subsystems for locomotives and transit vehicles. A fourth-tier, wholly owned subsidiary, Pioneer Friction Limited, based in Calcutta, India, made certain improper payments to Indian Railway Board (IRB) officials and other government entities in order to assist Pioneer in obtaining business during the IRB and Zonal Railway Contract tender process, scheduling preshipping product inspections, obtaining product delivery certificates, and curbing excise tax audits. The Indian government was Pioneer's largest customer. The NPA included monthly "facilitating payments" of $31.50 to Control Board of Excise and Customs personnel to stop the frequent audits. As a result, FCPA practitioners consider this case to represent the "vanishing facilitation payment" exception.

As part of its agreement with the DOJ, Wabtech agreed to pay a $300,000 penalty, implement rigorous internal controls, and cooperate fully with the DOJ. The agreement acknowledges Wabtech's voluntary disclosure of the conduct, its thorough self-investigation, full cooperation with the DOJ, and remedial efforts. These mitigating factors led the DOJ to agree not to prosecute Wabtech or Pioneer for making improper payments if Wabtech satisfied the obligations above for three years.

A settlement was reached in a related SEC matter.[114] In light of the business Pioneer obtained in exchange for unlawful payments to officials, Wabtech consented to the filing of an SEC complaint and agreed to pay approximately $288,000 in disgorgement of profits (including prejudgment interest) and approximately $89,000 in civil penalties. Instead of requiring an independent monitor, the SEC permitted Wabtech to retain an independent compliance consultant to renew the compliance program for 60 days.

Y.   United States v. Flowserve Corp.;[115] SEC v. Flowserve Corp.[116]

▶ **Misconduct Category:**	Surcharges and kickbacks disguised as inflated "after-sales service fees"
▶ **Countries:**	France, Iraq
▶ **Foreign Government Officials:**	Iraqi government
▶ **Improper Payment Dollar Value:**	$646,488
▶ **Combined Penalties:**	$10.5 million
▶ **Other:**	Oil-for-Food program; DPA

In February 2008, Flowserve Corporation (Flowserve), a Texas-based manufacturer of seals, valves, and pumps for the power, oil, gas, and chemical industries, agreed to pay a $4 million penalty as part of an agreement with the U.S. government regarding charges brought in connection with an ongoing investigation related to the United Nations Oil-for-Food program and the Iraqi government. The DOJ filed the DPA with Flowserve Corporation, as well as a criminal information against a French Flowserve subsidiary, Flowserve Pompes SAS (Flowserve Pompes), in the U.S. District Court for the District of Columbia. The criminal information charges that Flowserve Pompes engaged in a conspiracy to commit wire fraud and to violate the books and records provisions of the FCPA.[117]

Under the agreement, Flowserve has acknowledged responsibility for the actions of its subsidiary, whose employees and agents paid kickbacks to the Iraqi government in order to obtain contracts for the sale of large-scale water pumps and spare parts for use in Iraqi oil refineries. Between July 2002 and February 2003, employees of Flowserve Pompes paid a total of approximately $604,651 and offered to pay an additional $173,758 in kickbacks to the Iraqi government by inflating the price of contracts by approximately 10 percent before submitting them to the United Nations for approval; and concealed from the United Nations the fact that the contract prices contained a kickback to the Iraqi government. In recognition of Flowserve's review of the improper payments and the company's implementation of enhanced compliance policies and procedures, the DOJ agreed to defer prosecution of Flowserve Pompes for three years. If Flowserve and Flowserve Pompes abide by the terms of the DPA, the Department will dismiss the criminal information.

On the same date Flowserve also reached a books and records and internal controls settlement with the SEC under which it agreed to pay a $3 million civil penalty and approximately $3.5 million in disgorgement of all profits, including prejudgment interest, in connection with contracts for which the subsidiaries—Flowserve Pompes (French) and Flowserve B.V. (Dutch)—paid kickbacks to the Iraqi government.[118] In total, Flowserve agreed to pay approximately $10.5 million in penalties in the DOJ and SEC cases.

Z. United States v. Volvo Construction Equipment AB;[119] United States v. Renault Trucks SAS;[120] SEC v. Volvo AB[121]

▶ **Misconduct Category:**	Kickback payments disguised as "after-sales service fees"; Oil-for-Food program; use of agents and distributors
▶ **Countries:**	None
▶ **Foreign Government Officials:**	Iraqi government
▶ **Improper Payment Dollar Value:**	$6.3 million
▶ **Combined Penalties:**	$11 million plus $8.6 million in disgorgement of profits

▶ **Other:** DPAs with parent and two subsidiaries (Renault and Volvo Construction AB); separate conspiracies to commit wire fraud and violate the books and records provisions of the FCPA filed against subsidiaries; Oil-for-Food program

In March 2008, Volvo AB and two subsidiaries entered into a DPA whereby it agreed to a $7 million fine to the DOJ, a $4 million civil penalty to the SEC, and approximately $8.6 million in disgorgement in connection with U.N. Oil-for-Food program contracts for which its subsidiaries paid kickbacks to the Iraqi government. The informations charged that Renault Trucks and Volvo Construction Equipment AB (VCE) engaged in separate conspiracies to commit wire fraud and to violate the books and records provisions of the FCPA.

According to the letter agreement, AB Volvo acknowledged responsibility for the actions of its subsidiaries, whose employees, agents, and distributors paid kickbacks to the Iraqi government in order to obtain contracts for the sale of trucks and heavy commercial construction equipment. The DOJ alleged that between November 2000 and April 2003, employees and agents of Renault Trucks paid a total of approximately $5 million in kickbacks to the Iraqi government for a total of approximately 61 million euros' worth of contracts with various Iraqi ministries. To pay the kickbacks, Renault Trucks inflated the price of contracts by approximately 10 percent before submitting them to the United Nations for approval and concealed from the United Nations the fact that the contract prices contained a kickback to the Iraqi government. In some cases, Renault Trucks paid inflated prices to companies that outfitted the chassis and cabs produced by Renault Trucks. Those companies then used the excess funds to pay the kickbacks to the Iraqi government on behalf of Renault Trucks.

Further, between December 2000 and January 2003, Volvo Construction Equipment International AB (VCEI), the predecessor to VCE, and its distributors were awarded a total of approximately $13.8 million worth of contracts. During the same time period, employees, agents, and distributors of VCEI paid a total of approximately $1.3 million in kickbacks to the Iraqi government by inflating the price of contracts by approximately 10 percent before submitting them to the United Nations for approval and concealed from the United Nations the fact that the contract prices contained a kickback to the Iraqi government.

Beginning in 2000, the Iraqi government began requiring companies wishing to sell humanitarian goods to government ministries to pay a kickback, often mischaracterized as an "after-sales service fee," to the government in order to be granted a contract. The amount of that fee was usually 10 percent of the contract price. Such payments were not permitted under the Oil-for-Food program or other sanction regimes then in place.

In recognition of AB Volvo's thorough review of the improper payments and the company's implementation of enhanced compliance
policies and procedures, the DOJ agreed to defer prosecution of Renault
Trucks and VCE for three years. If AB Volvo, Renault Trucks, and VCE
abide by the terms of the agreement, the Department will dismiss the
criminal informations.

In a related matter, AB Volvo reached a settlement with the Securities
and Exchange Commission (SEC) under which it agreed to pay a $4 mil-
lion civil penalty and approximately $8.6 million in disgorgement of all
profits, including prejudgment interest, in connection with contracts for
which its subsidiaries paid kickbacks to the Iraqi government.

AA.   United States v. Self [122]

▶ **Misconduct Category:**	Sham marketing agreement with relative of a government official to obtain spare-parts contracts
▶ **Country:**	United Kingdom
▶ **Foreign Government Official:**	UK Ministry of Defence official
▶ **Improper Payment Dollar Value:**	$70,000
▶ **Combined Penalties:**	$20,000
▶ **Other:**	Two years' probation

In May 2008, Martin Self, a former president of Pacific Consolidated
Industries LP (PCI) of Santa Ana, California, pled guilty to charges related
to the bribery of a UK Ministry of Defence (UK-MOD) official in order to
obtain lucrative equipment contracts with the UK Royal Air Force. Self
pled guilty to a two-count information in U.S. District Court for the Central District of California, which charged him with violating the FCPA in
connection with the illicit payment of more than $70,000 in bribes for
the benefit of a UK-MOD official in exchange for obtaining and retaining
lucrative contracts for PCI.

PCI was a private company that manufactured air separation units
(ASUs) and other equipment for defense departments throughout the
world. ASUs generate oxygen in remote, extreme, and confined locations
for aircraft support and military hospitals. According to the plea agreement, in or about October 1999, Self as PCI's president and Leo Winston Smith,[123] PCI's then-executive vice president and director of sales
and marketing, caused PCI to enter into a marketing agreement with a
person Self understood to be a relative of the UK-MOD official. The official, as a result of his position within the UK-MOD, was able to influence the awarding of UK-MOD contracts for services and equipment.[124]
Self admitted that he was not aware of any genuine services provided by
the official's relative, and believed there was a high probability that the

payments were being made to the official's relative in order to benefit the official in exchange for obtaining and retaining the ASU contracts. Despite these beliefs, Self initiated several improper wire transfers to the relative of the UK-MOD official and deliberately avoided learning the true facts relating to the nature and purpose of the payments.

Self was sentenced to a prison term of eight months. In late 2003, after the conduct alleged in the information, PCI was acquired by a group of investors and renamed Pacific Consolidated Industries, LLC. The acquirer referred the matter to the Department of Justice and fully cooperated in the government's investigation.

BB.   United States v. Willbros Group Inc. & Willbros International Inc.;[125] SEC v. Willbros Group, Inc.[126]

▶ **Misconduct Category:**	Consultant contracts; cash bribes
▶ **Countries:**	Bolivia, Ecuador, Nigeria
▶ **Foreign Government Officials:**	Senior officials in executive branch; officials at state-owned oil company
▶ **Improper Payment Dollar Value:**	$6.3 million
▶ **Combined Penalties:**	$31.5 million
▶ **Other:**	Voluntary disclosure of 10-year scheme; termination of 15 officers or employees; $1 million improper payment during government investigation; corporate cooperation resulted in indictment of five individuals; DPAs for both parent and international subsidiary as a result of "exceptional cooperation"; $10.3 million in disgorgement of profits; fines to be paid over a three-year period

In May 2008, Willbros Group, Inc. (WGI) and its wholly owned subsidiary Willbros International, Inc. (WII) entered into a DPA with the DOJ for violations of the Foreign Corrupt Practices Act in Nigeria, Bolivia, and Ecuador.[127] WGI and WII jointly and severally agreed to pay $32.3 million: a $22 million criminal penalty in four installments to the DOJ and $10.3 million in disgorgement and prejudgment interest to the SEC. Willbros, which had incurred significant losses over the previous four years, was also allowed to pay its DOJ penalty over three years.

The DOJ filed a DPA and a criminal information against WGI and WII (collectively "Willbros") in the U.S. District Court for the Southern District of Texas. This six-count criminal information included one count of conspiracy to bribe Nigerian and Ecuadorian officials; two counts of violating the FCPA by authorizing specific corrupt payments to Nigerian and Ecuadorian officials; and three counts of violating the FCPA by falsifying books and records relating to corrupt payments and a tax fraud scheme.

WGI is a provider of construction, engineering, and other services in the oil and gas industry. It conducted international operations through WII. Willbros conspired with others to make corrupt payments to government officials abroad to assist Willbros in obtaining and retaining business, to secure improper advantages, and to induce officials to provide preferential treatment to them. Moreover, Willbros conspired to falsify books, records, and accounts to make these payments appear legitimate when they were actually bribes.

Three subsidiaries of WII conducted most of Willbros's Nigerian business. From the 1990s through 2005, these subsidiaries performed work on joint venture and other Nigerian oil and gas projects. One Nigerian project for Willbros was the Eastern Gas Gathering System (EGGS) project, which aimed to construct a major natural gas pipeline system through remote, swampy terrain in the Niger Delta. Through certain consultants and others, Willbros made a series of corrupt payments totaling more than $6.3 million to assist in obtaining this $387 million project. These payments were made and authorized to be made to officials of the Nigerian National Petroleum Corporation (NNPC), the Nigerian state-owned oil company; NNPC's subsidiary, the National Petroleum Investment Management Services; a senior official in the executive branch of the Nigerian federal government; officials of a multinational oil company operating the EGGS joint venture; and a political party.

In Ecuador, through certain consultants and others, Willbros agreed to make approximately $300,000 in corrupt payments to Ecuadorian government officials of the state-owned oil company PetroEcuador and its subsidiary PetroComercial, in order to assist in obtaining and retaining business. The business sought was a $3 million contract for the rehabilitation of approximately 16 kilometers of a gas pipeline, known as the Santo Domingo project.

In a related proceeding, the SEC filed a settled FCPA action in May 2008 against WGI and several former employees.[128] The complaint alleged that WGI engaged in multiple schemes to bribe foreign officials, including schemes to pay over $6 million to Nigerian government officials and employees to obtain contracts resulting in net profits of approximately $8.9 million; the aforementioned scheme to bribe Ecuadorian government officials to obtain a $3 million contract; and a scheme to avoid taxes fraudulently in Bolivia. In so doing, WGI violated the improper payment to foreign officials, books and records, internal controls, and false statement provisions. WGI agreed to entry of a judgment permanently enjoining it from future violations of these provisions. WGI must also pay disgorgement of the $8.9 million in profits, plus prejudgment interest of $1.4 million.

Aggravating facts against Willbros included the following. First, a payment was made to a senior official in the executive branch of the federal government of Nigeria. This was part of a series of corrupt payments that Willbros conspired to make and made through sham "consultancy agreements," and through the knowing payment of false invoices. Second, bribes were paid in three countries on two continents for 10 years. Third, a million-dollar bribe by a Willbros country manager was paid during the government investigation.

Upon discovering officer misconduct in Bolivia, Willbros took numerous remedial steps enabling it to obtain a DPA, including:

- Commencing a thorough audit committee internal investigation within 24 hours of notice of allegations of corporate tax fraud committed by employees and purported consultants working on behalf of the Willbros subsidiary's Bolivian subsidiary;
- Quickly expanding the scope of the internal investigation, which included extensive forensic analysis, into alleged misconduct in other international locations, primarily Nigeria and Ecuador, and promptly and voluntarily reporting the results of its investigation to the DOJ and the SEC;
- Severing its employment relationship with a senior international executive within 10 days of receiving allegations of his involvement in the Bolivian tax scheme, and seizing from him critical encrypted electronic evidence at the time of his severance;
- Taking prompt and appropriate disciplinary actions, without regard to rank, against 18 additional employees;
- Voluntarily agreeing, as to the DOJ only, to a limited waiver of attorney-client privilege with respect to certain specific subject matters important to the DOJ's understanding of the internal investigation;
- Promptly terminating commercial relationships with purported "consulting" companies based in Nigeria, which companies Willbros suspected of assisting in making improper payments to Nigerian government officials;
- Promptly reporting the misconduct of certain WII employees who, along with others, made additional improper payments in Nigeria after WGI and the government had begun investigations, which reporting was a substantial factor in causing the guilty pleas of two of the responsible individuals;
- Upon conclusion of the internal investigation, continuing to cooperate with the DOJ and SEC in their parallel investigations, which cooperation included making numerous current and former employees available for interviews and testimony in the United States and abroad, and responding promptly to requests for docu-

mentary evidence, much of which was located in remote international locations;

- Expanding, enhancing, and, where appropriate, centralizing its worldwide legal, accounting, and international audit functions;
- Issuing an enhanced, stand-alone FCPA policy and conducting worldwide training upon implementation of that policy;
- Retaining new senior management with substantial international experience and understanding of FCPA requirements;
- Acknowledging responsibility for the misconduct; and
- Delaying pursuit of civil remedies against certain former employees so as not to prejudice the DOJ's criminal investigation of the individuals.

The above cooperative and remedial steps were specifically outlined in the DPA and represent model remedial steps by a company discovering and promptly investigating bribery conduct. The Willbros resolution offers important guidance on how midsize companies uncovering serious misconduct by senior management in multiple countries can still manage to avoid a felony conviction for both the parent and its subsidiaries.

CC.   United States v. AGA Medical Corp.[129]

▶ **Misconduct Category:**	Kickback payments to physicians at state-owned hospitals
▶ **Country:**	China
▶ **Foreign Government Officials:**	High-ranking officials at state-owned hospital
▶ **Improper Payment Dollar Value:**	$480,000
▶ **Combined Penalties:**	$2 million
▶ **Other:**	DPA; use of Chinese distributor to make payments; prosecution of small U.S. company

In June 2008, AGA Medical Corporation of Plymouth, Minnesota, agreed to pay the Department of Justice a $2 million criminal penalty in connection with corrupt payments made to Chinese government officials. AGA is a privately held medical device manufacturer with about $150 million in annual sales.

The criminal information alleged two series of corrupt payments.[130] First, between 1997 and 2005, AGA, one of its high-ranking officers, and other employees agreed to make improper payments to doctors in China through AGA's local distributor. The doctors involved were employed by government-owned hospitals. Second, from 2000 to 2002, as it sought patents for its products, AGA and one of its high-ranking officers agreed to make corrupt payments to Chinese government officials through their local Chinese distributor.

The DOJ entered into a DPA with AGA and filed a criminal information against it in the U.S. District Court for the District of Minnesota. AGA, which voluntarily disclosed and thoroughly reviewed the improper payments, cooperated fully with the U.S. government, enhanced its corporate compliance policies and procedures, and engaged an independent corporate monitor. In recognition of these efforts, the DOJ agreed to a three-year DPA. The case makes clear that the DOJ will fully pursue small companies for anti-bribery conduct even if such companies have small overseas sales and limited compliance resources.

DD. U.S. Department of Justice—Faro Technologies, Inc;[131] *In re* Faro Technologies, Inc. Agreement[132] SEC v. Oscar H. Meza[133]

▶ **Misconduct Category:**	"Referral fees;" use of shell company to pay Chinese officials to "avoid exposure"
▶ **Country:**	China
▶ **Foreign Government Officials:**	Employees of state-owned or controlled companies
▶ **Improper Payment Dollar Value:**	$44,482
▶ **Combined Penalties:**	Faro: $2.95 million; Meza: $30,000 civil penalty and $26,707 in disgorgement of profits and prejudgement interest
▶ **Other:**	Two-year NPA; small company; voluntary disclosure and cooperation; independent monitor; disgorgement; Faro secured $4.5 million in sales and approximately $1.4 million in net profit.

In June 2008, Faro Technologies, Inc. entered into an NPA and agreed to pay the DOJ a $1.1 million penalty in connection with corrupt payments to Chinese government officials. Faro, a Florida-based public company, specializes in computerized measurement devices and software and had a net income of $18 million in 2007. It began selling its products in China in 2003 through a subsidiary, Faro China. In 2004 and 2005, in order to secure business there, a Faro employee authorized other Faro employees to make corrupt payments to employees of Chinese state-owned or state-controlled entities. These payments were internally termed "referral fees" and disguised as such, and helped to secure contracts worth approximately $4.5 million. In addition, in 2005, Faro employees began routing the corrupt payments to Chinese officials through a shell company, and wrote internal e-mails explaining that they did so to "avoid exposure." Faro falsely recorded at least $238,000 in improper payments in its books and records, terming the bribe payments "referral fees." Moreover, between May 2003 and February 2006, Faro did not maintain a system of internal controls regarding foreign sales sufficient to comply with the FCPA.

Faro voluntarily disclosed the improper payments and made a thorough review of them, cooperated with the DOJ investigation, implemented and committed to implement enhanced compliance policies and procedures, and agreed to engage an independent corporate monitor. In recognition of its voluntary disclosure and other efforts, the DOJ agreed to a two-year NPA. The SEC simultaneously instituted a settled enforcement action against Faro whereby Faro agreed to pay approximately $1.85 million in disgorgement of profits and prejudgment interest, and consented to the entry of a cease and desist order.

In August, 2009, the SEC filed a settled enforcement action against Oscar H. Meza, formerly the Director of Asia Pacific Sales for Faro. The Commission alleged that beginning in 2004, Meza authorized a former Faro subsidiary employee to make improper payments totaling $444,492 over the next two years, generating $4.5 million in sales and approximately $1.4 million in net profit. Meza agreed to pay a $30,000 civil penalty as well as $26,707 in disgorgement of profits and prejudgement interest. Meza was charged with anti-bribery books and records and internal controls violations, and aiding and abetting Faro's violations of the same.

EE.   United States v. Nexus Technologies[134]

▶ **Misconduct Category:**	Payments to secure supply contracts described as "commissions" in company records
▶ **Country:**	Vietnam
▶ **Foreign Government Officials:**	Ministries of Transport, Industry, and Public Safety
▶ **Improper Payment Dollar Value:**	$150,000
▶ **Combined Penalties:**	To be determined
▶ **Other:**	Three individual defendants and company awaiting trial; plea by Lukas

In September 2008, U.S. citizens Nam Nguyen, 52, of Houston; Joseph Lukas, 59, of Smithville, N.J.; Kim Nguyen, 39, of Philadelphia; and An Nguyen, 32, of Philadelphia were charged, along with Nexus Technologies Inc., a privately owned export company with offices in Philadelphia, New Jersey, and Vietnam that purchased a wide variety of equipment and technology, on one count of conspiracy to bribe Vietnamese public officials in violation of the FCPA and four substantive counts of violating the FCPA.

According to the indictment, Nexus Technologies Inc. sold equipment, including underwater mapping equipment, bomb containment equipment, helicopter parts, chemical detectors, satellite communication parts, and air tracking systems, for export to agencies of the government of Vietnam. The indictment alleged that from approximately 1999 through 2008, the defendants engaged in a conspiracy to pay Vietnamese government officials bribes in order to secure lucrative contracts for Nexus Technologies Inc. Over the course of the scheme, the defendants are alleged to have paid at least $150,000 in bribes to foreign officials in Vietnam. The defendants' customers in Vietnam are alleged to have included multiple Vietnamese government agencies, including the commercial branches of Vietnam's Ministries of Transport, Industry, and Public Safety. Nam Nguyen allegedly negotiated contracts and bribes with officials of Vietnamese government agencies, while Lukas negotiated with vendors in the United States. Kim Nguyen and An Nguyen allegedly arranged for the transfer of funds at Nam Nguyen's direction. In June 2009, Lukas pled guilty to one conspiracy count and one substantive FCPA count. Cases are still pending against the company and the remaining three individual defendants.

FF.   United States v. Stanley;[135] SEC v. Stanley[136]

▶ **Misconduct Category:**   Consultants (from UK and Japan)

▶ **Country:**   Nigeria

▶ **Foreign Government Officials:** Executive branch

▶ **Improper Payment Dollar Value:** $182 million

▶ **Combined Penalties:**   Restitution of $10.8 million

▶ **Other:**   Engineering, procurement, and construction contracts in Nigeria worth $6 billion; seven-year incarceration plea agreement; $10.8 million in restitution

In September 2008, Albert "Jack" Stanley, a former officer and director of Kellogg, Brown & Root, Inc. (KBR), a Texas-based global engineering and construction company, pled guilty to conspire to violate the FCPA and to violate the federal fraud statutes. The decade-long conspiracy included two separate schemes: bribery of Nigerian officials to obtain engineering, procurement, and construction contracts worth more than $6 billion, and conspiring to commit mail and wire fraud as part of a separate kickback scheme.

Between 1995 and 2004, KBR was part of a joint venture with three other companies awarded contracts by the government-owned company Nigeria LNG Ltd. (NLNG), to build liquefied natural gas (LNG) facilities on Bonny Island, Nigeria. Stanley was the senior representative of KBR on the joint venture's steering committee. He admitted that he authorized the joint venture to hire "agents" (Consulting Companies A and B) to bribe Nigerian officials, and that he met with senior officials in the executive branch of the Nigerian government to ask them to designate a representative with whom the joint venture could negotiate bribes. The joint venture paid $132 million to Consulting Company A and over $50 million to Consulting Company B during the bribery scheme; Stanley admitted that he intended for the agents' fees to be used, in part, to bribe Nigerian government officials. In a separate action, Stanley pled guilty to conspiracy to commit mail and wire fraud to defraud KBR and others. He admitted to receiving about $10.8 million in kickbacks from a consultant he caused KBR and its predecessor company to hire in connection with worldwide LNG projects.

Stanley, who awaits sentencing on May 26, 2010, faces a maximum penalty of 10 years in prison and a $500,000 fine. Under his plea agreement, he faces a seven-year sentence and the payment of $10.8 million in restitution. In a separate civil action, the SEC charged Stanley with violating the anti-bribery provisions of the FCPA and related provisions of the federal securities laws.

GG. United States v. Green & Green[137]

▶ **Misconduct Category:**   Sham contracts and sales commissions

▶ **Country:**   Thailand

▶ **Foreign Government Official:**   Former governor of Tourism Authority

▶ **Improper Payment Dollar Value:** $1.8 million

▶ **Combined Penalties:**   N/A

▶ **Other:**   Contract's value $14 million; tax and money laundering counts; two officers awaiting trial (small private company not charged)

In October 2008, the United States charged Gerald and Patricia Green, a film producer and his wife of West Hollywood, California, in the Central District of California, with paying bribes totaling $1.8 million to obtain contracts worth $14 million. The same couple had been indicted in January on federal charges of bribing a Thai government official, the former governor of the Tourism Authority of Thailand. The Greens allegedly paid these bribes during 2002 to 2007. As charged in the superseding indictment, the Greens conspired with others to make the bribes and used different business entities, some with phony business addresses and telephone numbers, in order to conceal the large sums they were being paid under the contracts. They disguised these bribes as "sales commissions." The indictment, which seeks forfeiture, charges the Greens with one count of conspiracy to violate the FCPA by paying bribes to a foreign public official and by engaging in money laundering; 10 substantive counts of violating the FCPA; seven counts of money laundering; one count of a transaction in criminally derived property; and two counts of false subscription of tax returns. The Greens were convicted by a jury in September, 2009, and await sentencing.

HH.   United States v. Aibel Group Ltd.[138]

▶ **Misconduct Category:**   Use of major international freight forwarder

▶ **Country:**   Nigeria

▶ **Foreign Government Officials:**   Customs Service

▶ **Improper Payment Dollar Value:** $2.1 million

▶ **Combined Penalties:** $4.2 million (with Aibel's guilty plea and sentence, the combined penalties paid by Vetco entities for the 2004, 2007, and 2008 guilty pleas now exceed $46 million)

▶ **Other:**   Plea to FCPA conspiracy and money laundering; violation of 2007 DPA resulting in an additional two-year reporting obligation to the U.S. government

In November 2008, Aibel Group Ltd., a United Kingdom corporation, pled guilty to a two-count superseding information charging a conspiracy to violate the FCPA and a substantive anti-money laundering in the Southern District of Texas. At the same time, Aibel Group admitted that it was not in compliance with a DPA it had entered into with the DOJ in February 2007 regarding the same underlying conduct. As part of the plea agreement, Aibel Group agreed to pay a $4.2 million criminal fine.

Beginning in February 2001, Aibel Group's predecessor company and several affiliated companies began providing engineering and procurement services, as well as subsea construction equipment, for Nigeria's first deepwater oil drilling operation, known as the Bonga Project. From at least September 2002 to at least April 2005, Aibel Group admitted to conspiring with others to make at least 378 corrupt payments totaling approximately $2.1 million to Nigerian customs service officials in an effort to induce those officials to give the defendants preferential treatment during the customs process. These corrupt payments were paid through a major international freight forwarding and customs clearance company to the Nigerian officials, and were coordinated largely through an affiliated company's offices in Houston.

This is the third time since July 2004 that entities affiliated with Aibel Group have pled guilty to violating the FCPA. On July 6, 2004, Vetco Gray UK Ltd., previously named ABB Vetco Gray UK Ltd., and an affiliated company pled guilty to violating the anti-bribery provisions of the FCPA in connection with the payment of more than $1 million in bribes to officials of the National Petroleum Investment Management Services, a Nigerian government agency that evaluates and approves potential bidders for contract work on oil exploration projects. ABB Vetco Gray UK Ltd. was renamed Vetco Gray UK Ltd. after its upstream oil and gas businesses and assets of its parent corporation, ABB Handels-und Verwaltungs AG (ABB), were acquired by a group of private equity entities.

In February 2007, Vetco Gray Controls Inc., Vetco Gray Controls Ltd. and Vetco Gray UK Ltd. (collectively referred to as the Vetco Gray entities), wholly owned subsidiaries of Vetco International Ltd., pled guilty to violating the anti-bribery provisions, *infra*. At the same time, Aibel Group, another wholly owned subsidiary of Vetco International Ltd., entered into the 2004 DPA with which Aibel Group admitted it was not in compliance. As part of the February 2007 plea, Vetco Gray Controls Inc., Vetco Gray Controls Ltd., and Vetco Gray UK Ltd. agreed to pay a combined $26 million criminal fine. Subsequent to the 2007 guilty pleas, the Vetco Gray entities were sold. The Vetco Gray entities have been in compliance with the terms of their respective plea agreements.

The resolution of the criminal investigation against Aibel Group in November 2008 and its affiliates in 2007 resulted, in large part, from the actions of the companies in voluntarily disclosing the matter to the Justice Department and the companies' agreement to take significant remedial steps. In addition to the $4.2 million criminal fine, Aibel Group was ordered in 2008 to serve a two-year term of organizational probation that requires, among other things, that it submit periodic reports regarding its progress in implementing anti-bribery compliance measures. The combined penalties paid by Vetco entities in 2004, 2007, and 2008 now exceed $46 million.

II.   United States v. Siemens AG;[139] SEC v. Siemens[140]

▶ **Misconduct Category:**	Consulting firm; cash payments; off the books slush funds; shell companies
▶ **Countries:**	Argentina, Bangladesh, China, France, Iraq, Isreal, Mexica, Russia, Turkey, Venezuela, Vietnam
▶ **Foreign Government Officials:**	Governmental officials; officials of state-owned telegraph & telephone board
▶ **Improper Payment Dollar Value:**	$1.3 billion

▶ **Combined Penalties:** $1.7 billion

▶ **Other:**   Largest FCPA fine ever; first criminal
                                   plea to books and records and
                                   internal controls violations (avoidance
                                   of government debarment and
                                   suspension); joint announcement
                                   of resolution by German and U.S.
                                   law enforcement officials; four-year
                                   monitorship—foreign national to
                                   serve as monitor; massive global
                                   internal investigation (34 countries,
                                   1,750 interviews, and 800 informational
                                   meetings); state of the art 10-element
                                   compliance model; $100 million World
                                   Bank settlement and up to four-year
                                   Russian ban

In December 2008, Siemens AG of Munich, Germany, and three subsidiaries (Siemens Argentina, Siemens Bangladesh, and Siemens Venezuela) pled guilty in Washington, D.C., to various FCPA violations and agreed to pay DOJ, SEC, and German authorities over $1.6 billion in penalties in the largest FCPA anti-bribery enforcement case to date. Siemens AG pled guilty to a two-count indictment charging criminal violations of the FCPA's internal controls and books and records provisions. By pleading guilty to the Act's accounting provisions, the parent company avoided a corruption-conviction government debarment in numerous jurisdictions. Further, pleas by three non-European subsidiaries likely avoided government debarment of Siemens in the European Community. The U.S. and German authorities concluded that Siemens and various subsidiaries had made improper payments exceeding $1.3 billion at various locations including Argentina, Bangladesh, France, Iraq, Turkey, and Venezuela. Siemens agreed to pay U.S. authorities penalties totaling $450 million and $350 million in disgorgement of profits through the SEC. The company agreed to pay German authorities $850 million in similar penalties and disgorgement.

In the wake of multiple searches of officers' and employees' homes in Germany, Siemens AG and its subsidiaries discovered FCPA violations after initiating an internal investigation of unprecedented scope. According to the DOJ, from the 1990s through 2007 Siemens engaged in a "systematic and widespread effort to make and to hide hundreds of millions of dollars in bribe payments across the globe."[141] From 2001 to 2007 Siemens and various subsidiaries paid more than $800 million in bribes. Efforts by Siemens executives involved off-the-books slush fund accounts and shell companies to facilitate bribes, and false entries on the company's books and records, for example, falsely recording bribes as consulting fees and accumulating profit reserves as a liability on company books and then using these funds to facilitate bribe payments.[142]

The company shared the results of its investigation with DOJ and SEC officials and continuously cooperated extensively and authentically with the DOJ in its ongoing investigation; took appropriate disciplinary actions against individual wrongdoers, including senior management; and took remedial action, including the complete restructuring of Siemens AG and the implementation of a sophisticated compliance program and organization. The 10 minimum elements of the compliance program required under the plea agreement are:

1. A compliance code with a clearly articulated corporate policy against violations of the FCPA, including its anti-bribery, books and records, and internal controls provisions, and other applicable counterparts (collectively, the "anti-corruption laws").

2. A system of financial and accounting procedures, including a system of internal accounting controls, designed to ensure the maintenance of fair and accurate books, records, and accounts.

3. Promulgation of compliance standards and procedures designed to reduce the prospect of violations of the anti-corruption laws and Siemens's compliance code. These standards and procedures shall apply to all directors, officers, and employees and, where necessary and appropriate, outside parties acting on behalf of Siemens in foreign jurisdictions, including agents, consultants, representatives, distributors, teaming partners, and joint venture partners (collectively referred to as "agents and business partners").

4. The assignment of responsibilities to one or more senior corporate officials of Siemens AG for the implementation and oversight of compliance with policies, standards, and procedures regarding the anti-corruption laws. Such corporate official(s) shall have the authority to report matters directly to the Audit or Compliance Committee of Siemens AG's Supervisory Board.

5. Mechanisms designed to ensure that the policies, standards, and procedures of Siemens regarding the anti-corruption laws are effectively communicated to all directors, officers, employees, and, where necessary and appropriate, agents and business partners. These mechanisms shall include (a) periodic training for all such directors, officers, employees, and, where necessary and appropriate, agents and business partners; and (b) annual certifications by all such directors, officers, employees, and, where necessary and appropriate, agents and business partners, certifying compliance with the training requirements.

6. An effective system for reporting suspected criminal conduct and/or violations of the compliance policies, standards, and

procedures regarding the anti-corruption laws for directors, officers, and, as necessary and appropriate, agents and business partners.

7. Appropriate disciplinary procedures to address, among other things, violations of the anti-corruption laws of Siemens's compliance code by directors, officers, and employees.

8. Appropriate due diligence requirements pertaining to the retention and oversight of agents and business partners.

9. Standard provisions in agreements, contracts, and renewals thereof with all agents and business partners that are designed to prevent violations of the FCPA and other applicable anti-corruption laws, which provisions may, depending upon the circumstances, include (a) anti-corruption representations and undertakings related to compliance with the anti-corruption laws; (b) rights to conduct audits of the books and records of the agent or business partner to ensure compliance with the foregoing; and (c) rights to terminate an agent or business partner as a result of any breach of anti-corruption laws, and regulations or representations and undertakings related to such matters.

10. Periodic testing of the compliance code, standards, and procedures designed to evaluate their effectiveness in detecting and reducing violations of the anti-corruption laws and Siemens's internal controls system and compliance code.

There are several significant features about the *Siemens* settlement in addition to the massive $1.7 billion in penalties. First, the parent company was not charged with bribery, enabling it to likely avoid government debarment in a large number of jurisdictions. Second, Siemens AG pled guilty to the FCPA's internal controls provision—the first time this section has been charged criminally. Third, while monitorships have become standard FCPA resolutions, the Siemens one is four years—a year longer than the common three-year terms, and the monitor will for the first time be a non-U.S. citizen, Dr. Theo Waizul, the former German Minister of Finance. Fourth, the announcement of the *Siemens* resolution was a joint one by the DOJ, SEC, and Munich prosecutors, signaling even greater coordination with foreign authorities in the anti-bribery arena. Fifth, the penalty, while massive by any measure, could have been more severe. Under the applicable corporate guidelines,[143] Siemens's criminal fine range was $1.35 billion to $2.7 billion.

The company received credit at sentencing for (1) substantial assistance in the investigation; (2) extraordinary efforts to uncover evidence of prior corrupt activities (34 countries, 1,750 interviews, and 800 informational meetings, and 1.5 million hours of billable time by outside counsel and accounting professionals); and (3) extensive commitment to restructure and remediate its operations to make it a worldwide leader in transparent and responsible corporate practices going forward. The company collected and preserved over 100 million documents and produced to the DOJ over 24,000 documents, amounting to over 100,000 pages. The *Siemens* case makes clear that there is almost no limit to corporate penalties, that companies will be expected to conduct thorough internal investigations, that multijurisdictional cooperation is here to stay, and that remedial measures must be thorough, global, and real.

In July 2009, Siemens AG reached a settlement with the World Bank, agreeing to pay $100 million over the next 15 years to aid anti-corruption efforts and agreeing to forgo bidding on any of the development bank's projects for two years. The World Bank's investigation focused on an urban-transport project the bank financed in Moscow. Under the agreement, Siemens's Russian unit faces a ban of up to four years on projects there, but the comprehensive settlement means the company will not face additional World Bank sanctions involving subsidiaries in other countries.[144]

JJ. United States v. Hioki[145]

▶ **Misconduct Category:**	Local sales agent payments to state-owned customers
▶ **Countries:**	Argentina, Brazil, Ecuador, Mexico, Venezuela
▶ **Foreign Government Officials:**	Officials of state-owned companies
▶ **Improper Payment Dollar Value:**	$1 million plus
▶ **Combined Penalties:**	$80,000
▶ **Other:**	Parallel antitrust division investigation of bid rigging; plea to conspiracy to violate both the FCPA and antitrust law

In December 2008, Misao Hioki, a Japanese marine hose executive with Bridgestone Corporation, pled guilty to both antitrust and FCPA violations and was sentenced to two years in jail and fined $80,000 for his participation in the conspiracies. With respect to his FCPA misconduct, the United States charged that from January 2004 through in or around May 2007, Hioki and his co-conspirators:

- Supervised Bridgestone's International Engineered Products (IEP) Department employees both in Japan and in regional subsidiaries, including a U.S. subsidiary of the company in the United States, who were responsible for selling the company's products in Latin America;
- Contracted with local sales agents in many of the Latin American countries where Bridgestone sought IEP sales;

- Developed relationships with employees of the government-owned enterprises with which Bridgestone sought to do business;
- Negotiated with employees of government-owned businesses in Argentina, Brazil, Ecuador, Mexico, Venezuela, and possibly other countries to make corrupt payments to those foreign officials to secure business for Bridgestone and its U.S. subsidiary;
- Approved the making of corrupt payments to the foreign government officials through the local sales agents, to secure business for Bridgestone and its U.S. subsidiary;
- Paid the local sales agents a commission for each sale and, if a corrupt payment to the customer through the local sales agent was involved with the sale, concealed that payment within the commission payment made to the local sales agent; and
- Coordinated these corrupt payments in Latin America through the U.S. subsidiary's offices in the United States including its Houston office.

The *Hioki* case demonstrates how different arms of the DOJ can work closely together. Here, the Antitrust Division was investigating marine hose cartel activity in Europe and Japan and later discovered information of possible FCPA violations in Latin America. The Antitrust Division shared the information with the Fraud Section of the DOJ, which supervises FCPA matters nationwide. Hioki was induced to cooperate in both investigations, which are continuing, and agreed to a two-year sentence.

KK.   United States v. Fiat S.p.A. Agreement;[146] United States v. Iveco S.p.A.;[147] United States v. CNH Italia S.p.A.;[148] United States v. CNH France S.A.;[149] SEC v. Fiat S.p.A & CNH Global N.V.[150]

▶ **Misconduct Category:**	Use of agents and distributor in Jordan and Lebanon to make payments to Iraqi government to obtain truck and truck parts contracts
▶ **Country:**	Iraq
▶ **Foreign Government Officials:**	None
▶ **Improper Payment Dollar Value:**	$4.4 million
▶ **Combined Penalties:**	$17.8 million
▶ **Other:**	Oil-for-Food program; none of the charged entities incorporated or headquartered in the United States; three-year DPA; use of conspiracy to commit wire fraud charges; exceptional international law enforcement cooperation

In December 2008, the DOJ and SEC announced that Fiat, the Italian automobile manufacturer, agreed to enter into a three-year DPA and to pay a total of $17.8 million to resolve an FCPA investigation. Fiat first agreed to pay $7 million in criminal penalties to the DOJ for improper payments to Iraqi ministers in connection with the U.N. Oil-for-Food program. Fiat and CNH Global, its Netherlands subsidiary, reached an SEC settlement whereby they agreed to pay $3.6 million in civil penalties and $7.2 million in disgorgement. In addition to demonstrating international law enforcement cooperation, the *Fiat* resolution is noteworthy for the fact that none of the entities charged was incorporated or headquartered in the United States, and very little of the misconduct occurred in the United States.

LL.   United States v. Kellogg, Brown & Root LLC;[151] SEC v. KBR[152]

▶ **Misconduct Category:**	Joint venture partners' payments to agents in UK and Japan
▶ **Country:**	Nigeria
▶ **Foreign Government Officials:**	High-level officials
▶ **Improper Payment Dollar Value:**	$180 million
▶ **Combined Penalties:**	$579 million
▶ **Other:**	Second largest FCPA fine—$402 million; appointment of a monitor

In February 2009, Texas-headquartered Kellogg Brown & Root (KBR) pled guilty to conspiring to violate the FCPA and four substantive violations of the anti-bribery provisions. Houston-based KBR is engaged in the business of providing engineering, procurement, and construction (EPC) services around the world, including designing and building liquefied natural gas (LNG) production plants. The criminal information alleged that beginning in 1994 and to 2004, KBR, along with other joint venture partners, paid bribes to high-level Nigerian government officials to win EPC contracts to build the Bonny Island LNG Project in the Delta Region of Nigeria. Members of the four-company joint venture paid two agents— one based in the United Kingdom and one in Japan—over $180 million to funnel bribes to Nigerian officials and win construction contracts worth more than $6 billion.[153] Under its plea agreement, KBR is required to pay a criminal fine of $402 million and to retain a monitor. This fine is the second largest FCPA criminal fine—behind only the Siemens $450 million criminal fine of December 2008.

In a related proceeding, the SEC charged KBR, an agent of U.S. issuer Halliburton, with violations of the anti-bribery provisions, and KBR and Halliburton Co., KBR's former parent company, with engaging in books and records and internal controls violations related to the bribery. KBR and Halliburton agreed to pay $177 million in disgorgement to settle the SEC's charges. The SEC $177 million sanction and the DOJ $402 million criminal penalty, totaling $579 million, represent the largest combined settlement ever paid by U.S. companies. In addition to a three-year monitor, the settlement imposes an independent consultant for Halliburton to review its policies and procedures as they relate to compliance with the FCPA.

MM.   United States v. Tesler & Chodan[154]

▶ **Misconduct Category:**	Consulting contracts
▶ **Country:**	Nigeria
▶ **Foreign Government Officials:**	Executive-branch officials and officials of state-owned oil company
▶ **Improper Payment Dollar Value:**	Up to $180 million
▶ **Combined Penalties:**	
▶ **Other:**	EPC contracts valued at $6 billion; UK extradition proceedings against Tesler in 2009; $130 million forfeiture

In February 2009, Jeffrey Tesler of London and Wojciech Chodan of Maidenhead, England, were charged with one count of conspiracy to violate the FCPA and 10 substantive violations under a sealed indictment filed in U.S. District Court for the Southern District of Texas.[155] Specifically, the two UK citizens were charged with a decade-long scheme to bribe Nigerian government officials to obtain engineering, procurement and construction (EPC) contracts. The EPC contracts to build liquefied natural gas (LNG) facilities on Bonny Island, Nigeria, were valued at more than $6 billion. The indictment also seeks forfeiture of more than $130 million from the defendants. In March 2009, Tesler was arrested by the London Metropolitan Police, and there is an outstanding arrest warrant in the United States for Chodan. The DOJ is seeking the defendants' extradition from the United Kingdom to the United States to stand trial.

Tesler was hired in 1995 as an agent of a four-company joint venture that was awarded four EPC contracts by Nigeria LNG Ltd. (NLNG) between 1995 and 2004 to build LNG facilities on Bonny Island. The government-owned Nigerian National Petroleum Corporation (NNPC) was the largest shareholder of NLNG, owning 49 percent of the company. Chodan was a former salesperson and consultant of a United Kingdom subsidiary of Kellogg, Brown & Root Inc. (KBR), one of the four joint venture companies. At so-called "cultural meetings," Chodan and other co-conspirators allegedly discussed the use of Tesler and other agents to pay bribes to Nigerian officials to secure the officials' support for awarding the EPC contracts to the joint venture.

The indictment alleges that the joint venture hired Tesler to bribe high-level Nigerian government officials, including top-level executive branch officials, and another agent to bribe lower-level Nigerian government officials, including employees of NLNG. At crucial junctures before the award of the EPC contracts, KBR's former CEO, Albert "Jack" Stanley, and others allegedly met with three successive former holders of a top-level office in the executive branch of the Nigerian government to ask the office holder to designate a representative with whom the joint venture should negotiate the bribes. Stanley and others allegedly negotiated bribe amounts with the office holders' representatives and agreed to hire Tesler and the other agent to pay the bribes. Stanley's sentencing is currently scheduled for August 27, 2009. The joint venture entered into a series of consulting contracts with a Gibraltar corporation allegedly controlled by Tesler to which the joint venture paid approximately $132 million for Tesler to use to bribe Nigerian government officials. On behalf of the joint venturers, Tesler wire-transferred bribe payments to or for the benefit of various Nigerian government officials, including officials of the executive branch, NNPC, and NLNG, and for the benefit of a political party in Nigeria. In a related criminal case, KBR's successor company, Kellogg, Brown & Root LLC, of Texas, pled guilty in February 2009 to charges related to the FCPA for its participation in the scheme to bribe Nigerian government officials. An extradition hearing for Tesler is under way.

NN.   United States v. Latin Node, Inc.[156]

▶ **Misconduct Category:**   Payments to third parties to obtain interconnection agreement and reduced rates

▶ **Countries:**   Honduras, Yemen

▶ **Foreign Government Officials:** Officials of state-owned telecommunication company; officials at the Ministry of Telecommunications; son of the president of Yemen

▶ **Improper Payment Dollar Value:** $2,250,000

▶ **Combined Penalties:** $2 million

▶ **Other:** Inadequate pre-closing due diligence; misconduct discovered during Elandia International Inc.'s post-closing discovery; post-acquisition voluntary disclosure to DOJ, and full cooperation and remedial actions, including termination of senior Latin Node management who had knowledge of or involvement in violations; plea by non-operating subsidiary may have avoided government debarment; no independent monitor

In April 2009, Latin Node Inc. (Latinode), a privately held Florida corporation, pled guilty to violation of the FCPA in connection with improper payments in Honduras and Yemen. The company agreed to pay a $2 million fine during a three-year period.[157]

Latinode, a wholesale telecommunications provider of protocol technology, admitted that from March 2004 to June 2007, it paid or caused to be paid $1,099,899 in payments to third parties, knowing that some or all of those funds would be passed on as bribes to officials of Hondutel, the state-owned telecom of Honduras. Latinode admitted it paid bribes to obtain an interconnection agreement and to reduce the rate per minute under the interconnection agreement. The payments were made through a Miami bank account with the knowledge and approval of senior Latinode executives. Recipients of the payments included a member of the interconnection agreement award evaluation committee, the deputy general manager of Hondutel, and a senior Hondutel in-house attorney.

Latinode also admitted that from July 2005 to April 2006, it made 17 payments totaling approximately $1,150,654 to Yemeni officials and to a third-party consultant with the knowledge that some or all of the funds would be passed on to Yemeni officials in exchange for favorable interconnection rates in Yemen. Intended payment recipients included the son of the Yemeni president, the vice president of operations at Tele Yemen, the Yemeni government-owned telecommunications company, other officials of Tele Yemen, and officials of the Yemeni Ministry of Telecommunications.

Elandia International Inc. first learned of the improper payments during post-closing discovery after it acquired Latinode and disclosed the misconduct to the DOJ. Further, it conducted an internal investigation, shared the factual results with the DOJ, and terminated senior Latinode management who had involvement in or knowledge of the improper payments. While no monitor requirement was imposed, Latinode was dissolved, negating any need for a monitor.

OO. United States v. Carson, Carson, Cosgrove, Edmonds, Ricotti, & Han Yong Kim; United States v. Covino & Morlock;[158] United States v. Control Components, Inc.[159]

▶ **Misconduct Category:** 263 corrupt payments to obtain contracts in over 30 countries

▶ **Countries:** China, Korea, Malaysia, United Arab Emirates

▶ **Foreign Government Officials:** State-owned company officials

▶ **Improper Payment Dollar Value:** $49 million in bribes to officials and $1.95 million in bribes to officers and employees of private companies

▶ **Combined Penalties:** CCI Corporate Fine of $18.2 million

▶ **Other:** Charging of six executives is an FCPA record, demonstrating DOJ commitment to pursue individual wrongdoers; destruction of records count against former director of sales for China and Taiwan; private bribes charged under the Travel Act; independent corporate compliance for three years

In April 2009, the DOJ charged six former executives of Control Components Inc. (CCI), an Orange County, California-based valve company, with a conspiracy to secure contracts by paying bribes to officials of foreign state-owned energy companies, as well as officers and employees of foreign and domestic private companies. According to the press release, bribes totaling $6.85 million resulted in net profits to the company of approximately $46.5 million. The indictment alleged that from approximately 2003 to 2007, the defendants and others caused 263 corrupt payments in more than 30 countries. Alleged corrupt payments were made to foreign officials of state-owned entities, including Jiangsu Nuclear Power Corp. (China), Guohua Electric Power (China), China Petroleum Materials and Equipment Corp., Petro China, Dongfang Electric Corporation (China), China National Offshore Oil Corporation, Korea Hydro and Nuclear Power, Petronas (Malaysia), and National Petroleum Construction Company (UAE).

The charges against the six executives include conspiracy to violate the FCPA and the Travel Act, substantive FCPA and Travel Act violations, and the destruction of records in connection with a matter within the jurisdiction of a department or agency of the United States. Earlier in 2009, former CCI executives Mario Covino and Richard Morlock pled guilty to the conspiracy charge and substantive FCPA charges and are expected to testify in the 2010 trial of the six executives.

In July 2009, CCI pled guilty to violations of the FCPA and the Travel Act in a bribery scheme to secure contracts in approximately 30 countries. CCI admitted it paid approximately $4.9 million to officials of state-owned companies and approximately $1.95 million in bribes to officers and employees of foreign privately owned companies. As part of a plea agreement, CCI agreed to pay a criminal fine of $18.2 million; to create, implement, and maintain a comprehensive anti-bribery compliance program; to retain an independent compliance monitor for a three-year term; to review the design and implementation of CCI's anti-bribery compliance program; to make periodic reports to the DOJ; to serve a three-year term of organized probation; and to continue to cooperate with the DOJ in its ongoing investigation.

PP. United States: Helmerich & Payne Inc.;[160] In the Matter of Helmerich & Payne, Inc.[161]

▶ **Misconduct Category:**

Bribes to import and export goods that were not within regulation, to import goods that could not be lawfully exported and to evade higher duties

▶ **Countries:** Argentina and Venezuela

▶ **Foreign Government Officials:** Customs Officials

▶ **Improper Payment Dollar Value:** Unknown

▶ **Combined Penalties:** $1.375 Million ($1 Million Penalty Plus $375,000 Disgorgement of Profits Including Prejudgment Interest)

▶ **Other:** Two Year DOJ Non-Prosecution Agreement; sec consent decree

In July 2009, Helmerich & Payne ("H&P"), a Tulsa-based contract supplier of oil drilling rigs, equipment, and personnel to the U.S. and South America, entered into a non-prosecution agreement with the Department of Justice relating to improper payments by H&P to Argentine and Venezuelan government officials. H&P is required to pay a $1 million penalty to resolve the allegations, to continue to cooperate, and to take future remedial steps. In a related matter, H&P settled with the SEC and agreed to pay $375,000 disgorgement of profits, including prejudgment interest.

H&P acknowledged that its subsidiaries, employees, and agents paid Argentine and Venezuelan customs officials in order to import and export goods that were not within regulation, to import goods that could not lawfully be imported, and to evade higher duties. As a result of H&P's voluntary disclosure and thorough self-investigation of the underlying conduct, the cooperation provided to the DOJ, and its extensive remedial efforts, the DOJ agreed not to prosecute H&P or its subsidiaries for making improper payments, provided the company pays the penalty, continues to cooperate, and implements further remedial measures under the two-year agreement.

QQ. United States v. AGCO Corporation;[162] SEC v. AGCO Corporation[163]

▶ **Misconduct Category:**	U.N. Oil for Food Program
▶ **Countries:**	Iraq
▶ **Foreign Government Officials:**	Ministry of Agriculture
▶ **Improper Payment Dollar Value:**	$5.9 Million
▶ **Combined Penalties:**	$19.9 Million ($4 Million and Disgorgement of $13.9 Million Plus $2 Million in Pre-Judgment Interest)
▶ **Other:**	DOJ deferred prosecution agreement (dpa); lax internal Audit and Legal Department oversight; use of fictitious "after sales service funds" to generate 40% kickbacks to government ministry

In September 2009, AGCO Corporation, a Duluth, Georgia, manufacturer and supplier of agricultural equipment and its subsidiaries, entered into a Deferred Prosecution Agreement relating to $5.9 million in kickback payments in connection with foreign sales of equipment under sixteen contracts to Iraq under the U.N. Oil for Food Program. The kickbacks were characterized as "after sales service funds ("ASSFs"), but no bona fide services were performed.

In 2000, AGCO's Iraq business manager learned from its Jordanian agent that the Iraqi Ministry of Agriculture was demanding a ten percent kickback as a condition of awarding contracts to AGCO, which sought to increase its market share in Iraq. To conceal the scheme, AGCO's employees created a fictional account denoted as "Ministry Accrual." The kickbacks were recorded in this account, which AGCO employees made appear was being used to pay an agent for his After Sales Commissions. The accrual account was created by AGCO Ltd.'s marketing staff had virtually no oversight from its finance department. Marketing and finance employees in the United Kingdom, France, and Denmark were instrumental in concealing the scheme whereby some contract prices were inflated by ten percent to cover the kickbacks to the Iraqi Ministry. One AGCO employee described the Finance Department employees as "blind leaders" who input information into AGCO's books without any adequate oversight role. Not only did AGCO's Internal Audit Department ignore newer problems with the sales process, but AGCO's legal department was aware that the company was conducting sales under the program into Iraq, a sanctioned country, but failed to ensure that the sanctions of the U.N. rules and regulations were followed.

Pursuant to the DPA, AGCO agreed to a $1.6 million penalty with the SEC. The parent company consented to a government injunction from future violations of Section 13(b)(2)(A) and Section 13(b)(2)(B) of the Securities Exchange Act of 1934, and ordered AGCO to disgorge $13,907,393 in profits, plus $2 million in prejudgment interest plus a civil penalty of $2.4 million.

RR. United States v. Joel Esquenazi, Carlos Rodriguez, Robert Antoine, Jean Rene Duperval, and Marguerite Grandison[164]

▶ **Misconduct Category:**   Use of Shell Companies to Receive and
                                     Forward Improper Payments to Haiti
                                     government officials to Obtain Preferred
                                     Telecommunications Rates

▶ **Countries:**   Haiti

▶ **Foreign Government Officials:** Haiti Teleco, Telecommunications
                                     Directors of International Relations

▶ **Improper Payment Dollar Value:** $800,000

▶ **Combined Penalties:**   Awaiting Trial

▶ **Other:**   First use of conspiracy and money
                                     laundering statutes to charge foreign
                                     officials

In December 2009, the DOJ unsealed a Southern District of Florida indictment charging two Florida executives of a Miami-based telecommunications company, the president of a Florida-based Telecom Consulting Services Corporation, and two former Haitian government officials for their alleged role in a foreign bribery, wire fraud, and money laundering scheme. The indictment alleged that the defendants participated in a scheme from November 2001 through March 2005, during which time the Florida telecommunications company paid more than $800,000 to shell companies to be used to bribe foreign officials of the Republic of Haiti's state-owned telecommunications company, Telecommunications D'Haiti (Haiti Teleco).

The telecommunications company executed a series of contracts with Haiti Teleco that allowed the company's customers to place telephone calls to Haiti. The alleged corrupt payments were authorized by the telecommunication company's president and vice president and were allegedly paid to successive Haitian government officials at Haiti Teleco. The purpose of the bribes was to obtain various business advantages from the Haitian officials for the telecommunications company, including issuing preferred telecommunications rates, reducing the number of minutes for which payment was owed, and giving a variety of credits towards sums owed, as well as to defraud the Republic of Haiti of revenue. To conceal the bribe payments, the defendants allegedly used shell companies to receive and forward on payments. In addition, they allegedly created false records claiming that the payments were for "consulting services," which were never intended or performed.

Signally, the former Haitian officials were charged with conspiracy to commit money laundering. The two, Robert Antoine and Jean Rene Duperval, had been directors of international relations for telecommunications at Haiti Teleco. While foreign officials may not be charged with substantive FCPA violations, there is no prohibition against charging a federal conspiracy to commit money laundering. This is the first time the DOJ has charged foreign officials in an FCPA matter.

The DOJ commended Haiti's financial intelligence unit, the Unité Centrale de Renseignements Financiers (UCREF), the Bureau des Affaires Financières et Economiques (BAFE), and the Haiti Ministry of Justice and Public Security. The prosecution is further indication of increased international law enforcement cooperation in anti-bribery investigations.

SS.   United States v. UTStarcom, Inc.[165]; SEC v. UTStarcom[166]

▶ **Misconduct Category:**	Improper Travel and Entertainment Expenses; Improper Executive Training Programs at U.S. Universities; Sham Consultants, Work Visas Issued under False Pretenses
▶ **Countries:**	China, Mongolia, and Thailand
▶ **Foreign Government Officials:**	Employees of State-Owned Telecommunications Companies
▶ **Improper Payment Dollar Value:**	$11 Million Plus
▶ **Combined Penalties:**	$3 Million
▶ **Other:**	DOJ non-prosecution agreement and sec consent decree; sightseeing trips under the guise of training; $600 bottles of wine; bribe to obtain a Mongolian licensee fee; voluntary disclosure and full cooperation; worldwide investigation, FCPA training and other proactive remedial efforts; annual compliance reports and certifications to the SEC for four years

In December 2009, UTStarcom Inc. (UTSI) entered into a non-prosecution agreement with the DOJ, agreeing to pay a $1.5 million fine for violations of the FCPA by providing travel and other things of value to foreign officials, specifically employees at state-owned telecommunications companies in the People's Republic of China (PRC). At the same time, the SEC obtained an identical penalty and obtained permanent injunctive relief. UTSI, a publicly traded Delaware-based corporation headquartered in California, is a global telecommunications company that designs, manufactures, and sells network equipment and handsets and has historically done most of its business in China with government-controlled municipal and provincial telecommunications companies through its wholly owned subsidiary UTStarcom China, Co. Ltd. (UTS-China).

The SEC alleged that UTStarcom's wholly owned subsidiary in China paid nearly $7 million between 2002 and 2007 for hundreds of overseas trips by employees of Chinese government-controlled telecommunications companies that were customers of UTStarcom, purportedly to provide customer training. It is part of UTS-China's standard practice to include as part of its internal sales contracts for wireless networks a provision for UTS-China to pay for some of the customer's employees to attend the purported training overseas after installation of the network. In reality, the trips were entirely or primarily for sightseeing popular tourist attractions in the United States, including Hawaii, Las Vegas, and New York City. Most trips lasted two weeks and cost $5,000 per customer employee. Also the trips were supposed to be for training at UTSI training facilities when UTSI had no training facilities at the purported training locations and conducted no training.

On at least seven occasions between 2002 and 2004, UTSI allegedly paid for executive training programs at U.S. universities that were attended by managers and other employees of government customers in China. The programs covered general management topics and were not specifically related to UTSI's products or business. UTSI paid for all expenses associated with the program, which totaled more than $4 million and included travel, tuition, room and board, field trips to tourist destinations, and a cash allowance of between $800 and $3,000 per person. UTSI accounted for the cost of the programs as "marketing expenses." The company's senior management believed that the executive training programs helped it obtain or retain business.

On at least ten occasions between 2001 and 2005, UTSI provided or offered full-time employment with UTSI in the U.S., including salaries and other benefits to employees of government customers or their family members in China and Thailand. In reality, these individuals never worked for UTSI in any capacity. However, phony annual performance reviews were placed in personnel files for the individuals to document their employment and UTSI improperly accounted for the payments to the individuals as "employee compensation." UT Starcom provided the individuals with work visas, when in reality the individuals did not work for UTStarcom.

In 2004, UTSI submitted a bid for a sales contract to a government-controlled telecommunications company in Thailand. While its bid was under consideration, UTSI's general manager in Thailand spent nearly $10,000 on French wine as a gift to agents of the government, including rare bottles that cost more than $600 each. The manager also spent $13,000 for entertainment expenses to secure the same contract. UTSI's former chief executive officer and executive vice president of UTS China approved the payments. UTSI reimbursed the expenditures and accounted for them as marketing expenses. In 2005, UTSI attempted to expand its business into Mongolia, and UTSI's EVP and the CEO of UTS-China authorized a $1.5 million payment to a Mongolian company pursuant to a purported consulting agreement and told UTSI's board of directors the $1.5 million was a license fee paid to the Mongolian government. In reality, the license fee was only $50,000 and the Mongolian company used a portion of that $1.5 million to make payments to at least one Mongolian government official to help UTSI obtain a favorable ruling in a dispute over its license. In 2007, the former parent EVP and CEO of its Chinese subsidiary authorized a $200,000 payment to a Chinese company pursuant to a purported consulting agreement. Although the payment was accounted for as a consulting expense, in reality there was a sham consulting company and the payment was made as part of an effort to obtain contracts from a Chinese government customer.

In 2006, after learning of alleged bribe payments, the parent company's audit committee initiated an internal investigation into potential FCPA violations, which UTSI expanded in 2007 and 2008 to cover all of its operations worldwide. UTSI adopted new FCPA-related policies and procedures, hired additional finance and internal compliance personnel, implemented stronger internal accounting controls, and conducted FCPA training at all of its major offices around the world. In reaching its NPA resolution, the DOJ recognized UTSI's voluntary disclosure, thorough self-investigation of the underlying conduct, the cooperation provided by the company to the department, and the company's remedial efforts. In the related administrative proceeding, UT Starcom agreed to settle SEC charges and pay a $1.5 million penalty and to provide the SEC with annual FCPA compliance reports and certifications for four years.[167]

TT. United States v. Alvarez (One of Sixteen Indictments in FBI Sting Operations)[168]

▶ **Misconduct Category:**   Scheme to pay bribes to Minister of Defense in African Country

▶ **Countries:**   Unidentified African Nation

▶ **Foreign Government Officials:** Minister of Defense

▶ **Improper Payment Dollar Value:** $3 Million Commission (20% to win $15 Million Deal)

▶ **Combined Penalties:**   Awaiting Trial

▶ **Other:**
Largest Single Investigation and Prosecution Against Individuals in FCPA History; 21 Search Warrants Executed in United States and United Kingdom by 150 FBI Agents and others; criminal forfeiture claim; mass arrests while attending las vegas industry trade show

In January 2010, twenty-two executives and employees of companies in military and law enforcement products industry were arrested for engaging in schemes to bribe foreign government officials to obtain and retain business. All but one of the defendants were arrested in Las Vegas while attending an industry trade show.[169] The sixteen indictments stemmed from an FBI undercover operation that focused on allegations of foreign bribery in the military and law enforcement products industry.

The sixteen indictments represent the largest single investigation and prosecution against individuals in the history of DOJ's enforcement of the FCPA. The indictments were returned on December 11, 2009, by a grand jury in Washington, D.C., but filed under seal until the arrests in January 2010. In connection with these indictments, approximately 150 FBI agents executed fourteen search warrants in locations across the country, including Bull Shoals, Ark.; San Francisco; Miami; Ponte Vedra Beach, Fla.; Sarasota, Fla.; St. Petersburg, Fla.; Sunrise, Fla.; University Park, Fla.; Decatur, Ga.; Stearns, Ky.; Upper Darby, Penn.; and Woodbridge, Va. Additionally, the United Kingdom's City of London Police executed seven search warrants in connection with their own investigations into companies involved in the foreign bribery conduct that formed the basis for the indictments.

The indictments allege that the defendants engaged in a scheme to pay bribes to the minister of defense for an unidentified country in Africa. In fact, the scheme was part of the undercover operation, with no actual involvement from any minister of defense. As part of the undercover operation, the defendants allegedly agreed to pay twenty percent "commission" to a sales agent who the defendants believed represented the minister of defense for a country in Africa in order to win a portion of a $15 million deal to outfit the country's presidential guard. In reality, the "sales agent" was an undercover FBI agent. The defendants were told that half of that "commission" would be paid directly to the minister of defense. The defendants allegedly agreed to create two price quotations in connection with the deals, with one quote representing the true cost of the goods and the second quote representing the true cost, plus the twenty percent "commission." The defendants also allegedly agreed to engage in a small "test" deal to show the minister of defense that he would personally receive the ten percent bribe. The defendants purportedly sent e-mail messages that confirmed their decisions.[170]

The indictments charged the following executives and employees of the various companies in the military and law enforcement product industries:

- Daniel Alvirez, 32, and Lee Allen Tolleson, 25, the president and director of acquisitions and logistics at a company in Bull Shoals, Ark., that manufactures and sells law enforcement and military equipment;
- Helmie Ashiblie, 44, the vice president and founder of a company in Woodbridge, Va., that supplies tactical bags and other security-related articles for law enforcement agencies and governments worldwide;
- Andrew Bigelow, 40, the managing partner and director of government programs for a Sarasota, Fla., company that sells machine guns, grenade launchers, and other small arms and accessories;
- R. Patrick Caldwell, 61, and Stephen Gerard Giordanella, 50, the current and former chief executive officers of a Sunrise, Fla., company that designs and manufactures concealable and tactical body armor;
- Yochanan R. Cohen, a/k/a Yochi Cohen, 47, the chief executive officer of a San Francisco company that manufactures security equipment, including body armor and ballistic plates;
- Haim Geri, 50, the president of a North Miami Beach, Fla., company that serves as a sales agent for companies in the law enforcement and military products industries;
- Amaro Goncalves, 49, the vice president of sales for Smith & Wesson, a Springfield, Mass., company that designs and manufactures firearms, firearm safety/security products, rifles, firearms systems, and accessories;
- John Gregory Godsey, a/k/a Greg Godsey, 37, and Mark Frederick Morales, 37, the owner and agent of a Decatur, Ga., company that sells ammunition and other law enforcement and military equipment;
- Saul Mishkin, 38, the owner and chief executive officer of an Aventura, Fla., company that sells law enforcement and military equipment;
- John M. Mushriqui, 28, and Jeana Mushriqui, 30, the director of international development and general counsel/U.S. manager of an Upper Darby, Penn., company that manufactures and exports bulletproof vests and other law enforcement and military equipment;
- David R. Painter, 56, and Lee M. Wares, 43, the chairman and director of a United Kingdom company that markets armored vehicles;
- Pankesh Patel, 43, the managing director of a United Kingdom company that acts as sales agent for companies in the law enforcement and military products industries;

- Ofer Paz, 50, the president and chief executive officer of an Israeli company that acts as a sales agent for companies in the law enforcement and military products industries;
- Jonathan M. Spiller, 58, the owner and president of a Ponte Vedra Beach, Fla., company that markets and sells law enforcement and military equipment;
- Israel Weisler, a/k/a Wayne Weisler, 63, and Michael Sachs, 66, owners and co-chief executive officers of a Stearns, Ky, company that designs, manufactures, and sells armor products, including body armor;
- John Benson Wier III, 46, the president of a St. Petersburg, Fla., company that sells tactical and ballistic equipment.

Each of the indictments allege that the defendants conspired to violate the FCPA, conspired to engage in money laundering, and engaged in substantive violations of the FCPA. The indictments also seek criminal forfeiture of the defendants' ill gotten gains.

UU.   United States v. Richard T. Bistrong[171]

▶ **Misconduct Category:**	"Success Fee" to Agent for the United Nations to Obtain Body Armor; Rigging of Pepper Spray Bid Specifications in the Netherlands and Advising a Colleague to the Use of Nigerian National Shell Company for Kickbacks to Secure Fingerprint Ink Contract
▶ **Countries:**	United Nations (A "Public International Organization);" Netherlands and Nigeria; Iraq (Export Violations)
▶ **Foreign Government Officials:**	U.N. Procurement Official; National Police Services Agency of the Netherlands (KLPD) Procurement Officer; and Nigerian National Independent Election commission (NIEC) Official
▶ **Improper Payment Dollar Value:**	$4.4 Million
▶ **Combined Penalties:**	Unknown
▶ **Other:**	Defendant is Reportedly "Individual 1" in the 22 Defendant FBI Sting of the military and law enforcement equipment industry

In January 2010, the DOJ charged Richard T. Bistrong in the U.S. District Court for the District of Columbia with conspiracy to make corrupt payments to foreign officials, to falsify books and records, and to export controlled goods without authorization. Bistrong, a former vice president for international sales at Armor Holdings of Jacksonville, Florida, is accused of paying bribes to get contracts to supply helmets, armored vests, pepper spray, and other protective gear to United Nations peacekeeping authorities and a Dutch law enforcement agency.

Specifically, beginning in July 2001, Bistrong's employer allegedly paid a U.N. agent more than $200,000 in commissions under a "success fee" arrangement for U.N. contracts, knowing a portion of the payments would go to a U.N. procurement official to induce that official to provide non-public inside information to the U.N. agent and to cause the U.N. to award body armor contracts to Bistrong's employer.

Further, the information charges that beginning in 2001, Bistrong allegedly schemed with a Dutch agent to rig a bid on a tender issued by the National Police Services Agency of the Netherlands ("KPLD") for a supply of pepper spray. At the request of a Norwegian sales agent and a Dutch agent, a KPLD procurement officer used his influence within KPLD to cause the KPLD to issue a tender specifying a specific type of pepper spray manufactured by Bistrong's employer and no other bidder, as opposed to an alternative pepper spray manufactured by a competitor that the KPLD was considering. After the award of the pepper spray contract to his employer, Bistrong and the Norwegian sales agent caused the company to pay the Dutch agent $15,000 for "marketing services," knowing some or all of that money would be passed onto the Dutch procurement officer.

Finally, the information charges that as part of the conspiracy, in 2006 Bistrong urged a fellow employee who was a Colombian citizen to not pay directly a Nigerian official of the Independent National Election Commission (INEC) to secure the sales of fingerprint inkpads to INEC, but instead to arrange for the official to designate a company to which a kickback should be paid. INEC never in fact purchased the inkpads.

Bistrong is also charged with conspiring to violate export control laws and specifically to export without a proper license ballistic armor, vests, and helmets to the Kurdistan Regional Government ("KRG"), which was located in Iraq. Armor reportedly disclosed the matter to the DOJ and SEC, and Bistrong was terminated before BAE Systems acquired the company in 2007.[172] In January 2010, the *New York Times* reported that Bistrong is "Individual 1" in the FBI's sting of the military and law enforcement supply industry.[173]

VV. United States v. BAE Systems plc[174]

▶ **Misconduct Category:**   Use of "Marketing Advisors" through Offshore Shell Companies to Ensure Favoritism in Foreign Government Sales

▶ **Countries:**   Kingdom of Saudi Arabia, Hungary, and Czech Republic

▶ **Foreign Government Officials:**   KSA Public Officials Who Would Influence KSA Fighter Jet Sales: Gain to BAES from False Statements to U.S. Government $200 million

▶ **Improper Payment Dollar Value:** $200 Million Plus

▶ **Combined Penalties:** $450 Million ($400 Million to U.S. and £30 Million to U.K. Authorities and Tanzania)

▶ **Other:**   False statements made to the U.S. secretary of defense and the DOJ regarding BAES' anti-corruption compliance measures and failure to honor certain compliance undertakings; despite the third largest criminal penalty ever imposed in an FCPA matter, no FCPA count charged; U.K. citizen to serve as corporate monitor for three-year period

In February 2010, the United States charged BAE Systems plc (BAES), formerly known as British Aerospace, with a conspiracy to: (a) knowingly impair the lawful functions of the Department of Defense and the Department of State; and (b) commit offenses against the United States, to wit: knowingly and willfully make false or fraudulent statements[175] and knowingly and willfully cause to be filed export license applications with the State Department's Directorate of Defense Trade Controls, that is, applications that failed to properly disclose fees on commissions made, offered and agreed to be made, directly or indirectly, in connection with sales of defense articles.[176] The improper payments furthered deals to lease SAAB/Grippen fighter jets to Hungary and the Czech Republic. In March 2010, BAES pled guilty and agreed to pay a $400 million fine,[177] the third largest criminal penalty in an FCPA investigation. BAES also agreed to the appointment of a monitor, a U.K. citizen acceptable to the DOJ for a period not to exceed three years.

Simultaneously with the filing of criminal information in the U.S., Britain's Serious Fraud Office (SFO) announced that it had reached an agreement with the BAES whereby the company will plead guilty to failing to keep reasonably accurate accounting records in relation to its activities in Tanzania. BAES agreed to pay £30 million comprising a financial order to be determined by a Crown Court judge, with the balance to be paid "as an *ex gratia* payment for the benefit of the people of Tanzania."[178]

The U.S. and U.K. resolutions with Europe's largest military contractor end two long-running investigations. While the criminal information filed in the U.S. did not name any individuals, prior published reports have indicated that BAES made payments exceeding $2 billion to Prince Bandar bin Sultan, the Kingdom's former ambassador to the United States, and to Prince Turki bin Nasser, who controlled the Saudi air force.[179] The criminal information stated that BAES' U.S. subsidiary was not involved in any of the illegal activities.[180]

The absence of a substantive FCPA count will likely aid BAES in avoiding a government debarment or suspension. The use of a conspiracy count predicated on false statements to U.S. government agencies also may have avoided problematic FCPA jurisdictional bases as most payments in the case appear to have been made wholly outside the United States. Still, the DOJ case serves as a warning that companies who pledge a compliance program and significant reforms to the DOJ or other government agencies should ensure that such promises are monitored, maintained and kept.

VII. PRACTICAL ADVICE IN INTERPRETING FCPA PROSECUTIONS, ENFORCEMENT ACTIONS, DOJ FCPA OPINION RELEASES, AND DOJ AND SEC CHARGING CRITERIA

Because there is a dearth of FCPA case law, counsel must carefully review DOJ prosecutions, DPAs, and NPAs, and SEC enforcement actions in the FCPA area. While not controlling as a matter of law, these resolutions can help guide clients through a challenging and evolving enforcement area. Some rules of thumb in reviewing the growing number of government charges, resolutions, and opinion releases include:

- Read each DOJ press release or SEC litigation release and DOJ information or SEC complaint for what it says and does not say. For example, does the resolution require a monitorship or simply impose an independent consultant? Does it suggest an ongoing investigation of the company's executives, or the industry, or a crossover into a related industry? For example, the Vetco Gray 2007 settlement spawned an investigation of a major international freight forwarder and its customers.
- Review favorable DOJ resolutions for their recognition of important compliance program and remedial measure efforts, e.g., Siemens and Willbros.
- Review the resolutions for language that portends follow-on individual DOJ prosecutions and/or SEC enforcement actions, e.g., the Schnitzer Steel criminal resolution led to a later SEC enforcement action against CEO Robert Philip.
- Do not ignore the lessons of seemingly minor resolutions; for example, the SEC's Delta & Pine Land Co. settlement signals a low dollar enforcement threshold for improper payments ($8,300/year), notwithstanding the company's voluntary disclosure and complete cooperation with the U.S. government.
- Assume that some of the DOJ and/or SEC settlement total dollar figures are approximations or estimates and may reflect what

the U.S. government thought it could prove in court as opposed to what it believes the actual figures may have been.

- Review what role a company's settlement with a foreign government authority may have played in the U.S. law enforcement settlement, for example, the Statoil settlement with Norway.
- Consider how the DOJ penalties in a published settlement correspond to U.S. Sentencing Guideline calculations under the Alternative Fines Act.
- Contrast the improper payment totals and resulting criminal penalties in first-offender cases versus recidivist cases (e.g., Baker Hughes and Vetco Gray), to see the fine multiplier the government uses against recidivists.
- Consider what types of misconduct are increasingly the focus of DOJ and SEC authorities, for example, Chinese travel and entertainment in the Lucent resolution, or merger and acquisition activity in the Titan, InVision, and Latin Node cases.
- Review the jurisdictional basis and theory underlying any DOJ or SEC action against foreign nationals or subsidiaries; for example, act in furtherance may be as insignificant as an e-mail in the United States.
- Consider why FCPA accounting provision charges were brought and not more egregious bribery violations; was there insufficient proof of bribes, or credit for exceptional cooperation?
- Review the SEC filings of any public company whose conduct is similar to the client's.
- Determine what specific remedial actions led the DOJ to not insist on a felony conviction; for example, Willbros's FCPA cooperation against former employees resulted in DPAs for both the parent and subsidiary.
- Consider whether a resolution required the imposition of a monitor. For example, the vast majority of oil for food prosecution settlements did not require an independent monitor. In Ingersoll Rand and Paradigm, the federal authorities permissed a "monitor-lite."
- Consider whether potential government debarment played a role in which charges were ultimately filed; for example, Siemens was not charged with any bribes but rather criminal books and records and internal controls violations, thereby avoiding mandatory EU debarment.
- Ascertain any industry, government program, or regional enforcement patterns. For example, the U.N. Oil-for-Food program cases did not result in FCPA bribery charges, because improper payments were made to a foreign government (Iraq) and not foreign government officials.
- Scan the index of DOJ FCPA Opinion Releases (Appendix 5) and consider any factually similar opinions.

- Consider whether the settlement or underlying document gives guidance on a particular foreign operation issue on policy; for example, the Wabtech NPA indicates that a $31.50 monthly payment to avoid recurrent audits may *not* be a legal "facilitating payment."
- Review the nine corporate charging criteria and commentary in *Principles of Federal Prosecution of Business Organizations* (Appendix 8).
- Review the thirteen SEC *Seaboard* charging criteria in any SEC investigation (Appendix 10).
- Consider any Section 20(a) Reports of the SEC, for example, Titan and Halliburton cases offering guidance to securities counsel handling mergers and acquisitions.

VIII.   ADDITIONAL RESOURCES

Ayres & Hipp, *Selected Trends in Enforcement of Anti-Corruption Laws throughout the World, in* THE FOREIGN CORRUPT PRACTICES ACT 2009: COPING WITH HEIGHTENED ENFORCEMENT RISKS (PLI Course Handbook B-1737, 2009).

Clark & Suprenant, *Siemens—Potential Interplay of FCPA Charges and Mandatory Debarment Under the Public Procurement Directive of the European Union*, presentation at the National Institute on White Collar Crime 2009 (San Francisco, March 5–6, 2009).

Press releases and litigation releases involving FCPA cases at Department of Justice and Securities and Exchange Commission Web sites (http://www.justice.gov and http://www.sec.gov).

Gibson, Dunn & Crutcher LLP, *2008 Year-End FCPA Update* (Jan. 25, 2009), available at http://www.gibsondunn.com/publications.

Martin, *Compliance with the Foreign Corrupt Practices Act and the Developing International Anti-Corruption Environment* (© 2009 Jay G. Martin) (unpublished manuscript on file at Baker Hughes Inc.).

Shearman & Sterling, FCPA DIGEST (October 2009) (comprehensive listing of every FCPA case since 1977), *available at* http://www.shearman.com.

Urofsky & Newcomb, *Recent Trends and Patterns in the Enforcement of the Foreign Corrupt Practices Act* (© 2009 Shearman & Sterling LLP), available at http://www.shearman.com.

NOTES

1. *United States v. Jefferson*, No. 1:07-CR-00209 (E.D. Va. June 2007).

2. *United States v. Smith*, No. 8:07-CR-00069 (C.D. Cal. Apr. 2007).

3. *United States v. Ott*, Crim. No. 07-CR-608 (D.N.J. July 2007); *U.S. v. Roger Michael Young*, No. 07-CR-609 (D.N.J. July 2007).

4. *United States v. Si Chan Wooh*, No. 07-CR-244-KI (D. Or. June 2007).

5. Press Release, U.S. Dep't of Justice, Four Executives Agree to Plead Guilty in Global LCD Price-Fixing Conspiracy (Jan. 15, 2009), http://www .usdoj.gov/opa/pr/2009/January/09-at-046.html.

6. Press Release, U.S. Dep't of Justice, Six Former Executives of California Valve Company Charged in $46 Million Foreign Bribery Conspiracy (Apr. 8, 2009).

7. Press Release, U.S. Dept. of Justice, *Twenty-Two Executives and Employees of Military and Law Enforcement Products Companies Charged in Foreign Bribery Scheme* (January 19, 2010), http://www.justice.gov/opa/pr/2010/January/ 10-crm-048.html.

8. Mark Mendelsohn, Deputy Chief, Fraud Section, U.S. Dep't of Justice, The Foreign Corrupt Practices Act: Current SEC and DOJ Enforcement Initiatives, Presentation at Am. Bar Ass'n Conference, Washington, D.C., Sept. 11, 2008.

9. *United States v. Monsanto Co.*, No. 05 CR 00008 (D.D.C. Jan. 6, 2005).

10. *SEC v. Ingersoll-Rand Co.*, No. 107 CV 01955 (D.D.C. Oct. 31, 2007).

11. *SEC v. York Int'l Corp.*, No. 07 CV 01750 (D.D.C. Oct. 1, 2007).

12. *See, e.g., In re Delta & Pine Land Co. & Turk Deltapure, Inc.*, SEC Release No. 56,138, Admin. Proceeding No. 3-12712 (July 26, 2007).

13. Press Release, U.S. Dep't of Justice, Aibel Group Ltd. Pleads Guilty to Foreign Bribery and Agrees to Pay $4.2 Million in Criminal Fines (Nov. 21, 2008), http://www.usdoj.gov/opa/pr/2008/November/08-crm-1041.html.

14. Memorandum from Craig S. Morford, Acting Deputy Att'y Gen., U.S. Dep't of Justice, to Heads of Department Components and United States Attorneys, Selection and Use of Monitors in Deferred Prosecution Agreements and Non-Prosecution Agreements with Corporations (Mar. 7, 2008), http:// www.usdoj.gov/dag/morford-useofmonitorsmemo-03072008.pdf. *See* Appendix 9.

15. Richard Grime & Alison Fischer, *Obvious and Not-So-Obvious Consequences for the Risk of FCPA Enforcement*, ABA Nat'l Inst. on White Collar Crime (San Francisco, Mar. 5–6, 2009), citing Judith Burns, *U.S. Justice Department Probing Oil Operation in Nigeria*, Dow JONES NEWS WIRE, July 25, 2007; *Oil Field Services Firm under Fire in Africa*, PETROLEUM INTELLIGENCE WEEKLY, Oct. 22. 2007.

16. THOMAS W. GOLDEN, STEVEN L. SKALAK & MONA M. CLAYTON, A GUIDE TO FORENSIC ACCOUNTING INVESTIGATION (2006).

17. *SEC v. Int'l Business Machs. Corp.*, Litig. Release No. 16,839, 73 S.E.C. Docket 3049 (Dec. 21, 2000).

18. *In re Baker Hughes Inc.*, Exchange Act Release No. 44,784, 75 S.E.C. Docket 1808 (Sep. 12, 2001).

19. No. 01-CV-3105 (S.D. Tex. 2001).

20. No. 01-CV-3106 (S.D. Tex. 2001).

21. *In re Chiquita Brands Int'l, Inc.,* Exchange Act Release No. 44,902, 75 S.E.C. Docket 2308 (Oct. 3, 2001).

22. *In re Bellsouth Corp.,* Exchange Act Release No. 45,279 (Jan. 15, 2002).

23. *In re BJ Servs. Co.,* Exchange Act Release No. 49,390 (Mar. 10, 2004).

24. *In re Schering-Plough Corp.,* Exchange Act Release No. 49,838, 82 S.E.C. Docket 3644 (Jun. 09, 2004).

25. *SEC v. The Dow Chem. Co.,* Litig. Release No. 20,000 (Feb. 13, 2007), Civil Action No. 07 CV 0033 (D.D.C.).

26. SEC Release No. 53,732 (Apr. 27, 2006).

27. *SEC v. Dow Chem. Co.,* Litig. Release No. 20,000 (Feb. 13, 2007), Civil Action No. 07 CV 0033 (D.D.C.).

28. SEC Release No. 56,138, Admin. Proceeding File No. 3-12712 (July 26, 2007).

29. *SEC v. Delta & Pine Land Co.,* No. 1:07-CV-01352 (RWR) (D.D.C. July 25, 2007).

30. Litig. Release No. 20,251 (Aug. 23, 2007), http://sec.gov/litigation/litreleases/2007/lr20251.htm.

31. SEC Release No. 56,533, Admin. Proceeding File No. 3-12833 (Sept. 26, 2007).

32. *SEC v. Srinivasan,* 07-CV-1699 (D.D.C. 2007).

33. *SEC v. Srinivasan,* Civil Action No. 1:07-CV-01699 (RBW) (D.D.C.) (Sept. 25, 2007).

34. *In re Elec. Data Sys. Corp.,* SEC Release No. 20,296, Admin. Proceeding No. 3-12825 (Sept. 25, 2007).

35. *SEC v. Chevron Corp.,* Litig. Release No. 20,363 (Nov. 14, 2007).

36. Litig. Release No. 20,410 (Dec. 20, 2007), http://www.sec.gov/litigation/litreleases/2007/lr20410.htm.

37. Civil Action No. 1:08-CV-01478 (EGS) (D.D.C.), http://www.sec.gov/litigation/litreleases/2008/lr20690.htm. (Aug. 27, 2008)

38. *SEC v. ITT Corporation,* Civil Action No. 1:09-CV-00272 (RJL) (D.D.C. 2009), http://www.sec.gov/litigation/complaints/2009/comp20896.pdf.

39. SEC v. Nature's Sunshine Products, Inc., SEC Litig. Release No. 21162 (July 31, 2009).

40. http://www.sec.gov/litigation/litreleases/2008/lr20690.htm.

41. SEC v. Avery Denison Corp.; SEC Litigation Release No. 21156 (July 28, 2009).

42. *Securities and Exchange Commission v. Bobby Benton,* Civ. Action No. 4:09-CV-03963 (S.D. Tex., Dec. 11, 2009), Lit. Rel. No. 21335 (Dec. 14, 2009). http://www.sec.gov/litreleases/2009/lr21335.htm

43. *Securities and Exchange Commission v. NATCO Group Inc.,* Civ. Action No. 4:10-CV-98 (S.D. Tex), Lit. Rel. No. 21374 January 11, 2010, http://www.sec.gov/litigation/lit releases/2010/lr21374.htm.

44. S. Rep. No. 95-1114, at 11 (1977), reprinted in 1977 U.S.C.C.A.N. 4098, 4108.

45. *United States v. Metcalf & Eddy, Inc.*, No. 99 Civ. 12566 (D. Mass. Dec. 14, 1999).

46. *Consent and Undertaking of Metcalf & Eddy, Inc.*, No. 99 Civ. 12566-NG (D. Mass. filed Dec. 14, 1999).

47. *Id.* ¶¶ 4, 7.

48. No. 02-CR-40 (D.D.C. 2002).

49. Press Release, U.S. Dep't of Justice, Former World Bank Employee Sentenced for Taking Kickbacks and Assisting in the Bribery of a Foreign Official (Apr. 25, 2008), http://www.usdoj.gov/opa/pr/2008/April/08-crm-341 .html.

50. *United States v. Basu*, Cp. No. 02-475 (D.D.C. Nov. 18, 2002).

51. *United States v. Basu*, Cri. No. 02-475-RWR (D.D.C. Nov. 2002).

52. *United States v. Sengupta*, Cr. No. 02-40 (D.D.C. Jan. 2002).

53. *United States v. Syncor Taiwan, Inc.*, No. 02 CR 01244 (C.D. Cal. Dec. 5, 2002).

54. *See SEC v. Syncor Int'l Corp.*, CA No. 1:02 CV O2421 (EGS) (D.D.C. filed Dec. 10, 2002).

55. *SEC v. Fu*, CA No. 1:07 CV 01735 (EGS) (D.D.C. filed Sept. 28, 2007).

56. *SEC v. Fu*, SEC Litig. Release No. 200310 (filed Sept. 28, 2007), Civil Action No. 1:07-cv-01735 (D.D.C.).

57. *United States v. Giffen*, 326 F. Supp. 2d 497 (S.D.N.Y. 2004).

58. No. 03-CR-406 (S.D.N.Y. 2003).

59. *United States v. Bodmer*, 342 F. Supp. 2d 176 (S.D.N.Y. 2004).

60. Press Release, U.S. Attorney for S. Dist. of New York, U.S. Announces Charges in Massive Bribe Scheme to Bribe Senior Government Officials in the Republic of Azerbaijan (Oct. 6, 2005).

61. *United States v. ABB Vetco Gray, Inc. & ABB Vetco Gray UK Ltd.*, No. 04 CR 27901 (S.D. Tex. 2004).

62. Case No. 1.04 CV 1141 (RBW) (D.D.C. July 6, 2009).

63. *United States v. Monsanto Co.*, No. 05 CR 00008 (D.D.C. Jan. 6, 2005).

64. *SEC v. Monsanto*, No. 05-CV-14 (D.D.C. 2005).

65. Press Release, U.S. Dept. of Justice, Invision Technologies, Inc. Enters into Agreement with United States (Dec. 6, 2004), http://www.usdoj .gov/opa/pr/2004/December/04_crm_70.htm.

66. *SEC v. GE InVision, Inc.*, No. 3:05-CV-00660 (N.D. Cal. Feb. 14, 2005).

67. *United States v. Titan Corp.*, No. 05 CR 0314 BEN (S.D. Cal. Mar. 1, 2005).

68. *SEC v. Titan Corp.*, 05-CV-0411 (D.D.C. 2005).

69. *United States v. Head*, No. 06-CR-01380 (S.D. Cal. 2006).

70. *SEC v. Titan Corp.*, Civil Action No. 05-0411 (JR) (D.D.C. filed Mar. 1, 2005).

71. Exchange Act Release No. 51283 (March 1, 2005), Report of Investigation Pursuant to Section 21(a) of the Securities Exchange Act of 1934 and Commission Statement on Potential Exchange Act 10(b) and Section 14(a) Liability, http://www.sec.gov/litigation/investreport/34-51238.htm.

72. Section 21(a) of the Exchange Act allows the Commission, in its discretion, to "make such investigations as it deems necessary to determine whether any person has violated, is violating or is about to violate any provision of this title" and "to publish information concerning any such violation." Such reports enable the Commission to broadly discuss its position regarding the conduct in question.

73. Bruce V. Bigelow, *Titan Ex-Exec Admits Role in Benin Bribery*, SAN DIEGO UNION-TRIBUNE, June 24, 2006, *available at* http://www.signonsandiego.com/uniontrib/20060624/news_1b24plea.html.

74. Press Release, U.S. Dep't of Justice, Micrus Corp. Enters into Agreement to Resolve Potential Foreign Corrupt Practices Act Liability (Mar. 2, 2005), http://www.usdoj.gov/opa/pr/2005/March/05_crm_090.htm.

75. *U.S. v. Diagnostic Products Corp.*, No. 05-CR-482 (C.D. Cal. 2005).

76. SEC Admin. Proceeding File No. 3-11933 (May 20, 2005).

77. Press Release, U.S. Dep't of Justice, DPC (Tianjin) Ltd. Charged with Violating the Foreign Corrupt Practices Act (May 20, 2005), http://www.usdoj.gov/opa/pr/2005/May/05_crm_282.htm.

78. Press Release, U.S. Attorney for S. District of New York, U.S. Announces Charges in Massive Scheme to Bribe Senior Government Officials in the Republic of Azerbaijan (Oct. 6, 2005).

79. *U.S. v. Kozeny*, 541 F. 3d 166 (2d Cir. 2008).

80. Memorandum Opinion and Order dated Oct. 21, 2008, *United States v. Kozeny et al.*, 05 CR 518 (SAS), citing S. REP. No. 95-114, at 10–11 (1977), *reprinted in* 1977 U.S.C.C.A.N. 4098, 4108.

81. Press Release, U.S. Dep't of Justice, Former Alcatel CIT Executive Sentenced for Paying $2.5 Million in Bribes to Senior Costa Rican Officials (Sept. 23, 2008), http://www.usdoj.gov/criminal/pr/ press_releases/2008/09/09-23-08alcatel-sentenced.pdf.

82. *United States v. Statoil ASA*, No. 06-CR-00960 (S.D.N.Y. 2006).

83. SEC Admin. Proceeding File No. 3-12453 (Oct. 13, 2006).

84. SEC Admin. Proceeding File No. 2-17456 (Oct. 16, 2006).

85. *SEC v. Robert W. Philip*, No. 07-CV-1836 (D. Or. 2007).

86. *SEC v. Philip*, No. 07-CV-1836 (D. Or. filed Dec. 13, 2007); SEC Litig. Release No. 20,397 (Dec. 13, 2007).

87. *United States v. Vetco Gray Controls Inc.*, No. 4:07-CR-00004 (S.D. Tex. 2007).

88. *United States v. Baker Hughes Svcs. Int'l, Inc.*, No. H-07-129 (S.D. Tex. 2007).

89. No. 4:07-CV-01408 (S.D. Tex. 2007).

90. Press Release, SEC No. 2007-77, SEC Charges Baker Hughes with Foreign Bribery and with Violating 2001 Commission Cease-and-Desist Order (April 26, 2007), http://www.sec.gov/news/press/2007/2007-77.htm.

91. Press Release, U.S. Dep't of Justice, Baker Hughes Subsidiary Pleads Guilty to Bribing Kazakh Official and Agrees to Pay $11 Million Criminal Fine as Part of the Largest Combined Sanction Ever Imposed in FCPA Case (Apr. 26, 2007), http://www.usdoj.gov/opa/pr/2007/April/07_crm_296.html.

92. Id.

93. Press Release, U.S. Dept. of Justice, *Congressman William Jefferson Indicted on Bribery, Racketeering, Money Laundering, Obstruction of Justice and Related Charges* (June 4, 2007), http://www.justice.gov/opa/pr/2007/June/07-crm-402.

94. Press Release, U.S. Dept. of Justice, *Former Congressman Sentenced to 13 Years in Prison for Bribery and Other Charges* (Nov. 13, 2009), http://www.justive.gov/opa/pr/2009/ November/09-crm-231.html.

95. Press Release, U.S. Dep't of Justice, Paradigm B.V. Agrees to Pay $1 Million Penalty to Resolve Foreign Bribery Issues in Multiple Countries (Sept. 24, 2007), http://www.usdoj.gov/opa/pr/2007/September/07_crm_751.html.

96. Press Release, U.S. Dep't of Justice, Ingersoll-Rand Agrees to Pay $2.5 Million Fine in Connections with Payment of Kickbacks under the U.N. Oil for Food Program.

97. *SEC v. Ingersoll-Rand Co.*, No. 07-CV-1955 (D.D.C. 2007).

98. *United States v. Thermo King Ireland Ltd.*, No. 1:07 CR-00296 (D.D.C. 2007); *United States v. Ingersoll-Rand Italiana SpA*, No. 1:07 CR-00294 (D.D.C. 2007).

99. *SEC v. Ingersoll-Rand Co.*, No. 107-CV-01955 (D.D.C. Oct. 31, 2007).

100. Press Release, U.S. Dep't of Justice, Justice Department Agrees to Defer Prosecution of York International Corporation in Connection with Payment of Kickbacks under the U.N. Oil for Food Program (Oct. 1, 2007), http://www.usdoj.gov/opa/pr/2007/October/07_crm_283.html.

101. Id.

102. *SEC v. York Int'l Corp.*, No. 07 CV 01750 (D.D.C. Oct. 1, 2007).

103. *United States v. Steph*, Criminal No. H-07 307 (S.D. Tex. Nov. 5, 2007).

104. *United States v. Tillery & Novak*, Criminal No. H-08 022 (S.D. Tex. Jan. 17, 2008).

105. Press Release, U.S. Dept. of Justice, *Former Willbros International Consultant Pleads Guilty to $6 Million Foreign Bribery Scheme* (November 12, 2009), http://www.justice.gov/opa/pr/2009/November/09-crm-1220.html.

106. Press Release, U.S. Dep't of Justice, Former Willbros International Executive and Consultant Charged in $6 Million Foreign Bribery Conspiracy (Dec. 19, 2008), http://www.usdoj.gov/opa/pr/2008/December/08-crm-1137.html.

107. Press Release, U.S. Dep't of Justice, Lucent Technologies Inc. Agrees to Pay $1 Million Fine to Resolve FCPA Allegations (Dec. 21, 2007), http://www.justice.gov/opa/pr/2007/December/07_crm_1028.html.

108. No. 07-CV-02301 (D.D.C. 2007).

109. In December 2006, Lucent merged with Alcatel SA of France to form Alcatel-Lucent, headquartered in Paris.

110. Press Release, U.S. Dep't of Justice, Lucent Technologies Inc. Agrees to Pay $1 Million Fine to Resolve FCPA Allegations (Dec. 21, 2007), http://www.usdoj.gov/opa/pr/2007/December/07_crm_1028.html.

111. *SEC v. Lucent Techs. Inc.*, Civil Action No. 1:07-CV-02301, Litig. Release No. 20,414 (D.D.C. filed Dec. 21, 2007) (RBW).

112. Press Release, U.S. Dep't of Justice, Westinghouse Air Brake Technologies Corporation Agrees to Pay $300,000 Penalty to Resolve Foreign Bribery Violations in India (Feb. 14, 2008). http://www.usdoj.gov/opa/pr/2008/February/08_crm_116.html.

113. No. 08-CV-706 (E.D. Pa. 2008).

114. *SEC v. Westinghouse Air Brake Techs. Corp.*, Civil Action No. 08-CV-706, SEC Litig. Release No. 20,457 (E.D. Pa. Feb. 14, 2008).

115. Press Release, U.S. Dep't of Justice, Flowserve Corp. to Pay $4 Million Penalty for Kickback Payments to the Iraqi Government Under the U.N. Oil for Food Program (Feb. 21, 2008), http://www.usdoj.gov/criminal/npftf/pr/press_releases/2008/feb/02-21-08flowserv-agree.pdf.

116. No. 1:08 CV-00294 (D.D.C. 2008).

117. No. 1:08-CR-00035 (D.D.C. 2008).

118. *SEC v. Flowserve Corp.*, Civil Action No. 08 CV00294, Litig. Release No. 20461 (D.D.C. Feb. 21, 2008) (EGS).

119. Press Release, U.S. Dep't of Justice, AB Volvo to Pay $7 Million Penalty for Kickback Payments to the Iraqi Government under the U.N. Oil for Food Program (March 20, 2008), http://www.usdoj.gov/opa/pr/2008/March/08_crm_220.html.

120. *Id.*

121. Press Release, U.S. Dep't of Justice, AB Volvo to Pay $7 Million Penalty for Kickback Payments for the Iraqi Government under the U.N. Oil for Food Program (Mar. 20, 2008); *SEC v. AB Volvo*, Civil Action No. 08 CV 00473 (D.D.C.) (JB), Litig. Release No. 20,504 (Mar. 20, 2008).

122. Press Release, U.S. Dep't of Justice, Former Pacific Consolidated Industries LP Executive Pleads Guilty in Connection with Bribes Paid to UK Ministry of Defence Official (May 8, 2008), http://www.usdoj.gov/opa/pr/2008/May/08-crm-394.html.

123. Winston Smith was indicted in April 2007 for his role in the scheme and pled guilty on September 3, 2009. Sentencing is set for December 18, 2009.

124. The UK-MOD official was investigated by UK authorities and has pled guilty in the United Kingdom to accepting bribes from PCI and was sentenced to two years in prison.

125. Press Release, U.S. Dep't of Justice, Former World Bank Employee Sentenced for Taking Kickbacks and Assisting in the Bribery of a Foreign Official (Apr. 25, 2008), http://www.usdoj.gov/opa/pr/2008/April/08-crm-341.html.

126. No. 08 CV-1494 (S.D. Tex. 2008).

127. Press Release, U.S. Dep't of Justice, Willbros Group Inc. Enters Deferred Prosecution Agreement and Agrees to Pay $22 Million Penalty for FCPA Violations (May 14, 2008), http://www.usdoj.gov/opa/pr/2008/May/08-crm-417.html. Mr. Tarun represented Willbros Group Inc. and Willbros International Inc. before the Department of Justice and guided the company during the three-year DOJ-SEC investigation.

128. *SEC v. Willbros Group Inc.*, Civil Action No. 4:08-CV-01494, SEC Litig. Release No. 20,571 (S.D. Tex. Houston Div. May 14, 2008).

129. Press Release, U.S. Dep't of Justice, AGA Medical Corporation Agrees to Pay $2 Million Penalty and Enter Deferred Prosecution Agreement for FCPA Violations (June 3, 2008), http://www.usdoj.gov/opa/pr/2008/June/08-crm-491.html.

130. No. 0:08-CR-00172 (D. Minn. 2008).

131. Press Release, U.S. Dep't of Justice, Faro Technologies Inc. Agrees to Pay $1.1 Million Penalty and Enter Non-Prosecution Agreement for FCPA Violations (June 5, 2008), http://www.usdoj.gov/opa/pr/2008/June/08-crm-505.html.

132. SEC Admin. Proceeding File No. 3-13059 (June 5, 2008).

133. SEC v. Oscar H. Meza, Litig. Release No. 21190 (August 29, 2009) Civil Action No. 1:09-CV-01648 (D.D.C.).

134. Press Release, U.S. Dep't of Justice, Philadelphia Export Company and Employees Indicted for Paying Bribes to Foreign Officials (Sept. 5, 2008), http://www.usdoj.gov/opa/pr/2008/September/08-crm-782.html.

135. *United States v. Stanley*, CR. No. 8-597 (S.D. Tex.), *available at* http://s3.amazonaws.com/propublica/assets/docs/stanley_information_080829.pdf.

136. *SEC v. Stanley*, No. 08CR-697 (S.D. Tex. 2008).

137. Press Release, U.S. Att'y's Office for the Central Dist. of Cal., Film Executive and Spouse Indicted for Paying Bribes to a Thai Tourism Official to Obtain Lucrative Contracts (Oct. 2, 2008), http://www.usdoj.gov/usao/cac/pressroom/pr2008/134.html.

138. Press Release, U.S. Dep't of Justice, Aibel Group Ltd. Pleads Guilty to Foreign Bribery and Agrees to Pay $4.2 Million in Criminal Fines (Nov. 21, 2008), http://www.usdoj.gov/opa/pr/2008/November/08-crm-1041.html.

139. No. 08-CR-367 (D.D.C. 2008).

140. *SEC v. Siemens AG*, No. 08-CV-02167 (D.D.C. 2008).

141. Press Release, U.S. Dep't of Justice, Transcript of Press Conference Announcing Siemens AG and Three Subsidiaries Plead Guilty to Foreign Corrupt Practices Act Violations (Dec. 15, 2008), http://www.usdoj.gov/opa/pr/2008/December/08-crm-1105.html.

142. *Id.*

143. U.S. SENTENCING GUIDELINES MANUAL § 8C2.7.

144. Vanessa Fuhrmans, *Siemens Settles with World Bank on Bribes*, WALL ST. J., July 3, 2009, at B1.

145. Press Release, U.S. Dep't of Justice, Japanese Executive Pleads Guilty, Sentenced to Two Years in Jail for Participating in Conspiracies to Rig Bids and Bribe Foreign Officials to Purchase Marine Hose and Related Products (Dec. 10, 2008), http://www.usdoj.gov/opa/pr/2008/December/08-at-1084 .html.

146. Press Release, U.S. Dep't of Justice, Fiat Agrees to $7 Million Fine in Connection with Payment of $4.4 Million in Kickbacks by Three Subsidiaries under U.N. Oil for Food Program (December 22, 2008), http://www.usdoj .gov/opa/pr/2008/December/08_crm_1140.html.

147. No. 1:08-CR-00377-RJL (D.D.C. 2008).

148. No. 1:08-CR-00378-RJL (D.D.C. 2008).

149. No. 1:08-CR-00379-RJL (D.D.C. 2008).

150. No. 1:08-CV-02211 (D.D.C. 2008).

151. *United States v. Kellogg Brown & Root LLC*, H-09-071 (S.D. Tex.-Houston Div. information filed Feb. 6, 2009).

152. *SEC v. Halliburton Co. & KBR Inc.*, Civil Action No. 4:09-0399 (S.D. Tex. February 11, 2009).

153. The former CEO of KBR is Albert Jack Stanley, *supra*.

154. Press Release, U.S. Dep't of Justice, Two UK Citizens Charged by United States with Bribing Nigerian Government Officials to Obtain Lucrative Contracts as Part of KBR Joint Venture Scheme (Mar. 5, 2009), http:// www.usdoj.gov/criminal/pr/press_releases/2009/03/03-05-09tesler-charged .pdf.

155. *United States v. Tesler & Chodan*, H-09-098 (S.D. Tex. February 17, 2009).

156. *United States v. Latin Node, Inc.*, Case No. 1:09-CR-20239-PCH (S.D. Fla. filed Mar. 23, 2009).

157. Press Release, U.S. Dep't of Justice, Latin Node Inc. Pleads Guilty to Foreign Corrupt Practices Act Violation and Agrees to Pay a $2 Million Criminal Fine (Apr. 7, 2009), http://www.usdoj.gov/opa/pr/2009/April/09_ crm_318.html.

158. Press Release, U.S. Dep't of Justice, Six Former Executives of California Valve Company Charged in $46 Million Foreign Bribery Conspiracy (Apr. 8, 2009).

159. *Id.*

160. Press Release, U.S. Dept. of Justice, Helmerich & Payne Agrees to Pay $1 Million Penalty to Resolve Allegations of Foreign Bribery in South America (July 30, 2009). http://www.justice.gov/opa/pr/2009/July/09-crm-741.html.

161. Exchange Act Release No. 60400 (July 30, 2009) http://www.sec .gov/litigation/admin/2009/34-60400.pdf.

162. Press Release, U.S. Dept. of Justice, AGCO Corp. to Pay $1.6 Million in Connection with Payments to the Former Iraqi Government under the U.N. Oil-for-Food Program (September 30, 2009), http://www.justice.gov/ opa/pr/2009/September/ 09-crm-1056.html

163. *SEC v. AGCO Corporation*, Civ. Act. No. 1:09-CV-01865 (D.D.C.) (RMU), Lit. Rel. No. 21229 (September 30, 2009).

164. *United States v. Joel Esquenazi, Carlos Rodriguez, Robert Antoine, Jean Rene Duperval, and Marguerite Grandison*, 1:09-cr 21010-JEM-1, U.S.D.C. S.D. Fl. (Miami) (filed 12/04/09), http://www.justice.gov/opa/pr/2009/December/09-crm-1307.html.

165. Press Release, U.S. Dept. of Justice, UTStarcom Agrees to Pay $1.5 Million Penalty for Acts of Foreign Bribery in China (December 31, 2009) http://www.justice.gov/opa/pr/2009/ December/09-CRM-1390.html.

166. *Securities and Exchange Commission v. UTStarcom Inc.*, Case No. CV/09 6094 (JSW), U.S.D.C. N.D. Cal. Lit. Rel. No. 21357 (December 31, 2009); http://www.sec.gov/litreleases/ 2009/lr 21357.htm.

167. *Id.*

168. Press Release, U.S. Dept. of Justice, Twenty-Two Executives and Employees of Military and Law Enforcement Products Companies Charged in Foreign Bribery Scheme (January 19, 2010), http://www.justice.gov/opa/pr/2010/January/10-crm-048.html.

169. Diana B. Henriques, *FBI Snares Weapons Executives in Bribery Sting*, N.Y. Times, Jan. 21, 2010, at A3.

170. *Id.*

171. Information. 1:10-CR-00021-RJL-1, U.S.D.C. (D.D.C.) (Jan. 21, 2010).

172. Diana B. Henriques, *Supplier Accused of Bribes for U.N. Contracts*, N.Y. Times, January 23, 2010, http://www.nytimes.com/2010/01/23/business/23sting.html.

173. *Id. See* TT, *supra*, and discussion of *United States v. Alvarez*.

174. *United States v. BAE Systems plc.*, 1:10-cr-00035-JDB-1 U.S.D.C. D.D.C. (filed February 5, 2010).

175. 18 U.S.C. § 1001.

176. 22 U.S.C. § 1778.

177. Press Release, U.S. Dept. of Justice, BAE Systems plc Pleads Guilty and Ordered to Pay $400 Million Criminal Fine (March 1, 2010), http://www.justice.gov/opa/pr/2010/March/10-CRM-209.html.

178. Press Release, United Kingdom Serious Fraud Office, BAE Systems plc (February 5, 2010), http://www.sfo.uk/press-room/latest-press-releases/press-releases-2010/bae-systems-plc.

179. Christopher Drew and Nicola Clark, *BAE Settles Corruption Charges*, Feb. 6, 2010, www.nytimes.com/2010/02/06/business/global/06bribe.html.

180. Criminal Information at ¶ 2.

Conclusion

In an era of increasing globalized trade, anti-bribery conventions, international law enforcement cooperation, multijurisdictional government investigations, corporate governance initiatives, and greater public company reporting responsibilities, Department of Justice prosecutions and Securities and Exchange Commission enforcement actions against U.S. companies, their U.S. and foreign employees, and foreign nationals and entities for Foreign Corrupt Practices Act violations are on the rise and the stakes are far greater. Monetary sanctions in the tens and hundreds of millions of dollars—and, in the case of Siemens, $1.7 billion—as well as impositions of three-year monitorships are no longer rare and are essentially the rule for repeat offenders. With the prosecution of Siemens in both the United States and Germany, there is now precedent for criminal charges and billion-dollar penalties being simultaneously secured by law enforcement authorities in multiple jurisdictions.

To minimize the risk of FCPA violations, multinational companies can design quality compliance programs and internal controls that greatly reduce the risk of corrupt payments *and* earn the company significant credit if misconduct occurs and the DOJ and SEC investigate. Key compliance initiatives include custom codes of conduct and FCPA policies; regular live training for senior executives and for managers in international sales, finance, and legal roles; FCPA risk-based audits; and a sound protocol for addressing allegations of misconduct. Companies must conduct thorough due diligence of mergers, acquisitions, joint ventures, and third-party contractors; this due diligence can avert a disastrous business decision or establish the best defense against successor liability. Companies should continue post-transaction due diligence and take appropriate steps in the wake of telltale red flags. Corporate counsel are well advised to use experienced FCPA counsel for consultation, privileged audits, and investigations, and to secure written legal opinions.

When serious FCPA or related allegations arise, responsible companies, boards of directors, audit committees, and special committees promptly investigate and, if necessary, take swift disciplinary and other remedial actions. In some circumstances, public companies may choose to voluntarily report misconduct and to cooperate with the DOJ, the SEC, and foreign regulators in return for more lenient treatment by both the United States government and foreign governments. In other cases, an investigation may fail to sustain FCPA allegations but nonetheless lead to improved controls and other remedial measures.

Unless investigation or defense counsel promptly conduct a thorough factual investigation in the country or countries before or parallel to any U.S. government investigation and expand the scope of the investigation, as appropriate, the opportunity to persuade DOJ prosecutors or SEC staff attorneys to not return FCPA criminal charges, to file less serious criminal charges, to obtain a deferred prosecution agreement, or to bring only a civil enforcement action will almost surely be undermined. If the DOJ or SEC learns that a company has sat on sensitive payment allegations and done little, if any, quality investigation, their view of the company, its management, and its legal department will be dramatically different. A public company's management team and board may in select circumstances elect not to disclose or report misconduct, but if they ignore misconduct and take no corrective actions, and the United States government later discovers the misconduct, they can expect a very long, painful, and expensive investigation of the company—and possibly its management team.

Prompt disciplinary actions and implementation of constructive remedial measures in the wake of FCPA violations can in some circumstances help a company and its employees avoid criminal charges or enforcement actions altogether. Timely and thoughtful responses to FCPA misconduct can reduce the risk of costly litigation, government suspension and debarment, incarceration of executives, large fines, foreign government investigations, onerous injunctive relief, and the adverse effects of a lengthy, distracting, time-consuming, and uncertain government investigation.

Appendices

APPENDIX 1

Foreign Corrupt Practices Act

TEXT OF THE FOREIGN CORRUPT PRACTICES ACT
Current through Pub. L. 105-366 (November 10, 1998)
UNITED STATES CODE
TITLE 15. COMMERCE AND TRADE
CHAPTER 2B–SECURITIES EXCHANGES

§ 78M. PERIODICAL AND OTHER REPORTS

(a) Reports by issuer of security; contents

Every issuer of a security registered pursuant to section 78l of this title shall file with the Commission, in accordance with such rules and regulations as the Commission may prescribe as necessary or appropriate for the proper protection of investors and to insure fair dealing in the security—

(1) such information and documents (and such copies thereof) as the Commission shall require to keep reasonably current the information and documents required to be included in or filed with an application or registration statement filed pursuant to section 78l of this title, except that the Commission may not require the filing of any material contract wholly executed before July 1, 1962.

(2) such annual reports (and such copies thereof), certified if required by the rules and regulations of the Commission by independent public accountants, and such quarterly reports (and such copies thereof), as the Commission may prescribe. Every issuer of a security registered on a national securities exchange shall also file a duplicate original of such information, documents, and reports with the exchange.

(b) Form of report; books, records, and internal accounting; directives

(2) Every issuer which has a class of securities registered pursuant to section 78l of this title and every issuer which is required to file reports pursuant to section 78o(d) of this title shall—

   (A) make and keep books, records, and accounts, which, in reasonable detail, accurately and fairly reflect the transactions and dispositions of the assets of the issuer; and

   (B) devise and maintain a system of internal accounting controls sufficient to provide reasonable assurances that—

   (i) transactions are executed in accordance with management's general or specific authorization;

   (ii) transactions are recorded as necessary (I) to permit preparation of financial statements in conformity with generally accepted accounting principles or any other criteria applicable to such statements, and (II) to maintain accountability for assets;

   (iii) access to assets is permitted only in accordance with management's general or specific authorization; and

   (iv) the recorded accountability for assets is compared with the existing assets at reasonable intervals and appropriate action is taken with respect to any differences.

(3) (A) With respect to matters concerning the national security of the United States, no duty or liability under paragraph (2) of this subsection shall be imposed upon any person acting in cooperation with the head of any Federal department or agency responsible for such matters if such act in cooperation with such head of a department or agency was done upon the specific, written directive of the head of such department or agency pursuant to Presidential authority to issue such directives. Each directive issued under this paragraph shall set forth the specific facts and circumstances with respect to which the provisions of this paragraph are to be invoked. Each such directive shall, unless renewed in writing, expire one year after the date of issuance.

   (B) Each head of a Federal department or agency of the United States who issues such a directive pursuant to this paragraph shall maintain a complete file of all such directives and shall, on October 1 of each year, transmit a summary of matters covered by such directives in force at any time during the previous year to the Permanent Select Committee on Intelligence of the House of Representatives and the Select Committee on Intelligence of the Senate.

(4) No criminal liability shall be imposed for failing to comply with the requirements of paragraph (2) of this subsection except as provided in paragraph (5) of this subsection.

(5) No person shall knowingly circumvent or knowingly fail to implement a system of internal accounting controls or knowingly falsify any book, record, or account described in paragraph (2).

(6) Where an issuer which has a class of securities registered pursuant to section 78l of this title or an issuer which is required to file reports pursuant to section 78o(d) of this title holds 50 per centum or less of the voting power with respect to a domestic or foreign firm, the provisions of paragraph (2) require only that the issuer proceed in good faith to use its influence, to the extent reasonable under the issuer's circumstances, to cause such domestic or foreign firm to devise and maintain a system of internal accounting controls consistent with paragraph (2). Such circumstances include the relative degree of the issuer's ownership of the domestic or foreign firm and the laws and practices governing the business operations of the country in which such firm is located. An issuer which demonstrates good faith efforts to use such influence shall be conclusively presumed to have complied with the requirements of paragraph (2).

(7) For the purpose of paragraph (2) of this subsection, the terms "reasonable assurances" and "reasonable detail" mean such level of detail and degree of assurance as would satisfy prudent officials in the conduct of their own affairs.

§ 78DD-1. PROHIBITED FOREIGN TRADE PRACTICES BY ISSUERS

(a) Prohibition

It shall be unlawful for any issuer which has a class of securities registered pursuant to section 78l of this title or which is required to file reports under section 78o(d) of this title, or for any officer, director, employee, or agent of such issuer or any stockholder thereof acting on behalf of such issuer, to make use of the mails or any means or instrumentality of interstate commerce corruptly in furtherance of an offer, payment, promise to pay, or authorization of the payment of any money, or offer, gift, promise to give, or authorization of the giving of anything of value to—

(1) any foreign official for purposes of—

(A) (i) influencing any act or decision of such foreign official in his official capacity, (ii) inducing such foreign official to do or omit to do any act in violation of the lawful duty of such official, or (iii) securing any improper advantage; or

(B) inducing such foreign official to use his influence with a foreign government or instrumentality thereof to affect or influence any act or decision of such government or instrumentality, in order to assist such issuer in obtaining or retaining business for or with, or directing business to, any person;

(2) any foreign political party or official thereof or any candidate for foreign political office for purposes of—

(A) (i) influencing any act or decision of such party, official, or candidate in its or his official capacity, (ii) inducing such party, official, or candidate to do or omit to do an act in violation of the lawful duty of such party, official, or candidate, or (iii) securing any improper advantage; or

(B) inducing such party, official, or candidate to use its or his influence with a foreign government or instrumentality thereof to affect or influence any act or decision of such government or instrumentality.

in order to assist such issuer in obtaining or retaining business for or with, or directing business to, any person; or

(3) any person, while knowing that all or a portion of such money or thing of value will be offered, given, or promised, directly or indirectly, to any foreign official, to any foreign political party or official thereof, or to any candidate for foreign political office, for purposes of—

(A) (i) influencing any act or decision of such foreign official, political party, party official, or candidate in his or its official capacity, (ii) inducing such foreign official, political party, party official, or candidate to do or omit to do any act in violation of the lawful duty of such foreign official, political party, party official, or candidate, or (iii) securing any improper advantage; or

(B) inducing such foreign official, political party, party official, or candidate to use his or its influence with a foreign government or instrumentality thereof to affect or influence any act or decision of such government or instrumentality,

in order to assist such issuer in obtaining or retaining business for or with, or directing business to, any person.

(b) Exception for routine governmental action

Subsections (a) and (g) of this section shall not apply to any facilitating or expediting payment to a foreign official, political party, or party official the purpose of which is to expedite or to secure the performance of a routine governmental action by a foreign official, political party, or party official.

(c) Affirmative defenses

It shall be an affirmative defense to actions under subsection (a) or (g) of this section that—

    (1) the payment, gift, offer, or promise of anything of value that was made, was lawful under the written laws and regulations of the foreign official's, political party's, party official's, or candidate's country; or

    (2) the payment, gift, offer, or promise of anything of value that was made, was a reasonable and bona fide expenditure, such as travel and lodging expenses, incurred by or on behalf of a foreign official, party, party official, or candidate and was directly related to—

        (A) the promotion, demonstration, or explanation of products or services; or

        (B) the execution or performance of a contract with a foreign government or agency thereof.

(d) Guidelines by Attorney General

Not later than one year after August 23, 1988, the Attorney General, after consultation with the Commission, the Secretary of Commerce, the United States Trade Representative, the Secretary of State, and the Secretary of the Treasury, and after obtaining the views of all interested persons through public notice and comment procedures, shall determine to what extent compliance with this section would be enhanced and the business community would be assisted by further clarification of the preceding provisions of this section and may, based on such determination and to the extent necessary and appropriate, issue—

    (1) guidelines describing specific types of conduct, associated with common types of export sales arrangements and business contracts, which for purposes of the Department of Justice's present enforcement policy, the Attorney General determines would be in conformance with the preceding provisions of this section; and

    (2) general precautionary procedures which issuers may use on a voluntary basis to conform their conduct to the Department of Justice's present enforcement policy regarding the preceding provisions of this section.

The Attorney General shall issue the guidelines and procedures referred to in the preceding sentence in accordance with the provisions of subchapter II of chapter 5 of Title 5 and those guidelines and procedures shall be subject to the provisions of chapter 7 of that title.

(e) Opinions of Attorney General

(1) The Attorney General, after consultation with appropriate departments and agencies of the United States and after obtaining the views of all interested persons through public notice and comment procedures, shall establish a procedure to provide responses to specific inquiries by issuers concerning conformance of their conduct with the Department of Justice's present enforcement policy regarding the preceding provisions of this section. The Attorney General shall, within 30 days after receiving such a request, issue an opinion in response to that request. The opinion shall state whether or not certain specified prospective conduct would, for purposes of the Department of Justice's present enforcement policy, violate the preceding provisions of this section. Additional requests for opinions may be filed with the Attorney General regarding other specified prospective conduct that is beyond the scope of conduct specified in previous requests. In any action brought under the applicable provisions of this section, there shall be a rebuttable presumption that conduct, which is specified in a request by an issuer and for which the Attorney General has issued an opinion that such conduct is in conformity with the Department of Justice's present enforcement policy, is in compliance with the preceding provisions of this section. Such a presumption may be rebutted by a preponderance of the evidence. In considering the presumption for purposes of this paragraph, a court shall weigh all relevant factors, including but not limited to whether the information submitted to the Attorney General was accurate and complete and whether it was within the scope of the conduct specified in any request received by the Attorney General. The Attorney General shall establish the procedure required by this paragraph in accordance with the provisions of subchapter II of chapter 5 of Title 5 and that procedure shall be subject to the provisions of chapter 7 of that title.

(2) Any document or other material which is provided to, received by, or prepared in the Department of Justice or any other department or agency of the United States in connection with a request by an issuer under the procedure established under paragraph (1), shall be exempt from disclosure under section 552 of Title 5 and shall not, except with the consent of the issuer, be made publicly available, regardless of whether the Attorney General responds to such a request or the issuer withdraws such request before receiving a response.

(3) Any issuer who has made a request to the Attorney General under paragraph (1) may withdraw such request prior to the time the Attorney General issues an opinion in response to such request. Any request so withdrawn shall have no force or effect.

(4) The Attorney General shall, to the maximum extent practicable, provide timely guidance concerning the Department of Justice's present enforcement policy with respect to the preceding provisions of this section to potential exporters and small businesses that are unable to obtain specialized counsel on issues pertaining to such provisions. Such guidance shall be limited to responses to requests under paragraph (1) concerning conformity of specified prospective conduct with the Department of Justice's present enforcement policy regarding the preceding provisions of this section and general explanations of compliance responsibilities and of potential liabilities under the preceding provisions of this section.

(f) Definitions

For purposes of this section

(1) (A) The term "foreign official" means any officer or employee of a foreign government or any department, agency, or instrumentality thereof, or of a public international organization, or any person acting in an official capacity for or on behalf of any such government or department, agency, or instrumentality, or for or on behalf of any such public international organization.

(B) For purposes of subparagraph (A), the term "public international organization" means—

(i) an organization that is designated by Executive Order pursuant to section 1 of the International Organizations Immunities Act (22 U.S.C. § 288); or

(ii) any other international organization that is designated by the President by Executive Order for the purposes of this section, effective as of the date of publication of such order in the Federal Register.

(2) (A) A person's state of mind is "knowing" with respect to conduct, a circumstance, or a result if—

(i) such person is aware that such person is engaging in such conduct, that such circumstance exists, or that such result is substantially certain to occur; or

(ii) such person has a firm belief that such circumstance exists or that such result is substantially certain to occur.

(B) When knowledge of the existence of a particular circumstance is required for an offense, such knowledge is established if a person is aware of a high probability of the existence of such circumstance, unless the person actually believes that such circumstance does not exist.

(3) (A) The term "routine governmental action" means only an action which is ordinarily and commonly performed by a foreign official in—

(i) obtaining permits, licenses, or other official documents to qualify a person to do business in a foreign country;

(ii) processing governmental papers, such as visas and work orders;

(iii) providing police protection, mail pick-up and delivery, or scheduling inspections associated with contract performance or inspections related to transit of goods across country;

(iv) providing phone service, power and water supply, loading and unloading cargo, or protecting perishable products or commodities from deterioration; or

(v) actions of a similar nature.

(B) The term "routine governmental action" does not include any decision by a foreign official whether, or on what terms, to award new business to or to continue business with a particular party, or any action taken by a foreign official involved in the decision-making process to encourage a decision to award new business to or continue business with a particular party.

(g) Alternative Jurisdiction

(1) It shall also be unlawful for any issuer organized under the laws of the United States, or a State, territory, possession, or commonwealth of the United States or a political subdivision thereof and which has a class of securities registered pursuant to section 12 of this title or which is required to file reports under section 15(d) of this title, or for any United States person that is an officer, director, employee, or agent of such issuer or a stockholder thereof acting on behalf of such issuer, to corruptly do any act outside the United States in furtherance of an offer, payment, promise to pay, or authorization of the payment of any money, or offer, gift, promise to give, or authorization of the giving of anything of value to any of the persons or entities set forth in paragraphs (1), (2), and (3) of this subsection (a) of this section for the purposes set forth therein, irrespective of whether such issuer or such officer, director, employee, agent or stockholder

makes use of the mails or any means or instrumentals of interstate commerce in furtherance of such offer, gift payment promise, or authorization.

(2) As used in this subsection, the term "United States person"
means a national of the United States (as defined in section 101
of the Immigration and Nationality Act (8 U.S.C. § 1101)) or
any corporation, partnership, association, joint-stock company,
business trust, unincorporated organization, or sole proprietorship organized under the laws of the United States or any State,
territory, possession, or commonwealth of the United States, or
any political subdivision thereof.

§ 78DD-2. PROHIBITED FOREIGN TRADE PRACTICES BY DOMESTIC CONCERNS

(a) Prohibition

It shall be unlawful for any domestic concern, other than an issuer which
is subject to section 78dd-1 of this title, or for any officer, director,
employee, or agent of such domestic concern or any stockholder thereof
acting on behalf of such domestic concern, to make use of the mails or
any means or instrumentality of interstate commerce corruptly in furtherance of an offer, payment, promise to pay, or authorization of the
payment of any money, or offer, gift, promise to give, or authorization of
the giving of anything of value to—

(1) any foreign official for purposes of—
    (A) (i) influencing any act or decision of such foreign official in
his official capacity, (ii) inducing such foreign official to do
or omit to do any act in violation of the lawful duty of such
official, or (iii) securing any improper advantage; or
    (B) inducing such foreign official to use his influence with a
foreign government or instrumentality thereof to affect
or influence any act or decision of such government or
instrumentality,

in order to assist such domestic concern in obtaining or retaining business for or with, or directing business to, any person;

(2) any foreign political party or official thereof or any candidate for
foreign political office for purposes of—
    (A) (i) influencing any act or decision of such party, official, or
candidate in its or his official capacity, (ii) inducing such
party, official, or candidate to do or omit to do an act in

violation of the lawful duty of such party, official, or candidate, or (iii) securing any improper advantage; or

(B) inducing such party, official, or candidate to use its or his influence with a foreign government or instrumentality thereof to affect or influence any act or decision of such government or instrumentality,

in order to assist such domestic concern in obtaining or retaining business for or with, or directing business to, any person;

(3) any person, while knowing that all or a portion of such money or thing of value will be offered, given, or promised, directly or indirectly, to any foreign official, to any foreign political party or official thereof, or to any candidate for foreign political office, for purposes of—

(A) (i) influencing any act or decision of such foreign official, political party, party official, or candidate in his or its official capacity, (ii) inducing such foreign official, political party, party official, or candidate to do or omit to do any act in violation of the lawful duty of such foreign official, political party, party official, or candidate, or (iii) securing any improper advantage; or

(B) inducing such foreign official, political party, party official, or candidate to use his or its influence with a foreign government or instrumentality thereof to affect or influence any act or decision of such government or instrumentality,

in order to assist such domestic concern in obtaining or retaining business for or with, or directing business to, any person.

(b) Exception for routine governmental action

Subsections (a) and (i) of this section shall not apply to any facilitating or expediting payment to a foreign official, political party, or party official the purpose of which is to expedite or to secure the performance of a routine governmental action by a foreign official, political party, or party official.

(c) Affirmative defenses

It shall be an affirmative defense to actions under subsection (a) or (i) of this section that—

(1) the payment, gift, offer, or promise of anything of value that was made, was lawful under the written laws and regulations of the foreign official's, political party's, party official's, or candidate's country; or

(2) the payment, gift, offer, or promise of anything of value that was made, was a reasonable and *bona fide* expenditure, such as travel and lodging expenses, incurred by or on behalf of a foreign official, party, party official, or candidate and was directly related to

    (A) the promotion, demonstration, or explanation of products or services; or

    (B) the execution or performance of a contract with a foreign government or agency thereof.

(d) Injunctive relief

(1) When it appears to the Attorney General that any domestic concern to which this section applies, or officer, director, employee, agent, or stockholder thereof, is engaged, or about to engage, in any act or practice constituting a violation of subsection (a) or (i) of this section, the Attorney General may, in his discretion, bring a civil action in an appropriate district court of the United States to enjoin such act or practice, and upon a proper showing, a permanent injunction or a temporary restraining order shall be granted without bond.

(2) For the purpose of any civil investigation which, in the opinion of the Attorney General, is necessary and proper to enforce this section, the Attorney General or his designee are empowered to administer oaths and affirmations, subpoena witnesses, take evidence, and require the production of any books, papers, or other documents which the Attorney General deems relevant or material to such investigation. The attendance of witnesses and the production of documentary evidence may be required from any place in the United States, or any territory, possession, or commonwealth of the United States, at any designated place of hearing.

(3) In case of contumacy by, or refusal to obey a subpoena issued to, any person, the Attorney General may invoke the aid of any court of the United States within the jurisdiction of which such investigation or proceeding is carried on, or where such person resides or carries on business, in requiring the attendance and testimony of witnesses and the production of books, papers, or other documents. Any such court may issue an order requiring such person to appear before the Attorney General or his designee, there to produce records, if so ordered, or to give testimony touching the matter under investigation. Any failure to obey such order of the court may be punished by such court as a contempt thereof.

All process in any such case may be served in the judicial district in which such person resides or may be found. The Attorney General may make such rules relating to civil investigations as may be necessary or appropriate to implement the provisions of this subsection.

(e) Guidelines by Attorney General

Not later than 6 months after August 23, 1988, the Attorney General, after consultation with the Securities and Exchange Commission, the Secretary of Commerce, the United States Trade Representative, the Secretary of State, and the Secretary of the Treasury, and after obtaining the views of all interested persons through public notice and comment procedures, shall determine to what extent compliance with this section would be enhanced and the business community would be assisted by further clarification of the preceding provisions of this section and may, based on such determination and to the extent necessary and appropriate, issue—

(1) guidelines describing specific types of conduct, associated with common types of export sales arrangements and business contracts, which for purposes of the Department of Justice's present enforcement policy, the Attorney General determines would be in conformance with the preceding provisions of this section; and

(2) general precautionary procedures which domestic concerns may use on a voluntary basis to conform their conduct to the Department of Justice's present enforcement policy regarding the preceding provisions of this section.

The Attorney General shall issue the guidelines and procedures referred to in the preceding sentence in accordance with the provisions of subchapter II of chapter 5 of Title 5 and those guidelines and procedures shall be subject to the provisions of chapter 7 of that title.

(f) Opinions of Attorney General

(1) The Attorney General, after consultation with appropriate departments and agencies of the United States and after obtaining the views of all interested persons through public notice and comment procedures, shall establish a procedure to provide responses to specific inquiries by domestic concerns concerning conformance of their conduct with the Department of Justice's present enforcement policy regarding the preceding provisions of this section. The Attorney General shall, within 30 days after receiving such a request, issue an opinion in response to that request. The opinion shall state whether or not certain specified prospective conduct would, for purposes of the Department of

Justice's present enforcement policy, violate the preceding provisions of this section. Additional requests for opinions may be filed with the Attorney General regarding other specified prospective conduct that is beyond the scope of conduct specified in previous requests. In any action brought under the applicable provisions of this section, there shall be a rebuttable presumption that conduct, which is specified in a request by a domestic concern and for which the Attorney General has issued an opinion that such conduct is in conformity with the Department of Justice's present enforcement policy, is in compliance with the preceding provisions of this section.

Such a presumption may be rebutted by a preponderance of the evidence. In considering the presumption for purposes of this paragraph, a court shall weigh all relevant factors, including but not limited to whether the information submitted to the Attorney General was accurate and complete and whether it was within the scope of the conduct specified in any request received by the Attorney General. The Attorney General shall establish the procedure required by this paragraph in accordance with the provisions of subchapter II of chapter 5 of Title 5 and that procedure shall be subject to the provisions of chapter 7 of that title.

(2) Any document or other material which is provided to, received by, or prepared in the Department of Justice or any other department or agency of the United States in connection with a request by a domestic concern under the procedure established under paragraph (1), shall be exempt from disclosure under section 552 of Title 5 and shall not, except with the consent of the domestic concern, be made publicly available, regardless of whether the Attorney General response to such a request or the domestic concern withdraws such request before receiving a response.

(3) Any domestic concern who has made a request to the Attorney General under paragraph (1) may withdraw such request prior to the time the Attorney General issues an opinion in response to such request. Any request so withdrawn shall have no force or effect.

(4) The Attorney General shall, to the maximum extent practicable, provide timely guidance concerning the Department of Justice's present enforcement policy with respect to the preceding provisions of this section to potential exporters and small businesses that are unable to obtain specialized counsel on issues pertaining to such provisions. Such guidance shall be limited to responses to requests under paragraph (1) concerning conformity of specified prospective conduct with the Department of Justice's present enforcement policy regarding the preceding provisions of

this section and general explanations of compliance responsibilities and of potential liabilities under the preceding provisions of this section.

(g) Penalties

(1) (A) Any domestic concern that is not a natural person and that violates subsection (a) or (i) of this section shall be fined not more than $2,000,000.

(B) Any domestic concern that is not a natural person and that violates subsection (a) or (i) of this section shall be subject to a civil penalty of not more than $10,000 imposed in an action brought by the Attorney General.

(2) (A) Any natural person that is an officer, director, employee, or agent of a domestic concern, or stockholder acting on behalf of such domestic concern, who willfully violates subsection (a) or (i) of this section shall be fined not more than $100,000 or imprisoned not more than 5 years, or both.

(B) Any natural person that is an officer, director, employee, or agent of a domestic concern, or stockholder acting on behalf of such domestic concern, who violates subsection (a) or (i) of this section shall be subject to a civil penalty of not more than $10,000 imposed in an action brought by the Attorney General.

(3) Whenever a fine is imposed under paragraph (2) upon any officer, director, employee, agent, or stockholder of a domestic concern, such fine may not be paid, directly or indirectly, by such domestic concern.

(h) Definitions

For purposes of this section:

(1) The term "domestic concern" means—

(A) any individual who is a citizen, national, or resident of the United States; and

(B) any corporation, partnership, association, joint-stock company, business trust, unincorporated organization, or sole proprietorship which has its principal place of business in the United States, or which is organized under the laws of a State of the United States or a territory, possession, or commonwealth of the United States.

(2) (A) The term "foreign official" means any officer or employee of a foreign government or any department, agency, or instrumentality thereof, or of a public international organization,

or any person acting in an official capacity for or on behalf of any such government or department, agency, or instrumentality, or for or on behalf of any such public international organization.

(B) For purposes of subparagraph (A), the term "public international organization" means—

   (i) an organization that has been designated by Executive order pursuant to Section 1 of the International Organizations Immunities Act (22 U.S.C. § 288); or

   (ii) any other international organization that is designated by the President by Executive order for the purposes of this section, effective as of the date of publication of such order in the Federal Register.

(3) (A) A person's state of mind is "knowing" with respect to conduct, a circumstance, or a result if—

   (i) such person is aware that such person is engaging in such conduct, that such circumstance exists, or that such result is substantially certain to occur; or

   (ii) such person has a firm belief that such circumstance exists or that such result is substantially certain to occur.

(B) When knowledge of the existence of a particular circumstance is required for an offense, such knowledge is established if a person is aware of a high probability of the existence of such circumstance, unless the person actually believes that such circumstance does not exist.

(4) (A) The term "routine governmental action" means only an action which is ordinarily and commonly performed by a foreign official in—

   (i) obtaining permits, licenses, or other official documents to qualify a person to do business in a foreign country;

   (ii) processing governmental papers, such as visas and work orders;

   (iii) providing police protection, mail pick-up and delivery, or scheduling inspections associated with contract performance or inspections related to transit of goods across country;

   (iv) providing phone service, power and water supply, loading and unloading cargo, or protecting perishable products or commodities from deterioration; or

   (v) actions of a similar nature.

(B) The term "routine governmental action" does not include any decision by a foreign official whether, or on what terms, to award new business to or to continue business with a particular party, or any action taken by a foreign official involved in the decision-making process to encourage a decision to award new business to or continue business with a particular party.

(5) The term "interstate commerce" means trade, commerce, transportation, or communication among the several States, or between any foreign country and any State or between any State and any place or ship outside thereof, and such term includes the intrastate use of—

(A) a telephone or other interstate means of communication, or

(B) any other interstate instrumentality.

(i) Alternative Jurisdiction

(1) It shall also be unlawful for any United States person to corruptly do any act outside the United States in furtherance of an offer, payment, promise to pay, or authorization of the payment of any money, or offer, gift, promise to give, or authorization of the giving of anything of value to any of the persons or entities set forth in paragraphs (1), (2), and (3) of subsection (a), for the purposes set forth therein, irrespective of whether such United States person makes use of the mails or any means or instrumentality of interstate commerce in furtherance of such offer, gift, payment, promise, or authorization.

(2) As used in this subsection, a "United States person" means a national of the United States (as defined in section 101 of the Immigration and Nationality Act (8 U.S.C. § 1101)) or any corporation, partnership, association, joint-stock company, business trust, unincorporated organization, or sole proprietorship organized under the laws of the United States or any State, territory, possession, or commonwealth of the United States, or any political subdivision thereof.

§78DD-3. PROHIBITED FOREIGN TRADE PRACTICES BY PERSONS OTHER THAN ISSUERS OR DOMESTIC CONCERNS

(a) Prohibition

It shall be unlawful for any person other than an issuer that is subject to section 30A of the Securities Exchange Act of 1934 or a domestic concern, as defined in section 104 of this Act, or for any officer, director, employee, or agent of such person or any stockholder thereof acting on behalf of such person, while in the territory of the United States, corruptly to make use of the mails or any means or instrumentality of interstate commerce or to do any other act in furtherance of an offer, payment, promise to pay, or authorization of the payment of any money, or offer, gift, promise to give, or authorization of the giving of anything of value to

(1) any foreign official for purposes of—

    (A) (i) influencing any act or decision of such foreign official in his official capacity, (ii) inducing such foreign official to do or omit to do any act in violation of the lawful duty of such official, or (iii) securing any improper advantage; or

    (B) inducing such foreign official to use his influence with a foreign government or instrumentality thereof to affect or influence any act or decision of such government or instrumentality,

in order to assist such person in obtaining or retaining business for or with, or directing business to, any person;

(2) any foreign political party or official thereof or any candidate for foreign political office for purposes of—

    (A) (i) influencing any act or decision of such party, official, or candidate in its or his official capacity, (ii) inducing such party, official, or candidate to do or omit to do an act in violation of the lawful duty of such party, official, or candidate, or (iii) securing any improper advantage; or

    (B) inducing such party, official, or candidate to use its or his influence with a foreign government or instrumentality thereof to affect or influence any act or decision of such government or instrumentality,

in order to assist such person in obtaining or retaining business for or with, or directing business to, any person; or

(3) any person, while knowing that all or a portion of such money or thing of value will be offered, given, or promised, directly or indirectly, to any foreign official, to any foreign political party or official thereof, or to any candidate for foreign political office, for purposes of—

    (A) (i) influencing any act or decision of such foreign official, political party, party official, or candidate in his or its official capacity, (ii) inducing such foreign official, political party, party official, or candidate to do or omit to do any act in violation of the lawful duty of such foreign official, political party, party official, or candidate, or (iii) securing any improper advantage; or

    (B) inducing such foreign official, political party, party official, or candidate to use his or its influence with a foreign government or instrumentality thereof to affect or influence any act or decision of such government or instrumentality,

in order to assist such person in obtaining or retaining business for or with, or directing business to, any person.

(b) Exception for routine governmental action

Subsection (a) of this section shall not apply to any facilitating or expediting payment to a foreign official, political party, or party official the purpose of which is to expedite or to secure the performance of a routine governmental action by a foreign official, political party, or party official.

(c) Affirmative defenses

It shall be an affirmative defense to actions under subsection (a) of this section that—

(1) the payment, gift, offer, or promise of anything of value that was made, was lawful under the written laws and regulations of the foreign official's, political party's, party official's, or candidate's country; or

(2) the payment, gift, offer, or promise of anything of value that was made, was a reasonable and *bona fide* expenditure, such as travel and lodging expenses, incurred by or on behalf of a foreign official, party, party official, or candidate and was directly related to—

(A) the promotion, demonstration, or explanation of products or services; or

(B) the execution or performance of a contract with a foreign government or agency thereof.

(d) Injunctive relief

(1) When it appears to the Attorney General that any person to which this section applies, or officer, director, employee, agent, or stockholder thereof, is engaged, or about to engage, in any act or practice constituting a violation of subsection (a) of this section, the Attorney General may, in his discretion, bring a civil action in an appropriate district court of the United States to enjoin such act or practice, and upon a proper showing, a permanent injunction or a temporary restraining order shall be granted without bond.

(2) For the purpose of any civil investigation which, in the opinion of the Attorney General, is necessary and proper to enforce this

section, the Attorney General or his designee are empowered to administer oaths and affirmations, subpoena witnesses, take evidence, and require the production of any books, papers, or other documents which the Attorney General deems relevant or material to such investigation. The attendance of witnesses and the production of documentary evidence may be required from any place in the United States, or any territory, possession, or commonwealth of the United States, at any designated place of hearing,

(3) In case of contumacy by, or refusal to obey a subpoena issued to, any person, the Attorney General may invoke the aid of any court of the United States within the jurisdiction of which such investigation or proceeding is carried on, or where such person resides or carries on business, in requiring the attendance and testimony of witnesses and the production of books, papers, or other documents. Any such Court may issue an order requiring such person to appear before the Attorney General or his designee, there to produce records, if so ordered, or to give testimony touching the matter under investigation. Any failure to obey such order of the court may be punished by such court as a contempt thereof.

(4) All process in any such case may be served in the judicial district in which such person resides or may be found. The Attorney General may make such rules relating to civil investigations as may be necessary or appropriate to implement the provisions of this subsection.

(e) Penalties

(1) (A) Any juridical person that violates subsection (a) of this section shall be fined not more than $2,000,000.

(B) Any juridical person that violates subsection (a) of this section shall be subject to a civil penalty of not more than $10,000 imposed in an action brought by the Attorney General,

(2) (A) Any natural person who willfully violates subsection (a) of this section shall be fined not more than $100,000 or imprisoned not more than 5 years, or both.

(B) Any natural person who violates subsection (a) of this section shall be subject to a civil penalty of not more than $10,000 imposed in an action brought by the Attorney General.

(3) Whenever a fine is imposed under paragraph (2) upon any officer, director, employee, agent, or stockholder of a person, such fine may not be paid, directly or indirectly, by such person.

(f) Definitions

For purposes of this section:

(1) The term "person," when referring to an offender, means any natural person other than a national of the United States (as defined in 8 U.S.C. § 1101) or any corporation, partnership, association, joint-stock company, business trust, unincorporated organization, or sole proprietorship organized under the law of a foreign nation or a political subdivision thereof.

(2) (A) The term "foreign official" means any officer or employee of a foreign government or any department, agency, or instrumentality thereof, or of a public international organization, or any person acting in an official capacity for or on behalf of any such government or department, agency, or instrumentality, or for or on behalf of any such public international organization.

(B) For purposes of subparagraph (A), the term "public international organization" means—

(i) an organization that has been designated by Executive Order pursuant to Section 1 of the International Organizations Immunities Act (22 U.S.C. § 288); or

(ii) any other international organization that is designated by the President by Executive order for the purposes of this section, effective as of the date of publication of such order in the Federal Register.

(3) (A) A person's state of mind is "knowing" with respect to conduct, a circumstance, or a result if—

(i) such person is aware that such person is engaging in such conduct, that such circumstance exists, or that such result is substantially certain to occur; or

(ii) such person has a firm belief that such circumstance exists or that such result is substantially certain to occur.

(B) When knowledge of the existence of a particular circumstance is required for an offense, such knowledge is established if a person is aware of a high probability of the existence of such circumstance, unless the person actually believes that such circumstance does not exist.

(4) (A) The term "routine governmental action" means only an action which is ordinarily and commonly performed by a foreign official in—

(i) obtaining permits, licenses, or other official documents to qualify a person to do business in a foreign country;

(ii) processing governmental papers, such as visas and work orders;

      (iii) providing police protection, mail pickup and delivery, or scheduling inspections associated with contract performance or inspections related to transit of goods across country;

      (iv) providing phone service, power and water supply, loading and unloading cargo, or protecting perishable products or commodities from deterioration; or

      (v) actions of a similar nature.

    (B) The term "routine governmental action" does not include any decision by a foreign official whether, or on what terms, to award new business to or to continue business with a particular party, or any action taken by a foreign official involved in the decision-making process to encourage a decision to award new business to or continue business with a particular party.

  (5) The term "interstate commerce" means trade, commerce, transportation, or communication among the several States, or between any foreign country and any State or between any State and any place or ship outside thereof, and such term includes the intrastate use of—

    (A) a telephone or other interstate means of communication, or

    (B) any other interstate instrumentality.

§ 78FF. PENALTIES

(a) Willful violations; false and misleading statements

Any person who willfully violates any provision of this chapter (other than section 78dd-1 of this title), or any rule or regulation thereunder the violation of which is made unlawful or the observance of which is required under the terms of this chapter, or any person who willfully and knowingly makes, or causes to be made, any statement in any application, report, or document required to be filed under this chapter or any rule or regulation thereunder or any undertaking contained in a registration statement as provided in subsection (d) of section 78o of this title, or by any self-regulatory organization in connection with an application for membership or participation therein or to become associated with a member thereof, which statement was false or misleading with respect to any material fact, shall upon conviction be fined not more than $5,000,000, or imprisoned not more than 20 years, or both, except that when such person is a person other than a natural person, a fine not exceeding $25,000,000 may be imposed; but no person shall be subject to imprisonment under this section for the violation of any rule or regulation if he proves that he had no knowledge of such rule or regulation.

(b) Failure to file information, documents, or reports

Any issuer which fails to file information, documents, or reports required to be filed under subsection (d) of section 78o of this title or any rule or regulation thereunder shall forfeit to the United States the sum of $100 for each and every day such failure to file shall continue. Such forfeiture, which shall be in lieu of any criminal penalty for such failure to file which might be deemed to arise under subsection (a) of this section, shall be payable into the Treasury of the United States and shall be recoverable in a civil suit in the name of the United States.

(c) Violations by issuers, officers, directors, stockholders, employees, or agents of issuers

(1) (A) Any issuer that violates subsection (a) or (g) of section 78dd-1 of this title shall be fined not more than $2,000,000.

(B) Any issuer that violates subsection (a) or (g) of section 78dd-1 of this title shall be subject to a civil penalty of not more than $10,000 imposed in an action brought by the Commission.

(2) (A) Any officer, director, employee, or agent of an issuer, or stockholder acting on behalf of such issuer, who willfully violates subsection (a) or (g) of section 78dd-1 of this title shall be fined not more than $100,000, or imprisoned not more than 5 years, or both.

(B) Any officer, director, employee, or agent of an issuer, or stockholder acting on behalf of such issuer, who violates subsection (a) or (g) of section 78dd-1 of this title shall be subject to a civil penalty of not more than $10,000 imposed in an action brought by the Commission.

(3) Whenever a fine is imposed under paragraph (2) upon any officer, director, employee, agent, or stockholder of an issuer, such fine may not be paid, directly or indirectly, by such issuer.

APPENDIX 2

OECD Convention

Convention on Combating Bribery of Foreign
Officials in International Business Transactions[1]

Adopted by the Negotiating Conference on 21 November 1977

PREAMBLE

The Parties,

Considering that bribery is a widespread phenomenon in international business transactions, including trade and investment, which raises serious moral and political concerns, undermines good governance and economic development, and distorts international competitive conditions;

Considering that all countries share a responsibility to combat bribery in international business transactions;

Having regard to the Revised Recommendation on Combating Bribery in International Business Transactions, adopted by the Council of the Organisation for Economic Co-operation and Development (OECD) on 23 May 1977, C(97)123/FINAL, which, *inter alia*, called for effective measures to deter, prevent and combat the bribery of foreign public officials in connection with international business transactions, in particular the prompt criminalization of such bribery in an effective and coordinated manner and in conformity with the agreed common elements set out in that Recommendation and with the jurisdictional and other basic legal principles of each country;

Welcoming other recent developments which further advance international understanding and co-operation in combating bribery of public officials, including actions of the United Nations, the World Bank, the International Monetary Fund, the World Trade Organisation, the Organisation of American States, the Council of Europe and the European Union;

Welcoming the efforts of companies, business organisations and trade unions as well as other non-governmental organisations to combat bribery;

Recognising the role of governments in the prevention of solicitation of bribes from individuals and enterprises in international business transactions;

---

1. OECD Doc. DAFFE/IME/BR(97)20, *reprinted in* 37 I.L.M. 1 (1998).

Recognising that achieving progress in this field requires not only efforts on a national level but also multilateral co-operation, monitoring and follow-up;

Recognising that achieving equivalence among the measures to be taken by the Parties in an essential object and purpose of the Convention, which requires that the Convention be ratified without derogations affecting this equivalence;

Have agreed as follows:

ARTICLE 1—THE OFFICIAL BRIBERY OF FOREIGN PUBLIC OFFICIALS

1. Each Party shall take such measures as may be necessary to establish that it is a criminal offence under its law for any person intentionally to offer, promise or give any undue pecuniary or other advantage, whether directly or through intermediaries, to a foreign public official, for that official or for a third party, in order that the official act or refrain from acting in relation to the performance of official duties, in order to obtain or retain business or other improper advantage in the conduct of international business.

2. Each Party shall take any measures necessary to establish that complicity in, including incitement, aiding and abetting, or authorization of an act of bribery of a foreign public official shall be a criminal offence. Attempt and conspiracy to bribe a foreign public official shall be criminal offences to the same extent as attempt and conspiracy to bribe a public official of that Party.

3. The offences set out in paragraphs 1 and 2 above are hereinafter referred to as "bribery of a foreign public official".

4. For the purpose of this Convention:

   a. "foreign public official" means any person holding a legislative, administrative or judicial office of a foreign country, whether appointed or elected; any person exercising a public function for a foreign country, including for a public agency or public enterprise; and any official or agent of a public international organisation;

   b. "foreign country" includes all levels and subdivisions of government, from national to local;

   c. "act or refrain from acting in relation to the performance of official duties" includes any use of the public official's position, whether or not within the official's authorized competence.

ARTICLE 2—RESPONSIBILITY OF LEGAL PERSONS

Each Party shall take such measures as may be necessary, in accordance with its legal principles, to establish the liability of legal persons for the bribery of a foreign public official.

ARTICLE 3—SANCTIONS

1. The bribery of a foreign public official shall be punishable by effective, proportionate and dissuasive criminal penalties. The range of penalties shall be comparable to that applicable to the bribery of the Party's own public officials and shall, in the case of natural persons, include deprivation of liberty sufficient to enable effective mutual legal assistance and extradition.

2. In the event that, under the legal system of a Party, criminal responsibility is not applicable to legal persons, that Party shall ensure that legal persons shall be subject to effective, proportionate and dissuasive non-criminal sanctions, including monetary sanctions, for bribery of foreign public officials.

3. Each Party shall take such measures as may be necessary to provide that the bribe and the proceeds of the bribery of a foreign public official, or property the value of which corresponds to that of such proceeds, are subject to seizure and confiscation or that monetary sanctions of comparable effect are applicable.

4. Each Party shall consider the imposition of additional civil or administrative sanctions upon a person subject to sanctions for the bribery of a foreign public official.

ARTICLE 4—JURISDICTION

1. Each Party shall take such measures as may be necessary to establish its jurisdiction over the bribery of a foreign public official when the offence is committed in whole or in part in its territory.

2. Each Party which has jurisdiction to prosecute its nationals for offences committed abroad shall take such measures as may be necessary to establish its jurisdiction to do so in respect of the bribery of a foreign public official, according to the same principles.

3. When more than one Party has jurisdiction over an alleged offence described in this Convention, the Parties involved shall, at the request of one of them, consult with a view to determining the most appropriate jurisdiction for prosecution.

4. Each Party shall review whether its current basis for jurisdiction is effective in the fight against the bribery of foreign public officials and, if it is not, shall take remedial steps.

ARTICLE 5—ENFORCEMENT

Investigation and prosecution of the bribery of a foreign public official shall be subject to the applicable rules and principles of each Party. They shall not be influenced by considerations of national economic interest, the potential effect upon relations with another State or the identity of the natural or legal persons involved.

ARTICLE 6—STATUTE OF LIMITATIONS

Any statute of limitations applicable to the offence of bribery of a foreign public official shall allow an adequate period of time for the investigation and prosecution of this offence.

ARTICLE 7—MONEY LAUNDERING

Each Party which has made bribery of its own public official a predicate offence for the purpose of the application of its money laundering legislation shall do so on the same terms for the bribery of a foreign public official, without regard to the place where the bribery occurred.

ARTICLE 8—ACCOUNTING

1. In order to combat bribery of foreign public officials effectively, each Party shall take such measures as may be necessary, within the framework of its laws and regulations regarding the maintenance of books and records, financial statement disclosures, and accounting and auditing standards, to prohibit the establishment of off-the-books accounts, the making of off-the-books or inadequately identified transactions, the recording of non-existent expenditures, the entry of liabilities with incorrect identification of their object, as well as the use of false documents, by companies subject to those laws and regulations, for the purpose of bribing foreign public officials or of hiding such bribery.

2. Each Party shall provide effective, proportionate and dissuasive civil, administrative or criminal penalties for such omission and falsifications in respect of the books, records, accounts and financial statements of such companies.

ARTICLE 9—MUTUAL LEGAL ASSISTANCE

1. Each Party shall, to the fullest extent possible under its laws and relevant treaties and arrangements, provide prompt and effective legal assistance to another Party for the purpose of criminal investigations and proceedings brought by a Party concerning offenses within the scope of this Convention and for non-criminal proceedings within the scope of this Convention brought by a Party against a legal person. The requested Party

shall inform the requesting Party, without delay, of any additional information or documents needed to support the request for assistance and, where requested, of the status and outcome of the request for assistance.

2. Where a Party makes mutual legal assistance conditional upon the existence of dual criminality, dual criminality shall be deemed to exist if the offense for which the assistance is sought is within the scope of this Convention.

3. A Party shall not decline to render mutual legal assistance for criminal matters within the scope of this Convention on the ground of bank secrecy.

ARTICLE 10—EXTRADITION

1. Bribery of a foreign public official shall be deemed to be included as an extraditable offence under the laws of the Parties and the extradition treaties between them.

2. If a Party which makes extradition conditional on the existence of an extradition treaty receives a request for extradition from another Party with which it has no extradition treaty, it may consider this Convention to be the legal basis for extradition in respect of the offence of bribery of a foreign public official.

3. Each Party shall take any measures necessary to assure either that it can extradite its nationals or that it can prosecute its nationals for the offence of bribery of a foreign public official. A Party which declines to request to extradite a person for bribery of a foreign public official solely on the ground that the person is its national shall submit the case to its competent authorities for the purpose of prosecution.

4. Extradition for bribery of a foreign public official is subject to the conditions set out in the domestic law and applicable treaties and arrangements of each Party. Where a Party makes extradition conditional upon the existence of dual criminality, that condition shall be deemed to be fulfilled if the offence for which extradition is sought is within the scope of Article 1 of this Convention.

ARTICLE 11—RESPONSIBLE AUTHORITIES

For purposes of Article 4, paragraph 3, on consultation, Article 9, on mutual legal assistance and Article 10, on extradition, each Party shall notify to the Secretary-General of the OECD an authority or authorities responsible for making and receiving requests, which shall serve as channel of communication for these matters for that Party, without prejudice to other arrangements between Parties.

ARTICLE 12—MONITORING AND FOLLOW-UP

The Parties shall co-operate in carrying out a programme of systematic follow-up to monitor and promote the full implementation of this Convention. Unless otherwise decided by consensus of the Parties, this shall be done in the framework of the OECD Working Group on Bribery in International Business Transactions and according to its terms of reference, or within the framework and terms of reference of any successor to its functions, and Parties shall bear the costs of the programme in accordance with the rules applicable to that body.

ARTICLE 13—SIGNATURE AND ACCESSION

1. Until its entry into force, this Convention shall be open for signature by OECD members and by non-members which have been invited to become full participants in its Working Group on Bribery in International Business Transactions.

2. Subsequent to its entry into force, this Convention shall be open to accession by any nonsignatory which is a member of the OECD or has become a full participant in the Working Group on Bribery in International Business Transactions or any successor to its functions. For each such nonsignatory, the Convention shall enter into force on the sixtieth day following the date of deposit of its instrument of accession.

ARTICLE 14—RATIFICATION AND DEPOSITARY

1. This Convention is subject to acceptance, approval or ratification by the Signatories, in accordance with their respective laws.

2. Instruments of acceptance, approval, ratification or accession shall be deposited with the Secretary-General of the OECD, who shall serve as depositary of this Convention.

ARTICLE 15—ENTRY INTO FORCE

1. This convention shall enter into force on the sixtieth day following the date upon which five of the ten countries which have the ten largest export shares set out in (annexed),[2] and which represent by themselves at least sixty per cent of the combined total exports of those ten countries, have deposited their instruments of acceptance, approval, or ratification. For each signatory depositing its instrument after such entry into force, the Convention shall enter into force on the sixtieth day after deposit of its instrument.

---

2. The annex to the OECD Convention is not included in this appendix.

2. If, after 31 December 1998, the Convention has not entered into force under paragraph 1 above, any signatory which has deposited its instrument of acceptance, approval or ratification may declare in writing to the Depositary its readiness to accept entry into force of this Convention under this paragraph 2. The Convention shall enter into force for such a signatory on the sixtieth day following the date upon which such declarations have been deposited by at least two signatories. For each signatory depositing its declaration after such entry into force, the Convention shall enter into force on the sixtieth day following the date of deposit.

ARTICLE 16—AMENDMENT

Any Party may propose the amendment of this Convention. A proposed amendment shall be submitted to the Depositary which shall communicate it to the other Parties at least sixty days before convening a meeting of the Parties to consider the proposed amendment. An amendment adopted by consensus of the parties, or by such other means as the Parties may determine by consensus, shall enter into force sixty days after the deposit of an instrument of ratification, acceptance or approval by all of the Parties, or in such other circumstances as may be specified by the Parties at the time of adoption of the amendment.

ARTICLE 17—WITHDRAWAL

A Party may withdraw from this Convention by submitting written notification to the Depositary. Such withdrawal shall be effective one year after the date of the receipt of the notification. After withdrawal, co-operation shall continue between the Parties and the Party which has withdrawn on all requests for assistance or extradition made before the effective date of withdrawal which remain pending.

Concerning Belgium-Luxembourg: Trade statistics for Belgium and Luxembourg are available only on a combined basis for the two countries. For purposes of Article 15, paragraph 1 of the Convention, if either Belgium of Luxembourg deposits its instrument of acceptance, approval or ratification, or if both Belgium and Luxembourg deposit their instruments of acceptance, approval or ratification, it shall be considered that one of the countries which have the ten largest exports shares has deposited its instrument and the joint exports of both countries will be counted towards the 60 percent of combined total exports of those ten countries, which is required for entry into force under this provision.

APPENDIX 3

Preliminary Multinational Anti-Bribery/FCPA Compliance Risk Profile

© 2009 Robert W. Tarun

This Anti-Bribery/Foreign Corrupt Practices Act (FCPA) Risk Assessment is designed to give a multinational company a preliminary snapshot view of its potential risk for FCPA misconduct, to provide a framework on how it might improve its compliance efforts, and to ensure that there is a solid record of the company's compliance program if it is investigated by U.S. or other law enforcement authorities. It is not intended to be a substitute for consultation with an experienced FCPA counsel, an FCPA audit by counsel, an audit lite, or a particular country or industry risk analysis. To complete, first add scores in Section A and then subtract applicable scores in Section B. The net score in Section C will determine your company's risk category under the table below. Key factors for each criterion are italicized. You are encouraged to assess your company as objectively as possible.

High Risk	55–69
Moderate Risk	70–85
Low Risk	86–100

SECTION A: ADD

Code of Conduct and Separate FCPA Compliance Policy

Custom Code of Conduct that *in clear, simple language addresses problematic FCPA areas for the company, discusses consequences to employees who fail to comply with laws, rules and regulations,* and provides employees with *contact information for further guidance*   2

Code of Conduct or a separate FCPA Compliance policy that gives *concrete examples* of proscribed FCPA conduct and appropriate guidance, *e.g.,* gifts, travel and entertainment, agents, interface with foreign government officials   2

Code of Conduct and any separate FCPA Compliance Policy
are translated into *every* applicable foreign language of countries
where the company has foreign operations   2

Code of Conduct that requires *annual* certification of *every* officer
and manager who has any international responsibilities that he
or she has complied with FCPA *and* is aware of no violations the
past year   2

Code of Conduct and any separate FCPA Compliance Policy are
reviewed annually paragraph-by-paragraph by Legal Department
members and/or the Chief Compliance Officer in light of the
preceding year's internal compliance issues, industry best
practices, and legal cases and developments   2

Subtotal: ___ of 10

Board of Directors

Live substantive anti-bribery or FCPA training for the BOD
(one hour) every two years; signatures on training attendance
forms; and retention of training materials, *e.g.*, PowerPoints,
handouts, etc.   2

An Audit Committee or Compliance Committee *charter* whose
mandate encompasses anti-bribery and FCPA compliance   2

Audit Committee or BOD Minutes contain *specific* references
on anti-bribery or FCPA reporting issues *and* actions   2

Annual legal report to the BOD on *anti-bribery or FCPA legal
developments and best practices*   2

Each Director provided an *FCPA guide or booklet*   2

Subtotal: ___ of 10

CEO

Annual live substantive anti-bribery or FCPA training (one hour);
record of training, *e.g.*, signature on training attendance form;
and retention of training materials, *e.g.*, PowerPoints, handouts, etc.   2

Annual travel to 2 or more high-corruption risk operations if company
does business in more than 10 foreign countries   2

5 or more years senior managerial experience with multinational company
whose foreign operations are in *one or more BRICK[1]* countries   2

Resided and worked in foreign country with a *Transparency International
Corruption Perception Index (CPI)* ≤ 5.0   2

CEO that has specifically emphasized the importance of FCPA compliance to executive team, sales managers and finance staff in past 12 months   2

Subtotal: ___ of 10

CFO

Annual live substantive anti-bribery or FCPA training (one hour); record of training attendance; and retention of training materials, *e.g.*, PowerPoints, handouts, etc.   2

5 or more years senior level financial and controls experience with a multinational company   2

5 or more years senior level experience with multinational company whose foreign operations are *in one or more BRICK countries*   1

Resided and worked in foreign country with a *Transparency International* Corruption Perception Index (CPI) ≤ 5.0   1

Annual travel to 2 or more high-corruption risk operations if company does business in more than 10 foreign countries   2

Senior foreign financial managers or officers directly report to CFO rather than to in-country managers   2

Subtotal: ___ of 10

General Counsel

General Counsel who requires one annual hour of *live substantive anti-bribery or FCPA training for all* his or her legal staff who have international and/or M&A responsibilities; records of training attendance; and retention of training materials, *e.g.*, PowerPoints, handouts, etc.   2

General Counsel who has the *clear authority to nix a merger or acquisition* if he or she believes there is a *significant* risk of anti-bribery or FCPA violations by the target   3

General Counsel who designates at least one experienced lawyer to look into *any* anti-bribery or FCPA allegation (*e.g.*, within 5 days) *and* has implemented a formal investigatory protocol to review significant FCPA allegations   2

General Counsel who regularly consults or directs his or her staff to *consult anti-bribery or FCPA counsel* on M&A, third-party contracts, and common anti-bribery or FCPA issues, e.g., travel and entertainment, customs interface, etc.   2

General Counsel who has had his or her legal staff, finance and
audit groups conduct annual *ongoing* due diligence of joint
venturers, agents, consultants, distributors, and other
third-parties *after* the signing of a contract   2

General Counsel who annually conducts *legal "audit lites"* of
operations in select countries where there are significant
Transparency International Corruption Perception Index (CPI)
($\leq$ 5.0) problems or substantial corporate growth goals   2

General Counsel who regularly secures *written* opinions or
advice on FCPA issues   2

Subtotal: ___ of 15

Contracts

Contracts that *specify U.S. FCPA or other anti-bribery laws and
details what they prohibit and permit as affirmative defenses*—and do
not simply state that JV partners, agents, distributors, or other
third-parties must comply with "all applicable U.S. laws and
regulations"   2

Contracts that give company *the unqualified right to audit* joint
venture partner, agent, consultant, distributor, or other
third-party in every such contract   2

Audits rights as to *all* joint venture parties, agents, distributors,
or any major third-party contractors *exercised* at least every
three years   2

Contracts that give the company *clear grounds for termination* of
joint venture, agency, consultancy, or third-party contractor
including termination *for refusal to provide requested documents
or make managers available for interviews* if sensitive allegations
are made   2

Subtotal: ___ of 8

Internal Audits

Internal Audit staff or core staff dedicated to international
audits who are required to participate in annual *live anti-bribery
laws or FCPA* training; records of training attendance; and retention
of training materials, *e.g.*, PowerPoints, handouts, course
materials, etc.   2

Internal Audit staff or core staff dedicated to international audits
who *rotate foreign operation audits* based on *Transparency International*
rankings or similar criteria   2

Internal Audits required of *every* BRICK country *in which the company does business at least every two years*   2

Internal Audit Director who *directly reports to the Audit Committee at least twice a year*   2

Internal Audits where *all anti-bribery or FCPA-related interviews are conducted by and memorialized by lawyers*   3

Subtotal: ___ of 11

Compliance Culture and Senior Management

A *formally designated* Chief Compliance Officer (full-time in an organization with 10,000 or more employees) who reports directly to the General Counsel and Chief Executive Officer *and* has *unrestricted access* to the Audit Committee   2

Compliance Committee which meets quarterly to review *all* FCPA or anti-bribery allegations, industry standards, training and legal developments. (Compliance Committee members might include the General Counsel or Deputy General Counsel, Regional Counsel, Chief Financial Officer, Chief Accounting Officer, Director of Internal Audit, Director of Human Resources and Director of Security)   2

Perception that the *Code of Conduct and other ethics rules* for employees *fully apply to senior management as well*   2

International Hot Line   1

Annual written report or database summarizing company's anti-bribery or FCPA allegations and compliance that is distributed to General Counsel, Chief Compliance Officer and other appropriate officers   2

Subtotal: ___ of 9

Anti-Bribery or FCPA Training and Certification

Annual live anti-bribery or FCPA training for *all* senior sales, legal, senior financial and country managers in countries with a *Transparency International* Corrupt Perception Index (CPI) ≤ 5.0; records of training attendance; and retention of training materials, *e.g.*, PowerPoints, handouts, etc.   2

Live anti-bribery or FCPA training provided to all joint venture partners, management, agents, consultants, distributors, or third-party contractors (other than for Fortune 500 consultants, recognized law firms, accounting firms, etc. or day contractors, *e.g.*, hydraulic engineer to receive $175/hour or $1,600 maximum per day) every 18 months; records of training attendance; and retention of training materials, *e.g.*, PowerPoints, handouts, etc.   2

Annual specialized FCPA or anti-bribery training for personnel who interface with foreign government officials, such as customs, tax, visas, and logistics personnel; records of training attendance; and retention of training materials, *e.g.*, PowerPoints, handouts, etc.   2

Annual certification of reading and adherence to anti-bribery or FCPA policy by *all* country managers, foreign sales heads and finance managers; and five-year retention of certifications   2

Subtotal: ___ of 8

Due Diligence and Acquisition Practices

Substantial due diligence files for *all* joint venture partners, agents, consultants, distributors, or third-party contractors (other than for Fortune 500 consultants, recognized law firms, accounting firms, etc. or day contractors), including local reference checks contacted and memorialized in signed memoranda, multinational references, completed questionnaires, and a signed statement by sponsoring employee or officer describing the particular need for any agent, consultant, or third-party—and retention of—due diligence files for life of contracts plus five years   3

On-site visits to *all* foreign operations and interviews of managers and major agents, consultants, distributors, and other third-party contractors *as part of M&A due diligence and prior to closing*   3

Day One Compliance Program to assimilate all mergers and acquisitions into acquirer's compliance program and to *live* train *all* acquired managers on anti-bribery or FCPA compliance within 30 days of closing; and retention of all records establishing Day One Compliance Plan   3

Subtotal: ___ of 9

SECTION A TOTAL: _____

MAXIMUM: 100

SECTION B: **SUBTRACT**

FCPA Country Risk

25% of issuer's revenues are in countries where the *Transparency International* Corruption Perception Index (CPI) is 0.0 to 4.9   3

Annual growth plan of 20% or more revenue in two or more countries where the *Transparency International* Corruption Perception Index (CPI) is 0.0 to 4.9   3

If *15% or more of company's revenues* come from a BRICK country, add 4 points for *each* BRICK country   4

Subtotal: ___ of 10

Regional and/or In-Country Management Weaknesses

Regional or senior *in-country manager* who *lacks true commitment* to FCPA training and compliance ("old school" factor)   3

Regional or *senior financial officer* who *lacks true commitment* to FCPA training and compliance ("old school" factor)   3

Weak in-country accounting *staffs and internal controls*   2

No regional legal adviser or lawyer *directly responsible for emerging markets or BRICK countries*   2

Subtotal: ___ of 10

Prior and Current FCPA or Anti-Bribery Investigations

Prior DOJ and/or SEC FCPA investigation   3

Ongoing DOJ or SEC FCPA investigation or foreign government anti-bribery investigation   5

DOJ prosecution or SEC enforcement action involving FCPA matters in last decade   7

Subtotal: ___ of 15

SECTION B TOTAL: _____

SECTION C:

SECTION A TOTAL: _____

LESS SECTION B TOTAL: − _____

FCPA COMPLIANCE RISK PROFILE TOTAL SCORE   = _____

Your Company's Score:

High Risk   55–69

Moderate Risk   70–85

Low Risk   86–100

Officer/Councel:

Date:

Comments:

_____

_____

_____

_____

_____

_____

_____

_____

_____

_____

APPENDIX 4

U.S. Department of Justice
Lay-Person's Guide to FCPA

FOREIGN CORRUPT PRACTICES ACT
ANTIBRIBERY PROVISIONS

United States Department of Justice
Fraud Section, Criminal Division
10th & Constitution Ave. NW (Bond 4th fl.)
Washington, D.C. 20530
phone: (202) 514-7023
fax: (202) 514-7021
internet: www.usdoj.gov/criminal/fraud/fcpa
email: FCPA.fraud@usdoj.gov

United States Department of Commerce
Office of the Chief Counsel for International Commerce
14th Street and Constitution Avenue, NW
Room 5882
Washington, D.C. 20230
phone: (202) 482-0937
fax: (202) 482-4076
internet: www.ita.doc.gov/legal

INTRODUCTION

The 1988 Trade Act directed the Attorney General to provide guidance concerning the Department of Justice's enforcement policy with respect to the Foreign Corrupt Practices Act of 1977 ("FCPA"), 15 U.S.C. §§ 78dd-1, *et seq.*, to potential exporters and small businesses that are unable to obtain specialized counsel on issues related to the FCPA. The guidance is limited to responses to requests under the Department of Justice's

Foreign Corrupt Practices Act Opinion Procedure (described below at p. 345) and to general explanations of compliance responsibilities and potential liabilities under the FCPA. This brochure constitutes the Department of Justice's general explanation of the FCPA.

U.S. firms seeking to do business in foreign markets must be familiar with the FCPA. In general, the FCPA prohibits corrupt payments to foreign officials for the purpose of obtaining or keeping business. In addition, other statutes such as the mail and wire fraud statutes, 18 U.S.C. § 1341, 1343, and the Travel Act, 18 U.S.C. § 1952, which provides for federal prosecution of violations of state commercial bribery statutes, may also apply to such conduct.

The Department of Justice is the chief enforcement agency, with a coordinate role played by the Securities and Exchange Commission (SEC). The Office of General Counsel of the Department of Commerce also answers general questions from U.S. exporters concerning the FCPA's basic requirements and constraints.

This brochure is intended to provide a general description of the FCPA and is not intended to substitute for the advice of private counsel on specific issues related to the FCPA. Moreover, material in this brochure is not intended to set forth the present enforcement intentions of the Department of Justice or the SEC with respect to particular fact situations.

BACKGROUND

As a result of SEC investigations in the mid-1970's, over 400 U.S. companies admitted making questionable or illegal payments in excess of $300 million to foreign government officials, politicians, and political parties. The abuses ran the gamut from bribery of high foreign officials to secure some type of favorable action by a foreign government to so-called facilitating payments that allegedly were made to ensure that government functionaries discharged certain ministerial or clerical duties. Congress enacted the FCPA to bring a halt to the bribery of foreign officials and to restore public confidence in the integrity of the American business system.

The FCPA was intended to have and has had an enormous impact on the way American firms do business. Several firms that paid bribes to foreign officials have been the subject of criminal and civil enforcement actions, resulting in large fines and suspension and debarment from federal procurement contracting, and their employees and officers have gone to jail. To avoid such consequences, many firms have implemented detailed compliance programs intended to prevent and to detect any improper payments by employees and agents.

Following the passage of the FCPA, the Congress became concerned that American companies were operating at a disadvantage compared to foreign companies who routinely paid bribes and, in some countries, were permitted to deduct the cost of such bribes as business expenses on their taxes. Accordingly, in 1988, the Congress directed the Executive Branch to commence negotiations in the Organization of Economic Cooperation and Development (OECD) to obtain the agreement of the United States' major trading partners to enact legislation similar to the FCPA. In 1997, almost ten years later, the United States and thirty-three other countries signed the OECD Convention on Combating Bribery of Foreign Public Officials in International Business Transactions. The United States ratified this Convention and enacted implementing legislation in 1998. See Convention and Commentaries on the DOJ web site.

The antibribery provisions of the FCPA make it unlawful for a U.S. person, and certain foreign issuers of securities, to make a corrupt payment to a foreign official for the purpose of obtaining or retaining business for or with, or directing business to, any person. Since 1998, they also apply to foreign firms and persons who take any act in furtherance of such a corrupt payment while in the United States.

The FCPA also requires companies whose securities are listed in the United States to meet its accounting provisions. See 15 U.S.C. § 78m. These accounting provisions, which were designed to operate in tandem with the antibribery provisions of the FCPA, require corporations covered by the provisions to make and keep books and records that accurately and fairly reflect the transactions of the corporation and to devise and maintain an adequate system of internal accounting controls. This brochure discusses only the antibribery provisions.

ENFORCEMENT

The Department of Justice is responsible for all criminal enforcement and for civil enforcement of the antibribery provisions with respect to domestic concerns and foreign companies and nationals. The SEC is responsible for civil enforcement of the antibribery provisions with respect to issuers.

ANTIBRIBERY PROVISIONS
BASIC PROHIBITION

The FCPA makes it unlawful to bribe foreign government officials to obtain or retain business. With respect to the basic prohibition, there are five elements which must be met to constitute a violation of the Act:

A. Who—The FCPA potentially applies to any individual, firm, officer, director, employee, or agent of a firm and any stockholder acting on behalf of a firm. Individuals and firms may also be penalized if they order, authorize, or assist someone else to violate the antibribery provisions or if they conspire to violate those provisions.

Under the FCPA, U.S. jurisdiction over corrupt payments to foreign officials depends upon whether the violator is an "issuer," a "domestic concern," or a foreign national or business.

An "issuer" is a corporation that has issued securities that have been registered in the United States or who is required to file periodic reports with the SEC. A "domestic concern" is any individual who is a citizen, national, or resident of the United States, or any corporation, partnership, association, joint-stock company, business trust, unincorporated organization, or sole proprietorship which has its principal place of business in the United States, or which is organized under the laws of a State of the United States, or a territory, possession, or commonwealth of the United States.

Issuers and domestic concerns may be held liable under the FCPA under either territorial or nationality jurisdiction principles. For acts taken within the territory of the United States, issuers and domestic concerns are liable if they take an act in furtherance of a corrupt payment to a foreign official using the U.S. mails or other means or instrumentalities of interstate commerce. Such means or instrumentalities include telephone calls, facsimile transmissions, wire transfers, and interstate or international travel. In addition, issuers and domestic concerns may be held liable for any act in furtherance of a corrupt payment taken outside the United States. Thus, a U.S. company or national may be held liable for a corrupt payment authorized by employees or agents operating entirely outside the United States, using money from foreign bank accounts, and without any involvement by personnel located within the United States.

Prior to 1998, foreign companies, with the exception of those who qualified as "issuers," and foreign nationals were not covered by the FCPA. The 1998 amendments expanded the FCPA to assert territorial jurisdiction over foreign companies and nationals. A foreign company or person is now subject to the FCPA if it causes, directly or through agents, an act in furtherance of the corrupt payment to take place within the territory of the United States. There is, however, no requirement that such act make use of the U.S. mails or other means or instrumentalities of interstate commerce.

Finally, U.S. parent corporations may be held liable for the acts of foreign subsidiaries where they authorized, directed, or controlled the activity in question, as can U.S. citizens or residents, themselves "domestic concerns," who were employed by or acting on behalf of such foreign-incorporated subsidiaries.

B.   Corrupt intent—The person making or authorizing the payment must have a corrupt intent, and the payment must be intended to induce the recipient to misuse his official position to direct business wrongfully to the payer or to any other person. You should note that the FCPA does not require that a corrupt act succeed in its purpose. The *offer* or *promise* of a corrupt payment can constitute a violation of the statute. The FCPA prohibits any corrupt payment intended to *influence* any act or decision of a foreign official in his or her official capacity, to induce the official to do or omit to do any act in violation of his or her lawful duty, to obtain any improper advantage, or to *induce* a foreign official to use his or her influence improperly to affect or influence any act or decision.

C.   Payment—The FCPA prohibits paying, offering, promising to pay (or authorizing to pay or offer) money or anything of value.

D.   Recipient—The prohibition extends only to corrupt payments to a *foreign official, a foreign political party* or *party official*, or any *candidate* for foreign political office. A "foreign official" means any officer or employee of a foreign government, a public international organization, or any department or agency thereof, or any person acting in an official capacity. You should consider utilizing the Department of Justice's Foreign Corrupt Practices Act Opinion Procedure for particular questions as to the definition of a "foreign official," such as whether a member of a royal family, a member of a legislative body, or an official of a state-owned business enterprise would be considered a "foreign official."

The FCPA applies to payments to *any* public official, regardless of rank or position. The FCPA focuses on the *purpose* of the payment instead of the particular duties of the official receiving the payment, offer, or promise of payment, and there are exceptions to the antibribery provision for "facilitating payments for routine governmental action" (see below).

E.   Business Purpose Test—The FCPA prohibits payments made in order to assist the firm in *obtaining* or *retaining business* for or with, or *directing business* to, any person. The Department of Justice interprets "obtaining or retaining business" broadly, such that the term encompasses more than the mere award or renewal of a contract. It should be noted that the business to be obtained or retained does *not* need to be with a foreign government or foreign government instrumentality.

THIRD PARTY PAYMENTS

The FCPA prohibits corrupt payments through intermediaries. It is unlawful to make a payment to a third party, while knowing that all or a portion of the payment will go directly or indirectly to a foreign official. *The term "knowing" includes conscious disregard and deliberate ignorance.* The elements of an offense are essentially the same as described above, except that in this case the "recipient" is the intermediary who is making the payment to the requisite "foreign official."

Intermediaries may include joint venture partners or agents. To avoid being held liable for corrupt third party payments, U.S. companies are encouraged to exercise due diligence and to take all necessary precautions to ensure that they have formed a business relationship with reputable and qualified partners and representatives. Such due diligence may include investigating potential foreign representatives and joint venture partners to determine if they are in fact qualified for the position, whether they have personal or professional ties to the government, the number and reputation of their clientele, and their reputation with the U.S. Embassy or Consulate and with local bankers, clients, and other business associates. In addition, in negotiating a business relationship, the U.S. firm should be aware of so-called "red flags," i.e., unusual payment patterns or financial arrangements, a history of corruption in the country, a refusal by the foreign joint venture partner or representative to provide a certification that it will not take any action in furtherance of an unlawful offer, promise, or payment to a foreign public official and not take any act that would cause the U.S. firm to be in violation of the FCPA, unusually high commissions, lack of transparency in expenses and accounting records, apparent lack of qualifications or resources on the part of the joint venture partner or representative to perform the services offered, and whether the joint venture partner or representative has been recommended by an official of the potential governmental customer.

You should seek the advice of counsel and consider utilizing the Department of Justice's Foreign Corrupt Practices Act Opinion Procedure for particular questions relating to third party payments.

PERMISSIBLE PAYMENTS AND AFFIRMATIVE DEFENSES

The FCPA contains an explicit exception to the bribery prohibition for "facilitating payments" for "routine governmental action" and provides affirmative defenses which can be used to defend against alleged violations of the FCPA.

FACILITATING PAYMENTS FOR ROUTINE GOVERNMENTAL ACTIONS

There is an exception to the antibribery prohibition for payments to facilitate or expedite performance of a "routine governmental action."

The statute lists the following examples: obtaining permits, licenses, or other official documents; processing governmental papers, such as visas and work orders; providing police protection, mail pick-up and delivery; providing phone service, power and water supply, loading and unloading cargo, or protecting perishable products; and scheduling inspections associated with contract performance or transit of goods across country.

Actions "similar" to these are also covered by this exception. If you have a question about whether a payment falls within the exception, you should consult with counsel. You should also consider whether to utilize the Justice Department's Foreign Corrupt Practices Opinion Procedure, described below on p. 345.

"Routine governmental action" does *not* include any decision by a foreign official to award new business or to continue business with a particular party.

AFFIRMATIVE DEFENSES

A person charged with a violation of the FCPA's antibribery provisions may assert as a defense that the payment was lawful under the written laws of the foreign country or that the money was spent as part of demonstrating a product or performing a contractual obligation.

Whether a payment was lawful under the written laws of the foreign country may be difficult to determine. You should consider seeking the advice of counsel or utilizing the Department of Justice's Foreign Corrupt Practices Act Opinion Procedure when faced with an issue of the legality of such a payment.

Moreover, because these defenses are "affirmative defenses," the defendant is required to show in the first instance that the payment met these requirements. The prosecution does not bear the burden of demonstrating in the first instance that the payments did not constitute this type of payment.

SANCTIONS AGAINST BRIBERY

CRIMINAL

The following criminal penalties may be imposed for violations of the FCPA's antibribery provisions: corporations and other business entities are subject to a fine of up to $2,000,000; officers, directors, stockholders, employees, and agents are subject to a fine of up to $100,000 and imprisonment for up to five years. Moreover, under the Alternative Fines Act, these fines may be actually quite higher—the actual fine may be up to twice the benefit that the defendant sought to obtain by making the corrupt payment. You should also be aware that fines imposed on individuals may *not* be paid by their employer or principal.

CIVIL

The Attorney General or the SEC, as appropriate, may bring a civil action for a fine of up to $10,000 against any firm *as well as* any officer, director, employee, or agent of a firm, or stockholder acting on behalf of the firm, who violates the antibribery provisions. In addition, in an SEC enforcement action, the court may impose an additional fine not to exceed the greater of (i) the gross amount of the pecuniary gain to the defendant as a result of the violation, or (ii) a specified dollar limitation. The specified dollar limitations are based on the egregiousness of the violation, ranging from $5,000 to $100,000 for a natural person and $50,000 to $500,000 for any other person.

The Attorney General or the SEC, as appropriate, may also bring a civil action to enjoin any act or practice of a firm whenever it appears that the firm (or an officer, director, employee, agent, or stockholder acting on behalf of the firm) is in violation (or about to be) of the antibribery provisions.

OTHER GOVERNMENTAL ACTION

Under guidelines issued by the Office of Management and Budget, a person or firm found in violation of the FCPA may be barred from doing business with the Federal government. *Indictment alone can lead to suspension of the right to do business with the government.* The President has directed that no executive agency shall allow any party to participate in any procurement or nonprocurement activity if any agency has debarred, suspended, or otherwise excluded that party from participation in a procurement or nonprocurement activity.

In addition, a person or firm found guilty of violating the FCPA may be ruled ineligible to receive export licenses; the SEC may suspend or bar persons from the securities business and impose civil penalties on persons in the securities business for violations of the FCPA; the Commodity Futures Trading Commission and the Overseas Private Investment Corporation both provide for possible suspension or debarment from agency programs for violation of the FCPA; and a payment made to a foreign government official that is unlawful under the FCPA cannot be deducted under the tax laws as a business expense.

PRIVATE CAUSE OF ACTION

Conduct that violates the antibribery provisions of the FCPA may also give rise to a private cause of action for treble damages under the Racketeer Influenced and Corrupt Organizations Act (RICO), or to actions under other federal or state laws. For example, an action might be brought under RICO by a competitor who alleges that the bribery caused the defendant to win a foreign contract.

GUIDANCE FROM THE GOVERNMENT

The Department of Justice has established a Foreign Corrupt Practices Act Opinion Procedure by which any U.S. company or national may request a statement of the Justice Department's present enforcement intentions under the antibribery provisions of the FCPA regarding any proposed business conduct. The details of the opinion procedure may be found at 28 CFR Part 80. Under this procedure, the Attorney General will issue an opinion in response to a specific inquiry from a person or firm within thirty days of the request. (The thirty-day period does not run until the Department of Justice has received all the information it requires to issue the opinion.) Conduct for which the Department of Justice has issued an opinion stating that the conduct conforms with current enforcement policy will be entitled to a presumption, in any subsequent enforcement action, of conformity with the FCPA. Copies of releases issued regarding previous opinions are available on the Department of Justice's FCPA web site.

For further information from the Department of Justice about the FCPA and the Foreign Corrupt Practices Act Opinion Procedure, contact Mark F. Mendelsohn, Deputy Chief, Fraud Section, at (202) 514-1721; or William Jacobson, Assistant Chief, Fraud Section, at (202) 353-0449 .

Although the Department of Commerce has no enforcement role with respect to the FCPA, it supplies general guidance to U.S. exporters who have questions about the FCPA and about international developments concerning the FCPA. For further information from the Department of Commerce about the FCPA contact Eleanor Roberts Lewis, Chief Counsel for International Commerce, or Arthur Aronoff, Senior Counsel, Office of the Chief Counsel for International Commerce, U.S. Department of Commerce, Room 5882, 14th Street and Constitution Avenue, N.W., Washington, D.C. 20230, (202) 482-0937.

APPENDIX 5

DOJ FCPA Opinion Releases Index

Foreign Corrupt Practices Act
U.S. Department of Justice
Opinion Procedure Releases
1993 Through 2009

FCPA Opinion Procedure Release No.	Date	Subject	Country
93-01	04/20/1993	COMMERCIAL Major commercial organization proposing to supply management services to entity owned by government of a former Eastern Bloc country.	Former Eastern Bloc Country
93-02	05/11/1993	DEFENSE American company seeking to enter into a sales agreement to sell defense equipment to foreign country's armed forces.	Foreign Country
94-01	05/13/1994	CONSULTING American company and wholly-owned subsidiary seeking to enter into a consulting relationship with foreign individual who is general director of a state-owned enterprise.	Foreign Country

FCPA Opinion Procedure Release No.	Date	Subject	Country
95-01	01/11/1995	DONATION U.S.-based energy company planning to acquire and operate a plant in a South Asian country and make a prospective donation to charitable organization and foreign public limited liability company near the plant.	South Asian nation
95-02	09/14/1995	OFFSET OBLIGATIONS Two American companies seeking to enter into two transactions in a foreign country have to fulfill offset obligations in foreign country as a result of contracts entered.	Foreign Country
96-01	11/25/1996	NON-PROFIT FUNDING Non-profit corporation seeking to sponsor and provide funds to representatives from ten foreign countries to attend environmental protection training courses in the United States.	Ten regional nations
96-2	11/25/1996	MARKETING U.S. company seeking to manufacture and sell off equipment used in commercial and military aircraft to state-owned enterprise of foreign country.	Foreign Country

FCPA Opinion Procedure Release No.	Date	Subject	Country
97-01	02/27/1997	COMMERCIAL Wholly-owned subsidiary of U.S. Company submitting a bid to sell and service high technology equipment with private company in foreign country.	Foreign Country
97-2	11/05/1997	DONATION U.S.-based utility company seeking to donate funds to government entity in Asian country to build a school near plant to be built by U.S.-based utility company.	Asian nation
98-01	02/23/1998	ENVIRONMENTAL CLEAN-UP U.S.-based industrial and service company seeking to arrange to pay environmental contamination liability imposed on it by the Nigerian government and to clean up contaminated site.	Nigeria
98-2	08/05/1998	MILITARY Wholly-owned subsidiary of U.S. company submitting a bid to foreign-owned entity to sell and service military training program and enter into several agreements with private company in same foreign country.	Foreign Country

FCPA Opinion Procedure Release No.	Date	Subject	Country
00-01	03/29/2000	COMPENSATION U.S. law firm seeking to provide payments and benefits to foreign partner of a U.S. law firm, who took a leave of absence from the law firm to become a high-ranking Foreign Government Official.	Foreign Country
01-01	05/24/2001	COMMERCIAL U.S. company seeking to enter into a joint venture with a French company which is contributing pre-existing contracts and transactions to joint venture at risk if any of these contracts procured by French company was obtained or maintained through bribery.	France
01-02	07/18/2001	COMMERCIAL U.S. company seeking to avoid any impropriety in situation where chairman of foreign company (who is also an advisor to his country's senior government official) which will form a consortium with a partially owned U.S. company will be bidding on prospective government business.	Foreign Country

FCPA Opinion Procedure Release No.	Date	Subject	Country
01-03	12/11/2001	COMMERCIAL Wholly-owned U.S. subsidiary seeking to submit a bid to a foreign government for sale of equipment to government with the assistance of a foreign dealer who informed it that payments have been made or would be made by dealer to government officials so that bid is accepted.	Foreign Country
03-01	01/15/2003	ACQUISITION OF COMPANY U.S. issuer while acquiring another U.S. company with both U.S. and foreign subsidiaries learned that officers of foreign subsidiary authorized and made payments to foreign state owned entities to obtain or retain business.	Foreign Country
04-01	01/06/2004	EVENT SPONSORING U.S. law firm seeking to sponsor, present and pay costs for a Comparative Law Seminar on Labor & Employment Law in conjunction with a ministry of the People's Republic of China.	People's Republic of China

FCPA Opinion Procedure Release No.	Date	Subject	Country
04-02	07/12/2004	ACQUISITION OF COMPANIES Investment group acquiring certain companies and assets from ABB Ltd. relating to upstream oil, gas and petrochemical businesses, which had been charged with FCPA violations relating to transactions involving business in several foreign countries, including Nigeria.	Foreign Countries, including Nigeria
04-03	06/14/2004	EVENT SPONSORING American law firm sponsoring and paying for travel expenses related to a trip to U.S. for 12 ministry officials from the People's Republic of China to discuss employment issues.	People's Republic of China
04-04	09/03/2004	EVENT SPONSORING U. S. company providing funds for a Study Tour of foreign officials who are members of committee drafting insurance regulations in foreign country.	Foreign Country
06-01	10/16/2006	BENEVOLENT CONTRIBUTION Delaware corporation with headquarters in Switzerland seeking to contribute $25,000 to a regional Customs department or Ministry of Finance in an African country as part of a pilot project to improve local enforcement of anti-counterfeiting laws.	African nation

FCPA Opinion Procedure Release No.	Date	Subject	Country
06-02	12/31/2006	RETENTION OF LAW FIRM Wholly-owned U.S. subsidiary in foreign country seeking to retain law firm to aid in obtaining foreign exchange from government agency by preparing application and representing company for a substantial flat fee.	Foreign Country
07-01	07/24/2007	EDUCATIONAL FUNDING Issuer seeking to cover domestic expenses for a trip to U.S. of a six-person delegation of the government of an Asian country for educational and promotional tour of the Issuer's U.S. operations sites.	Asian nation
07-02	09/11/2007	EDUCATIONAL FUNDING U.S. insurance company proposing to pay domestic expenses of six junior mid-level officials of a foreign government for education programs at its U.S. headquarters in order to familiarize the officials with operation of the U.S. insurance company.	Foreign Country
07-03	12/21/2007	PAYMENT OF LEGAL EXPENSES Permanent resident of the U.S. proposing to make a payment required by a family court judge in an Asian country to cover litigation-related costs.	Asian nation

FCPA Opinion Procedure Release No.	Date	Subject	Country
08-01	01/15/2008	INVESTMENT Wholly-owned foreign subsidiary of U.S. issuer seeking to undertake a prospective majority investment in a foreign company which is responsible for managing certain public services for a major foreign municipality.	Foreign Country
08-02	06/13/2008	ACQUISITION OF COMPANY Halliburton Company and its subsidiaries considering making an additional bid to acquire the entire share capital of a company based in the United Kingdom, a company which is traded on the London Stock Exchange and operates in over 50 countries.	United Kingdom
08-03	07/11/2008	FUNDING FOR JOURNALISTS TRACE International, Inc. proposing to pay certain expenses for approximately 20 journalists employed by media outlets based in the People's Republic of China to enable them to attend a press conference being held by TRACE in Shanghai.	People's Republic of China
09-01	08/08/2009	A medical device designer and manufacturer proposing to provide a foreign government, not a foreign official, free sample devices, each worth $19,000.	Foreign country

APPENDIX 6

FCPA Acquisition Due Diligence Checklist

- Corporate Information
  - Names and Addresses of Target's Officers, Directors, Management Level Employees, Owners and Principal Shareholders (private company)
  - Names and Addresses of Target's Officers, Directors, Management Level Employees, Owners and Shareholders with Interests of 10% or More (public company)
  - Identification of any Officers, Directors, Management Level Employees, Owners or Principal Shareholders Who are:
    - Current or Former Government Officials or Employees
    - Close Family Members of Government Officials or Employees
- FCPA or Anti-Bribery Compliance Policies and Procedures
  - Statement of Corporate Compliance Policy
  - Internal FCPA or Anti-Bribery Compliance Procedures
  - FCPA or Anti-Bribery Compliance Training Materials
    - PowerPoint Presentations
    - Handouts
    - Attendance Lists
    - Acknowledgment Forms
  - Internal Accounting Control Procedures
  - Appropriate Translation of Compliance Policies and Procedures
- International Business Activities
  - Countries in which Target has Business Operations
  - Countries in which Target makes sales to Government Entities (including State-Owned Commercial Enterprises)
    - Evaluation of Countries against *Transparency International* Corruption Perception Index (CPI)
  - List of all Registrations, Licenses, Permits and other Government Approvals held by Target to do business in each Country
  - Identification of each Government Agency responsible for administering Registration, Licensing, Permits and Approvals
    - Copies of all Correspondence with Government Agencies relating to Registration, Licensing, Permits and Approvals

- List of all Consultants and other Intermediaries engaged to Perform Services in connection with Registration, Licensing, Permits or Approvals from Government Agencies
  - Copies of Contracts with those Consultants and other Intermediaries
  - Records of all Compensation paid to Consultants and other Intermediaries
- Sales to Government Entities (including State-Owned Commercial Enterprises)
  - List of all Government Entities to which Target Sells or Supplies Goods or Services
  - Percentage of Target's Total Business with Government Entities
  - Copies of all Contracts to Sell or Supply Goods or Services to Government Entities
    - Include Copies of Subcontracts to Supply Goods or Services to Government Contractors
    - Copies of Sales Records under Government Contracts
  - List of all Payments, along with Payment Records, to Third Parties, including Consultants, Sales Representatives, Agents, and Other Intermediaries, made in connection with any Government Contract or Subcontract
- Relationships with Intermediaries
  - List of all Distributors, Sales Representatives, Agents, Resellers, Freight Forwarders, Consultants, Customs Brokers and Other Intermediaries Retained by Target for any Purpose
    - List of Intermediaries Engaged by Target for the Purpose of Promoting Sales of the Target's Goods or Services to Government Entities (including State-Owned Commercial Enterprises)
    - Copies of Contracts with all Intermediaries
    - Description of Services Performed by each such Intermediary
    - Compensation Arrangements and Payment Records of all Payments to Intermediaries
  - Description of Approval Process for the Retention of Intermediaries
    - Background Check and Due Diligence Materials on each Intermediary
    - Records of Approval of each Intermediary
  - Records and Reports of any Investigation or Termination of any Intermediary based on Anti-Corruption Concerns
- Dealings with Government Officials
  - Records of all Payments and Gifts to any Government Officials
  - Records of all Hospitality (travel, meals, lodging) provided to any Government Officials

- Approval Process for Payments, Gifts and Hospitality for Government Officials
  - Purpose for each Payment, Gift or Hospitality
  - Actual Approvals for each Payment, Gift or Hospitality
  - Legal Opinions on Legality of each Payment, Gift or Hospitality
- Accounting Records Reflecting each Payment, Gift or Hospitality
- Contributions and Donations
  - Contributions to Political Parties
  - Contributions to Candidates for Political Office
  - Donations to Government Agencies
  - Donations to Charitable Organizations
  - Approval Process for Contributions and Donations
    - Purpose or Rationale for each Contribution and Donation
    - Actual Approvals for each Contribution and Donation
    - Legal Opinions on Legality of each Contribution and Donation (especially political contributions)
  - Accounting Records Reflecting each Contribution and Donation
- Compliance Reviews, Violations and Enforcement Actions
  - Internal Procedures on Compliance Reviews
    - Reports of Compliance Audits
    - Follow-Up Actions in Response to Compliance Audits
  - Records and Reports of Internal Compliance Investigations
  - Records and Reports of External (Government) Compliance Investigations
  - Documents relating to Threatened, Pending and Completed Administrative and Judicial Enforcement Actions and Proceedings
  - Voluntary Disclosures of Suspected Violations to Government Agencies
  - Local Legal Opinions Relating to Anti-Corruption Issues
- List of all Funds, Assets, Accounts, and Transactions not recorded or reflected on the Target's Books and Records
- Internet Searches
  - Target
  - Officers and Directors
  - Management Level Employees
  - Owners or Principal Shareholders (all private companies and 10% or more shareholders of public companies)

APPENDIX 7

American College of Trial Lawyers' *Recommended Practices for Companies and Their Counsel in Conducting Internal Investigations* (February 2008)

RECOMMENDED PRACTICES FOR COMPANIES AND THEIR COUNSEL IN CONDUCTING INTERNAL INVESTIGATIONS

Approved by the Board of Regents
February 2008

AMERICAN COLLEGE OF TRIAL LAWYERS

The American College of Trial Lawyers, founded in 1950, is composed of the best of the trial bar from the United States and Canada. Fellowship in the College is extended by invitation only, after careful investigation, to those experienced trial lawyers who have mastered the art of advocacy and those whose professional careers have been marked by the highest standards of ethical conduct, professionalism, civility and collegiality. Lawyers must have a minimum of 15 years' experience before they can be considered for Fellowship. Membership in the College cannot exceed 1% of the total lawyer population of any state or province. Fellows are carefully selected from among those who represent plaintiffs and those who represent defendants in civil cases; those who prosecute and those who defend persons accused of crime. The College is thus able to speak with a balanced voice on important issues affecting the administration of justice. The College strives to improve and elevate the standards of trial practice, the administration of justice and the ethics of the trial profession.

♦ ♦ ♦

"In this select circle, we find pleasure and charm in the illustrious company of our contemporaries and take the keenest delight in exalting our friendships."

—Hon. Emil Gumpert,
Chancellor-Founder, ACTL

American College of Trial Lawyers
19900 MacArthur Boulevard, Suite 610
Irvine, California 92612
Telephone: (949) 752-1801
Facsimile: (949) 752-1674
E-mail: nationaloffice@actl.com
Website: www.actl.com

AMERICAN COLLEGE OF TRIAL LAWYERS

PAST PRESIDENTS

1950-51 EMIL GUMPERT*
Los Angeles, California
1951-52 C. RAY ROBINSON*
Merced, California
1952-53 CODY FOWLER*
Tampa, Florida
1953-54 E. D. BRONSON*
San Francisco, California
1954-55 CODY FOWLER*
Tampa, Florida
1955-56 WAYNE E. STICHTER*
Toledo, Ohio
1956-57 JESSE E. NICHOLS*
Oakland, California
1957-58 LEWIS C. RYAN*
Syracuse, New York
1958-59 ALBERT E. JENNER, JR.*
Chicago, Illinois
1959-60 SAMUEL P. SEARS*
Boston, Massachusetts
1960-61 LON HOCKER*
Woods Hole, Massachusetts
1961-62 LEON JAWORSKI*
Houston, Texas
1962-63 GRANT B. COOPER*
Los Angeles, California
1963-64 WHITNEY NORTH SEYMOUR*
New York, New York
1964-65 BERNARD G. SEGAL*
Philadelphia, Pennsylvania
1965-66 EDWARD L. WRIGHT*
Little Rock, Arkansas
1966-67 FRANK G. RAICHLE*
Buffalo, New York
1967-68 JOSEPH A. BALL*
Long Beach, California
1968-69 ROBERT W. MESERVE*
Boston, Massachusetts
1969-70 HON. LEWIS F. POWELL, JR.*
Washington, District of Columbia
1970-71 BARNABAS F. SEARS*
Chicago, Illinois
1971-72 HICKS EPTON*
Wewoka, Oklahoma
1972-73 WILLIAM H. MORRISON*
Portland, Oregon
1973-74 ROBERT L. CLARE, JR.*
New York, New York
1974- AUSTIN W. LEWIS*
New Orleans, Louisiana
1975-76 THOMAS E. DEACY, JR.
Kansas City, Missouri
1976-77 SIMON H. RIFKIND*
New York, New York
1977-78 KRAFT W. EIDMAN*
Houston, Texas
1978-79 MARCUS MATTSON*
Los Angeles, California

1979-80 JAMES E. S. BAKER*
Chicago, Illinois
1980-81 JOHN C. ELAM*
Columbus, Ohio
1981-82 ALSTON JENNINGS*
Little Rock, Arkansas
1982-83 LEON SILVERMAN
New York, New York
1983-84 GAEL MAHONY
Boston, Massachusetts
1984-85 GENE W. LAFITTE
New Orleans, Louisiana
1985-86 GRIFFIN B. BELL
Atlanta, Georgia
1986-87 R. HARVEY CHAPPELL, JR.
Richmond, Virginia
1987-88 MORRIS HARRELL*
Dallas, Texas
1988-89 PHILIP W. TONE*
Chicago, Illinois
1989-90 RALPH I. LANCASTER, JR.
Portland, Maine
1990-91 CHARLES E. HANGER*
San Francisco, California
1991-92 ROBERT B. FISKE, JR.
New York, New York
1992-93 FULTON HAIGHT*
Santa Monica, California
1993-94 FRANK C. JONES
Atlanta, Georgia
1994-95 LIVELY M. WILSON
Louisville, Kentucky
1995-96 CHARLES B. RENFREW
San Francisco, California
1996-97 ANDREW M. COATS
Oklahoma City, Oklahoma
1997-98 EDWARD BRODSKY*
New York, New York
1998-99 E. OSBORNE AYSCUE, JR.
Charlotte, North Carolina
1999-2000 MICHAEL E. MONE
Boston, Massachusetts
2000-2001 EARL J. SILBERT
Washington, District of Columbia
2001-2002 STUART D. SHANOR
Roswell, New Mexico
2002-2003 WARREN B. LIGHTFOOT
Birmingham, Alabama
2003-2004 DAVID W. SCOTT, Q.C.
Ottawa, Ontario
2004-2005 JAMES W. MORRIS, III
Richmond, Virginia
2005-2006 MICHAEL A. COOPER,
New York, New York
2006-2007 DAVID J. BECK
Houston, Texas

* Deceased

TABLE OF CONTENTS

RECOMMENDED PRACTICES FOR
COMPANIES AND THEIR COUNSEL IN
CONDUCTING INTERNAL INVESTIGATIONS*

I.   Purpose of the Paper

Since 2001, over 2,500 public companies have retained outside counsel to conduct internal investigations into suspected wrong-doing by corporate executives and employees. These investigations have included inquiries into suspected violations of the Foreign Corrupt Practices Act; alleged options backdating activities; alleged violations of the antitrust, environmental, import/export, and other laws; and financial statement improprieties.[1] The Federal Criminal Procedure Committee of the American College of Trial Lawyers has observed counsel implementing a wide variety of procedures and protocols in conducting corporate internal investigations for issuers and public companies in particular. The result has been variances both in treatment of officers and employees and in outcomes of the investigations for such officers and employees and the corporations themselves. The Committee has sought to determine, and now recommends, what it believes to be the fairest and most effective practices for conducting internal investigations of possible corporate wrongdoing. Although the principles articulated in this paper are tailored to internal investigations by issuers and public companies where significant allegations of malfeasance are alleged or suspected, many of these principles may be applied in the context of other entities and smaller investigations.

---

[*]   The principal draftsman of this report was David M. Brodsky (New York, N.Y.). He was assisted by a subcommittee of the Federal Criminal Procedure Committee of the American College of Trial Lawyers consisting of its Chair Douglas R. Young (San Francisco, CA.), Fellows Nanci Clarence (San Francisco, CA.), James Brosnahan (San Francisco, CA.), John S. Siffert (New York, N.Y.), Robert G. Morvillo (New York, N.Y.), the Honorable Nancy Gertner (US District Court, District of Massachusetts), and Regent Liaison Robert W. Tarun (Chicago, IL.). Fellow Cristina Arguedas (Berkeley, CA.) also reviewed this report.

[1]   *See, e.g.,* the Wall Street Journal Options Scoreboard, where 143 public companies are listed as having conducted internal investigations into suspected options backdating, http://online.wsj.com/public/resources/documents/info-optionsscore06-full.html.

A sample of the internal investigations conducted by different law firms reveals the diversity of the matters under internal investigation since 2001:
  * representation of Fortune 100 Company in a Special Litigation Committee investigation involving derivative shareholder claims against directors and officers regarding false financial statements and conflicts of interest arising out of acquisitions;
  * representation of the Audit Committee of leading lessor of shipping containers and chassis in an internal investigation arising from an accounting restatement;
  * representation of the Corporate Governance Committee of a major transportation company in a review of its corporate governance structure;
  * representation of the Audit Committee of a large semiconductor company in an internal investigation involving alleged accounting improprieties and self-dealing;
  * representation of the Audit Committee of a major computer data storage company regarding an investigation involving revenue recognition issues at one of the companies subsidiaries;
  * representation of a leading fiber optics company in an internal investigation;
  * representation of an Audit Committee into allegations of insider trading by certain directors and those affiliated with them
  * representation of a U.S. public company and its U.S. subsidiary corresponding to the Japanese subsidiary in an investigation involving improper labeling of the grade and quality of plastics being used in computer monitors and other electronics equipment being shipped around the world, including the U.S.; and
  * representation of an Audit Committee of one of the world's largest industrial corporations into the activities of foreign subsidiaries relating to energy plant inspections.

II.   <u>Initial Organizational Issues</u>

A.   Factors to Consider When Evaluating Whether to Commence an Internal Investigation When Allegations Have Been Lodged of Significant Corporate Malfeasance Or Where an Outside Auditor Suspects Illegality

Internal investigations typically result from discovery -- by the Company, the media, an external auditor, or a whistleblower -- of circumstances that raise a serious concern of potential liability or financial misconduct. The investigations are thus meant to determine the validity and seriousness of the circumstances alleged or disclosed and what action, if any, the Company should take consistent with the best interests of the shareholders. Among the possible responsive actions are remediation, market disclosure, and preparation for, and defense of, potential prosecutorial and regulatory actions or civil lawsuits. Depending on whose conduct is the focus of the investigation, senior management, the Board of Directors, an audit committee or a special committee of disinterested directors may decide to commence an investigation. There are some respected corporate lawyers who counsel that Boards should resist the trend of having audit committees or special committees of independent directors routinely investigating whistleblower complaints and the like.[2]

Whether to commence an internal investigation may be a discretionary decision, *supra*, or in limited circumstances may be prescribed by statute. In the latter case, Section 10A of the Exchange Act requires external auditors, who detect or otherwise become aware that an illegal act has or may have occurred, to determine whether it is likely such an illegal act has occurred and the effect of any illegal act on the Company's financial statements. Auditors look to the Company to investigate and evaluate such possible illegalities and then assess whether the Company and the Board of Directors have taken "timely and appropriate remedial actions" regarding such possible illegalities. In this regard, the methodology used in "10A investigations" is not materially different from an internal investigation commenced on the company's own initiative, and therefore, for the purposes of this paper they will be treated collectively.

Outside of the 10A context, there are several circumstance that have traditionally triggered the initiation of internal investigations by senior management, a Board, audit committee or special committee:

        a.   Receipt of a whistleblower letter or communication that raises allegations of misconduct by senior or significant members of management;

        b.   Shareholder demand in the nature of an actual or threatened derivative action against directors and officers, possibly leading to formation of a Special Litigation Committee;

        c.   Allegations of misconduct raised by external auditor, internal auditor, or compliance;

        d.   Board member suspicion of misconduct by officers or employees;

        e.   Receipt of subpoena or informal request for information by a government or self-regulatory organization (SRO), or an announcement by a government agency or SRO of suspicions of misconduct by the Company or industry; or

        f.   Allegations of misconduct by the media, watchdog groups, or academics.

---

2   Andrew Ross Sorkin, *Questioning an Adviser's Advice*, N.Y. TIMES, Jan. 8, 2008 (interview of Martin Lipton).

In addition, although there have been no reported enforcement actions under the section yet, the "reporting up" provisions of the Sarbanes-Oxley Act of 2002 require in-house counsel to ensure that the corporation takes appropriate steps in response to allegations of wrongdoing.

B.   External Factors, Such as The Existence or Anticipated Existence of a Parallel Government Investigation or Shareholder Lawsuit, Should Be Considered When Making Decisions About How To Conduct and Document An Internal Investigation

There is a reasonable likelihood that any major internal investigation will be followed by, or conducted parallel to, an actual (or anticipated) external investigation by (one or more of): the Department of Justice, Securities and Exchange Commission, NYSE (or other self regulatory organization ("SRO")), a state attorney general or local district attorney, or other enforcement or regulatory authority. The Company and the Board may also be facing civil lawsuits, including shareholder class actions and derivative suits, pertaining to the alleged misconduct; and in certain instances, may be dealing with criminal investigations initiated by federal and, more recently, state prosecutors.[3]

The existence or threatened existence of any of these external events necessarily affects how the Company, Board, audit or independent committee, and outside counsel conduct and document an internal investigation. As discussed more fully below, counsel and the Company should anticipate that all documents created, facts uncovered, and witness statements made to them, may be disclosed to the government or regulator, and also may be discoverable by a private plaintiff. This assumption should be a factor in all major decisions about the procedure and protocol for any major internal investigation. In particular, the company, the Board or its independent committees, and counsel may want, or may be forced, to make an early determination about whether and how they will "cooperate" with government or regulatory investigations.

During approximately the last decade, driven by regulatory policies promulgated by the Department of Justice,[4] the Securities and Exchange Commission and other regulators,[5] and

---

3   *See, e.g.*, Mark Gimein, *Eliot Spitzer: The Enforcer*, Fortune, Sept. 16, 2002, at 77; Charles Gasparino & Paul Beckett, *Quick Fix May Elude Citigroup and Weill*, Wall St. J., Sept. 10, 2002, at C1; Gregory Zuckerman & Mitchell Pacelle, *Now, Telecom Deals Face Scrutiny*, Wall St. J., June 28, 2002, at C1.

4   *See* text, *infra* at n. 7-10, 13-14.

5   *See* "Report of Investigation Pursuant to Section 21(a) of the Securities Exchange Act of 1934 and Commission Statement on the Relationship of Cooperation to Agency Enforcement Decisions," issued on October 23, 2001 as Releases 44969 and 1470, available at http://www.sec.gov/litigation/investreport/34-44969.htm, and referred to as the "Seaboard Report." The Seaboard Report is the SEC's current policy regarding waiver of privilege and work product, and sets forth the criteria that it will consider in determining the extent to which organizations will be granted credit for cooperating with the agency's staff by discovering, self-reporting, and remedying illegal conduct, which cooperation, or lack thereof, in the eyes of the staff will be taken into consideration when the SEC decides what, if any, enforcement action to take. The Seaboard Report has been read by practitioners as encouraging companies not to assert, or to waive, their attorney-client privilege, work product, and other legal protections as a sign of full cooperation. *See* Seaboard Report at paragraph 8, criteria no. 11, and footnote 3.

Another example of a regulatory agency promulgating similar policies is the Commodity Futures Trading Commission ("CFTC"), the Enforcement Division of which issued an Enforcement Advisory on August 11, 2004, entitled "Cooperation Factors in Enforcement Division Sanction Recommendations," promoting the waiver of appropriate privileges. The CFTC issued a revised Enforcement Advisory eliminating the waiver language on March 1, 2007. *See* http://www.abanet.org/poladv/priorities/privilegewaiver/acprivilege.html.

the U.S. Sentencing Commission, the passage of federal legislation mandating certain activities by independent auditors and Audit Committees, and civil litigation, there has been a renewed emphasis on companies' expanding the scope of their cooperation with governmental investigations, and even initiating them, by conducting extensive internal investigations into perceived corporate misconduct in order to achieve longer-term benefits at the hands of such regulators and avoid what could be punitive reactions by regulators and auditors.

Since the mid-1990s, the principal focus of law enforcement and regulatory authorities in the United States has been to develop policies and guidelines designed to induce corporations and other business entities to waive, or not assert, applicable attorney-client and work-product privileges and protections.[6] In 1999, after several years of informal policies at various United States Attorney's Offices (principally the Southern District of New York), the Department of Justice formally adopted what came to be known as the "Holder Memorandum," after Eric Holder, then Deputy Attorney General of the United States. The Holder Memorandum, although advisory, set forth standards by which a corporation would be judged cooperative in a federal criminal investigation.[7] One factor was whether the corporation waived or did not assert privileges protecting the confidentiality of communications.

In 2002, then Deputy Attorney General Larry Thompson promulgated a revision of the Holder Memorandum, this time making mandatory the use of the factors in judging whether a corporation was sufficiently cooperative, including whether applicable privileges were waived or not asserted.[8] Among the most controversial of the nine additional factors in the Thompson Memorandum were those addressed to indicia of corporate "cooperation," including a willingness to waive or not assert the attorney-client privilege and the attorney work-product doctrine[9] and a willingness to deny advancement of fees and expenses and indemnification coverage.[10]

---

6   *See* United States Attorneys' Criminal Resource Manual, Art. 162, §VI.B; United States Sentencing Guidelines Manual §8C2.5(g)(2001); the SEC's Seaboard Report, http://www.sec.gov/litigation/investreport/34-44969.htm; *see also* the EPA Voluntary Disclosure Program, the HHS Provider Self-Disclosure Protocol, and the Department of Justice Antitrust Corporate Leniency Policy.

7   *See generally* Memorandum from Eric Holder, Jr., Deputy Attorney General, to All Heads of Department Components and U.S.Attorneys (June 16, 1999) (including attachment entitled "Federal Prosecution of Corporations"), *reprinted in* Criminal Resource Manual, arts. 161, 162, *available at* http://www.usdoj.gov/usao/eousa/foia_reading_room/usam/title9/crm00100.htm.

8   *See* US DOJ, Principles of Federal Prosecution of Business Organizations (Jan. 20, 2003) (the "Thompson Memorandum"), *available at* http://www.usdoj.gov/dag/cftf/business_organizations.pdf.

9   Regarding the attorney-client privilege and work-product doctrine, the Thompson Memorandum stated, in relevant part, that "[o]ne factor the prosecutor may weigh in assessing the adequacy of a corporation's cooperation is the completeness of its disclosure including, if necessary, a waiver of the attorney-client and work product protections, both with respect to its internal investigation and with respect to communications among specific officers, directors, and employees and counsel. Such waivers permit the government to obtain statements of possible witnesses, subjects and targets, without having to negotiate individual cooperation or immunity agreements."

10   Regarding denial of advancement of fees and expenses, the Thompson Memorandum stated, in relevant part, that "a corporation's promise of support to culpable employees and agents…through the advancing of attorneys' fees…may be considered by the prosecutor in weighing the extent and value of a corporation's cooperation."

In 2004, following the general trend of policy reflected in the Thompson Memorandum, the United States Sentencing Commission adopted an amendment that a corporation's waiver of the attorney-client privilege and work product protections would be a prerequisite for obtaining a reduction by a corporation in its culpability score.

The adoption of these policies by the Department of Justice and other regulatory entities have made inroads into historic policies protecting privilege and work-product in favor of policies promoting cooperation with governmental agencies and maximizing the effectiveness and efficiency of governmental investigations.[11] Companies formerly expected that the work product of their counsel prepared as a result of an internal investigation (and advice given as a result of such investigation) would be protected. Instead, however, many have come to learn that, upon the initiation of a governmental inquiry (formal or informal, and whether the company is a target or not) such expectations of confidentiality have in many cases been illusory. Internal investigations, conducted by and at the direction of legal counsel, are a critical tool by which companies and their boards learn about violations of law, breaches of duty and other misconduct that may expose the company to liability and damages. They are also an essential predicate to enabling companies to take remedial action and to formulate defenses, where appropriate. But internal investigations no longer have clear and predictable protections of confidentiality in the current environment, viewed as a "culture of waiver."[12]

Following significant criticism by business organizations and bar associations, these principles were superseded in 2006 by the so-called McNulty Memorandum.[13] The McNulty Memorandum reaffirms many of the factors to be considered by federal prosecutors when conducting corporate investigations and deciding whether to indict corporations or considering corporate plea agreements, but places some procedural restrictions and additional procedural reviews on prosecutors regarding their ability to request waivers of corporate attorney-client privileges or work-product

---

11   Joint Drafting Committee of the American College of Trial Lawyers, *The Erosion of the Attorney-Client Privilege and Work Product Doctrine in Federal Criminal Investigations* (March 2002), *available at* http://www.actl.com/AM/Template. cfm?Section=All_Publications&Template=/CM/ContentDisplay.cfm&ContentFileID=68.

12   "The Decline of the Attorney-Client Privilege in the Corporate Context," Survey Results, Presented to the United States Congress and the United States Sentencing Commission, March 2006, http://www.nacdl.org/public.nsf/whitecollar/wcnews024/ $FILE/A-C_PrivSurvey.pdf, and http://www.acca.com/public/attyclntprvlg/coalitionussctestimony031506.pdf ("Survey Results").

13   *See* Principles of Federal Prosecution of Business Organizations (December 12, 2006) (the "McNulty Memorandum"), *available at* http://www.usdoj.gov/dag/speech/2006/mcnulty_memo.pdf

protections.[14][15] Despite these additional restrictions and reviews, there is little practical difference between the McNulty Memorandum and its predecessors: all maintain the position that waivers of the privilege and work product protections will be bases for favorable treatment of corporations and thus will still provide significant motivation for defense attorneys zealously representing their corporate clients to offer waivers without prosecutors having to ask. Since the main focus of both DOJ Memoranda is an evaluation of how the DOJ evaluates the "authenticity of a corporation's cooperation with a government investigation," including waivers, the McNulty Memorandum will still provide significant motivation for defense attorneys zealously representing their corporate clients to offer waivers without prosecutors having to ask.

In 2001, the SEC announced its own cooperation policy when it decided to take no action against Seaboard Corporation despite evidence that its former controller had caused the company's books and records to be inaccurate and its financial reports misstated. The Commission outlined thirteen factors it would consider in determining cooperation.[16]

In 2006, the SEC updated its standards for imposing civil penalties on corporations.[17] As explained in the Commission's Statement,

---

14   The McNulty Memorandum lists nine factors that "prosecutors must consider…in reaching a decision as to the proper treatment of a corporate target":
(1)   the nature and seriousness of the offense including the risk of harm to the public and any policies and priorities relating to the particular categories of crime;
(2)   the pervasiveness of wrongdoing within the business organization including complicity in or condonation of the wrongdoing by management;
(3)   the history of similar conduct within the company including prior criminal, civil and regulatory enforcement actions against the company;
(4)   the timely and voluntary disclosure of wrongdoing and the company's willingness to cooperate in the investigation of its own agents;
(5)   the existence and adequacy of the company's pre-existing compliance program;
(6)   the company's remedial actions, including efforts to implement an effective compliance program or improve an existing one, efforts to replace responsible management, efforts to discipline or terminate wrongdoers, efforts to pay restitution, and efforts to cooperate with government agencies;
(7)   collateral consequences, including disproportionate harm to shareholders, pension holders and employees not proven personally culpable, and impact on the public arising from the prosecution;
(8)   the adequacy of the prosecution of individuals who are responsible for the corporation's malfeasance; and
(9)   adequacy of civil, regulatory enforcement actions or other remedies. *Id.*

15   We note also that as this paper is being published, Congress is considering the "Attorney-Client Privilege Protection Act," which would impose a bar on federal investigations requesting companies to waive privilege or to refuse to advance fees (H. 3013, passed by the U.S. House of Representatives on November 13, 2007; S.186, now before the U.S. Senate Judiciary Committee).

16   *Report of Investigation Pursuant to Section 21(a) of the Securities Exchange Act of 1934 and Commission Statement on the Relationship of Cooperation to Agency Enforcement Decisions*, Release No. 44969, Oct. 23, 2001, *available at* http://www.sec. gov/litigation/investreport/34-44969.htm.

17   Statement of the Securities and Exchange Commission Concerning Financial Penalties, January 4, 2006, *available at* http://www. sec.gov/news/press/2006-4.htm; *see also* Litigation Release No. 19520, January 4, 2006, *SEC v. McAfee, Inc.*, Civil Action No. 06-009 (PJH) (N.D. Cal. 2006); *see also* Baker and Holbrook, "SEC Statement Clarifies Corporate Penalties – A Bit," National Law Journal, March 13, 2006.

"whether, and if so to what extent, to impose civil penalties against a corporation… turns principally on two considerations: The presence or absence of a direct benefit to the corporation as a result of the violation…[and] [t]he degree to which the penalty will recompense or further harm the injured shareholders."

Several additional factors the Commission will take into account include:

(1)   The need to deter the particular type of offense;
(2)   The extent of injury to innocent parties;
(3)   Whether complicity in the violation is widespread throughout the corporation;
(4)   The level of intent on the part of the perpetrators;
(5)   The degree of difficulty in detecting the particular type of offense;
(6   Presence or lack of remedial steps by the corporation;
(7)   Extent of cooperation with the Commission and other law enforcement agencies.

Despite the DOJ memoranda and SEC guidance discussed above, in most cases, the precise benefits of the Company's cooperation, if any, cannot be known at the outset of an investigation. Indeed, many companies that have cooperated with the government have received stiff financial penalties, albeit perhaps lower than if no cooperation had been proffered.[18] In the area of enforcement of the Foreign Corrupt Practices Act, Assistant Attorney General Alice Fischer has stated that, although not in the "best interests of law enforcement to make promises about lenient treatment in cases where the magnitude, duration, or high-level management involvement in the disclosed conduct may warrant a guilty plea and a significant penalty,…there is *always a benefit* to corporate cooperation, including voluntary disclosure, as contemplated by the Thompson memo. …*[I]f you are doing the things you should be doing* – whether it is self-policing, self-reporting, conducting proactive risk assessments, improving your controls and procedures, training on the FCPA, or *cooperating with an investigation* after it starts – *you will get a benefit*. It may not mean that you or your client will get a complete pass, but *you will get a real, tangible benefit*" (emphasis added).[19] While the number of DOJ-deferred prosecution or non-prosecution agreements has increased recently, many corporations and their counsel continue to believe that the benefits of cooperation have not been tangible and have, with certain DOJ divisions and sections or U.S. Attorney offices, been far too unclear. Some companies, after due consideration, have decided, in the face of a grand jury subpoena or allegation of wrongdoing, neither to conduct an internal investigation nor to cooperate with government authorities.

Signally, the Antitrust Division has a very clear standard – that parties who cooperate fully receive amnesty and reduced civil penalties. The Antitrust Criminal Penalty Enhancement

---

18   For a discussion of the Securities and Exchange Commission's response to cooperation through the end of 2004, *see* Tim Reason, *The Limits of Mercy: The Cost of Cooperation with the SEC is High. The Cost of Not Cooperating is Even Higher,* CFO Magazine, April 2005, *available at* http://www.cfo.com/article.cfm/3804652/c_3805512?f=magazine_featured.

19   Prepared Remarks of Alice S. Fisher at the ABA National Institute on the Foreign Corrupt Practices Act, October 16, 2006, *available at* http://www.usdoj.gov/criminal/fraud/docs/reports/speech/2006/10-16-06AAGFCPASpeech.pdf.

and Reform Act, adopted in 2004, increases the criminal penalties for violations, but also increases the incentives for self-reporting and cooperation in criminal antitrust matters. Corporations and individuals reporting their involvement in antitrust violations may receive immunity from the DOJ's Antitrust Division under its leniency program, insulating successful applicants from criminal fines and imprisonment. The legislation thus creates strong incentives for antitrust violators to be the first to self-report their violations and thus insulate themselves from criminal prosecution, though not from the likely civil litigation to follow.[20] In a statement issued after the bill was signed into law, Assistant Attorney General for Antitrust R. Hewitt Pate stated that the Act would make the DOJ's Corporate Leniency Program "even more effective."[21]

As emphasized in the College's 2002 report *The Erosion of the Attorney-Client Privilege and Work Product Doctrine in Federal Criminal Investigations*,[22] the attorney-client privilege and work product doctrine play a central role in corporate governance and remain essential to the due administration of the American criminal justice system. A waiver of these protections should not be taken lightly. This paper assumes that while a company, board, or audit or independent committee will consider, first and foremost, whether and how to conduct an internal investigation so as to protect the interests of the company and its stakeholders, it will also be cognizant of the importance of the attorney-client privilege and work-product protections in our society. (See also footnote 15, preceding.)

C.   The Role of the Board and Management in Conducting and Overseeing the Investigation

The relative participation of management and the Board in an internal investigation is a function principally of the nature of the allegations. Where the alleged or suspected conduct involves senior officers or serious employee misconduct, or where the corporate entity is the focal point of a government inquiry, it is important that management, including usually the General Counsel's office, not be, and not be perceived to be, in charge of the internal investigation. An investigation carried out by management, or a corporate department (such as an internal audit department), likely will not be afforded credibility. Furthermore, the continuing involvement in the conduct of the investigation by board members and officers whose conduct is at issue may taint the ability to preserve the privilege as well as the appearance of impartiality.[23]

Rather, the Board of Directors should delegate the task of overseeing the conduct of the internal investigation and retaining counsel to conduct the investigation to the Audit Committee of the Board, the independent members of the Audit Committee, or alternatively, some group of independent Board members forming a Special Committee (hereinafter, jointly referred to as the "Independent Committee").

---

20   H.R. 1086, 108th Cong., Title II, §201-221(2004). The benefits to the second, third or fourth cooperating company in Antitrust Division investigations are significantly less.

21   Press Release, Department of Justice, Assistant Attorney General for Antitrust, R. Hewitt Pate, Issues Statement on Enactment of Antitrust Criminal Penalty Enhancement And Reform Act of 2004 (June 23, 2004), *available at* http://www.usdoj.gov/atr/public/press_releases/2004/204319.htm.

22   http://www.actl.com/AM/Template.cfm?Section=All_Publications&Template=/CM/ContentDisplay.cfm&ContentFileID=68

23   *See Ryan v. Gifford*, 2007 WL 4259557 (Del. Ch. Nov. 30, 2007) (*Ryan I*); *Ryan v. Gifford*, 2008 Del. Ch. LEXIS 2 (Del. Ch. Jan. 2, 2008) (*Ryan II*).

D.   Independent Outside Counsel Should Be Retained To Conduct Significant Internal Investigations

At least since the era of Enron, WorldCom, Adelphia, and other corporate scandals, government prosecutors, regulators,[24] and, increasingly, the Company's independent auditors, have looked askance at the choice of regular outside corporate counsel to conduct a sensitive inquiry. This skepticism is based on the fear that regular corporate counsel may have a motive to avoid criticizing, and thus alienating, senior management, the source of perhaps sizeable past and future law firm revenues. Regular counsel may also have given advice on matters related to the subject of the investigation and members of the firm may become witnesses in the internal, or subsequent external, investigation. Similarly, the government and outside auditors will likely be concerned that the Company's regular outside counsel's business and social familiarity with the Company's management or implicated directors will cause counsel to pull punches to avoid alienating friends. However, there may be select circumstances where regular outside counsel's knowledge of a corporation's business, special expertise, and distance from the core investigation issues and subjects permit it to conduct an objective investigation. In some cases, in fact, the government agency most interested in the investigation may agree in advance that regular counsel is the most viable choice to conduct the investigation so long as the objectivity of the effort is assured.

The Company is best served to portray itself to the government, its independent auditors, the investment community, and the media as having complete integrity and a commitment to uncovering the facts. Thus, choosing independent counsel with few if any prior ties to the Company ("Special Counsel")[25] has become commonplace and is generally regarded as the first step in convincing governmental authorities of the "authenticity" of its cooperation.[26] Such Special Counsel are perceived as not beholden to the Company and able to view facts in an objective manner, neither biased in favor of the Company or its management, nor, indeed, the governmental authorities.[27]

There are several consequences to the bias in favor of Special Counsel:

First, placing a higher value on the perception of independence than on the experience of existing counsel comes at a price: existing counsel's familiarity with the people and practices of the corporate client is lost, and the absence of such, while it might satisfy the perceptions

---

24   *See* speech by SEC Commissioner Campos, "How to be an Effective Board Member," August 15, 2006, at http://www.sec. gov/news/speech/2006/spch081506rcc.htm ("…when circumstances indicate possible wrongdoing, the audit committee and the board should have their own independent advisors, investigators, and lawyers. As guided by Sarbanes-Oxley, the board and its committees should 'engage independent counsel and other advisors, as it determines necessary to carry out its duties' and should not rely exclusively on the corporation's advisors and lawyers").

25   The term "Special Counsel" is used in the same sense as the term "independent counsel" is generally used by other authors and papers. In our view, counsel that have been used occasionally by companies for individual matters should not be precluded from being selected as Special Counsel; rather, we recommend that whatever counsel is chosen, such firm not have had a substantial prior relationship with the Company.

26   Bennett, Kriegel, Rauh, and Walker, "Internal Investigations and the Defense of Corporations in the Sarbanes-Oxley Era," 62 Bus.Law.55, 57 (Nov. 2006)(hereinafter, "Bennett").

27   Indeed, some firms have specialized in the conduct of internal investigations, at the possible risk that such consistent conducting of internal investigations may tend to align the Special Counsel regularly with the interests of the regulators, rather than the Company and its shareholders.

of the regulators and independent auditors, could well cause a consequential cost increase to the public company and its shareholders.[28]

        Second, the bias sometimes results in the self-perception that Special Counsel are hired in order to find wrongdoing and thus to justify the Special Committee's judgment that wrongdoing may have occurred. In this regard, it is incumbent on the Independent Committee, as well as the Special Counsel, to ensure that the Special Counsel mandate is to investigate the validity of the allegations and not to ferret out some perceived concerns for the sake of justifying what inevitably is the significant cost of the investigation.

        It should be the goal of the Independent Committee, in seeking to determine the truth of the underlying allegations, to safeguard and act in the best interests of the shareholders, as well as to prevent the internal investigation from impairing the reputations of employees, officers, and directors of the Company not found to have engaged in wrongdoing. To those ends, Special Counsel should be instructed to engage in investigative tactics designed to get at the truth, including using their investigative, technological, and professional capabilities.

        The Independent Committee should be aware that Special Counsel, left unchecked, could succumb to the abuses that are an occupational hazard of special prosecutors as described by then-Attorney General Robert Jackson, and cited by Justice Scalia:

> If the prosecutor is obliged to choose his case, it follows that he can choose his defendants. Therein is the most dangerous power of the prosecutor: that he will pick people that he thinks he should get, rather than cases that need to be prosecuted. With the law books filled with a great assortment of crimes, a prosecutor stands a fair chance of finding at least a technical violation of some act on the part of almost anyone. In [such cases], it is not a question of discovering the commission of a crime and then looking for the man who has committed it, it is a question of picking the man and then searching the law books, or putting investigators to work, to pin some offense on him.[29]

        Third, in the current and foreseeable regulatory environment, the findings of Special Counsel are more likely to be credited by prosecutors, regulators, or private counsel (*e.g.*, when justifying settlement of a class or derivative lawsuit) if the Special Counsel is independent – *i.e.*, without a substantial prior relationship with the company or its senior management.

---

28   *See* announcement by Dell Corporation of the cost of $135 million to it in retaining Special Counsel and forensic accountants to investigate issues resulting in a restatement of net income for 2003 through 2005 of between $50 and $150 million on total net income of $12 billion for that period. According to the Form 8-K, the investigation was done by 125 lawyers from Special Counsel and 250 accountants who conducted 233 interviews of 146 Dell employees and reviewed 5 million documents. *See* http://www.sec.gov/Archives/edgar/data/826083/000095013407018421/d49260e8vk.htm.

29   R. Jackson, The Federal Prosecutor, Address Delivered at the Second Annual Conference of United States Attorneys, April 1, 1940, quoted in *Morrison, Independent Counsel v. Olson, et al.*, 487 U.S. 654 (1988) (Scalia, J., dissenting).

E.   The Independent Committee and Special Counsel Should Determine The Appropriate Scope of the Inquiry and the Rules of the Road

The Board should pass a resolution broadly authorizing the Independent Committee to retain counsel and their agents (e.g., auditors or other experts), conduct an investigation, and report its ultimate findings to the Board. The Independent Committee should retain the Special Counsel in writing. Special Counsel's retention letter should state the allegations under review and the scope of the inquiry, and make clear that Counsel is to advise the Independent Committee of its legal rights and obligations, as well as potential liabilities. Absent a conflict, the general counsel or regular outside counsel will advise the Company of its related rights and obligations and liabilities. The scope of the Special Counsel's engagement can be expanded in appropriate circumstances, and that expansion should also be confirmed in writing by the Independent Committee.

The scope of Special Counsel's mandate as set forth in the retention letter should be determined by the Independent Committee, in consultation with the Board, and state whether the Committee shall act for the Board or investigate and report to the Board for action. In defining the scope of the investigation, the Independent Committee must decide whether to provide Special Counsel at the outset with a broad mandate to find any and all suspected corporate wrongdoing, or a narrower mandate, at least at the outset, to examine only specific allegations or suspicions. In the latter case, Special Counsel should reassess with the Independent Committee whether additional suspicions should form the basis for a separate investigation by this or other Special Counsel or by regular counsel.

The Independent Committee and Special Counsel should also agree upon specific reporting procedures and protocols for documenting the investigation (such as the designation of all communications with legends such as "ATTORNEY-CLIENT PRIVILEGED" and, where applicable, "ATTORNEY WORK PRODUCT"). The goal at the outset should be frequent updating by oral reporting. Careful consideration should be given to the extent to which written reports should be rendered, if at all, during or at the conclusion of the inquiry. There is typically limited utility and great risk in creating interim written reports of investigation. Such interim reports run the risk of creating confusion and credibility issues, as well as potential unfairness to officers or employees who are the subjects of the investigations, if facts discovered in the latter part of the investigation are inconsistent with preliminary factual determinations or interim substantive findings.

The Board of Directors, in consultation with the Independent Committee, should also determine whether and to what extent Special Counsel may waive the Company's attorney-client privilege or its own work product protections in its dealings with regulators or other third parties.[30] We question whether there are any circumstances where Special Counsel, either on its own or with the authority of the Independent Committee, but without specific authority from the Board of Directors, should waive the Company's attorney-client privilege. We recommend that the Special Counsel not be given the authority to make such waiver decisions without prior full deliberation by the Independent Committee and the full Board, with the latter being encouraged to take advice from regular or other counsel on this decision.[31]

Nor should Special Counsel be allowed to condition its retention by the Independent Committee upon a pre-retention decision by the Independent Committee to waive all privileges. Furthermore, the engagement letter for Special Counsel should make clear that Special Counsel's work product, data, and document collection and analysis belong to the Independent Committee and the Company, not to Special Counsel, and should be returned to the Independent Committee and Company upon completion of the investigation, for possible use by the Company in its defense of possible third party or government claims.

There are times when it is far more efficient in terms of both cost and time for an outside expert to assist Special Counsel in the course of its investigations. Under Sarbanes-Oxley, the Audit Committee (which may well be functioning as the Independent Committee) has the authority to retain expert assistance in the course of an investigation.[32] The Independent Committee should exercise that authority by permitting Special Counsel to retain additional professionals, including forensic auditors, investigators, and public relations advisers, where necessary and with appropriate consultation with the Committee.

The choice of a particular expert and the manner in which it is retained are critical junctures in an investigation. In order to protect the attorney-client privilege and general confidentiality of communications between Special Counsel and its additional professionals, it is not advisable to choose professionals who also regularly or generally are employed by the Company to perform similar services, unless a very convincing case can be made that the Special Counsel's professionals are different and separated from the Company's regular professionals. In some situations, Special Counsel have conferred with prosecutors and regulators and obtained the prior approval of experts well-known to the company.

---

30   *See In re Qwest Communications International Inc. Securities Litigation*, 450 F.3d 1179 (10 Cir. 2006), in which the Court held that a company's turning over to the SEC and DOJ of internal investigative documents, pursuant to a confidentiality agreement, constituted a waiver of the attorney-client and work product privileges, and rejected the doctrine of "selective waiver" or "limited waiver." *See also U.S. v. Reyes*, 2006 U.S. Dist. Lexis 94456 (N.D. Cal. Dec. 22, 2006), holding that investigating counsel's oral report to DOJ and SEC summarizing otherwise privileged internal investigation interviews created a waiver, and rejecting the concept of "selective waiver." In connection therewith, the Judicial Conference of the United .States proposed and the U.S. Senate Judiciary has reported favorably to the Senate for a floor vote S. 2450, which would enact new Rule 502 of the Federal Rules of Evidence, placing, *inter alia*, new restrictions on waivers of the attorney-client privilege, such as limitations on the scope of a waiver and inadvertent disclosure and new procedures on the effectiveness of confidentiality orders. See http://www. uscourts.gov/rules/index2.html#sen502. Notably, however, the Judicial Conference did not recommend and the Senate Judiciary Committee did not adopt any version of the "selective waiver" doctrine.

31   We note the possibility that Special Counsel may unintentionally induce an inadvertent waiver of the corporate attorney-client privilege if there are communications by Company's officers or Board members directly with Special Counsel, rather than through the Independent Committee. See *Ryan v. Gifford*, 2007 WL 4259557 (Del. Ch. Nov. 30, 2007) (*Ryan I*); see generally, Gregory P. Joseph, "Privilege Developments I," The National Law Journal, February 11, 2008. However, the confines of this paper do not allow for analysis and recommendations with respect to this circumstance.

32   15 U.S.C. 78f(m)(5) ("AUTHORITY TO ENGAGE ADVISERS- Each audit committee shall have the authority to engage independent counsel and other advisers, as it determines necessary to carry out its duties.")

Experts should sign retention agreements that make clear their engagement is in contemplation of providing assistance for legal advice. Conclusions of independent experts also improve the appearance to outsiders (*i.e.*, government agencies and auditors) that the investigation is in fact independent.

F.   Communications to, and Indemnification of, Company Employees

Numerous management and employee morale issues will likely arise during the course of an internal investigation, especially where long-standing practices or the conduct of senior employees are under investigation. These issues should be addressed promptly by the Independent Committee, usually by a memorandum to all affected employees to keep employees abreast of general information about the purpose and expected length of the inquiry, the expectation of the Audit Committee that all employees will cooperate with the inquiry and with Special Counsel, and the need to preserve all data related to the investigation.

Importantly, the Independent Committee should explicitly communicate what constitutes "cooperation" of an employee during an internal investigation, and that an employee's refusal to cooperate in this regard may result in dismissal. In most circumstances, the cooperation of employees should include: (1) the provision, upon request, of all documents related to company business whether kept in the employee's office, home, or personal computer; (2) strict compliance with all document hold and retention notices; and (3) submission to interviews by Special Counsel.[33]

The Independent Committee should make an early determination of the extent to which employees of the Company will be authorized to retain separate representation by counsel whose fees will be advanced or indemnified, either through existing indemnification policies or new policies designed for the scope of the internal investigation (a decision that is largely governed by state law and the entity's bylaws). The Company should give consideration to distributing a memorandum to employees notifying them of the nature of any prospective investigation, the possible need for witness interviews, the Company's ability to recommend counsel for individual employees, the possibility that the Company will be responsible for advancing fees and expenses for the employee's representation, and the absolute requirement that any employee being interviewed tell the truth to Special Counsel.[34]

Whether to indemnify or advance legal fees (and the scope of any such indemnification or advancement) to employees has become a significant area of controversy under the

---

33   We distinguish the situation where an employee must cooperate fully with an internal investigation, including making himself available for an interview , or be subject to employment sanctions including possible discharge, from the situation where an employee invokes constitutional protections under the Fifth Amendment not to testify before a governmental body. In the latter situation, we do not think it appropriate for a Company to sanction the employee's invocation of constitutional rights by penalty or discharge. Nor, importantly, do we think it appropriate for governmental bodies to consider a corporation non-cooperative if it does not discharge or sanction an employee who invokes such protections, see *infra* at 22. We note the observation of the U.S. Supreme Court in *Slochower v. Board of Higher Education*, 350 US 551, 557-58 (1956) that ". . . a witness may have a reasonable fear of prosecution and yet be innocent of any wrongdoing. The privilege serves to protect the innocent who might otherwise be ensnared by ambiguous circumstances..." and do not think a Company should be in any way penalized for respecting an employee's invocation of such constitutional right.

34   *See Bennett*, at 65.

Thompson Memorandum and will likely continue to be under the McNulty Memorandum.[35] Under the Thompson Memorandum, in making charging decisions with respect to entities, prosecutors were required to consider whether the entity was supporting "culpable employees and agents . . . through the advancing of attorney's fees."[36] In June 2006, just months before the Department of Justice issued revised guidelines through the McNulty Memorandum, a district court in the Southern District of New York held this provision of the Thompson Memorandum unconstitutional in connection with the government's prosecution of several former KPMG employees for participation in the creation of allegedly fraudulent tax shelters.[37] In that case, the court held that the government's exertion of pressure on KPMG to refuse to advance legal fees for certain of its former employees violated those employees' Fifth and Sixth Amendment rights.[38]

        In response, the McNulty Memorandum softened the DOJ's guidance. Under the McNulty Memorandum, federal prosecutors "*generally* should not take into account whether a corporation is advancing attorneys' fees to employees or agents under investigation and indictment;" but may take indemnification of employees into account in "extremely rare cases" in which "the totality of the circumstances show[s] that [the advancement of fees] was intended to impede a government investigation."[39] It is yet unclear whether a federal prosecutor's invocation of this aspect of the McNulty Memorandum in "extremely rare" circumstances would survive constitutional challenge. (Judge Kaplan's initial holdings with respect to the broader provisions of the Thompson Memorandum are currently before the Second Circuit.) It is also not clear the extent to which provisions of the McNulty Memorandum dealing with corporations' waiving the applicable privileges or not denying indemnity to employees under investigation are actually being followed by the line Assistant U.S. Attorneys, by whom most investigations are being conducted.[40]

        As a general matter, the SEC for its part has generally not considered, and in our view should not consider, whether an entity has chosen to indemnify or advance legal fees

---

35   *See generally, United States v. Stein,* 435 F.Supp.2d 330 (SDNY 2006); *see also United States v. Stein* 452 F. Supp. 2d 230 (S.D.N.Y. 2006), *vacated by Stein v. KPMG LLP)* 486 F.3d 753 (2d Cir. 2007); *United States v. Stein,* 488 F.Supp.2d 350 (S.D.N.Y. 2007); *see also SEC v. Lucent Technologies,* Litigation Release No. 18715 / May 17, 2004, *available at* http://www. sec.gov/litigation/litreleases/lr18715.htm (Lucent fined $25 million for non-cooperation in that, *inter alia,* after reaching an agreement in principle with the staff to settle the case, and without being required to do so by state law or its corporate charter, Lucent expanded the scope of employees who could be indemnified against the consequences of the SEC enforcement action and failed over a period of time to provide timely and full disclosure to the staff on a key issue concerning indemnification of employees.)

36   *Thompson Memorandum, supra* n. 8, at 7-8.

37   435 F. Supp. 2d at 365-69.

38   *Id.* at 356-360.

39   *Id.* at 360-365.

40   In a survey conducted in 2007 by the Association of Corporate Counsel and the National Association of Criminal Defense Lawyers, corporate members were contacted via email and invited to participate confidentially in a survey to determine whether there had been or continued to be instances of prosecutorial abuse in the coercion of the waiver of their clients' attorney-client privilege or work product protection or denial of the rights to counsel or job security protections for their employees in the corporate investigation process. In a report to the U.S. Senate Judiciary Committee by the former Chief Justice of the Delaware Supreme Court, E. Norman Veasey, numerous instances of such coerced waivers and other abuses were cited, including several where Assistant U.S. Attorneys either did not know of the McNulty Memorandum, or were unfamiliar with its modifications of prior Department of Justice Practices. *See* Letter to Senate Judiciary Committee, dated September 13, 2007, *available at* http://www. abanet.org/poladv/abaday07/acpresources.html

for its employees or former employees, in determining whether the entity has been sufficiently "cooperative." (However, in 2004, the SEC took action against Lucent in part because the company "expanded the scope of employees that could be indemnified against the consequences of this SEC enforcement action," after it had reached "an agreement in principle with the staff to settle the case, and without being required to do so by state law or its corporate charter."[41]) The SEC has explicitly barred settling parties from recovering penalty payments through indemnification agreements. This policy, adopted in 2004 to purportedly "enhance deterrence and accountability," "require[s] settling parties to forgo any rights they may have to indemnification, reimbursement by insurers, or favorable tax treatment of penalties."[42] We question whether such a policy is fair to employees who may have engaged in what the SEC perceives as wrongdoing but did not do so as so-called "rogue" employees, but rather in furtherance of what they may have mistakenly believed was corporate policy. We also question what legitimate interest the SEC or, for that matter, any agency of the government has in interfering in any way with a corporation's legal right to pay the legal fees and expenses of past and present employees in defense of an investigation, trial, or appeal; with the exception of making payments for the purpose of the employee's committing acts of obstruction of justice by, for example, destroying documents, threatening witnesses, or suborning perjury.

Based upon the treatment by the SEC and the courts of indemnification and advancement of fees issues, we recommend that Independent Committees adopt a written policy at the outset of an internal investigation regarding the scope of indemnity and advancement that will be followed, presumably in adherence to its by-laws, applicable state laws, and other corporate and regulatory governance policies. The policy should include the possibility that, at the outset, the Independent Committee could desire to expand the scope of indemnity to include employees who might not be covered by the by-laws but are likely witnesses, subjects or targets of the inquiry, as well as independent contractors or acting officers of companies or their subsidiaries who perform important executive functions but are not literally within the company's standard indemnity policies. It is not recommended that, to curry favor with the regulators or governmental authorities, those individuals performing such functions be excluded from indemnification or advancement.

III.   Creating an Accurate Factual Record: Document Review & Witness Interviews

Given the attention being given by prosecutors and regulators to document preservation and production, the expedient collection and review of relevant documents, and interviewing of relevant witnesses, are principal steps in ensuring an accurate factual record.

A.   Mechanics of a Litigation Hold

At the outset of an investigation, counsel (likely Special Counsel in collaboration with regular or internal counsel) should identify the universe of documents that must be *preserved*,

---

41   *"Lucent Settles SEC Enforcement Action Charging the Company with $1.1 Billion Accounting Fraud,"* http://www.sec.gov/news/press/2004-67.htm. ("Companies whose actions delay, hinder or undermine SEC investigations will not succeed," said Paul Berger, Associate Director of Enforcement. "Stiff sanctions and exposure of their conduct will serve as a reminder to companies that only genuine cooperation serves the best interests of investors.")

42   Speech by Stephen Cutler, Director of Division of Enforcement, 24th Annual Ray Garrett Jr. Corporate & Securities Law Institute, April 29, 2004, http://www.sec.gov/news/speech/spch042904smc.htm.

as opposed to the universe of documents that must be *collected.* Counsel should not send a blanket email request that all relevant documents be forwarded to a central source.

The first step should be the identification of all relevant employees who are the likely sources of documents; preliminary interviews should be conducted by regular outside counsel and internal counsel to determine such relevant employees. Then, internal counsel should send an email direction to relevant employees stating, in essence, that no documents, including electronic documents and attachments, may be destroyed without explicit approval of counsel, see *infra.*

Third, regular counsel should engage in an analysis of relevant documents to determine if others should be included in the "litigation hold." This is especially important when the organization affected by the internal inquiry is in many disparate locations. For electronic documents, this may include communicating with the "key players" to learn how they stored information. Because of the amendments to the Federal Rules of Civil Procedure pertaining to e-discovery that went into effect on December 1, 2006, internal counsel should already have prepared and have available guides to all sources of "electronically stored information" in the Company, *see* Rule 16(f), and should be prepared to institute a litigation hold on all such materials.[43]

External counsel should oversee compliance with a litigation hold, using reasonable efforts to continually monitor the party's retention and production of relevant documents.[44] Once the relevant documents are obtained, all documents should be logged in the same way that one would during traditional litigation. A revised document storage and retention policy should be established as early as possible following the collection of relevant documents. This should involve the segregation of relevant backup electronic media, which in some cases may necessitate counsel's taking physical possession of backup tapes.[45]

As with traditional litigation, care should be taken to avoid over- or under-production during discovery. Over-producing data, especially in light of the volume of electronic media, can greatly drive up fees without yielding additional relevant data. An even greater risk of over-production or uncontrolled production is the waiver of privilege, which can result when documents are produced in their native application formats without care being taken to reveal metadata or

---

43   Among the varieties of electronically stored information, or "ESI," is one particular type called "metadata," defined by one Federal Magistrate Judge, as "(i) information embedded in a ESI in Native File [the electronic format of the application in which such ESI is normally created, viewed and/or modified] that is not ordinarily viewable or printable from the application that generated, edited, or modified such Native File; and (ii) information generated automatically by the operation of a computer or other information technology system when a Native File is created, modified, transmitted, deleted or otherwise manipulated by a user of such system." Suggested Protocol for Discovery of Electronically Stored Information, *In re Electronically Stored Information,* U.S.D.C., D.Md (Magistrate Judge Paul Grimm)(2007), *available at* http://www.mdd.uscourts.gov/news/news/ESIProtocol.pdf at pgs. 2-3. Metadata has provided Special Counsel with the ability to view drafts of documents and emails, including electronic information concerning the creation, formation, editing of such document, as well as the author or viewer of such edits and the dates of creation and viewing.

44   *See Zubulake v. UBS Warburg,* 2004 WL 1620866 (S.D.N.Y. July 20, 2004) ("Zubulake V"). *See also Telecom International Am. Ltd. V. AT&T Corp.,* 189 F.R.D. 76, 81 (S.D.N.Y. 1999) ("Once on notice [that evidence is relevant], the obligation to preserve evidence runs first to counsel, who then has a duty to advise and explain to the client its obligations to retain pertinent documents that may be relevant to the litigation") (citing *Kansas-Nebraska Natural Gas Co. v. Marathon Oil Co.,* 109 F.R.D. 12, 18 (D.Neb. 1983)).

45   *In re Electronically Stored Information, supra* n. 41, at 10.

maintain relationships between attachments and emails. Under-production and spoliation during the discovery process may result in sanctions ranging from adverse inference instructions[46] to default judgments because of counsel's insufficient actions[47] to monetary fines.[48]

B.   Document Collection & Review

Document collection is usually accomplished by the Company's regular outside and internal counsel, and then review of the documents and interviewing of witnesses by Special Counsel. The relevant universe of hard-copy and electronic documents must be identified and collected as early as possible in the investigative process, even before Special Counsel is retained, so that all available information will be preserved and there will be a sufficient factual background to identify relevant witnesses and conduct efficient interviews by asking the appropriate questions and being able to refresh witnesses' recollections.

Inside counsel and internal technology experts can be particularly helpful in identifying processes and sources of documents, and in coordinating the document collection process; each should play a major role in supervising the gathering, production, and preservation of documents, including electronic documents. However, once the Independent Committee has been appointed and Special Counsel retained, we recommend that the function of document analysis should be that of the Special Counsel and retained technology professionals to retrieve, host, and analyze electronic and hard documents. Internal technology professionals should be used only in those circumstances in which the Company has a sufficiently sophisticated staff that is trained in issues that may become critical in a subsequent litigation (*i.e.*, chain of custody) or in a government investigation (*i.e.*, the preservation of metadata).

C.   Witness Interviews

After relevant documents are reviewed (assuming time permits), Special Counsel should identify the relevant witnesses and begin conducting the interviews. Investigating lawyers should be aware that they could become witnesses in a criminal or civil procedure where an issue arises as to what statements a witness made to them during the investigation. In certain cases, such as when the scope of the issues are unclear, it may make sense for Special Counsel to begin the interview process before all relevant documents can be digested. Careful consideration should be given as to who should attend each interview both for reasons of obtaining objective responses and for ensuring the appearance of obtaining objective responses. Whether inside counsel should be present during the employee interviews is an issue that should receive special attention. The risks of having internal counsel present at the interview include inadvertently chilling the employee's ability to be forthcoming and having the employee incorrectly perceive that she is represented personally

---

[46]   *See In Re Seroquel Products Liability Litigation,* 244 F.R.D. 650 (M.D.Fla., Aug. 21, 2007) (granting in part a motion for sanctions against the defendant for failure to produce the discovery in usable format).

[47]   *See Metropolitan Opera Assoc., Inc. v. Local 100, Hotel Employees & Restaurant Employees International Union,* 212 F.R.D. 178, 222 (S.D.N.Y. 2003).

[48]   *See In the Matter of Banc of America Securities LLC,* Admin. Proc. File No. 3-11425, Mar. 10, 2004, *available at* http://www. sec.gov/litigation/admin/34-49386.htm (fining Banc of America $10,000,000 for violating sections 17(a) and 17(b) of the Exchange Act for failure to produce documents during a Commission investigation).

by the internal counsel. It may also inadvertently trigger concerns by external auditors or regulators that inside counsel may herself be a potential wrongdoer, and thus inappropriately present when interviews are being conducted. At the very least, the issue should be thoroughly vetted with the Independent Committee before inside counsel takes a seat at the investigating table.

In some instances, it may be necessary for the Company to hire separate legal counsel for employees who are being interviewed that may have — or may appear to have — interests adverse to the Company. However, depending upon the Company's by-laws, it should not be necessary to retain such counsel until such adversity becomes sufficiently clear, or until an employee makes a reasonable request for separate counsel. An employee may on her own choose to seek the advice of counsel and ask that counsel be present for the interview. Absent exigent circumstances, *e.g.*, the need to immediately conduct interviews in order to qualify for corporate amnesty under Antitrust Division Corporate Leniency Program, a company should not refuse to grant such a request for counsel. However, as indicated earlier, an employee should be advised that his failure timely to cooperate – which includes fully submitting to interviews by Special Counsel – may result in adverse employment consequences including dismissal.

Special Counsel should be especially wary of the situation that arises frequently in the course of an internal investigation, when an employee who is otherwise without counsel is about to be interviewed and, before or as an interview is being conducted, asks whether she needs to consult counsel, or if she retains counsel, would the Company pay for such counsel. Special Counsel is best advised under these circumstances to remind the witness that he does not represent her and that if she wishes to speak to counsel, the Special Counsel would be willing to adjourn the interview for a reasonable time to allow such consultation, and, assuming that the Company's by-laws so allow, to consider the Company's indemnification of the employee's costs of counsel and advancement of fees and expenses.

As discussed above, advance preparation for such contingencies should include consultation with the Independent Committee at the outset of the engagement regarding the scope of the Company's obligations to indemnify and advance fees to categories of directors, officers, and employees.

The Independent Committee should also decide whether Special Counsel will agree with counsel for employees to make documents available to them for review before conducting interviews. Absent special circumstances such as valid concerns of possible witness tampering, obstruction of justice, other evidence of attempts to disrupt the integrity of the internal investigation, or an inability to retrieve and review voluminous documentation, Special Counsel generally should not interview witnesses before the witnesses have had a chance to review relevant documents. We specifically disapprove of Special Counsel's attempting to interview a witness who has not been given an adequate opportunity to refresh his recollection as to prior events by reviewing key hard or electronic documents, or Special Counsel's succumbing to pressure from prosecutors or regulators to attempt to do so, in an effort to trap a witness into a misstatement, which would otherwise not occur if the witness were properly refreshed with all relevant documents and electronic communications. This is particularly true since the government has indicted several executives in obstruction of justice cases in recent years based on alleged misstatements to outside counsel during the course of an investigation.[49] Accordingly, before interviews of officers and employees, and whenever practical, Special Counsel should make available to counsel for employees the topics and documents that will be covered in the interview, and allow employees to obtain copies of their documentary files, including calendars and electronic data.

At the outset of the interview, in addition to providing an overview of the investigation and the purpose of the interview, Special Counsel should make very clear that (1) Special Counsel represents the Company (or the Independent Committee, as the case may be); (2) Special Counsel is not the employee's lawyer and does not represent the employee's interests separate from those of its own client; (3) the conversation is protected by the attorney-client privilege, but the privilege belongs to the Company; and therefore (4) the Company can choose to waive its privilege and disclose all or part of what the employee has told Special Counsel during the interview to external auditors, the government, regulators, or others. Employees also should be apprised of their rights and responsibilities if they are contacted by regulators or prosecutors and asked to subject themselves to an interview, including the ability, without employment sanction, to invoke constitutional rights.

In light of the position taken by the DOJ, as indicated above, that an employee can be indicted for obstruction of justice under 18 U.S.C. 1512, if she lies to private counsel conducting an internal investigation, where she knows that her statements may be shared with a government agency such as the SEC or DOJ conducting its own investigation, we recommend that Special Counsel advise employees at the outset of the interview whether the Company has made a decision to waive the attorney-client privilege and work product protections, or is likely to do so, and to disclose the memorandum of interview to governmental authorities. In recent years, the government has brought several such cases.[50] It should be anticipated that an employee, being so advised, would seek individual counsel and Special Counsel should be prepared to accommodate the request for an adjournment to seek such counsel.

The interviews should be memorialized in a manner consistent with the attorney work-product doctrine and the ultimate purpose of the investigation. A memorandum should be prepared by Special Counsel of the substance of each witness's interview as close in time to the interview as possible. Ultimate decisions on the contents of the memorandum of a witness's interview should be Special Counsel's. However, fairness, and the possible use of such memoranda in follow-up inquiries by Special Counsel, regulators, or prosecutors, causes us to recommend that counsel for witnesses be given reasonable opportunity to review the memoranda for substance and to recommend possible modifications (which Special Counsel may, but is not compelled to, adopt, especially where the recommended modifications are, in Special Counsel's opinion, contrary to what was stated at the interview) so as to avoid misstating or mischaracterizing a witness's statements and

---

49   *See* text, *infra*, at n. 50.

50   *Id.*

to address adverse inferences that may be submitted in company proffers.[51] Special Counsel should consider reading, explaining the substance of, or showing a draft of the memorandum of interview of the witness to counsel for interviewed witnesses to review for accuracy but not to keep a copy thereof.[52]

In addition, if a final written report is to be prepared, we recommend that tentative conclusions as to witnesses' conduct should, as a matter of fairness and completeness, be shared with counsel for present or former employees whose conduct is under examination for possible correction, modification or explanation. Again, we do not suggest that Special Counsel is obligated to adopt any modification suggested, but rather only to give any suggestion whatever weight is in Special Counsel's opinion warranted under the circumstances.

The question of the extent to which, if at all, privileged and work-product protected material should be made available to the company's independent auditors, if, as would be expected, they so request, is highly complex.[53] There is little, if any, authority to support the view that dissemination of privileged information to an independent auditor does not create a waiver of the privilege. With respect to the production to external auditors of Special Counsel's work product prepared in anticipation of litigation, the decisions are inconsistent regarding whether doing so constitutes a waiver.[54] In the latter circumstance, we believe that entry into a written agreement with the independent auditor, acknowledging the confidentiality of the information shared and assuring that it will be held in confidence *might* be effective in some jurisdictions despite *Medinol*. However, under current case law, it is doubtful that any written confidentiality agreement with the independent auditor with respect to privileged material could prevent a waiver from being found. Notwithstanding

---

51   *See U.S. v. Kumar, E.D.N.Y., DOJ News Release, September 22, 2004* ("Former Computer Associates executives indicted on securities fraud, obstruction charges"), *available at* http://www.usdoj.gov/opa/pr/2004/September/04_crm_642.htm ("Shortly after being retained, the company's law firm met with [executives] in order to inquire into their knowledge of the practices that were the subject of the government investigations. During these meetings, the defendants ... allegedly presented to the law firm an assortment of false justifications to explain away evidence of the 35-day month practice. The indictment alleges that [the defendants] ... intended ... that the company's law firm would present these false justifications to the U.S. Attorney's Office, the SEC and the FBI in an attempt to persuade the government that the 35-day month practice never existed").

52   We note the possible argument that disclosure to a witness or her counsel of the substance of a draft memorandum of interview or of tentative conclusions as to a witness's conduct may be deemed a waiver of the corporate privilege and perhaps Special Counsel's work product. We believe that risk of the success of such argument may be able to be mitigated by conditioning such limited disclosure upon the execution of a narrow "common interest" agreement between Special Counsel and counsel for the witness, premised upon the common interest that exists to prevent inadvertent factual errors and conclusions based thereon from being made by Special Counsel and the Independent Committee. See *Ryan v. Gifford I, supra* ("Under [the common interest] exception [to the attorney-client privilege],... for the communication to remain privileged even after its disclosure to others, the "others [must] have interests that are 'so parallel and non-adverse that, at least with respect to the transaction involved, they may be regarded as acting as joint venturers.'" *Saito v. McKesson HBOC, Inc.*, No. 18553, 2002 WL 31657622, at *4 (Del. Ch. Nov. 13, 2002) (citing *Jedwab v. MGM Grand Hotels, Inc.*, No. 8077, 1986 WL 3426, at *2 (Del. Ch. Mar. 20, 1986))."

53   See Brodsky, Palmer, and Malionek, "The Auditor's Need For Its Client's Detailed Information vs. The Client's Need to Preserve the Attorney-Client Privilege and Work Product Protection: The Debate, The Problems, and Proposed Solutions," http://www.abanet.org/buslaw/attorneyclient/publichearing20050211/schedule.shtml

54   *See Medinol, Ltd. v. Boston Scientific Corp.*, 214 F.R.D. 113 (S.D.N.Y. 2002) (holding that the disclosure of an internal investigation report to outside auditors waives both the attorney-client and work-product privileges, because the auditor's interests are not necessarily aligned with the corporation's interests). *But see Merrill Lynch & Co., Inc. v. Allegheny Energy, Inc.*, 2004 WL 2389822 (S.D.N.Y. 2004) (holding that the disclosure of internal investigation reports to outside auditors, while waiving the attorney-client privilege, does not waive the work product privilege because under the facts of the case the auditor and the corporation is not the equivalent of the type of tangible adversarial relationship contemplated by the work product doctrine).

the resulting dilemma to the Independent Committee and the Board of Directors, we believe there may well be circumstances where the independent auditor will insist that presentation of privileged material is a *sine qua non* for the certification of financial statements. Under those circumstances, a Board may have no choice but to authorize the delivery of such materials. However, we recommend that all other alternative courses of action be first explored with the independent auditors before such an outcome. We further recommend that Special Counsel be advised by the Board and Independent Committee at the outset of the engagement not to share information with the Company's external auditors without the written, fully informed consent of both the Independent Committee and the Company's Board. We recommend that the Board formally consider and decide the production and waiver issue before any steps leading to waiver are taken.

IV.   Developing a Record of the Investigation

During the course of the investigation, we recommend that Special Counsel keep and continuously update a record of witnesses and documents examined, documents shown to witnesses, and issues being raised. We also recommend that the Independent Committee be regularly updated on the course of the investigation. Under certain circumstances, these updates, especially those being done in the early stages of an inquiry, should be made orally, because the possibility exists that preliminary information gathered or early conclusions formed may well prove to be inaccurate or incomplete; premature recording of such information or conclusions could well be prejudicial to the company as well as implicated employees. In particular, once the Special Counsel has conveyed early impressions to the Independent Committee (based on preliminary reviews of documents and early interviews), those impressions may, as a practical matter, prove embarrassing to modify or be impossible to eradicate from the minds of the Independent Committee.

Once the investigation has been completed, Special Counsel must report its findings, conclusions, and bases to the Board, the Audit Committee, or the Independent Committee, as the case may be. Careful and early consideration must be given to whether the ultimate form of the report will be written or oral, and the effect of preparing a report on issues concerning the corporate attorney-client privilege and work product protections. The form of the report and the nature of its preliminary dissemination should be analyzed because of the likelihood that some version of the report will likely make it into the hands of government authorities or plaintiffs' attorneys, resulting in the substantial risk of enhanced civil litigation against the Company, and the officers and directors. If the report is to be written, careful consideration must be given to whether it will be posted on a website[55], and whether it will be turned over to prosecutors, regulators, and the independent auditor. [56]

Special Counsel should be careful to remind the governing body that the report's conclusions are ultimately that of the Independent Committee, not just Special Counsel, and that the Board members have fiduciary responsibilities to draw their own conclusions as to the evidence presented, and should not simply accept the conclusions as drawn by Special Counsel without a full understanding of the bases for such conclusions.

V. The External Investigation

A. Role of Special Counsel in Follow-on Investigations and Civil Litigation.

The Company may be tempted to use the services or work product of its Special Counsel in connection with its defense of external investigations and civil litigation. However, many experienced General Counsel and practitioners believe that Special Counsel should not be used as Company defense counsel, lest the independence of the Special Counsel be brought into question, and the legitimacy of the inquiry be compromised. We recommend that such follow-up inquiries be handled by counsel other than Special Counsel; otherwise, the view of Special Counsel as being independent of management will likely be dissipated, and external auditors, as well as regulators or prosecutors, are likely to disregard the work of such Special Counsel as being the product of bias.

B. Use of Work Product of Special Counsel

As to whether the documents and database accumulated by the Special Counsel may be utilized by Company or employee counsel to minimize expenses to the Company and maximize the speed of preparation, we recommend that, absent genuine regulatory concerns regarding possible obstruction of justice, such documents and databases should be available for that use, once stripped of the evidence of the internal thought processes of Special Counsel.

Among the more difficult issues facing Company counsel that has inherited such document depository and work product is the extent to which such should be made available to counsel for present or former employees, who are likely also facing civil litigation and regulatory

---

55   Posting a copy of an internal investigative report to the Independent Committee on a website or otherwise making it available to the public runs the risk of waiving both the protections of the work product doctrine and the corporate attorney-client privilege. *In re Kidder Peabody Securities Litigation*, 168 F.R.D. 459, 467, 469-70 (SDNY 1996) ("The decision to release the report appears, in retrospect, to have been virtually a foregone conclusion from the outset since this was a crucial aspect of Kidder's public relations strategy… In practical terms this means that Kidder's waiver by publication requires disclosure of those portions of the interview documents that are specifically alluded to in the [Special Counsel] report.")

56   *See Ryan v. Gifford,* 2007 WL 4259557 (Del. Ch. Nov. 30, 2007) (*Ryan I*), where it was held that delivery of a report by a special investigative committee, set up following the filing of a derivative action, to a Board of Directors consisting of several directors who were also named as defendants in the derivative action, constituted a full waiver of the privilege as to all communications between the committee and its counsel, including all correspondence between the special committee and its counsel, the investigation report, and all correspondence between the company and counsel to the special committee. Several unusual factors contributed to the finding of waiver. For example, because the directors were present at the committee's report in their personal, not fiduciary, capacities, the Court found the privilege had been waived, particularly as their personal attorneys were present and they used the committee's findings in their individual defenses. Furthermore, the special committee lacked sufficient authority to take action independent of the other board members.

investigations. Although outside the strict boundaries of this paper, we again believe that, absent genuine concerns about obstruction of justice, fairness dictates that such materials be made available on an individualized basis to such present or former employees, especially since it is likely that they have also been made available already to the Department of Justice, SEC, or other regulators.[57] Accordingly, we also recommend that the presumption be that the work product of Special Counsel such as witness interviews conducted by Special Counsel should be made available, on an individualized basis, to counsel for present or former employees, again, absent genuine concerns of obstruction of justice.

VI.   Recommendations

1.   An organization should take steps to consider an internal investigation when allegations have been lodged of significant corporate malfeasance or where an outside auditor gives notice that it suspects the possibility of illegal corporate activity. A Board of Directors, an audit, or a special committee may in select circumstances conclude that it is not in the best interests of the Company to investigate, disclose to, or cooperate with the government. In reaching the decision as to what is in the best interests of the shareholders, the Board, audit committee, or special committee may weigh and consider published prosecutorial and regulatory policies, related cases and dispositions, DOJ and/or SEC statements and the impact and costs of actual or anticipated litigation on the Company.

2.   Where the alleged or suspected conduct involves senior officers or serious employee misconduct, or where the corporate entity is the focal point of a government inquiry, management, including usually the general counsel's office, should not be, and should not be perceived to be, in charge of the internal investigation.

3.   A committee of the Board of Directors consisting of the independent members of the Board (the "Independent Committee") should be delegated the task by the Board of Directors of overseeing the conduct of the internal investigation when allegations have been lodged of significant corporate malfeasance or where an outside auditor gives notice that it suspects the possibility of illegal corporate activity and retaining counsel to conduct the investigation.

4.   The goal of the Independent Committee should be to seek to determine the truth of the underlying allegations, to safeguard and act in the best interests of the shareholders, and to prevent the internal investigation from impairing the reputations of employees, officers, and directors of the Company not found to have engaged in wrongdoing.

5.   The Board should pass a resolution broadly authorizing the Independent Committee to retain counsel and their agents, conduct an investigation, and report its ultimate findings to the Board. In order to preserve communications between the Committee and the Board as privileged, the Committee should have authority to take action independent of the Board.

---

57   It should be noted that the Department of Justice is on record in at least one option backdating case that disclosure of witness interview memoranda of Special Counsel to counsel for derivative plaintiffs, and other parties, would constitute premature disclosure of the substance of testimony from potential Government witnesses and would facilitate efforts by subjects and potential criminal defendants to manufacture evidence and tailor their testimony and defenses to conform to the Government's proof. *In re UnitedHealth Group Shareholder Derivative Litigation*, USDC, D.Minn., Civil No. 06-1216JMR/FLN.

6.   Outside counsel which has not had a substantial prior relationship with the Company and its senior management ("Special Counsel") should be retained to conduct significant internal investigations.

7.   The Independent Committee should retain the Special Counsel in writing. Special Counsel's engagement letter should state the allegations under review, the scope of the inquiry, and make clear that Special Counsel is to advise the Company of its legal rights and obligations, as well as its potential liabilities.

8.   The scope of the Special Counsel's engagement can be expanded in appropriate circumstances, and that expansion should also be confirmed in writing by the Independent Committee.

9.   The Special Counsel should be instructed to engage in investigative tactics designed to get at the truth of the underlying allegations of wrongdoing, including using such investigative, technological, and professional techniques of which they are capable.

10.   It should not be the goal of the Special Counsel, absent specific mandate from the Independent Committee, to investigate any perceived wrongdoing by corporate officers or employees wherever it may occur.

11.   The Independent Committee and Special Counsel should also agree upon specific reporting procedures and protocols for documenting the investigation.

12.   The Independent Committee should also determine whether and to what extent Special Counsel may waive the Company's attorney-client privilege or its own work product protections in its dealings with regulators or other third parties. The waiver of these protections is a major corporate decision that requires full and frank discussion of the benefits of these privileges and the impact of a waiver on prosecutorial, regulatory or parallel proceedings. In few, if any, cases, should Special Counsel be given the authority to make such waiver decisions on its own without prior full deliberation by the Independent Committee and the full Board, with the latter being encouraged to take advice from regular or other counsel on this decision.

13.   Special Counsel should not be allowed to condition its retention by the Independent Committee upon a pre-retention decision by the Independent Committee to waive all privileges.

14.   The engagement letter for Special Counsel should make clear that Special Counsel's work product, data, and document collection and analysis belongs to the Independent Committee and their Special Counsel, and upon completion of the investigation, may, in appropriate circumstances, be shared under the common interest privilege with the Company for possible use in its defense of third party or government claims. Any sharing of the materials with any director-defendants should be done only if it is clear those directors are acting in their fiduciary, not individual, capacities; to this end, their individual counsel should not be present and the directors should not use those materials in their individual defenses, or else the common interest privilege could be waived.

15.   The Independent Committee should authorize the Special Counsel in writing to retain additional professionals, including forensic auditors, investigators, and public relations advisers, where necessary.

16.   Experts should sign retention agreements that make clear their engagement is in contemplation of providing assistance for legal advice.

17.   The Independent Committee should consider promptly addressing management and employee morale issues by a memorandum to all affected employees to keep employees abreast of general information about the purpose and expected length of the inquiry, and the expectation that all employees will cooperate with the inquiry and with Special Counsel.

18.   The Independent Committee should explicitly communicate what constitutes "cooperation" of an employee during an internal investigation, and that an employee's refusal timely to cooperate in this regard may result in dismissal. In most circumstances, the cooperation of employees should include: (1) the provision upon request of all documents related to company business whether kept in the employee's office, home, or personal computer; (2) strict compliance with all document hold and retention notices; and (3) submission to interviews by Special Counsel.

19.   At the outset of an investigation, the Independent Committee should adopt a written policy regarding the scope of indemnity and advancement to directors, officers and employees, or others affiliated with the Company, in adherence to its by-laws, other corporate governance policies or new policies designed for the scope of the internal investigation.

20.   The Independent Committee should also consider, at the outset of an internal investigation, adopting a written policy expanding the scope of indemnity to include employees otherwise not covered by normal indemnification policies, and independent contractors or acting officers of companies or their subsidiaries who perform important executive functions but are not literally within the company's standard indemnity policies. The adoption of any expanded indemnification or advancement policy should be adhered to, once adopted, and not thereafter expanded to include those originally excluded, unless the scope of the investigation is altered.

21.   The Independent Committee should give careful consideration to distributing a memorandum to affected employees notifying them of the nature of any prospective investigation, the possible need for witness interviews, the ability of the Company to recommend counsel for individual employees, the possibility that the Company will be responsible for advancing fees and expenses for the employee's representation, and the requirement that any employee asked to give an interview cooperate and tell the truth to Special Counsel.

22.   External counsel should oversee compliance with a litigation hold, using reasonable efforts to continually monitor the party's retention and production of relevant hard-copy and electronic documents.

23.   The relevant universe of hard-copy and electronic documents must be identified and collected as early as possible in the investigative process, even before Special Counsel is retained.

24.   Special Counsel and retained forensic professionals should conduct document review and analysis of electronic and hard documents.

25.   Assuming time permits, after review and analysis of documents, Special Counsel should identify the relevant witnesses and begin conducting the interviews.

26.   At the outset of the interview, Special Counsel should advise each witness that (1) the Special Counsel represents the Independent Committee, (2) Special Counsel is not the employee's lawyer and does not represent the employee's interests; (3) statements made to the Special Counsel should be truthful; (4) the interview is protected by the attorney-client privilege, but the privilege belongs to the Company; and (5) the Independent Committee can unilaterally choose to waive its privilege and disclose all or part of what the employee has told Special Counsel during the interview to external auditors, the government, regulators, or others.

27.   The Independent Committee and Special Counsel should give careful consideration as to whether inside counsel should attend witness interviews, with an eye to maximizing the possibility of obtaining objective responses and to ensuring the appearance of obtaining objective responses.

28.   Special Counsel should advise employees at the outset of the interview whether the Company has made a decision to waive the attorney-client privilege and work product protections, or is likely to do so, and to disclose the memorandum of interview to governmental agencies such as the SEC or DOJ that is conducting its own investigation.

29.   Special Counsel should tell witnesses at the outset of the interview that the Department of Justice has taken the position that an employee can be indicted for obstruction of justice under 18 U.S.C. § 1512, if he or she lies to private counsel conducting an internal investigation, where he or she knows that his or her statements may be shared with a government agency such as the SEC or DOJ that is conducting its own investigation.

30.   Absent special circumstances such as valid concerns of possible witness tampering, obstruction of justice, other evidence of attempts to disrupt the integrity of the internal investigation or the unavailability of hard-copy or electronic documents, Special Counsel should make available to witnesses or their counsel the topics and documents that will be covered in the interview, and allow employees to obtain copies of their documentary files, including calendars and electronic data.

31.   Absent special circumstances such as valid concerns of possible witness tampering, obstruction of justice, or other evidence of attempts to disrupt the integrity of the internal investigation, Special Counsel should not generally interview witnesses before they have had a reasonable opportunity to review relevant documents.

32.   Absent special circumstances such as valid concerns of possible witness tampering, obstruction of justice, or other evidence of attempts to disrupt the integrity of an investigation, Special Counsel should resist attempts by prosecutors or regulators to seek the Special Counsel's interview of a witness who has not been given an opportunity to refresh his recollection as to prior events.

33.   Special Counsel should not advise an employee whether he or she should seek the advice of individual counsel, lest the employee misunderstand the role of Special Counsel as being the exclusive representative of the Independent Committee. Under these circumstances Special Counsel should remind the witness that the Special Counsel does not represent the witness and that if he or she wishes to speak to counsel, the Special Counsel will adjourn the interview for a short time to allow such consultation, and, if previously authorized by the Independent Committee, to provide recommendations of counsel.

34.   Special Counsel should memorialize the substance of each witness interview as close in time to the interview as possible and in a manner consistent with the attorney work-product doctrine and the ultimate purpose of the investigation.

35.   Absent special circumstances such as valid concerns of possible witness tampering, obstruction of justice, or other evidence of attempts to disrupt the integrity of an investigation, Special Counsel should give counsel for witnesses an opportunity to suggest modifications to the memoranda so as to avoid misstating or mischaracterizing a witness's statements. Special Counsel should consider reading, explaining the substance of, or showing a draft of the memorandum of the interview of the witness to counsel for interviewed witnesses to review for accuracy, but not to keep a copy thereof.

36.   Absent special circumstances such as valid concerns of possible witness tampering, obstruction of justice, or other evidence of attempts to disrupt the integrity of an investigation, if a final written report is to be prepared, Special Counsel should share tentative conclusions as to witnesses' conduct with counsel for present or former employees whose conduct is under examination for possible correction or modification.

37.   If the company's independent auditors request access to privileged information or the Special Counsel's work product, the Independent Committee should first explore all other alternative courses of action, but should not have the power or authority to decide the issue on its own. The Independent Committee should give careful consideration to such request and make a recommendation to the Board. The Special Counsel should be advised by the Board and Independent Committee at the outset of the engagement not to share information with the Company's external auditors without the written, fully informed consent of both the Independent Committee and the Company's Board.

38.   We recommend that the Board formally consider and decide the issue of production to the independent auditors before any steps leading to waiver are taken. In light of inconsistent decisions regarding whether production of Special Counsel's work product to external auditors constitutes a waiver of the work product protections, it is important to enter into a written confidentiality and common interest agreement with external auditors that allows for work product information to be provided without a waiver issue arising.

39.   During the course of the investigation, Special Counsel should keep and continuously update a record of witnesses and documents examined, documents shown to witnesses, and issues raised.

40.   Special Counsel should regularly update the Independent Committee on the course of the investigation. In the early stages of an inquiry, updates should generally be made orally, because of the possibility that preliminary information gathered or early conclusions formed might prove to be inaccurate or incomplete, and prejudicial to the company as well as employees implicated by them.

41.   Upon the completion of the investigation, Special Counsel should report its findings and the conclusions, and the bases therefor, to the Board, the Audit Committee, or the Independent Committee, as the case may be. Special Counsel should be careful to remind the governing body that the report's conclusions are ultimately that of the Independent Committee, not just Special Counsel, and that the Board members have fiduciary responsibilities to draw their own conclusions as to the evidence presented.

42.   Before presentation of the final report, the Independent Committee and Special Counsel should again give careful consideration to whether the ultimate form of the report will be written, oral or PowerPoint, to whom it will be provided, and how it will be published.

43.   Special Counsel should not be used as Company defense counsel in civil or criminal litigation or investigations that follow the internal investigation.

44.   Absent genuine regulatory concerns regarding possible obstruction of justice, the database of documents and selected work product, once stripped of the evidence the internal thought processes of Special Counsel, should be made available for use by any Special Litigation Committee, counsel to the Company, and on an individualized basis, to counsel for present or former employees.

APPENDIX 8

Title 9, Chapter 9-28.000 Principles of Federal Prosecution of Business Organizations (U.S. Department of Justice)[1]

---

1. While these guidelines refer to corporations, they apply to the consideration of the prosecution of all types of business organizations, including partnerships, sole proprietorships, government entities, and unincorporated associations.

9-27.001   DUTIES OF FEDERAL PROSECUTORS AND DUTIES OF CORPORATE LEADERS

The prosecution of corporate crime is a high priority for the Department of Justice. By investigating allegations of wrongdoing and by bringing charges where appropriate for criminal misconduct, the Department promotes critical public interests. These interests include, to take just a few examples: (1) protecting the integrity of our free economic and capital markets; (2) protecting consumers, investors, and business entities that compete only through lawful means; and (3) protecting the American people from misconduct that would violate criminal laws safeguarding the environment.

In this regard, federal prosecutors and corporate leaders typically share common goals. For example, directors and officers owe a fiduciary duty to a corporation's shareholders, the corporation's true owners, and they owe duties of honest dealing to the investing public in connection with the corporation's regulatory filings and public statements. The faithful execution of these duties by corporate leadership serves the same values in promoting public trust and confidence that our criminal cases are designed to serve.

A prosecutor's duty to enforce the law requires the investigation and prosecution of criminal wrongdoing if it is discovered. In carrying out this mission with the diligence and resolve necessary to vindicate the important public interests discussed above, prosecutors should be mindful of the common cause we share with responsible corporate leaders. Prosecutors should also be mindful that confidence in the Department is affected both by the results we achieve and by the real and perceived ways in which we achieve them. Thus, the manner in which we do our job as prosecutors—including the professionalism we demonstrate, our willingness to secure the facts in a manner that encourages corporate compliance and self-regulation, and also our appreciation that corporate prosecutions can potentially harm blameless investors, employees, and others—affects public perception of our mission. Federal prosecutors recognize that they must maintain public confidence in the way in which they exercise their charging discretion. This endeavor requires the thoughtful analysis of all facts and circumstances presented in a given case. As always, professionalism and civility play an important part in the Department's discharge of its responsibilities in all areas, including the area of corporate investigations and prosecutions.

[new August 2008]

9-28.200   GENERAL CONSIDERATIONS OF CORPORATE LIABILITY

A.   General Principle: Corporations should not be treated leniently because of their artificial nature nor should they be subject to harsher treatment. Vigorous enforcement of the criminal laws against corporate wrongdoers, where appropriate, results in great benefits for law enforcement and the public, particularly in the area of white collar crime. Indicting corporations for wrongdoing enables the government to be a force for positive change of corporate culture, and a force to prevent, discover, and punish serious crimes.

B.   Comment: In all cases involving corporate wrongdoing, prosecutors should consider the factors discussed further below. In doing so, prosecutors should be aware of the public benefits that can flow from indicting a corporation in appropriate cases. For instance, corporations are likely to take immediate remedial steps when one is indicted for criminal misconduct that is pervasive throughout a particular industry, and thus an indictment can provide a unique opportunity for deterrence on a broad scale. In addition, a corporate indictment may result in specific deterrence by changing the culture of the indicted corporation and the behavior of its employees. Finally, certain crimes that carry with them a substantial risk of great public harm—e.g., environmental crimes or sweeping financial frauds—may be committed by a business entity, and there may therefore be a substantial federal interest in indicting a corporation under such circumstances.

In certain instances, it may be appropriate, upon consideration of the factors set forth herein, to resolve a corporate criminal case by means other than indictment. Non-prosecution and deferred prosecution agreements, for example, occupy an important middle ground between declining prosecution and obtaining the conviction of a corporation. These agreements are discussed further in USAM 9-28.1000. Likewise, civil and regulatory alternatives may be appropriate in certain cases, as discussed in USAM 9-28.1100.

Where a decision is made to charge a corporation, it does not necessarily follow that individual directors, officers, employees, or shareholders should not also be charged. Prosecution of a corporation is not a substitute for the prosecution of criminally culpable individuals within or without the corporation. Because a corporation can act only through individuals, imposition of individual criminal liability may provide the strongest deterrent against future corporate wrongdoing. Only rarely should provable individual culpability not be pursued, particularly if it relates to high-level corporate officers, even in the face of an offer of a corporate guilty plea or some other disposition of the charges against the corporation.

Corporations are "legal persons," capable of suing and being sued, and capable of committing crimes. Under the doctrine of *respondeat superior*, a corporation may be held criminally liable for the illegal acts of its directors, officers, employees, and agents. To hold a corporation liable for these actions, the government must establish that the corporate agent's actions (i) were within the scope of his duties and (ii) were intended, at least in part, to benefit the corporation. In all cases involving wrongdoing by corporate agents, prosecutors should not limit their focus solely to individuals or the corporation, but should consider both as potential targets.

Agents may act for mixed reasons—both for self-aggrandizement (both direct and indirect) and for the benefit of the corporation, and a corporation may be held liable as long as one motivation of its agent is to benefit the corporation. *See United States v. Potter*, 463 F.3d 9, 25 (1st Cir. 2006) (stating that the test to determine whether an agent is acting within the scope of employment is "whether the agent is performing acts of the kind which he is authorized to perform, and those acts are motivated, at least in part, by an intent to benefit the corporation."). In *United States v. Automated Medical Laboratories, Inc.*, 770 F.2d 399 (4th Cir. 1985), for example, the Fourth Circuit affirmed a corporation's conviction for the actions of a subsidiary's employee despite the corporation's claim that the employee was acting for his own benefit, namely his "ambitious nature and his desire to ascend the corporate ladder." *Id.* at 407. The court stated, "Partucci was clearly acting in part to benefit AML since his advancement within the corporation depended on AML's well-being and its lack of difficulties with the FDA." *Id.*; see also *United States v. Cincotta*, 689 F.2d 238, 241-42 (1st Cir. 1982) (upholding a corporation's conviction, notwithstanding the substantial personal benefit reaped by its miscreant agents, because the fraudulent scheme required money to pass through the corporation's treasury and the fraudulently obtained goods were resold to the corporation's customers in the corporation's name).

Moreover, the corporation need not even necessarily profit from its agent's actions for it to be held liable. In *Automated Medical Laboratories*, the Fourth Circuit stated:

> [B]enefit is not a "touchstone of criminal corporate liability; benefit at best is an evidential, not an operative, fact." Thus, whether the agent's actions ultimately redounded to the benefit of the corporation is less significant than whether the agent acted with the intent to benefit the corporation. The basic purpose of requiring that an agent have acted with the intent to benefit the corporation, however, is to insulate the corporation from criminal liability for actions of its agents which may be *inimical* to the interests of the corporation or which may have been undertaken solely to advance the interests of that agent or of a party other than the corporation.

770 F.2d at 407 (internal citation omitted) (quoting *Old Monastery Co. v. United States*, 147 F.2d 905, 908 (4th Cir. 1945)).

[new August 2008]

9-28.300   FACTORS TO BE CONSIDERED

A.   General Principle: Generally, prosecutors apply the same factors in determining whether to charge a corporation as they do with respect to individuals. *See* USAM 9-27.220 *et seq*. Thus, the prosecutor must weigh all of the factors normally considered in the sound exercise of prosecutorial judgment: the sufficiency of the evidence; the likelihood of success at trial; the probable deterrent, rehabilitative, and other consequences of conviction; and the adequacy of noncriminal approaches. *See id.* However, due to the nature of the corporate "person," some additional factors are present. In conducting an investigation, determining whether to bring charges, and negotiating plea or other agreements, prosecutors should consider the following factors in reaching a decision as to the proper treatment of a corporate target:

- the nature and seriousness of the offense, including the risk of harm to the public, and applicable policies and priorities, if any, governing the prosecution of corporations for particular categories of crime (see USAM 9-28.400);
- the pervasiveness of wrongdoing within the corporation, including the complicity in, or the condoning of, the wrongdoing by corporate management (see USAM 9-28.500);

- the corporation's history of similar misconduct, including prior criminal, civil, and regulatory enforcement actions against it (see USAM 9-28.600);
- the corporation's timely and voluntary disclosure of wrongdoing and its willingness to cooperate in the investigation of its agents (see USAM 9-28.700);
- the existence and effectiveness of the corporation's pre-existing compliance program (see USAM 9-28.800);
- the corporation's remedial actions, including any efforts to implement an effective corporate compliance program or to improve an existing one, to replace responsible management, to discipline or terminate wrongdoers, to pay restitution, and to cooperate with the relevant government agencies (see USAM 9-28.900);
- collateral consequences, including whether there is disproportionate harm to shareholders, pension holders, employees, and others not proven personally culpable, as well as impact on the public arising from the prosecution (see USAM 9-28.1000);
- the adequacy of the prosecution of individuals responsible for the corporation's malfeasance; and
- the adequacy of remedies such as civil or regulatory enforcement actions (see USAM 9-28.1100).

B. Comment: The factors listed in this section are intended to be illustrative of those that should be evaluated and are not an exhaustive list of potentially relevant considerations. Some of these factors may not apply to specific cases, and in some cases one factor may override all others. For example, the nature and seriousness of the offense may be such as to warrant prosecution regardless of the other factors. In most cases, however, no single factor will be dispositive. In addition, national law enforcement policies in various enforcement areas may require that more or less weight be given to certain of these factors than to others. Of course, prosecutors must exercise their thoughtful and pragmatic judgment in applying and balancing these factors, so as to achieve a fair and just outcome and promote respect for the law.

In making a decision to charge a corporation, the prosecutor generally has substantial latitude in determining when, whom, how, and even whether to prosecute for violations of federal criminal law. In exercising that discretion, prosecutors should consider the following statements of principles that summarize the considerations they should weigh and the practices they should follow in discharging their prosecutorial responsibilities. In doing so, prosecutors should ensure that the general purposes of the criminal law—assurance of warranted punishment, deterrence of further criminal conduct, protection of the public from dangerous and fraudulent conduct, rehabilitation of offenders, and restitution for victims and affected communities—are adequately met, taking into account the special nature of the corporate "person."

[new August 2008]

9-28.400   SPECIAL POLICY CONCERNS

A.   General Principle: The nature and seriousness of the crime, including the risk of harm to the public from the criminal misconduct, are obviously primary factors in determining whether to charge a corporation. In addition, corporate conduct, particularly that of national and multi-national corporations, necessarily intersects with federal economic, tax, and criminal law enforcement policies. In applying these Principles, prosecutors must consider the practices and policies of the appropriate Division of the Department, and must comply with those policies to the extent required by the facts presented.

B.   Comment: In determining whether to charge a corporation, prosecutors should take into account federal law enforcement priorities as discussed above. *See* USAM 9-27.230. In addition, however, prosecutors must be aware of the specific policy goals and incentive programs established by the respective Divisions and regulatory agencies. Thus, whereas natural persons may be given incremental degrees of credit (ranging from immunity to lesser charges to sentencing considerations) for turning themselves in, making statements against their penal interest, and cooperating in the government's investigation of their own and others' wrongdoing, the same approach may not be appropriate in all circumstances with respect to corporations. As an example, it is entirely proper in many investigations for a prosecutor to consider the corporation's pre-indictment conduct, e.g., voluntary disclosure, cooperation, remediation or restitution, in determining whether to seek an indictment. However, this would not necessarily be appropriate in an antitrust investigation, in which antitrust violations, by definition, go to the heart of the corporation's business. With this in mind, the Antitrust Division has established a firm policy, understood in the business community, that credit should not be given at the charging stage for a compliance program and that amnesty is available only to the first corporation to make full disclosure to the government. As another example, the Tax Division has a strong preference for prosecuting responsible individuals, rather than entities, for corporate tax offenses. Thus, in determining whether or not to charge a corporation, prosecutors must consult with the Criminal, Antitrust, Tax, Environmental and Natural Resources, and National Security Divisions, as appropriate.

[new August 2008]

9-28.500   PERVASIVENESS OF WRONGDOING WITHIN THE CORPORATION

A. General Principle: A corporation can only act through natural persons, and it is therefore held responsible for the acts of such persons fairly attributable to it. Charging a corporation for even minor misconduct may be appropriate where the wrongdoing was pervasive and was undertaken by a large number of employees, or by all the employees in a particular role within the corporation, or was condoned by upper management. On the other hand, it may not be appropriate to impose liability upon a corporation, particularly one with a robust compliance program in place, under a strict *respondeat superior* theory for the single isolated act of a rogue employee. There is, of course, a wide spectrum between these two extremes, and a prosecutor should exercise sound discretion in evaluating the pervasiveness of wrongdoing within a corporation.

B.   Comment: Of these factors, the most important is the role and conduct of management. Although acts of even low-level employees may result in criminal liability, a corporation is directed by its management and management is responsible for a corporate culture in which criminal conduct is either discouraged or tacitly encouraged. As stated in commentary to the Sentencing Guidelines:

> Pervasiveness [is] case specific and [will] depend on the number, and degree of responsibility, of individuals [with] substantial authority . . . who participated in, condoned, or were willfully ignorant of the offense. Fewer individuals need to be involved for a finding of pervasiveness if those individuals exercised a relatively high degree of authority. Pervasiveness can occur either within an organization as a whole or within a unit of an organization.

USSG § 8C2.5, cmt. (n. 4).

[new August 2008]

9-28.600   THE CORPORATION'S PAST HISTORY

A. General Principle: Prosecutors may consider a corporation's history of similar conduct, including prior criminal, civil, and regulatory enforcement actions against it, in determining whether to bring criminal charges and how best to resolve cases.

B.   Comment: A corporation, like a natural person, is expected to learn from its mistakes. A history of similar misconduct may be probative of a corporate culture that encouraged, or at least condoned, such misdeeds, regardless of any compliance programs. Criminal prosecution of a corporation may be particularly appropriate where the corporation previously had been subject to non-criminal guidance, warnings, or sanctions, or previous criminal charges, and it either had not taken adequate action to prevent future unlawful conduct or had continued to engage in the misconduct in spite of the warnings or enforcement actions taken against it. The corporate structure itself (e.g., the creation or existence of subsidiaries or operating divisions) is not dispositive in this analysis, and enforcement actions taken against the corporation or any of its divisions, subsidiaries, and affiliates may be considered, if germane. *See* USSG § 8C2.5(c), cmt. (n. 6).

[new August 2008]

9-28.700   THE VALUE OF COOPERATION

A.   General Principle: In determining whether to charge a corporation and how to resolve corporate criminal cases, the corporation's timely and voluntary disclosure of wrongdoing and its cooperation with the government's investigation may be relevant factors. In gauging the extent of the corporation's cooperation, the prosecutor may consider, among other things, whether the corporation made a voluntary and timely disclosure, and the corporation's willingness to provide relevant information and evidence and identify relevant actors within and outside the corporation, including senior executives.

Cooperation is a potential mitigating factor, by which a corporation—just like any other subject of a criminal investigation—can gain credit in a case that otherwise is appropriate for indictment and prosecution. Of course, the decision not to cooperate by a corporation (or individual) is not itself evidence of misconduct, at least where the lack of cooperation does not involve criminal misconduct or demonstrate consciousness of guilt (e.g., suborning perjury or false statements, or refusing to comply with lawful discovery requests). Thus, failure to cooperate, in and of itself, does not support or require the filing of charges with respect to a corporation any more than with respect to an individual.

B.   Comment: In investigating wrongdoing by or within a corporation, a prosecutor is likely to encounter several obstacles resulting from the nature of the corporation itself. It will often be difficult to determine which individual took which action on behalf of the corporation. Lines of authority and responsibility may be shared among operating divisions or departments, and records and personnel may be spread throughout the United States or even among several countries. Where the criminal conduct continued over an extended period of time, the culpable or knowledgeable personnel may have been promoted, transferred, or fired, or they may have quit or retired. Accordingly, a corporation's cooperation may be critical in identifying potentially relevant actors and locating relevant evidence, among other things, and in doing so expeditiously.

This dynamic—i.e., the difficulty of determining what happened, where the evidence is, and which individuals took or promoted putatively illegal corporate actions—can have negative consequences for both the government and the corporation that is the subject or target of a government investigation. More specifically, because of corporate attribution principles concerning actions of corporate officers and employees (see, e.g., supra section II), uncertainty about exactly who authorized or directed apparent corporate misconduct can inure to the detriment of a corporation. For example, it may not matter under the law which of several possible executives or leaders in a chain of command approved of or authorized criminal conduct; however, that information if known might bear on the propriety of a particular disposition short of indictment of the corporation. It may not be in the interest of a corporation or the government for a charging decision to be made in the absence of such information, which might occur if, for example, a statute of limitations were relevant and authorization by any one of the officials were enough to justify a charge under the law. Moreover, and at a minimum, a protracted government investigation of such an issue could, as a collateral consequence, disrupt the corporation's business operations or even depress its stock price.

For these reasons and more, cooperation can be a favorable course for both the government and the corporation. Cooperation benefits the government—and ultimately shareholders, employees, and other often blameless victims—by allowing prosecutors and federal agents, for example, to avoid protracted delays, which compromise their ability to quickly uncover and address the full extent of widespread corporate crimes. With cooperation by the corporation, the government may be able to reduce tangible losses, limit damage to reputation, and preserve assets for restitution. At the same time, cooperation may benefit the corporation by enabling the government to focus its investigative resources in a manner that will not unduly disrupt the corporation's legitimate business operations. In addition, and critically, cooperation may benefit the corporation by presenting it with the opportunity to earn credit for its efforts.

[new August 2008]

9-28.710   ATTORNEY-CLIENT AND WORK PRODUCT PROTECTIONS

The attorney-client privilege and the attorney work product protection serve an extremely important function in the American legal system. The attorney-client privilege is one of the oldest and most sacrosanct privileges under the law. *See Upjohn v. United States*, 449 U.S. 383, 389 (1981). As the Supreme Court has stated, "[i]ts purpose is to encourage full and frank communication between attorneys and their clients and thereby promote broader public interests in the observance of law and administration of justice." *Id.* The value of promoting a corporation's ability to seek frank and comprehensive legal advice is particularly important in the contemporary global business environment, where corporations often face complex and dynamic legal and regulatory obligations imposed by the federal government and also by states and foreign governments. The work product doctrine serves similarly important goals.

For these reasons, waiving the attorney-client and work product protections has never been a prerequisite under the Department's prosecution guidelines for a corporation to be viewed as cooperative. Nonetheless, a wide range of commentators and members of the American legal community and criminal justice system have asserted that the Department's policies have been used, either wittingly or unwittingly, to coerce business entities into waiving attorney-client privilege and work-product protection. Everyone agrees that a corporation may freely waive its own privileges if it chooses to do so; indeed, such waivers occur routinely when corporations are victimized by their employees or others, conduct an internal investigation, and then disclose the details of the investigation to law enforcement officials in an effort to seek prosecution of the offenders. However, the contention, from a broad array of voices, is that the Department's position on attorney-client privilege and work product protection waivers has promoted an environment in which those protections are being unfairly eroded to the detriment of all.

The Department understands that the attorney-client privilege and attorney work product protection are essential and long- recognized components of the American legal system. What the government seeks and needs to advance its legitimate (indeed, essential) law enforcement mission is not waiver of those protections, but rather the facts known to the corporation about the putative criminal misconduct under review. In addition, while a corporation remains free to convey non-factual or "core" attorney-client communications or work product—if and only if the corporation voluntarily chooses to do so—prosecutors should not ask for such waivers and are directed not to do so. The critical factor is whether the corporation has provided the facts about the events, as explained further herein.

[new August 2008]

9-28.720   COOPERATION: DISCLOSING
THE RELEVANT FACTS

Eligibility for cooperation credit is not predicated upon the waiver of attorney-client privilege or work product protection. Instead, the sort of cooperation that is most valuable to resolving allegations of misconduct by a corporation and its officers, directors, employees, or agents is disclosure of the relevant *facts* concerning such misconduct. In this regard, the analysis parallels that for a non-corporate defendant, where cooperation typically requires disclosure of relevant factual knowledge and not of discussions between an individual and his attorneys.

Thus, when the government investigates potential corporate wrongdoing, it seeks the relevant facts. For example, how and when did the alleged misconduct occur? Who promoted or approved it? Who was responsible for committing it? In this respect, the investigation of a corporation differs little from the investigation of an individual. In both cases, the government needs to know the facts to achieve a just and fair outcome. The party under investigation may choose to cooperate by disclosing the facts, and the government may give credit for the party's disclosures. If a corporation wishes to receive credit for such cooperation, which then can be considered with all other cooperative efforts and circumstances in evaluating how fairly to proceed, then the corporation, like any person, must disclose the relevant facts of which it has knowledge.[2]

(a) Disclosing the Relevant Facts—Facts Gathered Through Internal Investigation

Individuals and corporations often obtain knowledge of facts in different ways. An individual knows the facts of his or others' misconduct through his own experience and perceptions. A corporation is an artificial construct that cannot, by definition, have personal knowledge of the facts. Some of those facts may be reflected in documentary or electronic media like emails, transaction or accounting documents, and other records. Often, the corporation gathers facts through an internal investigation. Exactly how and by whom the facts are gathered is for the corporation to decide. Many corporations choose to collect information about potential misconduct through lawyers, a process that may confer attorney-client privilege or attorney work product protection on at least some of the information collected. Other corporations may choose a method of fact-gathering that does not have that effect—for example, having employee or other witness statements collected after interviews by non-attorney personnel. Whichever process the corporation selects, the government's key measure of cooperation must remain the same as it does for an individual: has the party timely disclosed the relevant facts about the puta-

---

2. There are other dimensions of cooperation beyond the mere disclosure of facts, of course. These can include, for example, providing non-privileged documents and other evidence, making witnesses available for interviews, and assisting in the interpretation of complex business records. This section of the Principles focuses solely on the disclosure of facts and the privilege issues that may be implicated thereby.

tive misconduct? That is the operative question in assigning cooperation credit for the disclosure of information—*not* whether the corporation discloses attorney-client or work product materials. Accordingly, a corporation should receive the same credit for disclosing facts contained in materials that are not protected by the attorney-client privilege or attorney work product as it would for disclosing identical facts contained in materials that are so protected.[3] On this point the Report of the House Judiciary Committee, submitted in connection with the attorney-client privilege bill passed by the House of Representatives (H.R. 3013), comports with the approach required here:

> [A]n . . . attorney of the United States may base cooperation credit on the facts that are disclosed, but is prohibited from basing cooperation credit upon whether or not the materials are protected by attorney-client privilege or attorney work product. As a result, an entity that voluntarily discloses should receive the same amount of cooperation credit for disclosing facts that happen to be contained in materials not protected by attorney-client privilege or attorney work product as it would receive for disclosing identical facts that are contained in materials protected by attorney-client privilege or attorney work product. There should be no differentials in an assessment of cooperation (i.e., neither a credit nor a penalty) based upon whether or not the materials disclosed are protected by attorney-client privilege or attorney work product.

H.R. Rep. No. 110-445 at 4 (2007).

In short, so long as the corporation timely discloses relevant facts about the putative misconduct, the corporation may receive due credit for such cooperation, regardless of whether it chooses to waive privilege or work product protection in the process.[4] Likewise, a corporation that does not disclose the relevant facts about the alleged misconduct—for

---

3. By way of example, corporate personnel are typically interviewed during an internal investigation. If the interviews are conducted by counsel for the corporation, certain notes and memoranda generated from the interviews may be subject, at least in part, to the protections of attorney-client privilege and/or attorney work product. To receive cooperation credit for providing factual information, the corporation need not produce, and prosecutors may not request, protected notes or memoranda generated by the lawyers' interviews. To earn such credit, however, the corporation does need to produce, and prosecutors may request, relevant factual information—including relevant factual information acquired through those interviews, unless the identical information has otherwise been provided—as well as relevant non-privileged evidence such as accounting and business records and emails between non-attorney employees or agents.

4. In assessing the timeliness of a corporation's disclosures, prosecutors should apply a standard of reasonableness in light of the totality of circumstances.

whatever reason—typically should not be entitled to receive credit for cooperation.

Two final and related points bear noting about the disclosure of facts, although they should be obvious. First, the government cannot compel, and the corporation has no obligation to make, such disclosures (although the government can obviously compel the disclosure of certain records and witness testimony through subpoenas). Second, a corporation's failure to provide relevant information does not mean the corporation will be indicted. It simply means that the corporation will not be entitled to mitigating credit for that cooperation. Whether the corporation faces charges will turn, as it does in any case, on the sufficiency of the evidence, the likelihood of success at trial, and all of the other factors identified in Section III above. If there is insufficient evidence to warrant indictment, after appropriate investigation has been completed, or if the other factors weigh against indictment, then the corporation should not be indicted, irrespective of whether it has earned cooperation credit. The converse is also true: The government may charge even the most cooperative corporation pursuant to these Principles if, in weighing and balancing the factors described herein, the prosecutor determines that a charge is required in the interests of justice. Put differently, even the most sincere and thorough effort to cooperate cannot necessarily absolve a corporation that has, for example, engaged in an egregious, orchestrated, and widespread fraud. Cooperation is a relevant potential mitigating factor, but it alone is not dispositive.

(b) Legal Advice and Attorney Work Product

Separate from (and usually preceding) the fact-gathering process in an internal investigation, a corporation, through its officers, employees, directors, or others, may have consulted with corporate counsel regarding or in a manner that concerns the legal implications of the putative misconduct at issue. Communications of this sort, which are both independent of the fact-gathering component of an internal investigation and made for the purpose of seeking or dispensing legal advice, lie at the core of the attorney-client privilege. Such communications can naturally have a salutary effect on corporate behavior—facilitating, for example, a corporation's effort to comply with complex and evolving legal and regulatory regimes.[5] Except as noted in subparagraphs (b)(i) and (b)(ii) below,

---

5. These privileged communications are not necessarily limited to those that occur contemporaneously with the underlying misconduct. The would include, for instance, legal advice provided by corporate counsel in an internal investigation report. Again, the key measure of cooperation is the disclosure of factual information known to the corporation, not the disclosure of legal advice or theories rendered in connection with the conduct at issue (subject to the two exceptions noted in U.S.A.M. 9-28.720(b)(i-ii)).

a corporation need not disclose and prosecutors may not request the disclosure of such communications as a condition for the corporation's eligibility to receive cooperation credit.

Likewise, non-factual or core attorney work product—for example, an attorney's mental impressions or legal theories—lies at the core of the attorney work product doctrine. A corporation need not disclose, and prosecutors may not request, the disclosure of such attorney work product as a condition for the corporation's eligibility to receive cooperation credit.

(i) Advice of Counsel Defense in the Instant Context

Occasionally a corporation or one of its employees may assert an advice-of-counsel defense, based upon communications with in- house or outside counsel that took place prior to or contemporaneously with the underlying conduct at issue. In such situations, the defendant must tender a legitimate factual basis to support the assertion of the advice-of-counsel defense. *See, e.g., Pitt v. Dist. of Columbia*, 491 F.3d 494, 504-05 (D.C. Cir. 2007); *United States v. Wenger*, 427 F.3d 840, 853-54 (10th Cir. 2005); *United States v. Cheek*, 3 F.3d 1057, 1061-62 (7th Cir. 1993). The Department cannot fairly be asked to discharge its responsibility to the public to investigate alleged corporate crime, or to temper what would otherwise be the appropriate course of prosecutive action, by simply accepting on faith an otherwise unproven assertion that an attorney—perhaps even an unnamed attorney—approved potentially unlawful practices. Accordingly, where an advice-of-counsel defense has been asserted, prosecutors may ask for the disclosure of the communications allegedly supporting it.

(ii) Communications in Furtherance of a Crime or Fraud

Communications between a corporation (through its officers, employees, directors, or agents) and corporate counsel that are made in furtherance of a crime or fraud are, under settled precedent, outside the scope and protection of the attorney-client privilege. *See United States v. Zolin*, 491 U.S. 554, 563 (1989); *United States v. BDO Seidman, LLP*, 492 F.3d 806, 818 (7th Cir. 2007). As a result, the Department may properly request such communications if they in fact exist.

[new August 2008]

9-28.730   OBSTRUCTING THE INVESTIGATION

Another factor to be weighed by the prosecutor is whether the corporation has engaged in conduct intended to impede the investigation. Examples of such conduct could include: inappropriate directions to employees or their counsel, such as directions not to be truthful or to conceal relevant facts; making representations or submissions that contain misleading assertions or material omissions; and incomplete or delayed production of records.

In evaluating cooperation, however, prosecutors should not take into account whether a corporation is advancing or reimbursing attorneys' fees or providing counsel to employees, officers, or directors under investigation or indictment. Likewise, prosecutors may not request that a corporation refrain from taking such action. This prohibition is not meant to prevent a prosecutor from asking questions about an attorney's representation of a corporation or its employees, officers, or directors, where otherwise appropriate under the law.[6] Neither is it intended to limit the otherwise applicable reach of criminal obstruction of justice statutes such as 18 U.S.C. § 1503. If the payment of attorney fees were used in a manner that would otherwise constitute criminal obstruction of justice—for example, if fees were advanced on the condition that an employee adhere to a version of the facts that the corporation and the employee knew to be false—these Principles would not (and could not) render inapplicable such criminal prohibitions.

Similarly, the mere participation by a corporation in a joint defense agreement does not render the corporation ineligible to receive cooperation credit, and prosecutors may not request that a corporation refrain from entering into such agreements. Of course, the corporation may wish to avoid putting itself in the position of being disabled, by virtue of a particular joint defense or similar agreement, from providing some relevant facts to the government and thereby limiting its ability to seek such cooperation credit. Such might be the case if the corporation gathers facts from employees who have entered into a joint defense agreement with the corporation, and who may later seek to prevent the corporation from disclosing the facts it has acquired. Corporations may wish to address this situation by crafting or participating in joint defense agreements, to the extent they choose to enter them, that provide such flexibility as they deem appropriate.

Finally, it may on occasion be appropriate for the government to consider whether the corporation has shared with others sensitive infor-

---

6. Routine questions regarding the representation status of a corporation and its employees, including how and by whom attorneys' fees are paid, sometimes arise in the course of an investigation under certain circumstances—to take one example, to assess conflict-of-interest issues. Such questions can be appropriate and this guidance is not intended to prohibit such limited inquiries.

mation about the investigation that the government provided to the corporation. In appropriate situations, as it does with individuals, the government may properly request that, if a corporation wishes to receive credit for cooperation, the information provided by the government to the corporation not be transmitted to others—for example, where the disclosure of such information could lead to flight by individual subjects, destruction of evidence, or dissipation or concealment of assets.

[new August 2008]

9-28.740   OFFERING COOPERATION: NO ENTITLEMENT TO IMMUNITY

A corporation's offer of cooperation or cooperation itself does not automatically entitle it to immunity from prosecution or a favorable resolution of its case. A corporation should not be able to escape liability merely by offering up its directors, officers, employees, or agents. Thus, a corporation's willingness to cooperate is not determinative; that factor, while relevant, needs to be considered in conjunction with all other factors.

[new August 2008]

9-28.750   QUALIFYING FOR IMMUNITY, AMNESTY, OR REDUCED SANCTIONS THROUGH VOLUNTARY DISCLOSURES

In conjunction with regulatory agencies and other executive branch departments, the Department encourages corporations, as part of their compliance programs, to conduct internal investigations and to disclose the relevant facts to the appropriate authorities. Some agencies, such as the Securities and Exchange Commission and the Environmental Protection Agency, as well as the Department's Environmental and Natural Resources Division, have formal voluntary disclosure programs in which self-reporting, coupled with remediation and additional criteria, may qualify the corporation for amnesty or reduced sanctions. Even in the absence of a formal program, prosecutors may consider a corporation's timely and voluntary disclosure in evaluating the adequacy of the corporation's compliance program and its management's commitment to the compliance program. However, prosecution and economic policies specific to the industry or statute may require prosecution notwithstanding a corporation's willingness to cooperate. For example, the Antitrust Division has a policy of offering amnesty only to the first corporation to agree to cooperate. Moreover, amnesty, immunity, or reduced sanctions may not be appropriate where the corporation's business is permeated with fraud or other crimes.

[new August 2008]

9-28.760   OVERSIGHT CONCERNING DEMANDS FOR WAIVERS OF ATTORNEY-CLIENT PRIVILEGE OR WORK PRODUCT PROTECTION BY CORPORATIONS CONTRARY TO THIS POLICY

The Department underscores its commitment to attorney practices that are consistent with Department policies like those set forth herein concerning cooperation credit and due respect for the attorney-client privilege and work product protection. Counsel for corporations who believe that prosecutors are violating such guidance are encouraged to raise their concerns with supervisors, including the appropriate United States Attorney or Assistant Attorney General. Like any other allegation of attorney misconduct, such allegations are subject to potential investigation through established mechanisms.

[new August 2008]

9-28.800   CORPORATE COMPLIANCE PROGRAMS

A.   **General Principle:**   Compliance programs are established by corporate management to prevent and detect misconduct and to ensure that corporate activities are conducted in accordance with applicable criminal and civil laws, regulations, and rules. The Department encourages such corporate self-policing, including voluntary disclosures to the government of any problems that a corporation discovers on its own. However, the existence of a compliance program is not sufficient, in and of itself, to justify not charging a corporation for criminal misconduct undertaken by its officers, directors, employees, or agents. In addition, the nature of some crimes, e.g., antitrust violations, may be such that national law enforcement policies mandate prosecutions of corporations notwithstanding the existence of a compliance program.

B.   **Comment:**   The existence of a corporate compliance program, even one that specifically prohibited the very conduct in question, does not absolve the corporation from criminal liability under the doctrine of *respondeat superior. See United States v. Basic Constr. Co.,* 711 F.2d 570, 573 (4th Cir. 1983) ("[A] corporation may be held criminally responsible for antitrust violations committed by its employees if they were acting within the scope of their authority, or apparent authority, and for the benefit of the corporation, even if . . . such acts were against corporate policy or express instructions."). As explained in *United States v. Potter*, 463 F.3d 9 (1st Cir. 2006), a corporation cannot "avoid liability by adopting abstract rules" that forbid its agents from engaging in illegal acts, because "[e]ven a specific directive to an agent or employee or honest efforts to police such rules do not automatically free the company for the wrongful acts of agents." *Id.* at 25-26. *See also United States v. Hilton Hotels Corp.*, 467 F.2d 1000, 1007 (9th Cir. 1972) (noting that a corporation "could not gain exculpation by issuing general instructions without undertaking to enforce those instructions by means commensurate with the obvious risks"); *United States v. Beusch*, 596 F.2d 871, 878 (9th Cir. 1979) ("[A] corporation may be liable for acts of its employees done contrary to express instructions and policies, but . . . the existence of such instructions and policies may be considered in determining whether the employee in fact acted to benefit the corporation.").

While the Department recognizes that no compliance program can ever prevent all criminal activity by a corporation's employees, the critical factors in evaluating any program are whether the program is adequately designed for maximum effectiveness in preventing and detecting wrongdoing by employees and whether corporate management is enforcing the program or is tacitly encouraging or pressuring employees to engage in misconduct to achieve business objectives. The Department has no formulaic requirements regarding corporate compliance programs. The fundamental questions any prosecutor should ask are: Is the corporation's compliance program well designed? Is the program being applied earnestly and in good faith? Does the corporation's compliance program work? In answering these questions, the prosecutor should consider the comprehensiveness of the compliance program; the extent and pervasiveness of the criminal misconduct; the number and level of the corporate employees involved; the seriousness, duration, and frequency of the misconduct; and any remedial actions taken by the corporation, including, for example, disciplinary action against past violators uncovered by the prior compliance program, and revisions to corporate compliance programs in light of lessons learned.[7] Prosecutors should also consider the promptness of any disclosure of wrongdoing to the government. In evaluating compliance programs, prosecutors may consider whether the corporation has established corporate governance mechanisms that can effectively detect and prevent misconduct. For example, do the corporation's directors exercise independent review over proposed corporate actions rather than unquestioningly ratifying officers' recommendations; are internal audit functions conducted at a level sufficient to ensure their independence and accuracy; and have the directors established an

---

7. For a detailed review of these and other factors concerning corporate compliance programs, see USSG § 8B2.1.

information and reporting system in the organization reasonably designed to provide management and directors with timely and accurate information sufficient to allow them to reach an informed decision regarding the organization's compliance with the law. *See, e.g., In re Caremark Int'l Inc. Derivative Litig.*, 698 A.2d 959, 968-70 (Del. Ch. 1996).

Prosecutors should therefore attempt to determine whether a corporation's compliance program is merely a "paper program" or whether it was designed, implemented, reviewed, and revised, as appropriate, in an effective manner. In addition, prosecutors should determine whether the corporation has provided for a staff sufficient to audit, document, analyze, and utilize the results of the corporation's compliance efforts. Prosecutors also should determine whether the corporation's employees are adequately informed about the compliance program and are convinced of the corporation's commitment to it. This will enable the prosecutor to make an informed decision as to whether the corporation has adopted and implemented a truly effective compliance program that, when consistent with other federal law enforcement policies, may result in a decision to charge only the corporation's employees and agents or to mitigate charges or sanctions against the corporation.

Compliance programs should be designed to detect the particular types of misconduct most likely to occur in a particular corporation's line of business. Many corporations operate in complex regulatory environments outside the normal experience of criminal prosecutors. Accordingly, prosecutors should consult with relevant federal and state agencies with the expertise to evaluate the adequacy of a program's design and implementation. For instance, state and federal banking, insurance, and medical boards, the Department of Defense, the Department of Health and Human Services, the Environmental Protection Agency, and the Securities and Exchange Commission have considerable experience with compliance programs and can be helpful to a prosecutor in evaluating such programs. In addition, the Fraud Section of the Criminal Division, the Commercial Litigation Branch of the Civil Division, and the Environmental Crimes Section of the Environment and Natural Resources Division can assist United States Attorneys' Offices in finding the appropriate agency office(s) for such consultation.

[new August 2008]

9-28.900   RESTITUTION AND REMEDIATION

A.   General Principle: Although neither a corporation nor an individual target may avoid prosecution merely by paying a sum of money, a prosecutor may consider the corporation's willingness to make restitution and steps already taken to do so. A prosecutor may also consider other remedial actions, such as improving an existing compliance program or disciplining wrongdoers, in determining whether to charge the corporation and how to resolve corporate criminal cases.

B. Comment: In determining whether or not to prosecute a corporation, the government may consider whether the corporation has taken meaningful remedial measures. A corporation's response to misconduct says much about its willingness to ensure that such misconduct does not recur. Thus, corporations that fully recognize the seriousness of their misconduct and accept responsibility for it should be taking steps to implement the personnel, operational, and organizational changes necessary to establish an awareness among employees that criminal conduct will not be tolerated.

Among the factors prosecutors should consider and weigh are whether the corporation appropriately disciplined wrongdoers, once those employees are identified by the corporation as culpable for the misconduct. Employee discipline is a difficult task for many corporations because of the human element involved and sometimes because of the seniority of the employees concerned. Although corporations need to be fair to their employees, they must also be committed, at all levels of the corporation, to the highest standards of legal and ethical behavior. Effective internal discipline can be a powerful deterrent against improper behavior by a corporation's employees. Prosecutors should be satisfied that the corporation's focus is on the integrity and credibility of its remedial and disciplinary measures rather than on the protection of the wrongdoers.

In addition to employee discipline, two other factors used in evaluating a corporation's remedial efforts are restitution and reform. As with natural persons, the decision whether or not to prosecute should not depend upon the target's ability to pay restitution. A corporation's efforts to pay restitution even in advance of any court order is, however, evidence of its acceptance of responsibility and, consistent with the practices and policies of the appropriate Division of the Department entrusted with enforcing specific criminal laws, may be considered in determining whether to bring criminal charges. Similarly, although the inadequacy of a corporate compliance program is a factor to consider when deciding whether to charge a corporation, that corporation's quick recognition of the flaws in the program and its efforts to improve the program are also factors to consider as to appropriate disposition of a case.

[new August 2008]

9-28.1000 COLLATERAL CONSEQUENCES

A. General Principle: Prosecutors may consider the collateral consequences of a corporate criminal conviction or indictment in determining whether to charge the corporation with a criminal offense and how to resolve corporate criminal cases.

B.   Comment: One of the factors in determining whether to charge a natural person or a corporation is whether the likely punishment is appropriate given the nature and seriousness of the crime. In the corporate context, prosecutors may take into account the possibly substantial consequences to a corporation's employees, investors, pensioners, and customers, many of whom may, depending on the size and nature of the corporation and their role in its operations, have played no role in the criminal conduct, have been unaware of it, or have been unable to prevent it. Prosecutors should also be aware of non-penal sanctions that may accompany a criminal charge, such as potential suspension or debarment from eligibility for government contracts or federally funded programs such as health care programs. Determining whether or not such non-penal sanctions are appropriate or required in a particular case is the responsibility of the relevant agency, and is a decision that will be made based on the applicable statutes, regulations, and policies.

Virtually every conviction of a corporation, like virtually every conviction of an individual, will have an impact on innocent third parties, and the mere existence of such an effect is not sufficient to preclude prosecution of the corporation. Therefore, in evaluating the relevance of collateral consequences, various factors already discussed, such as the pervasiveness of the criminal conduct and the adequacy of the corporation's compliance programs, should be considered in determining the weight to be given to this factor. For instance, the balance may tip in favor of prosecuting corporations in situations where the scope of the misconduct in a case is widespread and sustained within a corporate division (or spread throughout pockets of the corporate organization). In such cases, the possible unfairness of visiting punishment for the corporation's crimes upon shareholders may be of much less concern where those shareholders have substantially profited, even unknowingly, from widespread or pervasive criminal activity. Similarly, where the top layers of the corporation's management or the shareholders of a closely-held corporation were engaged in or aware of the wrongdoing, and the conduct at issue was accepted as a way of doing business for an extended period, debarment may be deemed not collateral, but a direct and entirely appropriate consequence of the corporation's wrongdoing.

On the other hand, where the collateral consequences of a corporate conviction for innocent third parties would be significant, it may be appropriate to consider a non-prosecution or deferred prosecution agreement with conditions designed, among other things, to promote compliance with applicable law and to prevent recidivism. Such agreements are a third option, besides a criminal indictment, on the one hand, and a

declination, on the other. Declining prosecution may allow a corporate criminal to escape without consequences. Obtaining a conviction may produce a result that seriously harms innocent third parties who played no role in the criminal conduct. Under appropriate circumstances, a deferred prosecution or non-prosecution agreement can help restore the integrity of a company's operations and preserve the financial viability of a corporation that has engaged in criminal conduct, while preserving the government's ability to prosecute a recalcitrant corporation that materially breaches the agreement. Such agreements achieve other important objectives as well, like prompt restitution for victims.[8] Ultimately, the appropriateness of a criminal charge against a corporation, or some lesser alternative, must be evaluated in a pragmatic and reasoned way that produces a fair outcome, taking into consideration, among other things, the Department's need to promote and ensure respect for the law.
[new August 2008]

9-28.1100 OTHER CIVIL OR REGULATORY ALTERNATIVES

A. General Principle: Non-criminal alternatives to prosecution often exist and prosecutors may consider whether such sanctions would adequately deter, punish, and rehabilitate a corporation that has engaged in wrongful conduct. In evaluating the adequacy of non-criminal alternatives to prosecution—e.g., civil or regulatory enforcement actions—the prosecutor may consider all relevant factors, including:

1. the sanctions available under the alternative means of disposition;
2. the likelihood that an effective sanction will be imposed; and
3. the effect of non-criminal disposition on federal law enforcement interests.

B. Comment: The primary goals of criminal law are deterrence, punishment, and rehabilitation. Non-criminal sanctions may not be an appropriate response to a serious violation, a pattern of wrongdoing, or prior non-criminal sanctions without proper remediation. In other cases, however, these goals may be satisfied through civil or regulatory actions. In determining whether a federal criminal resolution is appropriate, the prosecutor should consider the same factors (modified appropriately for the regulatory context) considered when determining whether to leave

---

8. Prosecutors should note that in the case of national or multi-national corporations, multi-district or global agreements may be necessary. Such agreements may only be entered into with the approval of each affected district or the appropriate Department official. See U.S.A.M. 9-27.641.

prosecution of a natural person to another jurisdiction or to seek non-criminal alternatives to prosecution. These factors include: the strength of the regulatory authority's interest; the regulatory authority's ability and willingness to take effective enforcement action; the probable sanction if the regulatory authority's enforcement action is upheld; and the effect of a non-criminal disposition on federal law enforcement interests. *See* USAM 9-27.240, 9-27.250.

[new August 2008]

9-28.1200   SELECTING CHARGES

A.   General Principle: Once a prosecutor has decided to charge a corporation, the prosecutor at least presumptively should charge, or should recommend that the grand jury charge, the most serious offense that is consistent with the nature of the defendant's misconduct and that is likely to result in a sustainable conviction.

B.   Comment: Once the decision to charge is made, the same rules as govern charging natural persons apply. These rules require "a faithful and honest application of the Sentencing Guidelines" and an "individualized assessment of the extent to which particular charges fit the specific circumstances of the case, are consistent with the purposes of the Federal criminal code, and maximize the impact of Federal resources on crime." *See* USAM 9-27.300. In making this determination, "it is appropriate that the attorney for the government consider, *inter alia*, such factors as the [advisory] sentencing guideline range yielded by the charge, whether the penalty yielded by such sentencing range . . . is proportional to the seriousness of the defendant's conduct, and whether the charge achieves such purposes of the criminal law as punishment, protection of the public, specific and general deterrence, and rehabilitation."

[new August 2008]

9-28.1300   PLEA AGREEMENTS WITH CORPORATIONS

A.   General Principle: In negotiating plea agreements with corporations, as with individuals, prosecutors should generally seek a plea to the most serious, readily provable offense charged. In addition, the terms of the plea agreement should contain appropriate provisions to ensure punishment, deterrence, rehabilitation, and compliance with the plea agreement in the corporate context. Although special circumstances may mandate a different conclusion, prosecutors generally should not agree to accept a corporate guilty plea in exchange for non-prosecution or dismissal of charges against individual officers and employees.

B   Comment: Prosecutors may enter into plea agreements with corporations for the same reasons and under the same constraints as apply to plea agreements with natural persons. *See* USAM 9-27.400-530. This means, *inter alia*, that the corporation should generally be required to plead guilty to the most serious, readily provable offense charged. In addition, any negotiated departures or recommended variances from the advisory Sentencing Guidelines must be justifiable under the Guidelines or 18 U.S.C. § 3553 and must be disclosed to the sentencing court. A corporation should be made to realize that pleading guilty to criminal charges constitutes an admission of guilt and not merely a resolution of an inconvenient distraction from its business. As with natural persons, pleas should be structured so that the corporation may not later "proclaim lack of culpability or even complete innocence." *See* USAM 9-27.420(b)(4), 9-27.440, 9-27.500. Thus, for instance, there should be placed upon the record a sufficient factual basis for the plea to prevent later corporate assertions of innocence.

A corporate plea agreement should also contain provisions that recognize the nature of the corporate "person" and that ensure that the principles of punishment, deterrence, and rehabilitation are met. In the corporate context, punishment and deterrence are generally accomplished by substantial fines, mandatory restitution, and institution of appropriate compliance measures, including, if necessary, continued judicial oversight or the use of special masters or corporate monitors. *See* USSG §§ 8B1.1, 8C2.1, *et seq.* In addition, where the corporation is a government contractor, permanent or temporary debarment may be appropriate. Where the corporation was engaged in fraud against the government (e.g., contracting fraud), a prosecutor may not negotiate away an agency's right to debar or delist the corporate defendant.

In negotiating a plea agreement, prosecutors should also consider the deterrent value of prosecutions of individuals within the corporation. Therefore, one factor that a prosecutor may consider in determining whether to enter into a plea agreement is whether the corporation is seeking immunity for its employees and officers or whether the corporation is willing to cooperate in the investigation of culpable individuals as outlined herein. Prosecutors should rarely negotiate away individual criminal liability in a corporate plea.

Rehabilitation, of course, requires that the corporation undertake to be law-abiding in the future. It is, therefore, appropriate to require the corporation, as a condition of probation, to implement a compliance program or to reform an existing one. As discussed above, prosecutors may consult with the appropriate state and federal agencies and components of the Justice

Department to ensure that a proposed compliance program is adequate and meets industry standards and best practices. *See* USAM 9-28.800.

In plea agreements in which the corporation agrees to cooperate, the prosecutor should ensure that the cooperation is entirely truthful. To do so, the prosecutor may request that the corporation make appropriate disclosures of relevant factual information and documents, make employees and agents available for debriefing, file appropriate certified financial statements, agree to governmental or third-party audits, and take whatever other steps are necessary to ensure that the full scope of the corporate wrongdoing is disclosed and that the responsible personnel are identified and, if appropriate, prosecuted. *See generally* USAM 9-28.700. In taking such steps, Department prosecutors should recognize that attorney-client communications are often essential to a corporation's efforts to comply with complex regulatory and legal regimes, and that, as discussed at length above, cooperation is not measured by the waiver of attorney-client privilege and work product protection, but rather is measured by the disclosure of facts and other considerations identified herein such as making witnesses available for interviews and assisting in the interpretation of complex documents or business records.

These Principles provide only internal Department of Justice guidance. They are not intended to, do not, and may not be relied upon to create any rights, substantive or procedural, enforceable at law by any party in any matter civil or criminal. Nor are any limitations hereby placed on otherwise lawful litigative prerogatives of the Department of Justice.

[new August 2008]

APPENDIX 9

Morford Memorandum on Monitors

U.S. Department of Justice
Office of the Deputy Attorney General

The Deputy Attorney General

Washington, D.C. 20530
March 7, 2008

MEMORANDUM FOR HEADS OF DEPARTMENT COMPONENTS
UNITED STATES ATTORNEYS

FROM: Craig S. Morford

SUBJECT: Acting Deputy Attorney General Initial of Craig S. Morford Selection and Use of Monitors in Deferred Prosecution Agreements and Non-Prosecution Agreements with Corporations[1]

I. INTRODUCTION

The Department of Justice's commitment to deterring and preventing corporate crime remains a high priority. The Principles of Federal Prosecution of Business Organizations set forth guidance to federal prosecutors regarding charges against corporations. A careful consideration of those principles and the facts in a given case may result in a decision to

---

1. As used in these Principles, the terms "corporate" and "corporation" refer to all types of business organizations, including partnerships, sole proprietorships, government entities, and unincorporated associations.

negotiate an agreement to resolve a criminal case against a corporation without a formal conviction—either a deferred prosecution agreement or a non-prosecution agreement.[2] As part of some negotiated corporate agreements, there have been provisions pertaining to an independent corporate monitor.[3] The corporation benefits from expertise in the area of corporate compliance from an independent third party. The corporation, its shareholders, employees and the public at large then benefit from reduced recidivism of corporate crime and the protection of the integrity of the marketplace.

The purpose of this memorandum is to present a series of principles for drafting provisions pertaining to the use of monitors in connection with deferred prosecution and non-prosecution agreements (hereafter referred to collectively as "agreements") with corporations.[4] Given the varying facts and circumstances of each case—where different industries, corporate size and structure, and other considerations may be at issue—any guidance regarding monitors must be practical and flexible. This guidance is limited to monitors, and does not apply to third parties, whatever their titles, retained to act as receivers, trustees, or perform other functions.

A monitor's primary responsibility is to assess and monitor a corporation's compliance with the terms of the agreement specifically designed to address and reduce the risk of recurrence of the corporation's misconduct, and not to further punitive goals. A monitor should only be used where appropriate given the facts and circumstances of a particular matter. For example, it may be appropriate to use a monitor where a company does not have an effective internal compliance program, or where it needs to establish necessary internal controls. Conversely, in a situation where a company has ceased operations in the area where the criminal misconduct occurred, a monitor may not be necessary.

In negotiating agreements with corporations, prosecutors should be mindful of both: (1) the potential benefits that employing a monitor may have for the corporation and the public, and (2) the cost of a monitor and its impact on the operations of a corporation. Prosecutors shall, at a

---

2. The terms "deferred prosecution agreement" and "non-prosecution agreement" have often been used loosely by prosecutors, defense counsel, courts and commentators. As the terms are used in these Principles, a deferred prosecution agreement is typically predicated upon the filing of a formal charging document by the government, and the agreement is filed with the appropriate court. In the non-prosecution agreement context, formal charges are not filed and the agreement is maintained by the parties rather than being filed with a court. Clear and consistent use of these terms will enable the Department to more effectively identify and share best practices and to track the use of such agreements. These Principles do not apply to plea agreements, which involve the formal conviction of a corporation in a court proceeding.

3. Agreements use a variety of terms to describe the role referred to herein as "monitor," including consultants, experts, and others.

4. In the case of deferred prosecution agreements filed with the court, these Principles must be applied with due regard for the appropriate role of the court and/or the probation office.

minimum, notify the appropriate United States Attorney or Department Component Head prior to the execution of an agreement that includes a corporate monitor. The appropriate United States Attorney or Department Component Head shall, in turn, provide a copy of the agreement to the Assistant Attorney General for the Criminal Division at a reasonable time after it has been executed. The Assistant Attorney General for the Criminal Division shall maintain a record of all such agreements.

This memorandum does not address all provisions concerning monitors that have been included or could appropriately be included in agreements. Rather this memorandum sets forth nine basic principles in the areas of selection, scope of duties, and duration.

This memorandum provides only internal Department of Justice guidance. In addition, this memorandum applies only to criminal matters and does not apply to agencies other than the Department of Justice. It is not intended to, does not, and may not be relied upon to create any rights, substantive or procedural, enforceable at law by any party in any matter civil or criminal. Nor are any limitations hereby placed on otherwise lawful litigative prerogatives of the Department of Justice.

II. SELECTION

1. <u>Principle:</u> **Before beginning the process of selecting a monitor in connection with deferred prosecution agreements and non-prosecution agreements, the corporation and the Government should discuss the necessary qualifications for a monitor based on the facts and circumstances of the case. The monitor must be selected based on the merits. The selection process must, at a minimum, be designed to: (1) select a highly qualified and respected person or entity based on suitability for the assignment and all of the circumstances; (2) avoid potential and actual conflicts of interests;; and (3) otherwise instill public confidence by implementing the steps set forth in this Principle.**

To avoid a conflict, first, Government attorneys who participate in the process of selecting a monitor shall be mindful of their obligation to comply with the conflict-of interest guidelines set forth in 18 U.S.C. § 208 and 5 C.F.R. Part 2635. Second, the Government shall create a standing or ad hoc committee in the Department component or office where the case originated to consider monitor candidates. United States Attorneys and Assistant Attorneys General may not make, accept, or veto the selection of monitor candidates unilaterally. Third, the Office of the Deputy Attorney General must approve the monitor. Fourth, the Government should decline to accept a monitor if he or she has an interest in, or relationship with, the corporation or its employees, officers or directors that would cause a reasonable

person to question the monitor's impartiality. Finally, the Government should obtain a commitment from the corporation that it will not employ or be affiliated with the monitor for a period of not less than one year from the date the monitorship is terminated.

Comment: Because a monitor's role may vary based on the facts of each case and the entity involved, there is no one method of selection that should necessarily be used in every instance. For example, the corporation may select a monitor candidate, with the Government reserving the right to veto the proposed choice if the monitor is unacceptable. In other cases, the facts may require the Government to play a greater role in selecting the monitor. Whatever method is used, the Government should determine what selection process is most effective as early in the negotiations as possible, and endeavor to ensure that the process is designed to produce a high-quality and conflict-free monitor and to instill public confidence. If the Government determines that participation in the selection process by any Government personnel creates, or appears to create, a potential or actual conflict in violation of 18 U.S.C. § 208 and 5 C.F.R. Part 2635, the Government must proceed as in other matters where recusal issues arise. In all cases, the Government must submit the proposed monitor to the Office of the Deputy Attorney General for review and approval before the monitorship is established.

Ordinarily, the Government and the corporation should discuss what role the monitor will play and what qualities, expertise, and skills the monitor should have. While attorneys, including but not limited to former Government attorneys, may have certain skills that qualify them to function effectively as a monitor, other individuals, such as accountants, technical or scientific experts, and compliance experts, may have skills that are more appropriate to the tasks contemplated in a given agreement.

Subsequent employment or retention of the monitor by the corporation after the monitorship period concludes may raise concerns about both the appearance of a conflict of interest and the effectiveness of the monitor during the monitorship, particularly with regard to the disclosure of possible new misconduct. Such employment includes both direct and indirect, or subcontracted, relationships.

Each United States Attorney's Office and Department component shall create a standing or ad hoc committee ("Committee") of prosecutors to consider the selection or veto, as appropriate, of monitor candidates. The Committee should, at a minimum, include the office ethics advisor, the Criminal Chief of the United States Attorney's Office or relevant Section Chief of the Department component, and at least one other experienced prosecutor.

Where practicable, the corporation, the Government, or both parties, depending on the selection process being used, should consider a pool of at least three qualified monitor candidates. Where the selection process calls for the corporation to choose the monitor at the outset, the corporation should submit its choice from among the pool of candidates to the Government. Where the selection process calls for the Government to play a greater role in selecting the monitor, the Government should, where practicable, identify at least three acceptable monitors from the pool of candidates, and the corporation shall choose from that list.

III.   SCOPE OF DUTIES

A. Independence

2. Principle: A monitor is an independent third-party, not an employee or agent of the corporation or of the Government.

Comment: A monitor by definition is distinct and independent from the directors, officers, employees, and other representatives of the corporation. The monitor is not the corporation's attorney. Accordingly, the corporation may not seek to obtain or obtain legal advice from the monitor. Conversely, a monitor also is not an agent or employee of the Government.

While a monitor is independent both from the corporation and the Government, there should be open dialogue among the corporation, the Government and the monitor throughout the duration of the agreement.

B. Monitoring Compliance With The Agreement

3. Principle: A monitor's primary responsibility should be to assess and monitor a corporation's compliance with those terms of the agreement that are specifically designed to address and reduce the risk of recurrence of the corporation's misconduct, including, in most cases, evaluating (and where appropriate proposing) internal controls and corporate ethics and compliance programs.

Comment: At the corporate level, there may be a variety of causes of criminal misconduct, including but not limited to the failure of internal controls or ethics and compliance programs to prevent, detect, and respond to such misconduct. A monitor's primary role is to evaluate whether a corporation has both adopted and effectively implemented ethics and compliance programs to address and reduce the risk of recurrence of the corporation's misconduct. A well-designed ethics and compliance program that is not effectively implemented will fail to lower the risk of recidivism.

A monitor is not responsible to the corporation's shareholders. Therefore, from a corporate governance standpoint, responsibility for designing an ethics and compliance program that will prevent misconduct should remain with the corporation, subject to the monitor's input, evaluation and recommendations.

4.   Principle: In carrying out his or her duties, a monitor will often need to understand the full scope of the corporation's misconduct covered by the agreement, but the monitor's responsibilities should be no broader than necessary to address and reduce the risk of recurrence of the corporation's misconduct.

Comment: The scope of a monitor's duties should be tailored to the facts of each case to address and reduce the risk of recurrence of the corporation's misconduct. Among other things, focusing the monitor's duties on these tasks may serve to calibrate the expense of the monitorship to the failure that gave rise to the misconduct the agreement covers.

Neither the corporation nor the public benefits from employing a monitor whose role is too narrowly defined (and, therefore, prevents the monitor from effectively evaluating the reforms intended by the parties) or too broadly defined (and, therefore, results in the monitor engaging in activities that fail to facilitate the corporation's implementation of the reforms intended by the parties).

The monitor's mandate is not to investigate historical misconduct. Nevertheless, in appropriate circumstances, an understanding of historical misconduct may inform a monitor's evaluation of the effectiveness of the corporation's compliance with the agreement.

C.   Communications and Recommendations by the Monitor

5.   Principle: Communication among the Government, the corporation and the monitor is in the interest of all the parties. Depending on the facts and circumstances, it may be appropriate for the monitor to make periodic written reports to both the Government and the corporation.

Comment: A monitor generally works closely with a corporation and communicates with a corporation on a regular basis in the course of his or her duties. The monitor must also have the discretion to communicate with the Government as he or she deems appropriate. For example, a monitor should be free to discuss with the Government the progress of, as well as issues arising from, the drafting and implementation of an ethics and compliance program. Depending on the facts and circumstances, it may be appropriate for the monitor to make periodic written reports to both the Government and the corporation regarding, among other things: (1) the monitor's activities; (2) whether the corporation is complying with the terms of the agreement; and (3) any changes that are necessary to foster the corporation's compliance with the terms of the agreement.

6.   Principle: If the corporation chooses not to adopt recommendations made by the monitor within a reasonable time, either the

monitor or the corporation, or both, should report that fact to the Government, along with the corporation's reasons. The Government may consider this conduct when evaluating whether the corporation has fulfilled its obligations under the agreement.

Comment: The corporation and its officers and directors are ultimately responsible for the ethical and legal operations of the corporation. Therefore, the corporation should evaluate whether to adopt recommendations made by the monitor. If the corporation declines to adopt a recommendation by the monitor, the Government should consider both the monitor's recommendation and the corporation's reasons in determining whether the corporation is complying with the agreement. A flexible timetable should be established to ensure that both a monitor's recommendations and the corporation's decision to adopt or reject them are made well before the expiration of the agreement.

D. Reporting of Previously Undisclosed or New Misconduct

7. Principle: The agreement should clearly identify any types of previously undisclosed or new misconduct that the monitor will be required to report directly to the Government. The agreement should also provide that as to evidence of other such misconduct, the monitor will have the discretion to report this misconduct to the Government or the corporation or both.

Comment: As a general rule, timely and open communication between and among the corporation, the Government and the monitor regarding allegations of misconduct will facilitate the review of the misconduct and formulation of an appropriate response to it. The agreement may set forth certain types of previously undisclosed or new misconduct that the monitor will be required to report directly to the Government. Additionally, in some instances, the monitor should immediately report other such misconduct directly to the Government and not to the corporation. The presence of any of the following factors militates in favor of reporting such misconduct directly to the Government and not to the corporation, namely, where the misconduct: (1) poses a risk to public health or safety or the environment; (2) involves senior management of the corporation; (3) involves obstruction of justice; (4) involves criminal activity which the Government has the opportunity to investigate proactively and/or covertly; or (5) otherwise poses a substantial risk of harm. On the other hand, in instances where the allegations of such misconduct are not credible or involve actions of individuals outside the scope of the corporation's business, the monitor may decide, in the exercise of his or her discretion, that the allegations need not be reported directly to the Government.

IV. DURATION

8.   **Principle: The duration of the agreement should be tailored to the problems that have been found to exist and the types of remedial measures needed for the monitor to satisfy his or her mandate.**

Comment: The following criteria should be considered when negotiating duration of the agreement (not necessarily in this order): (1) the nature and seriousness of the underlying misconduct; (2) the pervasiveness and duration of misconduct within the corporation, including the complicity or involvement of senior management; (3) the corporation's history of similar misconduct; (4) the nature of the corporate culture; (5) the scale and complexity of any remedial measures contemplated by the agreement, including the size of the entity or business unit at issue; and (6) the stage of design and implementation of remedial measures when the monitorship commences. It is reasonable to forecast that completing an assessment of more extensive and/or complex remedial measures will require a longer period of time than completing an assessment of less extensive and/or less complex ones. Similarly, it is reasonable to forecast that a monitor who is assigned responsibility to assess a compliance program that has not been designed or implemented may take longer to complete that assignment than one who is assigned responsibility to assess a compliance program that has already been designed and implemented.

9.   **Principle: In most cases, an agreement should provide for an extension of the monitor provision(s) at the discretion of the Government in the event that the corporation has not successfully satisfied its obligations under the agreement. Conversely, in most cases, an agreement should provide for early termination if the corporation can demonstrate to the Government that there exists a change in circumstances sufficient to eliminate the need for a monitor.**

Comment: If the corporation has not satisfied its obligations under the terms of the agreement at the time the monitorship ends, the corresponding risk of recidivism will not have been reduced and an extension of the monitor provision(s) may be appropriate. On the other hand, there are a number of changes in circumstances that could justify early termination of an agreement. For example, if a corporation ceased operations in the area that was the subject of the agreement, a monitor may no longer be necessary. Similarly, if a corporation is purchased by or merges with another entity that has an effective ethics and compliance program, it may be prudent to terminate a monitorship.

APPENDIX 10

Report of Investigation Pursuant to Section 21(a) of the Securities Exchange Act of 1934 and Commission Statement on the Relationship of Cooperation to Agency Enforcement Decisions (Exchange Act Release No. 44969, Accounting and Auditing Enforcement Release No. 1470, October 23, 2001) ("Cooperation Statement") (*Seaboard* Opinion)

SECURITIES AND EXCHANGE COMMISSION

SECURITIES EXCHANGE ACT OF 1934
Release No. 44969 / October 23, 2001

ACCOUNTING AND AUDITING ENFORCEMENT
Release No. 1470 / October 23, 2001

Report of Investigation Pursuant to Section 21(a) of the Securities Exchange Act of 1934 and Commission Statement on the Relationship of Cooperation to Agency Enforcement Decisions

Today, we commence and settle a cease-and-desist proceeding against Gisela de Leon-Meredith, former controller of a public company's subsidiary.[1] Our order finds that Meredith caused the parent company's books and records to be inaccurate and its periodic reports misstated, and then covered up those facts.

We are not taking action against the parent company, given the nature of the conduct and the company's responses. Within a week of learning about the apparent misconduct, the company's internal auditors had conducted a preliminary review and had advised company management who, in turn, advised the Board's audit committee, that Meredith had caused the company's books and records to be inaccurate and its financial reports to be misstated. The full Board was advised and authorized the company to hire an outside law firm to conduct a thorough inquiry. Four days later, Meredith was dismissed, as were two other employees who, in the company's view, had inadequately supervised Meredith; a day later, the company disclosed publicly and to us that its financial statements would be restated. The price of the company's shares did not decline after the announcement or after the restatement was published. The company pledged and gave complete cooperation to our staff. It provided the staff with all information relevant to the underlying violations. Among other things, the company produced the details of its internal investigation, including notes and transcripts of interviews of Meredith and others; and it did not invoke the attorney-client privilege, work product protection or other privileges or protections with respect to any facts uncovered in the investigation.

The company also strengthened its financial reporting processes to address Meredith's conduct—developing a detailed closing process for the subsidiary's accounting personnel, consolidating subsidiary accounting functions under a parent company CPA, hiring three new CPAs for the accounting department responsible for preparing the subsidiary's financial statements, redesigning the subsidiary's minimum annual audit requirements, and requiring the parent company's controller to interview and approve all senior accounting personnel in its subsidiaries' reporting processes.

Our willingness to credit such behavior in deciding whether and how to take enforcement action benefits investors as well as our enforcement program. When businesses seek out, self-report and rectify illegal conduct, and otherwise cooperate with Commission staff, large expenditures of government and shareholder resources can be avoided and investors can benefit more promptly.[2] In setting forth the criteria listed below, we think a few caveats are in order:

First, the paramount issue in every enforcement judgment is, and must be, what best protects investors. There is no single, or constant, answer to that question. Self-policing, self-reporting, remediation and cooperation with law enforcement authorities, among other things, are unquestionably important in promoting investors' best interests. But, so too are vigorous enforcement and the imposition of appropriate sanctions where the law has been violated. Indeed, there may be circumstances where conduct is so egregious, and harm so great, that no amount of cooperation or other mitigating conduct can justify a decision not to bring any enforcement action at all. In the end, no set of criteria can, or should, be strictly applied in every situation to which they may be applicable.

Second, we are not adopting any rule or making any commitment or promise about any specific case; nor are we in any way limiting our broad discretion to evaluate every case individually, on its own particular facts and circumstances. Conversely, we are not conferring any "rights" on any person or entity. We seek only to convey an understanding of the factors that may influence our decisions.

Third, we do not limit ourselves to the criteria we discuss below. By definition, enforcement judgments are just that—judgments. Our failure to mention a specific criterion in one context does not preclude us from relying on that criterion in another. Further, the fact that a company has satisfied all the criteria we list below will not foreclose us from bringing enforcement proceedings that we believe are necessary or appropriate, for the benefit of investors.

In brief form, we set forth below some of the criteria we will consider in determining whether, and how much, to credit self-policing, self-reporting, remediation and cooperation—from the extraordinary step of taking no enforcement action to bringing reduced charges, seeking lighter sanctions, or including mitigating language in documents we use to announce and resolve enforcement actions.

1. What is the nature of the misconduct involved? Did it result from inadvertence, honest mistake, simple negligence, reckless or deliberate indifference to indicia of wrongful conduct, willful

misconduct or unadorned venality? Were the company's auditors misled?

2. How did the misconduct arise? Is it the result of pressure placed on employees to achieve specific results, or a tone of lawlessness set by those in control of the company? What compliance procedures were in place to prevent the misconduct now uncovered? Why did those procedures fail to stop or inhibit the wrongful conduct?

3. Where in the organization did the misconduct occur? How high up in the chain of command was knowledge of, or participation in, the misconduct? Did senior personnel participate in, or turn a blind eye toward, obvious indicia of misconduct? How systemic was the behavior? Is it symptomatic of the way the entity does business, or was it isolated?

4. How long did the misconduct last? Was it a one-quarter, or one-time, event, or did it last several years? In the case of a public company, did the misconduct occur before the company went public? Did it facilitate the company's ability to go public?

5. How much harm has the misconduct inflicted upon investors and other corporate constituencies? Did the share price of the company's stock drop significantly upon its discovery and disclosure?

6. How was the misconduct detected and who uncovered it?

7. How long after discovery of the misconduct did it take to implement an effective response?

8. What steps did the company take upon learning of the misconduct? Did the company immediately stop the misconduct? Are persons responsible for any misconduct still with the company? If so, are they still in the same positions? Did the company promptly, completely and effectively disclose the existence of the misconduct to the public, to regulators and to self-regulators? Did the company cooperate completely with appropriate regulatory and law enforcement bodies? Did the company identify what additional related misconduct is likely to have occurred? Did the company take steps to identify the extent of damage to investors and other corporate constituencies? Did the company appropriately recompense those adversely affected by the conduct?

9. What processes did the company follow to resolve many of these issues and ferret out necessary information? Were the Audit Committee and the Board of Directors fully informed? If so, when?

10. Did the company commit to learn the truth, fully and expeditiously? Did it do a thorough review of the nature, extent, origins and consequences of the conduct and related behavior? Did management, the Board or committees consisting solely of

outside directors oversee the review? Did company employees or outside persons perform the review? If outside persons, had they done other work for the company? Where the review was conducted by outside counsel, had management previously engaged such counsel? Were scope limitations placed on the review? If so, what were they?

11. Did the company promptly make available to our staff the results of its review and provide sufficient documentation reflecting its response to the situation? Did the company identify possible violative conduct and evidence with sufficient precision to facilitate prompt enforcement actions against those who violated the law? Did the company produce a thorough and probing written report detailing the findings of its review? Did the company voluntarily disclose information our staff did not directly request and otherwise might not have uncovered? Did the company ask its employees to cooperate with our staff and make all reasonable efforts to secure such cooperation?[3]

12. What assurances are there that the conduct is unlikely to recur? Did the company adopt and ensure enforcement of new and more effective internal controls and procedures designed to prevent a recurrence of the misconduct? Did the company provide our staff with sufficient information for it to evaluate the company's measures to correct the situation and ensure that the conduct does not recur?

13. Is the company the same company in which the misconduct occurred, or has it changed through a merger or bankruptcy reorganization?

We hope that this Report of Investigation and Commission Statement will further encourage self-policing efforts and will promote more self-reporting, remediation and cooperation with the Commission staff. We welcome the constructive input of all interested persons. We urge those who have contributions to make to direct them to our Division of Enforcement. The public can be confident that all such communications will be fairly evaluated not only by our staff, but also by us. We continue to reassess our enforcement approaches with the aim of maximizing the benefits of our program to investors and the marketplace.

By the Commission (Chairman Pitt, Commissioner Hunt, Commissioner Unger).

Footnotes:

1. In the Matter of Gisela de Leon-Meredith, Exchange Act Release No. 44970 (October 23, 2001).

2. We note that the federal securities laws and other legal requirements and guidance also promote and even require a certain measure of self-policing, self-reporting and remediation. *See, e.g.*, Section 10A of the Securities Exchange Act of 1934, 15 U.S.C. § 78j-1 (requiring issuers and auditors to report certain illegal conduct to the Commission); In the Matter of W.R. Grace & Co., Exchange Act Release No. 39157 (Sept. 30, 1997) (emphasizing the affirmative responsibilities of corporate officers and directors to ensure that shareholders receive accurate and complete disclosure of information required by the proxy solicitation and periodic reporting provisions of the federal securities laws); In the Matter of Cooper Companies, Inc., Exchange Act Release No. 35082 (Dec. 12, 1994) (emphasizing responsibility of corporate directors in safeguarding the integrity of a company's public statements and the interests of investors when evidence of fraudulent conduct by corporate management comes to their attention); In the Matter of John Gutfreund, Exchange Act Release No. 31554 (Dec. 3, 1992) (sanctions imposed against supervisors at broker-dealer for failing promptly to bring misconduct to attention of the government). *See also* Federal Sentencing Guidelines § 8C2.5(f) & (g) (organization's "culpability score" decreases if organization has an effective program to prevent and detect violations of law or if organization reports offense to governmental authorities prior to imminent threat of disclosure or government investigation and within reasonably prompt time after becoming aware of the offense); New York Stock Exchange Rules 342.21 & 351(e) (members and member organizations required to review certain trades for compliance with rules against insider trading and manipulation, to conduct prompt internal investigations of any potentially violative trades, and to report the status and/or results of such internal investigations).

3. In some cases, the desire to provide information to the Commission staff may cause companies to consider choosing not to assert the attorney-client privilege, the work product protection and other privileges, protections and exemptions with respect to the Commission. The Commission recognizes that these privileges, protections and exemptions serve important social interests. In this regard, the Commission does not view a company's waiver of a privilege as an end in itself, but only as a means (where necessary) to provide relevant and sometimes critical information to the Commission staff. Thus, the Commission recently filed an amicus brief arguing that the provision of privileged information to the Commission staff pursuant to a confidentiality agreement did not necessarily waive the privilege as to third parties. Brief of SEC as Amicus Curiae, McKesson HBOC, Inc., No. 99-C-7980-3 (Ga. Ct. App. Filed May 13, 2001). Moreover, in certain circumstances, the Commission staff has agreed that a witness' production of privileged information would not constitute a subject matter waiver that would entitle the staff to receive further privileged information.

http://www.sec.gov/litigation/investreport/34-44969.htm

APPENDIX 11

United States Sentencing Guidelines: Effective Compliance and Ethics Programs

CHAPTER 8–PART B–REMEDYING HARM FROM CRIMINAL CONDUCT, AND EFFECTIVE COMPLIANCE AND ETHICS PROGRAM

§ 8b2.1 Effective Compliance and Ethics Program

(a) To have an effective compliance and ethics program, for purposes of subsection (f) of § 8C2.5 (Culpability Score) and subsection (c)(1) of §8D1.4 (Recommended Conditions of Probation–Organizations), an organization shall—

(1) exercise due diligence to prevent and detect criminal conduct; and

(2) otherwise promote an organizational culture that encourages ethical conduct and a commitment to compliance with the law.

Such compliance and ethics program shall be reasonably designed, implemented and enforced so that the program is generally effective in preventing and detecting criminal conduct. The failure to prevent or detect the instant offense does not necessarily mean that the program is not generally effective in preventing and detecting criminal conduct.

(b) Due diligence and the promotion of an organizational culture that encourages ethical conduct and a commitment to compliance with the law within the meaning of subsection (a) minimally require the following:

(1) The organization shall establish standards and procedures to prevent and detect criminal conduct.

(2)(A) The organization's governing authority shall be knowledgeable about the content and operation of the compliance and ethics program and shall exercise reasonable oversight with respect to the implementation and effectiveness of the compliance and ethics program.

(B) High-level personnel of the organization shall ensure that the organization has an effective compliance and ethics program, as described in this guideline. Specific individual(s) within high-level personnel shall be assigned overall responsibility for the compliance and ethics program.

(C) Specific individual(s) within the organization shall be delegated day-to-day operational responsibility for the compliance and ethics program. Individual(s) with operational responsibility shall report periodically to high-level personnel and, as appropriate, to the governing authority, or an appropriate subgroup of the governing authority, on the effectiveness of the compliance and ethics program. To carry out such operational responsibility, such individual(s) shall be given adequate resources, appropriate authority, and direct access to the governing authority or an appropriate subgroup of the governing authority.

(3) The organization shall use reasonable efforts not to include within the substantial authority personnel of the organization any individual whom the organization knew, or should have known through the exercise of due diligence, has engaged in illegal activities or other conduct inconsistent with an effective compliance and ethics program.

(4)(A) The organization shall take reasonable steps to communicate periodically and in a practical manner its standards and procedures, and other aspects of the compliance and ethics program, to the individuals referred to in subdivision (B) by conducting effective training programs and otherwise disseminating information appropriate to such individuals' respective roles and responsibilities.

(B) The individuals referred to in subdivision (A) are the members of the governing authority, high-level personnel, substantial authority personnel, the organization's employees, and, as appropriate, the organization's agents.

(5) The organization shall take reasonable steps—

(A) to ensure that the organization's compliance and ethics program is followed, including monitoring and auditing to detect criminal conduct.

(B) to evaluate periodically the effectiveness of the organization's compliance and ethics program; and

(C) to have and publicize a system, which may include mechanisms that allow for anonymity or confidentiality, whereby the organization's employees and agents may report or seek guidance regarding potential or actual criminal conduct without fear of retaliation.

(6) The organization's compliance and ethics programs shall be promoted and enforced consistently throughout the organization through (A) appropriate incentives to perform in accordance with the compliance and ethics program; and (B) appropriate disciplinary measures for engaging in criminal conduct and for failing to take reasonable steps to prevent or detect criminal conduct.

(7) After criminal conduct has been detected, the organization shall take reasonable steps to respond appropriately to the criminal conduct and to prevent further similar criminal conduct, including making any necessary modifications to the organization's compliance and ethics program.

(c) In implementing subsection (b), the organization shall periodically assess the risk of criminal conduct and shall take appropriate steps to design, implement or modify each requirement set forth in subsection (B) to reduce the risk of criminal conduct identified through this process.

COMMENTARY

Application Notes:

1. **Definitions**—For purposes of this guideline:
"Compliance and ethics program" means a program designed to prevent and detect criminal conduct.

"Governing authority" means the (A) Board of Directors; or (B) if the organization does not have a Board of Directors, the highest-level governing body of the organization.

"High-level personnel of the organization" and "substantial authority personnel" have the meaning given those terms in the Commentary to § 8A1.2 (Application Instructions - Organizations).

"Standard and procedures" means standards of conduct and internal controls that are reasonably capable of reducing the likelihood of criminal conduct.

2. *Factors to Consider in Meeting Requirements of this Guideline*—

(A) *In General*—Each of the requirements set forth in this guideline shall be met by an organization; however, in determining what specific actions are necessary to meet those requirements, factors that shall be considered include: (i) applicable industry practice or the standards called for by any applicable governmental regulation; (ii) the size of the organization; and (iii) similar misconduct.

(B) *Applicable Governmental Regulation and Industry Practice*—An organization's failure to incorporate and follow applicable industry practice or the standards called for by any applicable governmental regulation weighs against a finding of an effective compliance and ethics program.

(C) *The Size of the Organization*—

(i) *In General*—The formality and scope of actions that an organization shall take to meet the requirements of this guideline, including the necessary features of the organization's standards and procedures, depend on the size of the organization.

(ii) *Large Organizations*—A large organization generally shall devote more formal operations and greater resources in meeting the requirements of this guideline than shall a small organization. As appropriate, a large organization should encourage small organizations (especially those that have, or seek to have, a business relationship with the large organization) to implement effective compliance and ethics programs.

(iii) *Small Organizations*—In meeting the requirements of this guideline, small organizations shall demonstrate the same degree of commitment to ethical conduct and compliance with the law as large organizations. However, a small organization may meet the requirements of this guideline with less formality and fewer resources than would be expected of large organizations. In appropriate circumstances, reliance on existing resources and simple systems can demonstrate a degree of commitment that, for a large organization, would only be demonstrated through more formally planned and implemented systems.

Examples of the informality and use of fewer resources with which a small organization may meet the requirements of this guideline include the following: (I) the governing authority's discharge of its responsibility for oversight of the compliance and ethics program by directly managing the organization's compliance and ethics efforts; (II) training employees through informal staff meetings, and monitoring through regular "walk arounds" or continuous observation while managing the organization; (III) using available personnel, rather than employing separate staff, to carry out the compliance and ethics program; and (IV) modeling its own compliance and ethics program on existing, well-regarded compliance and ethics programs and best practices of other similar organizations.

(D) *Recurrence of Similar Misconduct*—Recurrence of similar misconduct creates doubt regarding whether the organization took reasonable steps to meet the requirements of this guideline. For purposes of this subdivision, "similar misconduct" has the meaning given that term in the Commentary to § 8A1.2 (Application Instructions—Organizations).

3. *Application of Subsection (b)(2)*—High-level personnel and substantial authority personnel of the organization shall be knowledgeable about the content and operation of the compliance and ethics program, shall perform their assigned duties consistent with the exercise of due diligence, and shall promote an organizational culture that encourages ethical conduct and a commitment to compliance with the law.

If the specific individual(s) assigned overall responsibility for the compliance and ethics program does not have day-to-day operational responsibility for the program, then the individual(s) with day-to-day operational responsibility for the program typically should, no less than annually, give the governing authority or an appropriate subgroup thereof information on the implementation and effectiveness of the compliance and ethics program.

4. *Application of Subsection (b)(3)*—

(A) *Consistency with Other Law*—Nothing in subsection (b)(3) is intended to require conduct inconsistent with any Federal, State or local law, including any law governing employment or hiring practices.

(B) *Implementation*—In implementing subsection (b)(3), the organization shall hire and promote individuals so as to ensure that all individuals within the high-level personnel and substantial authority personnel of the organization will perform their assigned duties in a manner consistent with the exercise of due diligence and the promotion of an organizational culture that encourages ethical conduct and a commitment to compliance with the law under subsection (a). With respect to the hiring or promotion of such individuals, an organization shall consider the relatedness of the individual's illegal activities and other misconduct (i.e., other conduct inconsistent with an effective compliance and ethics program) to the specific responsibilities the individual is anticipated to be assigned and other factors such as: (i) the recency of the individual's illegal activities and other misconduct; and (ii) whether the individual has engaged in other such illegal activities and other such misconduct.

5. *Application of Subsection(b)(6)*—Adequate discipline of individuals responsible for an offense is a necessary component of enforcement; however, the form of discipline that will be appropriate will be case specific.

6. *Application of Subsection (c)*—To meet the requirements of subsection (c), an organization shall:

(A) Assess periodically the risk that criminal conduct will occur, including assessing the following:

(i) The nature and seriousness of such criminal conduct.

(ii) The likelihood that certain criminal conduct may occur because of the nature of the organization's business. If, because of the nature of an organization's business, there is a substantial risk that certain types of criminal conduct may occur, the organization shall take reasonable steps to prevent and detect that type of criminal conduct. For example, an organization that, due to the nature of its business, employs sales personnel who have flexibility to set prices shall establish standards and procedures designed to prevent and detect price-fixing. An organization that, due to the nature of its business, employs sales personnel who have flexibility to represent the material characteristics of a product shall establish standards and procedures designed to prevent and detect fraud.

(iii) The prior history of the organization. The prior history of an organization may indicate types of criminal conduct that it shall take actions to prevent and detect.

(B) Prioritize periodically, as appropriate, the actions taken pursuant to any requirement set forth in subsection (b), in order to focus on preventing and detecting the criminal conduct identified under subdivision (A) of this note as most serious, and most likely, to occur.

(C) Modify, as appropriate, the actions taken pursuant to any requirement set forth in subsection (b) to reduce the risk of criminal conduct identified under subdivision (A) of this note as most serious, and most likely, to occur.

Background: This section sets forth the requirements for an effective compliance and ethics program. This section responds to section 805(a) (2)(5) of the Sarbanes-Oxley Act of 2002, Public Law 107-204, which directed the Commission to review and amend, as appropriate, the guidelines and related policy statements to ensure that the guidelines that apply to organizations in this chapter "are sufficient to deter and punish organizational criminal misconduct."

The requirements set forth in this guideline are intended to achieve reasonable prevention and detection of criminal conduct for which the organization would be vicariously liable. The prior diligence of an organization in seeking to prevent and detect criminal conduct has a direct bearing on the appropriate penalties and probation terms for the organization if it is convicted and sentenced for a criminal offense.

APPENDIX 12

SEC Policy Statement Concerning Cooperation by Individuals in Its Investigations and Related Enforcement Actions

17 C.F.R. § 200.12 (2010)

Title 17: Commodity and Securities Exchanges
Part 202 – Informal and Other Procedures

202.12   Policy statement concerning cooperation by individuals in its investigations and related enforcement actions.

Cooperation by individuals and entities in the Commission's investigations and related enforcement actions can contribute significantly to the success of the agency's mission. Cooperation can enhance the Commission's ability to detect violations of the federal securities laws, increase the effectiveness and efficiency of the Commission's investigations, and provide important evidence for the Commission's enforcement actions. There is a wide spectrum of tools available to the Commission and its staff for facilitating and rewarding cooperation by individuals, ranging from taking no enforcement action to pursuing reduced charges and sanctions in connection with enforcement actions. As with any cooperation program, there exists some tension between the objectives of holding individuals fully accountable for their misconduct and providing incentives for individuals to cooperate with law enforcement authorities. This policy statement sets forth the analytical framework employed by the Commission and its staff for resolving this tension in a manner that ensures that potential cooperation arrangements maximize the Commission's law enforcement interests. Although the evaluation of cooperation requires a case-by-case analysis of the specific circumstances presented, as described in greater detail below, the Commission's general approach is to determine whether, how much, and in what manner to credit cooperation by individuals by evaluating four considerations: the assistance provided by the cooperating individual in the Commission's investigation or related enforcement actions ("Investigation"); the importance of the underlying matter in which the individual cooperated; the societal interest in ensuring that the cooperating individual is held accountable for his or her misconduct; and the appropriateness of cooperation credit based upon the profile of the cooperating individual. In the end, the goal of the Commission's analysis is to protect the investing public by determining whether the public interest in facilitating and rewarding an individual's cooperation in order to advance the Commission's law enforcement interests justifies the credit awarded to the individual for his or her cooperation.

(a) *Assistance provided by the individual.* The Commission assesses the assistance provided by the cooperating individual in the Investigation by considering, among other things:

(1) The value of the individual's cooperation to the Investigation including, but not limited to:

(i) Whether the individual's cooperation resulted in substantial assistance to the Investigation;

(ii) The timeliness of the individual's cooperation, including whether the individual was first to report the misconduct to the Commission or to offer his or her cooperation in the Investigation, and whether the cooperation was provided before he or she had any knowledge of a pending investigation or related action;

(iii) Whether the Investigation was initiated based on information or other cooperation provided by the individual;

(iv) The quality of cooperation provided by the individual, including whether the cooperation was truthful, complete, and reliable; and

(v) The time and resources conserved as a result of the individual's cooperation in the Investigation.

(2) The nature of the individual's cooperation in the Investigation including, but not limited to:

(i) Whether the individual's cooperation was voluntary or required by the terms of an agreement with another law enforcement or regulatory organization;

(ii) The types of assistance the individual provided to the Commission;

(iii) Whether the individual provided non-privileged information, which information was not requested by the staff or otherwise might not have been discovered;

(iv) Whether the individual encouraged or authorized others to assist the staff who might not have otherwise participated in the Investigation; and

(v) Any unique circumstances in which the individual provided the cooperation.

(b) *Importance of the underlying matter.* The Commission assesses the importance of the Investigation in which the individual cooperated by considering, among other things:

(1) The character of the Investigation including, but not limited to:

(i) Whether the subject matter of the Investigation is a Commission priority;

(ii) The type of securities violations;

(iii) The age and duration of the misconduct;

(iv) The number of violations; and

(v) The isolated or repetitive nature of the violations.

(2) The dangers to investors or others presented by the underlying violations involved in the Investigation including, but not limited to:

(i) The amount of harm or potential harm caused by the underlying violations;

(ii) The type of harm resulting from or threatened by the underlying violations; and

(iii) The number of individuals or entities harmed.[1]

[1] Cooperation in Investigations that involve priority matters or serious, ongoing, or widespread violations will be viewed most favorably.

(c) *Interest in holding the individual accountable.* The Commission assesses the societal interest in holding the cooperating individual fully accountable for his or her misconduct by considering, among other things:

(1) The severity of the individual's misconduct assessed by the nature of the violations and in the context of the individual's knowledge, education, training, experience, and position of responsibility at the time the violations occurred;

(2) The culpability of the individual, including, but not limited to, whether the individual acted with scienter, both generally and in relation to others who participated in the misconduct;

(3) The degree to which the individual tolerated illegal activity including, but not limited to, whether he or she took steps to prevent the violations from occurring or continuing, such as notifying the Commission or other appropriate law enforcement agency of the misconduct or, in the case of a violation involving a business organization, by notifying members of management not involved in the misconduct, the board of directors or the equivalent body not involved in the misconduct, or the auditors of such business organization of the misconduct;

(4) The efforts undertaken by the individual to remediate the harm caused by the violations including, but not limited to, whether he or she paid or agreed to pay disgorgement to injured investors and other victims or assisted these victims and the authorities in the recovery of the fruits and instrumentalities of the violations; and

(5) The sanctions imposed on the individual by other federal or state authorities and industry organizations for the violations involved in the Investigation.

(d) *Profile of the individual.* The Commission assesses whether, how much, and in what manner it is in the public interest to award credit for cooperation, in part, based upon the cooperating individual's personal and professional profile by considering, among other things:

(1) The individual's history of lawfulness, including complying with securities laws or regulations;

(2) The degree to which the individual has demonstrated an acceptance of responsibility for his or her past misconduct; and

(3) The degree to which the individual will have an opportunity to commit future violations of the federal securities laws in light of his or her occupation—including, but not limited to, whether he or she serves as: A licensed individual, such as an attorney or accountant; an associated person of a regulated entity, such as a broker or dealer; a fiduciary for other individuals or entities regarding financial matters; an officer or director of public companies; or a member of senior management—together with any existing or proposed safeguards based upon the individual's particular circumstances.

Note to §202.12: Before the Commission evaluates an individual's cooperation, it analyzes the unique facts and circumstances of the case. The above principles are not listed in order of importance nor are they intended to be all-inclusive or to require a specific determination in any particular case. Furthermore, depending upon the facts and circumstances of each case, some of the principles may not be applicable or may deserve greater weight than others. Finally, neither this statement, nor the principles set forth herein creates or recognizes any legally enforceable rights for any person.

[75 FR 3123, Jan. 19, 2010]

Table of Cases

Index